ENGLISH VOCABULARY QUICK REFERENCE

A Comprehensive Dictionary Arranged by Word Roots

Roger S. Crutchfield

Publisher's Cataloging-in-Publication
(Provided By Quality Books, Inc.)

Crutchfield, Roger S.
    English vocabulary quick reference: a comprehensive
dictionary arranged by word roots / Roger S. Crutchfield. -- 1st
ed.
    p. cm.
    Includes index.
    Preassigned LCCN: 97-94069
    ISBN: 0965913805
    1. English language--Roots--Dictionaries. 2. Vocabulary--
Dictionaries. 3. English language--Foreign elements--Greek--
Dictionaries. 4. English language--Foreign elements--Latin--
Dictionaries. 5. English language--Etymology--Dictionaries.
I. Title.

PE1580.C78 1997   422'.4803
                           QBI98-276

LexaDyne Publishing, Inc.
P.O. Box 4498
Leesburg, VA 20177-8564

Web site: http://www.quickreference.com
E-mail: vocabulary@quickreference.com

Library of Congress Catalog Card Number: 97-94069

ISBN: 0-9659138-0-5

Printed in the United States of America

✪ Printed on recycled paper using soy-based inks

ATTENTION EDUCATORS AND CORPORATIONS:

This book may be purchased in quantity at discount for
business or educational use. Call 1-888-599-4700

Cover design and Illustration: Jim's Studio - Fairfax, VA
http://home.earthlink.net/~jimstudio/

TABLE OF CONENTS

INTRODUCTION

Your vocabulary is extremely important! The words you use in speaking and writing create a window through which others view your knowledge. If this window is too small, others may never know your abilities and potential and may never understand your opinions and insights. The Vocabulary Quick Reference will make this window much larger by allowing you to increase your knowledge of word roots and begin the lifelong process of vocabulary building.

The Vocabulary Quick Reference is the only book of its kind. It was produced to meet the following, and previously unfulfilled, requirements of an effective vocabulary learning tool:

- List all the words that contain each root with a complete definition for each word.
- Show the complete etymology for each word.
- Show which words are most frequently used. This is important to students preparing for the SAT and other college entrance exams.
- Highlight the most important portion of each definition so the user has a short and easy-to-learn definition embedded within each complete definition.
- Create an alphabetical list of these highlighted words that will group related words together so they can be learned together.
- Develop a pronunciation technique that has no special characters and is easy to use.

For a detailed description of how this is done see the How To Use This Book section.

Learning vocabulary through memorization is very difficult and often temporary. However, learning becomes more meaningful through the study of roots. Once you understand the roots, you can dissect a word and use the roots to learn the meaning of the word. For instance, triskaidekaphobia can be dissected as follows: tris means **three**, kai means **and**, deka means **ten**, and phobia means **fear**. Therefore, triskaidekaphobia means **fear of the number 13**.

Words that sound alike are often confused. For example, bisect and dissect are similar in sound and are often misused and misspelled. Bisect [bi-,two + sect,to cut] means "to cut into two equal parts." Dissect [dis-,apart + sect,to cut] means "to cut apart." The prefix dis- in dissect means **apart**, but is often confused with the prefix di- which means two. Since dissect consists of two roots, the first ending in "s" and the second beginning with "s," it must be spelled with two s's. Once you understand the etymology you will never misuse or misspell bisect or dissect. This spelling rule also applies to many other words. In interrupt, irrupt, and corrupt, the first root ends with "r" and the following root begins with "r" so they must be spelled with two r's. The roots tell you how to spell the word. See page 200.

Another example of the power of etymology is in learning million, billion, trillion, etc., which all contain the root mill, meaning 1,000. Most people know how to spell and use million, billion, and trillion, but what comes after trillion? The root for million is mill, which means 1,000. Since million doesn't have a prefix a **1 is understood**. So one million is written as one set of three zeros after 1,000 or 1,000,000. In billion and trillion the **m** for mill **is understood** and the prefix indicates how many sets of three zeros are to be written after 1,000. Thus the etymology for billion is [bi-,two + [m]ill,thousand + -ion] which is written as 1,000,000,000 or **two** sets of three zeros after 1,000. The etymology for trillion is [tri-,three + [m]ill,thousand + -ion] which is written as 1,000,000,000,000 or **three** sets of three zeros after 1,000. After trillion comes quadrillion [quadr-,four + [m]ill,thousand + -ion] which is **four** sets of three zeros after 1,000 or

1,000,000,000,000,000. These prefixes continue through viginti which in Latin means twenty. You simply write down 1,000 and then add as many sets of three zeros as the prefix indicates. See pages 116 and 282. Centillion is written as 100 sets of three zeros after 1,000 or 1 followed by 303 zeros.

Words such as pneumonia can be very annoying because the first letter is silent. However, when you understand the root it is easy to see why the "p" in pneumonia is silent. Pneumo and the suffix -pnea are forms of the same root. In cases like apnea, the "p" is necessary and is pronounced. Therefore the pronunciations for pneumonia and apnea are (noo MOHN yuh) and (AP nee uh). See pages 193 and 194. The same is true for pter on page 196. The "p" is pronounced in helicopter (HEL ih kop' ter) and is silent in pterodactyl (tehr' uh DAK tul).

The roots ann meaning **year** and enn meaning **years** are an excellent example of how helpful roots can be in determining the correct word to use. For instance, if you are looking for a word that means "occurring once every two years" do you want to use biannual or biennial? Bi- means two and enn means years so the correct word is biennial. Biannual can't be correct because if the word contains the root ann it has to mean something that occurs within a one year period. Therefore, biannual means something that occurs twice a year. If the word contains the root enn it has to mean something that occurs once in two or more years. Once you understand that ann means **year** and enn means **years**, you will never confuse the annuals in your flower garden with the perennials. Since ann always pertains to something that occurs within a one year period, the annuals are the flowers that last only one season, while the perennials bloom year after year. See pages 73 and 283.

To see a few examples of words that should be learned together turn to the following pages in the keywords section:

> The keywords for utopia and dystopia on page 259 beginning with "imaginary."
> The keywords for grapheme, phoneme, morpheme, lexeme, semanteme, and taxeme on page 304 beginning with "smallest."
> The keywords for alexia and agraphia on page 270 beginning with "loss of the ability to."
> The keywords for cum laude, magna cum laude, and summa cum laude on page 324 beginning with "with praise for."
> The keywords for agnostic and atheist on page 284 beginning with "one who believes."
> See the keywords on page 285 beginning with "orbit."
> See the keywords on page 249 and 250 beginning with "fear."
> See the keywords on page 251 beginning with "figure of speech."

There are hundreds of words in this book that are just as easy and fun to learn as the examples presented here. Read through the dictionary and keyword sections and you will be amazed at how many words can be learned together, and their etymology makes learning and remembering them almost effortless.

This book contains 260 primary roots. When a root is given, every word that contains that root is listed so the user will know how many words contain the root and will have a complete definition for each word. The etymology is listed immediately after each word so the roots and the definition can be seen together at a glance. The keywords in the definition that reflect the etymology are also highlighted in blue so a direct connection can be made between the meaning and the etymology. This makes the meaning easy to understand and recall.

Remember, an impressive vocabulary will strengthen your self-confidence and give you a distinct advantage in an increasingly competitive world. The vocabulary you build with the Vocabulary Quick Reference will improve your quality of life as it opens new doors and prepares you for future opportunities.

HOW TO USE THIS BOOK

The Vocabulary Quick Reference begins with a primary root index that lists 260 word roots. All prefixes and suffixes are considered to be roots. They are simply roots that occur at the beginning or end of a word. Each root in this section is followed by a page number that indicates the page in the dictionary section where the root can be found.

In the dictionary section, each root is followed by a comprehensive list of words that contain that root. The number of words following each root varies and is limited to those words found in a standard desk dictionary such as Webster's New World, American Heritage, or Webster's 10th New Collegiate. The words in the lists that follow each root are referred to as main entries. If a main entry contains more than one primary root, that main entry appears in more than one list. The secondary root index in the last section of the book includes a list of over 500 additional roots for which no lists were made. These are generally less common roots, but still very important to the etymology of the main entries in the dictionary section.

For each main entry in the dictionary section, the etymology follows the word and the definition follows the etymology. The pronunciation is located after the definition. If the main entry is in **red**, it was found in a student dictionary such as Webster's High School Dictionary, Thorndike-Barnhart Student Dictionary, or Macmillan's Dictionary for Students and is therefore considered to be a very common word. The main entries in **red** are very likely to appear on the SAT and other college entrance exams.

The words in blue within each definition are called keywords because they are the most important part of the definition. They are essentially a shorter definition imbedded within the complete definition. These keywords in blue are compiled into a long alphabetical list that comprises the keyword section of the Vocabulary Quick Reference. This comprehensive list of keywords brings the meanings of all the main entries in the dictionary section into one list that groups many related words together.

The red keywords in the keyword section correspond to the red main entries in the dictionary section. If the main entry was red in the dictionary section, its keywords will be red in the keywords section. This is to enable the user to easily pick out the more common words while reading through the keyword section.

The main entry index lists all the main entries and the page numbers they appear on in the dictionary section. This list can be used when the user knows the word to be looked up and just needs the page number.

Braces { } are used in the dictionary section to indicate a short definition or explanation for the preceding word or syllable. See decare on page 163 and the pronunciation for regress on page 97.

Colored tabs are provided for quick access to the dictionary, keywords, and main entry index sections.

The introduction to the Vocabulary Quick Reference appears on page i and the pronunciation key appears on page iv.

PRONUNCIATION KEY

The pronunciation key is a phonics-based system that was developed especially for the Vocabulary Quick Reference. This simple yet thorough methodology uses no special characters and is being accepted by users at all levels of education as an easy-to-use alternative to complicated pronunciation schemes that use numerous esoteric symbols.

ay	=	long a	as in late
a	=	short a	as in hat
ah	=	a	as in father
ee	=	long e	as in heat
e or eh	=	short e	as in get (eh at the end of a syllable)
eye	=	long i	as in hide
i or ih	=	short i	as in hit (ih at the end of a syllable)
oh	=	long o	as in coat
o	=	short o	as in hot
yoo	=	long u	as in cute
u	=	short u	as in cut

aer		
ar	ehr	as in care
er		
er		
ir	ihr	as in sphere
yr		
ar	ahr	as in car

u or uh	=	schwa	as the a in along (uh LONG)
			as the 3rd e in eleven (ee LEV un)
			as the i in vanity (VAN uh tee)
			as the 1st o in compose (cum POHZ)

A schwa is defined as a neutral vowel sound that, in most unstressed syllables, receives the least amount of stress. It is commonly represented in dictionaries as an inverted "e." It will be written here as "u" at the beginning or in the middle of a syllable and as "uh" at the end of a syllable or when standing alone.

Capital letters indicate a primary accent. A secondary accent is indicated by an accent mark.

PRIMARY ROOT INDEX

hepat/o..........liver 100 (Greek)

hepta-, hept-..........seven 161 (Greek)

hetero..........different, other 102 (Greek)

hexa-, hex-..........six 161 (Greek)

homo, homoio, homeo..........same, similar, equal 100 (Greek)

hydr/o..........water, hydrogen, liquid 20 (Greek)

hyp-, hypo-..........under, below, less 109 (Greek)

hyper-..........above, excessive, beyond, over 108 (Greek)

iatr/o..........healing, medical treatment 110 (Greek)

icon/o..........image 111 (Greek)

-ics..........study of, science, skill, practice, knowledge 130 (Greek)

idio-..........peculiar, personal, distinct 111 (Greek)

ig-, il-, in-, im-, ir-..........not, without 4 (Latin)

inter-..........between, among 111 (Latin)

intra-, intro-..........within, inward, inside, into 80 (Latin)

iso-..........equal, same 103 (Greek)

-itis..........inflammation 112 (Greek)

ject..........to throw 114 (Latin)

junct..........to join 114 (Latin)

kilo-..........thousand (10^3) 115 (Greek)

kine, kinet, kinemat..........motion, division 116 (Greek)

-latry..........worship 117 (Greek)

leuk/o, leuc/o..........white, colorless 117 (Greek)

lex..........word, law, reading 66 (Latin)

lingu..........language, tongue 118 (Latin)

lip/o..........fat 118 (Greek)

-lite, -ite..........mineral, rock, stone, fossil 118 (Greek)

a-, an-   not, without

abiogenesis [*a-, without + bio, living organisms + -genesis, generation*] The now discredited theory that living organisms can be spontaneously generated directly from nonliving matter. Opposed to biogenesis. (ay' beye' oh JEN uh sis)

abiotic [*a-, without + bio, life + -tic*] Referring to the absence of life or specific life conditions. See biotic. (ay' beye OT ik)

abranchiate [*a-, without + branchi, gill + -ate*] Without gills. (ay BRANG kee it)

abulia [*a-, without + -bulia, will*] Lack of willpower and the ability to make decisions. (uh BYOO lee uh)

abysmal [*a-, without + Grk > byssos, bottom + -al*] Not capable of being measured or understood. Extreme. See incomprehensible and inscrutable. (uh BIZ mul)

abyss [*a-, without + Grk > byssos, bottom*] 1.A deep or seemingly bottomless chasm, gulf, or space. 2.Anything immeasurably deep, infinite, or unfathomable. 3.The primeval chaos before the Creation. (uh BIS)

abyssal [*a-, without + Grk > byssos, bottom + -al*] Pertaining to the bottom waters of the ocean depths or floor. (uh BIS ul)

acarpous [*a-, without + carp, fruit + -ous*] Not bearing fruit. Sterile. (ay KAHR pus)

acaudate [*a-, without + Ltn > cauda, tail + -ate*] Without a tail. (ay KAW dayt')

acaulescent [*a-, without + Ltn > caulis, stem + -escent*] Without a stem or having a very short stem. (ay' kaw LES ent)

acedia [*a-, without + Grk > kedos, care + -ia*] Spiritual apathy or boredom. (uh SEE dee uh)

acentric [*a-, without + centr, center + -ic*] Without a center. (ay SEN trik)

acephalous [*a-, without + cephal, head + -ous*] 1.Having no distinguishable head. 2.Having no leader or ruler. (ay SEF uh lus)

achene [*a-, not + Grk > chainein, to gape*] A small, dry fruit that is formed from a simple ovary bearing a single seed and ripens without splitting open its sheath. (uh KEEN)

achlamydeous [*a-, without + Grk > chlamys, cloak + -eous*] Without a calyx or corolla. See perianth. (ak' luh MID ee us)

achondroplasia [*a-, without + chondro, cartilage + plas, development + -ia*] A congenital bone disorder caused by abnormal conversion of cartilage into bone, resulting in deformities and dwarfism. (ay kon' druh PLAY zhuh)

achromatic [*a, without + chromat, color + ic*] 1.Without color. 2.Transmitting light without constituent color separation, as a lens. (ak' roh MAT ik)

achromatin [*a-, without + chromat, color + -in*] The part of a cell nucleus that does not stain readily with basic dyes. See chromatin. (ay KROH muh tin)

achromic [*a-, without + chrom, color + -ic*] 1.Without color. 2.Lacking normal pigmentation. See leukoderma. (ay KROH mik)

acotyledon [*a-, without & cotyledon [seed leaves]*] Any plant without seed leaves. (ay KOT l eed' n)

acyclic [*a-, not + cycl, circle + -ic*] Not cyclic. (ay SEYE klik)

adiabatic [*a-, not + dia, through + Grk > bainein, to go + -ic*] Occurring without gaining or losing heat. (ad' ee uh BAT ik)

adynamic [*a-, without + dynam, strength + -ic*] Characterized by or causing weakness. See dynamic. (ay' deye NAM ik)

adytum [*a-, not + Grk > dyein, enter + -um*] The sanctum in certain ancient temples open only to priests. (AD ih tum)

aedes [*a-, not + Grk > edos, pleasure + -es*] Any of a genus of mosquitos, including a mosquito that transmits yellow fever and dengue. (ay EE deez)

afebrile [*a-, without + Ltn > febris, fever + -ile*] Without fever. (ay FEE brul)

agamete [*a-, without & gamete*] An asexual reproductive cell that progresses directly into an adult, as a spore. (ay GAM eet)

agamic [*a-, without + gam, sexual union + -ic*] Reproducing without sexual union. Asexual. Opposed to gamic. (ay GAM ik)

agamogenesis [*a-, without + gamo, sexual union + -genesis, production*] Asexual reproduction by budding, fission, cell division, etc. See monogenesis (def. 2). (ay gam' uh JEN uh sis)

agenesis [*a-, without + -genesis, formation*] Lack of development or absence of an organ or other body part. (ay JEN uh sis)

agnosia [*a-, without + gnos, knowledge + -ia*] Total or partial loss of the ability to recognize familiar objects, often resulting from brain damage. (ag NOH zhuh)

agnostic [*a-, without + gnos, knowledge + -tic*] One who believes the existence of God is unknown, but does not deny the possibility that God exists. See atheist and infidel (def. 1). (ag NOS tik)

agonic [*a-, not + gon, angle + -ic*] Not having or forming an angle. (ay GON ik)

agonic line [*a-, not + gon, angle + -ic & line*] A line on a map connecting points on the earth's surface with zero magnetic declination. See isogonal line and isoclinic line. (ay GON ik leyen)

agranulocyte [*a-, without & granul(e) & -cyte, cell*] Either of two types of mature white blood cells that have only very minute granules in the cytoplasm. See granulocyte and leukocyte. (ay GRAN yuh loh seyet')

agrapha [*a-, not + graph, written + -a*] Sayings attributed to Jesus, but not in the Bible. See logion. (AG ruh fuh)

agraphia [*a-, not + graph, writing + -ia*] The total or partial loss of the ability to write, usually resulting from a pathological condition. See alexia, dyslexia, and dysgraphia. (ay GRAF ee uh)

ahimsa [*a-, without + Sanskrit > himsa, injury*] The Hindu, Buddhist, and Jainist doctrine of respect for and nonviolence toward all living creatures. (uh HIM sah')

alexia [*a-, not + lex, reading + -ia*] A neurological disorder caused by brain lesions that results in loss of the ability to read. See agraphia, dysgraphia, and dyslexia. (uh LEK see uh)

amaranth [*a-, not + Grk > marainein, to fade away + anth, flower*] 1.A legendary flower that never fades or dies. 2.Any plant of the genus Amaranthus, some of which are grown for their flowers and colored leaves. (AM uh ranth')

ambrosia [*a-, not + Grk > brotos, mortal + -ia*] 1.In Greek and Roman mythology, the food or drink of the gods thought to bestow immortality. 2.Something that tastes or smells especially delicious. (am BROH zhuh)

amenorrhea [*a-, without + meno, menstruation + rrhea, flow*] Abnormal absence or suppression of menstruation. (ay men' uh REE uh)

amethyst [*a-, not + Grk > methystos, drunken*] 1.A violet or purple variety of quartz used as a gem. So named from the belief that it prevented intoxication. 2.A violet or purple color. (AM uh thist)

ametropia [*a-, not + metr, measure + -opia, visual condition*] Any visual condition resulting from abnormal refraction of the eye, such as astigmatism, nearsightedness, or farsightedness. (am' ih TROH pee uh)

amnesia [*a-, without + mne, memory + -ia*] Total or partial loss of memory due to brain injury, disease, shock, etc. (am NEE zhuh)

amnesty [*a-, without + mne, memory + -ty*] A general pardon, especially for political offenses against a government. (AM nuh stee)

amoral [*a-, not & moral*] 1.Neither moral nor immoral. 2.Lacking moral principles. (ay MOR ul)

amorphous [*a-, without + morph, form + -ous*] 1.Without distinct form or shape. Shapeless. 2.Not belonging to a particular type or pattern. Anomalous. 3.Without crystalline form or structure. (uh MOR fus)

amyotonia [*a-, without + myo, muscle + Grk > tonos, tone + -ia*] Lacking muscle tone. (ay' meye uh TOH nee uh)

anacoluthon [*an-, not + Grk > akolouthos, following*] An abrupt change within a sentence from one grammatical construction to another, sometimes used for rhetorical effect. (an' uh kuh LOO thon')

anaemia [*an-, without + -aemia, blood condition*] 1.A condition in which there is an abnormal decrease in total blood volume, hemoglobin, or the number of red blood cells, resulting in pallor of the skin, shortness of breath, and lethargy. 2.Lack of vitality or vigor. Same as anemia. (uh NEE mee uh)

anaerobe [*an-, without + aero, air + bio, life*] A microorganism that does not require free oxygen to live. Opposed to aerobe. (AN uh rohb')

anaerobic [*an-, without + aero, air + bio, life + -ic*] Living without air or free oxygen. Opposed to aerobic (def. 1). (an' uh ROH bik)

anaesthesia [*an-, without + aesthes, feeling + -ia*] Total or partial loss of sensibility to pain and other sensations, produced by disease, drugs, hypnosis, etc. Same as anesthesia. (an' es THEE zhuh)

analcite [*an-, not + Grk > alkimos, strong + -ite, mineral*] A white or light-colored zeolite mineral. So named for its weak electric power when rubbed. (uh NAL seyet')

analgesia [*an-, without + alg, pain + -ia*] Absence of sensibility to pain while in a fully conscious state. (an' l JEE zee uh)

analgesic [*an-, without + alg, pain + -ic*] A drug or remedy that relieves pain, as aspirin. (an' l JEE zik)

analphabetic [*an-, not & alphabet & -ic*] Not able to read or write. See literate (def. 1), illiterate (def. 1), and semiliterate. (an' al' fuh BET ik)

anaphrodisia [*an-, without + Grk > aphrodisia, sexual pleasure*] Decline or absence of sexual desire. (an af' ruh DIZ ee uh)

anarchy [*an-, without + arch, rule + -y*] 1.The absence of any form of government. 2.Political and social disorder and confusion. Lawlessness. (AN ur kee)

anarthria [*an-, without + Grk > arthron, articulation + -ia*] Loss of the ability to articulate speech. See dysarthria, aphasia, and dysphasia. (an AHR three uh)

anecdote [*an-, not + Grk > ekdotos, published*] 1.Originally, secret or little-known items of biography or history. 2.A short narrative of an entertaining or interesting incident or event. (AN ik doht')

anemia [*an-, without + -emia, blood condition*] 1.A condition in which there is an abnormal decrease in total blood volume, hemoglobin, or the number of red blood cells, resulting in pallor of the skin, shortness of breath, and lethargy. 2.Lack of vitality or vigor. (uh NEE mee uh)

anencephaly [*an-, without + encephal, brain + -y*] Partial or total absence of the brain at birth. (an' en SEF uh lee)

aneroid [*a-, without + Grk > neros, fluid + -oid*] Not using fluid. (AN uh roid')

aneroid barometer [*a-, without + Grk > neros, fluid + -oid & barometer*] A barometer that measures atmospheric pressure by measuring the movement of a thin metal disk rather than the movement of a column of fluid. (AN uh roid' buh ROM et er)

anesthesia [*an-, without + esthes, feeling + -ia*] Total or partial loss of sensibility to pain and other sensations, produced by disease, drugs, hypnosis, etc. (an' es THEE zhuh)

anesthesiology [*anesthesi(a) & -ology, study of*] The branch of medicine dealing with the study and use of anesthesia and anesthetics. See anesthesia. (an' es thee' zee OL uh jee)

anhydride [*an-, without + hydr, water + -ide*] A compound derived by the removal of water from an acid or other compound. (an HEYE dreyed')

anhydrite [*an-, without + hydr, water + -ite, mineral*] A usually white to gray mineral composed of anhydrous calcium sulfate that is similar to gypsum, but does not contain water. (an HEYE dreyet')

anhydrous [*an-, without + hydr, water + -ous*] Pertaining to a compound without water in its composition, especially water of crystallization. (an HEYE drus)

aniso- [*an-, not + iso-, equal*] A word root meaning "not equal." (an EYE soh)

aniseikonia [*aniso-, not equal + icon, image + -ia*] An abnormal visual condition in which the image is not the same size in both eyes. Opposed to iseikonia. (an eye' seye KOH nee uh)

anisogamous [*aniso-, not equal + gam, sexual union + -ous*] Characterized by the fusion of heterogametes. Same as heterogamous (def. 1). (an' eye SOG uh mus)

anisogamy [*aniso-, not equal + -gamy, sexual union*] The union of two dissimilar gametes, as in form, size, or function. See isogamy. (an' eye SOG uh mee)

anisometric [*aniso-, not equal + metr, measure + -ic*] Not having or exhibiting equality in dimensions or measurements. Not isometric. See isometric (def. 1). (an eye' suh MET rik)

anisometropia [*aniso-, not equal + metr, measure + -opia, visual condition*] An abnormal visual condition in which the refractive power is not equal in both eyes. See isometropia. (an eye' soh mih TROH pee uh)

anisotropic [*aniso-, not equal + trop, responding to a stimulus + -ic*] 1.Having unequal responses to external stimuli. 2.Having properties that vary depending on the direction of measurement. See isotropic. (an eye' suh TROP ik)

anodyne [*an-, without + odyn, pain*] A medicine or remedy that soothes or relieves pain. (AN uh deyen')

anomalous [*an-, not + homo, same + -ous*] Deviating from the normal rule, method, or arrangement. Irregular. Abnormal. (uh NOM uh lus)

anomaly [*an-, not + homo, same + -y*] 1.Deviation from the normal rule, method, or arrangement. 2.The angular distance of an orbiting body, as a planet or satellite, from its previous perihelion or perigee. See perihelion and perigee. (uh NOM uh lee)

anomie [*a-, without + nom, system of laws + -ie*] A lack of standards and values, resulting in social or personal instability. (AN uh mee)

anomy [*a-, without + -nomy, system of laws*] A lack of standards and values, resulting in social or personal instability. Same as anomie. (AN uh mee)

anonym [*an-, without + onym, name*] 1.An anonymous person. 2.Pseudonym. See pseudonym and nom de guerre. (AN uh nim')

anonymous [*an-, without + onym, name + -ous*] 1.Without a known or acknowledged name. 2.Of unknown source or origin. 3.Without individuality or distinct characteristics. (uh NON uh mus)

anorexia [*an-, without + Grk > orexis, appetite + -ia*] 1.Lack of or diminished appetite. 2.Short for anorexia nervosa. (an' uh REK see uh)

anorexia nervosa [*an-, without + Grk > orexis, appetite + -ia & Ltn > nervosus, nervous*] A psychological eating disorder, usually occurring in young women, characterized by aversion to food and pathological fear of obesity and resulting in life-threatening weight loss. See bulimia nervosa. (an' uh REK see uh nur VOH suh)

anorthite [*an-, not + ortho, straight + -ite, rock*] A white, gray, or pink plagioclase feldspar found in many igneous rocks. So named for its oblique crystals. (an OR theyet')

anorthosite [*an-, not + ortho, straight + -ite, rock*] A plutonic igneous rock, chiefly plagioclase feldspar. So named for its oblique crystals. (an OR thuh seyet')

anosmia [*an-, without + osm, smell + -ia*] Partial or total absence of the sense of smell. (an OZ mee uh)

anoxemia [*an-, without + ox, oxygen + -emia, blood condition*] An abnormally low level of oxygen in the blood. See anoxia, hypoxia, and hypoxemia. (an' ok SEE mee uh)

anoxia [*an-, without + ox, oxygen + -ia*] 1.Absence or deficiency of oxygen in body tissues. 2.Hypoxia. See anoxemia, hypoxia, and hypoxemia. (an OK see uh)

anuran [*an-, without + Grk > oura, tail*] Pertaining to frogs and toads, all of which have no tail and are highly specialized for jumping. (uh NOOR un)

anuria [*an-, without + -uria, urine*] Absence of the formation or excretion of urine. (uh NOOR ee uh)

aorist [*a-, without + Grk > horos, boundary + -ist*] A verb tense that denotes past action with no indication of the action being completed, continued, or repeated. (AY uh rist)

apathy [*a-, without + -pathy, feeling*] 1.Lack of emotion or feeling. 2.Lack of interest or concern. Indifference. See lethargy. (AP uh thee)

aperiodic [*a-, not + peri, around + Grk > hodos, journey + -ic*] 1.Not characterized by periods or repeated cycles. 2.Not occurring at regular intervals. Irregular. Opposed to periodic. (ay' pihr ee OD ik)

apetalous [*a-, without & petal & -ous*] Without petals. (ay PET l us)

aphanite [*a-, not + Grk > phainein, to show + -ite, rock*] A fine-grained rock with constituents so small they cannot be seen with the naked eye. (AF uh neyet')

aphasia [*a-, without + -phasia, speech*] Total or partial loss of the ability to understand or use spoken or written language, usually resulting from brain injury. See dysphasia, anarthria, and dysarthria. (uh FAY zhuh)

aphonia [*a-, without + phon, voice + -ia*] Loss of voice due to disease, injury, or structural abnormality. (ay FOH nee uh)

aphotic [*a-, without + phot, light + -ic*] Without light; specifically, the lower part of the ocean that does not receive enough light for photosynthesis. (ay FOHT ik)

aphyllous [*a-, without + phyll, leaf + -ous*] Without leaves. (ay FIL us)

aplastic anemia [*a-, not + plast, forming cells or tissue + -ic & anemia*] Anemia that results from defective blood-producing bone marrow. See anemia. (ay PLAS tik uh NEE mee uh)

apnea [*a-, not + -pnea, breathing*] Temporary cessation of breathing. See dyspnea and eupnea. (AP nee uh)

apnoea [*a-, not + -pnoea, breathing*] Temporary cessation of breathing. Same as apnea. (AP nee uh)

apodal [*a-, without + pod, feet + -al*] Without feet or legs. (AP uh dul)

apraxia [*a-, without + Grk > praxis, action + -ia*] Other than with paralysis or other motor or sensory impairment, the total or partial loss of the ability to execute purposeful voluntary movements. (ay PRAK see uh)

apteral [*a-, without + pter, wing + -al*] Pertaining to a structure with columns on each end, but none along the sides. See peripteral. (AP ter ul)

apterous [*a-, without + pter, wing + -ous*] Without wings or winglike appendages. (AP ter us)

apteryx [*a-, without + pteryx, wing*] A New Zealand bird with undeveloped wings and no tail. Kiwi. (AP ter iks')

arrhythmia [*a-, without & rhythm & -ia*] Any irregularity of the heart's normal rhythm. (uh RITH mee uh)

aseptic [*a-, not + Grk > septos, putrid + -ic*] Free from microorganisms that produce disease, fermentation, or putrefaction. (ay SEP tik)

asexual [*a-, without & sex & -ual*] 1.Lacking a sex or sexual organs. Sexless. 2.Pertaining to reproduction from a single individual without the involvement of male or female gametes, as in fission, budding, spore production, etc. (ay SEK shoo ul)

asocial [*a-, not & social*] 1.Antisocial. Not gregarious. 2.Not considerate of others. Selfish. See gregarious. (ay SOH shul)

aspheric [*a-, not & spher(e) & -ic*] Having a nearly perfect spherical shape with only slight aberrations, as a lens. (ay SFIHR ik)

asphyxia [*a-, without + Grk > sphyxis, pulse + -ia*] Lack of oxygen in the blood, causing death or unconsciousness. (as FIK see uh)

a-, an-

astatic [*a-, not + stat, stationary + -ic*] 1.Not steady or stable. 2.Not taking a particular direction or position. See static. (ay STAT ik)

astatine [*a-, not + stat, stationary + -ine*] A highly unstable radioactive chemical element that occurs naturally in the thyroid gland and is also produced artificially by bombarding bismuth with alpha particles. (AS tuh teen')

asthenia [*a-, without + sthen, strength + -ia*] Loss or lack of strength or energy. Debility. Weakness. (as THEE nee uh)

asthenopia [*a-, without + sthen, strength + -opia, visual condition*] Eye weakness or strain, often causing headache, ocular discomfort, etc. (as thuh NOH pee uh)

asthenosphere [*a-, without + stheno, strength & sphere*] A zone beneath the earth's surface that lies beneath the lithosphere and consists of several hundred kilometers of weak material that readily yields to persistent stresses. (as THEN uh sfihr')

astigmatism [*a-, not + Grk > stigma, point + -tism*] A refractive error of a lens, including the lens of the eye, that prevents light rays from meeting at a common focal point, resulting in a blurred or distorted image. (uh STIG muh tiz' um)

astomatous [*a-, without + stomat, mouth + -ous*] Without a mouth or stomata. (ay STOM uh tus)

asymmetry [*a-, without & symmetry*] Without symmetry. See symmetry. (ay SIM ih tree)

asymptote [*a-, not + sym, together + Grk > ptotos, falling*] A straight line that a curve continually approaches, but never meets, even if the curve is extended to infinity. (AS im toht')

asynchronous [*a-, not + syn, same + chron, time + -ous*] 1.Not occurring at the same time. 2.Not occurring at the same rate. See synchronous. (ay SING kruh nus)

asyndeton [*a-, not + syn, together + Grk > dein, to bind + -on*] The omission of one or more conjunctions between sentence elements for rhetorical effect. See polysyndeton. (uh SIN dih tahn')

ataractic [*a-, not + Grk > taraktos, disturbed + -ic*] 1.A tranquilizer. 2.Having a tranquilizing or calming effect. (at' uh RAK tik)

ataraxia [*a-, not + Grk > taraktos, disturbed + -ia*] Calmness and peace of mind. Tranquility. (at' uh RAK see uh)

ataxia [*a-, without + tax, arrangement + -ia*] Total or partial loss of the ability to coordinate voluntary muscle action, especially in the extremities. (uh TAK see uh)

atheist [*a-, not + the, God + -ist*] One who believes there is no God. See agnostic and infidel (def. 1). (AY thee ist)

atom [*a-, not + tom, to cut*] 1.Anything considered to be an irreducible constituent of a specified system. 2.The smallest component of an element having all the properties of the element, with protons and neutrons at its positively charged nucleus surrounded by a complex arrangement of revolving electrons. (AT um)

atonal [*a-, without + Grk > tonos, tone + -al*] Lacking a tone center or key. (ay TOHN l)

atonic [*a-, without + Grk > tonos, accent + -ic*] Not accented or stressed, as a word or syllable. (ay TON ik)

atony [*a-, without + Grk > tonos, tone + -y*] Lack of normal muscle tone. (AT n ee)

atrophy [*a-, without + -trophy, nourishment*] A wasting away or failure to properly develop due to insufficient nutrition, as of organs, tissues, or other body parts. (AT ruh fee)

avitaminosis [*a-, without & vitamin & -osis, diseased condition*] Any disease caused by vitamin deficiency. See hypervitaminosis. (ay veyet' uh mih NOH sis)

axenic [*a-, without + xen, foreign + -ic*] 1.Raised under germ-free conditions, as a laboratory animal. 2.Not contaminated by any other organisms, as a laboratory culture. (ay ZEN ik)

azo- [*a-, without + zo, life*] A word root meaning "lifeless" or "containing nitrogen." So named because nitrogen does not support life. (AY zoh)

azygous [*a-, not + zyg, pair + -ous*] Not occurring as one of a pair. Having no mate. Single. (ay ZEYE gus)

deuteranopia [*deuter, second + an-, without + -opia, visual condition*] A visual defect in which the retina fails to respond to the color green. So named from the blindness to green, which is regarded as the second primary color. See protanopia and tritanopia. (doot' uh ruh NOH pee uh)

myasthenia [*my, muscle + a-, without + sthen, strength + -ia*] Abnormal muscle fatigue or weakness. (meye' us THEE nee uh)

neurasthenia [*neur, nerve + a-, without + sthen, strength + -ia*] A disorder originally thought to result from neural exhaustion, including such symptoms as chronic fatigue, weakness, and irritability. (noor' us THEE nee uh)

protanopia [*prot-, first + an-, without + -opia, visual condition*] A visual defect in which the retina fails to respond to the color red. So named from the blindness to red, which is regarded as the first primary color. See deuteranopia and tritanopia. (proht' n OH pee uh)

tritanopia [*Grk > tritos, third + an-, without + -opia, visual condition*] A visual defect in which the retina fails to respond to the color blue. So named from the blindness to blue, which is regarded as the third primary color. See protanopia and deuteranopia. (treye' tuh NOH pee uh)

ig-, il-, in-, im-, ir- not, without

ignoble [*ig-, not + Ltn > nobilis, noble*] 1.Not of noble birth, reputation, or position. 2.Without honor, character, or worth. Base. (ig NOH bul)

ignominy [*ig-, without + nomin, name + -y*] 1.Loss of one's good name and reputation. 2.Great personal shame and dishonor. (IG nuh min' ee)

ignorant [*ig-, without + gnos, knowledge + -ant*] Without knowledge or training. Not educated. Illiterate. See illiterate (def. 1). (IG nuh runt)

ignore [*ig-, without + gnos, knowledge*] To refuse to notice or recognize. (ig NOR)

illegal [*il-, not + lex, law + -al*] 1.Not legal. Prohibited by law. 2.Unauthorized according to official rules or regulations. See illicit. (ih LEE gul)

illegible [*il-, not + Ltn > legere, read + -ible*] Impossible or difficult to read. (ih LEJ uh bul)

illegitimate [*il-, not + lex, law + -ate*] 1.Born out of wedlock. 2.Not lawful or acceptable. 3.Improper, incorrect, or contrary to good usage. (il' ih JIT uh mut)

illiberal [*il-, not + Ltn > liber, free + -al*] 1.Intolerant. Narrow-minded. 2.Not generous. Stingy. (ih LIB ur ul)

illicit [*il-, not + Ltn > licere, to be permitted + -it*] Not permitted by law or custom. Illegal. Forbidden. See illegal. (ih LIS it)

illiterate [*il-, not & literate*] 1.Having little or no formal education, especially not able to read or write. See analphabetic and semiliterate. 2.Displaying a lack of culture, especially in literature and language. See literate. (ih LIT ur it)

immaculate [*im-, without + Ltn > macula, spot + -ate*] 1.Without spot or stain. Extremely clean. 2.Without fault or error. 3.Without sin. Pure. See impeccable. (ih MAK yuh lut)

immediate [*im-, without + medi, middle + -ate*] 1.Without delay. 2.Without intervention. Direct. 3.Next in line or order. (ih MEE dee it)

immense [*im-, not + Ltn > mensus, measured*] 1.Very large. See infinite (def. 2). 2.Very good. Excellent. (ih MENS)

immiscible [*im-, not + Ltn > miscere, mix + -ible*] Not capable of being mixed. (ih MIS uh bul)

immortal [*im-, not + mort, dead + -al*] 1.Not subject to death. 2.Living or lasting forever. 3.Having everlasting fame. (ih MORT l)

immune [*im-, without + Ltn > munia, services*] 1.Protected from infection or disease. 2.Exempt, as from punishment or taxation. (ih MYOON)

immutable [*im-, not + mut, change + -able*] Not changeable. (ih MYOOT uh bul)

impalpable [*im-, not + Ltn > palpare, touch + -able*] 1.Not capable of being felt by touching. Intangible. 2.Not readily grasped by the mind. Vague. See intangible. (im PAL puh bul)

impeccable [*im-, without + Ltn > peccare, sin + -able*] 1.Without fault or error. 2.Not capable of sin or wrongdoing. See immaculate. (im PEK uh bul)

impecunious [*im-, without + Ltn > pecunia, money + -ous*] Having little or no money. Poor. (im' pih KYOO nee us)

impenitent [*im , without + Ltn > paenitere, regret + -ent*] Without shame or regret. (im PEN ih tent)

impermeable [*im-, not & perme(ate) & -able*] 1.Not able to be penetrated. 2.Not permitting the passage of fluid. See permeate. (im PER mee uh bul)

imperturbable [*im-, not + per, through + turb, agitate + -able*] Not capable of being disturbed or upset. Calm. See equanimity and equable (def. 2). (im' per TUR buh bul)

impervious [*im-, not + per, through + via, way + -ous*] 1.Not capable of being penetrated. Impenetrable. Impermeable. 2.Not disturbed or affected by. See pervious. (im PER vee us)

implacable [*im-, not + plac, please + -able*] Not capable of being appeased or pacified. See inexorable. (im PLAK uh bul)

implausible [*im-, not + Ltn > plaudere, applaud + -ible*] Not believable or reasonable. Improbable. (im PLAW zuh bul)

imponderable [*im-, not + Ltn > ponderare, weigh + -able*] Not capable of being precisely weighed or evaluated. (im PON der uh bul)

impotent [*im-, not + Ltn > potens, having power*] 1.Lacking in power. Ineffective. 2.Lacking physical strength. Weak. 3.Not capable of engaging in sexual intercourse; said usually of the male. (IM puh tent)

impregnable [*im-, not + Ltn > prehendere, grasp + -able*] Not capable of being taken by force. (im PREG nuh bul)

impropriety [*im-, not + Ltn > proprius, proper + -ty*] 1.Improper action or behavior. 2.Improper use of a word or phrase in speech or writing. (im' pruh PREYE ih tee)

improvise [*im-, not + pro-, before + vis, to see*] 1.To compose, sing, or recite without preparation. 2.To make or invent from readily available materials. (IM proh veyez')

imprudent [*im-, not + Ltn > prudens, showing foresight*] Lacking discretion. Unwise. Not prudent. (im' PROOD nt)

impudent [*im-, not + Ltn > pudens, shameful*] Offensively bold or forward. Saucy. Insolent. See insolent. (IM pyuh dent)

impunity [*im-, without + Ltn > poena, penalty + -ity*] Exemption from punishment, injury, or loss. (im PYOO nih tee)

inadvertent [*in-, not & advertent*] 1.Not attentive. Heedless. 2.Unintentional. Accidental. See advertent. (in' uhd VURT nt)

inalienable [*in-, not + Ltn > alius, other + -able*] Not capable of being taken away or transferred. (in AYL yuh nuh bul)

inane [*Ltn > inanis, empty*] 1.Empty. Void. 2.Lacking meaning or significance. Silly. (in AYN)

inanimate [*in-, not + anim, spirit + -ate*] 1.Not living. Lifeless. 2.Without liveliness or energy. Dull. (in AN uh mut)

inapt [*in-, not + apt, fit*] 1.Not suitable. Inappropriate. 2.Awkward. Clumsy. See inept. (in APT)

inauspicious [*in-, not & auspicious*] Unfavorable. Unlucky. Not auspicious. See auspicious. (in' aw SPISH us)

incessant [*in-, not + Ltn > cessare, to stop + -ant*] Continuing without interruption. (in SES unt)

incest [*in-, not + Ltn > castus, chaste*] Sexual intercourse between persons too closely related to be legally married. (IN sest)

incognito [*in-, without + cogn, knowledge*] 1.With one's true identity concealed or disguised. 2.Disguised identity. (in' kog NEE toh)

incognizant [*in-, without + cogn, knowledge + -ize + -ant*] Without knowledge or awareness. (in KOG nuh zunt)

incommensurate [*in-, not + com-, together + Ltn > mensus, measured + -ate*] Not proportionate. Inadequate. (in' kuh MEN sur it)

incommodious [*in-, not + Ltn > commodus, convenient + -ous*] Inconvenient. Uncomfortable. (in' kuh MOHD ee us)

incompetent [*in-, not + Ltn > competere, adequate + -ent*] 1.Not able to meet requirements in skill, knowledge, etc. 2.Not legally qualified. (in KOM puh tent)

incomprehensible [*in-, not + com-, together + Ltn > prehendere, grasp + -ible*] Not capable of being comprehended or understood. Inconceivable. See inscrutable. (in' kom prih HEN suh bul)

inconclusive [*in-, not & conclusive*] Not leading to a clear, convincing, or definite result. Opposed to conclusive. (in' kun KLOO siv)

incongruous [*in-, not + Ltn > congruere, come together + -ous*] 1.Not compatible or harmonious. 2.Out of place. Absurd. (in KONG groo us)

inconsonant [*in-, not + con-, together + son, sound + -ant*] Not in agreement or harmony. (in KON suh nunt)

inconspicuous [*in-, not & conspicuous*] 1.Not easily noticed. 2.Attracting little or no attention. See conspicuous. (in' kun SPIK yoo us)

incorporeal [*in-, without + corpor, body + -eal*] 1.Lacking material substance. Spiritual. 2.Lacking physical existence, but regarded by the law as existing, as a right or privilege. Intangible. Opposed to corporeal. (in' kor POR ee ul)

incorrigible [*in-, not + Ltn > corrigere, correct + -ible*] Not capable of being corrected, reformed, or controlled. (in KOR ih juh bul)

incorrupt [*in-, not & corrupt*] 1.Not corrupt. 2.Not subject to decay or contamination. 3.Error-free. (in' kuh RUPT)

incredible [*in-, not + cred, believe + -ible*] 1.Not believable. 2.Seeming impossible. Amazing. (in KRED uh bul)

incredulous [*in-, not + cred, believe + -ulous*] 1.Unbelieving. Skeptical. 2.Showing an unwillingness to believe. (in KREJ uh lus)

indecorous [*in-, not + Ltn > decorus, proper*] Not in accordance with accepted standards of behavior and good taste. Improper. (in DEK ur us)

indefeasible [*in-, not + dis-, away + fac, to do + -ible*] Not capable of being annulled or terminated. (in' dih FEE zuh bul)

indelible [*in-, not + Ltn > delebilis, perishable*] Not capable of being removed or erased. (in DEL uh bul)

indemnify [*in-, not + Ltn > damnum, harm + -ify, to make*] 1.To compensate for loss, damage, or hardship. 2.To insure against future loss, damage, or hardship. (in DEM nih feye)

indescribable [*in-, not + de-, down + scrib, to write + -able*] Not able to be described. (in' dih SKREYE buh bul)

indignant [*in-, not + dign, worthy + -ant*] Feeling or showing anger, especially at unfair or unjust treatment or conduct. (in DIG nunt)

indispose [*in-, not + Ltn > disponere, arrange*] 1.To make unwilling. 2.To make incapable or unfit. Disqualify. (in' dis POHZ)

indocile [*in-, not + Ltn > docere, teach + -ile*] Not easily taught or disciplined. Recalcitrant. Intractable. See intractable. (in DOS ul)

indolent [*in-, not + Ltn > dolere, feel pain + -ent*] Disliking work or exertion. Lazy. Idle. (IN duh lent)

indomitable [*in-, not + Ltn > domare, tame + -able*] Not easily subdued, conquered, or discouraged. See invincible. (in DOM it uh bul)

indubitable [*in-, not + Ltn > dubitare, doubt + -able*] Not to be doubted. Unquestionable. (in DOO bit uh bul)

inedible [*in-, not + Ltn > edere, eat + -ible*] Not fit to be eaten. Not edible. (in ED uh bul)

ineffable [*in-, not + ef-, out + Ltn > fari, speak + -able*] Not capable of being expressed in words. Indescribable. Unutterable. (in EF uh bul)

inefficacious [*in-, not + Ltn > efficere, bring about + -acious*] Not capable of producing the desired effect. Ineffective. Inadequate. (in' ef' ih KAY shus)

ineloquent [*in-, not + e-, out + loqu, to speak + -ent*] Not exercising forceful, persuasive, or fluent speech. (in EL uh kwent)

ineluctable [*in-, not + Ltn > eluctari, escape + -able*] Not able to be avoided. Inescapable. Inevitable. See inevitable. (in' ih LUK tuh bul)

inept [*in-, not + ept, fit*] 1.Not suitable. Inappropriate. 2.Awkward. Clumsy. Incompetent. 3.Not fitting. Unfit. See inapt. (in EPT)

inequality [*in-, not & equal & -ity*] The condition of being unequal or uneven. (in' ih KWOL ih tee)

inequity [*in-, not + equ, equal + -ity*] Lack of justice. Unfairness. See iniquity. (in EK wit ee)

ineradicable [*in-, not + e-, out + radic, root + -able*] Impossible to completely get rid of. Not eradicable. See eradicate. (in' ih RAD ih kuh bul)

inert [*in-, without + art, skill*] 1.Without the inherent ability to move or act. 2.Sluggish in motion or action. 3.Not able to readily combine or react with other elements, as certain gases. (in URT)

inevitable [*in-, not + Ltn > evitare, avoid + -able*] Not able to be avoided or prevented. Certain. See ineluctable. (in EV it uh bul)

inexorable [*in-, not + Ltn > exorare, prevail upon + -able*] Not capable of being persuaded or affected by appeal or entreaty. Unyielding. Unrelenting. See implacable. (in EKS ur uh bul)

inexpiable [*in-, not + Ltn > expiare, appease + -able*] Not capable of being expiated or atoned for. (in EKS pee uh bul)

inexplicable [*in-, not + Ltn > explicare, explain + -able*] Not capable of being explained, understood, or accounted for. (in' ik SPLIK uh bul)

infallible [*in-, not + Ltn > fallere, deceive + -ible*] 1.Not capable of error. 2.Not capable of failure. Certain. (in FAL uh bul)

infamous [*in-, without + Ltn > fama, fame + -ous*] 1.Having a bad reputation. Notorious. 2.Shamefully bad. Detestable. Despicable. (IN fuh mus)

infelicitous [*in-, not + Ltn > felix, happy + -it + -ous*] 1.Not suitable. Inappropriate. 2.Not happy. Unfortunate. (in' fuh LIS ih tus)

infidel [*in-, without + fid, faith*] 1.One who denies the existence of God. See agnostic and atheist. 2.A non-believer in a particular religion, especially Islam or Christianity. 3.A non-believer in a particular theory, doctrine, principle, etc. (IN fih del')

infidelity [*in-, without + fid, faith + -ity*] 1.Lack of faith in a particular religion. 2.Lack of faithfulness to a spouse. Adultery. (in' fih DEL ih tee)

infinite [*in-, without + Ltn > finis, limit*] 1.Without limits or bounds of any kind. 2.Extremely great. Immense. Vast. See immense (def. 1). (IN fuh nit)

infinitesimal [*in-, without + Ltn > finis, limit + -imal*] Incalculably or immeasurably small. (in' fin' uh TES uh mul)

infirmity [*in-, not + Ltn > firmus, strong + -ity*] 1.A physical or moral weakness or flaw. 2.An ailment or diseased condition. See dyscrasia. (in FUR muh tee)

inimical [*in-, not + Ltn > amicus, friendly + -al*] 1.Unfriendly. Hostile. Antagonistic. 2.Unfavorable. Harmful. Adverse. See adverse (def. 1). (in IM ih kul)

inimitable [*in-, not + Ltn > imitari, copy + -able*] Not capable of being imitated. Matchless. (in IM it uh bul)

iniquity [*in-, not + equ, equal + -ity*] Lack of righteousness. Wickedness. Gross injustice. See inequity. (in IK wit ee)

6

innocuous [*in-, not + noc, harmful + -ous*] Not harmful or injurious. (ih NOK yoo us)

innominate [*in-, without + nomin, name + -ate*] Without a name. Anonymous. See anonymous (def. 1). (ih NOM uh nit)

inordinate [*in-, without + Ltn > ordo, order + -ate*] Not within reasonable limits. Excessive. (in ORD n it)

insatiable [*in-, not + Ltn > satis, enough + -able*] Not capable of being satisfied or appeased. (in SAY shuh bul)

inscrutable [*in-, not + Ltn > scrutari, examine + -able*] Not easily understood. Obscure. Enigmatic. Incomprehensible. See perspicuous and incomprehensible. (in SKROOT uh bul)

insipid [*in-, not + Ltn > sapidus, tasty*] 1.Lacking taste or flavor. Tasteless. 2.Lacking excitement or interest. Dull. (in SIP id)

insolent [*in-, not + Ltn > solere, accustomed + -ent*] 1.Offensively arrogant or rude. 2.Boldly disrespectful. See impudent. (IN suh lent)

insomnia [*in-, not + somni, sleep + -ia*] Chronic inability to sleep. (in SOM nee uh)

insouciant [*in-, not + Ltn > soucier, care + -ant*] Without concern or worry. Carefree. Nonchalant. (in SOO see unt)

insuperable [*in-, not + super-, over + -able*] Not capable of being overcome or surmounted. Insurmountable. (in SOO per uh bul)

intangible [*in-, not + Ltn > tangere, touch + -ible*] 1.Not capable of being touched. Impalpable. 2.Not readily grasped by the mind. Vague. See impalpable. (in TAN juh bul)

intractable [*in-, not + tract, draw + -able*] 1.Not easily controlled or managed. Stubborn. 2.Not easily worked or handled. 3.Not easily treated or cured. See tractable. (in TRAK tuh bul)

intransigent [*in-, not + trans, through + ag, to drive + -ent*] Refusing to compromise. Uncompromising. Unyielding. (in TRAN sih jent)

intransitive [*in-, not + trans, across + it, go + -ive*] Pertaining to a verb that indicates a complete action without requiring a direct object to complete its meaning. See transitive. (in TRAN sih tiv)

intrepid [*in-, not + Ltn > trepidus, alarmed*] Not afraid in the presence of danger. Dauntless. (in TREP id)

inveracity [*in-, not + ver, true + -acity*] Lack of veracity. Untruthfulness. See veracity. (in' vuh RAS ih tee)

invincible [*in-, not + vinc, conquer + -ible*] Not capable of being conquered or overcome. See indomitable. (in VIN suh bul)

irradicable [*ir-, not + radic, root + -able*] Impossible to completely get rid of. Not eradicable. Same as ineradicable. (ihr RAD ih kul bul)

irrecusable [*ir-, not + Ltn > recusare, reject + -able*] Not capable of being rejected or refused. (ihr' rih KYOO zuh bul)

irrefutable [*ir-, not + Ltn > refutare, repel + -able*] Not capable of being disproved or refuted. Indisputable. (ihr REF yuh tuh bul)

irreparable [*ir-, not + Ltn > reparare, bring back + -able*] Not capable of being repaired, restored, or rectified. (ihr REP ur uh bul)

irrespective [*ir-, without & respect & -ive*] Without consideration for or regard to. Regardless. (ihr' rih SPEK tiv)

irreverent [*ir-, without + Ltn > revereri, respect + -ent*] Not showing or feeling proper reverence. Disrespectful. (ihr REV ur ent)

irrevocable [*ir-, not + re-, back + voc, to call + -able*] Not able to be called back or undone, as a decision. Unalterable. Final. (ihr REV uh kuh bul)

irrupt [*ir-, within + rupt, burst*] 1.To break or burst in suddenly or violently. Invade. 2.To increase abruptly in number, as a population. (ih RUPT)

terra incognita [*terra, land & in-, without + cogn, knowledge*] 1.An unknown land or territory. 2.An unexplored or unknown field of knowledge. (TEHR uh in' kog NEET uh)

acro   high, extremity, tip

acrobat [*acro, high + Grk > bainein, to walk*] A skilled performer of gymnastic feats on a tightrope, trapeze, etc. (AK ruh bat')

acrobatics [*acro, high + Grk > bainein, to walk + -ics, skill*] 1.The skill of performing gymnastic feats. 2.An impressive display of agility. (ak' ruh BAT iks)

acrocarpous [*acro, extremity + carp, fruit + -ous*] Bearing fruit at the tip of the stem or stalk, as certain ferns and mosses. (ak' roh KAHR pus)

acrocentric [*acro, extremity + centr, center + -ic*] Pertaining to a chromosome with the centromere closer to one end than the other. See telocentric. (ak' roh SEN trik)

acrocephaly [*acro, high + cephal, head + -y*] A congenital malformation of the skull that gives the head a peaked or conical shape. Same as oxycephaly. (ak' roh SEF uh lee)

acrodont [*acro, high + dont, teeth*] Having teeth fastened to the upper surface of the jaw without sockets, as some lower vertebrates. See pleurodont. (AK ruh dont')

acrogen [*acro, tip + gen, origin*] A flowerless plant having a stem with its growing point at the apex, as a moss or fern. (AK ruh jen)

acromegaly [*acro, extremity + -megaly, large*] A chronic disease caused by a disorder of the pituitary gland and marked by progressive enlargement of bones in the head, hands, and feet. (ak' roh MEG uh lee)

acromion [*acro, extremity + Grk > omos, shoulder + -ion*] The upper, outer extremity of the scapula. (uh KROH mee un)

acronym [*acro, high + onym, name*] A word formed from the first letter or group of letters from each word of a series of words, such as *radar* from (ra)dio (d)etecting (a)nd (r)anging. (AK ruh nim')

acropetal [*acro, high + -petal, moving toward*] Developing from the base of the stem upward toward the apex, as some leaves and flowers. (uh KROP ih tul)

acrophobia [*acro, high + -phobia, fear*] Abnormal fear of heights. (ak' ruh FOH bee uh)

acropolis [*acro, high + -polis, city*] A fortified hill of an ancient Greek city, especially the Acropolis in Athens. (uh KROP uh lis)

acrosome [*acro, tip* + *-some, body*] A saclike structure at the head of a sperm cell that releases egg-penetrating enzymes which dissolve the protective layers of an egg cell, thus allowing the sperm to enter the egg. (AK ruh sohm')

acrostic [*acro, high & stic(h) {line of verse}*] A poem or arrangement of words in which the first, last, or certain other letters in each line form a word, phrase, or message. See telestich. (uh KRAW stik)

aerobatics [*aero, air & (acro)batics*] The skill of performing difficult aerial maneuvers in an aircraft. See acrobatics. (ehr' uh BAT iks)

aero   air

aerate [*aero, air* + *-ate*] 1.To expose to the air. 2.To charge or mix a liquid with a gas. 3.To supply with oxygen, as the blood through respiration. (EHR ayt)

aerial [*aero, air* + *-ial*] 1.Pertaining to, occurring in, or caused by air. 2.Living, growing, or occurring in the air or atmosphere rather than in soil or water. See terrestrial (def. 3) and aquatic. 3.Performed from or by aircraft. (EHR ee ul)

aeroballistics [*aero(dynamics) & ballistics*] The combined science of aerodynamics and ballistics that deals with the flight of missiles, bombs, and other projectiles in the atmosphere. See aerodynamics and ballistics. (ehr' oh buh LIS tiks)

aerobatics [*aero, air & (acro)batics*] The skill of performing difficult aerial maneuvers in an aircraft. See acrobatics. (ehr' uh BAT iks)

aerobe [*aero, air* + *bio, life*] A microorganism that requires free oxygen to live. Opposed to anaerobe. (EHR ohb)

aerobic [*aero, air* + *bio, life* + *-ic*] 1.Living only in the presence of air or free oxygen. Opposed to anaerobic. 2.Pertaining to aerobics. 3.Pertaining to or produced by aerobes. (ehr OH bik)

aerobics [*aero, air* + *bio, life* + *-ics, practice*] A system of vigorous exercises designed to improve the body's ability to take in and utilize oxygen. (ehr OH biks)

aerobiology [*aero, air* + *bio, life* + *-logy, study of*] The study of the dispersion of air-borne biological materials such as microbes, pollen, and pollutants. (ehr' oh beye OL uh jee)

aerodrome [*aero, air* + *-drome, course*] British variant of airdrome. Airport. (EHR uh drohm')

aerodynamics [*aero, air* + *dynam, power* + *-ics, study of*] The branch of dynamics dealing with the study of the forces exerted by the motion of air and other gases. See aeromechanics and aerostatics. (ehr' oh deye NAM iks)

aerodyne [*aero, air* + *dyn, power*] An aircraft that is heavier than air and gets its lift from aerodynamic motion, as a conventional airplane, helicopter, glider, etc. See aerodynamics and aerostat. (EHR uh deyen')

aeroembolism [*aero, air & embolism*] An embolism caused by air bubbles that may occur as a result of head, neck, or heart surgery, induced abortion, or severe decompression sickness. (ehr' oh EM buh liz' um)

aerography [*aero, air* + *-graphy, writing*] The descriptive study of the atmosphere and its phenomena. See aerology. (ehr OG ruh fee)

aerolite [*aero, air* + *-lite, stone*] A stony meteorite. See chondrite. (EHR uh leyet')

aerolith [*aero, air* + *lith, stone*] A stony meteorite. Same as aerolite. (EHR uh lith')

aerology [*aero, air* + *-logy, study of*] The branch of meteorology dealing with the study of air in the atmosphere, especially in the upper levels. See aerography. (ehr OL uh jee)

aeromechanics [*aero, air & mechanics*] The science dealing with the motion and equilibrium of air and other gases, including aerodynamics and aerostatics. See aerodynamics and aerostatics. (ehr' oh muh KAN iks)

aerometeorograph [*aero, air & meteorograph*] A meteorograph modified for use in an aircraft. (ehr' oh meet' ee OR uh graf')

aerometer [*aero, air* + *meter, to measure*] An instrument for measuring the weight and estimating the density of air and other gases. (ehr OM et er)

aeronautics [*aero, air* + *naut, sailor* + *-ics, science*] The science dealing with the design, construction, performance, and flight characteristics of aircraft. (ehr' uh NOT iks)

aeroneurosis [*aero, air* + *neur, nerve* + *-osis, abnormal condition*] A neurosis in aircraft pilots characterized by insomnia, mild depression, and various physical symptoms. (ehr' oh noo ROH sis)

aeronomy [*aero, air* + *-nomy, system of laws*] The science dealing with the study of the physics and chemistry of the upper atmosphere. (ehr ON uh mee)

aeropause [*aero, air & pause*] The outermost boundary between the earth's atmosphere and outer space, above which the air is too thin for conventional aircraft to fly. (EHR uh poz')

aerophagia [*aero, air* + *phag, to eat* + *-ia*] Abnormal swallowing of air. (ehr' uh FAY juh)

aerophobia [*aero, air* + *-phobia, fear*] Abnormal fear of air, especially of drafts. (ehr' uh FOH bee uh)

aerophore [*aero, air* + *-phore, to carry*] A device, used by firemen, pilots, etc., for carrying air to the lungs in case of oxygen shortage or on newborn infants to stimulate breathing. (EHR uh for')

aeroplane [*aero, air & plane*] British variant of airplane. (EHR uh playn')

aerosol [*aero, air & sol(ution)*] A liquid substance packaged with a gas under pressure and dispersed through a valve, as deodorant, hair spray, etc. (EHR uh sol')

aerospace [*aero, air & space*] 1.The earth's atmosphere and the space beyond it, especially the space in which spacecraft operate. 2.Pertaining to the science or technology of aviation. See hydrospace. (EHR oh spays')

aerosphere [*aero, air & sphere*] The atmosphere surrounding the earth. (EHR oh sfihr')

aerostat [*aero, air* + *stat, stationary*] An aircraft, as a balloon or airship, that gets its lift from one or more containers filled with a gas lighter than air rather than from aerodynamic motion. See aerodyne. (EHR oh stat')

aerostatics [*aero, air* + *stat, stationary* + *-ics, study of*] The branch of statics dealing with the study of the equilibrium of air and other gases and the equilibrium of solid bodies immersed in them. See aeromechanics and aerodynamics. (ehr' oh STAT iks)

aerothermodynamics [*aero, air + thermo, heat + dynam, energy + -ics, study of*] The branch of dynamics dealing with the study of the relationship between heat and mechanical energy in air and other gases. See thermodynamics. (ehr' oh thur' moh deye NAM iks)

anaerobe [*an-, without + aero, air + bio, life*] A microorganism that does not require free oxygen to live. Opposed to aerobe. (AN uh rohb')

anaerobic [*an-, without + aero, air + bio, life + -ic*] Living without air or free oxygen. Opposed to aerobic (def. 1). (an' uh ROH bik)

agog   leader, to lead

anagoge [*ana-, again + agog, to lead*] A mystical or spiritual interpretation of a word or words, especially of the Scriptures. (AN uh goh' jee)

demagog [*dem, people + agog, leader*] 1.A leader who obtains power by appealing to the popular prejudices and emotions of the people. 2.Originally, a popular leader of the people. Same as demagogue. (DEM uh gog')

demagogue [*dem, people + agog, leader*] 1.A leader who obtains power by appealing to the popular prejudices and emotions of the people. 2.Originally, a popular leader of the people. (DEM uh gog')

emmenagogue [*en-, into + men, menstruation + agog, to lead*] An agent that stimulates menstrual flow. (uh MEN uh gog')

hypnagogic [*hypn, sleep + agog, to lead + -ic*] Pertaining to or associated with the state of drowsiness preceding sleep. See hypnopompic. (hip' nuh GOJ ik)

mystagogue [*myst(ery) & agog, leader*] A person who initiates candidates into religious mysteries or a mystery cult. (MIS tuh gog')

pedagog [*ped, child + agog, leader*] A schoolteacher, especially one who instructs in a pedantic, dogmatic, and formal manner. Same as pedagogue. (PED uh gog')

pedagogics [*ped, child + agog, leader + -ics, science*] The science, art, or profession of teaching. Same as pedagogy. (ped' uh GOJ iks)

pedagogue [*ped, child + agog, leader*] A schoolteacher, especially one who instructs in a pedantic, dogmatic, and formal manner. (PED uh gog')

pedagogy [*ped, child + agog, leader + -y*] The science, art, or profession of teaching. See didactics and pedagogics. (PED uh goh' jee)

sialagogue [*sial, saliva + agog, to lead*] An agent that stimulates the flow of saliva. (seye AL uh gog')

synagog [*syn-, together + agog, to lead*] 1.A Jewish house of worship and religious study. 2.A Jewish assemblage for worship and religious study. (SIN uh gog')

synagogue [*syn-, together + agog, to lead*] 1.A Jewish house of worship and religious study. 2.A Jewish assemblage for worship and religious study. Same as synagog. (SIN uh gog')

agr/o, agri   crop production, field

agrarian [*agr, field + -arian*] Pertaining to the ownership, management, and cultivation of land. (uh GREHR ee un)

agribusiness [*agri, crop production & business*] Large-scale farming and related businesses, including the processing and distribution of farm commodities. (AG rih biz' nis)

agriculture [*agri, crop production & culture*] The art or science of crop production and livestock management. Farming. See aquaculture, hydroponics, and geoponics. (AG rih kul' chur)

agrobiology [*agro, crop production + bio, life + -logy, science*] The quantitative science of plant growth and nutrition, as related to soil control and crop yield. (ag' roh beye OL uh jee)

agrology [*agr, crop production + -ology, science*] The science of soils dealing especially with crop production. (uh GROL uh jee)

agronomics [*agro, crop production + nom, system of laws + -ics, science*] The science of soil management and crop production. Same as agronomy. (ag' ruh NOM iks)

agronomy [*agro, crop production + -nomy, system of laws*] The science of soil management and crop production. (uh GRON uh mee)

agrostology [*Grk > agrostis, grass + -ology, study of*] The branch of botany dealing with the study of grasses. (ag' ruh STOL uh jee)

alg/o   pain

algolagnia [*algo, pain + -lagnia, lust*] Sexual pleasure obtained from experiencing or inflicting pain, as in masochism or sadism. (al' guh LAG nee uh)

algometer [*algo, pain + meter, to measure*] An instrument for measuring the degree of sensitivity to pain resulting from a stimulus such as pressure. (al GOM et er)

algophobia [*algo, pain + -phobia, fear*] Abnormal fear of pain. (al' guh FOH bee uh)

analgesia [*an-, without + alg, pain + -ia*] Absence of sensibility to pain while in a fully conscious state. (an' l JEE zee uh)

analgesic [*an-, without + alg, pain + -ic*] A drug or remedy that relieves pain, as aspirin. (an' l JEE zik)

arthralgia [*arthr, joint + alg, pain + -ia*] Pain in a joint. (ahr THRAL juh)

cardialgia [*cardi, heart + alg, pain + -ia*] Pain in or near the heart. (kahr' dee AL juh)

causalgia [*caust, to burn + alg, pain + -ia*] A severe, constant burning pain, usually resulting from a peripheral nerve injury. (koz AL juh)

coxalgia [*Ltn > coxa, hip + alg, pain + -ia*] 1.Pain in the hip joint. 2.Disease of the hip joint. (koks AL juh)

metralgia [*metr, uterus + alg, pain + -ia*] Pain in the uterus. (mih TRAL juh)

myalgia [*my, muscle + alg, pain + -ia*] Pain in a muscle. (meye AL juh)

nephralgia [*nephr, kidney + alg, pain + -ia*] Pain in the kidneys. (neh FRAL juh)

neuralgia [*neur, nerve + alg, pain + -ia*] Intense pain along the course of one or more nerves. (noo RAL juh)

nostalgia [*Grk > nostos, return home + alg, pain + -ia*] 1.Pathological homesickness. 2.A painful longing for persons, things, conditions, or situations of the past. (nos TAL juh)

odontalgia [*odont, tooth + alg, pain + -ia*] Toothache. (oh' don TAL juh)

otalgia [*ot, ear* + *alg, pain* + *-ia*] Pain in the ear. Earache.
(oh TAL juh)

ambi-, amphi   both, on both sides, around

ambiance [*ambi-, around* + *-ance*] The special mood, character, or atmosphere surrounding a person, place, or thing. (AM bee ens)

ambidextrous [*ambi-, both* + *Ltn > dexter, skillful* + *-ous*] 1.Able to use both hands equally well. 2.Very skillful. Adroit. Facile. (am' bih DEKS trus)

ambience [*ambi-, around* + *-ence*] The special mood, character, or atmosphere surrounding a person, place, or thing. Same as ambiance. (AM bee ens)

ambient [*ambi-, around* + *-ent*] Surrounding. Encompassing. Enclosing. See circumambient, circumfluent, and circumjacent. (AM bee ent)

ambiguous [*ambi, both* + *ag, to drive* + *-ous*] 1.Having more than one possible meaning or interpretation. Equivocal. See equivocal, unequivocal, and univocal (def. 1). 2.Unclear. Uncertain. Doubtful.
(am BIG yoo us)

ambisexual [*ambi-, both & sexual*] Bisexual.
(am' bih SEK shoo ul)

ambit [*ambi-, around* + *-it*] 1.The circumference of something. 2.The boundary or scope of something.
(AM bit)

ambivalent [*ambi-, both* + *Ltn > valere, to be strong* + *-ent*] Having simultaneous, conflicting feelings toward someone or something. Undecided. Wavering.
(am BIV uh lent)

ambivert [*ambi-, both* + *vert, turn*] A person with personality characteristics of both an introvert and an extrovert. See introvert and extrovert. (AM bih vurt')

amphiarthrosis [*amphi-, on both sides* + *arthr, joint* + *-osis, action*] Any articulation permitting only slight motion of a joint, as that between the vertebrae. See diarthrosis and synarthrosis. (am' fee ahr THROH sis)

amphibian [*amphi-, both* + *bio, life* + *-an*] 1.Any of various cold-blooded vertebrate animals, such as frogs and salamanders, the larvae of which breathe by gills and the adults of which breathe by lungs. See semiaquatic (def. 2) and semiterrestrial. 2.A vehicle that can operate both on water and on land. See amphibious (def. 2). 3.An aircraft that can take off and land either on land or water. (am FIB ee un)

amphibiotic [*amphi-, both* + *bio, life* + *-tic*] Pertaining to organisms that live in water in the larval stage and on land in the adult stage. (am' fih beye OT ik)

amphibious [*amphi-, both* + *bio, life* + *-ous*] Literally, "living a double life." 1.Able to live both in water and on land. See semiaquatic (def. 2) and semiterrestrial. 2.Able to operate both in water and on land. See amphibian (def. 2). 3.Pertaining to military operations involving both naval vessels and ground troops.
(am FIB ee us)

amphibole [*amphi-, around* + *Grk > ballein, to throw*] Silicate minerals consisting of various combinations of sodium, magnesium, calcium, iron, and aluminum. So named from the numerous varieties. (AM fuh bohl')

amphibolite [*amphibol(e) & -ite, rock*] A metamorphic rock consisting mainly of amphibole. (am FIB uh leyet')

amphibology [*amphi-, both* + *log, discourse* + *-y*] Ambiguity of speech, especially from uncertain grammatical construction. (am' fih BOL uh jee)

amphibrach [*amphi-, on both sides* + *brachy, short*] A trisyllabic metrical foot consisting of a long syllable between two short syllables in quantitative meter, and a stressed syllable between two unstressed syllables in accentual meter. See amphimacer. (AM fuh brak')

amphictyony [*amphi-, around* + *Grk > ktizein, to dwell* + *-y*] In ancient Greece, a group of states united around a common religious center, especially at Delphi.
(am FIK tee uh nee)

amphimacer [*amphi-, on both sides* + *macro, long* + *-er*] A trisyllabic metrical foot consisting of a short syllable between two long syllables in quantitative meter, and an unstressed syllable between two stressed syllables in accentual meter. See amphibrach. (am FIM uh sur)

amphimixis [*amphi-, both* + *Grk > mixis, mixing*] True sexual reproduction by fusion of male and female gametes. See apomixis and parthenogenesis.
(am' fih MIK sis)

amphipod [*amphi-, both* + *pod, feet*] Any of a large order of crustaceans with legs for walking and legs for swimming, as beach fleas and sand hoppers.
(AM fuh pod')

amphiprostyle [*amphi-, on both sides & prostyle*] Having columns along both fronts, but none along either side. See amphistylar, peristyle, and prostyle.
(am' fih PROH steyel)

amphisbaena [*amphi-, on both sides* + *Grk > bainein, to go* + *-a*] In Greek mythology, a serpent with a head at both ends of its body. (am' fis BEE nuh)

amphistylar [*amphi-, both* + *styl, column* + *-ar*] Having columns along both fronts or along both sides. See amphiprostyle, peristyle, and prostyle.
(am' fih STEYE lur)

amphitheater [*amphi-, around & theater*] A round or oval building with rising tiers of seats and an arena at the center. (AM fuh thee' uh ter)

amphitheatre [*amphi-, around & theatre*] A round or oval building with rising tiers of seats and an arena at the center. Same as amphitheater. (AM fuh thee' uh ter)

amphithecium [*amphi-, around* + *Grk > theke, case* + *-ium*] The outer layer of cells in the sporangium of a moss or liverwort. See endothecium (def. 2).
(am' fih THEE shee um)

amphora [*amphi-, on both sides* + *phor, to carry* + *-a*] A jar with a handle on each side and a narrow neck, used by the ancient Greeks to carry oil or wine. (AM fur uh)

amphoteric [*amphi-, both* + *Grk > terikos*] Reacting as or having the properties of both an acid and a base.
(am' fuh TEHR ik)

circumambient [*circum-, around & ambient {surrounding}*] Surrounding. Encompassing. Enclosing. See ambient, circumfluent, and circumjacent. (sur' kum AM bee ent)

triphibian [*tri-, three & (am)phibian*] Able to operate or function in water, on land, or in the air. See amphibian.
(treye FIB ee un)

ana- up, back, again, against, throughout

anabaena [*ana-, up + Grk > bainein, to go + -a*] Any of various freshwater blue-green algae, often occurring in drinking water and causing a bad taste and odor. (an' uh BEE nuh)

Anabaptist [*ana-, again & bapt(ize) & -ist*] Any member of the radical movements of the 16th century Reformation who denied the validity of infant baptism, opposed military service, and advocated the separation of church and state. (an' uh BAP tist)

anabatic [*ana-, up + Grk > bainein, to go + -ic*] Pertaining to wind caused by upward flowing air. See katabatic. (an' uh BAT ik)

anabiosis [*ana-, again + bio, life + -sis*] Restoration to life after apparent death. (an' uh beye OH sis)

anabolism [*ana-, up & (meta)bolism*] The constructive metabolic process in organisms by which food is changed into complex body substance. Opposed to catabolism. See metabolism. (uh NAB uh liz' um)

anachronism [*ana-, back + chron, time + -ism*] A chronological error in which someone or something is represented as existing or occurring out of its proper place in time. (uh NAK ruh niz' um)

anaclisis [*ana-, against + clin, to lean + -sis*] A strong emotional dependence on others for protection and gratification. (an' uh KLEYE sis)

anacrusis [*ana-, back + Grk > krouein, to strike + -sis*] An unaccented syllable or syllables at the beginning of a line of verse, preceding the normal meter. (an' uh KROO sis)

anadiplosis [*ana-, again + diplo, double + -sis*] Rhetorical repetition of the last word or words of one clause, phrase, etc., at the beginning of the next, as "She gave her time; time was all she had to give." (an' uh dih PLOH sis)

anadromous [*ana-, up + -dromous, moving*] Migrating up a river from a sea to spawn. See catadromous and diadromous. (uh NAD ruh mus)

anaglyph [*ana-, throughout & glyph {relief carving}*] An embossed ornament carved in low relief. (AN uh glif')

anagoge [*ana-, again + agog, to lead*] A mystical or spiritual interpretation of a word or words, especially of the Scriptures. (AN uh goh' jee)

anagram [*ana-, again + gram, to write*] 1.A word or phrase formed by rearranging the letters of another word or phrase. 2.A game in which words are formed from a group of randomly chosen letters. See logogriph. (AN uh gram')

analects [*ana-, up + Grk > legein, to gather*] Selected literary excerpts or passages from the writings of one or more authors. (AN l ekts')

analogy [*ana-, again + log, word + -y*] 1.Similarity in certain aspects or features between things otherwise dissimilar. 2.Similarity. 3.Similarity in function between anatomical organs or parts of different origin and structure. (uh NAL uh jee)

analysis [*ana-, up + -lysis, decomposition*] 1.The separation of a material or intellectual whole into its elements for individual study. 2.A detailed examination of something. (uh NAL uh sis)

analytics [*analy(sis) & -ics, science*] The branch of science dealing with logical analysis. (an' l IT iks)

analyze [*ana-, up + -lyze, decomposition*] To separate into constituent parts or basic principles so as to study the nature of the whole. (AN l eyez')

anamnesis [*ana-, again + mne, memory + -sis*] 1.A recalling to memory of past events. Reminiscence. 2.The complete medical history of a patient. (an' am' NEE sis)

anamorphic [*ana-, again + morph, form + -ic*] Producing optical magnification that is different from each of two perpendicular directions. (an' uh MOR fik)

anapest [*ana-, back + Grk > paiein, to strike*] A metrical foot consisting of two short syllables followed by one long syllable, or two unstressed syllables followed by one stressed syllable. So named from its being the reverse of a dactyl. See dactyl (def. 2) and tribrach. (AN uh pest')

anaphase [*ana-, again & phase*] In mitosis, the phase after the metaphase during which the chromosomes split and the two sets of daughter chromosomes move to opposite poles of the spindle. See prophase, metaphase, and telophase. (AN uh fayz')

anaphora [*ana-, again + phor, to produce + -a*] 1.The deliberate repetition of a word or words at the beginning of successive phrases, clauses, sentences, or verses. See epistrophe. 2.The use of a word or words to avoid repetition of a word or words used previously in the same sentence, as "I know it and *so do you*" vs. "I know it and *you know it too*." (uh NAF uh ruh)

anaphylaxis [*ana-, again + Grk > phylaxis, protection*] Hypersensitivity to a substance resulting from a previous inoculation against the substance. (an' uh fuh LAK sis)

anaplasia [*ana-, back + plas, forming cells or tissue + -ia*] The reversion of mature cells to a less differentiated form, as in most malignant tissue. See cataplasia. (an' uh PLAY zhuh)

anaptyxis [*ana-, back + Grk > ptyssein, to fold + -is*] The insertion of a vowel in a word to aid in pronunciation, as in "thisaway." See epenthesis. (an' up TIK sis)

anastomosis [*ana-, again + stomat, mouth + -sis*] 1.Interconnection between branches, as of rivers, nerves, blood vessels, etc. 2.The surgical connection of separate or severed hollow or tubular structures to form a continuous channel. (uh nas' tuh MOH sis)

anastrophe [*ana-, back + Grk > strophe, turning*] Reversal of the normal order of words in a phrase or sentence for rhetorical effect. (uh NAS truh fee)

anathema [*ana-, up + the, to put + -ma*] 1.A formal ecclesiastical ban or curse often followed by excommunication. 2.A person or thing intensely disliked. (uh NATH uh muh)

anatomy [*ana-, up + -tomy, to cut*] 1.The structural makeup of a plant or animal or any of its parts. 2.Dissection of all or part of a plant or animal to study its parts. 3.The science dealing with the structure of plants and animals. (uh NAT uh mee)

anatropous [*ana-, back + trop, turning + -ous*] In the ovary of an angiosperm, having the ovule inverted so that the micropyle lies near the base of the stalk. See orthotropous and campylotropous. (uh NAT ruh pus)

cryptanalysis [*crypt, secret & analysis*] The science of analyzing and deciphering code and other secret writings. See cryptography. (krip' tuh NAL uh sis)

DICTIONARY

neuroanatomy [*neuro, nerve & anatomy*] The branch of neurology dealing with the study of the anatomy of the nervous system. (noor' oh uh NAT uh mee)

psychoanalysis [*psycho, mental process & analysis*] A method of analyzing mental processes and treating mental disorders. (seye' koh uh NAL uh sis)

cata-
down, completely, thoroughly, against, intensive, according to

acatalectic [*a-, without & catalectic*] Pertaining to a line of verse with the complete number of syllables in the last foot. See catalectic and hypercatalectic. (ay' kat l EK tik)

anticatalyst [*anti-, against & catalyst*] A substance that retards or inhibits a chemical reaction. See catalyst (def. 1). (an' tee KAT l ist)

autocatalysis [*auto-, self & catalysis*] Acceleration of a chemical reaction due to one or more of its products themselves acting as catalysts. (awt' oh kuh TAL uh sis)

biocatalyst [*bio, life & catalyst*] An agent, such as an enzyme, that activates or speeds up a biochemical reaction. See catalyst (def. 1). (beye' oh KAT l ist)

catabolism [*cata-, down & (meta)bolism*] The destructive metabolic process in organisms by which complex body substance is changed into energy and waste products of a simpler composition. Opposed to anabolism. See metabolism. (kuh TAB uh liz' um)

catabolite [*catabol(ism) & -ite*] A waste product resulting from the process of catabolism. (kuh TAB uh leyet')

catachresis [*cata-, against + Grk > chresthai, to use + -sis*] 1.The incorrect or strained use of a word or words, as for rhetorical effect. 2.The use of a forced and deliberate paradoxical figure of speech. (kat' uh KREE sis)

cataclysm [*cata-, down + Grk > klyzein, to wash*] 1.A devastating flood. Deluge. See cataract (def. 2). 2.Any violent upheaval or disaster occurring in nature, as an earthquake, volcano, etc. See catastrophe (def. 1). 3.Any violent political or social upheaval, as a revolution, war, etc. (KAT uh kliz' um)

catadromous [*cata-, down + -dromous, moving*] Migrating down a river to a sea to spawn. See anadromous and diadromous. (kuh TAD ruh mus)

catafalque [*cata-, down + Ltn > fala, wooden scaffold*] A wooden framework that supports the coffin during a funeral. (KAT uh falk')

catalectic [*cata-, down + Grk > legein, to stop + -ic*] Pertaining to a line of verse lacking part of the last foot. See acatalectic and hypercatalectic. (kat' l EK tik)

catalepsy [*cata-, down + -lepsy, seizure*] A trancelike condition that may occur in various physical or psychological disorders such as epilepsy, schizophrenia, etc., characterized by muscular rigidity and loss of voluntary motion. See catatonia. (KAT l ep' see)

catalog [*cata-, completely + log, word*] A systematic list of items such as names, titles, or articles, usually in alphabetical order. (KAT l og')

catalogue [*cata-, completely + log, word*] A systematic list of items such as names, titles, or articles, usually in alphabetical order. Same as catalog. (KAT l og')

catalyst [*cata-, intensive + -lysis, decomposition + -ist*] 1.A substance that changes and especially increases the rate of a chemical reaction without being changed in the process. See anticatalyst. 2.A person who precipitates an event or change without being affected by the consequences. (KAT l ist)

catamenia [*cata-, according to + men, month + -ia*] Menstruation. (kat' uh MEE nee uh)

cataplasia [*cata-, down + plas, forming cells or tissue + -ia*] The degenerative reversion of cells or tissue to an earlier, more embryonic stage. See anaplasia. (kat' uh PLAY zhuh)

catapult [*cata-, against + Grk > pallein, to hurl*] 1.An ancient military device for hurling large stones, arrows, etc. 2.A mechanism for launching aircraft, as from the deck of an aircraft carrier. (KAT uh pult')

cataract [*Grk > katarassein, to dash down*] 1.A very large waterfall. 2.A strong downpour. Deluge. See cataclysm (def. 1). 3.A disease of the eye characterized by a clouding of the lens or capsule, causing partial or total blindness. (KAT uh rakt')

catarrh [*cata-, down + rrhea, excessive flow*] Inflammation of a mucous membrane, especially of the nose and throat, accompanied by increased discharge of mucous. (kuh TAHR)

catarrhine [*cata-, down + rhin, nose*] Having a nose with nostrils close together and directed downward, as in Old World monkeys, higher apes, and man. See platyrrhine. (KAT uh reyen')

catastasis [*cata-, down + Grk > histanai, to stand + -sis*] The part of a play, following the epitasis and preceding the catastrophe, during which the action is at its height. See protasis (def. 2), epitasis, and catastrophe (def. 2). (kuh TAS tuh sis)

catastrophe [*cata-, down + Grk > strophe, turning*] 1.A sudden and widespread disaster. See cataclysm (def. 2). 2.The part of a play following the catastasis during which the plot is resolved. See protasis (def. 2), epitasis, and catastasis. (kuh TAS truh fee)

catatonia [*cata-, down + tono, tension + -ia*] A condition usually associated with schizophrenia that is characterized by muscle rigidity and stupor, often alternating with excessive motor activity. See catalepsy. (kat' uh TOH nee uh)

catechesis [*cata-, thoroughly + Grk > echein, sound + -sis*] Oral instruction, especially as given to catechumens. (kat' ih KEE sis)

catechetical [*cata-, thoroughly + Grk > echein, sound + -ical*] Pertaining to teaching by the method of questions and answers. (kat' ih KET ih kul)

catechize [*cata-, thoroughly + Grk > echein, sound + -ize*] 1.To teach by the method of questions and answers, especially in religious principles. 2.To question closely or excessively. (KAT ih keyez')

catechumen [*cata-, thoroughly + Grk > echein, sound + -men*] 1.A person being taught the fundamentals of Christianity. 2.A person being taught the fundamentals of any subject. (kat' ih KYOO mun)

category [*cata-, completely + Grk > agora, assembly + -y*] 1.A division or class in a system of classification. 2.Any of various basic classes into which all knowledge can be placed. (KAT ih gor' ee)

cathedra [*cata-, down* + *Grk > hedra, seat*] 1.The official chair or throne of a bishop in a cathedral. 2.The official chair of a position or office. (kuh THEE druh)

cathedral [*cata-, down* + *Grk > hedra, seat* + *-al*] The principal church of a diocese that contains the bishop's official throne. (kuh THEE drul)

catheter [*cata-, down* + *Grk > hienai, to send* + *-er*] A hollow tube inserted into a body passage or cavity to remove fluids, make examinations, etc. (KATH ut ur)

cathexis [*cata-, down* + *Grk > echein, to hold* + *-is*] The concentration of psychic energy on some person, object, or idea. (kuh THEK sis)

catholic [*cata-, completely* + *hol, whole* + *-ic*] Of broad or general scope, especially in sympathies, tastes, or interests. Universal. (KATH lik)

Catholic [*cata-, completely* + *hol, whole* + *-ic*] 1.Pertaining to the Roman Catholic Church. 2.A member of the Catholic Church. (KATH lik)

hypercatalectic [*hyper-, over* & *catalectic*] Pertaining to a line of verse with one or more additional syllables after the last complete foot. See acatalectic and catalectic. (heye' per kat' l EK tik)

katabatic [*cata-, down* + *Grk > bainein, to go* + *-ic*] Pertaining to wind caused by downward flowing air. See anabatic. (kat' uh BAT ik)

andr/o   man, male, stamen

androecium [*andr, stamen* + *Grk > oikos, house* + *-ium*] The aggregate of male reproductive organs in a flower. The stamen or stamens considered collectively. See gynoecium. (an DREE shee um)

androgen [*andro, male* + *gen, formation*] Any of the steroid hormones that promote male characteristics. (AN druh jen)

androgenous [*andro, male* + *gen, production* + *-ous*] Producing male offspring only. (an DROJ uh nus)

androgynous [*andro, male* + *gyn, female* + *-ous*] 1.Exhibiting both male and female sexual characteristics. Hermaphroditic. 2.Bearing both staminate and pistillate flowers on the same stalk or in the same cluster. See synoecious (def. 2). (an DROJ uh nus)

android [*andr, man* + *-oid, resembling*] 1.Having a form or shape resembling that of a human. 2.A robot with the appearance of a human. (AN droid)

androphobia [*andro, man* + *-phobia, fear*] Abnormal fear of men. (an' druh FOH bee uh)

androsterone [*andro, male* & *ster(ol)* & *-one*] A weak androgenic steroid found in both male and female urine. (an DROS tuh rohn')

diandrous [*di-, two* + *andr, stamen* + *-ous*] Having two stamens. (deye AN drus)

gynandromorph [*gyn, female* + *andro, male* + *morph, form*] An abnormal individual exhibiting a mixture of male and female characteristics. (jih NAN druh morf')

gynandrous [*gyn, female* + *andr, male* + *-ous*] Pertaining to flowers having the stamens united with the pistils, as in certain orchids. (jih NAN drus)

misandry [*mis, to hate* + *andr, man* + *-y*] Hatred of, or animosity toward, men. See misogyny. (MIS an' dree)

monandry [*mon-, one* + *andr, man* + *-y*] The custom or practice of having only one husband at a time. See monogyny, polygyny, and polyandry. (muh NAN dree)

philander [*phil, love* + *andr, man* + *-er*] (of a man) To engage in a love affair with no intention of marriage. (fih LAN der)

polyandry [*poly, many* + *andr, man* + *-y*] 1.The custom or practice of having more than one husband at a time. 2.Having many stamens in one flower. See polygyny, monogyny, and monandry. (POL ee an' dree)

gyn/o, gyne, gynec/o   woman, female

androgynous [*andro, male* + *gyn, female* + *-ous*] 1.Exhibiting both male and female sexual characteristics. Hermaphroditic. 2.Bearing both staminate and pistillate flowers on the same stalk or in the same cluster. See synoecious (def. 2). (an DROJ uh nus)

epigynous [*epi-, upon* + *gyn, female* + *-ous*] Having floral parts or organs attached to the top of the gynoecium, as a daisy. See perigynous and hypogynous. (ih PIJ uh nus)

gynandromorph [*gyn, female* + *andro, male* + *morph, form*] An abnormal individual exhibiting a mixture of male and female characteristics. (jih NAN druh morf')

gynandrous [*gyn, female* + *andr, male* + *-ous*] Pertaining to flowers having the stamens united with the pistils, as in certain orchids. (jih NAN drus)

gynarchy [*gyn, woman* + *arch, rule* + *-y*] Government by women or a woman. Same as gynecocracy. (JIN ahr' kee)

gynecocracy [*gyneco, woman* + *-cracy, government*] Government by women or a woman. (jin' uh KOK ruh see)

gynecoid [*gynec, woman* + *-oid, resembling*] Resembling or characteristic of a woman. (JIN ih koid')

gynecology [*gynec, woman* + *-ology, study of*] The branch of medical science dealing with the study of disorders and diseases peculiar to women, especially those of the reproductive system. See gyniatrics. (geye' nuh KOL uh jee)

gynecomastia [*gyneco, female* + *mast, breast* + *-ia*] Abnormal overdevelopment of the male breasts. (geye' nuh koh MAS tee uh)

gynecopathy [*gyneco, woman* + *-pathy, disease*] Any of several diseases peculiar to women. (jin' uh KOP uh thee)

gynephobia [*gyne, woman* + *-phobia, fear*] Abnormal fear of women. (jin' uh FOH bee uh)

gyniatrics [*gyn, woman* + *iatr, healing* + *-ics, study of*] The branch of medical science dealing with the study and treatment of diseases peculiar to women. See gynecology. (jin' ee AT riks)

gynoecium [*gyn, female* + *Grk > oikos, house* + *-ium*] The aggregate of female reproductive organs in a flower, consisting of one or more carpels. The pistil or pistils considered collectively. See androecium. (jih NEE shee um)

gynophore [*gyno, female* + *-phore, to bear*] The floral stalk that bears the gynoecium. (JIN uh for')

heterogynous [*hetero, different* + *gyn, female* + *-ous*] Having two forms of female, one nonreproductive and the other reproductive, as bees. (het' uh ROJ uh nus)

hologynic [*holo, whole* + *gyn, female* + *-ic*] Pertaining to hereditary traits transmitted directly through the female line. (hol' uh JIN ik)

gyn/o, gyne, gynec/o

hypogynous [*hypo-, below + gyn, female + -ous*] Having floral parts or organs arranged below and out of contact with the gynoecium, as a buttercup. See epigynous and perigynous. (heye POJ uh nus)

misogynist [*miso, to hate + gyn, woman + -ist*] One who hates women. (mih SOJ uh nist)

misogyny [*miso, to hate + gyn, woman + -y*] Hatred of, or animosity toward, women. See misandry and philogyny. (mih SOJ uh nee)

monogyny [*mono-, one + gyn, woman + -y*] The custom or practice of having only one wife at a time. See monandry, polygyny, and polyandry. (muh NOJ uh nee)

perigynous [*peri-, around + gyn, female + -ous*] Having floral parts or organs arranged around the edge of a cuplike receptacle containing the gynoecium, as a rose. See epigynous and hypogynous. (puh RIJ uh nus)

philogyny [*philo, love + gyn, woman + -y*] Love and admiration of women. See misogyny. (fih LOJ uh nee)

polygyny [*poly, many + gyn, woman + -y*] 1.The custom or practice of having more than one wife at a time. 2.Having many pistils in one flower. See polyandry, monogyny, and monandry. (puh LIJ uh nee)

trichogyne [*tricho, hair + gyne, female*] A hairlike projection from the end of the female sex organ in certain red and green algae, lichens, and some fungi, that receives the male gamete. (TRIK uh jeyen')

anthrop/o   man, human

anthropocentric [*anthropo, man + centr, center + -ic*] 1.Considering human beings as the central fact and ultimate aim of the universe. 2.Interpreting everything in the universe in terms of the values and experiences of human beings. (an' thruh puh SEN trik)

anthropogenesis [*anthropo, man + -genesis, origin*] The scientific study of man's origin. (an' thruh puh JEN uh sis)

anthropography [*anthropo, man + -graphy, writing*] The branch of anthropology dealing with the descriptive study of the distribution of mankind according to physical characteristics, customs, language, etc. See anthropology. (an' thruh POG ruh fee)

anthropoid [*anthrop, human + -oid, resembling*] 1.Resembling a human. 2.Resembling an ape. (AN thruh poid')

anthropology [*anthrop, man + -ology, study of*] The study of the origin, distribution, and development of man. See anthropography. (an' thruh POL uh jee)

anthropometry [*anthropo, human + -metry, science of measuring*] The scientific study of human anatomical and physiological measurements for the purpose of analysis, comparison, and classification. (an' thruh POM ih tree)

anthropomorphism [*anthropo, human + morph, form + -ism*] The ascription of human form or characteristics to nonhuman things such as gods or animals. (an' thruh puh MOR fiz' um)

anthropopathism [*anthropo, human + path, feeling + -ism*] The ascription of human emotions to a nonhuman object or being. (an' thruh POP uh thiz' um)

anthropophagy [*anthropo, human + phag, to eat + -y*] Cannibalism. (an' thruh POF uh jee)

anthroposophy [*anthropo, man + -sophy, wisdom*] A religious philosophy, established by Rudolf Steiner, that emphasizes the study of the nature of man and is similar to theosophy. (an' thruh POS uh fee)

lycanthrope [*Grk > lykos, wolf + anthrop, man*] A werewolf. (LEYE kun throhp')

lycanthropy [*Grk > lykos, wolf + anthrop, man + -y*] 1.A mental disorder in which the patient believes he is a wolf. 2.The mythical belief in the ability to transform oneself into a wolf. (leye KAN thruh pee)

misanthrope [*mis, to hate + anthrop, man*] One who hates or distrusts mankind. (MIS un throhp')

misanthropy [*mis, to hate + anthrop, man + -y*] Hatred or distrust of mankind. (mis AN thruh pee)

paleoanthropic [*paleo, ancient + anthrop, man + -ic*] Pertaining to ancient forms of humans. (pay' lee oh' an THROP ik)

paleoanthropology [*paleo, ancient + anthrop, man + -ology, study of*] The branch of anthropology dealing with the study of prehistoric man prior to homo sapiens. (pay' lee oh an' thruh POL uh jee)

philanthropist [*phil, love + anthrop, man + -ist*] A lover of mankind and active promoter of goodwill. (fih LAN thruh pist)

philanthropy [*phil, love + anthrop, man + -y*] A love of and desire to help mankind, especially by doing good deeds. (fih LAN thruh pee)

Pithecanthropus [*Grk > pithekos, ape + anthrop, man + -us*] An extinct genus of humanoid primates whose classification was based on fossil remains found in Java, but are now classified in the extinct species Homo erectus. Java man. (pith' ih KAN thruh pus)

Sinanthropus [*Sino, Chinese + anthrop, man + -us*] An extinct genus of humanoid primates whose classification was based on fossil remains found near Peking, China, but are now classified in the extinct species Homo erectus. Peking man. (seye NAN thruh pus)

therianthropic [*Grk > therion, beast + anthrop, man + -ic*] Worshiping beings that are in a combined animal and human form. (thihr' ee an THROP ik)

zoanthropy [*zo, animal + anthrop, man + -y*] A form of mental disorder in which the patient believes he is an animal. (zoh AN thruh pee)

ante-   before

ancestry [*ante-, before + cede, to go + -ry*] 1.All past generations. 2.All the individuals in a person's line of descent. See posterity. (AN ses' tree)

ante meridiem [*ante-, before & Ltn > meridies, noon*] Before noon. Abbreviated A.M. or a.m. See post meridiem. (AN tee muh RID ee um)

antebellum [*ante-, before + bell, war + -um*] Occurring or existing before a war, specifically before the American Civil War. See postbellum. (an' tee BEL um)

antecede [*ante-, before + cede, to go*] To go before in rank, order, or time. Precede. See precede. (an' tuh SEED)

antecedent [*ante-, before + cede, to go + -ent*] 1.A word, phrase, or clause referred to by a relative or personal pronoun. 2.A preceding event, condition, or cause. (an' tuh SEED nt)

antecessor [*ante-, before + cess, to go + -or*] One who goes before. Predecessor. (an' tuh SES ur)

antechamber [*ante-, before & chamber*] A room leading into a larger or more important room. Same as anteroom. (AN tee chaym' ber)

antechoir [*ante-, before & choir*] A place reserved in front of the choir for the choir members and clergy. (AN tee kweyer')

antedate [*ante-, before & date*] 1.To date with a date that is earlier than the actual date, as on a document or check. Predate. 2.To precede in time. Opposed to postdate. (AN tih dayt')

antediluvian [*ante-, before + Ltn > diluvium, great flood*] 1.Occurring or existing before the time of the Biblical Flood. 2.Very old. Outdated. Old fashioned. See postdiluvian. (an' tee duh LOO vee un)

antemeridian [*ante-, before + Ltn > meridies, noon*] Occurring before noon. See postmeridian. (an' tee muh RID ee un)

antemortem [*ante-, before + mort, death + -em*] Occurring before death. See postmortem (def. 1). (an' tee MORT um)

antenatal [*ante-, before + nat, birth + -al*] Existing or occurring before birth. Same as prenatal. (an' tee NAYT l)

antependium [*ante-, before + Ltn > pendere, to hang + -ium*] A decorative veil for the front of an alter. (an' tee PEN dee um)

antepenult [*ante-, before + Ltn > paene, almost + Ltn > ultimus, last*] The third to the last syllable in a word. See penult, penultimate, and antepenultimate. (an' tee PEE nult')

antepenultimate [*ante-, before + Ltn > paene, almost + Ltn > ultimus, last + -ate*] The third to the last item in a series. See penult, penultimate, and antepenult. (an' tee pih NUL tuh mut)

anterior [*ante-, before + -er + -ior*] 1.Placed or located on or near the front. 2.Coming before in order or time. Previous. Opposed to posterior. (an TIHR ee ur)

anteroom [*ante-, before & room*] A room leading into a larger or more important room. (AN tee room')

post-   after, behind

ex post facto [*Ltn > ex post facto, from something done afterward*] Enacted or taking effect after the fact. Retroactive. See retroactive. (EKS pohst FAK toh)

post meridiem [*post-, after & Ltn > meridies, noon*] After noon. Abbreviated P.M. or p.m. See ante meridiem. (POHST muh RID ee um)

postaxial [*post-, behind + ax, axis + -ial*] Pertaining to or located behind an axis of the body, especially the medial aspect of the upper limb and the lateral aspect of the lower limb. (pohst AK see ul)

postbellum [*post-, after + bell, war + -um*] Occurring or existing after a war, specifically after the American Civil War. See antebellum. (pohst BEL um)

postdate [*post-, after & date*] 1.To date with a date that is later than the actual date, as on a document or check. 2.To follow in time. Opposed to antedate. (pohst DAYT)

postdiluvian [*post-, after + Ltn > diluvium, great flood*] Occurring or existing after the time of the Biblical Flood. See antediluvian (def. 1). (pohst' duh LOO vee un)

posterior [*post-, after + -er + -ior*] 1.Placed or located at or near the back. 2.Coming after in order or time. Subsequent. Opposed to anterior. (pos TIHR ee ur)

posterity [*post-, after + -er + -ity*] 1.All future generations. 2.All the offspring of one person. See ancestry. (pos TEHR ih tee)

postgraduate [*post-, after & graduate*] Pertaining to advanced study pursued after graduation from college or high school. (pohst' GRAJ oo it)

posthumous [*post-, after + Ltn > humus, earth + -ous*] 1.Arising, occurring, or continuing after a person's death. 2.Born after the death of the father. 3.Published after the death of the author. (POS choo mus)

posthypnotic [*post-, after + hypn, sleep + -otic*] 1.Occurring after hypnosis. 2.Pertaining to a suggestion given during hypnosis and intended for execution after awakening. (pohst' hip NOT ik)

postimpressionism [*post-, after & impressionism*] A French theory and technique of painting in the late 19th century that rejected the objectivity of impressionism and sought to use a less formal and precise representation of color, form, etc. (pohst' im PRESH uh niz' um)

postlude [*post-, after + lud, to play*] 1.A concluding piece of music, especially an organ voluntary at the end of a church service. 2.A closing phase. See prelude and interlude. (POHST lood)

postmeridian [*post-, after + Ltn > meridies, noon*] Occurring after noon. See antemeridian. (pohst' muh RID ee un)

postmillennial [*post-, after + mill, thousand + enn, years + -ial*] Occurring or existing after the millennium. See premillennial. (pohst' mih LEN ee ul)

postmortem [*post-, after + mort, death + -em*] 1.Occurring after death. See antemortem. 2.Autopsy. 3.Occurring after an event, as a game or political election. (pohst MORT um)

postnasal [*post-, behind & nasal*] Occurring or located behind the nasal cavity. (pohst NAY zul)

postnatal [*post-, after + nat, birth + -al*] Existing or occurring after birth. See prenatal, neonatal, and perinatal. (pohst NAYT l)

postnuptial [*post-, after + Ltn > nuptiae, wedding + -al*] Done or occurring after marriage. See prenuptial. (pohst NUP shul)

postpartum [*post-, after + Ltn > partum, birth*] Pertaining to or occurring after childbirth. See postnatal. (pohst PAHR tum)

postpone [*post-, after + pon, to put*] To change to a future time. Defer. (pohst POHN)

postprandial [*post-, after + Ltn > prandium, a meal + -al*] After a meal, especially dinner. (pohst PRAN dee ul)

postscript [*post-, after + script, to write*] A paragraph or message appended below the signature in a letter or at the end of a book, document, etc., as an afterthought or to give supplementary information. Abbreviated P.S. (POHST skript)

postvocalic [*post-, after + voc, voice + -al + -ic*] Pertaining to a consonant or other linguistic element that occurs immediately after a vowel. See vocalic, prevocalic, and intervocalic. (pohst' voh KAL ik)

preposterous [*pre-, before + post-, after + -er + -ous*] Literally, "with the back part in front." Contrary to reason, nature, or common sense. Absurd. (prih POS ter us)

pro-
before, forward, forth, in place of, in addition to

amphiprostyle [*amphi-, on both sides & prostyle*] Having columns along both fronts ,but none along either side . See amphistylar, peristyle, and prostyle.
(am' fih PROH steyel)

geometric progression [*geometric & pro-, forward + gress, to step + -ion*] A sequence of terms , as 2, 4, 8, 16, 32 or 1, 1/2, 1/4, 1/8, 1/16,in which any two adjacent terms have the same ratio . (jee' uh MET rik pruh GRESH un)

improvise [*im-, not + pro-, before + vis, to see*] 1.To compose , sing, or recite without preparation . 2.To make or invent from readily available materials .
(IM proh veyez')

philoprogenitive [*philo, love & progenitive*] 1Loving one's offspring . 2Producing many offspring . See progenitive and polytocous. (fil' oh proh JEN ih tiv)

pro bono [*Ltn > for the good*] Provided free of charge , especially for the public good. (proh BOH noh)

pro rata [*Ltn > according to the calculated portion*] Proportionately . In proportion. (proh RAYT uh)

proceed [*pro-, forward + ceed, to go*] 1.To go forward or onward, especially after a pause or interruption. Advance . 2.To go on or act in an orderly manner .
(proh SEED)

procephalic [*pro-, forward + cephal, head + -ic*] Pertaining to the anterior portion of the head . (proh' suh FAL ik)

proclaim [*pro-, before + Ltn > clamare, to call out*] To announce officially or publicly. Declare. See promulgate (def. 1) and enunciate (def. 2).
(proh KLAYM)

proclivity [*pro-, forward + clin, slope + -ity*] A natural or habitual inclination or tendency. Predisposition . Propensity. See propensity. (proh KLIV ih tee)

procrastinate [*pro-, forward + Ltn > cras, tomorrow + -ate*] To put off doing something until a later time , especially habitually. (proh KRAS tuh nayt')

procreate [*pro-, before & create*] 1.To produce offspring . Reproduce . See propagate (def. 1). 2.To produce . Beget . (PROH kree ayt')

procumbent [*pro-, forward + Ltn > cubare, lie down + -ent*] 1Lying face down . Prone. Prostrate. 2Trailing along the ground , but not putting down roots, as certain vines and trailing plants. (proh KUM bent)

procure [*pro-, before + Ltn > cura, care*] 1.To obtain by special effect or means. 2.To bring about . Cause . Effect. (proh KYOOR)

prodigal [*pro-, forward + ag, to drive + -al*] 1Carelessly or recklessly extravagant . Wasteful . See profligate (def. 2). 2Abundant . Lavish . Copious . Profuse. See profuse.
(PROD ih gul)

prodrome [*pro-, before + -drome, to run*] An early warning symptom indicating the onset of a disease or condition. (PROH drohm)

produce [*pro-, forward + duc, to lead*] To bring forward or into existence . Yield. Bear. (pruh DOOS)

proem [*pro-, before + Grk > oime, song*] An introductory comment or statement , as in a book or speech. Preface . See prolegomenon. (PRO em)

profess [*pro-, forth + Ltn > fateri, confess*] 1.To declare openly . Affirm . Avow. 2Pretend . (pruh FES)

proffer [*pro-, forth + French > affrir, to offer*] An offer or proposal. (PROF ur)

proficient [*pro-, forward + fic, to make + -ient*] Highly skilled , qualified, or capable. Competent . Adept. Expert. (pruh FISH ent)

profligate [*pro-, forward + Ltn > fligere, to dash + -ate*] 1Morally corrupt . 2Extremely wasteful . See prodigal (def. 1). (PROF lih gayt')

profound [*pro-, forward + Ltn > fundus, bottom*] 1.Very deep . 2.Very deeply felt . 3.Having or showing great knowledge and understanding . (proh FOUND)

profuse [*pro-, forth + fus, pour*] 1.Very or excessively generous . 2.Given or done freely and abundantly. 3Plentiful . Abundant . Copious . See prodigal.
(pruh FYOOS)

progenitive [*pro-, forward + gen, birth + -itive*] Capable of producing offspring . Reproductive. See philoprogenitive (def. 2) and polytocous.
(proh JEN ih tiv)

progenitor [*pro-, before + gen, birth + -itor*] 1.A direct ancestor in a line of descent. 2Predecessor or originator. (proh JEN ih tur)

progeny [*pro-, forward + gen, birth + -y*] Offspring . Descendants. Children. (PROJ uh nee)

prognathous [*pro-, forward + gnath, jaw + -ous*] Having the jaws projecting forward beyond the upper part of the face. See orthognathous. (PROG nuh thus)

prognosis [*pro-, before + gnos, knowledge + -is*] A prediction of the probable cause , course, and result of a disease . (prog NOH sis)

prognostic [*pro-, before + gnos, knowledge + -tic*] 1.A sign , omen, or other indication of things to come . 2.A prediction or forecast. (prog NOS tik)

prognosticate [*pro-, before + gnos, knowledge + -tic + -ate*] To predict using present indications as a guide.
(prog NOS tih kayt')

progress [*pro-, forward + gress, to go*] 1.Gradual improvement . (PROG res {noun}) 2.A moving forward toward a specific goal or more advanced stage.
(pruh GRES {verb})

progression [*pro-, forward + gress, to step + -ion*] 1Forward movement . 2.A sequence of numbers with a constant relation between each number and the one preceding it. (pruh GRESH un)

project [*pro-, forward + ject, to throw*] To throw or impel forward , outward, or upward. See protrude and protuberant. (pruh JEKT)

projectile [*pro-, forward + ject, to throw + -ile*] An object , such as a bullet, that is fired, thrown , or otherwise projected forward . (pruh JEKT ul)

prokaryote [*pro-, before + kary, nucleus + -ote*] An organism whose genetic material is not contained in a membrane-bound nucleus , as bacteria and blue-green algae. See eukaryote. (proh KEHR ee oht')

prolate [*pro-, forward + Ltn > ferre, to carry*] Lengthened at the poles , as a spheroid formed by revolving an ellipse around its longer axis. Opposed to oblate. (PROH layt)

prolegomenon [*pro-, before + Grk > legein, to say*] Introductory comments or remarks , especially when formal or critical. Preface . See proem.
(proh' lih GOM un non')

prolepsis [*pro-, before + Grk > lambanein, to seize + -sis*] 1.The anticipation and answering in advance of opposing arguments or objections. 2.The representation of something in the future as existing or occurring previously or presently. (proh LEP sis)

prolix [*pro-, forth + Ltn > liquere, to flow*] Very long and wordy . Verbose. Tedious. See verbose, diffuse (def. 2), and verbalize (def. 3). (proh LIKS)

prolocutor [*pro-, before + locu, to speak + -tor*] 1.A presiding officer or chairman of an assembly . 2.Spokesperson . (proh LOK yuh tur)

prologue [*pro-, before + log, discourse*] 1.An introduction to a discourse , poem, play, etc. 2.An introductory event , proceeding, etc. (PROH log)

prolusion [*pro-, before + lus, to play + -ion*] 1.An introductory essay or article. 2.A preliminary exercise or attempt . (proh LOO zhun)

prominent [*pro-, forward + Ltn > minere, project + -ent*] 1 Projecting beyond the surface . 2 Easily noticed . Conspicuous. See conspicuous (def. 1). 3 Well-known . Distinguished . Eminent. See eminent (def. 1). (PROM uh nent)

promiscuous [*pro-, forth + Ltn > miscere, mix + -ous*] 1 Composed of mixed and indiscriminate parts , things, or individuals . 2.Having frequent and indiscriminate sexual relations . 3 Casual . Irregular. (pruh MIS kyoo us)

promulgate [*pro-, forth + Ltn > vulgare, publish + -ate*] 1.To announce officially and formally . Proclaim. See proclaim and enunciate (def .2). 2.To put into effect by formal proclamation . 3.To make widespread . Disseminate . See propagate (def. 2). (PROM ul gayt')

pronephros [*pro-, before + nephr, kidney + -os*] One of the three embryonic excretory organ s of vertebrates that disappears during the embryonic development of higher vertebrates and becomes the adult kidney in certain lower fishes . See mesonephros and metanephros. (proh NEF ros)

pronominal [*pro-, in place of + nomin, noun + -al*] Pertaining to or functioning as a pronoun . See pronoun. (proh NOM uh nul)

pronoun [*pro-, in place of & noun*] A word used in place of a noun . See pronominal. (PROH noun)

propaedeutic [*pro-, before + Grk > paideia, education + -ic*] Pertaining to or having the nature of preliminary instruction . (proh' pih DOO tik)

propagate [*pro-, forward + Ltn > pangere, to fasten + -ate*] 1.To produce offspring .Breed . Multiply. See procreate (def. 1). 2.To spread to a larger number or a broader area.Disseminate . See promulgate (def. 3). (PROP uh gayt')

propel [*pro-, forward + pel, to drive*] To cause to move forward or onward. (pruh PEL)

propensity [*pro-, forward + Ltn > pendere, to hang + -ity*] A natural inclination or tendency.Bent . See proclivity. (pruh PEN sih tee)

prophase [*pro-, before & phase*] In mitosis ,the first phase during which the spindle and chromosomes form and the nuclear membrane disappears. See metaphase, anaphase, and telophase. (PROH fayz)

prophet [*pro-, before + Grk > phanai, to speak + -et*] 1.A person who speaks for God or a god. 2.A person who attempts to predict the future . 3.A spokesperson for a cause , movement, etc. (PROF it)

prophylactic [*pro-, before + Grk > phylax, guard + -tic*] 1 Protective or preventative, especially against disease . 2.A condom . (proh' fuh LAK tik)

propitiate [*pro-, forward + Ltn > petere, to seek + -ate*] To gain or regain the goodwill or favor of .Conciliate . Appease . (proh PISH ee ayt')

propitious [*pro-, forward + Ltn > petere, to seek + -ious*] 1 Favorable .Auspicious . See auspicious. 2 Favorably inclined .Gracious . (proh PISH us)

proponent [*pro-, forth + pon, to put + -ent*] 1.A person who supports something .Advocate . See advocate (def. 2). 2.A person who presents a proposal or proposition. (pruh POH nent)

propound [*pro-, forward + pon, to put*] To put forward for consideration .Propose . (proh POUND)

prorogue [*pro-, before + rog, to ask*] To discontinue a session of a legislature or parliament. (proh ROHG)

proscribe [*pro-, before + scrib, to write*] 1.To condemn as harmful or dangerous.Prohibit . 2.To forbid as unlawful.Outlaw . (proh SKREYEB)

prosector [*pro-, before + sect, to cut + -or*] A person who dissects cadavers in preparation for anatomical demonstrations . (proh SEK tur)

prosecute [*pro-, forth + secut, follow*] 1.To pursue . Follow up. 2.To bring legal action against . (PROS ih kyoot')

prospect [*pro-, forward + spect, to look*] 1.The act of looking forward .Anticipation . 2.A possible candidate or customer . 3.To explore , as for gold or other mineral deposits. (PROS pekt)

prospective [*pro-, forward + spect, to look + -ive*] 1.Pertaining to or in the future . 2 Likely to occur or become.Potential . Expected. (pruh SPEK tiv)

prospectus [*pro-, forward + spect, to look + -us*] A formal document describing a proposed commercial enterprise, literary work, or other project . (pruh SPEK tus)

prostyle [*pro-, before + styl, column*] Having a row of columns along the front only. See amphistylar, amphiprostyle, and peristyle. (PROH steyel)

protasis [*pro-, before + Grk > teinein, to stretch + -sis*] 1.The clause expressing the condition in a conditional sentence . Opposed to apodosis. 2.The first part of a play during which the characters are introduced . See epitasis, catastasis, and catastrophe (def. 2). (PROT uh sis)

prothesis [*pro-, in addition to + the, to put + -sis*] The addition of a letter, syllable, or phoneme to the beginning of a word to make it easier to pronounce or to make a new word. (PROTH uh sis)

prothorax [*pro-, before & thorax*] The anterior segment of the three thoracic segments of an insect , bearing the first pair of legs. See mesothorax and metathorax. (proh THOR aks')

protract [*pro-, forward + tract, draw*] To draw out or extend in time or space .Prolong .Lengthen . (proh TRAKT)

protrude [*pro-, forward + Ltn > trudere, thrust*] To stick out . Project . See project and protuberant. (proh TROOD)

protuberant [*pro-, forward + Ltn > tuber, swelling + -ant*] Sticking out .Bulging . Protruding. See project and protrude. (proh TOO ber unt)

proverb [*pro-, before + verb, word*] A short , popular saying that expresses a well-known truth or useful thought, usually about character or conduct.Adage . Maxim. See aphorism, apothegm, and gnome. (PROV urb)

proverbial [*pro-, before + verb, word + -ial*] 1.Pertaining to, resembling, or having the nature of a proverb . 2 Well-known and commonly spoken of.Notorious . 3 Expressed in a proverb . (pruh VUR bee ul)

pro-

provident [*pro-, before + Ltn > videre, see + -ent*]
1. Providing and preparing for the future. Prudent.
2. Thrifty. Frugal. (PROV ih dent)

proviso [*pro-, before + Ltn > videre, see*] 1. A clause in a legal document that specifies some condition. 2. A condition or stipulation. (proh VEYE zoh)

provitamin [*pro-, before & vitamin*] A precursor of a vitamin that an organism can convert into a vitamin, as carotene which is converted to vitamin A. (proh VEYET uh min)

provoke [*pro-, forth + vok, to call*] To incite to some action, feeling, or desire. Excite. Cause. (pruh VOHK)

provost [*pro-, before + pon, to put*] 1. An official in charge of an institution. 2. A high-ranking official in some colleges and universities. (PROH vohst)

anth/o flower

amaranth [*a-, not + Grk > marainein, to fade away + anth, flower*] 1. A legendary flower that never fades or dies.
2. Any plant of the genus Amaranthus, some of which are grown for their flowers and colored leaves.
(AM uh ranth')

anther [*anth, flower + -er*] The pollen-bearing part of the stamen of a flower, usually borne at the end of a stalk.
(AN ther)

antheridium [*anther & -idium*] The male reproductive organ of ferns, mosses, fungi, and algae. See archegonium. (an' thuh RID ee um)

anthesis [*anth, flower + -esis*] The blooming stage of a flower. (an THEE sis)

anthocyanin [*antho, flower + cyan, blue + -in*] A water-soluble, blue to red pigment found in plants, some insects, and especially flowers. (an' thuh SEYE uh nin)

anthodium [*anth, flower + -ode, like + -ium*] A flower head of composite plants, as in daisies, dandelions, or asters. (an THOH dee um)

anthology [*antho, flower + Grk > logia, collection + -y*] A collection of selected writings such as poems, short stories, or plays. (an THOL uh jee)

anthophore [*antho, flower + -phore, to bear*] A stalk between the calyx and corolla of certain flowers that supports the floral parts. (AN thuh for')

anthozoan [*antho, flower + zo, animal + -an*] Any of the marine organisms in the class Anthozoa with no medusoid stage and a dominant polyp stage, including the soft, stony, and horny corals, the sea pens, and the sea anemones. So named from their resemblance to flowers. (an' thuh ZOH un)

chrysanthemum [*chrys, yellow + anth, flower*] Any of a genus of plants of the composite family, commonly referred to as mums, that bear flowers in various colors, most commonly yellow, white, or red.
(krih SAN thuh mum)

dianthus [*Grk > Dios of Zeus + anth, flower + -us*] Any of a genus of flowering plants of the pink family, as the sweet william or carnation. (deye AN thus)

helianthus [*heli, sun + anth, flower + -us*] Any of a genus of plants including the sunflowers. (hee' lee AN thus)

hydranth [*hydr, water + anth, flower*] Any of the nutritive polyps in a hydroid colony that typically bear tentacles and a mouth. So named from their resemblance to a flower. (HEYE dranth)

hypanthium [*hyp-, under + anth, flower + -ium*] An expanded floral receptacle that bears the sepals, petals, and stamens. (heye PAN thee um)

monanthous [*mon-, one + anth, flower + -ous*] Bearing only one flower, as certain plants. (muh NAN thus)

perianth [*peri-, around + anth, flower*] The external envelope of a flower, consisting of the calyx or corolla or both. (PEHR ee anth')

polyanthus [*poly, many + anth, flower + -us*] 1. Any of a variety of primroses bearing multi-flowered umbels.
2. A narcissus bearing clusters of fragrant yellow or white flowers. (pol' ee AN thus)

flor, flori flower

effloresce [*ef-, out + flor, flower + -esce*] 1. To bloom. 2. To become a powder as a result of loss of water of crystallization. 3. To become covered with crust as a result of evaporation or chemical change. (ef' luh RES)

efflorescence [*ef-, out + flor, flower + -escence*] 1. The period or state of flowering. See florescence and inflorescence (def. 3). 2. The process of unfolding or developing. (ef' luh RES ens)

flora [*flor, flower + -a*] All the plant life of a particular region or period. See fauna and biota. (FLOR uh)

Flora [*flor, flower + -a*] In Roman mythology, the goddess of flowers. (FLOR uh)

floral [*flor, flower + -al*] Pertaining to, consisting of, or resembling flowers or flora. (FLOR ul)

florescence [*flor, flower + -escence*] The act, period, or state of blooming. See efflorescence (def. 1) and inflorescence (def. 3). (floh RES ens)

floret [*flor, flower + -et, diminutive*] A small flower, especially one of the small disk or ray flowers forming the head of a composite plant. (FLOR it)

floriated [*flori, flower + -ated*] Having floral decorations or designs. (FLOR ee ay' tid)

floribunda [*flori, flower + -bunda*] Any of a class of hybrid roses bearing numerous large flowers and characterized by a long blooming period.
(flor' uh BUN duh)

floriculture [*flori, flower & culture*] The cultivation of flowers and ornamental plants. (FLOR uh kul' chur)

florid [*flor, flower + -id*] 1. Flushed with a red or pink color. Ruddy. 2. Having an excessively flowery and showy style. Ornate. (FLOR id)

Florida [*Spanish > florida, land of flowers*] A state located in the southeastern United States between the Gulf of Mexico and the Atlantic Ocean. (FLOR ih duh)

floriferous [*flori, flower + fer, to bear + -ous*] Bearing flowers. (flor IF ur us)

florigen [*flori, flower + gen, to produce*] A plant hormone produced in the leaves that stimulates buds to flower.
(FLOR uh jen)

florin [*flor, flower + -in*] 1. A gold coin of Florence, Italy, issued in 1252. So named because it was originally stamped with the figure of a lily. 2. A British coin worth two shillings. 3. Any of various gold and silver coins issued in Europe, similar to the Florentine florin. (FLOR in)

florist [*flor, flower + -ist*] A grower and seller of flowers and ornamental plants. (FLOR ist)

floristics [*flor, flower* + *-ist* + *-ics, study of*] The branch of botany dealing with the study of the number and species of plants in a particular region. See flora. (flor IS tiks)

inflorescence [*in-, on* + *flor, flower* + *-escence*] 1.The arrangement of flowers on a plant. 2.A flower cluster. 3.Unfolding of blossoms. Blooming. See florescence and efflorescence (def. 1). (in' fluh RES ens)

multiflora rose [*multi-, many* + *flor, flower* + *-a* & *rose*] A vigorous thorny rose with dense clusters of small flowers, often used for hedges. (MUL tuh flor' uh rohz)

tubuliflorous [*tubul(ar)* & *flor, flower* + *-ous*] Having florets or flowers with tubular corollas, as some composite plants. (too' byuh luh FLOR us)

apo-   away, from, off, separate

aphaeresis [*apo-, off* + *Grk > hairein, to take* + *-sis*] The omission of one or more letters or sounds from the beginning of a word. Same as apheresis. (uh FEHR uh sis)

aphelion [*apo-, away* + *heli, sun* + *-on*] The point in a planet's orbit that is farthest from the sun. See perihelion. (uh FEE lee un)

apheresis [*apo-, off* + *Grk > hairein, to take* + *-sis*] The omission of one or more letters or sounds from the beginning of a word. See syncope (def. 1) and apocope. (uh FEHR uh sis)

aphesis [*apo-, away* + *Grk > hienai, to send* + *-sis*] A form of apheresis consisting of the gradual omission of an unstressed vowel at the beginning of a word. See apheresis. (AF uh sis)

aphorism [*apo-, from* + *Grk > horizein, to separate* + *-ism*] A short statement of a general truth or shrewd observation. Maxim. See apothegm, gnome, and proverb. (AF uh riz' um)

apocalypse [*apo-, from* + *Grk > kryptein, cover*] A prophetic revelation or disclosure. (uh POK uh lips')

apocarpous [*apo-, away* & *carp(el)* & *-ous*] Having individual carpels that are distinctly separate. See syncarpous. (ap' uh KAHR pus)

apochromatic [*apo-, away* + *chromat, color* + *-ic*] Pertaining to a lens with no chromatic or spherical aberration. (ap' uh kroh MAT ik)

apocope [*apo-, off* + *Grk > koptein, to cut*] The omission of one or more letters or sounds from the end of a word. See apheresis and syncope (def. 1). (uh POK uh pee)

apocrine [*apo-, off* + *Grk > krinein, to separate*] Pertaining to glands of the human body in which part of the secreting cell's cytoplasm is lost along with the secretion, as the large sweat glands in the armpit and anal areas that produce strong odor. See eccrine. (AP uh krin')

Apocrypha [*apo-, from* + *crypt, hidden* + *-a*] 1.Fourteen Biblical books included in the Vulgate and Septuagint, but excluded from the Hebrew and Protestant Scriptures. 2.Various religious writings excluded from the New Testament. 3.Writings or statements of dubious authorship or authenticity. (uh POK ruh fuh)

apocryphal [*apo-, from* + *crypt, hidden* + *-al*] 1.Of dubious authenticity. Spurious. Counterfeit. Not genuine. 2.Pertaining to the Apocrypha. (uh POK ruh ful)

apodictic [*apo-, from* + *Grk > deiknynai, to show* + *-ic*] 1.Clearly established or proved. Indisputable. 2.Expressing absolute certainty. (ap' uh DIK tik)

apodosis [*apo-, away* + *Grk > didonai, to give* + *-sis*] The clause expressing the consequence or conclusion in a conditional sentence. Opposed to protasis (def. 1). (uh POD uh sis)

apogamy [*apo-, away* + *-gamy, sexual union*] A situation in which the sporophyte develops directly from the gametophyte without fertilization, as in pteridophytes. See apospory. (uh POG uh mee)

apogee [*apo-, away* + *geo, earth*] The point at which the orbit of the moon or a satellite is farthest from the earth. See perigee. (AP uh jee)

apologetics [*apo-, from* + *log, discourse* + *-ics, study of*] The branch of theology dealing with the defense or proof of Christianity. (uh pol' uh JET iks)

apologia [*apo-, from* + *log, word* + *-ia*] A formal defense, especially of one's opinions, actions, or position. (ap' uh LOH jee uh)

apologue [*apo-, from* + *log, discourse*] A short allegorical story usually intended to express a moral. See parable. (AP uh log')

apology [*apo-, from* + *log, word* + *-y*] 1.A statement expressing regret or asking pardon for an error or discourtesy. 2.A formal written or spoken justification or defense. (uh POL uh jee)

apolune [*apo-, away* + *lun, moon*] The point in a satellite's lunar orbit that is farthest from the moon. See perilune. (AP uh loon')

apomixis [*apo-, separate* + *Grk > mixis, mixing*] An asexual reproductive process in certain plants that does not require fertilization or meiosis. See amphimixis and parthenogenesis. (ap' uh MIK sis)

aponeurosis [*apo-, from* + *Grk > neuron, sinew* + *-osis, formation*] A sheetlike, fibrous membrane resembling a flattened tendon that covers a muscle or connects it to its insertion. (ap' uh noo ROH sis)

apophthegm [*apo-, from* + *Grk > phthengesthai, to speak*] A short, witty, instructive saying. Maxim. Same as apothegm. (AP uh them')

apophyllite [*apo-, off* + *phyll, leaf* + *-ite, mineral*] A white, pale-pink, or pale-green crystalline mineral usually occurring in square transparent prisms or in white or grayish masses. So named from its tendency to flake off under intense heat. (uh POF uh leyet')

apoplexy [*apo-, off* + *Grk > plessein, to strike* + *-y*] Sudden loss of bodily function due to rupture or blockage of a blood vessel in the brain. Stroke. (AP uh plek' see)

apospory [*apo-, away* + *spor, spore* + *-y*] A situation in which the gametophyte develops directly from the sporophyte without spore formation or meiosis, as in certain bryophytes and pteridophytes. See apogamy. (AP uh spor' ee)

apostasy [*apo-, away* + *Grk > histanai, to stand* + *-y*] An abandonment of one's principles, cause, religion, etc. See tergiversate (def. 2). (uh POS tuh see)

apostle [*apo-, off* + *Grk > stellein, to send*] 1.One of twelve disciples chosen by Christ to teach the gospel. 2.The first Christian missionary in a region. 3.A pioneer of an important belief or great reform. (uh POS ul)

apostrophe [*apo-, away + Grk > strophe, turning*] 1.A mark used to show the omission of letters, the possessive case, or the plural of letters or numbers. 2. Words addressed to an absent or imaginary person or thing for rhetorical effect (uh POS truh fee)

apothecary [*apo-, away + the, to put + -ary*] A pharmacist or druggist licensed to prepare and sell drugs and medicines. (uh POTH uh kehr' ee)

apothecium [*apo-, away + Grk > theke, case + -ium*] An open, cup-shaped fruiting body of ascomycete fungi on which asci are borne. See cleistothecium and perithecium. (ap' uh THEE shee um)

apothegm [*apo-, from + Grk > phthengesthai, to speak*] A short, witty, instructive saying Maxim See aphorism, gnome, and proverb. (AP uh them')

apothem [*apo-, from + the, to put*] The perpendicular distance from the center of a regular polygon to one of its sides (AP uh them')

apotheosis [*apo-, from + theo, god + -sis*] 1.The elevating of a human being to the status of a god Deification 2.A glorified ideal (uh poth' ee OH sis)

apotropaic [*apo-, away + trop, turning + -ic*] Designed to ward off evil, as a symbol or ritual. (ap' uh troh PAY ik)

plasmapheresis [*plasm(a) & apo, away + Grk > hairein, to take + -sis*] A medical process in which blood is drawn from a donor, the plasma removed, and the blood cells returned to the circulatory system of the donor (plaz' muh FEHR uh sis)

zygapophysis [*zyg, pair + apo, from + Grk > phyein, to grow + -sis*] One of two paired natural outgrowths of a vertebra that serve to interlock each vertebra with the ones above and below. (zig' uh POF uh sis)

aqua   water

aqua [*aqua, water*] 1. Water 2.A light bluish-green color Aquamarine. (AK wuh)

aqua fortis [*aqua, water & Ltn > fortis, strong*] Nitric acid (AK wuh FORT is)

aqua pura [*aqua, water & Ltn > pura, pure*] Pure water (AK wuh PYOOR uh)

aqua regia [*aqua, water & reg, rule*] Literally, "royal water." A mixture of hydrochloric and nitric acids used for dissolving gold and platinum and for testing metals. Gold and platinum were once considered to be noble metals. (AK wuh REE jee uh)

aqua vitae [*aqua, water & vit, life*] Literally, "water of life." 1. Alcohol 2.Whiskey, brandy, or other strong liquor See aquavit. (AK wuh VEYET ee)

aquacade [*aqua, water & (caval)cade*] Aquatic entertainment consisting of divers and swimmers and often performed to music. (AK wuh kayd')

aquaculture [*aqua, water & culture*] The cultivation of water animals and plants in a controlled environment. Hydroponics. See agriculture, hydroponics, and geoponics. (AK wuh kul' chur)

aquamarine [*aqua, water + mar, sea + -ine*] 1.A transparent bluish-green variety of beryl 2.A bluish-green color (ak' wuh muh REEN)

aquanaut [*aqua, water + naut, sailor*] A person trained to live, explore, and work underwater to conduct scientific research. (AK wuh not')

aquaplane [*aqua, water & plane*] A board on which a person rides standing upright while it is being towed by a motorboat (AK wuh playn')

aquarelle [*Italian > acquarella, water color*] A painting done in thin transparent watercolors (ak' wuh REL)

aquarium [*aqua, water + -arium, a place for*] A place, especially a water-filled transparent tank, for keeping aquatic animals and plants See terrarium and vivarium. (uh KWEHR ee um)

Aquarius [*aqua, water + -ius*] 1.A zodiacal constellation located near the celestial equator that is pictured as a man pouring water Water Bearer. 2.In astrology, the eleventh sign of the zodiac (uh KWEHR ee us)

aquatic [*aqua, water + -tic*] Living growing, or occurring in or on water See aerial (def. 2) and terrestrial (def. 3). (uh KWOT ik)

aquatint [*aqua, water + Ltn > tintus, to tint*] An etching process that produces several tones similar to watercolor washes (AK wuh tint')

aquavit [*aqua, water + vit, life*] Literally, "water of life." A strong, dry Scandinavian liquor distilled from potatoes or grain and flavored with caraway seeds. See aqua vitae. (AK wuh veet')

aqueduct [*aqua, water + duct, to lead*] A large pipe or channel used to carry water from a remote supply. (AK wuh dukt')

aqueous [*aqua, water + -ous*] Pertaining to or containing water. Watery (AY kwee us)

aqueous humor [*aqueous & humor {body fluid}*] A watery fluid contained in the anterior and posterior chambers of the eye (AY kwee us HYOO mur)

aquifer [*aqua, water + fer, to bear*] An underground water-bearing rock formation (AK wuh fer)

semiaquatic [*semi-, partly & aquatic*] 1.Adapted for growing in or near water 2.Often found in water, but not entirely aquatic See semiterrestrial and amphibious (def. 1). (sem' ee uh KWOT ik)

subaquatic [*sub-, nearly & aquatic*] Not entirely aquatic See semiaquatic (def. 2). (sub' uh KWOT ik)

subaqueous [*sub-, under + aqua, water + -eous*] 1. Living occurring, or formed underwater 2. Adapted or suitable for use underwater (sub' AY kwee us)

terraqueous [*terr, land + aqua, water + -eous*] Composed of both land and water, as the earth. (tehr AY kwee us)

hydr/o   water, hydrogen, liquid

anhydride [*an-, without + hydr, water + -ide*] A compound derived by the removal of water from an acid or other compound. (an HEYE dreyd')

anhydrite [*an-, without + hydr, water + -ite, mineral*] A usually white to gray mineral composed of anhydrous calcium sulfate that is similar to gypsum, but does not contain water (an HEYE dreyet')

anhydrous [*an-, without + hydr, water + -ous*] Pertaining to a compound without water in its composition, especially water of crystallization. (an HEYE drus)

carbohydrate [*carbo, carbon & hydrate*] Any of numerous organic compounds, including starches, sugars, and cellulose, that consist of carbon combined with hydrogen and oxygen So named from the former belief that all carbohydrates could be represented as hydrates of carbon. (kahr' boh HEYE drayt')

dehydrate [*de-, remove + hydr, water + -ate*] To remove all or part of the water from See rehydrate. (dee HEYE drayt')

dehydrogenase [*de-, remove & hydrogen & -ase, enzyme*] Any of various enzymes that catalyze the removal of hydrogen from a donor and often the transfer of it to an acceptor. (dee' heye DROJ uh nayz')

dehydrogenate [*de-, remove & hydrogen & -ate*] To remove hydrogen from. (dee' heye DROJ uh nayt')

electrohydraulic [*electro, electric & hydraulic*] Pertaining to or involving both electric and hydraulic mechanisms (ih lek' troh heye DRAW lik)

glycogenolysis [*glyco, glycogen + gen, formation & (hydr)olysis*] The conversion of glycogen back to glucose by hydrolysis See glycogenesis and glyconeogenesis. (gleye' koh jen OL uh sis)

hemihydrate [*hemi-, half & hydrate*] A hydrate, such as plaster of paris, that contains two moles of compound for each mole of water (hem' ih HEYE drayt')

hydra [*Grk > Hydra, mythical water serpent*] Any fresh water polyp of the genus Hydra. So named in reference to the ability of the hydra to rapidly reproduce its cells, as the mythical Hydra could reproduce its heads. See Hydra (def. 1). (HEYE druh)

Hydra [*Grk > Hydra, mythical water serpent*] 1. In Greek mythology, a many-headed monster slain by Hercules, that grew back two heads for every one cut off. 2. A very large and long constellation in the Southern Hemisphere (HEYE druh)

hydrangea [*hydr, water + angi, vessel + -a*] Any of various trees or shrubs of the genus Hydrangea with large white, blue, or pink flower clusters. So named from the seed capsule being shaped like a water vessel or a cup (heye DRAYN juh)

hydrant [*hydr, water + -ant*] A vertical water pipe attached to a main line and used especially for fighting fires (HEYE drunt)

hydranth [*hydr, water + anth, flower*] Any of the nutritive polyps in a hydroid colony that typically bear tentacles and a mouth. So named from their resemblance to a flower (HEYE dranth)

hydrargyrum [*hydr, liquid + argyr, silver + -um*] A metallic element existing at room temperature as a silvery heavy liquid Mercury (heye DRAHR juh rum)

hydratase [*hydr, water + -ase, enzyme*] An enzyme that catalyzes the hydration or dehydration of a compound (HEYE druh tayz')

hydrate [*hydr, water + -ate*] A compound containing water and another substance chemically combined in a definite ratio. (HEYE drayt')

hydraulic [*hydr, liquid + Grk > aulos, pipe + -ic*] Operated by the pressure created by a liquid forced through a tube, pipe, aperture, etc., as a hydraulic jack or hydraulic brakes. (heye DRAW lik)

hydraulics [*hydr, liquid + Grk > aulos, pipe + -ics, science*] The science dealing with the laws governing the motion of water and other liquids (heye DRAW liks)

hydrazine [*hydr, hydrogen + azo, containing nitrogen + -ine*] A colorless liquid, N_2H_4 used chiefly as a reducing agent and as a jet and rocket propulsion fuel (HEYE druh zeen')

hydrazoic acid [*hydr, hydrogen + azo, containing nitrogen + -ic & acid*] A highly volatile liquid, NH_3 used in making explosives (heye' druh ZOH ik AS id)

hydric [*hydr, hydrogen + -ic*] 1. Pertaining to or containing hydrogen 2. Characterized by or requiring a substantial amount of moisture See mesic and xeric. (HEYE drik)

hydride [*hydr, hydrogen + -ide*] A binary compound of hydrogen and another element (HEYE dreyed)

hydriodic acid [*hydr, hydrogen & iodic & acid*] A colorless acid that is an aqueous solution of hydrogen iodide gas, HI. (heye' dree OD ik AS id)

hydrobromic acid [*hydro, hydrogen & bromic & acid*] A colorless or slightly yellow acid that is an aqueous solution of hydrogen bromide gas, HBr. (heye' druh BROH mik AS id)

hydrocarbon [*hydro, hydrogen & carbon*] Any of a large group of organic compounds that contain only hydrogen and carbon, as crude oil. (heye' druh KAHR bun)

hydrocele [*hydro, liquid + -cele, tumor*] A collection of serous fluid in a body cavity especially in the testes. (HEYE druh seel')

hydrocephalus [*hydro, liquid + cephal, head + -us*] An abnormal accumulation of cerebrospinal fluid in the ventricles of the brain, causing compression of the brain and enlargement of the head. (heye' druh SEF uh lus)

hydrochloric acid [*hydro, water & chloric & acid*] A strong colorless acid that is an aqueous solution of hydrogen chloride gas, HCl. (heye' druh KLOR ik AS id)

hydrocolloid [*hydro, water + coll, glue + -oid, resembling*] Any of various substances that form a gel when combined with water (heye' druh KOL oid')

hydrocortisone [*dihydro-, addition of two hydrogen atoms & cortisone*] A steroid hormone, $C_{21}H_{30}O_5$, produced by the adrenal cortex that has applications and effects similar to cortisone, $C_{21}H_{28}O_5$. So named because it contains two more hydrogen atoms than cortisone. (heye' druh KORT uh zohn')

hydrocyanic acid [*hydro, hydrogen & cyanic & acid*] A poisonous, colorless acid that is an aqueous solution of hydrogen cyanide gas or liquid, HCN. (heye' droh seye AN ik AS id)

hydrodynamics [*hydro, liquid + dynam, power + -ics, science*] The branch of hydromechanics dealing with the study of fluids in motion and of solid bodies immersed in them. See hydromechanics and hydrostatics. (heye' droh deye NAM iks)

hydroelectric [*hydro, water & electric*] Pertaining to the generation of electricity by water power (heye' droh ih LEK trik)

hydrofluoric acid [*hydro, hydrogen + fluor, fluorine + -ic & acid*] A strong, colorless acid that is an aqueous solution of hydrogen fluoride gas or liquid, HF (heye' druh FLOOR ik AS id)

hydrofoil [*hydro, water & (air)foil*] A winglike structure similar to an airfoil, but used on a ship or boat to lift the vessel out of the water while in motion. (HEYE druh foil')

hydrogen [*hydro, water + gen, to produce*] A highly flammable, gaseous chemical element that combines with oxygen to form water and is the lightest of the elements. So named from the generation of water during its combustion (HEYE druh jen)

hydrogenase [*hydrogen & -ase, enzyme*] Any of various enzymes that catalyze the oxidation of hydrogen. (heye DROJ uh nayz')

hydrogenate [*hydrogen & -ate*] To combine, reduce, or treat with hydrogen. (heye DROJ uh nayt')

hydrography [*hydro, water + -graphy, science*] The scientific study of water on the earth's surface, especially navigable waterways. See hydrology. (heye DROG ruh fee)

hydroid [*hydr(a) & -oid, resembling*] 1.Pertaining to or characteristic of a hydra. 2.The polyp stage of a hydrozoan. See hydromedusa. (HEYE droid)

hydrokinetics [*hydro, liquid + kinet, motion + -ics, science*] The branch of hydrodynamics dealing with the study of liquids in motion. See hydrodynamics. (heye' droh kih NET iks)

hydrology [*hydr, water + -ology, study of*] The study of the distribution, effects, and properties of water on and beneath the earth's surface and in the atmosphere. See hydrography. (heye DROL uh jee)

hydrolysis [*hydro, water + -lysis, decomposition*] The chemical decomposition of a compound resulting from reaction with water. (heye DROL uh sis)

hydromagnetics [*hydro, liquid & magnetics*] Magnetohydrodynamics. (heye' droh mag NET iks)

hydromancy [*hydro, water + -mancy, divination*] Divination by observing the motion of water. (HEYE druh man' see)

hydromechanics [*hydro, liquid & mechanics*] The science dealing with the motion and equilibrium of fluids and of solid bodies immersed in them, including hydrodynamics and hydrostatics. See hydrodynamics and hydrostatics. (heye' droh muh KAN iks)

hydromedusa [*hydr(a) & medusa*] The medusoid stage of a hydrozoan. See hydroid (def. 2). (heye' droh mih DOO suh)

hydromel [*hydro, water + meli, honey*] A liquor consisting of a mixture of honey and water that becomes mead when fermented. (HEYE druh mel')

hydrometallurgy [*hydro, water & metallurgy*] The process of removing metals from ores by treatment with a liquid, as by leaching. (heye' droh MET l ur' jee)

hydrometeor [*hydro, water + Grk > meteoron, atmospheric phenomenon*] Any form of precipitation, such as rain, sleet, snow, fog, etc., formed by the condensation of water vapor in the atmosphere. (heye' droh MEET ee ur)

hydrometeorology [*hydro, water + Grk > meteoron, atmospheric phenomenon + -ology, study of*] The branch of meteorology dealing with the study of water in the atmosphere. (heye' droh meet' ee uh ROL uh jee)

hydrometer [*hydro, water + meter, to measure*] A floating instrument for measuring the density or specific gravity of liquids. See densimeter. (heye DROM et er)

hydromorphic [*hydro, water + morph, form + -ic*] Being structurally adapted to an aquatic environment, as water plants. (heye' druh MOR fik)

hydronic [*hydr, liquid + -onic*] Pertaining to a system of heating or cooling that involves heat transfer by circulating liquids or vapors through a closed piping loop. (heye DRON ik)

hydropathy [*hydro, water + -pathy, disease*] The practice of treating disease with water; particularly, a science that claims to cure all diseases by the internal and external use of water. See hydrotherapy. (heye DROP uh thee)

hydrophane [*hydro, water + phan, to appear*] A variety of opal that is nearly opaque when dry, but transparent or translucent when wet. (HEYE druh fayn')

hydrophilic [*hydro, water + phil, affinity for + -ic*] Capable of absorbing or dissolving in water or having an affinity for water. (heye' druh FIL ik)

hydrophobia [*hydro, water + -phobia, fear*] 1.Abnormal fear of water. 2.Rabies. So named from the victim's inability to swallow liquids in spite of extreme thirst. (heye' druh FOH bee uh)

hydrophone [*hydro, water + -phone, sound*] A device for monitoring underwater sounds, as from a submarine. (HEYE druh fohn')

hydrophyte [*hydro, water + -phyte, plant*] A plant that grows only in water or extremely wet soil. See mesophyte and xerophyte. (HEYE druh feyet')

hydroplane [*hydro, water & plane*] 1.A watercraft that skims along the surface of the water at high speeds. 2.To skim along the surface of the water at high speeds. (HEYE druh playn')

hydroponics [*hydro, water & (geo)ponics*] The science of growing plants by placing the roots in nutrient-rich solutions rather than soil. See agriculture, aquaculture, and geoponics. (heye' druh PON iks)

hydroscope [*hydro, water + -scope, to view*] An optical instrument for viewing objects at considerable depths underwater. (HEYE druh skohp')

hydrosol [*hydro, water & sol(ution)*] A colloidal solution in which water is the dispersing medium. (HEYE druh sol')

hydrospace [*hydro, water & space*] The regions under the ocean, especially those being scientifically explored. See aerospace (def. 1). (HEYE druh spays')

hydrosphere [*hydro, water & sphere*] All the water on the surface of the earth. See lithosphere and atmosphere (def. 1). (HEYE druh sfihr')

hydrostatics [*hydro, liquid + stat, stationary + -ics, science*] The branch of hydromechanics dealing with the study of fluids at rest or in equilibrium, especially the pressure and equilibrium of liquids. See hydromechanics and hydrodynamics. (heye' druh STAT iks)

hydrotaxis [*hydro, water & taxis*] The movement of a freely moving organism in response to moisture. See hydrotropism. (heye' druh TAK sis)

hydrotherapeutics [*hydro, water & therapeutics*] Hydrotherapy. See hydrotherapy. (heye' droh thehr' uh PYOO tiks)

hydrotherapy [*hydro, water & therapy*] The scientific use of water to treat injury or disease, as with mineral baths, whirlpools, compresses, etc. See hydrotherapeutics and hydropathy. (heye' druh THEHR uh pee)

hydrothermal [*hydro, water + therm, heat + -al*] Pertaining to hot water on or beneath the surface of the earth. (heye' druh THUR mul)

hydrothorax [*hydro, liquid & thorax*] A collection of fluid in one or both pleural cavities, usually resulting from cardiac failure. (heye' druh THOR aks')

hydrotropism [*hydro, water + trop, responding to a stimulus + -ism*] The movement or growth of an organism or part in response to moisture, as the root of a plant. See hydrotaxis. (heye DROT ruh piz' um)

hydrous [*hydr, water + -ous*] Containing water. (HEYE drus)

hydroxide [*hydr, hydrogen* + *ox, oxygen* + *-ide*] An organic or inorganic compound containing the hydroxyl group or the hydroxyl ion. (heye DROK seyed')

hydroxy [*hydr, hydrogen* & *oxy(gen)*] Indicating the presence of the hydroxyl group. (heye DROK see)

hydroxyl [*hydr, hydrogen* & *ox(ygen)* & *-yl*] The univalent radical, OH, that consists of one atom of hydrogen and one atom of oxygen. (heye DROK sul)

hydrozoan [*hydro, water* + *zo, animal* + *-an*] Any of the small aquatic animals in the class Hydrozoa, including several corals, marine hydroids, fresh-water hydras, etc. (heye' druh ZOH un)

magnetohydrodynamics [*magneto, magnetic force* & *hydrodynamics*] The science dealing with the motion of water and other electrically conductive fluids in magnetic fields. See hydrodynamics. (mag NEET oh heye' droh deye NAM iks)

oxyhydrogen [*oxy, oxygen* & *hydrogen*] Pertaining to or using an oxygen and hydrogen mixture, as for producing a hot flame. (ok' see HEYE druh jen)

plasmasol [*plasma* & *(hydro)sol*] The fluid state of cytoplasm that is more liquid than plasmagel. See plasmagel. (PLAZ muh sol')

rehydrate [*re-, back* + *hydr, water* + *-ate*] To restore water to. See dehydrate. (ree HEYE drayt')

arch, archi, arche/o, archae/o
rule, chief, first, ancient

anarchy [*an-, without* + *arch, rule* + *-y*] 1.The absence of any form of government. 2.Political and social disorder and confusion. Lawlessness. (AN ur kee)

archaeology [*archae, ancient* + *-ology, study of*] The study of the life and history of ancient peoples. (ahr' kee OL uh jee)

archaeopteryx [*archaeo, first* + *pteryx, wing*] An extinct reptilelike bird, often called the first bird, that had feathers and well-developed wings. (ahr' kee OP ter iks)

archangel [*arch, chief* & *angel*] Chief angel. A high-ranking angel. (AHRK ayn' jul)

archbishop [*arch, chief* & *bishop*] The highest ranking bishop of an archdiocese. See archdiocese. (AHRCH bish' up)

archdiocese [*arch(bishop)* & *diocese*] A diocese under the authority of an archbishop. See archbishop. (ahrch' DEYE uh sis)

archegonium [*arche, first* + *gon, reproduction* + *ium*] The female reproductive organ of ferns, mosses, and related plants and of most gymnosperms. See antheridium. (ahr' kuh GOH nee um)

archenemy [*arch, chief* & *enemy*] Chief enemy. (ahrch' EN uh mee)

archenteron [*arch, first* & *enteron {alimentary canal}*] The primitive digestive cavity of a gastrula, formed by the invagination of the blastula. See blastula, gastrula, and blastopore. (ahr KEN ter on')

archeology [*arche, ancient* + *-ology, study of*] The study of the life and history of ancient peoples. Same as archaeology. (ahr' kee OL uh jee)

Archeozoic [*archeo, ancient* + *zo, life* + *-ic*] Designating the first geological era occurring between 5,000,000,000 and 1,500,000,000 years ago and characterized by the earliest datable formation of rocks and one-celled organisms. See Proterozoic. (ahr' kee uh ZOH ik)

archesporium [*arche, first* + *spor, spore* + *-ium*] The cell or cells in a sporangium that ultimately develop into spores. (ahr' kuh SPOR ee um)

archetype [*arche, first* & *type*] The original model of a piece of work after which subsequent copies are patterned. A prototype. See prototype. (AHR kih teyep')

archfiend [*arch, chief* & *fiend*] Chief fiend. (AHRCH feend)

archipelago [*archi, chief* + *Grk > pelagos, sea*] 1.A group or chain of islands. 2.A body of water containing many islands. (ahr' kuh PEL uh goh')

architect [*archi, chief* + *Grk > tekton, builder*] A professional designer of buildings or other large construction projects. (AHR kih tekt')

architectonics [*architect(ure)* & *-ics, study of*] 1.The scientific study of architecture. See tectonics (def. 1). 2.The scientific study of the systematization of knowledge. (ahr' kih tek TON iks)

archon [*arch, chief* + *-on*] A chief magistrate in ancient Athens. (AHR kon)

archpriest [*arch, chief* & *priest*] 1.Formerly, the chief priest of a cathedral chapter in the Roman Catholic Church. 2.The eldest priest of a diocese among the Orthodox Churches. (ahrch PREEST)

autarchy [*auto-, self* + *arch, rule* + *-y*] 1.Absolute rule or sovereignty. 2.A country or state under such rule. See autocracy. 3.A national policy of economic self-sufficiency. Same as autarky. (AW tahr' kee)

diarchy [*di-, two* + *arch, rule* + *-y*] Government by two rulers or authorities. (DEYE ahr' kee)

dyarchy [*dy-, two* + *arch, rule* + *-y*] Government by two rulers or authorities. Same as diarchy. (DEYE ahr' kee)

eparchy [*ep-, over* + *arch, rule* + *-y*] 1.A diocese or province in an Eastern Orthodox Church. 2.In modern Greece, a governmental subdivision of a province. 3.In ancient Greece, a governmental province or district. (EP ahr' kee)

gynarchy [*gyn, woman* + *arch, rule* + *-y*] Government by women or a woman. Same as gynecocracy. (JIN ahr' kee)

hagiarchy [*hagi, holy* + *arch, rule* + *-y*] Government by holy persons, as priests or saints. Same as hagiocracy. (HAG ee ahr' kee)

heptarchy [*hept-, seven* + *arch, rule* + *-y*] 1.Government by seven rulers. 2.The supposed seven Anglo-Saxon kingdoms existing in England during the 7th and 8th centuries. (HEP tahr' kee)

heresiarch [*heres(y)* & *arch, chief*] The founder or chief supporter of a heresy. (huh REE zee ahrk')

hierarchy [*hier, holy* + *arch, rule* + *-y*] 1.A group of persons or things classified according to successive rank. 2.A ruling group of clergy classified according to successive rank. (HEYE ur ahr' kee)

matriarch [*matri, mother* + *arch, rule*] 1.The mother and ruler of a family, clan, etc. 2.A well-respected elderly woman. See patriarch. (MAY tree ahrk')

menarche [*men, menstruation* + *arche, first*] The first occurrence of menstruation. (muh NAHR kee)

monarch [*mon-, one* + *arch, rule*] The sole ruler of a nation or state. (MON ahrk)

monarchy [*mon-, one* + *arch, rule* + *-y*] Government by one ruler. (MON ahr' kee)

oligarchy [*olig, few* + *arch, rule* + *-y*] Government by a few rulers. (OL uh gahr' kee)

arch, archi, arche/o, archae/o

patriarch [*patri, father* + *arch, rule*] 1.The father and ruler of a family, clan, etc. 2.A well-respected elderly man. See matriarch. (PAY tree ahrk')

pentarchy [*pent-, five* + *arch, rule* + *-y*] 1. Government by five rulers. 2.A group of five states, each having its own ruler. (PEN tahr' kee)

symposiarch [*symposi(um)* & *arch, chief*] 1.The director of a symposium in ancient Greece. 2.A toastmaster. (sim POH zee ahrk')

tetrarch [*tetra-, four* + *arch, rule*] 1.The ruler of one of four provinces in the ancient Roman Empire. 2.A subordinate governor, ruler, etc. (TET rahrk)

tetrarchy [*tetra-, four* + *arch, rule* + *-y*] 1. Government by four rulers. 2.The territory under the jurisdiction of a tetrarch. (TET rahr' kee)

thearchy [*the, god* + *arch, rule* + *-y*] Rule by a god or gods. (THEE ahr' kee)

triarchy [*tri-, three* + *arch, rule* + *-y*] Government by three rulers. Triumvirate. See triumvirate. (TREYE ahr' kee)

trierarch [*tri-, three* + *Grk* > *eres, to row* + *arch, chief*] The commander of a trireme. See trireme. (TREYE uh rahrk')

-cracy, crat   government, rule, power

aristocracy [*aristo, best* + *-cracy, government*] 1. Government by the elite or upper class. 2.A class given special privileges and status because of birth, rank, or wealth. Nobility. (ehr' ih STOK ruh see)

autocracy [*auto-, self* + *-cracy, government*] 1. Government by one person possessing absolute power. 2.A country or state with this form of government. See autarchy. (aw TOK ruh see)

bureaucracy [*French* > *bureau, office* + *-cracy, government*] Government characterized by hierarchical authority among numerous departments and subdivisions staffed with nonelected officials. (byoo ROK ruh see)

democracy [*demo, people* + *-cracy, government*] Government run by the people, exercised either directly by them or through elected officials. (dih MOK ruh see)

democrat [*demo, people* + *crat, government*] 1.A member or supporter of the Democratic Party. 2.A person who advocates government by the people. (DEM uh krat')

gerontocracy [*geronto, old age* + *-cracy, government*] Government by elders. (jehr' un TOK ruh see)

gynecocracy [*gyneco, woman* + *-cracy, government*] Government by women or a woman. (jin' uh KOK ruh see)

hagiocracy [*hagio, holy* + *-cracy, government*] Government by holy persons, as priests or saints. See theocracy. (hag' ee OK ruh see)

hierocracy [*hiero, holy* + *-cracy, government*] Government by the clergy or by priests. (heye' ur OK ruh see)

isocracy [*iso-, equal* + *-cracy, government*] Government in which all people share equal political power. (eye SOK ruh see)

meritocracy [*Ltn* > *meritus, earned* + *-cracy, rule*] 1.A system in which ability and achievement are the basis for advancement. 2. Leadership by an intellectual elite based on their own ability and talent rather than class privileges. (mehr' ih TOK ruh see)

mobocracy [*mob* & *-cracy, rule*] Rule by a mob. See ochlocracy. (mob OK ruh see)

monocracy [*mono-, one* + *-cracy, government*] Government by one person possessing absolute power. Same as autocracy (def. 1). (muh NOK ruh see)

ochlocracy [*Grk* > *ochlos, mob* + *-cracy, government*] Government by a mob. Mob rule. See mobocracy. (ok LOK ruh see)

physiocracy [*physio, nature* + *-cracy, government*] A school of political thought characterized by the belief that government policy should not interfere with natural economic laws. (fiz' ee OK ruh see)

plutocracy [*Grk* > *ploutos, wealth* + *-cracy, government*] 1. Government or rule by the wealthy. 2.A controlling class of wealthy people. (ploo TOK ruh see)

slavocracy [*slav(e)* & *-cracy, power*] The power structure formed by pro-slavery forces in America before the Civil War. (slay VOK ruh see)

stratocracy [*Grk* > *stratos, army* + *-cracy, government*] Government by the military. (struh TOK ruh see)

technocracy [*techno, skill* + *-cracy, government*] The management and control of government and social systems by technical experts and engineers. (tek NOK ruh see)

thalassocracy [*thalasso, sea* + *-cracy, rule*] Rule of the seas. (thal' uh SOK ruh see)

theocracy [*theo, God* + *-cracy, government*] A government by persons claiming to be representatives of God or a god. See hagiocracy. (thee OK ruh see)

timocracy [*Grk* > *time, honor* + *-cracy, government*] 1.A form of government in which officials must be property owners. 2.A form of government in which love of honor is the principal motivator. (teye MOK ruh see)

prot-, proto-   primitive, first, chief

protagonist [*prot-, chief* + *Grk* > *agonistes, actor*] 1.The leading character in a drama or story. 2.The leader or champion of a cause. (proh TAG uh nist)

protanopia [*prot-, first* + *an-, without* + *-opia, visual condition*] A visual defect in which the retina fails to respond to the color red. So named from the blindness to red, which is regarded as the first primary color. See deuteranopia and tritanopia. (proht' n OH pee uh)

prothonotary [*prot-, chief* + *Ltn* > *notarius, clerk* + *-y*] A chief clerk in some courts of law. (proh THON uh tehr' ee)

prothonotary warbler [*prothonotary* & *warbler*] A small bird with a deep-yellow head and breast and bluish-gray tail and wings. So named from the yellow hood worn by some prothonotaries. (proh THON uh tehr' ee WOR blur)

protist [*prot-, primitive* + *-ist*] Any of numerous simple organisms, including algae, fungi, bacteria, and protozoans, that have characteristics of both animals and plants. (PROHT ist)

protocol [*proto-, first* + *coll, glue*] 1.An original draft or record from which a document is prepared. So named from its originally being the first sheet glued onto the front of a manuscript describing the contents. 2.A code of etiquette and precedence observed by diplomats and heads of state. (PROHT uh kol')

protohistory [*proto-, primitive* & *history*] The historical period immediately preceding recorded history. (proht' oh HIS tree)

protohuman [*proto-, primitive & human*] Pertaining to humanlike primates resembling modern humans but more primitive in development. (proht' oh HYOO mun)

protolanguage [*proto-, first & language*] A language that is the ancestor of another language or languages. (PROHT oh lang' gwij)

protolithic [*proto-, first + lith, stone + -ic*] Early name for the Eolithic period. See Eolithic. (proht' uh LITH ik)

protomartyr [*proto-, first & martyr*] The first martyr in a cause or movement. (PROHT oh mahrt' ur)

proton [*prot-, primitive + -on, subatomic particle*] An elementary particle that is the fundamental constituent of the nucleus of an atom and has a positive charge equal in magnitude to the negative charge of an electron. (PROH tahn)

protonema [*proto-, primitive + nema, thread*] A green, primary threadlike structure produced in mosses and certain related plants that arises from a spore and eventually develops into a mature plant. (proht' uh NEE muh)

protonotary [*proto-, chief + Ltn > notarius, clerk + -y*] A chief clerk in some courts of law. Same as prothonotary. (proh TON uh tehr' ee)

protopathic [*proto-, chief + path, feeling + -ic*] Pertaining to certain sensory nerves that respond only to rather gross variations in pressure, pain, heat, or cold. Opposed to epicritic. (proht' uh PATH ik)

protoplasm [*proto-, primitive + plasm, forming cells or tissue*] A complex, jellylike colloidal substance conceived of as forming the essential living matter of all plant and animal cells. The protoplasm surrounding the nucleus is the cytoplasm and that composing the nucleus is the nucleoplasm. See nucleoplasm and cytoplasm. (PROHT uh plaz' um)

protoplast [*proto-, first + plast, form*] 1. A being or thing that is the first made or formed 2. The living portion of a plant or bacterial cell including the cytoplasm, nucleus, and plasma membrane, but not the cell wall. (PROHT uh plast')

protostele [*proto-, primitive & stele*] A primitive arrangement of vascular tissue in most roots and stems (PROHT uh steel')

prototrophic [*proto-, first + troph, nourishment + -ic*] Pertaining to bacteria with the same nutritional requirements as that of the normal wild type (proht' uh TROF ik)

prototype [*proto-, first & type*] 1. The original model or first functional version of a device, machine, etc. 2. An original being or thing from which others develop or are patterned. See archetype. (PROHT uh teyep')

protoxylem [*proto-, first & xylem*] The first formed xylem of a stem or root that develops from the procambium. (proht' uh ZEYE lum)

protozoan [*proto-, primitive + zo, animal + -an*] Any of the single-celled or acellular microorganisms with animal-like characteristics that occur in varied form, structure, and habitat. (proht' uh ZOH un)

protozoology [*protozo(a) & -ology, study of*] The branch of zoology dealing with the study of protozoans (proht' oh zoh OL uh jee)

pale/o   ancient

micropaleontology [*micro-, small + pale, ancient + ont, being + -ology, study of*] The branch of paleontology dealing with the study of microscopic plant and animal fossils See paleontology. (meye' kroh pay' lee on TOL uh jee)

paleethnology [*pale, ancient + ethn, race + -ology, study of*] The branch of ethnology dealing with the study of early races of mankind (pay' lee eth NOL uh jee)

paleoanthropic [*paleo, ancient + anthrop, man + -ic*] Pertaining to ancient forms of humans (pay' lee oh' an THROP ik)

paleoanthropology [*paleo, ancient + anthrop, man + -ology, study of*] The branch of anthropology dealing with the study of prehistoric man prior to homo sapiens. (pay' lee oh an' thruh POL uh jee)

paleobotany [*paleo, ancient + Grk > botane, plant + -y*] The branch of paleontology dealing with the study of ancient plant life through the study of fossil remains See paleozoology and paleontology. (pay' lee oh BOT n ee)

paleoecology [*paleo, ancient + eco, environment + -logy, study of*] The branch of ecology dealing with the study of the interrelations between ancient plants and animals and their environment (pay' lee oh' ih KOL uh jee)

paleogeography [*paleo, ancient + geo, earth + -graphy, science*] The scientific study of the geographic features of the earth as they existed in ancient times (pay' lee oh' jee OG ruh fee)

paleography [*paleo, ancient + -graphy, writing*] The scientific study of ancient forms of writing (pay' lee OG ruh fee)

Paleolithic [*paleo, ancient + lith, stone + -ic*] Pertaining to the second period of the Stone Age beginning with the use of crudely chipped stone tools (pay' lee uh LITH ik)

paleomagnetism [*paleo, ancient + magnet, magnetic force + -ism*] The magnetization of an ancient rock acquired at the time of its formation. (pay' lee oh MAG nuh tiz' um)

paleontography [*pale, ancient + onto, organism + -graphy, writing*] The descriptive study of plant and animal fossils See paleontology. (pay' lee on TOG ruh fee)

paleontology [*pale, ancient + ont, being + -ology, study of*] The science dealing with the study of ancient plant and animal life through the study of fossil remains See paleobotany and paleozoology. (pay' lee on TOL uh jee)

Paleozoic [*paleo, ancient + zo, animal + -ic*] Designating the third geological era occurring between 620,000,000 and 230,000,000 years ago and characterized by the first insects, fishes, amphibians, and reptiles See Mesozoic. (pay' lee uh ZOH ik)

paleozoology [*paleo, ancient + zo, animal + -ology, study of*] The branch of paleontology dealing with the study of ancient animal life through the study of fossil remains See paleobotany and paleontology. (pay' lee oh' zoh OL uh jee)

arbor   tree

arbor [*arbor, tree*] A shady area with the roof and sides formed by trees, shrubs, or a lattice covered with vines. (AHR bur)

Arbor Day [*arbor, tree & day*] A spring holiday for planting trees, observed individually by most states of the U.S. (AHR bur day)

arboreal [*arbor, tree + -eal*] 1.Resembling a tree. See arborescent and dendroid. 2.Living in trees. (ahr BOR ee ul)

arboreous [*arbor, tree + -eous*] 1.Having many trees. Wooded. 2.Treelike. (ahr BOR ee us)

arborescent [*arbor, tree + -escent*] Resembling a tree in structure, appearance, or growth. Branching. See arboreal (def. 1) and dendroid. (ahr' buh RES ent)

arboretum [*arbor, tree + -etum, place*] A place for the study and exhibition of trees and shrubs. (ahr' buh REET um)

arboriculture [*arbor, tree & culture*] The cultivation of trees and shrubs. (AHR bur ih kul' chur)

arbor vitae [*arbor, tree & vit, life*] The treelike structure of white nerve tissue seen in a cross section of the cerebellum. (AHR bur VEYET ee)

arborvitae [*arbor, tree + vit, life*] Any of various ornamental trees or shrubs of the pine family with small scalelike leaves, sometimes called the tree of life. (ahr' bur VEYET ee)

dendr/o, dendri   tree

dendriform [*dendri, tree & form*] Having the characteristic shape of a tree. (DEN druh form')

dendrite [*dendr, tree + -ite, mineral*] 1.A mineral or rock with branching, treelike markings. 2.One of the branching, treelike processes of a nerve cell that carries impulses toward the cell body. See axon and neuron. (DEN dreyet)

dendrochronology [*dendro, tree + chron, time + -ology, study of*] The study of the annular growth rings in trees for the purpose of dating and determining past events and climatic changes. (den' droh kruh NOL uh jee)

dendroid [*dendr, tree + -oid, resembling*] Resembling a tree in structure, growth, or appearance. Arborescent. Branching. See arborescent and arboreal (def. 1). (DEN droid)

dendrology [*dendr, tree + -ology, study of*] The botanical study of trees and shrubs. (den DROL uh jee)

epidendrum [*epi-, on + dendr, tree + -um*] Any of numerous small-flowered, mostly epiphytic orchids found mainly in tropical America. (ep' ih DEN drum)

philodendron [*philo, love + dendr, tree + -on*] Any of a genus of tree-climbing plants indigenous to tropical America and often grown as ornamental house plants. Literally means "loving trees," in reference to its climbing habit. (fil' uh DEN drun)

rhododendron [*rhodo, red + dendr, tree + -on*] Any of various evergreen trees and shrubs with pink, white, and purple flowers. (roh' duh DEN drun)

-arium, -orium, -ary   a place for

apiary [*api, bee + -ary, a place for*] A place for keeping bees. A collection of beehives. (AY pee ehr' ee)

aquarium [*aqua, water + -arium, a place for*] A place, especially a water-filled transparent tank, for keeping aquatic animals and plants. See terrarium and vivarium. (uh KWEHR ee um)

auditorium [*audit, hearing + -orium, a place for*] A place for the gathering of an audience, as in a theater, school, library, etc. (awd' ih TOR ee um)

aviary [*avi, bird + -ary, a place for*] A place for keeping birds, such as a building, large cage, or other enclosure. (AY vee ehr' ee)

cinerarium [*Ltn > cinis, ashes + -arium, a place for*] A place for keeping the ashes of the cremated dead. See columbarium (def. 1). (sin' uh REHR ee um)

columbarium [*columba, dove + -arium, a place for*] 1.A vault lined with niches for urns containing the ashes of the cremated dead. See cinerarium. 2.A pigeonhole in a dovecote. (kol' um BEHR ee um)

crematorium [*cremat(e) & -orium, a place for*] A place for the cremation of corpses. (kree' muh TOR ee um)

formicary [*Ltn > formica, ant + -ary, a place for*] A nest of ants. Anthill. (FOR mih kehr' ee)

herbarium [*herb & -arium, a place for*] A place for keeping a collection of dried plants mounted and labeled for scientific study. (hur BEHR ee um)

insectary [*insect & -ary, a place for*] A place for keeping, breeding, and studying live insects. (in SEK tuh ree)

mortuary [*mort, dead + -ary, a place for*] A place for keeping dead bodies prior to burial. (MOR choo ehr' ee)

natatorium [*Ltn > natare, to swim + -orium, a place for*] An indoor swimming pool. (nayt' uh TOR ee um)

oceanarium [*ocean & -arium, a place for*] A large aquarium for keeping and displaying marine life. (oh' shuh NEHR ee um)

ossuary [*osse, bone + -ary, a place for*] A place for holding the bones of the dead. A charnel house. (OSH oo ehr' ee)

piscary [*pisc, fish + -ary, a place for*] 1.Fishing rights in waters owned by another. Now usually referred to as "common of piscary." 2.A place for fishing. (PIS kuh ree)

planetarium [*planet & -arium, a place for*] A room or building containing a device for projecting the images, positions, and motions of celestial bodies. (plan' ih TEHR ee um)

polyzoarium [*polyzo(an) & -arium, a place for*] The skeletal system of a polyzoan colony. (pol' ee zoh EHR ee um)

sacrarium [*sacr, sacred + -arium, a place for*] 1.The sanctuary in a church. 2.A piscina in the Roman Catholic Church. (suh KREHR ee um)

sanatorium [*Ltn > sanare, cure + -orium, a place for*] 1.An institution for the treatment of chronic diseases. 2.A health resort. (san' uh TOR ee um)

sanitarium [*Ltn > sanare, cure + -arium, a place for*] 1.An institution for the treatment of chronic diseases. 2.A health resort. Same as sanatorium. (san' ih TEHR ee um)

scriptorium [*script, to write + -orium, a place for*] A writing room, especially in a monastery. (skrip TOR ee um)

solarium [*sol, sun + -arium, a place for*] A room or porch exposed to the sun. (suh LEHR ee um)

sudatorium [*Ltn > sudare, to sweat + -orium, a place for*] A heated room used for sweat baths. (soo' duh TOR ee um)

terrarium [*terr, land & (viv)arium*] A place, especially a small glass enclosure, for keeping small land animals and plants. See aquarium and vivarium. (tuh REHR ee um)

vespiary [*Ltn > vespa, wasp + -ary, a place for*] A nest of wasps. (VES pee ehr' ee)

vivarium [*viv, living + -arium, a place for*] An indoor place for raising and studying live animals and plants. See aquarium and terrarium. (veye VEHR ee um)

arthr/o   joint

amphiarthrosis [*amphi-, on both sides + arthr, joint + -osis, action*] Any articulation permitting only slight motion of a joint, as that between the vertebrae. See diarthrosis and synarthrosis. (am' fee ahr THROH sis)

arbovirus [*ar(thropod) & bo(rne) & virus*] Any of a group of arthropod-borne viruses, including the causative agents of yellow fever and encephalitis, that are transmitted to humans primarily by mosquitoes and ticks. (ahr' buh VEYE rus)

arthralgia [*arthr, joint + alg, pain + -ia*] Pain in a joint. (ahr THRAL juh)

arthritis [*arthr, joint + -itis, inflammation*] Inflammation of a joint, as in gout or rheumatoid arthritis. (ahr THREYE tis)

arthrodesis [*arthro, joint + Grk > desis, binding*] The surgical fixation of a joint. Artificial ankylosis. (ahr THROD uh sis)

arthropathy [*arthro, joint + -pathy, disease*] Any disease of the joints. (ahr THROP uh thee)

arthropod [*arthro, joint + pod, foot*] Any of the largest phylum of invertebrate animals, including crustaceans, arachnids, and insects, with jointed legs, an exoskeleton, and a segmented body. (AHR thruh pod')

arthroscope [*arthro, joint + -scope, to examine*] An endoscope for examining or performing surgery on the interior of a joint, as the knee. (AHR thruh skohp')

arthrosis [*arthr, joint + -osis, action*] 1. A joint between bones. 2. A degenerative disease of a joint. (ahr THROH sis)

arthrospore [*arthro, joint & spore*] A spore formed by filament segmentation in some blue-green algae and in the mycelium of a fungus. (AHR thruh spor')

diarthrosis [*dia-, through + arthr, joint + -osis, action*] Any articulation permitting free motion of a joint in any direction. See amphiarthrosis and synarthrosis. (deye' ahr THROH sis)

enarthrosis [*en-, in + arthr, joint + -osis, formation*] A joint in which the ball-shaped end of one bone fits into the socket-shaped end of another bone, as the hip or shoulder joint. Ball-and-socket joint. (en' ahr THROH sis)

osteoarthritis [*osteo, bone + arthr, joint + -itis, inflammation*] Inflammation caused by a slowly progressive disease marked by degeneration of the cartilage in joints. (os' tee oh' ahr THREYE tis)

rheumatoid arthritis [*rheumat(ism) & arthr, joint + -itis, inflammation*] A chronic disease marked by stiffness, pain, swelling, inflammation, and often deformity of joints. (ROO muh toid' ahr THREYE tis)

synarthrosis [*syn-, together + arthr, joint + -osis, action*] Any articulation in which the bones are rigidly joined permitting no motion of the joint. See diarthrosis and amphiarthrosis. (sin' ahr THROH sis)

astro, aster   star

aster [*aster, star*] 1. A star-shaped cytoplasmic cell structure that is formed around the centrosome during mitosis. 2. Any of various flowers having rayed, daisylike petals varying in color from white to bluish, purple, or pink. (AS ter)

asterisk [*aster, star + -isk*] A star-shaped sign (*) used in writing and printing to indicate footnote references, omissions, etc. (AS tuh risk')

asterism [*aster, star + -ism*] 1. A cluster of stars possibly forming a constellation. 2. A star-shaped figure optically produced in some crystal structures by transmitted or reflected light. (AS tuh riz' um)

asteroid [*aster, star + -oid, resembling*] 1. Any of numerous small celestial bodies ranging in diameter from 1 to 700 miles that orbit around the sun, usually between Jupiter and Mars. 2. Star-shaped. (AS tuh roid')

astrobiology [*astro, star + bio, living organisms + -logy, study of*] The branch of biology dealing with the search for and study of extraterrestrial living organisms. Same as exobiology. (as' troh beye OL uh jee)

astrocyte [*astro, star + -cyte, cell*] A star-shaped cell that is one of several types of neuroglial cells in the brain and spinal cord. (AS truh seyet')

astrocytoma [*astro, star + cyt, cell + -oma, tumor*] A malignant tumor of the brain or spinal cord composed of astrocytes. (as' troh seye TOH muh)

astrodome [*astro, star & dome*] A transparent dome mounted on top of an aircraft fuselage through which observations for celestial navigation are made. (AS truh dohm')

astrodynamics [*astro, star + dynam, power + -ics, science*] The science dealing with the dynamics of space vehicles and celestial bodies. (as' troh deye NAM iks)

astrogeology [*astro, star + geo, earth + -logy, study of*] The scientific study of the origin, history, and structure of celestial bodies in the solar system. (as' troh jee OL uh jee)

astrolabe [*astro, star + Grk > lambanein, to take*] An instrument used before the invention of the sextant for determining the altitude and position of celestial bodies. See sextant (def. 2). (AS truh layb')

astrology [*astro, star + -logy, study of*] The mathematical study of the supposed connection between the positions and aspects of heavenly bodies and the course of human affairs. See astronomy. (uh STROL uh jee)

astrometry [*astro, star + -metry, science of measuring*] The scientific study of the measurement of the relative brightness, motions, distances, and positions of celestial bodies. (uh STROM ih tree)

astronaut [*astro, star + naut, sailor*] A person trained as a pilot or crew member of a spacecraft. (AS truh not')

astronautics [*astro, star + naut, sailor + -ics, science*] The science dealing with spacecraft and space flight. (as' truh NOT iks)

DICTIONARY

astronavigation [*astro, star & navigation*] 1Navigation using the positions of the sun, moon,stars , or planets. Celestial navigation . 2Navigation of spacecraft . (as' troh nav' ih GAY shun)

astronomical [*astronom(y) & -ical*] 1.Having to do with astronomy. 2Extremely large , as the values used in astronomy. See enormous and cosmic (def. 2). (as' truh NOM ih kul)

astronomical unit [*astronomical & unit*] Aunit of length , approximately 93 million miles,equal to the average distance from the earth to the sun , used to express astronomical distances. (as' truh NOM ih kul YOO nit)

astronomy [*astro, star + -nomy, system of laws*] The scientificstudy of the universe . See astrology. (uh STRON uh mee)

astrophotography [*astro, star & photography*] Theart or practiceof photographing celestial objects . (as' troh fuh TOG ruh fee)

astrophysics [*astro, star & physics*] The branch of astronomy dealing with thestudy of the physical properties and characteristicsof stars, planets, and othercelestial bodies . (as' troh FIZ iks)

bioastronautics [*bio, life + astro, star + naut, sailor + -ics, science*] The branch ofscience dealing with the medical and biologicaleffects of space travel on living things . (beye' oh as' truh NOT iks)

disaster [*dis-, negative + aster, star*] Any occurrence causingwidespread damage or harm. Sonamed from the belief that these events are caused byan unfavorable aspect of the stars or planets. See astrology. (dih ZAS ter)

auto- self, same

autacoid [*auto-, same + Grk > akos, cure + -oid*] Any of various physiologically activesecretions in the body whose functional classification is uncertain. (AWT uh koid')

autarchy [*auto-, self + arch, rule + -y*] 1Absolute rule or sovereignty . 2.A country or state under such rule. See autocracy. 3.Anational policy of economicself-sufficiency . Same as autarky. (AW tahr' kee)

autarky [*auto-, self + Grk > arkein, suffice + -y*] Anational policy of economicself-sufficiency . (AW tahr' kee)

autecology [*auto-, same + eco, environment + -logy, study of*] Thestudy of ecology as it relates to an individual organism and its environment or toa species and its environment . See synecology and ecology. (awt' ih KOL uh jee)

autism [*auto-, self + -ism*] Amental disorder , characterized by extreme self-absorption , that includes fantasies, daydreaming, withdrawal from reality, and inability to relate to others. (AW tiz' um)

autoantibody [*auto-, self & antibody*] Anantibody that is produced by an individual's own body in response to an altered antigen that the body views as foreign. See autoimmunity. (awt' oh AN tih bod' ee)

autobiography [*auto-, self + bio, life + -graphy, written*] The story of one's life written by oneself . See biography. (awt' oh beye OG ruh fee)

autocatalysis [*auto-, self & catalysis*] Acceleration of a chemical reactiondue to one or more of itsproducts themselvesacting as catalysts . (awt' oh kuh TAL uh sis)

autocephalous [*auto-, self + cephal, head + -ous*] Pertaining especially to an EasternChurch whose bishop isnot governed by external authority . (awt' oh SEF uh lus)

autochthonous [*auto-, same + chthon, earth + -ous*] 1.Pertaining to a particularregion's original inhabitants .Aboriginal . 2.Pertaining to a particular region's indigenous plants and animals . (aw TOK thuh nus)

autocracy [*auto-, self + -cracy, government*] 1Government by one person possessing absolute power. 2.A country or state with this form of government. See autarchy. (aw TOK ruh see)

autodidact [*auto-, self & didact {teacher}*] Aself-educated person . (awt' oh DEYE dakt')

autoecious [*auto-, same + Grk > oikos, house + -ious*] Pertaining toparasites that spend their entirelife cycle on the same species of host , as certain fungi. See heteroecious. (aw TEE shus)

autoerotism [*auto-, self + eroto, sexual desire + -ism*] Sexual self-satisfaction , as by masturbation. (awt' oh EHR uh tiz' um)

autogamy [*auto-, self + -gamy, sexual union*] 1Self-fertilization in plants . 2Self-fertilization in certain fungi andprotozoans in which the pronuclei of a divided cell nucleus unite. Opposed to allogamy. (aw TOG uh mee)

autogenesis [*auto-, self + -genesis, generation*] The now discredited theory thatliving organisms can be spontaneously generated directlyfrom nonliving matter . Same as abiogenesis. (awt' oh JEN uh sis)

autogenous [*auto-, self + gen, generation + -ous*] 1Self-generating . 2Originating within the sameorganism . See heterogenous, endogenous, and exogenous. (aw TOJ uh nus)

autogiro [*auto-, self + gyro, circle*] Anaircraft with a horizontal rotating wing to provide liftand a conventionalengine-driven propeller to provide propulsion. See helicopter and gyroplane. (awt' oh JEYE roh)

autograft [*auto-, same & graft*] Anytissue or organ that is grafted from one location to anotheron the same body . See heterograft and homograft. (AWT uh graft')

autograph [*auto-, self + graph, written*] Written or made with one's own hand , as a signature or manuscript. See allograph (def. 2). (AWT uh graf')

autogyro [*auto-, self + gyro, circle*] Anaircraft with a horizontal rotating wing to provide liftand a conventionalengine-driven propeller to provide propulsion. Same as autogiro. (awt' oh JEYE roh)

autohypnosis [*auto-, self & hypnosis*] Self-induced hypnosis . (awt' oh hip NOH sis)

autoimmunity [*auto-, self & immunity*] A condition in which an individual's body mistakes its own antigens for foreign antigens and producesantibodies against them,resulting in various autoimmune diseases such as rheumatoid arthritis and multiple sclerosis. See autoantibody. (awt' oh ih MYOON ih tee)

autointoxication [*auto-, self & intoxication*] Poisoning by substances createdwithin the body . (awt' oh in tok' suh KAY shun)

autologous [*auto-, self + Grk > logos, relationship + -ous*] Derived from or originating inthe same organism . (aw TOL uh gus)

autolysis [*auto-, self* + *-lysis, decomposition*] The breakdown of tissues or cells by self-produced enzymes, as in some pathological conditions and after death. (aw TOL uh sis)

automatic [*auto-, self* + *Grk > matos, acting* + *-ic*] 1.Moving, regulating, or operating without external assistance. 2.Occurring involuntarily, as a reflex. (awt' uh MAT ik)

automobile [*auto-, self* & *mobile*] A four-wheeled, self-propelled vehicle. (AWT uh moh beel')

autonetics [*auto-, self* & *(cyber)netics*] The study of automatic control systems. See cybernetics. (awt' oh NET iks)

autonomic [*auto-, self* + *nom, management* + *-ic*] Functioning or occurring involuntarily. See autonomic nervous system. (awt' uh NOM ik)

autonomic nervous system The part of the nervous system that controls the activity of involuntary body functions, including cardiac, respiratory, glandular, and other automatic functions. See sympathetic nervous system and parasympathetic nervous system. (awt' uh NOM ik NUR vus SIS tum)

autonomous [*auto-, self* + *nom, law* + *-ous*] 1.Self-governing. Independent. See heteronomous and semiautonomous. 2.Functioning or developing independently. 3.Existing as an independent organism. (aw TON uh mus)

autonomy [*auto-, self* + *-nomy, law*] The right of self-government. Independence. (aw TON uh mee)

autophyte [*auto-, self* + *-phyte, plant*] A plant that produces its own food by using inorganic matter and photosynthesis. See heterophyte and saprophyte. (AWT uh feyet')

autoplasty [*auto-, self* + *-plasty, forming cells or tissue*] The surgical grafting of tissue taken from another part of the same body. See heteroplasty and autograft. (AWT uh plas' tee)

autopsy [*auto-, self* + *-opsy, inspection*] The examination of a dead body, including the internal organs and structures, to determine the cause of death or the nature of pathological conditions. See necropsy. (AW top see)

autoradiograph [*auto-, same* + *radio, radiation* + *graph, recording*] An x-ray photograph made by laying the film directly on the object, thus revealing the presence of radioactive material. See radiograph. (awt' oh RAY dee uh graf')

autosome [*auto-, same* & *(chromo)some*] Any chromosome other than a sex chromosome. See sex chromosome. (AWT uh sohm')

autotomy [*auto-, self* + *-tomy, to cut*] The self-amputation and later regeneration of a lost or damaged appendage such as a lizard's tail or a crab's leg. (aw TOT uh mee)

autotoxin [*auto-, self* & *toxin*] A poison created within the body. (AWT oh tok' sin)

autotroph [*auto-, self* + *troph, nourishment*] An organism that produces its own food by using inorganic materials and either photosynthesis or chemosynthesis, as most plants and certain bacteria. See heterotroph. (AWT uh trof')

chemoautotrophic [*chemo, chemical* & *autotrophic*] Pertaining to an organism that produces its own food using inorganic materials and chemosynthesis, as certain bacteria. See photoautotrophic and autotroph. (kee' moh ot' uh TROF ik)

photoautotrophic [*photo, light* & *autotrophic*] Pertaining to an organism that produces its own food using inorganic materials and photosynthesis, as most plants. See chemoautotrophic and autotroph. (foht' oh ot' uh TROF ik)

semiautomatic [*semi-, partly* & *automatic*] 1.Pertaining to a device that is partly automatic and partly operated by hand. 2.A firearm that automatically ejects and reloads, but requires manual squeezing of the trigger for each shot. (sem' ee ot' uh MAT ik)

semiautonomous [*semi-, partly* & *autonomous*] Self-governing only with regard to certain affairs. See autonomous (def. 1) and heteronomous. (sem' ee aw TON uh mus)

ego   self

alter ego [*Ltn > alter, other* & *ego, self*] 1.Another aspect of oneself. Another self. 2.A very intimate and trusted friend. (AHL ter EE goh)

ego [*ego, self*] 1.The self. The conscious, thinking, and feeling individual as a whole. 2.The part of the conscious mind that is most aware of reality. 3.Self-esteem. (EE goh)

egocentric [*ego, self* + *centr, center* + *-ic*] 1.Self-centered. 2.Regarding the ego as the center of everything. See egomania. (ee' goh SEN trik)

egoism [*ego, self* + *-ism*] 1.Selfishness. Conceit. Egotism. See egotism (def. 2). 2.The ethical doctrine that self-interest is the basis of morality. Opposed to altruism (def. 2). (EE goh iz' um)

egoist [*ego, self* + *-ist*] 1.A selfish or self-centered person. 2.A conceited person. Same as egotist. (EE goh ist)

egomania [*ego, self* + *-mania, excessive desire*] Abnormally excessive preoccupation with oneself. See egocentric. (ee' goh MAY nee uh)

egotism [*ego, self* + *-tism*] 1.Excessive reference to oneself in speaking or writing. 2.Selfishness. Conceit. Egoism. See egoism (def. 1). (EE goh tiz' um)

egotist [*ego, self* + *-tist*] 1.A selfish or self-centered person. 2.A conceited person. (EE guh tist)

egotistical [*ego, self* + *-tistic* + *-al*] 1.Concerned with the welfare of oneself only. Selfish. 2.Talking or thinking too much about oneself. Conceited. (ee' guh TIST ih kul)

avi   bird

auspices [*avi, bird* + *spic, to see* + *-es*] 1.Kindly patronage and support. 2.A usually favorable omen, especially when observed in the actions of birds. 3.Divination, especially from the actions of birds. (AW spuh siz')

auspicious [*avi, bird* + *spic, to see* + *-ious*] 1.Marked by success. Fortunate. 2.Of good omen. Favorable. See auspices. (aw SPISH us)

avian [*avi, bird* + *-an*] Pertaining to or derived from birds. (AY vee un)

aviary [*avi, bird* + *-ary, a place for*] A place for keeping birds, such as a building, large cage, or other enclosure. (AY vee ehr' ee)

avi

aviation [*avi, bird + -ation*] 1.The art or science of operating aircraft. 2.The designing and manufacturing of aircraft. (ay' vee AY shun)

aviator [*avi, bird + -ator*] An aircraft pilot. (AY vee ayt' ur)

aviatrix [*avi, bird + -trix, feminine*] A female aircraft pilot. (ay' vee AY triks)

aviculture [*avi, bird & culture*] The raising and keeping of birds. (AY vih kul' chur)

avifauna [*avi, bird & fauna*] All the birds of a particular region or period. See fauna. (ay' vuh FAW nuh)

ornith/o   bird

ornithic [*ornith, bird + -ic*] Pertaining to or characteristic of birds. (or NITH ik)

ornithine [*ornith, bird + -ine*] An amino acid found in the urine of birds and also obtained by hydrolysis of arginine. (OR nuh theen')

ornithischian [*ornith, bird & isch(ium) & -ian*] Any of the herbivorous dinosaurs of the order Ornithischia with a pelvis resembling that of a bird. See ornithopod. (or' nuh THIS kee un)

ornithoid [*ornith, bird + -oid, resembling*] Resembling a bird. (OR nuh thoid')

ornithology [*ornith, bird + -ology, study of*] The branch of zoology dealing with the study of birds. (or' nuh THOL uh jee)

ornithopod [*ornitho, bird + pod, feet*] Any herbivorous dinosaur of the suborder Ornithopoda and the order Ornithischia that walked upright on the hind feet. See ornithischian. (OR nuh thuh pod')

ornithopter [*ornitho, bird + pter, wing*] An early experimental aircraft designed to be lifted and propelled by flapping wings. (OR nuh thop' ter)

ornithosis [*ornith, bird + -osis, diseased condition*] An infectious disease that can be transmitted by birds to human beings. Psittacosis. (or' nuh THOH sis)

ax   axis

abaxial [*ab-, away + ax, axis + -ial*] Situated or facing away from the axis or stem. See adaxial. (ab AK see ul)

adaxial [*ad-, toward + ax, axis + -ial*] Situated on or facing the side toward the axis or stem. See abaxial. (ad AK see ul)

axial [*ax, axis + -ial*] 1.Pertaining to an axis. 2.Located on, in the direction of, or along an axis. (AK see ul)

axile [*ax, axis + -ile*] A plant part attached to or located along the central axis. (AK seyel)

axis [*ax, axis + -is*] 1.A real or imaginary line about which a body rotates. 2.The main stem of a plant around which leaves and branches are arranged. 3.An imaginary line that passes through the center of an anatomical structure or about which it moves. (AK sis)

axle [*ax, axis + -le*] A supporting rod on which a wheel or set of wheels revolve. (AK sul)

axon [*ax, axis + -on*] The long process of a nerve cell that carries impulses away from the cell body. See dendrite (def. 2) and neuron. (AK sahn)

biaxial [*bi-, two + ax, axis + -ial*] Having two axes, as certain crystals. (beye AK see ul)

coaxial [*co-, with + ax, axis + -ial*] Having a common axis. (koh AK see ul)

monaxial [*mon-, one + ax, axis + -ial*] Having only one axis, as a plant or crystal. Same as uniaxial. (mon AK see ul)

postaxial [*post-, behind + ax, axis + -ial*] Pertaining to or located behind an axis of the body, especially the medial aspect of the upper limb and the lateral aspect of the lower limb. (pohst AK see ul)

preaxial [*pre-, before + ax, axis + -ial*] Located in front of an axis of the body or a body part. (pree AK see ul)

triaxial [*tri-, three + ax, axis + -ial*] Having three axes, as certain crystals. (treye AK see ul)

uniaxial [*uni-, one + ax, axis + -ial*] Having only one axis, as a plant or crystal. (yoo' nee AK see ul)

x-axis [*x & axis*] 1.The horizontal axis in a plane Cartesian coordinate system. 2.One of the three axes in a three-dimensional Cartesian coordinate system. See y-axis and z-axis. (EKS ak' sis)

y-axis [*y & axis*] 1.The vertical axis in a plane Cartesian coordinate system. 2.One of the three axes in a three-dimensional Cartesian coordinate system. See x-axis and z-axis. (WEYE ak' sis)

z-axis [*z & axis*] One of the three axes in a three-dimensional Cartesian coordinate system. See x-axis (def. 2) and y-axis (def. 2). (ZEE ak' sis)

bar/o   pressure, weight

aneroid barometer [*a-, without + Grk > neros, fluid + -oid & barometer*] A barometer that measures atmospheric pressure by measuring the movement of a thin metal disk rather than the movement of a column of fluid. (AN uh roid' buh ROM et er)

bar [*bar, pressure*] A metric unit of pressure equal to 1,000,000 dynes per square centimeter. (bahr)

bariatrics [*bar, weight + iatr, healing + -ics, study of*] The branch of medicine dealing with the study and treatment of obesity. (behr' ee AT riks)

baric [*bar, pressure + -ic*] Pertaining to pressure or weight, especially that of the atmosphere. (BEHR ik)

barite [*bar, weight + -ite, mineral*] A usually white mineral with a high specific gravity, consisting mainly of barium sulfate. (BEHR eyet)

barograph [*baro, pressure + graph, recording*] An instrument for graphically recording variations in atmospheric pressure. (BEHR uh graf')

barometer [*baro, pressure + meter, to measure*] 1.An instrument for measuring atmospheric pressure. 2.Something that monitors changes. An indicator. (buh ROM et er)

baroreceptor [*baro, pressure & receptor*] A sensory nerve ending that is sensitive to pressure changes. (behr' oh rih SEP tur)

baryon [*bar, weight + -on, subatomic particle*] Any of a group of elementary particles, also called heavy particles, that includes protons and neutrons. (BEHR ee on')

centibar [*centi-, hundredth + bar, pressure*] A metric unit of pressure equal to one hundredth of a bar, or 10,000 dynes per square centimeter. (SENT ih bahr')

centrobaric [*centro, center + bar, weight + -ic*] Pertaining to the center of gravity. (sen' truh BEHR ik)

decibar [*deci-, tenth + bar, pressure*] A metric unit of pressure equal to one tenth of a bar, or 100,000 dynes per square centimeter. (DES uh bahr')

hyperbaric [*hyper-, above* + *bar, pressure* + *-ic*] Pertaining to or occurring at pressures greater than normal atmospheric pressure. (heye' per BEHR ik)

isallobar [*iso-, equal* + *allo, variation* + *bar, pressure*] A line on a map connecting points with equal change of barometric pressure over a given time period. (eye SAL uh bahr')

isobar [*iso-, equal* + *bar, pressure*] A line on a map connecting points of equal barometric pressure for a specific period or time. (EYE suh bahr')

kilobar [*kilo-, thousand* + *bar, pressure*] A metric unit of pressure equal to 1,000 bars. (KIL uh bahr')

microbar [*micro-, millionth* + *bar, pressure*] A metric unit of pressure equal to one millionth of a bar or one dyne per square centimeter. (MEYE kroh bahr')

microbarograph [*micro-, small* + *baro, pressure* + *graph, recording*] An instrument for making a continuous recording of minute changes in atmospheric pressure. (meye' kroh BEHR uh graf')

millibar [*milli-, thousandth* + *bar, pressure*] A metric unit of pressure equal to one thousandth of a bar, or 1,000 dynes per square centimeter. (MIL uh bahr')

bell   war

antebellum [*ante-, before* + *bell, war* + *-um*] Occurring or existing before a war, specifically before the American Civil War. See postbellum. (an' tee BEL um)

bellicose [*bell, war* + *-ic* + *-ose*] Warlike or hostile in nature. Eager to fight. Pugnacious. See belligerent. (BEL ih kohs')

belligerent [*bell, war* + *Ltn > gerere, to wage* + *-ent*] 1.Pertaining to or engaged in warfare. 2.Warlike. Combative. Pugnacious. See bellicose. (buh LIJ ur ent)

cobelligerent [*co-, together* + *bell, war* + *Ltn > gerere, to wage* + *-ent*] A nation that cooperates with another or others in waging war. (koh' buh LIJ ur ent)

postbellum [*post-, after* + *bell, war* + *-um*] Occurring or existing after a war, specifically after the American Civil War. See antebellum. (pohst BEL um)

rebel [*re-, against* + *bell, war*] 1.To oppose or resist authority or the generally accepted convention. (rih BEL {verb}) 2.Person who refuses to obey or recognize authority or tradition. (REB ul {noun})

rebellion [*re-, against* + *bell, war* + *-ion*] An organized armed resistance against an existing government or ruling authority. Revolt. (rih BEL yun)

bene-   good, well

benediction [*bene-, good* + *dict, to speak* + *-ion*] 1.A blessing. 2.An invocation of a blessing, especially at the end of a church service. See malediction. (ben' uh DIK shun)

benefactor [*bene-, good* + *fact, to do* + *-or*] A person who gives aid, especially in the form of a gift or donation. See benefactress. (BEN uh fak' tur)

benefactress [*bene-, good* + *fact, to do* + *-ess, feminine*] A female benefactor. See benefactor. (BEN uh fak' tres)

beneficent [*bene-, good* + *fic, to do* + *-ent*] Doing good through acts of kindness or charity. (buh NEF uh sent)

beneficiary [*bene-, good* + *fic, to do* + *-ary*] A person who receives benefits, profits, or advantages. (ben' uh FISH ee ehr' ee)

benefit [*bene-, well* + *fic, to do*] Something that is helpful, profitable, or promotes well-being. (BEN uh fit')

benevolent [*bene-, good* + *vol, to wish* + *-ent*] Showing kindness and good will toward others. See malevolent and malicious. (buh NEV uh lent)

benign [*bene-, good* & *genus {born}*] 1.Having a kind and gentle disposition. 2.Totally or nearly harmless. Not malignant. See malignant. (bih NEYEN)

nota bene [*Ltn > nota, note* & *bene, well*] Take notice. Observe what follows. Note well. (NOHT uh BEE nee)

mal-, male-   bad, evil, ill, wrong

dismal [*Ltn > dies, day* + *mal, bad*] Causing depression, misery, or gloom. So named from unlucky days marked on medieval calendars. (DIZ mul)

mal de mer [*mal-, ill* & *French > mer, sea*] Seasickness. (mal' duh MEHR)

mala fide [*mal-, bad* & *fid, faith*] Literally, "in bad faith." Acting in bad faith. Opposed to bona fide. (MAL uh feyed')

maladapted [*mal-, bad* & *adapted*] Not satisfactorily adapted or poorly suited to a particular situation, activity, or environment. (mal' uh DAP tid)

maladjusted [*mal-, bad* & *adjusted*] Not satisfactorily or adequately adjusted, especially to one's environment or to changing situations and circumstances. (mal' uh JUS tid)

maladminister [*mal-, bad* & *administer*] To manage poorly, dishonestly, or inefficiently. (mal' uhd MIN uh ster)

maladroit [*mal-, bad* & *adroit {skillful}*] Characterized by a lack of adroitness. Awkward. Clumsy. (mal' uh DROIT)

malady [*mal-, bad* + *Ltn > habitus, condition* + *-y*] A disease or illness of the body, especially a chronic and fatal one. (MAL uh dee)

malaise [*mal-, ill* + *French > aise, ease*] A vague feeling of illness, discomfort, or uneasiness. (muh LAYZ)

malapert [*mal-, bad* + *Ltn > apert, clever*] Inappropriately bold or forward. Saucy. Impudent. (mal' uh PERT)

malapportionment [*mal-, wrong* & *apportionment*] Unfair or inappropriate apportionment to a legislature. (mal' uh POR shun ment)

malapropism [*malaprop(os)* & *-ism*] The ludicrous misuse of a word, especially by confusing it with another word having the same or nearly the same sound, but different meaning. Named after Mrs. Malaprop, a character in Richard B. Sheridan's play *The Rivals*, for her ludicrous misuse of words. (MAL uh prop' iz' um)

malapropos [*mal-, bad* & *apropos {at the right time}*] Said or done at an inappropriate place or time. (mal' ap' ruh POH)

malaria [*mal-, bad* + *Italian > aria, air*] Literally, "bad air." An infectious disease transmitted to humans by the bite of an infected mosquito and characterized by intermittent chills and fever. So named from the former notion that it was caused from the bad air of swamps. (muh LEHR ee uh)

malcontent [*mal-, bad* & *content*] 1.Discontented with present conditions. 2.A discontented or rebellious person. (mal' kun TENT)

maldistribution [*mal-, bad* & *distribution*] Inadequate or unfair distribution, as of resources or wealth. (mal' dis' truh BYOO shun)

mal-, male-

malediction [*male-, evil + dict, to speak + -ion*] An invocation of evil or harm on someone. Curse. See benediction. (mal' uh DIK shun)

malefaction [*male-, wrong + fact, to do + -ion*] A crime. (mal' uh FAK shun)

malefactor [*male-, wrong + fact, to do + -or*] A criminal. (MAL uh fak' tur)

malefic [*male-, evil + fic, to do*] Having an evil, harmful, or disastrous influence. (muh LEF ik)

maleficence [*male-, evil + fic, to do + -ence*] Doing or causing evil or harm. (muh LEF uh sens)

maleficent [*male-, evil + fic, to do + -ent*] Doing or causing evil or harm. (muh LEF uh sent)

malevolent [*male-, evil + vol, to wish + -ent*] Wishing harm or evil on others or another. See benevolent and malicious. (muh LEV uh lent)

malfeasance [*mal-, wrong + fac, to do + -ance*] Misconduct, evil-doing, or wrong-doing by a public official. See malversation. (mal FEE zens)

malformation [*mal-, bad & formation*] Defective or abnormal formation. (mal' for MAY shun)

malfunction [*mal-, bad & function*] 1.Abnormal or improper function. 2.To function abnormally or improperly. See dysfunction. (mal FUNGK shun)

malice [*mal-, ill + -ice*] 1.Deliberate ill will or evil intent toward another. 2.Deliberate intent to do unjustifiable injury or harm to another. (MAL is)

malicious [*mal-, ill + -ic + -ious*] Showing strong ill will. See benevolent and malevolent. (muh LISH us)

malign [*mal-, ill & genus {born}*] To speak ill of. (muh LEYEN)

malignant [*mal-, bad & genus {born} & -ant*] 1.Having a dangerous or evil influence or effect. 2.Very harmful or injurious. Pernicious. See benign. (muh LIG nunt)

malinger [*mal-, ill & genus {born} & -er*] To pretend injury or illness to avoid work. (muh LING ger)

malnutrition [*mal-, bad & nutrition*] Poor or inadequate nutrition. (mal' noo TRISH un)

malocclusion [*mal-, bad & occlusion {closing}*] Abnormal closure of the upper and lower teeth. (mal' uh KLOO zhun)

malodorous [*mal-, bad & odor & -ous*] Having a distinctive bad odor. (mal OHD ur us)

malposition [*mal-, bad & position*] Improper or abnormal position, especially of a body part or organ. (mal' puh ZISH un)

malpractice [*mal-, bad & practice*] Injurious, negligent, or otherwise improper treatment of a person by a physician or other professional. (mal PRAK tis)

malversation [*mal-, bad + vers, turn + -ation*] Corrupt or improper conduct in a trusted position, especially in public office. See malfeasance. (mal' vur SAY shun)

eu-   good, well

dyslogistic [*dys-, bad & (eu)logistic*] Showing disapproval. See eulogy. (dis' luh JIS tik)

dysphemism [*dys-, bad & (eu)phemism*] The substitution of an offensive term for an inoffensive one. See euphemism. (DIS fuh miz' um)

eucalyptus [*eu-, well + Grk > kalyptos, covered + -us*] Any of numerous tall, aromatic, mainly Australian trees of the genus Eucalyptus that yield timber and a medicinal oil. So named from the covering of the buds. (yoo' kuh LIP tus)

eucaryote [*eu-, good + kary, nucleus + -ote*] An organism whose genetic material is contained in a membrane-bound nucleus, as all animals and plants except bacteria and blue-green algae. Same as eukaryote. (yoo KEHR ee oht')

Eucharist [*eu-, good + Grk > charis, grace*] The Christian sacrament of Holy Communion in which bread and wine represent the body and blood of Christ. (YOO kuh rist)

euchromatin [*eu-, good & chromatin*] The part of the chromatin in a cell nucleus that is more lightly stained when the nucleus is not in the state of division and is genetically active. See chromatin and heterochromatin. (yoo KROH muh tin)

eudaemonism [*eu-, good + Ltn > daimon, spirit + -ism*] The doctrine that ranks the morality of actions according to their ability to produce happiness. Same as eudemonism. (yoo DEE muh niz' um)

eudemon [*eu-, good + Ltn > daimon, spirit*] A benevolent spirit. (yoo DEE mun)

eudemonism [*eu-, good + Ltn > daimon, spirit + -ism*] The doctrine that ranks the morality of actions according to their ability to produce happiness. (yoo DEE muh niz' um)

eugenic [*eu-, good + gen, to produce + -ic*] Causing improvement in the hereditary qualities of offspring. See dysgenic. (yoo JEN ik)

eugenics [*eu-, good + gen, to produce + -ics, study of*] The study of the improvement of a species, especially the human species, by genetic control of hereditary factors in breeding. Opposed to dysgenics. See euphenics. (yoo JEN iks)

euglena [*eu-, good + Grk > glene, eyeball + -a*] Any of various green, unicellular, freshwater organisms characterized by a single anterior flagellum and a reddish eyespot. (yoo GLEE nuh)

eukaryote [*eu-, good + kary, nucleus + -ote*] An organism whose genetic material is contained in a membrane-bound nucleus, as all animals and plants except bacteria and blue-green algae. See prokaryote. (yoo KEHR ee oht')

eulogy [*eu-, good + log, discourse + -y*] 1.A speech or writing in praise of a person or thing, especially a formal speech praising a recently deceased person. 2.High praise. See panegyric and dyslogistic. (YOO luh jee)

eupatrid [*eu-, good + patr, father + -id*] Pertaining to the hereditary aristocracy who formed the ruling class of ancient Athens. (yoo PAT rid)

eupepsia [*eu-, good + peps, digestion + -ia*] Normal digestion. See dyspepsia. (yoo PEP shuh)

euphemism [*eu-, good + Grk > pheme, speech + -ism*] The substitution of an inoffensive term for an offensive one. See dysphemism. (YOO fuh miz' um)

euphenics [*eu-, good & phen(otype) & -ics, study of*] The study of biological improvement of humans either before or after birth, as through prenatal manipulation of genes. See eugenics. (yoo FEN iks)

euphonious [*eu-, good + phon, sound + -ious*] Having a pleasant or agreeable sound. Harmonious. See cacophony. (yoo FOH nee us)

euphoria [*eu-, good + phor, state + -ia*] A feeling of well-being. Opposed to dysphoria. (yoo FOR ee uh)

euphotic [*eu-, good + phot, light + -ic*] Pertaining to the uppermost zone in a body of water through which sunlight penetrates in sufficient amounts for photosynthesis to occur. (yoo FOHT ik)

euplastic [*eu-, well + plast, forming cells or tissue + -ic*] Healing readily and well, as a wound. (yoo PLAS tik)

euploid [*eu-, good + -ploid, number of chromosomes*] Pertaining to cells with a full complement of chromosomes that are an exact multiple of the normal haploid number for the species, as diploid, triploid, tetraploid, etc. See heteroploid and haploid. (YOO ploid)

eupnea [*eu-, good + -pnea, breathing*] Normal breathing. See apnea and dyspnea. (yoop NEE uh)

eurhythmics [*eu-, good & rhythm & -ics, skill*] The art of performing rhythmical body movements, usually in response to music. Same as eurythmics. (yoo RITH miks)

eurhythmy [*eu-, good & rhythm & -y*] 1.Harmony and proportion, especially in architecture. 2.Rhythmical body movement in response to the rhythm of spoken words. Same as eurythmy. (yoo RITH mee)

euripus [*eu-, good + Grk > rhipe, rush + -us*] A strait with very strong and violent currents. (yoo REYE pus)

eurythmics [*eu-, good & r(h)ythm & -ics, skill*] The art of performing rhythmical body movements, usually in response to music. (yoo RITH miks)

eurythmy [*eu-, good & r(h)ythm & -y*] 1.Harmony and proportion, especially in architecture. 2.Rhythmical body movement in response to the rhythm of spoken words. (yoo RITH mee)

eutectic [*eu-, well + Grk > tekein, to melt + -ic*] Pertaining to an alloy or solution whose melting point is lower than any other possible combination of its constituents and usually lower than any of its constituents taken separately. (yoo TEK tik)

euthanasia [*eu-, good + thanas, death + -ia*] The act or practice of killing an individual for merciful reasons. (yoo' thuh NAY zhuh)

euthenics [*Grk > euthenein, to prosper + -ics, study of*] The study of the improvement of human well-being by improvement of living conditions. (yoo THEN iks)

eutrophic [*eu-, good + troph, nourishment + -ic*] Pertaining to a body of water rich in nutrients for supporting plant life, but deficient in oxygen for supporting animal life. See oligotrophic. (yoo TROF ik)

euxenite [*eu-, good + xen, foreign + -ite, mineral*] A lustrous, brownish-black mineral consisting primarily of cerium, erbium, columbium, titanium, uranium, and yttrium. So named for the rare elements it contains. (YOOK suh neyet')

dys-   bad, difficult, abnormal, impaired

dysarthria [*dys-, bad + Grk > arthron, articulation + -ia*] Defective articulation of speech caused by damage or disease of the central nervous system. See anarthria, aphasia, and dysphasia. (dis AHR three uh)

dyscrasia [*dys-, abnormal + Grk > krasis, mixture + -ia*] A term formerly used to indicate an imbalance of the four humors of the body, but currently used to indicate a diseased or pathologic condition. See infirmity (def. 2). (dis KRAY zhuh)

dysentery [*dys-, bad + enter, intestine + -y*] An infectious disease marked by intestinal inflammation, resulting in abdominal pain, fever, and frequent stools containing blood and mucus. (DIS en tehr' ee)

dysfunction [*dys-, abnormal & function*] Impaired or abnormal function, especially of an organ or body part. See malfunction. (dis FUNGK shun)

dysgenic [*dys-, abnormal + gen, production + -ic*] Causing deterioration in the hereditary qualities of offspring. See eugenic. (dis JEN ik)

dysgenics [*dys-, abnormal + gen, production + -ics, study of*] The biological study of the deterioration of hereditary qualities that cause degeneration in offspring. Opposed to eugenics. (dis JEN iks)

dysgraphia [*dys-, impaired + graph, writing + -ia*] Impairment of the ability to write, usually resulting from a brain lesion. See dyslexia, alexia, and agraphia. (dis GRAF ee uh)

dyskinesia [*dys-, impaired + kine, motion + -ia*] Impairment of voluntary muscular movements. (dis' kih NEE zhuh)

dyslexia [*dys-, impaired + lex, reading + -ia*] Impairment of the ability to read, characterized by the inability to distinguish separate parts of a word and often the result of a brain injury or defect. See dysgraphia, agraphia, and alexia. (dis LEK see uh)

dyslogistic [*dys-, bad & (eu)logistic*] Showing disapproval. See eulogy. (dis' luh JIS tik)

dysmenorrhea [*dys-, difficult + meno, menstruation + rrhea, flow*] Painful menstruation. (dis' men' uh REE uh)

dyspepsia [*dys-, abnormal + peps, digestion + -ia*] Abnormal digestion. Indigestion. See eupepsia. (dis PEP shuh)

dysphagia [*dys-, difficult + phag, to eat + -ia*] Difficulty in swallowing. (dis FAY juh)

dysphasia [*dys-, impaired + -phasia, speech*] Impairment of speech, and sometimes the ability to understand words, due to brain injury. See aphasia, anarthria, and dysarthria. (dis FAY zhuh)

dysphemism [*dys-, bad & (eu)phemism*] The substitution of an offensive term for an inoffensive one. See euphemism. (DIS fuh miz' um)

dysphonia [*dys-, difficult + phon, sound + -ia*] Difficulty in producing articulate speech sounds. (dis FOH nee uh)

dysphoria [*dys-, bad + phor, state + -ia*] A general feeling of ill-being. Opposed to euphoria. (dis FOR ee uh)

dysplasia [*dys-, abnormal + plas, forming cells or tissue + -ia*] Abnormal growth or development of various cells or tissues. (dis PLAY zhuh)

dyspnea [*dys-, difficult + -pnea, breathing*] Difficult breathing, often resulting from lung or heart disease. See apnea and eupnea. (DISP nee uh)

dysprosium [*dys-, difficult + Grk > prositos, to approach + -ium*] A rare-earth chemical element that is highly magnetic. (dis PROH zee um)

dysrhythmia [*dys-, abnormal & rhythm & -ia*] Abnormal or disturbed rhythm, as of brain waves or speech patterns. (dis RITH mee uh)

dysteleology [*dys-, bad + teleo, end + log, doctrine + -y*] A philosophical doctrine that considers existence to have no purpose or final cause. See teleology (def. 2). (dis tel' ee OL uh jee)

dystopia [*dys-, bad + Grk > topos, place + -ia*] An imaginary, dreadful place of total misery. Opposed to utopia. (dis TOH pee uh)

dystrophy [*dys-, bad + -trophy, nourishment*] Any disorder caused by faulty or inadequate nutrition of a tissue or organ, as muscular dystrophy. (DIS truh fee)

dysuria [*dys-, difficult + -uria, urine*] Painful or difficult urination. (dis YOOR ee uh)

muscular dystrophy [*muscular & dys-, bad + -trophy, nourishment*] A group of chronic muscle diseases of genetic or unknown origin that cause irreversible muscle deterioration and may result in complete incapacitation. (MUS kyuh lur DIS truh fee)

bibli/o   book

Bible [*bibli, book*] 1.The sacred book of Christianity, including the Old and New Testaments. 2.A book containing the sacred writings of a religion. (BEYE bul)

biblical [*bibli, book + -ical*] Pertaining to or in accordance with the Bible. (BIB lih kul)

biblicist [*bibli, book + -icist*] 1.A person who interprets the words of the Bible literally. 2.An expert on the Bible. (BIB lih sist)

bibliography [*biblio, book + -graphy, writing*] 1.A list of writings by a particular writer, publisher, etc., or on a particular subject. 2.A list of sources used by an author in the production of a text. (bib' lee OG ruh fee)

bibliolatry [*biblio, book + -latry, worship*] 1.Excessive adherence to a literal interpretation of the Bible. 2.Excessive devotion to or dependence on books. (bib' lee OL uh tree)

bibliomancy [*biblio, book + -mancy, divination*] Divination by means of a book, especially a randomly chosen Bible verse or literary passage. (BIB lee uh man' see)

bibliomania [*biblio, book + mania, excessive desire*] An excessive fondness for collecting books, especially rare ones. (bib' lee uh MAY nee uh)

bibliopegy [*biblio, book + Grk > pegia, to bind + -y*] The art or practice of binding books. (bib' lee OP uh jee)

bibliophile [*biblio, book + -phile, love*] A lover or collector of books. (BIB lee uh feyel')

bibliophobia [*biblio, book + -phobia, fear*] Abnormal fear of or distaste for books. (bib' lee uh FOH bee uh)

bibliopole [*biblio, book + Grk > polein, to sell*] A bookseller who deals in rare books. (BIB lee uh pohl')

bibliotheca [*biblio, book + Grk > theke, case + -a*] 1.A book collection. Library. 2.A catalog of books. (bib' lee uh THEE kuh)

bibliotherapy [*biblio, book & therapy*] The use of books and other reading material for psychiatric therapy or to help solve personal problems. (bib' lee uh THEHR uh pee)

bibliotics [*biblio, book + -ics, knowledge*] The analysis of handwriting and written documents to determine origin or authenticity. (bib' lee OT iks)

discography [*disco, disk & (biblio)graphy*] 1.The cataloging and analysis of phonograph records. 2.A complete list of the recordings made by a particular artist or composer. (dis KOG ruh fee)

bio
life, living organisms, living tissue, mode of living

abiogenesis [*a-, without + bio, living organisms + -genesis, generation*] The now discredited theory that living organisms can be spontaneously generated directly from nonliving matter. Opposed to biogenesis. (ay' beye' oh JEN uh sis)

abiotic [*a-, without + bio, life + -tic*] Referring to the absence of life or specific life conditions. See biotic. (ay' beye OT ik)

aerobe [*aero, air + bio, life*] A microorganism that requires free oxygen to live. Opposed to anaerobe. (EHR ohb)

aerobic [*aero, air + bio, life + -ic*] 1.Living only in the presence of air or free oxygen. Opposed to anaerobic. 2.Pertaining to aerobics. 3.Pertaining to or produced by aerobes. (ehr OH bik)

aerobics [*aero, air + bio, life + -ics, practice*] A system of vigorous exercises designed to improve the body's ability to take in and utilize oxygen. (ehr OH biks)

aerobiology [*aero, air + bio, life + -logy, study of*] The study of the dispersion of air-borne biological materials such as microbes, pollen, and pollutants. (ehr' oh beye OL uh jee)

agrobiology [*agro, crop production + bio, life + -logy, science*] The quantitative science of plant growth and nutrition, as related to soil control and crop yield. (ag' roh beye OL uh jee)

amphibian [*amphi-, both + bio, life + -an*] 1.Any of various cold-blooded vertebrate animals, such as frogs and salamanders, the larvae of which breathe by gills and the adults of which breathe by lungs. See semiaquatic (def. 2) and semiterrestrial. 2.A vehicle that can operate both on water and on land. See amphibious (def. 2). 3.An aircraft that can take off and land either on land or water. (am FIB ee un)

amphibiotic [*amphi-, both + bio, life + -tic*] Pertaining to organisms that live in water in the larval stage and on land in the adult stage. (am' fih beye OT ik)

amphibious [*amphi-, both + bio, life + -ous*] Literally, "living a double life." 1.Able to live both in water and on land. See semiaquatic (def. 2) and semiterrestrial. 2.Able to operate both in water and on land. See amphibian (def. 2). 3.Pertaining to military operations involving both naval vessels and ground troops. (am FIB ee us)

anabiosis [*ana-, again + bio, life + -sis*] Restoration to life after apparent death. (an' uh beye OH sis)

anaerobe [*an-, without + aero, air + bio, life*] A microorganism that does not require free oxygen to live. Opposed to aerobe. (AN uh rohb')

anaerobic [*an-, without + aero, air + bio, life + -ic*] Living without air or free oxygen. Opposed to aerobic (def. 1). (an' uh ROH bik)

antibiosis [*anti-, against + bio, living organisms + -sis*] An association between two or more organisms in which at least one is adversely affected. See symbiosis (def. 1). (an' tee beye OH sis)

astrobiology [*astro, star + bio, living organisms + -logy, study of*] The branch of biology dealing with the search for and study of extraterrestrial living organisms. Same as exobiology. (as' troh beye OL uh jee)

autobiography [*auto-, self + bio, life + -graphy, written*] The story of one's life written by oneself. See biography. (awt' oh beye OG ruh fee)

bioassay [*bio, living organisms & assay*] A technique for determining the biological activity of a drug or other substance by testing its effect on a living organism. (beye' oh AS ay)

bioastronautics [*bio, life + astro, star + naut, sailor + -ics, science*] The branch of science dealing with the medical and biological effects of space travel on living things. (beye' oh as' truh NOT iks)

biocatalyst [*bio, life & catalyst*] An agent, such as an enzyme, that activates or speeds up a biochemical reaction. See catalyst (def. 1). (beye' oh KAT l ist)

biocenosis [*bio, life + ceno, common + -sis*] An association of plants and animals that forms an ecological community. (beye' oh sih NOH sis)

biochemistry [*bio, life & chemistry*] The branch of chemistry dealing with chemical and biological processes in plants and animals. (beye' oh KEM ih stree)

biocide [*bio, living organisms + -cide, to kill*] An agent capable of killing living organisms, as an insecticide, herbicide, or antibiotic. (BEYE uh seyed')

bioclimatology [*bio, living organisms + climat, climate + -ology, study of*] The scientific study of the impact of climate on living organisms. (beye' oh kleye' muh TOL uh jee)

bioconversion [*bio, living organisms & conversion*] The process of converting organic matter into fuels such as methane or ethanol. (beye' oh kun VUR zhun)

biocybernetics [*bio, life & cybernetics*] The study of biological control and communication systems. See cybernetics. (beye' oh seye' ber NET iks)

biodegradable [*bio, living organisms & degradable*] Capable of being decomposed by microorganisms such as bacteria. See biolysis. (beye' oh dih GRAY duh bul)

bioecology [*bio, living organisms + eco, environment + -logy, science*] The science dealing with the interrelations between living organisms and their environment. (beye' oh ih KOL uh jee)

bioelectric [*bio, living organisms & electric*] Pertaining to the phenomena of electrical energy in living organisms. (beye' oh ih LEK trik)

bioenergetics [*bio, living organisms & energetics*] The branch of biology dealing with the study of the conversion of sunlight, food, etc., into energy by living organisms. See energetics. (beye' oh en' ur JET iks)

bioengineering [*bio, life & engineering*] The application of engineering techniques and principles to the study of medicine and biology. (beye' oh en' juh NIHR ing)

bioethics [*bio, life & ethics*] The study of the moral and ethical ramifications of biological and medical research. See ethics. (beye' oh ETH iks)

biofeedback [*bio, life & feedback*] A technique that uses the aid of an electronic device to monitor and control certain involuntary body functions such as heartbeat and blood pressure. (beye' oh FEED bak')

biogas [*bio, life & gas*] A fuel gas composed of carbon dioxide and methane and derived from the bacterial decomposition of organic waste. (BEYE oh gas')

biogenesis [*bio, living organisms + -genesis, production*] The theory that living organisms are only produced from other living organisms. Opposed to abiogenesis. (beye' oh JEN uh sis)

biogenic [*bio, living organisms + gen, production + -ic*] Essential to or produced by living organisms. (beye' oh JEN ik)

biogeography [*bio, life + geo, earth + -graphy, science*] The branch of biology dealing with the study of the geographical distribution of plants and animals. See phytogeography and zoogeography. (beye' oh jee OG ruh fee)

biography [*bio, life + -graphy, written*] The story of one's life written by another person. See autobiography. (beye OG ruh fee)

biohazard [*bio, life & hazard*] A biological agent that endangers the life or health of humans or other living organisms, as an infectious microbe. (BEYE oh haz' urd)

bioinstrumentation [*bio, life & instrumentation*] The use of instruments and devices for detecting, measuring, recording, and transmitting data from specific body functions to remote receiving stations for analysis, as from astronauts in space. (beye' oh in' struh men TAY shun)

biological clock [*biological & clock*] An innate timing mechanism in living organisms that regulates various cyclical activities such as sleep. (beye' uh LOJ ih kul klok)

biology [*bio, life + -logy, study of*] The scientific study of the origin, history, habits, etc., of living organisms and life processes, including both botany and zoology. (beye OL uh jee)

bioluminescence [*bio, living organisms + Ltn > lumen, light + -escence*] The emission of light by a living organism, as a firefly or certain fungi. (beye' oh loo' muh NES ens)

biolysis [*bio, life + -lysis, decomposition*] Decomposition of organic material caused by the action of microorganisms. See biodegradable. (beye OL uh sis)

biomass [*bio, living organisms & mass*] The collective mass of living organisms in a given region, area, or volume. (BEYE oh mas')

biomaterial [*bio, life & material*] A material, either natural or synthetic, that is a viable replacement for body parts such as tissue or bone. (beye' oh muh TIHR ee ul)

biomathematics [*bio, life & mathematics*] The application of mathematical principles to the study of medicine and biology. (beye' oh math' uh MAT iks)

biome [*bio, living organisms + -ome, mass*] The ecological community of plants and animals in a given region, as grassland or desert. (BEYE ohm)

biomechanics [*bio, life & mechanics*] The application of mechanical principles to the study of medicine and biology. (beye' oh muh KAN iks)

biomedicine [*bio, life & medicine*] Clinical medicine based on aspects of the biological sciences. (beye' oh MED ih sin)

biometeorology [*bio, living organisms + Grk > meteoron, atmospheric phenomenon + -ology, study of*] The study of the impact of natural or artificial atmospheric conditions on living organisms. (beye' oh meet' ee uh ROL uh jee)

biometrics [*bio, life + metr, to measure + -ics, study of*] The branch of biology dealing with the statistical and mathematical study of biological data. (beye' oh MET riks)

biometry [*bio, life* + *-metry, science of measuring*] The scientific study of the measurement of the probable life span of humans. (beye OM ih tree)

bionics [*bio, life* & *(electr)onics*] The application of biological principles to the study of engineering, especially electrical engineering. (beye ON iks)

bionomics [*bio, life* + *nom, law* + *-ics, study of*] Ecology. (beye' uh NOM iks)

biophysics [*bio, life* & *physics*] The application of the techniques and principles of physics to the study of medicine and biology. (beye' oh FIZ iks)

biopsy [*bio, living tissue* + *-opsy, inspection*] The removal of a small sample of living tissue for examination and diagnosis. (BEYE op' see)

biorhythm [*bio, life* & *rhythm*] An innate cyclic pattern of changes to the biological processes of an organism that vary according to internal and external factors. (BEYE oh rith' um)

bioscience [*bio, life* & *science*] The application of all the sciences to the study of medicine and biology. (beye' oh SEYE ens)

biosocial [*bio, life* & *social*] Pertaining to the application of sociology to the study of medicine and biology. (beye' oh SOH shul)

biosphere [*bio, life* & *sphere*] The part of the earth's crust, water, and atmosphere that supports life. See ecosphere. (BEYE uh sfihr')

biostatistics [*bio, life* & *statistics*] The application of statistical principles and processes to the study of medicine and biology. (beye' oh stuh TIS tiks)

biosynthesis [*bio, life* + *syn, together* + *the, to put* + *-sis*] The production of chemical substances by a living organism. (beye' oh SIN thuh sis)

biota [*biot(ic)* & *-a*] The combined plant and animal life (flora and fauna) of a particular region or period. See flora and fauna. (beye OHT uh)

biotechnology [*bio, living organisms* + *techn, skill* + *-ology, science*] The science of using living organisms to make or improve products or to improve other living organisms. (beye' oh tek NOL uh jee)

biotelemetry [*bio, life* & *telemetry*] The remote monitoring of the physical activities, conditions, or functions of a human or animal. See telemetry. (beye' oh tuh LEM ih tree)

biotic [*bio, life* + *-tic*] Pertaining to life or living things. See abiotic. (beye OT ik)

biotin [*biot(ic)* & *-in*] A B-complex vitamin found in all living cells and present in large amounts in liver, eggs, and yeast. (BEYE uh tin)

biotope [*bio, life* + *Grk* > *topos, place*] A small ecological area with uniform environmental conditions suitable for certain plant and animal life. (BEYE uh tohp')

biotron [*bio, living organisms* + *-tron, chamber*] A chamber for studying plants and animals under controlled climatic conditions. (BEYE uh tron')

biotype [*bio, life* & *type*] A group of organisms with the same fundamental genetic characteristics, but different physical characteristics. See genotype. (BEYE uh teyep')

chronobiology [*chrono, time* + *bio, life* + *-logy, study of*] The study of how time affects life, as in various biological rhythms. (kron' oh beye OL uh jee)

cryobiology [*cryo, cold* + *bio, living organisms* + *-logy, study of*] The scientific study of the effects of below-normal temperatures on living organisms. (kreye' oh beye OL uh jee)

cryonics [*cryo, cold* & *(bio)nics*] The practice of freezing the body of a recently deceased person to preserve it for possible revival by future medical cures. See bionics. (kreye ON iks)

endobiotic [*endo-, inside* + *bio, life* + *-tic*] Pertaining to an organism living within the tissues or cells of a host organism. See ectogenous. (en' doh beye OT ik)

exobiology [*exo-, outside* + *bio, living organisms* + *-logy, study of*] The branch of biology dealing with the search for and study of extraterrestrial living organisms. (eks' oh beye OL uh jee)

gnotobiotics [*gnos, knowledge* + *bio, living organisms* + *-ics, study of*] The science dealing with the study of organisms living in an environment free from germs or other microorganisms, except those known to be present. (noht' oh beye OT iks)

macrobiotics [*macro-, long* + *bio, life* + *-ics, study of*] The science of extending longevity, as through nutritious diets, stress reduction, etc. (mak' roh beye OT iks)

microbe [*micro-, small* + *bio, life*] A microorganism; especially a virus, bacterium, protozoan, etc., that causes disease. Germ. (MEYE krohb)

microbicide [*microb(e)* & *-cide, to kill*] An agent for killing microbes. (meye KROH buh seyed')

microbiology [*micro-, small* + *bio, life* + *-logy, study of*] The study of microscopic forms of life, as viruses, bacteria, protozoans, and other microorganisms. (meye' kroh beye OL uh jee)

molecular biology [*molecular* & *biology*] The branch of biology dealing with the study of the molecular structure of biological systems. (muh LEK yuh lur beye OL uh jee)

necrobiosis [*necro, death* + *bio, living tissue* + *-sis*] The natural process of death or decay of cells and tissues not due to disease or injury. See necrosis. (nek' roh beye OH sis)

parabiosis [*para-, beside* + *bio, life* + *-sis*] The joining of two individuals, as Siamese twins or as laboratory animals by surgical operation. (pehr' uh beye OH sis)

polysaprobic [*poly, many* + *sapro, decomposed* + *bio, life* + *-ic*] Pertaining to a body of water containing rapidly decomposing organic matter and little or no free oxygen. (pol' ee suh PROH bik)

psychobiography [*psycho, mind* & *biography*] A biography that psychoanalyzes the subject. (seye' koh beye OG ruh fee)

psychobiology [*psycho, mind* + *bio, life* + *-logy, study of*] 1.The scientific study of the integration of mind and body. 2.The scientific study of the biology of the mind. (seye' koh beye OL uh jee)

radiobiology [*radio, radiation* + *bio, living organisms* + *-logy, study of*] The branch of biology dealing with the study of the effects of radiation on living organisms. (ray' dee oh' beye OL uh jee)

rhizobium [*rhizo, root* + *bio, life* + *-um*] Any of various rod-shaped bacteria living freely in soil or as symbiotic nitrogen fixers that form root nodules in some leguminous plants. (reye ZOH bee um)

saprobe [*sapro, decaying + bio, life*] A plant or microorganism that lives on decaying organic matter. (SAP rohb)

sociobiology [*socio, social + bio, life + -logy, study of*] The biological study of social organization and behavior in humans and animals. See sociology. (soh' see oh' beye OL uh jee)

symbiosis [*sym-, together + bio, mode of living + -sis*] 1.Two dissimilar species living together in close association, especially if such association is of mutual benefit to each. See antibiosis. 2.Any mutually beneficial relationship between persons, groups, etc. (sim' bee OH sis)

triphibian [*tri-, three & (am)phibian*] Able to operate or function in water, on land, or in the air. See amphibian. (treye FIB ee un)

viv, vivi, vit   life, living, live

aqua vitae [*aqua, water & vit, life*] Literally, "water of life." 1.Alcohol. 2.Whiskey, brandy, or other strong liquor. See aquavit. (AK wuh VEYET ee)

aquavit [*aqua, water + vit, life*] Literally, "water of life." A strong, dry Scandinavian liquor distilled from potatoes or grain and flavored with caraway seeds. See aqua vitae. (AK wuh veet')

arbor vitae [*arbor, tree & vit, life*] The treelike structure of white nerve tissue seen in a cross section of the cerebellum. (AHR bur VEYET ee)

arborvitae [*arbor, tree + vit, life*] Any of various ornamental trees or shrubs of the pine family with small scalelike leaves, sometimes called the tree of life. (ahr' bur VEYET ee)

avitaminosis [*a-, without & vitamin & -osis, diseased condition*] Any disease caused by vitamin deficiency. See hypervitaminosis. (ay veyet' uh mih NOH sis)

bon vivant [*French > bon, good & viv, living + -ant*] Literally, "good liver." A person with refined tastes who enjoys good food and drink. See joie de vivre. (bon' vee VONT)

convivial [*con-, together + viv, living + -ial*] 1.Fond of eating, drinking, and good companionship. Sociable. Jovial. 2.Festive. (kun VIV ee ul)

curriculum vitae [*curriculum {course} & vit, life*] Literally, "course of life." A brief account of a person's education, career, and qualifications. (kuh RIK yuh lum VEYET ee)

devitalize [*de-, away + vit, life + -al + -ize*] To lower or take away the vitality of. Weaken. See revitalize. (dee VEYET l eyez')

hypervitaminosis [*hyper-, above & vitamin & -osis, abnormal condition*] An abnormal condition resulting from taking excessive amounts of one or more vitamins. See avitaminosis. (heye' per veyet' uh mih NOH sis)

inter vivos [*inter-, between & viv, living*] Taking place between living persons, as a gift or trust. (IN ter VEE vohs)

joie de vivre [*French > joie, joy & viv, living*] Literally, "joy of living." Hearty enjoyment of life. See bon vivant. (zhwah' duh VEE vruh)

modus vivendi [*Ltn > modus, manner & viv, living*] 1.A manner of living. 2.A temporary agreement between disputing persons or parties pending a final settlement. (MOH dus vih VEN dee)

ovoviviparous [*ovo, egg + vivi, living + -parous, to produce*] Producing eggs that hatch internally, as certain fishes, certain reptiles, etc. See oviparous and viviparous. (oh' voh veye' VIP ur us)

provitamin [*pro-, before & vitamin*] A precursor of a vitamin that an organism can convert into a vitamin, as carotene which is converted to vitamin A. (proh VEYET uh min)

qui vive [*French > qui, who & viv, live*] 1."Who goes there?" 2.On the alert. Watchful. (kee VEEV)

redivivus [*red-, again + viv, live + -us*] Reborn. Revived. Restored. (red' uh VEYE vus)

revitalize [*re-, again + vit, live + -al + -ize*] To restore vitality to. See devitalize. (ree VEYET l eyez')

revive [*re-, again + viv, live*] 1.To bring back to consciousness or life. Resuscitate. 2.To make useful, healthy, active, or current again. (rih VEYEV)

revivify [*re-, again + viv, live + -ify, to make*] To restore new life, vigor, or activity to. See vivify. (ree VIV uh feye')

survive [*super-, beyond + viv, live*] 1.To continue to live or remain in existence. 2.To live or exist longer than. (sur VEYEV)

viable [*vit, life + -able*] 1.Workable. Feasible. Practicable. 2.Capable of living and developing outside the uterus, as a newborn child or sufficiently developed fetus. 3.Capable of living and growing, as a spore or seed. (VEYE uh bul)

vital [*vit, life + -al*] 1.Pertaining to or essential to life. 2.Essential to the continuation of something. (VEYET l)

vital signs [*vit, life + -al & signs*] An individual's body temperature, pulse rate, and respiratory rate. (VEYET l seyens)

vital statistics [*vit, life + -al & statistics*] Statistical data pertaining to human life, as births, deaths, marriages, etc. (VEYET l stuh TIS tiks)

vitalism [*vit, life + -al + -ism*] The philosophical doctrine that life is not totally the result of chemical and physical forces and is, at least in part, due to some vital principle. (VEYET l iz' um)

vitality [*vit, life + -al + -ity*] 1.Energy. Vigor. 2.The ability to survive and develop. 3.The power to continue, endure, or survive. (veye TAL ih tee)

vitals [*vit, life + -als*] 1.Body organs that are considered essential to life, as the heart, lungs, liver, and brain. 2.The essential parts required to maintain the continued function or existence of something. (VEYET lz)

vitamin [*vit, life & amin(e)*] Any of various organic substances necessary in small amounts for normal metabolism, that are found naturally in plant and animal tissue and are also produced synthetically. (VEYET uh min)

viva [*viv, life*] Long live (the person, place, or thing specified). Salute or acclamation originating from Spanish and Italian, used to express approval. See vive. (VEE vuh)

viva voce [*viv, living & voc, voice*] 1.By word of mouth. Orally. 2.An oral examination in British universities. (VEYE vuh VOH see)

viv, vivi, vit

vivace [*viv, life* + *-ce*] In a brisk and lively manner. Used as a direction in music. (vee VAH chay)

vivacious [*viv, life* + *-acious*] Lively and spirited. Animated. See ebullient (def. 1). (veye VAY shus)

vivarium [*viv, living* + *-arium, a place for*] An indoor place for raising and studying live animals and plants. See aquarium and terrarium. (veye VEHR ee um)

vive [*viv, life*] Long live (the person, place, or thing specified). Salute or acclamation originating from French, used to express approval. See viva. (veev)

vivid [*viv, life* + *-id*] 1.Full of life and vigor. Lively. 2.Producing a clear and distinct impression. Sharp. 3.Bright and distinct. Brilliant. (VIV id)

vivify [*viv, life* + *-ify, to make*] To give life, vigor, or activity to. See revivify. (VIV uh feye')

viviparous [*vivi, living* + *-parous, to produce*] Producing live young rather than eggs, as most mammals, certain fishes, certain reptiles, etc. See ovoviviparous and oviparous. (veye VIP ur us)

vivisection [*vivi, living* + *sect, to cut* + *-ion*] The practice of cutting into the body of a living animal, especially for scientific research. (viv' uh SEK shun)

blast/o
cell, cell layer, immature cell, primitive, bud

blastema [*blast, immature cell* + *-ma*] 1.The undifferentiated living substance from which cells develop. 2.The undifferentiated cells or tissues from which a body organ or part develops or from which a body part regenerates. (bla STEE muh)

blastocoel [*blasto, cell layer* + *-coel, cavity*] The fluid-filled cavity of a blastula. See blastoderm and blastula. (BLAS tuh seel')

blastocyst [*blasto, cell layer* + *cyst, sac*] The stage of mammalian embryonic development during which implantation of the embryo into the uterine wall occurs. (BLAS tuh sist')

blastoderm [*blasto, cell layer* + *derm, skin*] 1.The layer of cells surrounding the blastocoel of a blastula. 2.The cells covering the blastocoel of a heavily-yolked egg. See blastocoel and blastula. (BLAS tuh derm')

blastodisk [*blasto, cell & disk*] 1.A small, disklike region of embryonic cells on a fertilized ovum, from which the embryo begins to develop. 2.A small, disklike region of protoplasm that appears on the surface of a heavily-yolked egg after fertilization, as in bird or reptile eggs. (BLAS tuh disk')

blastogenesis [*blasto, bud* + *-genesis, production*] 1.Reproduction by budding. 2.The theory that hereditary characteristics are carried from parents to offspring by germ plasm. Opposed to pangenesis. (blas' tuh JEN uh sis)

blastomere [*blasto, cell* + *-mere, part*] Any of the cells formed by cleavage of a fertilized ovum. (BLAS tuh mihr')

blastopore [*blasto, primitive & pore {small opening}*] The opening into the archenteron of the gastrula. See archenteron and gastrula. (BLAS tuh por')

blastula [*blast, cell layer* + *-ule, small* + *-a*] An early stage of embryonic development in which the embryo consists of a single spherical layer of cells surrounding a fluid-filled cavity. The cell layer is the blastoderm and the fluid-filled cavity is the blastocoel. See gastrula, blastoderm, and blastocoel. (BLAS choo luh)

diploblastic [*diplo, double* + *blast, cell layer* + *-ic*] 1.Pertaining to animals whose body wall consists of two cell layers: the endoderm and ectoderm. Includes only the cnidarians. See triploblastic. 2.Having two germ layers. (dip' loh BLAS tik)

ectoblast [*ecto-, outside* + *blast, cell layer*] 1.Undifferentiated embryonic ectoderm. 2.Ectoderm. See ectoderm, endoblast, and mesoblast. (EK tuh blast')

ectomere [*ecto-, outside & (blasto)mere*] A blastomere that develops into ectoderm. See ectoderm. (EK tuh mihr')

endoblast [*endo-, inside* + *blast, cell layer*] 1.Undifferentiated embryonic endoderm. 2.Endoderm. See endoderm, mesoblast, and ectoblast. (EN duh blast')

epiblast [*epi-, outside* + *blast, cell layer*] The outer layer of the three primary germ cell layers of an embryo from which the nervous system, the epidermis and epidermal tissues, sense organs, and certain other body parts develop. Same as ectoderm. (EP ih blast')

erythroblast [*erythro, red* + *blast, immature cell*] An immature, nucleated red blood cell normally found in bone marrow. See erythrocyte. (ih RITH ruh blast')

erythroblastosis [*erythro, red* + *blast, cell* + *-osis, abnormal condition*] The presence of erythroblasts in the circulating blood, as in certain diseases. (ih rith' roh blas TOH sis)

fibroblast [*fibro, fiber* + *blast, cell*] A cell that develops into connective tissue. (FEYE bruh blast')

hematoblast [*hemato, blood* + *blast, immature cell*] An immature blood cell from which other immature blood cells such as lymphoblasts, myeloblasts, and erythroblasts are derived. (hih MAT uh blast')

holoblastic [*holo, whole* + *blast, cell* + *-ic*] Pertaining to a fertilized egg that undergoes complete cleavage into individual blastomeres. See meroblastic. (hol' uh BLAS tik)

hypoblast [*hypo-, below* + *blast, cell layer*] The inner layer of the three primary germ cell layers of an embryo from which the gastrointestinal tract, most of the respiratory system, and many other organs develop. Same as endoderm. (HEYE puh blast')

idioblast [*idio-, distinct* + *blast, cell*] A plant cell that differs markedly from surrounding cells within the same tissue. (ID ee uh blast')

lymphoblast [*lympho, lymph* + *blast, immature cell*] An immature cell that is the precursor to a lymphocyte. See lymphocyte. (LIM fuh blast')

megaloblast [*megalo, large* + *blast, cell*] An abnormally large, dysfunctional erythroblast present in the blood, especially in cases of pernicious anemia and folic acid deficiency. (MEG uh loh blast')

melanoblast [*melano, black* + *blast, immature cell*] An immature cell that is the precursor to a melanophore or melanocyte. See melanophore and melanocyte. (muh LAN uh blast')

meroblastic [*mero, part + blast, cell + -ic*] Pertaining to a fertilized egg that undergoes partial cleavage due to the presence of large amounts of yolk. See holoblastic. (mehr' uh BLAS tik)

mesoblast [*meso-, middle + blast, cell layer*]
1. Undifferentiated embryonic mesoderm.
2. Mesoderm. See mesoderm, endoblast, and ectoblast. (MEZ uh blast')

neuroblast [*neuro, nerve + blast, immature cell*] An immature nerve cell that develops into a neuron. (NOOR uh blast')

neuroblastoma [*neuro, nerve + blast, cell + -oma, tumor*] A malignant tumor composed of neuroblasts, most often affecting the adrenal medulla of infants and children. See neuroblast. (noor' oh blas TOH muh)

odontoblast [*odonto, tooth + blast, cell*] Any of the connective tissue cells that form the outer surface of dental pulp and produce dentin. See dentin. (oh DONT uh blast')

osteoblast [*osteo, bone + blast, cell*] A bone-forming cell arising from a fibroblast. (OS tee uh blast')

triploblastic [*tripl(e) & blast, cell layer + -ic*] Pertaining to animals, including humans, whose embryo consists of three germ cell layers: the endoderm, mesoderm, and ectoderm. Includes all animals except cnidarians, sponges, and mesozoans. See diploblastic (def. 1). (trip' loh BLAS tik)

trophoblast [*tropho, nourishment + blast, cell layer*] The cell layer that forms the outer wall of the blastocyst. It supplies the embryo with nutrients and aids in implanting the embryo in the uterine wall. (TROF uh blast')

cyt/o, -cyte   cell

agranulocyte [*a-, without & granul(e) & -cyte, cell*] Either of two types of mature white blood cells that have only very minute granules in the cytoplasm. See granulocyte and leukocyte. (ay GRAN yuh loh seyet')

amebocyte [*ameb(a) & -cyte, cell*] 1. An ameboid cell found in the body fluids of invertebrates. 2. Any ameboid cell capable of ameboid movement. (uh MEE buh seyet')

astrocyte [*astro, star + -cyte, cell*] A star-shaped cell that is one of several types of neuroglial cells in the brain and spinal cord. (AS truh seyet')

astrocytoma [*astro, star + cyt, cell + -oma, tumor*] A malignant tumor of the brain or spinal cord composed of astrocytes. (as' troh seye TOH muh)

cytochemistry [*cyto, cell & chemistry*] The branch of cytology dealing with the study of cell chemistry in plants and animals. (seyet' oh KEM ih stree)

cytochrome [*cyto, cell + -chrome, pigment*] A respiratory pigment widely distributed in plant and animal cells that plays an essential role in cell respiration by undergoing alternate reduction and oxidation. (SEYET uh krohm')

cytogenesis [*cyto, cell + -genesis, formation*] Cell formation and development. (seyet' oh JEN uh sis)

cytogenetics [*cyto(logy) & genetics*] The comparative study of heredity and variation using the principles of cytology and genetics. See cytology and genetics. (seyet' oh juh NET iks)

cytokinesis [*cyto, cell + kine, division + -sis*] The changes that occur in the cytoplasm during cell division after the division of the nucleus. See cytoplasm and karyokinesis. (seyet' oh kih NEE sis)

cytokinin [*cyto, cell + -kinin, hormone*] Any of various plant growth hormones that promote cell division. (seyet' uh KEYE nin)

cytology [*cyt, cell + -ology, study of*] The branch of biology dealing with the study of the origin, structure, function, and pathology of cells. (seye TOL uh jee)

cytolysis [*cyto, cell + -lysis, decomposition*] The destruction or decomposition of cells. (seye TOL uh sis)

cytomegalic [*cyto, cell + megal, large + -ic*] Characterized by an abnormal enlargement of cells. (seyet' oh mih GAL ik)

cytomegalovirus [*cyto, cell + megalo, large & virus*] Any of various herpesviruses that cause enlargement of cells in various organs, and in humans, cause cytomegalic inclusion disease. (seyet' uh meg' uh loh VEYE rus)

cytopathic [*cyto, cell + path, disease + -ic*] Pertaining to or causing pathological disorders or changes in a cell. (seyet' uh PATH ik)

cytophotometry [*cyto, cell & photometry*] The scientific study of cells using photometry. See photometry. (seyet' oh foh TOM ih tree)

cytoplasm [*cyto, cell + plasm, protoplasm*] The protoplasm of a cell outside the nucleus. See nucleoplasm and protoplasm. (SEYET uh plaz' um)

cytostatic [*cyto, cell + stat, stationary + -ic*] Suppressing or preventing the growth and division of cells. (seyet' uh STAT ik)

cytotaxonomy [*cyto, cell + taxo, arrangement + -nomy, system of laws*] The classification of organisms based on chromosome characteristics and cellular structure. See taxonomy. (seyet' oh taks ON uh mee)

cytotoxin [*cyto, cell + tox, poison + -in*] A toxin or antibody that destroys certain cells, as snake venom. See neurotoxin and hemotoxin. (SEYET oh tok' sin)

endocytosis [*endo-, inside + cyt, cell + -osis, action*] Incorporation of material from the environment into a cell by phagocytosis or pinocytosis. Opposed to exocytosis. (en' doh seye TOH sis)

erythrocyte [*erythro, red + -cyte, cell*] A mature red blood cell that has no nucleus. See leukocyte and erythroblast. (ih RITH ruh seyet')

erythrocytometer [*erythro, red + cyto, cell + meter, to measure*] An instrument for counting red blood cells. (ih rith' roh seye TOM et er)

exocytosis [*exo-, outside + cyt, cell + -osis, action*] The discharge of material from a cell that is too large to diffuse through the cell wall, as a large molecule, particle, etc. Opposed to endocytosis. (eks' oh seye TOH sis)

gametocyte [*gameto, gamete + -cyte, cell*] A male or female germ cell that produces gametes through division by meiosis. See spermatocyte and oocyte. (guh MEET uh seyet')

granulocyte [*granul(e) & -cyte, cell*] One of three types of mature, granular white blood cells that vary according to the specific granules in the cytoplasm. See agranulocyte and leukocyte. (GRAN yuh loh seyet')

cyt/o, -cyte

hemacytometer [*hema, blood + cyto, cell + meter, to measure*] An instrument for counting the number of blood cells in a sample. Same as hemocytometer. (hee' muh seye TOM et er)

hemocyte [*hemo, blood + -cyte, cell*] A mature blood cell. (HEE muh seyet')

hemocytometer [*hemo, blood + cyto, cell + meter, to measure*] An instrument for counting the number of blood cells in a sample. (hee' moh seye TOM et er)

histiocyte [*histio, tissue + -cyte, cell*] A phagocyte found in connective tissue. (HIST ee uh seyet')

leukocyte [*leuko, white + -cyte, cell*] A mature white blood cell. Leukocytes are divided into granulocytes (neutrophils, eosinophils, and basophiles) and agranulocytes (monocytes and lymphocytes). See erythrocyte, granulocyte, and agranulocyte. (LOO kuh seyet')

leukocytosis [*leuko, white + cyt, cell + -osis, increase*] An abnormal increase in the number of white blood cells in the blood, resulting from various conditions or diseases, as infection or leukemia. (loo' koh seye TOH sis)

lymphocyte [*lympho, lymph + -cyte, cell*] A nongranular white blood cell that is present in the blood and lymphatic system and aids in the production of antibodies. See monocyte, agranulocyte, and leukocyte. (LIM fuh seyet')

macrocyte [*macro-, large + -cyte, cell*] An abnormally large red blood cell occurring in certain anemias and associated with folic acid deficiency. See microcyte. (MAK roh seyet')

megakaryocyte [*mega-, large + karyo, nucleus + -cyte, cell*] A large platelet-producing cell in the bone marrow with a highly lobulated nucleus. See thrombocyte. (meg' uh KEHR ee oh seyet')

melanocyte [*melano, black + -cyte, cell*] A melanin-producing epidermal cell responsible for skin color variations. (muh LAN uh seyet')

microcyte [*micro-, small + -cyte, cell*] An abnormally small mature red blood cell, occurring mainly in anemias, that is five microns or less in diameter. See macrocyte. (MEYE kroh seyet')

monocyte [*mono-, one + -cyte, cell*] A nongranular white blood cell with a single nucleus. See lymphocyte, agranulocyte, and leukocyte. (MON uh seyet')

oocyte [*oo, egg + -cyte, cell*] A female germ cell that undergoes a primary and secondary meiotic division to produce an ovum. See spermatocyte, oogonium (def. 1), and ovum. (OH uh seyet')

osteocyte [*osteo, bone + -cyte, cell*] A mature bone cell embedded within the bone matrix. (OS tee uh seyet')

phagocyte [*phago, to eat + -cyte, cell*] A white blood cell that protects the body against infection and disease by ingesting and destroying harmful foreign material such as cell debris, microorganisms, etc. See macrophage and microphage. (FAG uh seyet')

phagocytosis [*phagocyt(e) & -osis, action*] The ingestion and destruction of cells, microorganisms, and other foreign matter by phagocytes. See phagocyte. (fag' uh seye TOH sis)

pinocytosis [*Grk > pinein, to drink + cyt, cell + -osis, action*] The intake of fluids by a cell through invagination and the pinching off of the plasma membrane. (pin' uh seye TOH sis)

polycythemia [*poly, many + cyt, cell + -emia, blood condition*] A condition in which there is an abnormal increase in the number of red blood cells. (pol' ee seye THEE mee uh)

spermatocyte [*spermato, sperm + -cyte, cell*] A male germ cell that undergoes a primary and secondary meiotic division, thus forming four spermatids, which later become spermatozoa. See oocyte, spermatogonium, spermatid, and spermatozoon. (spur MAT uh seyet')

sporocyte [*sporo, spore + -cyte, cell*] The spore mother cell that gives rise to four haploid spores during meiosis. (SPOR uh seyet')

syncytium [*syn-, together + cyt, cell + -ium*] A multinucleate mass of protoplasm without distinct cellular boundaries, as in a muscle fiber. (sin SISH ee um)

thrombocyte [*thrombo, blood clot + -cyte, cell*] A blood platelet. See megakaryocyte. (THROM boh seyet')

thrombocytopenia [*thrombo, blood clot + cyto, cell + -penia, lacking*] An abnormal decrease in the number of blood platelets. (throm' boh seyet' uh PEE nee uh)

cardi/o   heart, orifice

bradycardia [*brady, slow + cardi, heart + -a*] Abnormal slowness of the heartbeat, usually less than 60 beats per minute. See tachycardia. (brad' ih KAHR dee uh)

cardia [*cardi, orifice + -a*] The portion of the stomach that connects to the esophagus. (KAHR dee uh)

cardiac [*cardi, heart + -ac*] 1.Pertaining to or involving the heart. 2.Pertaining to the orifice that connects the stomach to the esophagus. 3.A person with a heart disease or disorder. (KAHR dee ak')

cardialgia [*cardi, heart + alg, pain + -ia*] Pain in or near the heart. (kahr' dee AL juh)

cardiogenic [*cardio, heart + gen, origin + -ic*] Originating in the heart or resulting from a heart malfunction. (kahr' dee oh JEN ik)

cardiograph [*cardio, heart + graph, recording*] An instrument for graphically recording the movements of the heart. (KAHR dee oh graf')

cardioid [*cardi, heart + -oid, resembling*] A mathematical heart-shaped curve generated by tracing a fixed point on the circumference of a circle completely around the circumference of another circle of the same size. (KAHR dee oid')

cardiology [*cardi, heart + -ology, study of*] The study of the functions and diseases of the heart. (kahr' dee OL uh jee)

cardiomegaly [*cardio, heart + megal, large + -y*] Enlargement of the heart. (kahr' dee oh MEG uh lee)

cardiomyopathy [*cardio, heart + myo, muscle + -pathy, disease*] Any disease or disorder of the heart muscle. See cardiopathy. (kahr' dee oh' meye OP uh thee)

cardiopathy [*cardio, heart + -pathy, disease*] Any disease, disorder, or condition of the heart. See cardiomyopathy. (kahr' dee OP uh thee)

cardiophobia [*cardio, heart + -phobia, fear*] Abnormal fear of heart disease. (kahr' dee oh FOH bee uh)

cardiopulmonary [*cardio, heart + pulmon, lung + -ary*] Pertaining to or involving the heart and lungs. (kahr' dee oh PUL muh nehr' ee)

cardiorespiratory [*cardio, heart & respiratory*] Pertaining to or involving the heart and respiratory system. (kahr' dee oh RES per uh tor' ee)

cardiovascular [*cardio, heart & vascular*] Pertaining to or involving the heart and blood vessels. (kahr' dee oh VAS kyuh lur)

carditis [*cardi, heart + -itis, inflammation*] Inflammation of the heart. (kahr DEYE tis)

electrocardiograph [*electro, electric + cardio, heart + graph, recording*] An instrument for graphically recording small electric currents originating in the heart. (ih lek' troh KAHR dee uh graf')

endocardial [*endo-, inside + cardi, heart + -al*] 1.Located inside the heart. 2.Pertaining to the endocardium. (en' doh KAHR dee ul)

endocarditis [*endo-, inside + cardi, heart + -itis, inflammation*] Inflammation of the endocardium. (en' doh kahr DEYE tis)

endocardium [*endo-, inside + cardi, heart + -um*] The thin serous membrane lining the chambers of the heart. (en' doh KAHR dee um)

epicardium [*epi-, outside + cardi, heart + -um*] The innermost layer of the pericardium that touches the heart. See pericardium. (ep' ih KAHR dee um)

intracardiac [*intra-, within + cardi, heart + -ac*] Occurring or located within the heart. (in' truh KAHR dee ak')

megalocardia [*megalo, large + cardi, heart + -a*] Enlargement of the heart. Same as cardiomegaly. (meg' uh loh KAHR dee uh)

myocardiograph [*myo, muscle + cardio, heart + graph, recording*] An instrument for graphically recording the muscular activity of the heart. (meye' uh KAHR dee uh graf')

myocarditis [*myo, muscle + cardi, heart + -itis, inflammation*] Inflammation of the myocardium. (meye' oh kahr DEYE tis)

myocardium [*myo, muscle + cardi, heart + -um*] The middle layer of muscle in the walls of the heart. (meye' uh KAHR dee um)

pericarditis [*peri-, around + cardi, heart + -itis, inflammation*] Inflammation of the pericardium. (pehr' ih kahr DEYE tis)

pericardium [*peri-, around + cardi, heart + -um*] The double-layered sac surrounding the heart and the ends of the large vessels attached to the heart. (pehr' ih KAHR dee um)

phonocardiograph [*phono, sound + cardio, heart + graph, recording*] An instrument for graphically recording the sounds of the heartbeat. (foh' nuh KAHR dee uh graf')

tachycardia [*tachy, rapid + cardi, heart + -a*] Abnormally rapid heartbeat. See bradycardia. (tak' ih KAHR dee uh)

carn, carni   flesh, meat

carnage [*carn, flesh + -age*] Bloody slaughter of many people, as in battle. (KAHR nij)

carnal [*carn, flesh + -al*] 1.Pertaining to the body or flesh. 2.Sensual. Sexual. 3.Not spiritual. Worldly. (KAHRN l)

carnassial [*carn, flesh + -ial*] Pertaining to teeth adapted for cutting flesh. (kahr NAS ee ul)

carnation [*carn, flesh + -ation*] 1.A perennial plant of the pink family bearing red, white, and pink flowers. 2.A rosy-pink color. 3.A flesh-colored tint formerly used in painting. (kahr NAY shun)

carnelian [*carn, flesh + -ian*] A red to dark-red variety of chalcedony, often used as a gem. (kahr NEEL yun)

carnival [*carni, meat + Ltn > levare, to remove*] 1.The time of feasting and merrymaking just before Lent. 2.A traveling amusement show. (KAHR nuh vul)

carnivore [*carni, flesh + vor, to eat*] 1.Any of an order of flesh-eating mammals. 2.A plant that feeds on insects. (KAHR nuh vor')

carnivorous [*carni, flesh + vor, to eat + -ous*] 1.Feeding on flesh. See zoophagous. 2.Feeding on insects, as certain plants. See insectivorous. (kahr NIV ur us)

carrion [*carn, flesh + -ion*] 1.Dead and decaying flesh. 2.Something very disgusting or repulsive. 3.Feeding on dead or decaying flesh. See necrophagous. (KEHR ee un)

caruncle [*carn, flesh + -cle*] 1.A normal or abnormal fleshy outgrowth on a human or animal. 2.A fleshy outgrowth of the seed coat in certain seeds that develops at or near the hilum. (KEHR ung' kul)

charnel house [*carn, flesh + -al & house*] A building or vault where dead bodies are placed. (CHAHRN l hous)

chili con carne [*chili & con-, with & carn, meat*] Chili with meat. (CHIL ee kon KAHR nee)

incarnadine [*in-, in + carn, flesh + -ine*] 1.Flesh-colored. 2.Blood-red. Crimson. (in KAHR nuh deyen')

incarnate [*in-, in + carn, flesh + -ate*] 1.Endowed with bodily nature and form, especially of a human body. 2.Personified. Typified. Embodied. (in KAHR nit)

reincarnation [*re-, again + in-, in + carn, flesh + -ation*] The belief that after death the soul reappears in another body. (ree' in kahr NAY shun)

carp/o   fruit

acarpous [*a-, without + carp, fruit + -ous*] Not bearing fruit. Sterile. (ay KAHR pus)

acrocarpous [*acro, extremity + carp, fruit + -ous*] Bearing fruit at the tip of the stem or stalk, as certain ferns and mosses. (ak' roh KAHR pus)

apocarpous [*apo-, away & carp(el) & -ous*] Having individual carpels that are distinctly separate. See syncarpous. (ap' uh KAHR pus)

carpel [*carp, fruit*] The female reproductive organ in a flower, consisting of the ovary, a style, and the stigma. The entire female reproductive structure is the gynoecium which consists of one or more carpels. (KAHR pul)

carpogonium [*carpo, fruit + gon, reproduction + -ium*] The female egg-bearing organ in red algae from which a carpospore develops. (kahr' puh GOH nee um)

carpology [*carp, fruit + -ology, study of*] The branch of botany dealing with the study of fruits and seeds. (kahr POL uh jee)

carpophagous [*carpo, fruit + phag, to eat + -ous*] Feeding on fruit. Same as frugivorous. (kahr POF uh gus)

carpophore [*carp(el) & -phore, to bear*] The extended receptacle that attaches to the carpels in certain flowering plants. (KAHR puh for')

carpospore [*carpo, fruit & spore*] A nonmotile spore developed from the carpogonium in red algae. (KAHR puh spor')

carp/o

endocarp [*endo-, inside + carp, fruit*] The inner layer of the pericarp of a fruit, as the stone surrounding the seed of a cherry. See mesocarp, epicarp, and pericarp. (EN duh kahrp')

epicarp [*epi-, outside + carp, fruit*] The outer layer of the pericarp of a fruit, as the skin of a cherry. See endocarp, mesocarp, and pericarp. (EP ih kahrp')

exocarp [*exo-, outside + carp, fruit*] The outer layer of the pericarp of a fruit, as the skin of a cherry. Same as epicarp. (EKS uh kahrp')

mesocarp [*meso-, middle + carp, fruit*] The middle layer of the pericarp of a fruit, as the meat of a cherry. See endocarp, epicarp, and pericarp. (MEZ uh kahrp')

monocarpellary [*mono-, single & carpel & -ary*] Having one carpel only. (mon' uh KAHR puh lehr' ee)

monocarpic [*mono-, one + carp, fruit + -ic*] Capable of flowering or fruiting only once, as annual and biennial plants. See polycarpic. (mon' uh KAHR pik)

parthenocarpy [*Grk > parthenos, virgin + carp, fruit + -y*] The development of fruit without fertilization, as in the pineapple or banana. (PAHR thuh noh kahr' pee)

pericarp [*peri-, around + carp, fruit*] The ripened wall of a fruit that matures from the ovary wall following fertilization and consists of the endocarp, mesocarp, and epicarp. See endocarp, mesocarp, and epicarp. (PEHR ih kahrp')

polycarpellary [*poly, many & carpel & -ary*] Having many carpels. (pol' ee KAHR puh lehr' ee)

polycarpic [*poly, many + carp, fruit + -ic*] Capable of flowering or fruiting many times, as perennial plants. See monocarpic. (pol' ee KAHR pik)

pseudocarp [*pseudo, false + carp, fruit*] A fruit produced from other parts in addition to the ovary, as an apple. False fruit. Also referred to as accessory fruit. (SOOD uh kahrp')

rhizocarpous [*rhizo, root + carp, fruit + -ous*] Pertaining to perennial herbs with perennial roots and annual stems. (reye' zoh KAHR pus)

sarcocarp [*sarco, flesh + carp, fruit*] 1.The fleshy part of a drupaceous fruit such as the apricot or cherry. 2.Any fleshy fruit. (SAHR kuh kahrp')

schizocarp [*schizo, split + carp, fruit*] A dry fruit that splits at maturity into several closed, one-seeded carpels. (SKIZ uh kahrp')

syncarpous [*syn-, together & carp(el) & -ous*] Pertaining to a flower with the carpels united. See apocarpous. (sin KAHR pus)

caust, caut   to burn

causalgia [*caust, to burn + alg, pain + -ia*] A severe, constant burning pain, usually resulting from a peripheral nerve injury. (koz AL juh)

caustic [*caust, to burn + -ic*] 1.Capable of burning, eating away, or otherwise destroying by chemical action. Corrosive. 2.Very sarcastic. (KOS tik)

cauterize [*caut, to burn + -er + -ize*] To burn with a hot instrument such as a laser, electric current, or caustic substance, usually to destroy aberrant tissue. (KOT uh reyez')

encaustic [*en-, in + caust, to burn + -ic*] Painted by a process of mixing the colors with wax before burning in or applying heat. (en KOS tik)

holocaust [*holo, whole + caust, to burn*] 1.Great or total devastation involving loss of life, especially by fire. 2.A sacrificial offering consumed by fire. (HOL uh kost')

hypocaust [*hypo-, below + caust, to burn*] A space beneath the floor of an ancient Roman building that when filled with hot air provided a central heating system. (HEYE puh kost')

cede, ceed, cess   to go, to yield

accede [*ac-, to + cede, to go*] 1.To agree to. 2.To take control of an office or dignity. (ak SEED)

ancestry [*ante-, before + cede, to go + -ry*] 1.All past generations. 2.All the individuals in a person's line of descent. See posterity. (AN ses' tree)

antecede [*ante-, before + cede, to go*] To go before in rank, order, or time. Precede. See precede. (an' tuh SEED)

antecedent [*ante-, before + cede, to go + -ent*] 1.A word, phrase, or clause referred to by a relative or personal pronoun. 2.A preceding event, condition, or cause. (an' tuh SEED nt)

antecessor [*ante-, before + cess, to go + -or*] One who goes before. Predecessor. (an' tuh SES ur)

cede [*cede, to yield*] To give up, as rights or possessions. Relinquish. (seed)

concede [*con-, completely + cede, to go*] 1.To acknowledge as true. 2.To yield or grant, as a right or privilege. (kun SEED)

exceed [*ex-, out + ceed, to go*] 1.To go beyond a set limit. 2.To be greater than. (ek SEED)

intercede [*inter-, between + cede, to go*] 1.To act as a go-between in a disagreement. Mediate. 2.To plead in behalf of another. See intervene, mediate, and intermediary. (in' ter SEED)

precede [*pre-, before + cede, to go*] To go or be before in position, time, or importance. See antecede. (prih SEED)

proceed [*pro-, forward + ceed, to go*] 1.To go forward or onward, especially after a pause or interruption. Advance. 2.To go on or act in an orderly manner. (proh SEED)

recede [*re-, back + cede, to go*] 1.To move back or away. 2.To slope backward. (rih SEED)

retrocede [*retro-, back + cede, to go*] 1.To go back. Recede. See recede. 2.To give back. See cede. (ret' roh SEED)

secede [*se-, apart + cede, to go*] To withdraw formally from an organization such as a country, political party, church, etc. (sih SEED)

succeed [*sub-, beneath + ceed, to go*] 1.To replace another. Follow. 2.To accomplish what is intended or attempted. (suk SEED)

cent   hundred
centi-   hundredth

bicentennial [*bi-, two + cent, hundred + enn, years + -ial*] Occurring once every two hundred years. See semicentennial. (beye' sen TEN ee ul)

cent [*cent, hundred*] A monetary unit of the United States equal to one hundredth of a dollar. Penny. (sent)

cental [*cent, hundred + -al*] A unit of weight equal to one hundred pounds. Hundredweight. (SENT l)

centavo [*centi-, hundredth + -avo*] A monetary unit of various Spanish speaking countries equal to one hundredth of the basic unit. (sen TAH voh)

centenarian [*cent, hundred + enn, years + -arian*] A person who is at least 100 years of age. (sent' n EHR ee un)

centennial [*cent, hundred + enn, years + -ial*] Occurring once every one hundred years. (sen TEN ee ul)

centesimal [*Ltn > centesimus, hundredth + -al*] 1.Hundredth. 2.Divided into hundredths. (sen TES uh mul)

centesimo [*Ltn > centesimus, hundredth*] 1.A monetary unit of Uruguay and Chile equal to one hundredth of a peso. 2.A monetary unit of Italy equal to one hundredth of a lira. (sen TES uh moh')

centibar [*centi-, hundredth + bar, pressure*] A metric unit of pressure equal to one hundredth of a bar, or 10,000 dynes per square centimeter. (SENT ih bahr')

centigrade [*centi-, hundredth + -grade, to step*] A thermometer scale whose markings at 0 and 100 degrees mark the freezing point and boiling point of water. (SENT ih grayd')

centigram [*centi-, hundredth & gram*] A metric unit of weight equal to one hundredth of a gram. (SENT ih gram')

centiliter [*centi-, hundredth & liter*] A metric unit of volume equal to one hundredth of a liter. (SENT l ee' ter)

centillion [*cent, hundred + (m)ill, thousand + -ion*] A number expressed as 1 followed by 303 zeros, which is 100 groups of three zeros after 1,000. (sen TIL yun)

centime [*centi-, hundredth*] A monetary unit in France, Switzerland, and Belgium equal to one hundredth of a franc. (SAHN teem)

centimeter [*centi-, hundredth & meter*] A metric unit of length equal to one hundredth of a meter. (SENT ih mee' ter)

centimetre [*centi-, hundredth & metre*] A metric unit of length equal to one hundredth of a meter. Same as centimeter. (SENT ih mee' ter)

centimo [*centi-, hundredth*] A monetary unit of various Spanish speaking countries equal to one hundredth of the basic unit. (SENT ih moh')

centipede [*cent, hundred + -pede, feet*] Any of numerous elongated, flattened, predaceous arthropods of the class Chilopoda with numerous body segments each having one pair of legs, the front pair being modified into poisonous biting organs. See millipede and myriapod. (SENT ih peed')

centipoise [*centi-, hundredth & poise*] A unit of measure of viscosity equal to one hundredth of a poise. (SENT ih poiz')

centurion [*centur(y) & -ion*] An officer in the Roman army commanding a unit of one hundred men. (sen TOOR ee un)

century [*cent, hundred + -ury*] 1.A period of one hundred years. 2.A unit in the Roman army consisting of one hundred soldiers. 3.A group of one hundred. (SEN chuh ree)

cinquecento [*mill, thousand + quinque, five + cent, hundred*] Short for millecinquecento. The 16th century (1500-1599) period of Italian art and literature. See trecento, quattrocento, and seicento. (ching' kwih CHEN toh)

percent [*Ltn > per centum, by the hundred*] One hundredth part. (per SENT)

percentage [*Ltn > per centum, by the hundred + -age*] A given proportion of one hundred. (per SENT ij)

percentile [*Ltn > per centum, by the hundred + -ile*] Any of the ninety-nine values that divide a statistical frequency distribution into one hundred equal parts. See quartile, quintile (def. 2), and decile. (per SEN teyel')

quadricentennial [*quadri, four + cent, hundred + enn, years + -ial*] Occurring once every four hundred years. (kwod' ruh sen TEN ee ul)

quattrocento [*mill, thousand + quattro, four + cent, hundred*] Short for millequattrocento. The 15th century (1400-1499) period of Italian art and literature. See trecento, cinquecento, and seicento. (kwot' roh CHEN toh)

quincentennial [*quin, five + cent, hundred + enn, years + -ial*] Occurring once every five hundred years. (kwin' sen TEN ee ul)

seicento [*mill, thousand + sex, six + cent, hundred*] Short for milleseicento. The 17th century (1600-1699) period of Italian art and literature. See trecento, quattrocento, and cinquecento. (say CHEN toh)

semicentennial [*semi-, half + cent, hundred + enn, years + -ial*] Occurring once every fifty years. See bicentennial. (sem' ee sen TEN ee ul)

sesquicentennial [*sesqui-, one and a half + cent, hundred + enn, years + -ial*] Occurring once every one hundred and fifty years. (ses' kwih sen TEN ee ul)

sexcentenary [*sex-, six + cent, hundred + enn, years + -ary*] Occurring once every six hundred years. (seks' sen TEN uh ree)

tercentenary [*Ltn > tres, three + cent, hundred + enn, years + -ary*] Occurring once every three hundred years. Same as tricentennial. (tur' sen TEN uh ree)

trecento [*mill, thousand + Ltn > tres, three + cent, hundred*] Short for milletrecento. The 14th century (1300-1399) period of Italian art and literature. See quattrocento, cinquecento, and seicento. (tray CHEN toh)

tricentennial [*tri-, three + cent, hundred + enn, years + -ial*] Occurring once every three hundred years. (treye' sen TEN ee ul)

hect-, hecto-, hecat-   hundred

hecatomb [*hecat-, hundred + Grk > bous, ox*] 1.In ancient Greece and Rome, a public sacrifice to the gods of 100 oxen or cattle. 2.Any large-scale slaughter or sacrifice. (HEK uh tohm')

hectare [*hect-, hundred & are {100 square meters}*] A metric unit of area equal to 100 ares, 2.471 acres, or 10,000 square meters. (HEK tehr)

hectogram [*hecto-, hundred & gram*] A metric unit of weight equal to 100 grams. (HEK tuh gram')

hectograph [*hecto-, hundred + graph, recording*] A device that uses a glycerin coated sheet of gelatin to make multiple copies of written or typed material. (HEK tuh graf')

hectoliter [*hecto-, hundred & liter*] A metric unit of volume equal to 100 liters. (HEK tuh lee' ter)

hectometer [*hecto-, hundred & meter*] A metric unit of length equal to 100 meters. (HEK tuh mee' ter)

centr/o, centri   center

acentric [*a-, without* + *centr, center* + *-ic*] Without a center.
(ay SEN trik)

acrocentric [*acro, extremity* + *centr, center* + *-ic*] Pertaining to a chromosome with the centromere closer to one end than the other. See telocentric. (ak' roh SEN trik)

anthropocentric [*anthropo, man* + *centr, center* + *-ic*]
1.Considering human beings as the central fact and ultimate aim of the universe. 2.Interpreting everything in the universe in terms of the values and experiences of human beings. (an' thruh puh SEN trik)

areocentric [*areo, Mars* + *centr, center* + *-ic*] Centered on or originating from the planet Mars.
(ahr' ee oh SEN trik)

central [*centr, center* + *-al*] 1.Located or occurring at or near the center. 2.Easily accessible from all points.
(SEN trul)

central angle [*central & angle*] An angle formed by two radii of a circle and whose vertex is at the center of the circle. (SEN trul ANG gul)

centralism [*central & -ism*] The assignment of power in an organization to a central authority. (SEN truh liz' um)

centralize [*central & -ize*] 1.To gather about or focus on a center. 2.To bring under a central authority.
(SEN truh leyez')

centre [*centr, center*] A variant of center that is chiefly British. (SENT ur)

centric [*centr, center* + *-ic*] Located or occurring at or near the center. Same as central (def. 1). (SEN trik)

centrifugal [*centri, center* + *fug, to flee* + *-al*] Moving or tending to move outward away from a center or axis. Opposed to centripetal. (sen TRIF yuh gul)

centrifugal force [*centrifugal & force*] An inertial force that pulls a rotating body outward from a rotating center. See centripetal force. (sen TRIF yuh gul fors)

centrifuge [*centri, center* + *fug, to flee*] A device that uses centrifugal force to separate materials of different density, as cream from milk. (SEN truh fyooj')

centriole [*centri, center* + *-ole*] One of a pair of minute structures within a centrosome that forms the center of an aster during mitosis. (SEN tree ohl')

centripetal [*centri, center* + *-petal, moving toward*] Moving or tending to move inward toward a center or axis. Opposed to centrifugal. (sen TRIP ih tul)

centripetal force [*centripetal & force*] A radial force that pulls a rotating body inward towards the center of rotation. See centrifugal force. (sen TRIP ih tul fors)

centrist [*centr, center* + *-ist*] A person whose political views are considered to be in the center of the political spectrum. (SEN trist)

centrobaric [*centro, center* + *bar, weight* + *-ic*] Pertaining to the center of gravity. (sen' truh BEHR ik)

centroid [*centr, center* + *-oid*] 1.The center of mass of an object of constant density. 2.The point of intersection of the medians of a triangle. (SEN troid)

centromere [*centro, center* + *-mere, part*] The specialized structure on a chromosome that attaches to the spindle fiber during mitosis. (SEN truh mihr')

centrosome [*centro, center* + *-some, body*] A small cytoplasmic structure found near the nucleus of a cell that contains the centrioles and divides during mitosis into two centers that migrate to opposite poles.
(SEN truh sohm')

centrosphere [*centro, center & sphere*] 1.The cytoplasm that surrounds a centriole in the centrosome of a cell. 2.The interior central portion of the earth.
(SEN truh sfihr')

centrum [*centr, center* + *-um*] 1.A center, especially of an anatomical structure. 2.The body of a vertebra.
(SEN trum)

concentrate [*con-, together* + *centr, center* + *-ate*] To draw or direct toward a common center or objective.
(KON sen trayt')

concentric [*con-, together* + *centr, center* + *-ic*] Having a common center, as two or more circles. Opposed to eccentric (def. 2). See homocentric. (kun SEN trik)

dicentric [*di-, two* + *centr, center* + *-ic*] Having two centromeres. (deye SEN trik)

eccentric [*ec-, out* + *centr, center* + *-ic*] 1.Deviating from normal behavior or appearance. 2.Not having a common center, as two or more circles. Opposed to concentric. (ik SEN trik)

egocentric [*ego, self* + *centr, center* + *-ic*] 1.Self-centered. 2.Regarding the ego as the center of everything. See egomania. (ee' goh SEN trik)

endocentric [*endo-, inside* + *centr, center* + *-ic*] Pertaining to a grammatical construction that as a unit has the same syntactic function in the sentence as one or more of its immediate components, as *hot water*, which functions as the noun *water*. See exocentric.
(en' doh SEN trik)

epicenter [*epi-, on & center*] 1.The point directly above the center of an earthquake. 2.The focal point of a crisis, activity, etc. (EP ih sent' ur)

ethnocentric [*ethno, race* + *centr, center* + *-ic*] Excessive favoritism for one's own ethnic group.
(eth' noh SEN trik)

exocentric [*exo-, outside* + *centr, center* + *-ic*] Pertaining to a grammatical construction that as a unit does not have the same syntactic function in the sentence as any of its components, as *in the tree* which does not function as the noun *tree*. See endocentric.
(eks' oh SEN trik)

geocentric [*geo, earth* + *centr, center* + *-ic*] 1.Pertaining to or calculated from the center of the earth. 2.Having the earth as the center. See heliocentric.
(jee' oh SEN trik)

heliocentric [*helio, sun* + *centr, center* + *-ic*] 1.Pertaining to or calculated from the center of the sun. 2.Having the sun as the center. See geocentric.
(hee' lee oh SEN trik)

homocentric [*homo, same* + *centr, center* + *-ic*] Having a common center. See concentric. (hoh' muh SEN trik)

hypocenter [*hypo-, below & center*] The point on the earth's surface directly beneath the center of a nuclear explosion. (HEYE puh sent' ur)

metacenter [*meta-, between & center*] The point of intersection in a floating body of two vertical lines that are drawn through the center of buoyancy when the body is upright and when it is tilted.
(MET uh sent' ur)

orthocenter [*ortho, perpendicular & center*] The point where the three altitudes of a triangle intersect.
(OR thuh sent' ur)

polycentrism [*poly, many + centr, center + -ism*] The existence of two or more centers of power or authority within a political system, especially in the Communist world. (pol' ee SEN triz' um)

subcentral [*sub-, below + centr, center + -al*] Near or beneath the center. (sub' SEN trul)

telocentric [*telo, end + centr, center + -ic*] Pertaining to a chromosome with the centromere at one end. See acrocentric. (tel' uh SEN trik)

theocentric [*theo, God + centr, center + -ic*] Having God as the center of interest and concern. (thee' oh SEN trik)

ultracentrifuge [*ultra-, beyond & centrifuge*] A high speed centrifuge used for separating minute particles. (ul' truh SEN truh fyooj')

cephal/o   head
encephal/o   brain

acanthocephalan [*acantho, thorn + cephal, head + -an*] Any of various thorny-headed parasitic worms that attach to the digestive tract of the host by means of an anterior protruding proboscis. (uh kan' thuh SEF uh lun)

acephalous [*a-, without + cephal, head + -ous*] 1.Having no distinguishable head. 2.Having no leader or ruler. (ay SEF uh lus)

acrocephaly [*acro, high + cephal, head + -y*] A congenital malformation of the skull that gives the head a peaked or conical shape. Same as oxycephaly. (ak' roh SEF uh lee)

anencephaly [*an-, without + encephal, brain + -y*] Partial or total absence of the brain at birth. (an' en SEF uh lee)

autocephalous [*auto-, self + cephal, head + -ous*] Pertaining especially to an Eastern Church whose bishop is not governed by external authority. (awt' oh SEF uh lus)

bicephalous [*bi-, two + cephal, head + -ous*] Having two heads. (beye SEF uh lus)

brachycephalic [*brachy, short + cephal, head + -ic*] Having a comparatively short head with a cephalic index greater than 80. See cephalic index, mesocephalic, and dolichocephalic. (brak' ee suh FAL ik)

cephalad [*cephal, head + -ad, toward*] Toward the head. (SEF uh lad')

cephalic [*cephal, head + -ic*] Pertaining to the head or skull. (suh FAL ik)

cephalic index [*cephal, head + -ic & index*] An index of cranial capacity derived by dividing the head's maximum width by its maximum length and multiplying by 100. (suh FAL ik IN deks)

cephalin [*cephal, head + -in*] Pertaining to or situated near the head. (SEF uh lin)

cephalization [*cephal, head + -ization*] The gradual evolutionary tendency toward concentration of the brain and important sense organs in the head. (sef' uh luh ZAY shun)

cephalometer [*cephalo, head + meter, to measure*] An instrument for measuring the dimensions of the head. See craniometer. (sef' uh LOM et er)

cephalometry [*cephalo, head + -metry, science of measuring*] The scientific measurement of the dimensions of the head. See craniometry. (sef' uh LOM ih tree)

cephalopod [*cephalo, head + pod, foot*] Any of various marine mollusks that have a large, distinct head with tentacles around the mouth and well-developed eyes, as the octopus or squid. (SEF uh luh pod')

cephalothorax [*cephalo, head & thorax*] The combined head and thorax of many arthropods, as in arachnids and certain crustaceans. (sef' uh luh THOR aks')

dicephalous [*di-, two + cephal, head + -ous*] Having two heads. Same as bicephalous. (deye SEF uh lus)

diencephalon [*di-, two + encephal, brain + -on*] The posterior portion of the prosencephalon, including the epithalamus, thalamus, metathalamus, and hypothalamus. See telencephalon and prosencephalon. (deye' en SEF uh lon')

dolichocephalic [*dolicho, long + cephal, head + -ic*] Having a comparatively long head with a cephalic index less than 76. See cephalic index, brachycephalic, and mesocephalic. (dol' ih koh' suh FAL ik)

electroencephalograph [*electro, electric + encephalo, brain + graph, recording*] An instrument for graphically recording small electric currents in the brain. (ih lek' troh en SEF uh luh graf')

encephalic [*encephal, brain + -ic*] Pertaining to the brain. (en' suh FAL ik)

encephalitis [*encephal, brain + -itis, inflammation*] Inflammation of the brain. (en sef' uh LEYE tis)

encephalograph [*encephalo, brain + graph, recording*] An x-ray photograph of the brain taken after the cerebrospinal fluid has been removed and replaced with air. (en SEF uh luh graf')

encephalomyelitis [*encephalo, brain + myel, spinal cord + -itis, inflammation*] Any of various viral diseases resulting in acute inflammation of the brain and spinal cord. (en sef' uh loh meye' uh LEYE tis)

encephalon [*en-, in + cephal, head + -on*] The brain, composed of the prosencephalon, mesencephalon, and rhombencephalon. See prosencephalon, mesencephalon, and rhombencephalon. (en SEF uh lon')

encephalopathy [*encephalo, brain + -pathy, disease*] Any disease or disorder of the brain. (en sef' uh LOP uh thee)

hydrocephalus [*hydro, liquid + cephal, head + -us*] An abnormal accumulation of cerebrospinal fluid in the ventricles of the brain, causing compression of the brain and enlargement of the head. (heye' druh SEF uh lus)

leptocephalus [*lepto, thin + cephal, head + -us*] The thin, small-headed, transparent larva of certain eels. (lep' tuh SEF uh lus)

macrocephaly [*macro-, large + cephal, head + -y*] A condition characterized by an abnormally large head. See microcephaly. (mak' roh SEF uh lee)

mesencephalon [*meso-, middle + encephal, brain + -on*] 1.The embryonic midbrain from which the corpora quadrigemina, the cerebral peduncles, and the aqueduct of Sylvius develop. 2.Midbrain. See prosencephalon and rhombencephalon. (mez' en SEF uh lon')

mesocephalic [*meso-, middle + cephal, head + -ic*] Having a head of average length with a cephalic index between 76 and 80. See cephalic index, brachycephalic, and dolichocephalic. (mez' oh suh FAL ik)

cephal/o, encephal/o

metencephalon [*meta-, after* + *encephal, brain* + *-on*] The anterior portion of the rhombencephalon from which the cerebellum and pons develop. See myelencephalon and rhombencephalon. (met' en SEF uh lon')

microcephaly [*micro-, small* + *cephal, head* + *-y*] A condition characterized by an abnormally small head. See macrocephaly. (meye' kroh SEF uh lee)

myelencephalon [*myel, spinal cord* + *encephal, brain* + *-on*] The posterior portion of the rhombencephalon from which the medulla oblongata develops. See metencephalon and rhombencephalon. (meye' uh len SEF uh lon')

orthocephalous [*ortho, correct* + *cephal, head* + *-ous*] Having a normally proportioned head. (or' thuh SEF uh lus)

oxycephaly [*oxy, pointed* + *cephal, head* + *-y*] A congenital malformation of the skull that gives the head a peaked or conical shape. (ok' see SEF uh lee)

procephalic [*pro-, forward* + *cephal, head* + *-ic*] Pertaining to the anterior portion of the head. (proh' suh FAL ik)

prosencephalon [*pros, in front of* + *encephal, brain* + *-on*] 1.The embryonic forebrain from which the telencephalon and diencephalon develop. 2.Forebrain. See mesencephalon, rhombencephalon, diencephalon, and telencephalon. (pros' en SEF uh lon')

rhombencephalon [*rhomb(us) & encephal, brain* + *-on*] 1.The embryonic hindbrain from which the metencephalon and myelencephalon develop. 2.Hindbrain. See prosencephalon, mesencephalon, metencephalon, and myelencephalon. (rom' ben SEF uh lon')

telencephalon [*tel, end* + *encephal, brain* + *-on*] The anterior portion of the prosencephalon from which the cerebrum develops. See diencephalon and prosencephalon. (tel' en SEF uh lon')

cerebr/o   brain

cerebellum [*cerebr, brain* + *-um*] The portion of the brain that lies below the posterior part of the cerebrum, consists of three lobes, and functions to maintain equilibrium and control muscle coordination. (sehr' uh BEL um)

cerebral [*cerebr, brain* + *-al*] 1.Pertaining to the brain or cerebrum. 2.Intellectual. Requiring thought and reason. Not emotional. (suh REE brul)

cerebral cortex [*cerebral & cortex*] The thin, convoluted outer layer of gray matter of the cerebrum that is principally responsible for higher mental functions. (suh REE brul KOR teks)

cerebral palsy [*cerebral & palsy {paralysis}*] A form of paralysis usually caused by a prenatal brain defect or by brain injury during birth and characterized by impaired muscular power and coordination. (suh REE brul POL zee)

cerebrate [*cerebr, brain* + *-ate*] To use the mind. Think. (SEHR uh brayt')

cerebroside [*cerebr, brain* + *-ose* + *-ide*] Any of various galactose-containing lipids found mainly in nerve tissue. (SEHR uh bruh seyed')

cerebrospinal [*cerebro, brain & spinal*] Pertaining to or involving the brain and spinal cord. (suh ree' broh SPEYE nul)

cerebrovascular [*cerebro, brain & vascular*] Pertaining to or involving the blood vessels and blood supply of the brain. (suh ree' broh VAS kyuh lur)

cerebrum [*cerebr, brain* + *-um*] The largest portion of the brain that consists of two hemispheres and controls conscious and voluntary mental processes. (suh REE brum)

craniocerebral [*cranio, skull* + *cerebr, brain* + *-al*] Pertaining to or involving the skull and the brain. (kray' nee oh suh REE brul)

decerebrate [*de-, remove* + *cerebr, brain* + *-ate*] 1.Lacking cerebral functions due to injury or surgery. 2.Having the cerebrum inactivated or removed. (dee SEHR uh brayt')

crani/o   skull, cranium

cranial [*crani, skull* + *-al*] Pertaining to the skull. (KRAY nee ul)

craniate [*crani, skull* + *-ate*] Having a skull. (KRAY nee it)

craniocerebral [*cranio, skull* + *cerebr, brain* + *-al*] Pertaining to or involving the skull and the brain. (kray' nee oh suh REE brul)

craniology [*crani, skull* + *-ology, study of*] The branch of anatomy dealing with the study of skull characteristics, especially human skulls. (kray' nee OL uh jee)

craniometer [*cranio, skull* + *meter, to measure*] An instrument for measuring the dimensions of skulls. See cephalometer. (kray' nee OM et er)

craniometry [*cranio, skull* + *-metry, science of measuring*] The scientific measurement of the dimensions of skulls. See cephalometry. (kray' nee OM ih tree)

craniotomy [*cranio, skull* + *-tomy, to cut*] Surgical cutting into the skull, as for brain surgery. (kray' nee OT uh mee)

cranium [*crani, skull* + *-um*] The vertebrate skull. (KRAY nee um)

extracranial [*extra-, outside* + *crani, cranium* + *-al*] Occurring or located outside the cranium. (eks' truh KRAY nee ul)

intracranial [*intra-, within* + *crani, cranium* + *-al*] Occurring or located within the cranium. (in' truh KRAY nee ul)

pericranium [*peri-, around* + *crani, skull* + *-um*] The fibrous membrane of connective tissue covering the outer surface of the skull. (pehr' ih KRAY nee um)

chrom/o, chromat/o, chros, -chrome
color, pigment, chromium, chromatin

achromatic [*a-, without* + *chromat, color* + *-ic*] 1.Without color. 2.Transmitting light without constituent color separation, as a lens. (ak' roh MAT ik)

achromatin [*a-, without* + *chromat, color* + *-in*] The part of a cell nucleus that does not stain readily with basic dyes. See chromatin. (ay KROH muh tin)

achromic [*a-, without* + *chrom, color* + *-ic*] 1.Without color. 2.Lacking normal pigmentation. See leukoderma. (ay KROH mik)

apochromatic [*apo-, away* + *chromat, color* + *-ic*] Pertaining to a lens with no chromatic or spherical aberration. (ap' uh kroh MAT ik)

autosome [*auto-, same & (chromo)some*] Any chromosome other than a sex chromosome. See sex chromosome. (AWT uh sohm')

bichromate [*bi-, two + chrom, chromium + -ate*] An orange to red chemical compound containing two chromium atoms. Same as dichromate. (beye KROH mayt')

chroma [*chrom, color + -a*] The intensity and purity of color. (KROH muh)

chromaffin [*chrom, chromium + Ltn > affinis, related*] Staining readily with chromium salts. (KROH muh fin)

chromate [*chrom, chromium + -ate*] An ester or salt of chromic acid. (KROH mayt)

chromatic [*chromat, color + -ic*] 1.Pertaining to or having color. 2.Intensely colored. 3.Readily stained with dyes. (kroh MAT ik)

chromatic aberration [*chromat, color + -ic & aberration*] The color distortion created by a lens due to the refractive differences between wavelengths of light. (kroh MAT ik ab' uh RAY shun)

chromatics [*chromat, color + -ics, study of*] The study of colors. (kroh MAT iks)

chromatid [*chromat, chromatin + -id*] Either of two identical longitudinal strands resulting from chromosome reduplication during cell division. (KROH muh tid)

chromatin [*chromat, color + -in*] The part of a cell nucleus that stains readily with basic dyes and contains the genetic material that forms the chromosomes; it is composed of euchromatin and heterochromatin. See euchromatin, heterochromatin, and achromatin. (KROH muh tin)

chromatolysis [*chromato, chromatin + -lysis, decomposition*] The decomposition of chromatin or other stainable material in the nucleus of a cell, especially in a nerve cell as a result of injury or fatigue. (kroh' muh TOL uh sis)

chromatophore [*chromato, pigment + -phore, to produce*] A pigment-containing dermal cell found mostly in lower animals that causes skin color changes by contracting or expanding. (kroh MAT uh for')

chrome [*chrom, chromium*] 1.Chromium. 2.A shiny chromium alloy plating. 3.A chromium-containing pigment. (krohm)

chrome green [*chrom, pigment & green*] 1.Green pigments composed of a mixture of blue and chrome yellow. 2.Green pigment made from chromic oxide. See chrome red and chrome yellow. (krohm green)

chrome red [*chrom, pigment & red*] A red pigment containing basic lead chromate. See chrome green and chrome yellow. (krohm red)

chrome yellow [*chrom, pigment & yellow*] A yellow pigment containing normal lead chromate. See chrome red and chrome green. (krohm YEL oh)

chromic [*chrom, chromium + -ic*] Containing or derived from trivalent chromium. See chromous. (KROH mik)

chrominance [*chrom, color & (lum)inance*] The difference in purity between a color and a specific reference color of equal intensity. (KROH muh nens)

chromite [*chrom, chromium + -ite, mineral*] A metallic black or brownish-black mineral, ferrous chromate, that is an important ore of chromium. (KROH meyet)

chromium [*chrom, color + -ium, chemical element*] A blue-white, very hard metallic chemical element with a high resistance to corrosion, used especially in alloys and for plating. So named from the bright colors of its compounds. (KROH mee um)

chromodynamics [*chromo, color + dynam, energy + -ics, knowledge*] The theory dealing with the strong interactive forces that bind quarks together. These forces are characterized by three seemingly distinct, nonelectrical charges known as colors that are completely unrelated to real, visible colors. (kroh' moh deye NAM iks)

chromogen [*chromo, pigment + gen, production*] 1.A substance that can be chemically converted into a dye or pigment. 2.A pigment-producing bacterium. (KROH muh jen)

chromolithography [*chromo, color + litho, stone + -graphy, recording*] The process of producing colored pictures from a set of stone, aluminum, or zinc plates using lithography. See lithography. (kroh' moh lith OG ruh fee)

chromomere [*chromo, chromatin + -mere, part*] Any of the small particles of chromatin arranged linearly to form a chromosome. (KROH muh mihr')

chromonema [*chromo, chromatin + nema, thread*] The coiled, threadlike filamentous core that contains the genes and extends the entire length of a chromosome. (kroh' muh NEE muh)

chromophil [*chromo, color + phil, affinity for*] Capable of being readily stained with dyes. (KROH muh fil')

chromophore [*chromo, color + -phore, to produce*] A group of atoms in an organic compound whose arrangement gives rise to color. (KROH muh for')

chromoplast [*chromo, color & plast(id)*] A colored, pigment-containing plastid that contains either the green pigment chlorophyll or variously colored carotenoid pigments. See chloroplast and leucoplast. (KROH muh plast')

chromoprotein [*chromo, pigment & protein*] A protein with a metal-containing pigment, such as hemoglobin. (kroh' muh PROH teen')

chromosome [*chromo, chromatin + -some, body*] The elongated bodies in a cell nucleus that contain the genes and are responsible for determining and transmitting hereditary characteristics. See gene. (KROH muh sohm')

chromosphere [*chromo, color & sphere*] A gaseous, glowing zone surrounding the photosphere of the sun or other stars. See photosphere. (KROH muh sfihr')

chromous [*chrom, chromium + -ous*] Containing or derived from divalent chromium. See chromic. (KROH mus)

cytochrome [*cyto, cell + -chrome, pigment*] A respiratory pigment widely distributed in plant and animal cells that plays an essential role in cell respiration by undergoing alternate reduction and oxidation. (SEYET uh krohm')

dichroism [*di-, two + chros, color + -ism*] 1.The property of some crystals to display two different colors when viewed from two different directions. See trichroism and pleochroism. 2.The property of a substance to reflect light in one color and transmit light in another color. (DEYE kroh iz' um)

chrom/o, chromat/o, chros, -chrome

dichromate [*di-, two + chrom, chromium + -ate*] An orange to red chemical compound containing two chromium atoms. (deye KROH mayt')

dichromatic [*di-, two + chromat, color + -ic*] 1.Having or displaying two colors. 2.Displaying two distinct adult color phases that are unrelated to sex or age, as certain insects or birds. 3.Capable of distinguishing only two of the three primary colors. Red, green, and blue are the three primary colors. (deye' kroh MAT ik)

dichroscope [*di-, two + chros, color + -scope, to view*] An instrument for viewing the dichroism of crystals. See dichroism (def. 1). (DEYE kruh skohp')

episome [*epi-, on & (chromo)some*] A genetic element in some bacterial cells that can replicate independently in the cytoplasm or in association with the chromosomes. See plasmid. (EP ih sohm')

euchromatin [*eu-, good & chromatin*] The part of the chromatin in a cell nucleus that is more lightly stained when the nucleus is not in the state of division and is genetically active. See chromatin and heterochromatin. (yoo KROH muh tin)

genome [*gen(e) & (chromos)ome*] A complete haploid set of chromosomes with its full complement of genes. (JEE nohm)

hemachrome [*hema, blood + -chrome, color*] The red coloring matter in blood. (HEE muh krohm')

hemochromatosis [*hemo, blood + chromat, color + -osis, diseased condition*] A disease of iron metabolism characterized by excess accumulation of iron in the tissues of various organs, especially the skin, pancreas, and liver, causing bronze skin pigmentation, diabetes, and liver enlargement. (hee' muh kroh' muh TOH sis)

heterochromatic [*hetero, different + chromat, color + -ic*] Having several different colors. See monochromatic (def. 1). (het' uh roh' kroh MAT ik)

heterochromatin [*hetero, other & chromatin*] The part of the chromatin in a cell nucleus that is more darkly stained when the nucleus is not in the state of division and is genetically inactive. See chromatin and euchromatin. (het' uh roh KROH muh tin)

heterochromosome [*hetero, different & chromosome*] Either of two chromosomes in the germ cells of humans, animals, and some plants, that together determine an individual's sex. Same as sex chromosome. (het' uh roh KROH muh sohm')

homochromatic [*homo, same + chromat, color + -ic*] Pertaining to or having one color. Same as monochromatic (def. 1). (hoh' moh kroh MAT ik)

isochromatic [*iso-, equal + chromat, color + -ic*] 1.Of uniform color or tint. 2.Orthochromatic. See orthochromatic. (eye' soh kroh MAT ik)

isochrous [*iso-, equal + chros, color + -ous*] Having identical color or tint throughout. (eye SOK roh us)

metachromatism [*meta-, change + chromat, color + -ism*] A color change, especially as the result of a temperature change. (met' uh KROH muh tiz' um)

monochromatic [*mono-, one + chromat, color + -ic*] 1.Pertaining to or having one color. See heterochromatic. 2.Pertaining to light or other radiation that consists of a very narrow range of wavelengths or of a single wavelength. (mon' oh kroh MAT ik)

monochromatism [*mono-, one + chromat, color + -ism*] Complete color blindness in which all objects and colors appear as various shades of gray. (mon' uh KROH muh tiz' um)

monochrome [*mono-, one + -chrome, color*] A photograph, painting, or drawing done in various shades of a single color. (MON uh krohm')

monosome [*mono-, one & (chromo)some*] 1.An unpaired sex chromosome. 2.An unpaired X chromosome. (MON uh sohm')

orthochromatic [*ortho, correct + chromat, color + -ic*] 1.Correctly representing the relative intensity of colors. 2.Pertaining to films and plates treated to correctly represent all colors except red. See panchromatic. (or' thoh kroh MAT ik)

panchromatic [*pan, all + chromat, color + -ic*] Pertaining to films or plates that correctly represent all visible colors in the spectrum. See orthochromatic (def. 2). (pan' kroh MAT ik)

photochromic [*photo, light + chrom, color + -ic*] Pertaining to materials that change color when exposed to light or other radiant energy and in some cases return to their original color upon removal of the radiation source. (foht' oh KROH mik)

phytochrome [*phyto, plant + -chrome, pigment*] A protein pigment in plants that regulates growth and other physiological processes by responding to variations of red light. (FEYET uh krohm')

pleochroism [*pleo, more + chros, color + -ism*] The property of some crystals to display different colors when viewed from different directions. See dichroism (def. 1) and trichroism. (plee OK roh iz' um)

polychromatic [*poly, many + chromat, color + -ic*] Having or displaying many colors. (pol' ee kroh MAT ik)

polychrome [*poly, many + -chrome, color*] Done or decorated in many colors. (POL ee krohm')

polychromy [*poly, many + chrom, color + -y*] The art of painting or decorating in many colors. (POL ee kroh' mee)

rhodochrosite [*rhodo, red + chros, color + -ite, mineral*] A vitreous, impure mineral, chiefly manganese carbonate, with a rose-red color. (roh' duh KROH seyet')

sex chromosome [*sex & chromosome*] Either of two chromosomes in the germ cells of humans, animals, and some plants, that together determine an individual's sex. See autosome. (seks KROH muh sohm')

trichroism [*tri-, three + chros, color + -ism*] The property of some crystals to display three different colors when viewed from three different directions. See dichroism (def. 1) and pleochroism. (TREYE kroh iz' um)

trichromatic [*tri-, three + chromat, color + -ic*] 1.Having or displaying three colors, as in color photography and printing. 2.Capable of distinguishing all three primary colors, as in normal vision. The three primary colors are red, green, and blue. (treye' kroh MAT ik)

urochrome [*uro, urine + -chrome, pigment*] A pigment that produces the normal yellow color of urine. (YOOR uh krohm')

chron/o   time

anachronism [*ana-, back + chron, time + -ism*] A chronological error in which someone or something is represented as existing or occurring out of its proper place in time. (uh NAK ruh niz' um)

asynchronous [*a-, not + syn, same + chron, time + -ous*] 1.Not occurring at the same time. 2.Not occurring at the same rate. See synchronous. (ay SING kruh nus)

chronaxy [*chron, time + Grk > axia, value + -y*] The minimum time interval required to electrically stimulate nerve or muscle tissue with a current of twice the rheobase. (KROH nak' see)

chronic [*chron, time + -ic*] Lasting a long time, as a disease or disorder. Habitual. Lingering. (KRON ik)

chronicle [*chron, time + -icle*] A record of events given in the order of their occurrence. See annals. (KRON ih kul)

chronobiology [*chrono, time + bio, life + -logy, study of*] The study of how time affects life, as in various biological rhythms. (kron' oh beye OL uh jee)

chronograph [*chrono, time + graph, recording*] 1.An instrument for measuring and recording brief time intervals, as the duration of the occurrence of an event. 2.An instrument for measuring time intervals. Stopwatch. See chronoscope and chronometer. (KRON uh graf')

chronology [*chron, time + -ology, science*] 1.The science of measuring time and arranging events in time. See horology. 2.An order of events from earliest to latest. (kruh NOL uh jee)

chronometer [*chrono, time + meter, to measure*] An instrument for measuring extremely accurate time, as for science or navigation. See chronograph and chronoscope. (kruh NOM et er)

chronoscope [*chrono, time + -scope, to view*] An optical instrument for measuring brief time intervals. See chronograph and chronometer. (KRON uh skohp')

dendrochronology [*dendro, tree + chron, time + -ology, study of*] The study of the annular growth rings in trees for the purpose of dating and determining past events and climatic changes. (den' droh kruh NOL uh jee)

diachronic [*dia-, through + chron, time + -ic*] Pertaining to the study of the historical changes in a language. See synchronic. (deye' uh KRON ik)

geochronology [*geo, earth + chron, time + -ology, study of*] The study of the earth's age, history, developmental stages, etc. See geochronometry. (jee' oh kruh NOL uh jee)

geochronometry [*geo, earth + chrono, time + -metry, science of measuring*] The scientific measurement of geologic time, as from radioactive decay of isotopes. See geochronology. (jee' oh kruh NOM ih tree)

geosynchronous [*geo, earth + syn, same + chron, time + -ous*] Pertaining to a satellite whose orbit is approximately 23,000 miles above the earth, resulting in a rate of speed synchronous with the earth's rotation, thus making it seem to remain stationary. (jee' oh SING kruh nus)

glottochronology [*glotto, language + chron, time + -ology, study of*] The comparative study of two or more related languages to determine the time of their divergence from the parent language. See lexicostatistics. (glot' oh kruh NOL uh jee)

isochronal [*iso-, equal + chron, time + -al*] Characterized by equal duration or intervals of time. (eye SOK ruh nul)

synchro- [*syn-, same + chron, time*] A word root meaning "synchronous" or "synchronized." (SING kroh)

synchromesh [*synchro-, synchronous & mesh*] Designating a transmission in which gears are meshed by first synchronizing their speed of rotation. (SING kroh mesh')

synchronic [*syn-, same + chron, time + -ic*] Pertaining to the study of a language during a given time period in its development without concern for historical antecedents. See diachronic. (sin KRON ik)

synchronize [*syn-, same + chron, time + -ize*] To cause to occur at the same time or at the same rate. (SING kruh neyez')

synchronous [*syn-, same + chron, time + -ous*] 1.Occurring at the same time. 2.Occurring at the same rate. See asynchronous. (SING kruh nus)

synchroscope [*synchro-, synchronous + -scope, to observe*] An instrument for determining the degree of synchronism between associated machines, as two or more aircraft engines. (SING kruh skohp')

chrys/o   gold, yellow

chrysalis [*Ltn > crysallis, gold-colored sheath of a butterfly*] The hard-shelled pupa of a butterfly or moth between the larval and adult stages. (KRIS uh lis)

chrysanthemum [*chrys, yellow + anth, flower*] Any of a genus of plants of the composite family, commonly referred to as mums, that bear flowers in various colors, most commonly yellow, white, or red. (krih SAN thuh mum)

chrysarobin [*chrys, yellow & (ar)arob(a) & -in*] An orange-yellow crystalline substance derived from a deposit found in the wood of the araroba tree and used for the treatment of chronic skin disorders. (kris' uh ROH bin)

chryselephantine [*chrys, gold + Grk > elephas, ivory + -ine*] Made of or overlaid with gold and ivory, as certain statues and other objects in ancient Greece. (kris' el' uh FAN tin)

chrysoberyl [*chryso, yellow & beryl*] A vitreous mineral, beryllium aluminate, that is yellow or green in color and used as a gemstone. (KRIS uh behr' ul)

chrysolite [*chryso, yellow + -lite, mineral*] A yellowish-green transparent olivine used as a gem. (KRIS uh leyet')

chrysophyte [*chryso, yellow + -phyte, plant*] Any of a large group of golden-brown and yellowish-green algae with xanthophyll and carotene pigments in addition to chlorophyll pigments. (KRIS uh feyet')

chrysoprase [*chryso, yellow & praso*] An apple-green chalcedony sometimes used as a gem. (KRIS uh prayz')

xanth/o   yellow

xanthein [*xanth, yellow + -in*] A water-soluble yellow coloring matter found in the cell sap of some plants. (ZAN thee in)

xanthene [*xanth, yellow + -ene*] A yellow crystalline compound used in making various dyes and as a fungicide. (ZAN theen)

xanthic [*xanth, yellow + -ic*] Having a yellow or yellowish color. (ZAN thik)

xanthine [*xanth, yellow + -ine*] A yellowish-white purine base occurring in blood, urine, and some plants. (ZAN theen)

xanthoma [*xanth, yellow + -oma, tumor*] A small tumor of the skin composed of a yellowish mass of lipid-laden tissue cells. (zan THOH muh)

xanthophyll [*xantho, yellow + phyll, leaf*] Any of a group of carotenoid pigments in certain green plants that is responsible for the yellow to orange coloration in some autumn leaves. (ZAN thuh fil')

xanthous [*xanth, yellow + -ous*] Yellow. (ZAN thus)

-cide   to kill

algicide [*alg(ae) & -cide, to kill*] An agent for killing algae. (AL juh seyed')

bactericide [*bacteri, bacteria + -cide, to kill*] An agent for killing bacteria. (bak TIHR uh seyed')

biocide [*bio, living organisms + -cide, to kill*] An agent capable of killing living organisms, as an insecticide, herbicide, or antibiotic. (BEYE uh seyed')

ecocide [*eco, environment + -cide, to kill*] The destruction of the environment, as by defoliants, pollutants, chemical wastes, etc. (EK oh seyed')

fratricide [*Ltn > frater, brother + -cide, to kill*] The killing of one's own brother or sister. (FRAT ruh seyed')

fungicide [*fungi & -cide, to kill*] An agent for killing or inhibiting the growth of fungi. (FUN juh seyed')

genocide [*geno, race + -cide, to kill*] The deliberate and systematic killing of a racial, cultural, or political group. (JEN uh seyed')

germicide [*germ & -cide, to kill*] An agent for killing germs or other microorganisms. (JUR muh seyed')

herbicide [*herb & -cide, to kill*] An agent for killing or inhibiting the growth of plants, especially weeds. (HUR buh seyed')

homicide [*homo, same + -cide, to kill*] The killing of another human being. (HOM uh seyed')

infanticide [*infant & -cide, to kill*] The killing of an infant. (in FANT uh seyed')

insecticide [*insect & -cide, to kill*] An agent for killing insects. (in SEK tuh seyed')

larvicide [*larv(ae) & -cide, to kill*] An agent for killing harmful larvae. (LAHR vuh seyed')

matricide [*matri, mother + -cide, to kill*] The killing of one's own mother. (MAT ruh seyed')

microbicide [*microb(e) & -cide, to kill*] An agent for killing microbes. (meye KROH buh seyed')

ovicide [*ovi, egg + -cide, to kill*] An insecticide that is especially effective at killing the egg stage of an insect. (OH vuh seyed')

parasiticide [*parasit(e) & -cide, to kill*] An agent for killing plant or animal parasites. (pehr' uh SIT uh seyed')

parricide [*Ltn > peos, relative + -cide, to kill*] The killing of one's parent or close relative. (PEHR uh seyed')

patricide [*patri, father + -cide, to kill*] The killing of one's own father. (PAT ruh seyed')

pesticide [*pest & -cide, to kill*] An agent for killing pests such as rodents, insects, etc. (PES tuh seyed')

raticide [*rat & -cide, to kill*] An agent for killing rats. (RAT uh seyed')

regicide [*reg, rule + -cide, to kill*] The killing of a monarch, especially of one's own country. (REJ uh seyed')

rodenticide [*rodent & -cide, to kill*] An agent for killing rodents. (roh DENT uh seyed')

sororicide [*Ltn > soro, sister + -cide, to kill*] The killing of one's own sister. (suh ROR uh seyed')

spermicide [*spermi, sperm + -cide, to kill*] An agent for killing sperm. (SPUR muh seyed')

sporicide [*spori, spore + -cide, to kill*] An agent for killing spores. (SPOR uh seyed')

suicide [*Ltn > sui, oneself + -cide, to kill*] 1.The act of intentionally killing oneself. 2.The ruin or destruction of one's own prospects or interests through failed policies, decisions, etc. (SOO uh seyed')

taeniacide [*taenia {tapeworm} & -cide, to kill*] A drug or agent for killing tapeworms. (TEE nee uh seyed')

teniacide [*t(a)enia {tapeworm} & -cide, to kill*] A drug or agent for killing tapeworms. Same as taeniacide. (TEE nee uh seyed')

tyrannicide [*Grk > tyrannos, tyrant + -cide, to kill*] The act of killing a tyrant. (teye RAN uh seyed')

uxoricide [*Ltn > uxor, wife + -cide, to kill*] The act of killing one's wife. (uk SOR uh seyed')

vermicide [*vermi, worm + -cide, to kill*] A drug or agent for killing worms, especially parasitic intestinal worms. (VUR muh seyed')

viricide [*vir(us) & -cide, to kill*] An agent for killing or inhibiting viruses. Same as virucide. (VEYE ruh seyed')

virucide [*viru(s) & -cide, to kill*] An agent for killing or inhibiting viruses. (VEYE ruh seyed')

circum-   around

circumambient [*circum-, around & ambient {surrounding}*] Surrounding. Encompassing. Enclosing. See ambient, circumfluent, and circumjacent. (sur' kum AM bee ent)

circumambulate [*circum-, around & ambulate {walk}*] To walk around, especially ritualistically. See perambulate. (sur' kum AM byuh layt')

circumcise [*circum-, around + cis, cut*] 1.To remove the foreskin of a male. 2.To remove the clitoris of a female. (SUR kum seyez')

circumference [*circum-, around + fer, to carry + -ence*] 1.The boundary of a circle. 2.The distance around a figure, body, etc. (sur KUM fer ens)

circumflex [*circum-, around + flex, to bend*] 1.In the orthography of certain languages, a mark placed above a vowel to indicate sound or quality of pronunciation. See macron. 2.Winding or bending around. (SUR kum fleks')

circumfluent [*circum-, around + Ltn > fluere, to flow + -ent*] Surrounding. Flowing around. Encompassing. See ambient, circumambient, and circumjacent. (sur KUM floo ent)

circumfuse [*circum-, around + fus, pour*] 1.To pour or spread around. 2.To surround, as with a fluid. (sur' kum FYOOZ)

circumjacent [*circum-, around & (ad)jacent*] Surrounding. Adjacent on all sides. See ambient, circumambient, and circumfluent. (sur' kum JAY sent)

circumlocution [*circum-, around + locu, to speak + -tion*] 1.A roundabout, evasive, or long-winded way of speaking. 2.A roundabout expression. See periphrasis. (sur' kum loh KYOO shun)

circumlunar [*circum-, around* + *lun, moon* + *-ar*] Revolving around or surrounding the moon. See circumsolar and circumterrestrial. (sur' kum LOO nur)

circumnavigate [*circum-, around & navigate*] To sail or fly completely around, especially the earth. (sur' kum NAV ih gayt')

circumpolar [*circum-, around & polar*] 1.Found near or surrounding the North or South Pole. 2.Pertaining to a star or other celestial object that is continually visible above the horizon. (sur' kum POH lur)

circumscissile [*circum-, around* + *Ltn > scindere, to split* + *-ile*] Splitting along a traverse circular line, as some seed pods or capsules. (sur' kum SIS ul)

circumscribe [*circum-, around* + *scrib, to write*] 1.To draw a line around. Encircle. 2.To enclose within a boundary. Limit. Restrict. (SUR kum skreyeb')

circumsolar [*circum-, around* + *sol, sun* + *-ar*] Revolving around or surrounding the sun. See circumlunar and circumterrestrial. (sur' kum SOH lur)

circumspect [*circum-, around* + *spect, to look*] Careful to consider all possible consequences before judging, acting, etc. Prudent. Cautious. (SUR kum spekt')

circumstance [*circum-, around* + *Ltn > stare, to stand*] 1.A fact or condition that must be considered in determining a course of action. 2.The sum of conditions beyond willful control. (SUR kum stans')

circumterrestrial [*circum-, around* + *terr, earth* + *-ial*] Revolving around or surrounding the earth. See circumsolar and circumlunar. (sur' kum tuh RES tree ul)

circumvallate [*circum-, around* + *Ltn > vallum, rampart {defensive barrier}*] To surround by, or as if by, a rampart or other defensive obstruction. (sur' kum VAL ayt')

circumvent [*circum-, around* + *vent, to go*] 1.To bypass or go around. 2.To avoid or escape from, especially by artful maneuvering. See evade and elude. (sur' kum VENT)

circumvolution [*circum-, around* + *volu, turn* + *-tion*] The act of turning or winding about an axis. See vertiginous (def. 2). (sur' kum vuh LOO shun)

peri- around

aperiodic [*a-, not* + *peri, around* + *Grk > hodos, journey* + *-ic*] 1.Not characterized by periods or repeated cycles. 2.Not occurring at regular intervals. Irregular. Opposed to periodic. (ay' pihr ee OD ik)

perianth [*peri-, around* + *anth, flower*] The external envelope of a flower, consisting of the calyx or corolla or both. (PEHR ee anth')

periapt [*peri-, around* + *Grk > haptein, to fasten*] A small object worn as a charm to protect against evil, disease, etc. (PEHR ee apt')

pericarditis [*peri-, around* + *cardi, heart* + *-itis, inflammation*] Inflammation of the pericardium. (pehr' ih kahr DEYE tis)

pericardium [*peri-, around* + *cardi, heart* + *-um*] The double-layered sac surrounding the heart and the ends of the large vessels attached to the heart. (pehr' ih KAHR dee um)

pericarp [*peri-, around* + *carp, fruit*] The ripened wall of a fruit that matures from the ovary wall following fertilization and consists of the endocarp, mesocarp, and epicarp. See endocarp, mesocarp, and epicarp. (PEHR ih kahrp')

perichondrium [*peri-, around* + *chondr, cartilage* + *-ium*] The fibrous membrane of connective tissue covering the cartilage, except at the joint surfaces. (pehr' ih KON dree um)

pericranium [*peri-, around* + *crani, skull* + *-um*] The fibrous membrane of connective tissue covering the outer surface of the skull. (pehr' ih KRAY nee um)

pericycle [*peri-, around* + *cycl, circle*] The layer of parenchyma cells within the endodermis, that forms the outermost part of the stele in the stems and roots of most plants. (PEHR ih seye' kul)

periderm [*peri-, around* + *derm, skin*] The outer layers of tissue in roots and stems that consist of the cork cambium and other tissues arising from it. (PEHR ih derm')

perigee [*peri-, around* + *geo, earth*] The point at which the orbit of the moon or a satellite is nearest the earth. See apogee. (PEHR ih jee)

perigynous [*peri-, around* + *gyn, female* + *-ous*] Having floral parts or organs arranged around the edge of a cuplike receptacle containing the gynoecium, as a rose. See epigynous and hypogynous. (puh RIJ uh nus)

perihelion [*peri-, around* + *heli, sun* + *-on*] The point in a planet's orbit that is nearest the sun. See aphelion. (pehr' ih HEE lee un)

perikaryon [*peri-, around* + *kary, nucleus* + *-on*] The cytoplasm surrounding the nucleus of a nerve cell. (pehr' ih KEHR ee on')

perilune [*peri-, around* + *lun, moon*] The point in a satellite's lunar orbit that is nearest the moon. See apolune. (PEHR ih loon')

perimenopause [*peri-, around & menopause*] The frequently tumultuous and often unrecognized transition into menopause that for some women begins in their late thirties. (pehr' ih MEN uh poz')

perimeter [*peri-, around* + *meter, to measure*] 1.The outer boundary of an area. 2.The length of the outer boundary of a closed plane figure. (puh RIM et er)

perimorph [*peri-, around* + *morph, form*] A mineral enclosing a different kind of mineral. See endomorph. (PEHR ih morph')

perimysium [*peri-, around* + *my, muscle* + *-ium*] The sheath of connective tissue surrounding each primary bundle of muscle fibers. See endomysium and epimysium. (pehr' ih MIZ ee um)

perinatal [*peri-, around* + *nat, birth* + *-al*] Existing or occurring during the period near the time of birth; specifically, the period from the 28th week after gestation through the 7th week after birth. See prenatal, postnatal, and neonatal. (pehr' ih NAYT l)

perinephrium [*peri-, around* + *nephr, kidney* + *-ium*] The fatty and connective tissue surrounding a kidney. (pehr' ih NEF ree um)

perineurium [*peri-, around* + *neur, nerve* + *-ium*] The protective covering of connective tissue surrounding each bundle of nerve fibers in a peripheral nerve. See endoneurium and epineurium. (pehr' ih NOOR ee um)

period [*peri-, around* + *Grk > hodos, journey*] An interval of time between repeated cycles. (PIHR ee uhd)

periodic [*peri-, around* + *Grk > hodos, journey* + *-ic*] 1.Characterized by periods or repeated cycles. 2.Occurring at regular intervals. Opposed to aperiodic. (pihr' ee OD ik)

periodontal [*peri-, around + odont, tooth + -al*] Pertaining to the bone and tissue around a tooth. (pehr' ee oh DONT l)

periodontics [*peri-, around + odont, teeth + -ics, practice*] The branch of dentistry dealing with diseases of the bone and tissue surrounding and supporting the teeth. (pehr' ee oh DONT iks)

periodontitis [*peri-, around + odont, tooth + -itis, inflammation*] Inflammation of the tissues surrounding a tooth, which may result in pus-filled abscesses forming in the gums and spreading into the tooth socket, causing eventual tooth loss. See gingivitis and pyorrhea. (pehr' ee oh don TEYE tis)

perionychium [*peri-, around + onych, nail + -ium*] The border tissue around the back and sides of a fingernail or toenail. (pehr' ee oh NIK ee um)

periosteum [*peri-, around + oste, bone + -um*] The fibrous membrane of connective tissue covering every bone in the body, but not covering the joint surfaces. (pehr' ee OS tee um)

periostitis [*peri-, around + oste, bone + -itis, inflammation*] Inflammation of the periosteum. (pehr' ee os TEYE tis)

periotic [*peri-, around + ot, ear + -ic*] Located around the ear, especially the inner ear. (pehr' ee OH tik)

peripatetic [*peri-, around + Grk > patein, to walk + -ic*] 1.Pertaining to the philosophy of Aristotle, who taught while walking around in the Lyceum of ancient Athens. 2.Traveling around from place to place. (pehr' ih puh TET ik)

peripeteia [*peri-, around + Grk > ptotos, falling + -ia*] An abrupt or unexpected turn of events, especially in a literary work. (pehr' ih puh TEE uh)

peripheral [*peri-, around + Grk > pherein, to bear + -al*] 1.Lying at the outside or away from the center. 2.Serving an auxiliary function. (puh RIF ur ul)

peripheral nervous system One of two major divisions of the nervous system consisting of all parts of the nervous system except the brain and spinal cord, including the cranial and spinal nerves and the autonomic nervous system. See central nervous system and autonomic nervous system. (puh RIF ur ul NUR vus SIS tum)

periphery [*peri-, around + Grk > pherein, to bear + -y*] 1.The outermost part of an area within a boundary line. 2.Perimeter. 3.The area lying near the outer limits of something. (puh RIF uh ree)

periphrasis [*peri-, around + Grk > phrasis, speech*] A roundabout way of speaking or writing that uses many more words than necessary. See circumlocution. (puh RIF ruh sis)

periphrastic [*peri-, around + Grk > phrasis, speech + -ic*] Formed by using a word or phrase rather than an inflected form. Using an inflected form requires fewer words, such as "the story's end" instead of "the end of the story." (pehr' ih FRAS tik)

periphyton [*peri-, around + phyt, plant + -on*] Organisms that spend their life cycle attached to aquatic plants and other underwater surfaces, as snails and algae. (puh RIF ih tahn')

peripteral [*peri-, around + pter, wing + -al*] Pertaining to a structure with a row of columns on every side. See apteral. (puh RIP ter ul)

periscope [*peri-, around + -scope, to view*] A tubular optical instrument for viewing objects that are not in the direct line of sight, as on a submerged submarine. (PEHR ih skohp')

peristalsis [*peri-, around + Grk > stellein, to place + -sis*] A tubular muscular system that propels contained matter with wavelike muscular contractions, as the alimentary canal. (pehr' ih STOL sis)

peristome [*peri-, around + -stome, mouth*] 1.The fringe of toothlike appendages surrounding the opening of a moss capsule. 2.The structures surrounding the mouth of certain invertebrates. (PEHR ih stohm')

peristyle [*peri-, around + styl, column*] A row of columns surrounding a building or open space. See amphistylar, amphiprostyle, and prostyle. (PEHR ih steyel')

perithecium [*peri-, around + Grk > theke, case + -ium*] A small, flask-shaped fruiting body of ascomycete fungi in which asci are borne and which releases ascospores through an apical pore. See apothecium and cleistothecium. (pehr' ih THEE shee um)

peritoneum [*peri-, around + Grk > teinein, to stretch + -um*] The serous membrane lining the abdominal cavity and enclosing the viscera. (pehr' ih tuh NEE um)

peritonitis [*periton(eum) & -itis, inflammation*] Inflammation of the peritoneum. (pehr' ih tuh NEYE tis)

clud, clus   to close

conclude [*con-, completely + clud, to close*] 1.To bring to an end. Finish. 2.To form an opinion or reach a decision about. Decide. (kun KLOOD)

conclusive [*con-, completely + clus, to close + -ive*] Leading to a clear, convincing, or definite result. Opposed to inconclusive. (kun KLOO siv)

exclude [*ex-, out + clud, to close*] 1.To shut out. Refuse to admit, include, or consider. 2.To put out. Banish. Expel. See expel. (eks KLOOD)

include [*in-, in + clud, to close*] 1.To bring in as a part of a whole. 2.To add to a total, a class, etc. (in KLOOD)

inconclusive [*in-, not & conclusive*] Not leading to a clear, convincing, or definite result. Opposed to conclusive. (in' kun KLOO siv)

malocclusion [*mal-, bad & occlusion {closing}*] Abnormal closure of the upper and lower teeth. (mal' uh KLOO zhun)

occlude [*oc-, over + clud, to close*] 1.To close. 2.To prevent the passage of. Obstruct. 3.In chemistry, to absorb without changing the properties of. (uh KLOOD)

preclude [*pre-, before + clud, to close*] 1.To prevent from ever happening. Make impossible. 2.To exclude. See exclude. (prih KLOOD)

recluse [*re-, back + clus, to close*] A person who withdraws from society. (REK loos)

seclude [*se-, apart + clud, to close*] 1.To keep apart from others. Isolate. 2.To make private. Hide from view. (sih KLOOD)

cogn   knowledge

cognition [*cogn, knowledge + -ition*] 1.The act or process by which knowledge is acquired, including perception, memory, and judgment. 2.Something known, perceived, or recognized. (kog NISH un)

cognizance [*cogn, knowledge + -ize + -ance*] Conscious knowledge or awareness, especially the range or scope of knowledge possible through observation. (KOG nuh zuns)

cognoscente [*cogn, knowledge + -ent*] A person with superior knowledge of a subject, especially in the fine arts, literature, or fashion. Expert. Connoisseur. (kon' yuh SHEN tee)

cognoscible [*cogn, knowledge + -ible*] Capable of being known, perceived, or recognized. Knowable. (kog NOS uh bul)

incognito [*in-, without + cogn, knowledge*] 1.With one's true identity concealed or disguised. 2.Disguised identity. (in' kog NEE toh)

incognizant [*in-, without + cogn, knowledge + -ize + -ant*] Without knowledge or awareness. (in KOG nuh zunt)

precognition [*pre-, before + cogn, knowledge + -ition*] Knowledge of an event before its occurrence, especially through extrasensory means. Clairvoyance. See telegnosis and telepathy. (pree' kog NISH un)

recognizance [*re-, again + cogn, knowledge + -ize + -ance*] A legal bond or obligation requiring a person to perform a particular act, as to appear in court. (rih KOG nuh zuns)

recognize [*re-, again + cogn, knowledge + -ize*] 1.To know from past experience or awareness. 2.To acknowledge the significance, worthiness, or validity of. (REK ig neyez')

terra incognita [*terra, land & in-, without + cogn, knowledge*] 1.An unknown land or territory. 2.An unexplored or unknown field of knowledge. (TEHR uh in' kog NEET uh)

gnos, gnom, gnomon   knowledge

agnosia [*a-, without + gnos, knowledge + -ia*] Total or partial loss of the ability to recognize familiar objects, often resulting from brain damage. (ag NOH zhuh)

agnostic [*a-, without + gnos, knowledge + -tic*] One who believes the existence of God is unknown, but does not deny the possibility that God exists. See atheist and infidel (def. 1). (ag NOS tik)

diagnosis [*dia-, through + gnos, knowledge + -is*] 1.The process of learning the nature of a disease or condition by examining all of the symptoms. 2.The critical analysis of a situation, occurrence, or problem. 3.A brief description of the characteristics of an organism, species, etc. (deye' ig NOH sis)

diagnostics [*diagnos(is) & -ics, science*] The science or practice of diagnosis. (deye' ig NOS tiks)

geognosy [*geo, earth + gnos, knowledge + -y*] The study of the composition and structure of the earth. (jee OG nuh see)

gnome [*gnom, knowledge*] A short, pithy saying expressing a general truth. Maxim. See aphorism, apothegm, and proverb. (nohm)

gnomon [*gnomon, knowledge*] 1.A vertical object whose shadow indicates the time of day, as the style of a sundial. 2.The figure remaining in a parallelogram after a similar but smaller parallelogram has been removed from one of its corners. (NOH mon)

gnosis [*gnos, knowledge + -is*] An esoteric, allegedly superior knowledge of spiritual truths, as claimed by the Gnostics. (NOH sis)

gnostic [*gnos, knowledge + -tic*] Pertaining to or having intellectual or spiritual knowledge. (NOS tik)

Gnosticism [*gnos, knowledge + -tic + -ism*] A religious and philosophical doctrine of early Christianity that emphasized knowledge rather than faith as the key to salvation. (NOS tuh siz' um)

gnotobiotics [*gnos, knowledge + bio, living organisms + -ics, study of*] The science dealing with the study of organisms living in an environment free from germs or other microorganisms, except those known to be present. (noht' oh beye OT iks)

ignorant [*ig-, without + gnos, knowledge + -ant*] Without knowledge or training. Not educated. Illiterate. See illiterate (def. 1). (IG nuh runt)

ignore [*ig-, without + gnos, knowledge*] To refuse to notice or recognize. (ig NOR)

pathognomonic [*patho, disease + gnomon, knowledge + -ic*] Characteristic or indicative of a particular disease or condition. (puh thog' nuh MON ik)

pharmacognosy [*pharmaco, drug + gnos, knowledge + -y*] The science dealing with natural drugs of plant, animal, or mineral origin. (fahr' muh KOG nuh see)

physiognomy [*physio, nature + gnom, knowledge + -y*] 1.The art or practice of judging character from body form or facial features. 2.Facial features, especially when taken as a sign of character. (fiz ee OG nuh mee)

prognosis [*pro-, before + gnos, knowledge + -is*] A prediction of the probable cause, course, and result of a disease. (prog NOH sis)

prognostic [*pro-, before + gnos, knowledge + -tic*] 1.A sign, omen, or other indication of things to come. 2.A prediction or forecast. (prog NOS tik)

prognosticate [*pro-, before + gnos, knowledge + -tic + -ate*] To predict using present indications as a guide. (prog NOS tih kayt')

pyrognostics [*pyro, fire + gnos, knowledge + -tic*] The properties exhibited by a mineral when heated. (peye' rog NOS tiks)

serodiagnosis [*sero, serum & diagnosis*] Diagnosis by means of testing blood serum reactions. (sihr' oh deye' ig NOH sis)

telegnosis [*tele, distant + gnos, knowledge + -is*] Knowledge of distant happenings obtained by supernatural means. Clairvoyance. See precognition and telepathy. (tel' uh NOH sis)

corp/o, corpor, corpus   body

corporal [*corpor, body + -al*] Pertaining to the body. Bodily. (KOR pur ul)

corporate [*corpor, body + -ate*] 1.United into one body. 2.Having the nature of or belonging to a corporation. (KOR pur it)

corporation [*corpor, body + -ation*] A body of one or more persons granted a charter which recognizes it as a separate entity with many of the legal powers given to individuals. (kor' puh RAY shun)

corporeal [*corpor, body + -eal*] 1.Pertaining to the physical body. Not spiritual. 2.Of a material nature. Tangible. Opposed to incorporeal. (kor POR ee ul)

corp/o, corpor, corpus

corposant [*corpo, body* + *Ltn* > *sanctum, holy*] A glowing ball of electrical discharge seen on pointed objects, such as the tip of a ship's mast, trees, etc., during electrical storms. Sometimes called Saint Elmo's fire after Saint Elmo, the patron saint of sailors. (KOR puh sant')

corps [*corp, body*] 1.A body of people associated or acting together under common direction. 2.A separate branch or department of the military having some specialized function. (kor)

corpse [*corp, body*] A dead body, usually that of a human being. (korps)

corpulent [*corp, body* + *-ulent*] Excessively fat and fleshy. Obese. Stout. (KOR pyuh lent)

corpus [*corpus, body*] 1.A complete collection of writings on a particular subject or by a particular author. 2.The body of an animal or human, especially when dead. 3.The main body or substance of something. (KOR pus)

corpus callosum [*corpus, body & Ltn* > *callosum, callous*] The band of transverse nerve fibers connecting the cerebral hemispheres of the brain. (KOR pus kuh LOH sum)

Corpus Christi [*corpus, body & Ltn* > *Christi, Christ*] Literally, "body of Christ." In the Roman Catholic Church, a feast celebrated on the first Thursday following Trinity Sunday in honor of the Eucharist. (KOR pus KRIS tee)

corpus delicti [*corpus, body & Ltn* > *delictum, crime*] 1.The facts and material evidence that prove the commission of a crime. 2.The body of a murder victim. (KOR pus dih LIK teye')

corpus juris [*corpus, body & Ltn* > *juris, law*] Literally, "body of law." A collection of all the laws of a nation, state, etc. (KOR pus JOOR is)

Corpus Juris Canonici [*corpus, body & Ltn* > *juris, law & Ltn* > *canonicus, canon*] Literally, "body of canon law." The body of canon law of the Roman Catholic Church up to 1918, which was replaced by the Codex Juris Canonici. See Codex Juris Canonici. (KOR pus JOOR is kuh NON uh seye')

Corpus Juris Civilis [*corpus, body & Ltn* > *juris, law & Ltn* > *civilis, civil*] Literally, "body of civil law." The body of ancient Roman law that was issued during the reign of the emperor Justinian and forms the basis of most European law. (KOR pus JOOR is sih VIL is)

corpus luteum [*corpus, body & Ltn* > *luteus, yellow*] A yellow mass of tissue formed in an ovarian follicle after the release of an ovum. (KOR pus LOOT ee um)

corpus striatum [*corpus, body & Ltn* > *striatus, grooved*] Either of two striated ganglionic masses in front of and lateral to the thalamus in each cerebral hemisphere. (KOR pus streye AYT um)

corpuscle [*corpus, body* + *-cle, small*] 1.A minute particle. 2.A free-moving cell, especially a red or white blood cell. See erythrocyte and leukocyte. (KOR pus' ul)

habeas corpus [*Ltn* > *habere, to have & corpus, body*] Literally, "you may have the body," which are the opening words of the writ. Any of various writs issued to bring a prisoner before a court for the purpose of determining if he or she is being lawfully held. (HAY bee us KOR pus)

incorporate [*in-, into* + *corpor, body* + *-ate*] 1.To combine into one body so as to form an indistinguishable whole. 2.To form into a legal corporation. (in KOR puh rayt')

incorporeal [*in-, without* + *corpor, body* + *-eal*] 1.Lacking material substance. Spiritual. 2.Lacking physical existence, but regarded by the law as existing, as a right or privilege. Intangible. Opposed to corporeal. (in' kor POR ee ul)

cosm/o universe, world

cosmic [*cosm, universe* + *-ic*] 1.Pertaining to the universe. 2.Extremely large. Vast. See enormous and astronomical (def. 2). (KOZ mik)

cosmochemistry [*cosmo, universe & chemistry*] The science dealing with the chemical composition of the universe. (koz' moh KEM ih stree)

cosmogony [*cosmo, universe* + *-gony, origination*] The study or a theory of the origin of the universe. (koz MOG uh nee)

cosmography [*cosmo, universe* + *-graphy, science*] 1.The study of the structure and composition of nature, including astronomy, geography, and geology. 2.The descriptive study of the universe. See cosmology. (koz MOG ruh fee)

cosmology [*cosm, universe* + *-ology, science*] The science of the origin, structure, and development of the universe. See cosmography. (koz MOL uh jee)

cosmonaut [*cosmo, universe* + *naut, sailor*] A Russian astronaut. (KOZ muh not')

cosmopolis [*cosmo, world* + *-polis, city*] A large cosmopolitan city. (koz MOP uh lis)

cosmopolitan [*cosmo, world* + *-polis, city* + *-an*] 1.Belonging to or representative of the whole world. 2.Composed of persons from many different parts of the world. (koz' muh POL ih tun)

cosmos [*cosm, universe* + *-os*] 1.The universe regarded as an orderly and harmonious system. 2.Order and harmony. 3.Any orderly and harmonious system. (KOZ mus)

macrocosm [*macro-, large* + *cosm, universe*] The entire universe. See microcosm. (MAK roh koz' um)

microcosm [*micro-, small* + *cosm, world*] 1.A miniature world or system sometimes representative of a larger system. 2.Something viewed as the epitome of the world or universe. See macrocosm. (MEYE kroh koz' um)

cred belief, believe

accredit [*ac-, to & credit*] 1.To attribute or ascribe to. 2.To certify as meeting certain prescribed standards. (uh KRED it)

Apostles' Creed [*Apostle & Creed*] A Christian statement of belief, originally ascribed to the twelve Apostles, that begins "I believe in God the Father Almighty." See Nicene Creed. (uh POS ulz kreed)

credence [*cred, belief* + *-ence*] Validity. Belief. Credentials. (KREED ens)

credentials [*cred, belief* + *-ent* + *-ial*] Evidence attesting to one's achievements, confidence, or trustworthiness. (krih DEN shuls)

credibility gap [*cred, believe* + *-ible* + *-ity & gap*] The extent or degree to which a person, institution, etc., cannot be believed or trusted. (kred' uh BIL ih tee gap)

credible [*cred, believe* + *-ible*] Believable. (KRED uh bul)

credit [*cred, belief* + *-it*] 1.Belief, trust, confidence, or faith in the truth of something. 2.A reputation in good standing. (KRED it)

creditable [*cred, belief* + *-it* + *-able*] Worthy of belief or honor. (KRED it uh bul)

creditor [*credit & -or*] A person or firm to whom a debt is owed. (KRED ih tur)

credo [*Ltn > credo, I believe*] 1.A creed, especially the Apostles' Creed or the Nicene Creed. 2.The accompanying music to the Apostles' Creed or the Nicene Creed. (KREE doh)

credulous [*cred, believe* + *-ulous*] Apt to believe too easily without proper evidence. (KREJ uh lus)

creed [*cred, belief*] 1.A brief, formal statement of the religious beliefs of a church. 2.A set of guiding beliefs, principles, opinions, etc. (kreed)

discredit [*dis-, not* + *cred, believe* + *-it*] 1.To reject as not believable. 2.To cause to be doubted. (dis KRED it)

incredible [*in-, not* + *cred, believe* + *-ible*] 1.Not believable. 2.Seeming impossible. Amazing. (in KRED uh bul)

incredulous [*in-, not* + *cred, believe* + *-ulous*] 1.Unbelieving. Skeptical. 2.Showing an unwillingness to believe. (in KREJ uh lus)

miscreant [*mis-, bad* + *cred, believe* + *-ant*] 1.A very bad person. Villain. 2.Evil. Villainous. (MIS kree unt)

Nicene Creed [*Nicene & Creed*] A Christian statement of belief, adopted by the first Council of Nicaea in 325 A.D., that begins "We believe in one God." See Apostles' Creed. (NEYE seen kreed)

recreant [*re-, back* + *cred, believe* + *-ant*] 1.Cowardly. Faithless. Disloyal. 2.Coward. Traitor. (REK ree unt)

dox   belief, praise

doxology [*doxo, praise* + *log, discourse* + *-y*] A hymn or other expression of praise to God. (dok SOL uh jee)

heterodox [*hetero, different* + *dox, belief*] Not conforming to established doctrines or beliefs, especially in theology. Unorthodox. Heretical. See orthodox and unorthodox. (HET ur uh doks')

neoorthodoxy [*neo, new* + *ortho, correct* + *dox, belief* + *-y*] A 20th century movement in Protestant theology that opposes liberalism and adheres to certain doctrines of the Reformation. (nee' oh OR thuh dok' see)

orthodox [*ortho, correct* + *dox, belief*] Conforming to established doctrines or beliefs. See unorthodox and heterodox. (OR thuh doks')

paradox [*para, beyond* + *dox, belief*] 1.A statement that is true, but seems unbelievable, contradictory, or absurd, as "Water water everywhere, but not a drop to drink." 2.A statement that is self-contradictory and false. (PEHR uh doks')

unorthodox [*un-, not* + *ortho, correct* + *dox, belief*] Not conforming to established doctrines or beliefs. See orthodox and heterodox. (un' OR thuh doks')

cryo   cold

cryobiology [*cryo, cold* + *bio, living organisms* + *-logy, study of*] The scientific study of the effects of below-normal temperatures on living organisms. (kreye' oh beye OL uh jee)

cryogen [*cryo, cold* + *gen, to produce*] A liquefied gas used to produce very low temperatures. (KREYE uh jen)

cryogenics [*cryo, cold* + *gen, to produce* + *-ics, science*] The science dealing with the production and effects of very low temperatures. (kreye' oh JEN iks)

cryolite [*cryo, cold* + *-lite, mineral*] A vitreous mineral, sodium aluminum fluoride, that is found in Greenland and used in the production of aluminum. So named for its clear, icy appearance. (KREYE uh leyet')

cryometer [*cryo, cold* + *meter, to measure*] A thermometer for measuring very low temperatures, usually using alcohol in place of mercury. (kreye OM et er)

cryonics [*cryo, cold & (bio)nics*] The practice of freezing the body of a recently deceased person to preserve it for possible revival by future medical cures. See bionics. (kreye ON iks)

cryophilic [*cryo, cold* + *phil, a natural liking* + *-ic*] Existing or thriving at low temperatures. See psychrophilic. (kreye' uh FIL ik)

cryophyte [*cryo, cold* + *-phyte, plant*] A plant that grows on snow or ice, as mosses, algae, fungi, or bacteria. (KREYE uh feyet')

cryoprobe [*cryo, cold & probe*] An instrument for applying extreme cold to body tissues during cryosurgery. See cryosurgery. (KREYE uh prohb')

cryoscope [*cryo, cold* + *-scope, to observe*] An instrument for measuring the freezing points of liquids and solutions. (KREYE uh skohp')

cryoscopy [*cryo, cold* + *-scopy, to observe*] The scientific study of the freezing points of liquids and solutions. (kreye OS kuh pee)

cryostat [*cryo, cold* + *stat, stationary*] A device for maintaining a very low constant temperature. (KREYE uh stat')

cryosurgery [*cryo, cold & surgery*] Surgery that uses extreme cold temperatures to destroy abnormal cells or tissue. See cryoprobe. (kreye' oh SUR jer ee)

cryotherapy [*cryo, cold & therapy*] Medical treatment using low temperatures obtained through the application of ice, liquid nitrogen, etc. (kreye' oh THEHR uh pee)

crypt/o   secret, hidden

Apocrypha [*apo-, from* + *crypt, hidden* + *-a*] 1.Fourteen Biblical books included in the Vulgate and Septuagint, but excluded from the Hebrew and Protestant Scriptures. 2.Various religious writings excluded from the New Testament. 3.Writings or statements of dubious authorship or authenticity. (uh POK ruh fuh)

apocryphal [*apo-, from* + *crypt, hidden* + *-al*] 1.Of dubious authenticity. Spurious. Counterfeit. Not genuine. 2.Pertaining to the Apocrypha. (uh POK ruh ful)

crypt [*crypt, hidden*] 1.An underground room or vault, especially one under the floor of a church used as a burial place. 2.A small glandular sac or cavity. (kript)

crypt/o

cryptanalysis [*crypt, secret & analysis*] The science of analyzing and deciphering code and other secret writings. See cryptography. (krip' tuh NAL uh sis)

cryptic [*crypt, hidden + -ic*] 1.Having a hidden, ambiguous, or mysterious meaning. 2.Secret. Mysterious. Occult. 3.Using or involving cipher or code. (KRIP tik)

cryptoclastic [*crypto, hidden + Grk > klastos, broken + -ic*] Consisting of microscopic fragments. (krip' toh KLAS tik)

cryptocrystalline [*crypto, hidden + crystall, crystal + -ine*] Having a crystalline structure of such a fine grain as to be unrecognizable even under a microscope. (krip' toh KRIS tuh lin)

cryptogam [*crypto, hidden + gam, sexual union*] An obsolete term for any plant that does not produce flowers or seeds. So named from the less prominent reproductive organs of the plants in this group. (KRIP tuh gam')

cryptogenic [*crypto, hidden + gen, origin + -ic*] Of uncertain or unknown origin, as a disease. See idiopathy. (krip' tuh JEN ik)

cryptogram [*crypto, secret + gram, to write*] A message written in code or cipher. (KRIP tuh gram')

cryptography [*crypto, secret + -graphy, writing*] The art or science of writing and deciphering secret codes. See cryptanalysis. (krip TOG ruh fee)

cryptomeria [*crypto, hidden + mer, part + -ia*] A Japanese cedar tree with short inward-curving needles and soft fragrant wood. So named from the seeds being hidden by scales within the cones. (krip' tuh MIHR ee uh)

cryptozoite [*crypto, hidden & (sporo)zoite*] The exoerythrocyte stage of a malaria parasite during which it lives in tissue cells before entering the blood. See sporozoite. (krip' tuh ZOH eyet')

decrypt [*de-, remove + crypt, secret*] To translate secret code into understandable language. Decode. (dee KRIPT)

encrypt [*en-, into + crypt, secret*] To convert into secret code. Encode. (en KRIPT)

procryptic [*pro(tect) & crypt, hidden + -ic*] Having a camouflaged coloring or pattern, as certain animals. (proh KRIP tik)

cyan/o   blue

anthocyanin [*antho, flower + cyan, blue + -in*] A water-soluble, blue to red pigment found in plants, some insects, and especially flowers. (an' thuh SEYE uh nin)

cyan [*cyan, blue*] A moderate greenish-blue color. (SEYE an)

cyanic [*cyan, blue + -ic*] Blue or bluish in color. (seye AN ik)

cyanine [*cyan, blue + -ine*] A blue dye used to extend the range of color sensitivity of photographic film. (SEYE uh neen')

cyanite [*cyan, blue + -ite, mineral*] A mineral, aluminum silicate, sometimes used as a gemstone and usually blue in color. (SEYE uh neyet')

cyanobacteria [*cyano, blue & bacteria*] Blue-green algae. (seye' uh noh' bak TIHR ee uh)

cyanosis [*cyan, blue + -osis, abnormal condition*] A bluish or purplish coloration of the skin caused by insufficient oxygenation of the blood. (seye' uh NOH sis)

hemocyanin [*hemo, blood + cyan, blue + -in*] A blue respiratory pigment similar to hemoglobin, found in the blood of many arthropods and mollusks. See hemoglobin. (hee' muh SEYE uh nin)

cycl/o   circle, wheel

acyclic [*a-, not + cycl, circle + -ic*] Not cyclic. (ay SEYE klik)

bicycle [*bi-, two + cycl, wheel*] A vehicle with two large wire-spoked wheels in tandem, usually propelled by the rider pushing pedals. (BEYE sih' kul)

cycle [*cycl, circle*] A recurring time period during which the same event or sequence of events occur. (SEYE kul)

cycloid [*cycl, circle + -oid, resembling*] 1.Resembling a circle. 2.A curve generated by the motion of a point on the circumference of a circle rolled along a straight line that is in the same plane as the circle. See epicycloid and hypocycloid. 3.Pertaining to a cyclothymic person. See cyclothymic. (SEYE kloid)

cyclometer [*cyclo, circle + meter, to measure*] 1.An instrument for measuring circular arcs. 2.An instrument for measuring distance traveled by recording the revolutions of a wheel. (seye KLOM et er)

cyclone [*cycl, circle + -one*] A wind system, rotating clockwise in the southern hemisphere and counterclockwise in the northern hemisphere, characterized by rapidly circulating air about a low pressure center. Severe tropical cyclones are referred to as typhoons or hurricanes depending on their location. (SEYE klohn)

cyclopaedia [*cyclo, circle + Grk > paideia, education*] A book or group of books containing detailed information on a wide variety of subjects, usually arranged alphabetically. Same as encyclopedia. (seye' kluh PEE dee uh)

cyclopedia [*cyclo, circle + Grk > paideia, education*] A book or group of books containing detailed information on a wide variety of subjects, usually arranged alphabetically. Same as encyclopedia. (seye' kluh PEE dee uh)

cyclops [*cycl, circle + ops, eye*] In Greek mythology, any of the giants with a single eye located in the middle of the forehead. (SEYE klops)

cyclorama [*cycl, circle & (pan)orama*] A pictorial representation consisting of large pictures or projections on the inside wall of a circular room, creating a natural perspective for an observer standing in or near the center. See panorama. (seye' kluh RAM uh)

cyclosis [*cycl, circle + -osis, action*] The streaming movement of protoplasm within certain cells. (seye KLOH sis)

cyclostome [*cyclo, circle + -stome, mouth*] Any of a class of primitive vertebrates with a circular mouth and no jaws. (SEYE kluh stohm')

cyclothymia [*cyclo, circle + -thymia, mental disorder*] An emotional disorder characterized by recurring cycles of elation and mild depression. (seye' kluh THEYE mee uh)

encyclical [*en-, in + cycl, circle + -ical*] 1.Intended for wide circulation. 2.A letter from the pope addressed to all the bishops of the Church. (en SIK lih kul)

encyclopaedia [*en-, in + cyclo, circle + Grk > paideia, education*] A book or group of books containing detailed information on a wide variety of subjects, usually arranged alphabetically. Same as encyclopedia. (en seye' kluh PEE dee uh)

encyclopedia [*en-, in + cyclo, circle + Grk > paideia, education*] A book or group of books containing detailed information on a wide variety of subjects, usually arranged alphabetically. (en seye' kluh PEE dee uh)

epicycle [*epi-, outside + cycl, circle*] In Ptolemaic astronomy, a circle whose center moves around the circumference of a larger circle, simulating the orbit of a heavenly body around the earth. (EP ih seye' kul)

epicycloid [*epi-, outside + cycl, circle + -oid, resembling*] A curve generated by the motion of a point on the circumference of a circle rolled around the outside of a fixed circle. See cycloid (def. 2) and hypocycloid. (ep' ih SEYE kloid')

gigahertz [*giga-, billion (10^9) & hertz*] One billion cycles per second. Gigacycle. (GIG uh hurts')

hemicycle [*hemi-, half + cycl, circle*] A semicircular arrangement or structure. (HEM ih seye' kul)

heterocyclic [*hetero, other + cycl, circle + -ic*] Pertaining to a compound having a ring structure composed of atoms of more than one kind. (het' uh roh SEYE klik)

homocyclic [*homo, same + cycl, circle + -ic*] Pertaining to a compound having a ring structure composed of only one kind of atom. (hoh' muh SEYE klik)

hypocycloid [*hypo-, below + cycl, circle + -oid, resembling*] A curve generated by the motion of a point on the circumference of a circle rolled around the inside of a fixed circle. See cycloid (def. 2) and epicycloid. (heye' puh SEYE kloid')

isocyclic [*iso-, same + cycl, circle + -ic*] Having a ring composed of atoms of the same element. (eye' soh SEYE klik)

kilohertz [*kilo-, thousand & hertz*] One thousand cycles per second. Kilocycle. (KIL uh hurts')

megahertz [*mega-, million & hertz*] One million cycles per second. Megacycle. (MEG uh hurts')

monocyclic [*mono-, one + cycl, circle + -ic*] 1.Forming only one cycle or circle. 2.Having one ring of atoms in a molecule. See polycyclic. (mon' uh SEYE klik)

pericycle [*peri-, around + cycl, circle*] The layer of parenchyma cells within the endodermis, that forms the outermost part of the stele in the stems and roots of most plants. (PEHR ih seye' kul)

polycyclic [*poly, many + cycl, circle + -ic*] Having more than one ring of atoms in a molecule. See monocyclic (def. 2). (pol' ee SEYE klik)

recycle [*ro , again & cycle*] To put through a cycle, or a portion of a cycle, again in order to reuse. (ree' SEYE kul)

terahertz [*tera-, trillion (10^{12}) & hertz*] One trillion cycles per second. (TEHR uh hurts')

tricycle [*tri-, three + cycl, wheel*] A vehicle with three wheels, usually propelled by the rider pushing pedals. (TREYE sik' ul)

unicycle [*uni-, one + cycl, wheel*] A vehicle with one wheel, usually propelled by the rider pushing pedals. (YOO nih seye' kul)

gyr, gyro   circle

autogiro [*auto-, self + gyro, circle*] An aircraft with a horizontal rotating wing to provide lift and a conventional engine-driven propeller to provide propulsion. See helicopter and gyroplane. (awt' oh JEYE roh)

autogyro [*auto-, self + gyro, circle*] An aircraft with a horizontal rotating wing to provide lift and a conventional engine-driven propeller to provide propulsion. Same as autogiro. (awt' oh JEYE roh)

gyral [*gyr, circle + -al*] 1.Moving in a spiral or circular path. 2.Pertaining to a gyrus. (JEYE rul)

gyrate [*gyr, circle + -ate*] To move in a spiral or circular path. Rotate. (JEYE rayt)

gyre [*gyr, circle*] 1.Having a circular or swirling motion. Vortex. 2.A spiral or circular motion, especially a circular system of ocean currents. (jeyer)

gyro [*gyro, circle*] 1.A gyroscope. 2.A gyrocompass. (JEYE roh)

gyrocompass [*gyro(scope) & compass*] A navigational device containing a gyroscope with a rotating axis parallel to the earth's axis and thus pointing to true north instead of magnetic north. (JEYE roh kum' pus)

gyromagnetic [*gyro, circle + magnet, magnetic force + -ic*] Pertaining to or resulting from the magnetic properties of a rotating electrically charged particle. (jeye' roh mag NET ik)

gyroplane [*gyro, circle & plane*] Any aircraft that uses a horizontal rotating wing, as a helicopter or autogiro. See autogiro and helicopter. (JEYE ruh playn')

gyroscope [*gyro, circle & scope*] An apparatus with a wheel mounted so that its axis of rotation is able to turn freely in any direction and when spun rapidly keeps its original direction irrespective of the position of the mountings. (JEYE ruh skohp')

gyrus [*gyr, circle + -us*] One of the convoluted ridges on the surface of the brain caused by infolding of the cerebral cortex. See convolution (def. 2). (JEYE rus)

spirogyra [*spiro, coil + gyr, circle + -a*] Any of various green, filamentous freshwater algae with spiral chlorophyll bands in each cell. (speye' ruh JEYE ruh)

helic/o   spiral, circular

helical [*helic, spiral + -al*] Pertaining to or having the shape of a helix. Spiral. (IIEL ih kul)

helicoid [*helic, spiral + -oid, resembling*] 1.Shaped like a flattened spiral, as a snail shell. 2.A geometrical surface shaped like a coil or screw. (HEL ih koid')

helicon [*helic, circular + -on*] A large circular tuba carried around the player's shoulder. (HEL ih kon')

helicopter [*helico, circular + pter, wing*] An aircraft with a horizontal rotating wing that provides both lift and propulsion. See autogiro and gyroplane. (HEL ih kop' ter)

helix [*helic, spiral*] 1.Anything spiral in form or structure, as a snail shell, screw thread, etc. 2.The incurved rim of skin and cartilage around the outer ear. (HEE liks)

dactyl/o

dactyl/o   finger, toe, digit

artiodactyl [*artio, even number + dactyl, toe*] Any of various herbivorous hoofed mammals with an even number of toes on each foot. (ahr' tee oh DAK tul)

brachydactylous [*brachy, short + dactyl, finger + -ous*] Having abnormally short fingers or toes. (brak' ee DAK tuh lus)

dactyl [*dactyl, finger*] 1.A finger or toe. 2.A metrical foot consisting of one long syllable followed by two short syllables, or one stressed syllable followed by two unstressed syllables. So named from the three joints of the finger, the first of which is the longest. See anapest and tribrach. (DAK tul)

dactylogram [*dactylo, finger + gram, to record*] A fingerprint. (dak TIL uh gram')

dactylography [*dactylo, finger + -graphy, science*] The scientific study of fingerprints for the purpose of identification. (dak' tuh LOG ruh fee)

dactylology [*dactylo, finger + log, discourse + -y*] The art of communicating using a finger alphabet, as among the deaf. (dak' tuh LOL uh jee)

pentadactyl [*penta-, five + dactyl, finger*] Having five fingers or toes on each hand or foot. (pent' uh DAK tul)

perissodactyl [*Grk > perissos, uneven + dactyl, toe*] Any of various herbivorous, hoofed mammals with an uneven number of toes on each foot. (puh ris' oh DAK tul)

polydactyl [*poly, many + dactyl, finger*] Having more than the normal number of fingers or toes. (pol' ee DAK tul)

pterodactyl [*ptero, wing + dactyl, finger*] Any of an order of extinct flying reptiles with featherless wings of skin extending from the elongated fourth digit, along the forelimb to the back of the body. See pterosaur. (tehr' uh DAK tul)

syndactyl [*syn-, together + dactyl, digit*] Having two or more digits joined together, as by webbing. (sin DAK tul)

zygodactyl [*zygo, pair + dactyl, toe*] Having a pair of toes pointing forward and a pair pointing backward, as some birds. (zeye' guh DAK tul)

dem/o, demi   people

demagog [*dem, people + agog, leader*] 1.A leader who obtains power by appealing to the popular prejudices and emotions of the people. 2.Originally, a popular leader of the people. Same as demagogue. (DEM uh gog')

demagogue [*dem, people + agog, leader*] 1.A leader who obtains power by appealing to the popular prejudices and emotions of the people. 2.Originally, a popular leader of the people. (DEM uh gog')

demiurge [*demi, people + erg, work*] 1.The Gnostic creator of the material world, sometimes considered to be the creator of evil. 2.The Platonic creator of the material universe. 3.A magistrate or other public official in certain ancient Greek states. (DEM ee urj')

democracy [*demo, people + -cracy, government*] Government run by the people, exercised either directly by them or through elected officials. (dih MOK ruh see)

democrat [*demo, people + crat, government*] 1.A member or supporter of the Democratic Party. 2.A person who advocates government by the people. (DEM uh krat')

demographics [*demo, people + graph, recording + -ics, knowledge*] The statistical data of human populations, used to identify age, sex, education, income, etc. (dem' uh GRAF iks)

demography [*demo, people + -graphy, science*] The study of vital statistics, density, growth, etc., of human populations. (dih MOG ruh fee)

endemic [*en-, in + dem, people + -ic*] Peculiar to a particular people or locality, as a disease, species, etc. Native. (en DEM ik)

epidemic [*epi-, among + dem, people + -ic*] 1.Rapidly spreading disease among people in a region. 2.The rapid spread or sudden development of something, as crime, an idea, etc. See pandemic. (ep' ih DEM ik)

epidemiology [*epi-, among + demi, people + -ology, study of*] The study of the causes, prevention, and control of epidemic diseases among people. See epizootiology. (ep' ih dee' mee OL uh jee)

pandemic [*pan, all + dem, people + -ic*] A disease that is prevalent over a very large area, a continent, or the entire world. See epidemic. (pan DEM ik)

demi-   half, less than

demigod [*demi-, less than & god*] 1.A lesser or inferior god. 2.The offspring of a mortal and a god or goddess. 3.A superior person who seems like a god. (DEM ih god')

demimonde [*demi-, less than + Ltn > mundus, world*] 1.A class of women of dubious social standing because of their sexual promiscuity or indiscreet behavior. 2.A group engaged in an activity of dubious legality or respectability. (DEM ih mond')

demisemiquaver [*demi-, half + semi-, half & quaver {eighth note}*] In music, a thirty-second note denoted by a solid, oval-shaped character with a three-hooked vertical stem. See semiquaver and hemidemisemiquaver. (dem' ee SEM ee kway' vur)

demitasse [*demi-, less than + French > tasse, cup*] 1.A small cup of black coffee usually served after dinner. 2.A small cup for serving black coffee. (DEM ih tas')

hemidemisemiquaver [*hemi-, half + demi-, half + semi-, half & quaver {eighth note}*] In music, a sixty-fourth note denoted by a solid, oval-shaped character with a four-hooked vertical stem. See semiquaver and demisemiquaver. (hem' ee dem' ee SEM ee kway' vur)

hemi-   half, partly

hemicellulose [*hemi-, half & cellulose*] Any of a group of polysaccharide carbohydrates that are less complex and more easily hydrolyzed than cellulose. (hem' ih SEL yuh lohs')

hemicycle [*hemi-, half + cycl, circle*] A semicircular arrangement or structure. (HEM ih seye' kul)

hemidemisemiquaver [*hemi-, half + demi-, half + semi-, half & quaver {eighth note}*] In music, a sixty-fourth note denoted by a solid, oval-shaped character with a four-hooked vertical stem. See semiquaver and demisemiquaver. (hem' ee dem' ee SEM ee kway' vur)

hemihedral [*hemi-, half + -hedral, surface*] Having only half the number of plane surfaces needed for complete symmetry. (hem' ih HEE drul)

hemihydrate [*hemi-, half & hydrate*] A hydrate, such as plaster of paris, that contains two moles of compound for each mole of water. (hem' ih HEYE drayt')

hemimetabolic [*hemi-, half & metabolic*] Experiencing incomplete metamorphosis, as certain insects. See holometabolic. (hem' ih met' uh BOL ik)

hemimorphic [*hemi-, half + morph, form + -ic*] Pertaining to a crystal that is not symmetric at opposite axial ends. (hem' ih MOR fik)

hemiola [*hemi-, half + hol, whole + -a*] Occurring in a ratio of one and one half to one. In early music, a rhythmic alteration consisting of time units or measures in the ratio of three to two or two to three. (hem' ee OH luh)

hemiparasite [*hemi-, partly & parasite*] A plant or animal that is partially parasitic. (hem' ih PEHR uh seyet')

hemiplegia [*hemi-, half + -plegia, paralysis*] Total paralysis of one side of the body. (hem' ih PLEE jee uh)

hemipterous [*hemi-, half + pter, wing + -ous*] Any of a large number of insects belonging to the order Hemiptera that are commonly referred to as the true bugs. The order Hemiptera is composed of the suborders Homoptera and Heteroptera. See homopterous and heteropterous. (hih MIP ter us)

hemisphere [*hemi-, half & sphere*] 1.Half of the earth divided into north and south by the equator or east and west by a meridian. 2.One of the two halves of a sphere formed by a plane passing through its center. (HEM ih sfihr')

hemistich [*hemi-, half & stich {line of verse}*] Half of a poetic line of verse, usually on either side of the main caesura. (HEM ih stik')

semi-   half, partly

demisemiquaver [*demi-, half + semi-, half & quaver {eighth note}*] In music, a thirty-second note denoted by a solid, oval-shaped character with a three-hooked vertical stem. See semiquaver and hemidemisemiquaver. (dem' ee SEM ee kway' vur)

hemidemisemiquaver [*hemi-, half + demi-, half + semi-, half & quaver {eighth note}*] In music, a sixty-fourth note denoted by a solid, oval-shaped character with a four-hooked vertical stem. See semiquaver and demisemiquaver. (hem' ee dem' ee SEM ee kway' vur)

semiannual [*semi-, half + ann, year + -ual*] Occurring twice a year. Same as biannual. (sem' ee AN yoo ul)

semiaquatic [*semi-, partly & aquatic*] 1.Adapted for growing in or near water. 2.Often found in water, but not entirely aquatic. See semiterrestrial and amphibious (def. 1). (sem' ee uh KWOT ik)

semiarid [*semi-, partly & arid*] Pertaining to a climate having little annual rainfall. (sem' ee EHR id)

semiautomatic [*semi-, partly & automatic*] 1.Pertaining to a device that is partly automatic and partly operated by hand. 2.A firearm that automatically ejects and reloads, but requires manual squeezing of the trigger for each shot. (sem' ee ot' uh MAT ik)

semiautonomous [*semi-, partly & autonomous*] Self-governing only with regard to certain affairs. See autonomous (def. 1) and heteronomous. (sem' ee aw TON uh mus)

semicentennial [*semi-, half + cent, hundred + enn, years + -ial*] Occurring once every fifty years. See bicentennial. (sem' ee sen TEN ee ul)

semicolon [*semi-, partly & colon*] A punctuation mark that indicates more separation than a comma and less separation than a colon or period. (SEM ih koh' lun)

semiconductor [*semi-, partly & conductor*] Any of several substances, such as silicon or germanium, whose electrical conductivity ranges between that of a conductor and an insulator and is usually highly dependent on temperature. (SEM ee kun duk' tur)

semidiameter [*semi-, half & diameter*] 1.Half of a diameter. Radius. 2.The perceived radius of a spherical celestial body observed from the earth. (sem' ee deye AM et er)

semidiurnal [*semi-, half + Ltn > dies, day + -al*] 1.Completed in half a day. 2.Occurring once every twelve hours. (sem' ee deye URN l)

semifinal [*semi-, half & final*] The next to the last round in a contest of elimination. (sem' ee FEYE nul)

semiliterate [*semi-, partly & literate*] 1.Having limited ability to read and write. 2.Able to read, but not able to write. See literate (def. 1), illiterate (def. 1), and analphabetic. (sem' ee LIT ur it)

semilogarithmic [*semi-, half & logarithmic*] Having one logarithmic scale and one arithmetic scale. (sem' ee log' uh RITH mik)

semilunar [*semi-, half + lun, moon + -ar*] Having the shape of a half-moon or crescent. (sem' ee LOO nur)

semimonthly [*semi-, half & month & -ly*] Occurring twice a month. See bimonthly. (sem' ee MUNTH lee)

semiparasite [*semi-, partly & parasite*] A plant or animal that is partially parasitic. Same as hemiparasite. (sem' ee PEHR uh seyet')

semipermeable [*semi-, partly & permeable*] Partially permeable, as a membrane that allows only smaller molecules to pass through. See permeate. (sem' ee PUR mee uh bul)

semiprecious [*semi-, partly & precious*] Pertaining to a gem with less commercial value than a precious gem, as the garnet. (sem' ee PRESH us)

semiprofessional [*semi-, partly & professional*] Engaging in a profession or activity on a part-time basis. (sem' ee pruh FESH uh nul)

semiquaver [*semi-, half & quaver {eighth note}*] In music, a sixteenth note denoted by a solid, oval-shaped character with a two-hooked vertical stem. See demisemiquaver and hemidemisemiquaver. (SEM ee kway' vur)

semiterrestrial [*semi-, partly & terrestrial*] Often found on land, but not entirely terrestrial, as most amphibians. See semiaquatic (def. 2) and amphibian (def. 1). (sem' ee tuh RES tree ul)

semitone [*semi-, half & tone*] A musical tone halfway between two major tones. (SEM ee tohn')

semitransparent [*semi-, partly & transparent*] Not entirely transparent. See transparent (def. 1) and translucent. (sem' ee trans PEHR ent)

semivowel [*semi-, half & vowel*] A letter or speech sound with the sound of a vowel, but the function of a consonant, as the "w" in *well* or the "y" in *toy*. (SEM ih vou' ul)

semiweekly [*semi-, half & week & -ly*] Occurring twice a week. See biweekly. (sem' ee WEEK lee)

semiyearly [*semi-, half & year & -ly*] Occurring twice a year. Same as biannual. (sem' ee YIHR lee)

dent, denti tooth, teeth

bidentate [*bi-, two + dent, teeth + -ate*] Having two teeth or toothlike processes. (beye DEN tayt')

dental [*dent, teeth + -al*] 1.Pertaining to the teeth or to dentistry. 2.Articulated with the tip of the tongue on or above the upper front teeth. See interdental and labiodental. (DENT l)

dental hygienist [*dental & hygienist*] A dental assistant who cleans and polishes teeth, takes x-rays, etc. (DENT l heye JEEN ist)

dentate [*dent, teeth + -ate*] Having teeth or notches resembling teeth. Notched. (DEN tayt)

denticle [*denti, tooth + -cle, small*] 1.A small tooth or toothlike process. 2.A small calcified body that develops within the pulp cavity of a tooth. (DEN tih kul)

dentiform [*denti, tooth & form*] Tooth-shaped. (DEN tih form')

dentifrice [*denti, teeth + Ltn > fricare, to rub*] Any substance for cleaning teeth, as a powder or paste. (DEN tih fris)

dentigerous [*denti, teeth + -gerous, bearing*] Bearing teeth. (den TIJ ur us)

dentil [*dent, teeth + -il*] Any of a series of small, closely spaced, rectangular blocks projecting like teeth beneath a cornice. (DEN til)

dentin [*dent, tooth + -in*] The hard bony tissue that forms the main body of a tooth and surrounds the pulp cavity. It is covered by cementum below the gumline and enamel above the gumline. (DEN tin)

dentine [*dent, tooth + -ine*] The hard bony tissue that forms the main body of a tooth and surrounds the pulp cavity. It is covered by cementum below the gumline and enamel above the gumline. Same as dentin. (DEN teen)

dentistry [*dent, teeth + -ist + -ry*] The branch of medical science dealing with the diagnosis, prevention, and treatment of diseases and disorders of the teeth and associated structures. (DENT ih stree)

dentition [*denti, teeth + -tion*] 1.The teething process. 2.The kind, number, and arrangement of teeth. (den TISH un)

dentoid [*dent, tooth + -oid, resembling*] Tooth-shaped. Same as dentiform. (DEN toid)

denture [*dent, teeth + -ure*] A partial or complete set of removable artificial teeth. (DEN chur)

edentate [*e-, out + dent, teeth + -ate*] 1.Without teeth. 2.Any of an order of New World mammals with no teeth, as anteaters, armadillos, and sloths. (ee DEN tayt')

edentulous [*e-, out + dent, teeth + -ulous*] Without teeth, especially as a result of disease or injury. (ee DEN chuh lus)

interdental [*inter-, between + dent, teeth + -al*] 1.Located between the teeth. 2.Articulated with the tip of the tongue between the upper and lower front teeth. See dental and labiodental. (in' ter DENT l)

labiodental [*labio, lip + dent, teeth + -al*] Articulated with the participation of the lower lip and the upper front teeth. See dental and interdental. (lay' bee oh DENT l)

tridentate [*tri-, three + dent, teeth + -ate*] Having three teeth or toothlike processes. (treye DEN tayt')

dont, odont/o tooth, teeth

acrodont [*acro, high + dont, teeth*] Having teeth fastened to the upper surface of the jaw without sockets, as some lower vertebrates. See pleurodont. (AK ruh dont')

diphyodont [*di-, two + Grk > phyein, to grow + odont, teeth*] Developing two sets of teeth, the first set deciduous and the second set permanent, as in humans. (DIF ee oh dont')

endodontics [*endo-, inside + dont, tooth + -ics, practice*] The branch of dentistry dealing with the prevention and treatment of diseases and disorders of the tooth pulp. (en' doh DONT iks)

exodontics [*exo-, out + dont, tooth + -ics, practice*] The branch of dentistry dealing with the extraction of teeth. (eks' oh DONT iks)

microdont [*micro-, small + dont, teeth*] Having small teeth. (MEYE kroh dont')

odontalgia [*odont, tooth + alg, pain + -ia*] Toothache. (oh' don TAL juh)

odontoblast [*odonto, tooth + blast, cell*] Any of the connective tissue cells that form the outer surface of dental pulp and produce dentin. See dentin. (oh DONT uh blast')

odontoid [*odont, tooth + -oid, resembling*] Tooth-shaped. Same as dentiform. (oh DON toid')

odontology [*odont, teeth + -ology, science*] The branch of medical science dealing with the diagnosis, prevention, and treatment of diseases and disorders of the teeth and associated structures. Same as dentistry. (oh' don TOL uh jee)

odontophore [*odonto, teeth + -phore, to bear*] A structure at the base of the mouth of most mollusks that supports the radula, which is drawn back and forth to break up food. (oh DONT uh for')

orthodontics [*ortho, straight + dont, teeth + -ics, practice*] The branch of dentistry dealing with the straightening of abnormally aligned or positioned teeth. (or' thuh DONT iks)

periodontal [*peri-, around + odont, tooth + -al*] Pertaining to the bone and tissue around a tooth. (pehr' ee oh DONT l)

periodontics [*peri-, around + odont, teeth + -ics, practice*] The branch of dentistry dealing with diseases of the bone and tissue surrounding and supporting the teeth. (pehr' ee oh DONT iks)

periodontitis [*peri-, around + odont, tooth + -itis, inflammation*] Inflammation of the tissues surrounding a tooth, which may result in pus-filled abscesses forming in the gums and spreading into the tooth socket, causing eventual tooth loss. See gingivitis and pyorrhea. (pehr' ee oh don TEYE tis)

pleurodont [*pleur, side + odont, teeth*] Having teeth fastened to the inside of the jaw without sockets, as certain lizards. See acrodont. (PLOOR uh dont')

prosthodontics [*prosth(esis) & odont, teeth + -ics, practice*] The branch of dentistry dealing with the replacement of teeth with synthetic substitutes. (pros' thuh DONT iks) dia-

derma, derm, dermat/o   skin

blastoderm [*blasto, cell layer + derm, skin*] 1.The layer of cells surrounding the blastocoel of a blastula. 2.The cells covering the blastocoel of a heavily-yolked egg. See blastocoel and blastula. (BLAS tuh derm')

dermal [*derm, skin + -al*] Pertaining to the skin. Cutaneous. (DER mul)

dermatitis [*dermat, skin + -itis, inflammation*] Inflammation of the skin. (der' muh TEYE tis)

dermatogen [*dermato, skin + gen, to produce*] The outer layer of cells in embryonic plants and growing plant parts that gives rise to the epidermis. (der MAT uh jen)

dermatology [*dermat, skin + -ology, study of*] The branch of medical science dealing with the study of the functions and diseases of the skin. (der' muh TOL uh jee)

dermatome [*derma, skin + -tome, to cut*] 1.A surgical instrument for cutting thin slices of skin, as for grafting. 2.An area of the skin innervated by nerves from a single spinal nerve root. 3.The lateral portion of an embryonic somite from which the skin is derived. (DER muh tohm')

dermatophyte [*dermato, skin + -phyte, plant*] Any parasitic fungus of the skin, hair, or nails, such as athlete's foot or ringworm. (der MAT uh feyet')

dermatoplasty [*dermato, skin + -plasty, to form*] Skin grafting in plastic surgery operations. (der MAT uh plas' tee)

dermatosis [*dermat, skin + -osis, abnormal condition*] Any disease or disorder of the skin. (der' muh TOH sis)

dermis [*derm, skin + -is*] The layer of skin immediately below the epidermis, consisting of nerves, glands, blood and lymph vessels, and hair follicles. See epidermis (def. 1). (DER mis)

dermoid [*derm, skin + -oid, resembling*] 1.A benign tumor consisting of tissues derived from the ectoderm, such as skin, hair, or teeth. 2.Resembling skin. (DER moid)

echinoderm [*echino, spiny + derm, skin*] Any of numerous marine animals, including sea urchins and starfishes, that are often covered with spines and typically have five similar body parts extending symmetrically. (ih KEYE nuh derm')

ectoderm [*ecto-, outside + derm, skin*] The outer layer of the three primary germ cell layers of an embryo from which the nervous system, the epidermis and epidermal tissues, sense organs, and certain other body parts develop. See ectoblast, endoderm, and mesoderm. (EK tuh derm')

endermic [*en-, into + derm, skin + -ic*] Pertaining to a medicine, chemical, etc., that is absorbed through the skin. (en DER mik)

endoderm [*endo-, inside + derm, skin*] The inner layer of the three primary germ cell layers of an embryo from which the gastrointestinal tract, most of the respiratory system, and many other organs develop. See endoblast, mesoderm, and ectoderm. (EN duh derm')

endodermis [*endo-, inside + derm, skin + -is*] The innermost layer of cells in the cortex of the roots and stems of vascular plants. (en' doh DER mis)

epidermis [*epi-, outside + derm, skin + -is*] 1.The protective outer layer of skin that covers the dermis. See dermis. 2.The protective outer layer or layers of cells in plants. (ep' ih DER mis)

hypodermic [*hypo-, under + derm, skin + -ic*] 1.Injected under the skin. 2.Relating to parts under the skin. Subcutaneous. (heye' puh DER mik)

hypodermis [*hypo-, under + derm, skin + -is*] 1.The cell layer of a plant that lies immediately below the epidermis. 2.The cell layer in arthropods and certain other organisms that secretes and underlies the cuticle. (heye' puh DER mis)

intradermal [*intra-, within + derm, skin + -al*] Occurring or located within or between the layers of skin. (in' truh DER mul)

leukoderma [*leuko, white + derma, skin*] Partial or total absence of skin pigmentation. See achromic (def. 2). (loo' kuh DER muh)

mesoderm [*meso-, middle + derm, skin*] The middle layer of the three primary germ cell layers of an embryo, lying between the ectoderm and the endoderm, from which bones, connective tissue, muscles, and the vascular and urogenital systems develop. See mesoblast, endoderm, and ectoderm. (MEZ uh derm')

ostracoderm [*Grk > ostrakon, shell + derm, skin*] Any of an order of extinct jawless fish covered with an armor consisting of bony plates and scales. (os TRAK uh derm')

pachyderm [*pachy, thick + derm, skin*] Any of several large, thick-skinned, hoofed mammals, as the hippopotamus, elephant, or rhinoceros. (PAK ih derm')

periderm [*peri-, around + derm, skin*] The outer layers of tissue in roots and stems that consist of the cork cambium and other tissues arising from it. (PEHR ih derm')

pyoderma [*pyo, pus + derma, skin*] Any disease or infection of the skin that produces pus. (peye' uh DER muh)

scleroderma [*sclero, hard + derma, skin*] A disease marked by chronic thickening and hardening of the skin, caused by abnormal growth or swelling of fibrous tissues. (sklehr' uh DER muh)

sclerodermatous [*sclero, hard + dermat, skin + -ous*] Having a hard outer covering consisting of horny or bony tissue. (sklehr' uh DER muh tus)

taxidermy [*taxi, arrangement + derm, skin + -y*] The art of preparing and mounting the skins of animals to give them a lifelike appearance. (TAKS ih der' mee)

xeroderma [*xero, dry + derma, skin*] Abnormal dryness and roughness of the skin. (zihr' uh DER muh)

dia-   through, apart, across

adiabatic [*a-, not + dia, through + Grk > bainein, to go + -ic*] Occurring without gaining or losing heat. (ad' ee uh BAT ik)

bidialectal [*bi-, two & dialect & -al*] Having the ability to use two dialects of the same language. (beye' deye uh LEK tul)

diabetes [*dia-, through + Grk > bainein, to go + -es*] Any of several diseases characterized by an excessive discharge of urine and persistent thirst, especially diabetes mellitus. (deye' uh BEET eez)

diabetes insipidus [*diabetes & insipid & -us*] A rare form of diabetes caused by a disorder of the pituitary gland and characterized by intense thirst and excessive discharge of urine. (deye' uh BEET eez in SIP ih dus)

diabetes mellitus [*diabetes & meli, honey + -us*] A common form of diabetes characterized by deficiency of insulin, a high concentration of sugar in the blood and urine, thirst, hunger, and weight loss. (deye' uh BEET eez MEL ih tus)

diachronic [*dia-, through + chron, time + -ic*] Pertaining to the study of the historical changes in a language. See synchronic. (deye' uh KRON ik)

diacritic [*dia-, apart + Grk > krinein, to separate + -ic*] A mark used with a letter to indicate a special phonic value, stress, etc. (deye' uh KRIT ik)

diacritical [*dia-, apart + Grk > krinein, to separate + -ical*] Indicating a distinction. Distinguishing. (deye' uh KRIT ih kul)

diacritical mark [*dia-, apart + Grk > krinein, to separate + -ical & mark*] A mark used with a letter to indicate a special phonic value, stress, etc. Same as diacritic. (deye' uh KRIT ih kul mahrk)

diadromous [*dia-, through + -dromous, moving*] Migrating between salt and fresh waters, as some fishes. See catadromous and anadromous. (deye AD ruh mus)

diagenesis [*dia-, through + -genesis, formation*] The chemical and physical changes that occur during the conversion of sediment to sedimentary rock. (deye' uh JEN uh sis)

diageotropism [*dia-, through + geo, earth + trop, turning + -ism*] The tendency of certain plants or plant parts to grow or orient themselves at right angles to the direction of the earth's gravitational force. See diatropism. (deye' uh jee OT ruh piz' um)

diagnosis [*dia-, through + gnos, knowledge + -is*] 1.The process of learning the nature of a disease or condition by examining all of the symptoms. 2.The critical analysis of a situation, occurrence, or problem. 3.A brief description of the characteristics of an organism, species, etc. (deye' ig NOH sis)

diagnostics [*diagnos(is) & -ics, science*] The science or practice of diagnosis. (deye' ig NOS tiks)

diagonal [*dia-, through + gon, angle + -al*] A straight line going through the vertices of any two nonadjacent angles of a polygon or through any two vertices not in the same face of a polyhedron. (deye AG uh nul)

diagram [*dia-, through + gram, to write*] A graphic design used to illustrate how something works or to show the relationship and arrangement of parts. (DEYE uh gram')

diagraph [*dia-, across + graph, drawing*] An instrument for making scaled drawings. (DEYE uh graf')

diakinesis [*dia-, through + kine, motion + -sis*] The last stage of the prophase in meiosis, characterized by the homologous chromosomes repelling each other and the disappearance of the nucleolus. (deye' uh kih NEE sis)

dialect [*dia-, apart + lect, choose*] The characteristics of a language in a certain region distinguished by combinations of pronunciation, grammar, and vocabulary. (DEYE uh lekt')

dialectology [*dialect & -ology, study of*] The branch of linguistics dealing with the study of dialects. (deye' uh lek' TOL uh jee)

dialog [*dia-, through + log, discourse*] 1.A conversation between two or more people. 2.The passage of conversation in a play, story, etc. Same as dialogue. (DEYE uh log')

dialogue [*dia-, through + log, discourse*] 1.A conversation between two or more people. See duologue and trialogue. 2.The passage of conversation in a play, story, etc. (DEYE uh log')

dialysis [*dia-, apart + -lysis, decomposition*] The separation of particles in a solution by selective diffusion through a semipermeable membrane. (deye AL uh sis)

diameter [*dia-, through + meter, to measure*] A straight line that measures the distance through the center of a circle, sphere, etc. (deye AM et er)

diapason [*dia-, through + Grk > pason chordon, all the notes*] 1.The entire range of a voice or instrument. 2.A full, deep outburst of melodious sound. 3.Either of the two principal stops of an organ. (deye' uh PAY zun)

diapause [*dia-, through & pause*] A dormant period in the life cycle of certain insects during which metabolic activity is greatly reduced and growth and development cease. (DEYE uh poz')

diapedesis [*dia-, through + Grk > pedan, to leap + -sis*] The passage of blood cells, especially white blood cells, through the intact blood vessel walls. (deye' uh pih DEE sis)

diaphanous [*dia-, through + phan, to appear + -ous*] Being so fine in texture as to be translucent or transparent. (deye AF uh nus)

diaphoresis [*dia-, through + phor, to produce + -esis*] Copious perspiration. (deye' uh fuh REE sis)

diaphragm [*dia-, apart + Grk > phrassein, to enclose*] 1.A muscular partition that separates the abdominal and chest cavities in mammals. 2.A thin vibrating disk in a telephone receiver, microphone, etc. 3.A device for varying the aperture of a camera lens. (DEYE uh fram')

diarrhea [*dia-, through + rrhea, excessive flow*] Abnormally excessive and frequent fluid bowl movements, often a symptom of a gastrointestinal disorder. (deye' uh REE uh)

diarrhoea [*dia-, through + rrhoea, excessive flow*] Abnormally excessive and frequent fluid bowl movements, often a symptom of a gastrointestinal disorder. Same as diarrhea. (deye' uh REE uh)

diarthrosis [*dia-, through + arthr, joint + -osis, action*] Any articulation permitting free motion of a joint in any direction. See amphiarthrosis and synarthrosis. (deye' ahr THROH sis)

diaspora [*dia-, through + spor, to sow + -a*] The dispersion of a homogeneous group of people. (deye AS pur uh)

Diaspora [*dia-, through + spor, to sow + -a*] The dispersion of colonies of Jews after the Babylonian exile in the sixth century B.C. (deye AS pur uh)

diastole [*dia-, apart + Grk > stellein, to place*] Rhythmic relaxation of the heart after each systole, causing the cavities to fill with blood. See systole. (deye AS tuh lee)

diastrophism [*dia-, through + Grk > strophe, turning + -ism*] The process of deformation of the earth's surface, creating continents, mountains, and other surface features. (deye AS truh fiz' um)

diathermy [*dia-, through + therm, heat + -y*] The use of high-frequency sound, high-frequency current, or microwaves to produce heat in body tissue for medical treatment and therapy. (DEYE uh thur' mee)

diathesis [*dia-, apart + the, to put + -sis*] A hereditary predisposition to certain disorders or diseases. (deye ATH uh sis)

diatom [*dia-, through + tom, to cut*] Unicellular, aquatic algae with a two-part, overlapping, symmetrical cell wall containing silica. (DEYE uh tom')

diatribe [*dia-, through + Grk > tribe, rub*] A bitter and abusive criticism or condemnation. (DEYE uh treyeb')

diatropism [*dia-, through + trop, turning + -ism*] The tendency of certain plants or plant parts to grow or orient themselves at right angles to the force of a stimulus. See diageotropism. (deye AT ruh piz' um)

dieresis [*dia-, apart + Grk > hairein, to take + -sis*] 1.The separation of two adjacent vowels, especially of a diphthong, to form two syllables. See syneresis (def. 1) and diphthong. 2.Two dots placed over the second of two adjacent vowels to indicate that they are to be pronounced separately. 3.A pause in a line of verse caused by the end of a metrical foot coinciding with the end of a word. (deye EHR uh sis)

diopter [*dia-, through + opt, sight + -er*] A unit of measure of the refractive power of a lens equal to the reciprocal of its focal length expressed in meters. (deye OP ter)

dioptometer [*dia-, through + opto, eye + meter, to measure*] An optical instrument for measuring and testing the refraction and accommodation of the eye. (deye' op TOM et er)

dioptrics [*dia-, through + opt, sight + -ics, study of*] The branch of optics dealing with the study of refracted light. See optics. (deye OP triks)

diorama [*dia-, through + orama, view*] 1.A scene painted on partially transparent cloth and viewed through a small aperture. 2.A scene with lifelike figures or objects placed against a painted background. (deye' uh RAM uh)

epidiascope [*epi-, on + dia, through + -scope, to view*] A projector for displaying a magnified image of a transparency or an opaque object on a screen. (ep' ih DEYE uh skohp')

hemodialysis [*hemo, blood & dialysis*] Dialysis of the circulating blood for the purpose of removing impurities and waste. (hee' moh deye AL uh sis)

idiolect [*idio-, personal & (dia)lect*] The speech pattern of an individual, considered to be unique among users of the same dialect or language. (ID ee uh lekt')

isodiametric [*iso-, equal & diamet(e)r & -ic*] Having equal diameters or dimensions in all directions. (eye' soh deye' uh MET rik)

semidiameter [*semi-, half & diameter*] 1.Half of a diameter. Radius. 2.The perceived radius of a spherical celestial body observed from the earth. (sem' ee deye AM et er)

serodiagnosis [*sero, serum & diagnosis*] Diagnosis by means of testing blood serum reactions. (sihr' oh deye' ig NOH sis)

trans-   across, through, change, beyond

intransigent [*in-, not + trans, through + ag, to drive + -ent*] Refusing to compromise. Uncompromising. Unyielding. (in TRAN sih jent)

intransitive [*in-, not + trans, across + it, go + -ive*] Pertaining to a verb that indicates a complete action without requiring a direct object to complete its meaning. See transitive. (in TRAN sih tiv)

neurotransmitter [*neuro, nerve & transmitter*] A chemical substance that transmits impulses between two nerve cells. (noor' oh TRANS mit ur)

semitransparent [*semi-, partly & transparent*] Not entirely transparent. See transparent (def. 1) and translucent. (sem' ee trans PEHR ent)

traduce [*trans-, change + duc, to lead*] To harm the reputation of through false and malicious statements. (truh DOOS)

traject [*trans-, across + ject, to throw*] To transmit. (truh JEKT)

trajectory [*trans-, across + ject, to throw + -ory*] The path of a moving projectile, rocket, particle, etc. (truh JEKT uh ree)

transact [*trans-, through + act, to drive*] To conduct or negotiate, especially business affairs. (trans AKT)

transceiver [*trans(mitter) & (re)ceiver*] A radio consisting of a transmitter and receiver. (tran SEE vur)

transcend [*trans-, beyond + Ltn > scandere, to climb*] To go beyond or rise above the limits of. Exceed. Surpass. (tran SEND)

transcribe [*trans-, change + scrib, to write*] 1.To write or type a copy of spoken material, as dictation, lectures, court proceedings, etc. 2.To arrange a musical composition for another voice or instrument. 3.To represent speech sounds using phonetic symbols. (tran SKREYEB)

transcript [*trans-, change + script, to write*] 1.A written, typewritten, or printed copy of spoken material. 2.An official copy, as of court proceedings, a student's academic record, etc. (TRAN skript)

transducer [*trans-, change + duc, to lead + -er*] A device that converts energy from one form to another, as a cell that converts sunlight to electricity. (trans DOOS ur)

transduction [*trans-, change + duct, to lead + -ion*] The process of altering a bacterial cell's genetic makeup by the transfer of DNA from another bacterial cell by a bacterial virus. (trans DUK shun)

transect [*trans-, across + sect, to cut*] To divide by cutting across. (tran SEKT)

transept [*trans-, across & (s)ept(um) {partition}*] The shorter arms of a cross-shaped church that lie perpendicular to the main section. (TRAN sept)

transfer [*trans-, across + fer, to carry*] To move from one place or person to another. (trans FER)

transfigure [*trans-, change & figure*] 1.To profoundly change the form or appearance of. 2.To change the appearance of so as to glorify, exalt, or idealize. See transform. (trans FIG yur)

transfix [*trans-, through + Ltn > figere, pierce*] 1.To pierce through with, or as if with, a pointed object. 2.To hold motionless, as with terror, wonderment, astonishment, etc. Impale. (trans FIKS)

transform [*trans-, change & form*] 1.To profoundly change the form or appearance of. 2.To change the function, condition, or character of. Convert. See transfigure. (trans FORM)

trans-

transfuse [*trans-, across + fus, pour*] 1.To cause to flow from one source to another. 2.To transfer blood, blood plasma, etc., into the vessels of a person or animal. (trans FYOOZ)

transgress [*trans-, beyond + gress, to go*] 1.To go beyond, as a boundary, limit, etc. 2.To violate, as the law, a command, etc. (trans GRES)

transient [*trans-, through + Ltn > ire, to go + -ent*] Staying or lasting for only a short time. (TRAN shent)

transit [*trans-, through + it, go*] The process of moving across, over, or through. (TRAN sit)

transition [*trans-, across + it, go + -ion*] Moving or changing from one state, position, or subject to another. (tran ZISH un)

transitive [*trans-, across + it, go + -ive*] Pertaining to a verb that requires a direct object to complete its meaning. See intransitive. (TRAN sih tiv)

translate [*trans-, change + fer, to carry*] 1.To change from one language or set of symbols to another. 2.To change from one form or state to another. See transmute. 3.To express in simpler terms. (trans LAYT)

transliterate [*trans-, change + liter, letter + -ate*] To write letters or words in the corresponding characters of another alphabet. (trans LIT ur ayt')

translucent [*trans-, through + luc, light + -ent*] Allowing light to pass through, but sufficiently diffusing it so that objects on the other side cannot be clearly distinguished. See semitransparent and transparent (def. 1). (trans LOO sent)

transmarine [*trans-, across + mar, sea + -ine*] 1.Crossing over the sea. 2.Coming from or going across the sea. (trans' muh REEN)

transmit [*trans-, across + mit, to send*] To send or pass from one place to another. (trans MIT)

transmute [*trans-, across + mut, change*] To change from one form, substance, species, etc., to another. See translate (def. 2). (trans MYOOT)

transnational [*trans-, beyond & national*] Extending beyond the boundaries or interests of a nation. (trans NASH uh nul)

transonic [*trans-, across + son, sound + -ic*] Pertaining to, involving, or occurring at speeds near the speed of sound. (tran SON ik)

transparent [*trans-, through + Ltn > parere, to appear + -ent*] 1.Allowing light to pass through without diffusing it so that objects on the other side can be clearly distinguished. See semitransparent and translucent. 2.Easily understood or detected. Obvious. See perspicuous and transpicuous. (trans PEHR ent)

transpicuous [*trans-, through + spic, to see + -ous*] Easily understood. Transparent. See perspicuous and transparent (def. 2). (tran SPIK yoo us)

transpire [*trans-, through + spir, breathe*] 1.To take place or occur. Happen. 2.To become known. 3.To give off vapor containing waste products through a membrane or pores, as from the human body or from leaves. See transude. (tran SPEYER)

transplant [*trans-, across & plant*] 1.To uproot a plant and replant it in another location. 2.To surgically move an organ from one part of the body to another or from one individual to another. 3.To move from one place to another. (trans PLANT)

transport [*trans-, across + port, to carry*] To carry, move, or convey from one place to another, especially over long distances. (trans PORT)

transpose [*trans-, change + pos, to put*] To change the position or order of. (trans POHZ)

transsexual [*trans-, change & sex & -ual*] A person with a strong desire to identify with the opposite sex and who sometimes elects to undergo sex change surgery. See transvestite. (trans SEK shoo ul)

transude [*trans-, through + Ltn > sudare, to sweat*] To pass or exude through a permeable substance or pores, as a fluid. See transpire (def. 3). (tran SOOD)

transuranic [*trans-, beyond & uran(ium) + -ic*] Pertaining to an element with an atomic number greater than that of uranium. (trans' yoo RAN ik)

transverse [*trans-, across + vers, turn*] Lying or situated across. Set crosswise. (trans VURS)

transvestite [*trans-, change + Ltn > vestire, to clothe + -ite*] A person who dresses and behaves in the manner of the opposite sex. See transsexual. (trans VES teyet')

traverse [*trans-, across + vers, turn*] To travel over, along, or through. (truh VURS)

dic, dict
speech, to speak,
to proclaim {declare officially}, word

abdicate [*ab-, away + dic, to proclaim + -ate*] To formally declare the relinquishment of power, authority, or duty. Resign. Renounce. (AB dih kayt')

benediction [*bene-, good + dict, to speak + -ion*] 1.A blessing. 2.An invocation of a blessing, especially at the end of a church service. See malediction. (ben' uh DIK shun)

contradict [*contra-, opposite + dict, to speak*] 1.To express the opposite of. 2.To be contrary to. (kon' truh DIKT)

contraindicate [*contra-, against & indicate*] To advise against, as a particular treatment or procedure. (kon' truh IN dih kayt')

dedicate [*de-, away + dic, to speak + -ate*] 1.To set apart for a special use. Devote. 2.To address as a compliment to a person, cause, etc., as a mark of respect or affection. (DED ih kayt')

Dictaphone [*dict, to speak + -phone, sound*] Trademark for a device for recording dictation so it may be transcribed later. (DIK tuh fohn')

dictate [*dict, to speak + -ate*] 1.To speak or read aloud for another person to record or write down. 2.To prescribe or command with authority. (DIK tayt)

diction [*dict, to speak + -ion*] 1.Manner of expression in speech or writing. 2.Clarity and correctness in speaking or singing. Enunciation. Articulation. See phraseology, locution, and verbiage. (DIK shun)

dictionary [*dict, word + -ion + -ary*] A book composed of alphabetically listed words with information given for each word, including meaning, pronunciation, and etymology. (DIK shuh nehr' ee)

Dictograph [*dict, speech + graph, recording*] Trademark for a device for reproducing or recording telephone conversations. (DIK tuh graf')

dictum [*dict, to speak + -um*] 1.An authoritative formal statement. Pronouncement. 2.A popular saying. Maxim. (DIK tum)

edict [*e-, out + dict, to speak*] An official public order or decree. (EE dikt)

indicate [*in-, to + dic, proclaim + -ate*] 1.To point out or direct attention to. 2.To serve as a hint or sign of something. (IN dih kayt')

indict [*in-, to + dict, proclaim*] To charge with a crime or other offense, as by the findings of a grand jury. Accuse. (in DEYET)

interdict [*inter-, between + dict, to speak*] 1.To prohibit or forbid, usually in an official manner. (in' ter DIKT {verb}) 2.A disciplinary action in the Roman Catholic Church prohibiting certain privileges and functions. (IN ter dikt' {noun})

jurisdiction [*Ltn > juris, law + dict, to proclaim + -ion*] 1.The authority and power to administer justice. 2.The boundaries or limits within which authority may be applied. (joor' is DIK shun)

malediction [*male-, evil + dict, to speak + -ion*] An invocation of evil or harm on someone. Curse. See benediction. (mal' uh DIK shun)

obiter dictum [*Ltn > obiter, by the way & dict, to speak + -um*] 1.An incidental remark or observation. 2.An incidental opinion from a judge that is not essential to a case and is not binding. (OHB ih ter DIK tum)

predicate [*Ltn > praedicare, to proclaim*] 1.To proclaim or affirm as true. (PRED ih kayt' {verb}) 2.In grammar, the part of a sentence that expresses what is said about the subject. (PRED ih kut {noun})

predict [*pre-, before + dict, to speak*] To say or make known in advance. (prih DIKT)

syndicate [*syn-, same + dic, to speak + -ate*] 1.To sell for publication in many newspapers, periodicals, radio stations, or television stations at once. (SIN dih kayt' {verb}) 2.An association of individuals or companies formed to carry out some undertaking usually requiring a large amount of capital. (SIN dih kut {noun})

valediction [*Ltn > vale, farewell + dict, to speak + -ion*] A bidding or saying farewell. (val' uh DIK shun)

valedictorian [*Ltn > vale, farewell + dict, speech + -orian*] A graduating student, usually of the highest rank in the class, who delivers the farewell speech at commencement. (val' uh dik TOR ee un)

verdict [*ver, true + dict, to speak*] 1.The formal decision of a judge or jury. 2.An expressed conclusion. (VUR dikt)

veridical [*ver, true + dic, to speak + -al*] 1.Speaking the truth. Veracious. Truthful. 2.Genuine. (vuh RID ih kul)

vindicate [*Ltn > vindicare, to avenge + -ate*] 1.To provide supporting argument or evidence to clear from guilt, suspicion, blame, etc. Exonerate. 2.Justify. (VIN dih kayt')

vindictive [*Ltn > vindicare, to avenge + -ive*] 1.Feeling or showing a strong inclination toward revenge. 2.Intended to cause pain or suffering. (vin DIK tiv)

loqu, locu   to speak

allocution [*al-, to + locu, to speak + -tion*] A formal authoritative or hortatory speech. (al' uh KYOO shun)

circumlocution [*circum-, around + locu, to speak + -tion*] 1.A roundabout, evasive, or long-winded way of speaking. 2.A roundabout expression. See periphrasis. (sur' kum loh KYOO shun)

colloquial [*col-, together + loqu, to speak + -ial*] Pertaining to language suitable for informal conversation, but not appropriate for use in formal speech or writing. (kuh LOH kwee ul)

colloquium [*col-, together + loqu, to speak + -ium*] 1.A group discussion or informal meeting. 2.An academic seminar or conference led by several lecturers. (kuh LOH kwee um)

colloquy [*col-, together + loqu, to speak + -y*] A conversation or conference, especially one that is formal. (KOL uh kwee)

elocution [*e-, out + locu, to speak + -tion*] 1.Style or manner of public speaking. 2.The art of public speaking or reading. (el' uh KYOO shun)

eloquence [*e-, out + loqu, to speak + -ence*] The art of using forceful, persuasive, and fluent speech. (EL uh kwens)

eloquent [*e-, out + loqu, to speak + -ent*] 1.Exercising forceful, persuasive, and fluent speech. 2.Vividly expressive or revealing. (EL uh kwent)

grandiloquence [*grandi(ose) {great} & loqu, to speak + -ence*] Speech that uses lofty, pompous, or grandiose words or expressions. See magniloquent. (gran DIL uh kwens)

ineloquent [*in-, not + e-, out + loqu, to speak + -ent*] Not exercising forceful, persuasive, or fluent speech. (in EL uh kwent)

interlocution [*inter-, between + locu, to speak + -tion*] Dialogue or conversation between two or more people. (in' ter loh KYOO shun)

interlocutor [*inter-, between + locu, to speak + -tor*] One who takes part in a conversation or dialogue. (in' ter LOK yuh tur)

locution [*locu, to speak + -tion*] 1.A particular word, phrase, or form of expression. 2.A particular style of speaking. See diction, phraseology, verbiage. (loh KYOO shun)

loquacious [*loqu, to speak + -acious*] Tending to be very talkative. Garrulous. Opposed to taciturn. See voluble (def. 2). (loh KWAY shus)

magniloquent [*magni, great + loqu, to speak + -ent*] Grandiose, lofty, or pompous speech. See grandiloquence. (mag NIL uh kwent)

obloquy [*ob-, against + loqu, to speak + -y*] 1.The state of being verbally abused or spoken ill of. 2.Damage to one's reputation. (OB luh kwee)

prolocutor [*pro-, before + locu, to speak + -tor*] 1.A presiding officer or chairman of an assembly. 2.Spokesperson. (proh LOK yuh tur)

soliloquy [*soli, alone + loqu, to speak + -y*] 1.The act of talking to oneself. 2.The part of a drama in which a character talks to himself and reveals his thoughts to the audience without addressing a listener. (suh LIL uh kwee)

ventriloquism [*ventri, abdomen + loqu, to speak + -ism*] Literally, "to speak from the belly." The art of speaking so that the voice does not seem to come from the speaker, but from another source. (ven TRIL uh kwiz' um)

lex   word, law, reading

alexia [*a-, not* + *lex, reading* + *-ia*] A neurological disorder caused by brain lesions that results in loss of the ability to read. See agraphia, dysgraphia, and dyslexia. (uh LEK see uh)

dyslexia [*dys-, impaired* + *lex, reading* + *-ia*] Impairment of the ability to read, characterized by the inability to distinguish separate parts of a word and often the result of a brain injury or defect. See dysgraphia, agraphia, and alexia. (dis LEK see uh)

illegal [*il-, not* + *lex, law* + *-al*] 1.Not legal. Prohibited by law. 2.Unauthorized according to official rules or regulations. See illicit. (ih LEE gul)

illegitimate [*il-, not* + *lex, law* + *-ate*] 1.Born out of wedlock. 2.Not lawful or acceptable. 3.Improper, incorrect, or contrary to good usage. (il' ih JIT uh mut)

lex [*lex, law*] Law. (leks)

lex non scripta [*lex, law* & *Ltn > non scripta, unwritten*] Unwritten, or common law. See lex scripta. (leks non SKRIP tuh)

lex scripta [*lex, law* & *Ltn > scripta, written*] Written, or statute law. See lex non scripta. (leks SKRIP tuh)

lex talionis [*lex, law* & *Ltn > talionis, talion {retaliation}*] The law of retaliation, which requires that the punishment match the crime, as an eye for an eye. (leks tay' lee OH nis)

lexeme [*lex, word* + *-eme, structural unit*] The smallest meaningful linguistic unit that is a vocabulary item of a language. (LEKS eem)

lexical [*lex, word* + *-ical*] Pertaining to the vocabulary of a language. (LEKS ih kul)

lexicography [*lex, word* + *-ic* + *-graphy, writing*] The branch of linguistics dealing with the writing or compiling of dictionaries. See lexicology. (leks' ih KOG ruh fee)

lexicology [*lex, word* + *-ic* + *-ology, study of*] The branch of linguistics dealing with the study of the history and meanings of words. See lexicography. (leks' ih KOL uh jee)

lexicon [*lex, word* + *-ic* + *-on*] 1.A dictionary, especially of Latin, Greek, or Hebrew. 2.The vocabulary of a language or of a particular subject, author, profession, etc. See terminology. (LEKS ih kon')

lexicostatistics [*lex, word* + *-ic* & *statistics*] The statistical study of the vocabulary of languages to determine when the languages under study separated. See glottochronology. (leks' ih koh' stuh TIS tiks)

lexis [*lex, word* + *-is*] The vocabulary of a language. (LEKS is)

lexophobia [*lexo, reading* + *-phobia, fear*] Hatred or fear of reading. (leks' uh FOH bee uh)

log/o   word, discourse, doctrine

amphibology [*amphi-, both* + *log, discourse* + *-y*] Ambiguity of speech, especially from uncertain grammatical construction. (am' fih BOL uh jee)

analogy [*ana-, again* + *log, word* + *-y*] 1.Similarity in certain aspects or features between things otherwise dissimilar. 2.Similarity. 3.Similarity in function between anatomical organs or parts of different origin and structure. (uh NAL uh jee)

apologetics [*apo-, from* + *log, discourse* + *-ics, study of*] The branch of theology dealing with the defense or proof of Christianity. (uh pol' uh JET iks)

apologia [*apo-, from* + *log, word* + *-ia*] A formal defense, especially of one's opinions, actions, or position. (ap' uh LOH jee uh)

apologue [*apo-, from* + *log, discourse*] A short allegorical story usually intended to express a moral. See parable. (AP uh log')

apology [*apo-, from* + *log, word* + *-y*] 1.A statement expressing regret or asking pardon for an error or discourtesy. 2.A formal written or spoken justification or defense. (uh POL uh jee)

brachylogy [*brachy, short* + *log, discourse* + *-y*] 1.Brevity and over-conciseness of speech. 2.A condensed phrase or expression. (bra KIL uh jee)

catalog [*cata-, completely* + *log, word*] A systematic list of items such as names, titles, or articles, usually in alphabetical order. (KAT l og')

catalogue [*cata-, completely* + *log, word*] A systematic list of items such as names, titles, or articles, usually in alphabetical order. Same as catalog. (KAT l og')

collogue [*col-, together* + *log, discourse*] 1.To talk secretly. Confer. 2.Conspire. Intrigue. See conspire. (kuh LOG)

dactylology [*dactylo, finger* + *log, discourse* + *-y*] The art of communicating using a finger alphabet, as among the deaf. (dak' tuh LOL uh jee)

Decalog [*deca, ten* + *log, discourse*] The Ten Commandments. Same as Decalogue. (DEK uh log')

Decalogue [*deca, ten* + *log, discourse*] The Ten Commandments. (DEK uh log')

dialog [*dia-, through* + *log, discourse*] 1.A conversation between two or more people. 2.The passage of conversation in a play, story, etc. Same as dialogue. (DEYE uh log')

dialogue [*dia-, through* + *log, discourse*] 1.A conversation between two or more people. See duologue and trialogue. 2.The passage of conversation in a play, story, etc. (DEYE uh log')

doxology [*doxo, praise* + *log, discourse* + *-y*] A hymn or other expression of praise to God. (dok SOL uh jee)

duologue [*duo-, two* + *log, discourse*] A conversation between two people. See dialogue (def. 1) and trialogue. (DOO uh log')

dyslogistic [*dys-, bad* & *(eu)logistic*] Showing disapproval. See eulogy. (dis' luh JIS tik)

dysteleology [*dys-, bad* + *teleo, end* + *log, doctrine* + *-y*] A philosophical doctrine that considers existence to have no purpose or final cause. See teleology (def. 2). (dis tel' ee OL uh jee)

epilogue [*epi-, upon* + *log, discourse*] 1.A short poem or speech delivered by one of the actors directly to the audience following the conclusion of a play. 2.A concluding section at the end of a literary work. (EP ih log')

eulogy [*eu-, good* + *log, discourse* + *-y*] 1.A speech or writing in praise of a person or thing, especially a formal speech praising a recently deceased person. 2.High praise. See panegyric and dyslogistic. (YOO luh jee)

hagiology [*hagio, holy* + *log, word* + *-y*] 1.A collection of sacred writings. 2.The branch of literature dealing with writings about the lives of saints. See hagiography. (hag' ee OL uh jee)

haplology [*haplo-, single + log, word + -y*] The shortening of a word by omitting one of two identical or similar successive sounds or syllables. (hap LOL uh jee)

heterology [*hetero, different & (ana)logy*] A difference in structure or arrangement between apparently similar anatomical organs or parts, resulting from differences in origin. Opposed to homology. (het' uh ROL uh jee)

homologate [*homo, same + log, discourse + -ate*] 1.To confirm or approve. 2.To confirm or approve officially. (hoh MOL uh gayt')

homology [*homo, similar & (ana)logy*] A similarity in structure or arrangement, but not necessarily in function, of organs or parts found in organisms of common origin. Opposed to heterology. (hoh MOL uh jee)

horologe [*Grk > hora, hour + log, discourse*] Any device for indicating time, as a clock, sundial, hourglass, etc. A timepiece. (HOR uh lohj')

logaoedic [*log, word & ode & -ic*] Pertaining to verse that is composed of both dactyls and trochees or anapests and iambs. (log' uh EED ik)

logic [*log, discourse + -ic*] 1.The science dealing with the principles of correct and reliable reasoning. 2.Correct and reliable reasoning. (LOJ ik)

logion [*log, word + -on*] A saying attributed to Jesus, but not in the Gospels. See agrapha. (LOH gee on')

logo [*logo(type)*] A company name, symbol, or trademark. Short for logotype. See logotype (def. 2). (LOH goh)

logogram [*logo, word + gram, to write*] A letter, special character, or symbol representing a word, such as "$" for dollar. (LOG uh gram')

logography [*logo, word + -graphy, recording*] 1.Printing and designing with logotypes. 2.A method of longhand reporting in which several reporters take turns writing down a few words each. (loh GOG ruh fee)

logogriph [*logo, word + Grk > griphos, riddle*] A word puzzle, such as an anagram. See anagram (def. 2). (LOG uh grif')

logomachy [*logo, word + -machy, struggle*] 1.An argument about or concerning words. 2.A verbal controversy. (loh GOM uh kee)

logophile [*logo, word + -phile, love*] A lover of words. (LOG uh feyel')

logorrhea [*logo, discourse + rrhea, excessive flow*] Pathologically excessive, repetitious, and often incoherent speech. (log' uh REE uh)

Logos [*log, word + -os*] 1.The rational principle that governs the universe. 2.The divine Word of God incarnated in Jesus Christ. (LOH gohs)

logotype [*logo, word & type*] 1.A single piece of type containing more than one letter or a word. 2.A company name, symbol, or trademark. See logo. (LOG uh teyep')

Mariology [*Mar(y) & log, doctrine + -y*] The body of belief, doctrine, and opinion relating to the Virgin Mary. (mehr' ee OL uh jee)

martyrology [*martyr & log, discourse + -y*] 1.A list of martyrs, especially religious martyrs. 2.The history of martyrs. (mahrt' uh ROL uh jee)

misology [*miso, to hate + log, discourse + -y*] Hatred or distrust of argument, reasoning, or enlightenment. (mih SOL uh jee)

monologue [*mono-, one + log, discourse*] A long speech by one speaker. (MON uh log')

necrology [*necro, dead + log, discourse + -y*] A list of persons who have recently died. Obituary. (nuh KROL uh jee)

neologism [*neo, new + log, word + -ism*] 1.A new word, phrase, or expression. 2.An established word used in a new sense. (nee OL uh jiz' um)

nosology [*noso, disease + log, discourse + -y*] The branch of medicine dealing with the systematic classification of diseases. (noh SOL uh jee)

philology [*philo, love + log, discourse + -y*] 1.An early name for linguistics, especially historical and comparative linguistics. 2.Love of literature and learning. 3.The scientific study of written records to determine meaning, authenticity, etc. (fih LOL uh jee)

phraseology [*phrase & log, discourse + -y*] 1.Manner of using words and phrases in speech or writing. 2.Choice and arrangement of words and phrases. See diction, locution, and verbiage. (fray' zee OL uh jee)

prologue [*pro-, before + log, discourse*] 1.An introduction to a discourse, poem, play, etc. 2.An introductory event, proceeding, etc. (PROH log)

soteriology [*Grk > soteria, salvation + log, doctrine + -y*] The theological doctrine of salvation through Jesus Christ. (soh tihr' ee OL uh jee)

syllogism [*syl-, together + log, discourse + -ism*] A scheme of deductive reasoning with two premises and a conclusion. If both premises are true, then the conclusion is true, as "All people are important; you are a person; therefore, you are important." (SIL uh jiz' um)

tautology [*tauto, same + log, discourse + -y*] Needless repetition of an idea in different words. See pleonasm. (taw TOL uh jee)

terminology [*Ltn > terminus, term + log, discourse + -y*] The vocabulary of terms belonging to a particular science, art, or subject. See lexicon (def. 2). (tur' mih NOL uh jee)

tetralogy [*tetra-, four + log, discourse + -y*] A series of four related plays, novels, or other literary works. See trilogy. (teh TROL uh jee)

trialogue [*tri-, three & (di)alogue*] A conversation between three people or three groups of people. See duologue and dialogue (def. 1). (TREYE uh log')

trilogy [*tri-, three + log, discourse + -y*] A series of three related plays, novels, or other literary works. See tetralogy. (TRIL uh jee)

tropology [*tropo, figure of speech + log, discourse + -y*] 1.The figurative use of words in speech or writing. See trope. 2.The interpretation of the Scriptures in a figurative sense rather than a literal sense. (troh POL uh jee)

verb   word

ad verbum [*ad-, to & verb, word + -um*] Word for word. Verbatim. See verbatim. (ad VUR bum)

adverb [*ad-, toward + verb, word*] A word used to modify a verb, adjective, or another adverb by indicating time, place, manner, degree, etc. (AD vurb)

auxiliary verb [*auxiliary {helping} & verb*] A word, such as have, can, shall, may, or do, used with a main verb to help form a verbal unit expressing tense, mood, or voice. Helping verb. (og ZIL uh ree vurb)

verb

proverb [*pro-, before + verb, word*] A short, popular saying that expresses a well-known truth or useful thought, usually about character or conduct. Adage. Maxim. See aphorism, apothegm, and gnome. (PROV urb)

proverbial [*pro-, before + verb, word + -ial*] 1.Pertaining to, resembling, or having the nature of a proverb. 2.Well-known and commonly spoken of. Notorious. 3.Expressed in a proverb. (pruh VUR bee ul)

verb [*verb, word*] A part of speech that expresses action, state, or occurrence and usually functions as the main element of a predicate. (vurb)

verbal [*verb, word + -al*] 1.Expressed in words. Oral. 2.Consisting of words only, rather than meaning, substance, or action. 3.Derived from or relating to a verb. (VUR bul)

verbal noun [*verb, word + -al & noun*] A noun derived from a verb. Gerund. (VUR bul noun)

verbalism [*verb, word + -al + -ism*] 1.A verbal expression. 2.A word, phrase, or sentence with little or no meaning. (VUR buh liz' um)

verbalist [*verb, word + -al + -ist*] 1.A person skilled in the use of words. 2.A person who is more concerned with words than with reality or ideas. (VUR buh list)

verbalize [*verb, word + -al + -ize*] 1.To express in words. 2.To change into or use as a verb. 3.To be verbose. See verbose, diffuse (def. 2), and prolix. (VUR buh leyez')

verbatim [*verb, word + -atim*] Word for word. Literal. See ad verbum and literatim. (vur BAYT um)

verbatim et literatim [*verb, word + -atim & liter, letter + -atim*] Word for word and letter for letter. See verbatim and literatim. (vur BAYT um et lit' uh RAYT um)

verbiage [*verb, word + -age*] 1.An excess of words beyond what is necessary to show clear and concise meaning. 2.Manner or style of speaking or writing. See diction, phraseology, and locution. (VUR bee ij)

verbify [*verb, word + -ify, to make*] To change into or use as a verb. Same as verbalize (def. 2). (VUR buh feye')

verbose [*verb, word + -ose*] Using or containing more words than necessary. Wordy. See diffuse (def. 2), verbalize (def. 3), and prolix. (vur BOHS)

verbum sap [*Ltn > verbum sapienti sat est, a word to the wise is sufficient*] Expressing that nothing further needs to be said. (VUR bum sap')

verve [*verb, word*] 1.Vigor. Energy. 2.Spirit and enthusiasm, especially in literary or artistic work. (vurv)

liter   letter

alliteration [*al-, toward + liter, letter + -ation*] The repetition of the same initial sound in two or more words of a phrase, line of verse, etc., as in "wild, wonderful West Virginia." (uh lit' uh RAY shun)

belles-lettres [*French > beautiful letters*] Literature having aesthetic rather than didactic value, including drama, poetry, fiction, etc. (bel LET ruh)

illiterate [*il-, not & literate*] 1.Having little or no formal education, especially not able to read or write. See analphabetic and semiliterate. 2.Displaying a lack of culture, especially in literature and language. See literate. (ih LIT ur it)

literal [*liter, letter + -al*] 1.Following the usual meaning of a word or words. 2.Taking words in their exact or primary sense. Denotation. (LIT ur ul)

literary [*liter, letter + -ary*] 1.Pertaining to literature. 2.Occupied or engaged in the field of literature. 3.Well-informed about literature. (LIT uh rehr' ee)

literate [*liter, letter + -ate*] 1.Able to read and write. See analphabetic and semiliterate. 2.Displaying knowledge and culture. See illiterate. (LIT ur it)

literati [*liter, letter*] 1.Men of letters. Scholars. 2.Persons of literary or scholarly achievement. Literary intelligentsia. Intellectuals. (lit' uh ROT ee)

literatim [*liter, letter + -atim*] Letter for letter. Literally. See verbatim. (lit' uh RAYT um)

literature [*liter, letter + -ature*] 1.The entire body of writings in prose or verse of a specific period or country. 2.Creative writings recognized as having lasting and widespread interest. (LIT ur uh chur')

nonliterate [*non-, not & literate*] Without a written language. (non LIT ur it)

obliterate [*ob-, over + liter, letter + -ate*] To destroy leaving no traces. Erase. Efface. Wipe out. (uh BLIT uh rayt')

preliterate [*pre-, before & literate*] Pertaining to a culture or society without a written language. (pree LIT ur it)

semiliterate [*semi-, partly & literate*] 1.Having limited ability to read and write. 2.Able to read, but not able to write. See literate (def. 1), illiterate (def. 1), and analphabetic. (sem' ee LIT ur it)

transliterate [*trans-, change + liter, letter + -ate*] To write letters or words in the corresponding characters of another alphabet. (trans LIT ur ayt')

triliteral [*tri-, three + liter, letter + -al*] Consisting of three letters, especially of three consonants, as most roots of Semitic languages. (treye LIT ur ul)

verbatim et literatim [*verb, word + -atim & liter, letter + -atim*] Word for word and letter for letter. See verbatim and literatim. (vur BAYT um et lit' uh RAYT um)

duc, duct   to lead

abduct [*ab-, away + duct, to lead*] To lead away unlawfully by force or deceit. Kidnap. (ab DUKT)

abductor [*ab-, away + duct, to lead + -or*] A muscle that pulls a body part away from the median plane of the body. See adductor. (ab DUK tur)

adduce [*ad-, toward + duc, to lead*] To present as an example or as evidence or proof. (uh DOOS)

adductor [*ad-, toward + duct, to lead + -or*] A muscle that pulls a body part toward the median plane of the body. See abductor. (uh DUK tur)

aqueduct [*aqua, water + duct, to lead*] A large pipe or channel used to carry water from a remote supply. (AK wuh dukt')

conduce [*con-, together + duc, to lead*] To lead to or play a significant part in producing a particular result. (kun DOOS)

conducive [*con-, together + duc, to lead + -ive*] Contributing to or producing a usually favorable result. (kun DOO siv)

conduct [*con-, together + duct, to lead*] 1.The act of leading, controlling, or managing. (KON dukt {noun}) 2.To lead or carry out. (kun DUKT {verb})

deduce [*de-, away + duc, to lead*] To draw a conclusion through knowledge-based reasoning. (dih DOOS)

deduct [*de-, away + duct, to lead*] To take away one quantity from another. Subtract. (dih DUKT)

duce [*duc, to lead*] A leader or commander, especially the title of the leader of the Italian Fascist party, Benito Mussolini. (DOO chay)

duct [*duct, to lead*] 1.A narrow tube or channel for carrying body fluid, as from an exocrine gland. 2.A pipe or channel for carrying a fluid. (dukt)

ductile [*duct, to lead + -ile*] 1.Easily stretched, hammered thin, or drawn out. 2.Easily shaped or molded. 3.Easily led or persuaded. Gullible. Tractable. (DUK tul)

ductule [*duct & -ule, small*] A small duct for carrying body fluid. (DUK tool)

educate [*e-, out + duc, to lead + -ate*] To give training or knowledge to, especially as a formal and prolonged process. Teach. (EJ uh kayt')

educe [*e-, out + duc, to lead*] 1.To bring out or develop. Elicit. See evoke and elicit. 2.To deduce or infer, as from knowledge or experience. (ih DOOS)

induce [*in-, in + duc, to lead*] 1.To lead on, persuade, or otherwise influence to do something. 2.To cause. (in DOOS)

induct [*in-, in + duct, to lead*] 1.To formally place in an office, position, etc. 2.To recruit into the armed forces. (in DUKT)

introduce [*intro-, inward + duc, to lead*] To present for the first time. (in' truh DOOS)

oviduct [*ovi, egg & duct*] One of two ducts through which eggs pass from the ovary to the uterus. Also known in mammals as the fallopian tube. (OH vih dukt')

produce [*pro-, forward + duc, to lead*] To bring forward or into existence. Yield. Bear. (pruh DOOS)

reduce [*re-, back + duc, to lead*] To diminish in size, price, degree, etc. (rih DOOS)

seduce [*se-, away + duc, to lead*] 1.To lead astray from proper conduct, responsibility, loyalty, etc. 2.To entice someone to participate in sexual intercourse, especially for the first time. (sih DOOS)

traduce [*trans-, change + duc, to lead*] To harm the reputation of through false and malicious statements. (truh DOOS)

transducer [*trans-, change + duc, to lead + -er*] A device that converts energy from one form to another, as a cell that converts sunlight to electricity. (trans DOOS ur)

transduction [*trans-, change + duct, to lead + -ion*] The process of altering a bacterial cell's genetic makeup by the transfer of DNA from another bacterial cell by a bacterial virus. (trans DUK shun)

viaduct [*via, road + duct, to lead*] A highway or railroad bridge spanning a road, gorge, dip, etc. (VEYE uh dukt')

dyn, dyna, dynam/o   power, energy, strength

adynamic [*a-, without + dynam, strength + -ic*] Characterized by or causing weakness. See dynamic. (ay' deye NAM ik)

aeroballistics [*aero(dynamics) & ballistics*] The combined science of aerodynamics and ballistics that deals with the flight of missiles, bombs, and other projectiles in the atmosphere. See aerodynamics and ballistics. (ehr' oh buh LIS tiks)

aerodynamics [*aero, air + dynam, power + -ics, study of*] The branch of dynamics dealing with the study of the forces exerted by the motion of air and other gases. See aeromechanics and aerostatics. (ehr' oh deye NAM iks)

aerodyne [*aero, air + dyn, power*] An aircraft that is heavier than air and gets its lift from aerodynamic motion, as a conventional airplane, helicopter, glider, etc. See aerodynamics and aerostat. (EHR uh deyen')

aerothermodynamics [*aero, air + thermo, heat + dynam, energy + -ics, study of*] The branch of dynamics dealing with the study of the relationship between heat and mechanical energy in air and other gases. See thermodynamics. (ehr' oh thur' moh deye NAM iks)

astrodynamics [*astro, star + dynam, power + -ics, science*] The science dealing with the dynamics of space vehicles and celestial bodies. (as' troh deye NAM iks)

chromodynamics [*chromo, color + dynam, energy + -ics, knowledge*] The theory dealing with the strong interactive forces that bind quarks together. These forces are characterized by three seemingly distinct, nonelectrical charges known as colors that are completely unrelated to real, visible colors. (kroh' moh deye NAM iks)

dynameter [*dyna, power + meter, to measure*] An instrument for measuring the power of a telescope. (deye NAM et er)

dynamic [*dynam, energy + -ic*] 1.Having physical energy and power. Vigorous. Active. 2.Having the ability to change or progress. See static and adynamic. (deye NAM ik)

dynamics [*dynam, power + -ics, study of*] The branch of mechanics dealing with the study of force, mass, and motion. See statics, kinetics, and kinematics. (deye NAM iks)

dynamism [*dynam, energy + -ism*] 1.The theory that all phenomena of nature can be explained in terms of force or energy. 2.Vigor. Forcefulness. (DEYE nuh miz' um)

dynamite [*dynam, power + -ite*] A powerful explosive consisting of a porous material soaked with nitroglycerin. (DEYE nuh meyet')

dynamo [*dynam, energy*] 1.An electric generator, especially one that produces direct current. 2.An energetic and forceful person. (DEYE nuh moh')

dynamoelectric [*dynamo, energy & electric*] Pertaining to the production of electrical energy from mechanical energy or vice versa. (deye' nuh moh' ih LEK trik)

dynamometer [*dynamo, power + meter, to measure*] An instrument for measuring mechanical power or force. (deye' nuh MOM et er)

dynamotor [*dyna, power & motor*] A combined electric motor and generator for converting direct current to alternating current and vice versa. (DEYE nuh moht' ur)

dyne [*dyn, power*] The standard unit of force equal to the amount of force required to accelerate a mass of one gram by one centimeter per second per second. (deyen)

electrodynamics [*electro, electric + dynam, power + -ics, study of*] The branch of physics dealing with the study of the relationships between electric currents and associated magnetic forces. (ih lek' troh deye NAM iks)

electrodynamometer [*electro, electricity* + *dynamo, power* + *meter, to measure*] An instrument for measuring current by using the interaction between the magnetic fields of fixed and movable sets of coils to move an indicator. (ih lek' troh deye' nuh MOM et er)

geodynamics [*geo, earth* + *dynam, power* + *-ics, study of*] The branch of geology dealing with the study of forces within the earth. (jee' oh deye NAM iks)

hemodynamics [*hemo, blood* + *dynam, power* + *-ics, study of*] A branch of physiology dealing with the study of blood circulation. (hee' moh deye NAM iks)

heterodyne [*hetero, different* + *dyn, power*] Pertaining to the combination of two different radio frequencies to generate an intermediate frequency, which is the difference of the original frequencies. (HET ur uh deyen')

hydrodynamics [*hydro, liquid* + *dynam, power* + *-ics, science*] The branch of hydromechanics dealing with the study of fluids in motion and of solid bodies immersed in them. See hydromechanics and hydrostatics. (heye' droh deye NAM iks)

isodynamic [*iso-, equal* + *dynam, power* + *-ic*] 1.Having equal force, strength, or intensity. 2.Pertaining to an imaginary line connecting points on the earth's surface with equal magnetic intensity. (eye' soh deye NAM ik)

magnetohydrodynamics [*magneto, magnetic force & hydrodynamics*] The science dealing with the motion of water and other electrically conductive fluids in magnetic fields. See hydrodynamics. (mag NEET oh heye' droh deye NAM iks)

pharmacodynamics [*pharmaco, drug* + *dynam, strength* + *-ics, study of*] The branch of pharmacology dealing with the study of the effects and actions of drugs on living organisms. (fahr' muh koh' deye NAM iks)

photodynamic [*photo, light* + *dynam, energy* + *-ic*] Pertaining to, operated by, or reacting to the energy of light. (foht' oh deye NAM ik)

photodynamics [*photo, light* + *dynam, power* + *-ics, study of*] The study of the effects of light on plants and animals. (foht' oh deye NAM iks)

psychodynamics [*psycho, mental process* + *dynam, power* + *-ics, study of*] The study of mental or emotional processes or forces and their relation to human behavior and metal states. (seye' koh deye NAM iks)

telodynamic [*telo, distant* + *dynam, power* + *-ic*] Pertaining to the transmission of power over a distance, specifically mechanical power by cables and pulleys. (tel' uh deye NAM ik)

tetradynamous [*tetra-, four* + *dynam, strength* + *-ous*] Having four long stamens and two somewhat shorter stamens. (tet' ruh DEYE nuh mus)

thermodynamics [*thermo, heat* + *dynam, energy* + *-ics, study of*] The branch of physics dealing with the study of the relationships between heat and other forms of energy. See aerothermodynamics. (thur' moh deye NAM iks)

e-   out

e pluribus unum [*Ltn > out of many, one*] Out of many, one. Motto of the United States. (ee PLOOR uh bus YOO num)

ebullient [*e-, out* + *Ltn > bullire, boil* + *-ent*] 1.Overflowing with enthusiasm or excitement. Exuberant. Vivacious. See vivacious. 2.Boiling. Bubbling. (ih BOOL yent)

edentate [*e-, out* + *dent, teeth* + *-ate*] 1.Without teeth. 2.Any of an order of New World mammals with no teeth, as anteaters, armadillos, and sloths. (ee DEN tayt')

edentulous [*e-, out* + *dent, teeth* + *-ulous*] Without teeth, especially as a result of disease or injury. (ee DEN chuh lus)

edict [*e-, out* + *dict, to speak*] An official public order or decree. (EE dikt)

educate [*e-, out* + *duc, to lead* + *-ate*] To give training or knowledge to, especially as a formal and prolonged process. Teach. (EJ uh kayt')

educe [*e-, out* + *duc, to lead*] 1.To bring out or develop. Elicit. See evoke and elicit. 2.To deduce or infer, as from knowledge or experience. (ih DOOS)

egregious [*e-, out* + *greg, flock* + *-ious*] 1.Extremely bad. Flagrant. 2.Extraordinary or remarkable in a bad way. (ih GREE jus)

egress [*e-, out* + *gress, to go*] 1.The act or right of going out or forth. Emergence. See ingress (def. 1) and regress (def. 1). 2.A way or means of going out. Exit. Opposed to ingress. (EE gres)

ejaculate [*e-, out* + *Ltn > jaculari, to throw* + *-ate*] 1.To utter suddenly and forcefully. Exclaim. 2.To discharge suddenly, especially semen. (ih JAK yuh layt')

eject [*e-, out* + *ject, to throw*] 1.To throw out forcefully. Discharge. 2.To dismiss, as from competition, occupancy, office, etc. (ih JEKT)

elaborate [*e-, out* + *labor, work* + *-ate*] 1.To work out with care and in detail. 2.To add detail or embellishment to. (ih LAB uh rayt')

elan [*e-, out* + *Ltn > lancea, lance*] Enthusiasm. Verve. Dash. (ay LON)

elate [*e-, out* + *Ltn > ferre, to carry*] To raise the spirits of. (ih LAYT)

elect [*e-, out* + *leg, choose*] 1.To choose by vote. 2.To make a choice. Choose. (ih LEKT)

elicit [*e-, out* + *Ltn > lacere, entice* + *-it*] To draw out or bring forth. Evoke. Educe. See evoke and educe (def. 1). (ih LIS it)

elide [*e-, out* + *Ltn > laedare, strike*] 1.To omit a vowel or syllable in pronunciation. 2.To omit. Ignore. Suppress. (ih LEYED)

eligible [*e-, out* + *leg, choose* + *-ible*] 1.Qualified or worthy to be chosen. 2.Suitable or desirable, especially for marriage. (EL ih juh bul)

elite [*e-, out* + *leg, choose*] The group regarded as the most talented, superior, etc., in a country, society, or organization. (ih LEET)

elocution [*e-, out* + *locu, to speak* + *-tion*] 1.Style or manner of public speaking. 2.The art of public speaking or reading. (el' uh KYOO shun)

elongate [*e-, out* + *Ltn > longus, long* + *-ate*] To make longer. Lengthen. (ih LONG gayt')

eloquence [*e-, out* + *loqu, to speak* + *-ence*] The art of using forceful, persuasive, and fluent speech. (EL uh kwens)

eloquent [*e-, out* + *loqu, to speak* + *-ent*] 1.Exercising forceful, persuasive, and fluent speech. 2.Vividly expressive or revealing. (EL uh kwent)

elucidate [*e-, out* + *Ltn > lucidus, clear* + *-ate*] To make clear. Explain. (ih LOO sih dayt')

elude [*e-, out + lud, to play*] To escape from or avoid skillfully, cleverly, etc. See evade and circumvent (def. 2). (ee LOOD)

emaciate [*e-, out + Ltn > macies, leanness + -ate*] To make abnormally thin through illness or starvation. (ih MAY shee ayt')

emanate [*e-, out + Ltn > manare, to flow + -ate*] To originate or come forth from a source. (EM uh nayt')

emancipate [*e-, out + manu, hand + Ltn > capere, to take + -ate*] 1.To release from slavery or bondage. Liberate. See manumit. 2.To free from control or restraint. (ih MAN suh payt')

emasculate [*e-, out + Ltn > masculus, male + -ate*] 1.To deprive of the power to reproduce. Castrate. 2.To deprive of strength, vigor, or spirit. Weaken. See enervate. (ih MAS kyuh layt')

emend [*e-, out + Ltn > menda, fault*] To make corrections or improvements to by critical editing. (ih MEND)

emerge [*e-, out + merg, to dip*] 1.To come forth or into view. 2.To become known or apparent. (ih MURJ)

emigrate [*e-, out + Ltn > migrare, to move + -ate*] To move out of a country or region to settle in another. See immigrate. (EM ih grayt')

eminent [*e-, out + Ltn > minere, project + -ent*] 1.Superior, as in power, rank, or achievement. Distinguished. Prominent. See prominent (def. 3). 2.A high elevation. Hill. (EM ih nent)

emissary [*e-, out + miss, to send + -ary*] A person sent to represent a government, organization, or another person. (EM ih sehr' ee)

emit [*e-, out + mit, to send*] 1.Give off. Discharge. Utter. 2.To issue or put into circulation with authority, especially currency. (ee MIT)

emollient [*e-, out + Ltn > mollire, soften + -ent*] Softening. Soothing. Relaxing. (ih MOL yent)

emolument [*e-, out + Ltn > molere, grind + -ent*] Payment from an office, position, or employment. Wages. Compensation. (ih MOL yuh ment)

emulsion [*e-, out + Ltn > mulgere, milk + -sion*] A mixture of two liquids, one of which consists of small, fatty or resinous globules and is suspended, rather than dissolved, in the other. (ih MUL shun)

enervate [*e-, out + Ltn > nervus, nerve + -ate*] To reduce the strength or vigor of. Debilitate. Weaken. Emasculate. See emasculate (def. 2). (EN ur vayt')

enormous [*e-, out + Ltn > norma, a pattern + -ous*] Extremely or unusually large. Huge. See astronomical (def. 2) and cosmic (def. 2). (ih NOR mus)

enumerate [*e-, out + numer, number + -ate*] 1.To name one by one. List. 2.To determine the number of. Count. (ih NOO mer ayt')

enunciate [*e-, out + Ltn > nuntius, messenger + -ate*] 1.To pronounce, especially clearly and distinctly. Articulate. 2.To announce. Proclaim. See proclaim and promulgate (def. 1). (ee NUN see ayt')

eradicate [*e-, out + radic, root + -ate*] 1.To get rid of completely. Exterminate. 2.To pull out by, or as if by, the roots. Uproot. See ineradicable. (ih RAD ih kayt')

erase [*e-, out + Ltn > radere, scrape*] 1.To cause to disappear by rubbing, scratching, or scraping. 2.To remove all traces of. Obliterate. (ih RAYS)

erode [*e-, out + Ltn > rodere, gnaw*] 1.To eat into or wear away gradually. Corrode. 2.To destroy gradually. (ih ROHD)

eruct [*e-, out + Ltn > ructare, belch*] To belch. (ih RUKT)

erudite [*e-, out + Ltn > rudis, rude + -ite*] Very learned. Scholarly. (EHR yoo deyet')

erupt [*e-, out + rupt, burst*] To burst or break out violently from limits or restraint. (ih RUPT)

evacuate [*e-, out + Ltn > vacuus, empty + -ate*] 1.To empty out. 2.To remove persons from an area of danger. (ih VAK yoo ayt')

evade [*e-, out + vas, to go*] 1.To avoid skillfully or cleverly. 2.To avoid responsibility, confrontation, answering, etc. See elude and circumvent (def. 2). (ih VAYD)

evaluate [*e-, out + Ltn > valare, worth + -ate*] 1.To determine the value, quality, or amount of. Appraise. 2.To determine the numerical value of. (ih VAL yoo ayt')

evanesce [*e-, out + Ltn > vanus, vanish + -esce*] To disappear gradually, as vapor or smoke. (ev' uh NES)

evanescent [*e-, out + Ltn > vanus, vanish + -escent*] Disappearing quickly. Occurring for only a brief period. Fleeting. (ev' uh NES ent)

event [*e-, out + vent, to come*] A usually important occasion, contest, etc. (ih VENT)

eventuate [*e-, out + vent, to come + -ate*] To ultimately come about. Result. Culminate. (ih VENT choo ayt')

evert [*e-, out + vert, turn*] Turn outward or inside out. (ih VURT)

evict [*e-, out + vict, conquer*] To expel from a building, land, etc., by a legal process. (ih VIKT)

evident [*e-, out + vid, to see + -ent*] Easily seen or understood. Clear. Obvious. Manifest. See perspicuous and manifest. (EV ih dent)

evocative [*e-, out + voc, to call + -ative*] Tending to evoke. (ih VOK uh tiv)

evoke [*e-, out + vok, to call*] To bring out or call forth, as feelings, memories, etc. See educe (def. 1) and elicit. (ih VOHK)

evolute [*e-, out + volut, roll*] The locus of the centers of curvature of a curve known as the involute. See involute (def. 3). (EV uh loot')

evolution [*e-, out + volut, roll + -ion*] A gradual process of developmental change into a different and usually more complex form. See evolve. (ev' uh LOO shun)

evolve [*e-, out + volv, roll*] To develop gradually. (ih VOLV)

ineloquent [*in-, not + e-, out + loqu, to speak + -ent*] Not exercising forceful, persuasive, or fluent speech. (in EL uh kwent)

ineradicable [*in-, not + e-, out + radic, root + -able*] Impossible to completely get rid of. Not eradicable. See eradicate. (in' ih RAD ih kuh bul)

endo-   inside

endergonic [*endo-, inside + erg, work + -onic*] Pertaining to a biochemical reaction that requires the absorption of energy, as photosynthesis. Opposed to exergonic. (en' der GON ik)

endobiotic [*endo-, inside + bio, life + -tic*] Pertaining to an organism living within the tissues or cells of a host organism. See ectogenous. (en' doh beye OT ik)

endoblast [*endo-, inside + blast, cell layer*] 1.Undifferentiated embryonic endoderm. 2.Endoderm. See endoderm, mesoblast, and ectoblast. (EN duh blast')

endocardial [*endo-, inside* + *cardi, heart* + *-al*] 1.Located inside the heart. 2.Pertaining to the endocardium. (en' doh KAHR dee ul)

endocarditis [*endo-, inside* + *cardi, heart* + *-itis, inflammation*] Inflammation of the endocardium. (en' doh kahr DEYE tis)

endocardium [*endo-, inside* + *cardi, heart* + *-um*] The thin serous membrane lining the chambers of the heart. (en' doh KAHR dee um)

endocarp [*endo-, inside* + *carp, fruit*] The inner layer of the pericarp of a fruit, as the stone surrounding the seed of a cherry. See mesocarp, epicarp, and pericarp. (EN duh kahrp')

endocentric [*endo-, inside* + *centr, center* + *-ic*] Pertaining to a grammatical construction that as a unit has the same syntactic function in the sentence as one or more of its immediate components, as *hot water*, which functions as the noun *water*. See exocentric. (en' doh SEN trik)

endocrine [*endo-,* inside + *Grk* > *krinein, to separate*] Pertaining to glands that secrete directly into the blood or lymph, as the thyroid or adrenal. Opposed to exocrine. (EN duh krin')

endocrinology [*endocrin(e)* & *-ology, study of*] The branch of medical science dealing with the study of the endocrine system. See endocrine. (en' doh krih NOL uh jee)

endocytosis [*endo-, inside* + *cyt, cell* + *-osis, action*] Incorporation of material from the environment into a cell by phagocytosis or pinocytosis. Opposed to exocytosis. (en' doh seye TOH sis)

endoderm [*endo-, inside* + *derm, skin*] The inner layer of the three primary germ cell layers of an embryo from which the gastrointestinal tract, most of the respiratory system, and many other organs develop. See endoblast, mesoderm, and ectoderm. (EN duh derm')

endodermis [*endo-, inside* + *derm, skin* + *-is*] The innermost layer of cells in the cortex of the roots and stems of vascular plants. (en' doh DER mis)

endodontics [*endo-, inside* + *dont, tooth* + *-ics, practice*] The branch of dentistry dealing with the prevention and treatment of diseases and disorders of the tooth pulp. (en' doh DONT iks)

endoenzyme [*endo-, inside* & *enzyme*] An enzyme that functions within the cell that produced it. (en' doh EN zeyem)

endogamy [*endo-, inside* + *-gamy, marriage*] 1.The custom of marrying within one's clan, tribe, etc. 2.Self-pollination. Opposed to exogamy. (en DOG uh mee)

endogenous [*endo-, inside* + *gen, origin* + *-ous*] 1.Produced or originating from within. 2.Originating or developing from within the organism. See exogenous, autogenous, and heterogenous. (en DOJ uh nus)

endometrium [*endo-, inside* + *metr, uterus* + *-ium*] The mucous membrane that forms the inner lining of the uterus. (en' doh MEE tree um)

endomorph [*endo-, inside* + *morph, form*] A mineral enclosed inside another mineral. See perimorph. (EN duh morf')

endomorphic [*endo-, inside* + *morph, form* + *-ic*] Having a generally round and soft body build characterized by the prominence of structures derived from the embryonic endoderm. See mesomorphic and ectomorphic. (en' doh MOR fik)

endomysium [*endo-, inside* + *my, muscle* + *-ium*] The sheath of connective tissue surrounding each muscle fiber. See perimysium and epimysium. (en' doh MIZ ee um)

endoneurium [*endo-, inside* + *neur, nerve* + *-ium*] The protective covering of connective tissue surrounding each individual nerve fiber in a peripheral nerve. See perineurium and epineurium. (en' doh NOOR ee um)

endoparasite [*endo-, inside* & *parasite*] A parasite that lives inside the body of its host. See ectoparasite and entozoon. (en' doh PEHR uh seyet')

endophyte [*endo-, inside* + *-phyte, plant*] A parasitic or symbiotic plant growing within another plant. See epiphyte. (EN duh feyet')

endoplasm [*endo-, inside* + *plasm, protoplasm*] The inner, more fluid portion of the cytoplasm of a cell. See ectoplasm. (EN duh plaz' um)

endorphins [*endo-, inside* & *(m)orphin(e)*] Chemical substances produced in the brain that have a pain-relieving effect similar to morphine. See morphine. (en DOR fins)

endoscope [*endo-, inside* + *-scope, to examine*] A tubular optical instrument for examining the interior of a cavity, organ, or other body part. (EN duh skohp')

endoskeleton [*endo-, inside* & *skeleton*] The internal skeleton of the body of an animal. See exoskeleton. (en' doh SKEL ih tun)

endosmosis [*endo-, inside* & *osmosis*] 1.Osmosis in an inward direction. 2.Osmosis from a region of lower concentration to a region of higher concentration. Opposed to exosmosis. (en' doz MOH sis)

endosperm [*endo-, inside* + *sperm, seed*] A nutritive tissue that surrounds and nourishes the developing embryo in seed plants. (EN duh sperm')

endospore [*endo-, inside* & *spore*] 1.A spore formed within the cell membrane of a parent cell. 2.The innermost layer of the wall of a spore. See exospore. (EN duh spor')

endosteum [*endo-, inside* + *oste, bone* + *-um*] A layer of connective tissue lining the inner surface of the medullary cavity of a bone. (en DOS tee um)

endothecium [*endo-, inside* + *Grk* > *theke, case* + *-ium*] 1.The inner layer of tissue of a mature anther. 2.The inner layer of cells in the sporangium of a moss or liverwort. See amphithecium. (en' doh THEE shee um)

endotherm [*endo-, inside* + *therm, temperature*] A warm-blooded animal, such as a bird or mammal, whose body temperature remains relatively constant. Same as homoiotherm. (EN duh thurm')

endothermic [*endo-, inside* + *therm, heat* + *-ic*] Pertaining to a chemical reaction that causes the absorption of heat. See exothermic. (en' doh THUR mik)

endotoxin [*endo-, inside* & *toxin*] A toxin produced in some bacteria and released upon disintegration of the cell, as in bubonic plague or whooping cough. See exotoxin. (EN doh tok' sin)

endotracheal [*endo-, inside* + *trache, trachea* + *-al*] Placed inside the trachea, as an endotracheal tube used to maintain an open airway. (en' doh TRAY kee ul)

ecto-   outside

ectoblast [*ecto-, outside + blast, cell layer*]
1.Undifferentiated embryonic ectoderm. 2.Ectoderm.
See ectoderm, endoblast, and mesoblast. (EK tuh blast')

ectocommensal [*ecto-, outside & commensal*] An organism
living on the outer body surface of a host organism,
but not as a parasite. (ek' toh kuh MEN sul)

ectoderm [*ecto-, outside + derm, skin*] The outer layer of
the three primary germ cell layers of an embryo from
which the nervous system, the epidermis and
epidermal tissues, sense organs, and certain other
body parts develop. See ectoblast, endoderm, and
mesoderm. (EK tuh derm')

ectogenous [*ecto-, outside + gen, formation + -ous*] Capable
of developing and living outside the body of a host, as
certain parasitic bacteria. See endobiotic.
(ck TOJ uh nus)

ectomere [*ecto-, outside & (blasto)mere*] A blastomere that
develops into ectoderm. See ectoderm. (EK tuh mihr')

ectomorphic [*ecto-, outside + morph, form + -ic*] Having a
lean and slightly muscular body build characterized
by the prominence of structures derived from the
embryonic ectoderm. See endomorphic and
mesomorphic. (ek' toh MOR fik)

ectoparasite [*ecto-, outside & parasite*] A parasite that
lives on the outer surface of its host. See endoparasite
and epizoon. (ek' toh PEHR uh seyet')

ectoplasm [*ecto-, outside + plasm, protoplasm*] The outer,
more rigid portion of the cytoplasm of a cell. See
endoplasm. (EK tuh plaz' um)

ectotherm [*ecto-, outside + therm, temperature*] A cold-
blooded animal, such as a fish or reptile, whose body
temperature varies with the environment. Same as
poikilotherm. (EK tuh thurm')

ann   year
enn   years

annals [*ann, year + -als*] 1.A yearly chronological record
of events. 2.Historical records. Chronicles. See
chronicle. 3.Records of the proceedings and activities
of an organization or field of learning. (AN ulz)

anniversary [*ann, year + vers, turn + -ary*] The yearly
recurrence of a past event, as the date of a wedding.
(an' uh VUR suh ree)

anno Domini [*ann, year & Ltn > dominicus, of the Lord*]
Literally, "the year of our Lord." Used mainly in the
abbreviated form A.D. to indicate a specified year in
the Christian era. (AN oh DOM uh nee)

annual [*ann, year + ual*] 1.Occurring once a year. See
per annum. 2.Living only one season or year, as
certain plants or insects. (AN yoo ul)

annual ring [*ann, year + -ual & ring*] A concentric layer of
wood produced by one year's growth of a tree or other
woody plant. (AN yoo ul ring)

annuity [*ann, year + -ity*] An allowance or income paid
yearly or at other regular intervals. (uh NOO ih tee)

annus mirabilis [*ann, year & Ltn > mirabilis, wonders*]
Literally, "year of wonders." A year regarded as
pivotal, fateful, notable, etc. (AN us mih RAB uh lis)

biannual [*bi-, two + ann, year + -ual*] Occurring twice a
year. See biennial (def. 1). (beye AN yoo ul)

bicentennial [*bi-, two + cent, hundred + enn, years + -ial*]
Occurring once every two hundred years. See
semicentennial. (beye' sen TEN ee ul)

biennial [*bi-, two + enn, years + -ial*] 1.Occurring once
every two years. See biannual. 2.Lasting or living for
two years. (beye EN ee ul)

biennium [*bi-, two + enn, years + -ium*] A period of two
years. (beye EN ee um)

centenarian [*cent, hundred + enn, years + -arian*] A person
who is at least 100 years of age. (sent' n EHR ee un)

centennial [*cent, hundred + enn, years + -ial*] Occurring
once every one hundred years. (sen TEN ee ul)

decennial [*dec, ten + enn, years + -ial*] 1.Occurring once
every ten years. 2.Lasting or continuing for ten years.
(dih SEN ee ul)

decennium [*dec, ten + enn, years + -ium*] A period of ten
years. Decade. (dih SEN ee um)

millenarian [*mill, thousand + enn, years + -arian*]
1.Pertaining to one thousand, especially one thousand
years. 2.Pertaining to belief in the millennium.
(mil' uh NEHR ee un)

millennium [*mill, thousand + enn, years + -ium*] 1.A period
of one thousand years. 2.The period of one thousand
years mentioned in the Bible during which Christ will
rule on earth. (mih LEN ee um)

octennial [*oct-, eight + enn, years + -ial*] 1.Occurring once
every eight years. 2.Lasting or continuing for eight
years. (ok TEN ee ul)

per annum [*per {by} & ann, year + -um*] By the year.
Yearly. Annually. See annual (def. 1). (per AN um)

perennate [*per-, through + enn, years + -ate*] To last from
year to year or for many years. (PEHR uh nayt')

perennial [*per-, through + enn, years + -ial*] Lasting or
continuing through the year or through many years.
(puh REN ee ul)

postmillennial [*post-, after + mill, thousand + enn, years + -
ial*] Occurring or existing after the millennium. See
premillennial. (pohst' mih LEN ee ul)

premillennial [*pre-, before + mill, thousand + enn, years + -
ial*] Occurring or existing before the millennium. See
postmillennial. (pree' mih LEN ee ul)

quadrennial [*quadr, four + enn, years + -ial*] 1.Occurring
once every four years. 2.Lasting or continuing for four
years. (kwah DREN ee ul)

quadrennium [*quadr, four + enn, years + -ium*] A period of
four years. (kwah DREN ee um)

quadricentennial [*quadri, four + cent, hundred + enn, years
+ -ial*] Occurring once every four hundred years.
(kwod' ruh sen TEN ee ul)

quincentennial [*quin, five + cent, hundred + enn, years + -
ial*] Occurring once every five hundred years.
(kwin' sen TEN ee ul)

quindecennial [*quin, five + dec, ten + enn, years + -ial*]
1.Occurring once every fifteen years. 2.Lasting or
continuing for fifteen years. (kwin' dih SEN ee ul)

quinquennial [*quinque, five + enn, years + -ial*]
1.Occurring once every five years. 2.Lasting or
continuing for five years. (kwin KWEN ee ul)

quinquennium [*quinque, five + enn, years + -ium*] A period
of five years. (kwin KWEN ee um)

semiannual [*semi-, half + ann, year + -ual*] Occurring
twice a year. Same as biannual. (sem' ee AN yoo ul)

semicentennial [*semi-, half + cent, hundred + enn, years + -ial*] Occurring once every fifty years. See bicentennial. (sem' ee sen TEN ee ul)

septennial [*sept-, seven + enn, years + -ial*] 1.Occurring once every seven years. 2.Lasting or continuing for seven years. (sep TEN ee ul)

sesquicentennial [*sesqui-, one and a half + cent, hundred + enn, years + -ial*] Occurring once every one hundred and fifty years. (ses' kwih sen TEN ee ul)

sexcentenary [*sex-, six + cent, hundred + enn, years + -ary*] Occurring once every six hundred years. (seks' sen TEN uh ree)

sexennial [*sex-, six + enn, years + -ial*] 1.Occurring once every six years. 2.Lasting or continuing for six years. (seks EN ee ul)

superannuated [*super-, beyond + ann, year + -ated*] 1.Ineffective or retired because of old age or infirmity. 2.To set aside or discard as antiquated or obsolete. (soo' per AN yoo ay' tid)

tercentenary [*Ltn > tres, three + cent, hundred + enn, years + -ary*] Occurring once every three hundred years. Same as tricentennial. (tur' sen TEN uh ree)

tricentennial [*tri-, three + cent, hundred + enn, years + -ial*] Occurring once every three hundred years. (treye' sen TEN ee ul)

triennial [*tri-, three + enn, years + -ial*] 1.Occurring once every three years. 2.Lasting or continuing for three years. (treye EN ee ul)

triennium [*tri-, three + enn, years + -ium*] A period of three years. (treye EN ee um)

vicennial [*Ltn > viginti, twenty + enn, years + -ial*] 1.Occurring once every twenty years. 2.Lasting or continuing for twenty years. (veye SEN ee ul)

ep-, epi-
on, upon, outside, over, among, at, after, to

epact [*ep-, to + Grk > agein, to lead*] The nearly eleven day period of time by which the solar year leads the lunar year. (EE pakt)

eparchy [*ep-, over + arch, rule + -y*] 1.A diocese or province in an Eastern Orthodox Church. 2.In modern Greece, a governmental subdivision of a province. 3.In ancient Greece, a governmental province or district. (EP ahr' kee)

epenthesis [*ep-, among + en-, in + the, to put + -sis*] The insertion of a letter or sound into a word. See anaptyxis. (ih PEN thuh sis)

epexegesis [*ep-, over & exegesis {explanation}*] The addition of words for further explanation or clarification. (ep' ek' suh JEE sis)

ephebe [*ep-, at + Grk > hebe, early manhood*] A youth in ancient Greece enrolled in military training. (EF eeb)

ephemeral [*ep-, on + hemer, day + -al*] 1.Lasting for one day only. 2.Lasting for only a brief period of time. Transitory. Short-lived. (ih FEM ur ul)

ephemeris [*ep-, on + hemer, day + -is*] A table showing the precomputed positions of a satellite or other celestial body at regular intervals for a given period. (ih FEM ur is)

ephor [*ep-, over + Grk > horan, to see*] In ancient Sparta, one of a body of five annually elected magistrates having power over the king. (EF ur)

epiblast [*epi-, outside + blast, cell layer*] The outer layer of the three primary germ cell layers of an embryo from which the nervous system, the epidermis and epidermal tissues, sense organs, and certain other body parts develop. Same as ectoderm. (EP ih blast')

epicalyx [*epi-, outside & calyx*] An involucre below the calyx that resembles an extra outer calyx. (ep' ih KAY liks)

epicanthus [*epi-, over & canthus*] A vertical fold of skin that extends from the upper eyelid to the root of the nose, covering the inner canthus. It occurs normally in people of Asian descent and sometimes as a congenital abnormality, as in Down's syndrome. (ep' ih KAN thus)

epicardium [*epi-, outside + cardi, heart + -um*] The innermost layer of the pericardium that touches the heart. See pericardium. (ep' ih KAHR dee um)

epicarp [*epi-, outside + carp, fruit*] The outer layer of the pericarp of a fruit, as the skin of a cherry. See endocarp, mesocarp, and pericarp. (EP ih kahrp')

epicene [*epi-, on + -cene, common*] 1.A noun having only one form to denote both sexes. 2.Having characteristics of the other sex. 3.Having characteristics of both sexes or of neither sex. (EP ih seen')

epicenter [*epi-, on & center*] 1.The point directly above the center of an earthquake. 2.The focal point of a crisis, activity, etc. (EP ih sent' ur)

epicotyl [*epi-, upon & cotyl(edon)*] The portion of an embryonic plant stem located above the cotyledons. See hypocotyl. (ep' ih KOT l)

epicritic [*epi-, upon + Grk > kritikos, able to discern + -ic*] Pertaining to sensory nerve fibers in the skin that respond to small variations in pressure, pain, heat, or cold. Opposed to protopathic. (ep' ih KRIT ik)

epicycle [*epi-, outside + cycl, circle*] In Ptolemaic astronomy, a circle whose center moves around the circumference of a larger circle, simulating the orbit of a heavenly body around the earth. (EP ih seye' kul)

epicycloid [*epi-, outside + cycl, circle + -oid, resembling*] A curve generated by the motion of a point on the circumference of a circle rolled around the outside of a fixed circle. See cycloid (def. 2) and hypocycloid. (ep' ih SEYE kloid')

epidemic [*epi-, among + dem, people + -ic*] 1.Rapidly spreading disease among people in a region. 2.The rapid spread or sudden development of something, as crime, an idea, etc. See pandemic. (ep' ih DEM ik)

epidemiology [*epi-, among + demi, people + -ology, study of*] The study of the causes, prevention, and control of epidemic diseases among people. See epizootiology. (ep' ih dee' mee OL uh jee)

epidendrum [*epi-, on + dendr, tree + -um*] Any of numerous small-flowered, mostly epiphytic orchids found mainly in tropical America. (ep' ih DEN drum)

epidermis [*epi-, outside + derm, skin + -is*] 1.The protective outer layer of skin that covers the dermis. See dermis. 2.The protective outer layer or layers of cells in plants. (ep' ih DER mis)

epidiascope [*epi-, on + dia, through + -scope, to view*] A projector for displaying a magnified image of a transparency or an opaque object on a screen. (ep' ih DEYE uh skohp')

epididymis [*epi-, upon + Grk > didymoi, testicles + -is*] An oval-shaped structure containing a long tube in which sperm is stored and attached to the back side of each testis. (ep' ih DID uh mis)

epigastrium [*epi-, over + gastr, stomach + -ium*] The uppermost of the three middle regions of the abdomen, between the right hypochondriac region and the left hypochondriac region. See hypogastrium and hypochondrium. (ep' ih GAS tree um)

epigeal [*epi-, on + geo, earth + -al*] Growing on or near the surface of the ground. (ep' ih JEE ul)

epigene [*epi-, on + -gene, formation*] Formed or occurring on or near the surface of the earth. See hypogene. (EP ih jeen')

epigenesis [*epi-, after + -genesis, formation*] 1.The theory that the embryo develops by structural elaboration of organs and parts that do not pre-exist in the fertilized egg, rather than by preformation. 2.Alteration of the mineral content of a rock attributed to outside influences. (ep' ih JEN uh sis)

epigenous [*epi-, upon + gen, formation + -ous*] Developing or growing on the upper surface of a leaf or other plant part, as certain fungi. See hypogenous. (ih PIJ uh nus)

epiglottis [*epi-, over + glott, tongue + -is*] The thin, valvelike, cartilaginous structure at the base of the tongue that folds over the glottis during swallowing to prevent food from entering the windpipe. (ep' ih GLOT is)

epigram [*epi-, on + gram, to write*] 1.A short poem with a witty, ingenious, or pointed ending. 2.A short, witty, or pointed saying. (EP ih gram')

epigraph [*epi-, on + graph, writing*] 1.An inscription on a statue, monument, building, etc. 2.A brief quotation preceding the text of a book, chapter, or other literary work to introduce the theme. (EP ih graf')

epigraphy [*epi-, on + -graphy, writing*] The scientific study and interpretation of inscriptions, especially ancient inscriptions. (ih PIG ruh fee)

epigynous [*epi-, upon + gyn, female + -ous*] Having floral parts or organs attached to the top of the gynoecium, as a daisy. See perigynous and hypogynous. (ih PIJ uh nus)

epilepsy [*epi-, upon + -lepsy, seizure*] A disorder of the nervous system marked by recurrent episodes of convulsive seizures and loss of consciousness. (EP ih lep' see)

epilimnion [*epi-, upon + Grk > limne, lake + -ion*] In a stratified lake, the warmer uppermost layer of water that lies above the thermocline. See hypolimnion and thermocline. (ep' ih LIM nee on')

epilogue [*epi-, upon + log, discourse*] 1.A short poem or speech delivered by one of the actors directly to the audience following the conclusion of a play. 2.A concluding section at the end of a literary work. (EP ih log')

epimysium [*epi-, outside + my, muscle + -ium*] The sheath of connective tissue surrounding each individual muscle. See endomysium and perimysium. (ep' ih MIZ ee um)

epinasty [*epi-, over + -nasty, growth in a specific direction*] The condition in which leaves or other plant parts turn downward due to more rapid growth on the upper side. Opposed to hyponasty. (EP ih nas' tee)

epineurium [*epi-, outside + neur, nerve + -ium*] The protective covering of connective tissue surrounding a peripheral nerve. See endoneurium and perineurium. (ep' ih NOOR ee um)

Epiphany [*epi-, upon + phan, to appear + -y*] 1.An appearance or manifestation of a god or divine being. 2.In many Christian churches, a festival held on January 6th celebrating the three wise men coming to honor the baby Jesus in Bethlehem. (ih PIF uh nee)

epiphysis [*epi-, outside + Grk > phyein, to grow + -sis*] The end portion of a long bone that initially develops separated from it by cartilage, but subsequently unites with it through further ossification. (ih PIF uh sis)

epiphyte [*epi-, upon + -phyte, plant*] A plant growing independently on the surface of another plant on which it is dependent for support only. See endophyte. (EP ih feyet')

episode [*epi-, upon + Grk > eisodios, entry*] 1.A profound incident or event in the life or history of a person, country, etc. 2. An incident, scene, etc., that is integral to, but separated from, a continuous narrative. (EP ih sohd')

episome [*epi-, on & (chromo)some*] A genetic element in some bacterial cells that can replicate independently in the cytoplasm or in association with the chromosomes. See plasmid. (EP ih sohm')

epistasis [*epi-, over + -stasis, stoppage*] The suppression of the action of one gene by another nonallelic gene. (ih PIS tuh sis)

epistaxis [*epi-, on + Grk > stazein, to drip + -is*] Nosebleed. (ep' ih STAK sis)

epistemic [*Grk > episteme, knowledge + -ic*] Pertaining to or involving knowledge. (ep' ih STEE mik)

epistemology [*Grk > episteme, knowledge + -ology, study of*] The study of human knowledge and its limitations. (ih pis' tuh MOL uh jee)

epistle [*epi-, on + Grk > stellein, to send*] 1.A letter, especially a long, formal, and eloquently written one. 2.Any of the letters in the New Testament written by the Apostles. (ih PIS ul)

epistolary [*epi-, on + Grk > stellein, to send + -ary*] 1.Carried on by letters, as an epistolary correspondence. 2.Composed of a series of letters, as an epistolary novel. 3.Pertaining to or suitable for writing letters. (ih PIS tuh lehr' ee)

epistrophe [*epi-, on + Grk > strophe, turning*] The deliberate repetition of a word or words at the end of successive phrases, clauses, sentences, or verses. See anaphora (def. 1). (ih PIS truh fee)

epitaph [*epi-, on + Grk > taphos, tomb*] An inscription on a gravestone in memory of the person buried there. (EP ih taf')

epitasis [*epi-, after + Grk > teinein, to stretch + -sis*] The main part of a play, following the protasis and preceding the catastasis, that develops the plot and leads to the catastrophe. See protasis (def. 2), catastasis, and catastrophe (def. 2). (ih PIT uh sis)

epithalamium [*epi-, at + Grk > thalamos, bridal chamber + -ium*] A poem or song in honor of a bride and bridegroom. (ep' ih thuh LAY mee um)

epithelioma [*epitheli(um) & -oma, tumor*] A malignant tumor composed mainly of epithelial cells. See mesothelioma. (ep' ih thee' lee OH muh)

epithelium [*epi-, upon + thel, nipple + -ium*] Any tissue that covers a surface or organ, lines a tube or cavity, etc., and performs protective functions, as the skin. See mesothelium. (ep' ih THEE lee um)

epithet [*epi-, upon + the, to put*] 1.A word or phrase used to characterize a person or thing. 2.An abusive, insulting, or disparaging word or phrase. (EP ih thet')

epitome [*epi-, upon + -tome, to cut*] 1.A person or thing that is typical or a perfect example of something. See quintessence (def. 2). 2.A brief summary of a literary work. (ih PIT uh mee)

epizoite [*epi-, outside + zo, animal + -ite*] A nonparasitic animal that is attached to the body of another living animal, as for protection. (ep' ih ZOH eyet')

epizoon [*epi-, outside + zo, animal + -on*] An animal parasite that lives on the outside of the body of its host. See entozoon and ectoparasite. (ep' ih ZOH on)

epizootic [*epi-, among + zo, animal + -otic*] Pertaining to a rapidly spreading disease among animals of one kind. See epidemic and epizootiology. (ep' ih zoh OT ik)

epizootiology [*epi-, among + zo, animal + -ology, study of*] The study of the causes, prevention, and control of epidemic diseases among animals. See epidemiology. (ep' ih zoh ot' ee OL uh jee)

epoch [*ep-, at + Grk > echein, to hold*] 1.One of the subdivisions of a period in geologic time. 2.A period in history in which important or unusual events occurred. (EP uk)

epode [*ep-, after & ode*] 1.A lyric poem in which a short verse follows a longer one. 2.The part of an ancient Greek or Pindaric ode that follows the strophe and antistrophe. (EP ohd)

eponym [*ep-, upon + onym, name*] A real or mythical person after whom something, such as a place, period, theory, discovery, etc., is named. (EP uh nim')

mesothelium [*meso-, middle & (epi)thelium*] The layer of cells that forms the epithelium and is derived from the mesoderm. See epithelium. (mez' uh THEE lee um)

pseudepigraphy [*pseud, false + epi, upon + -graphy, writing*] 1.The false attribution of a novel, poem, etc., to a certain writer. 2.Spurious religious writings professing to be ascribed to Biblical characters. (sood' ih PIG ruh fee)

equ, equi   equal

adequate [*ad-, to + equ, equal + -ate*] 1.Enough. Sufficient. 2.Barely satisfactory. (AD ih kwit)

equable [*equ, equal + -able*] 1.Not varying. Even. Uniform. 2.Not easily disturbed. Calm. Tranquil. See imperturbable and equanimity. (EK wuh bul)

equal [*equ, equal + -al*] Exactly the same in amount, number, rank, size, etc. (EE kwul)

equanimity [*equ, equal + anim, mind + -ity*] The quality of remaining calm and even-tempered. Composure. See imperturbable and equable (def. 2). (ee' kwuh NIM ih tee)

equate [*equ, equal + -ate*] To make or consider equal. (ih KWAYT)

equation [*equ, equal + -ation*] 1.The process of equating. 2.A statement of the equality of two mathematical expressions. (ih KWAY zhun)

equator [*equ, equal + -ator*] An imaginary circle around the circumference of the earth equidistant from the North and South Poles. (ih KWAY tur)

equiangular [*equi, equal & angular*] Having all angles equal. (ee' kwih ANG gyuh lur)

equidistant [*equi, equal & distant*] Equally distant. (ee' kwih DIS tunt)

equilateral [*equi, equal + Ltn > latus, side + -al*] 1.Having all sides equal. 2.A closed plane figure with all sides equal. See isogon. (ee' kwuh LAT ur ul)

equilibrium [*equi, equal + Ltn > libra, balance + -ium*] 1.A state of balance between opposing forces. See equipoise (def. 1). 2.Mental and emotional balance. (ee' kwuh LIB ree um)

equinox [*equi, equal + Ltn > nox, night*] Either of the two times during the year when the sun crosses the celestial equator and day and night are of equal length in all parts of the earth. The vernal equinox occurs on March 21st and the autumnal equinox occurs on September 22nd. (EE kwuh noks')

equipoise [*equi, equal & poise (balance)*] 1.State of balance. Equilibrium. See equilibrium (def. 1). 2.Equal distribution of weight. See equiponderance. (EK wuh poiz')

equipollent [*equi, equal + Ltn > pollere, be strong + -ent*] Equal in force, effect, or significance. (ee' kwuh POL ent)

equiponderance [*equi, equal + Ltn > ponderare, weigh + -ance*] Equality of weight. See equipoise (def. 2). (ee' kwuh PON der ens)

equitable [*equi, equal + -able*] Fair. Just. Impartial. (EK wit uh bul)

equity [*equi, equal + -ity*] 1.Fairness. Justness. Impartiality. 2.The value of a property in excess of liens against it. (EK wit ee)

equivalent [*equi, equal + -valent, having a specified valence*] 1.Equal in value, number, measure, significance, etc. 2.Having the same chemical combining weight. (ih KWIV uh lent)

equivocal [*equi, equal + voc, voice + -al*] Having more than one meaning and often intended to deceive or mislead. Ambiguous. See ambiguous (def. 1), unequivocal, and univocal (def. 1). (ih KWIV uh kul)

equivocate [*equi, equal + voc, voice + -ate*] To use ambiguous or unclear expressions, usually to mislead, deceive, or to avoid giving a direct answer. Quibble. See tergiversate (def. 1). (ih KWIV uh kayt')

equivoke [*equi, equal + vok, voice*] An ambiguous word, phrase, or expression. (EK wuh vohk')

inadequate [*in-, not & adequate*] Not adequate. See adequate. (in AD ih kwit)

inequality [*in-, not & equal & -ity*] The condition of being unequal or uneven. (in' ih KWOL ih tee)

inequity [*in-, not + equ, equal + -ity*] Lack of justice. Unfairness. See iniquity. (in EK wit ee)

iniquity [*in-, not + equ, equal + -ity*] Lack of righteousness. Wickedness. Gross injustice. See inequity. (in IK wit ee)

unequal [*un-, not & equal*] 1.Not equal. 2.Not balanced. 3.Not adequate. See adequate. (un EE kwul)

unequivocal [*un-, not + equi, equal + voc, voice + -al*] Not ambiguous. Unmistakable. Clear. See ambiguous (def. 1), equivocal, and univocal (def. 1). (un' ih KWIV uh kul)

erg/o   work

allergy [*allo, other* + *erg, work* + *-y*] An abnormal reaction, as sneezing or itching, to certain substances such as pollen, dust, dander, etc. (AL ur jee)

bioenergetics [*bio, living organisms & energetics*] The branch of biology dealing with the study of the conversion of sunlight, food, etc., into energy by living organisms. See energetics. (beye' oh en' ur JET iks)

demiurge [*demi, people* + *erg, work*] 1.The Gnostic creator of the material world, sometimes considered to be the creator of evil. 2.The Platonic creator of the material universe. 3.A magistrate or other public official in certain ancient Greek states. (DEM ee urj')

dramaturge [*drama & erg, work*] A writer or producer of plays. A playwright. (DRAM uh turj')

dramaturgy [*drama & erg, work* + *-y*] The art or technique of writing or producing dramas. (DRAM uh tur' jee)

endergonic [*endo-, inside* + *erg, work* + *-onic*] Pertaining to a biochemical reaction that requires the absorption of energy, as photosynthesis. Opposed to exergonic. (en' der GON ik)

energetics [*en-, at* + *erg, work* + *-ics, science*] The science dealing with the laws that govern all forms of energy and the transformation from one form to another. (en' ur JET iks)

energy [*en-, at* + *erg, work* + *-y*] 1.The vigor, power, or capacity for doing work. 2.Usable power. (EN ur jee)

erg [*erg, work*] A unit of work equal to the amount of work done by a force of one dyne acting through a distance of one centimeter. (urg)

ergograph [*ergo, work* + *graph, recording*] An instrument for measuring and recording a muscle's work capacity while under exertion. (UR guh graf')

ergometer [*ergo, work* + *meter, to measure*] An apparatus for measuring the work done by a muscle or muscle group over a given period of time. (ur GOM et er)

ergonomics [*erg, work & (ec)onomics*] The study of the relationship between people and their working environment. (ur' guh NOM iks)

ergophobia [*ergo, work* + *-phobia, fear*] Abnormal fear of work. (ur' guh FOH bee uh)

exergonic [*exo-, outside* + *erg, work* + *-onic*] Pertaining to a biochemical reaction that releases energy, as catabolism. Opposed to endergonic. (eks' ur GON ik)

exoergic [*exo-, outside* + *erg, work* + *-ic*] Pertaining to a chemical reaction that causes the liberation of heat, as combustion. Same as exothermic. (eks' oh UR jik)

lethargy [*Grk > lethe, forgetfulness* + *a-, not* + *erg, work* + *-y*] Abnormal drowsiness or lack of energy. Apathetic inactivity. See apathy. (LETH ur jee)

liturgics [*Grk > leos, people* + *erg, work* + *-ics, study of*] The study of prescribed forms of formal public worship. (lih TUR jiks)

liturgy [*Grk > leos, people* + *erg, work* + *-y*] 1.A prescribed form for public worship. 2.The Eucharist in the Eastern Orthodox Church. 3.The Book of Common Prayer in the Episcopal Church. (LIT ur jee)

metallurgy [*metal & erg, work* + *-y*] The science or technique of working with and extracting metals. See metallography. (MET l ur' jee)

synergism [*syn-, together* + *erg, work* + *-ism*] The combined effect of the cooperative action of separate entities that is greater than the sum of their individual effects, as certain drugs, body parts, etc. (SIN ur jiz' um)

synergy [*syn-, together* + *erg, work* + *-y*] The combined effect of the cooperative action of separate entities that is greater than the sum of their individual effects, as certain drugs, body parts, etc. Same as synergism. (SIN ur jee)

thaumaturgy [*thaumat, miracle* + *erg, work* + *-y*] The working of miracles or magic. (THAW muh tur' jee)

zymurgy [*zym, fermentation* + *erg, work* + *-y*] The branch of chemistry dealing with the study of fermentation processes, as in winemaking, brewing, etc. See zymology. (ZEYE mur jee)

erythr/o   red

erythema [*erythr, red* + *-ma*] Abnormal redness of the skin, as from sunburn or inflammation. (ehr' uh THEE muh)

erythrism [*erythr, red* + *-ism*] Unusual redness, as of feathers or hair. (EHR uh thriz' um)

erythrite [*erythr, red* + *-ite, mineral*] A mineral, hydrous cobalt arsenate, usually rose-colored and used for coloring glass. (EHR uh threyet')

erythroblast [*erythro, red* + *blast, immature cell*] An immature, nucleated red blood cell normally found in bone marrow. See erythrocyte. (ih RITH ruh blast')

erythroblastosis [*erythro, red* + *blast, cell* + *-osis, abnormal condition*] The presence of erythroblasts in the circulating blood, as in certain diseases. (ih rith' roh blas TOH sis)

erythrocyte [*erythro, red* + *-cyte, cell*] A mature red blood cell that has no nucleus. See leukocyte and erythroblast. (ih RITH ruh seyet')

erythrocytometer [*erythro, red* + *cyto, cell* + *meter, to measure*] An instrument for counting red blood cells. (ih rith' roh seye TOM et er)

erythroid [*erythr, red* + *-oid, resembling*] 1.Having a reddish color. 2.Pertaining to red blood cells or their precursors. (ih RITH roid')

erythrophobia [*erythro, red* + *-phobia, fear*] Abnormal fear of anything red, or of blushing. (ih rith' roh FOH bee uh)

erythropoiesis [*erythro, red* + *-poiesis, production*] The production and development of red blood cells. See leukopoiesis. (ih rith' roh poi EE sis)

rhod/o   red

rhodamine [*rhod, red & amine*] Any of several synthetic dyes ranging in color from red to pink. (ROH duh meen')

rhodium [*rhod, red* + *-ium, chemical element*] A hard, durable, gray-white metallic chemical element that is used to form high temperature alloys with platinum, as an electrical contact material, and as plating on other metals to produce a corrosion-resistant coating. So named for the reddish color of a solution of its salts. (ROH dee um)

rhodochrosite [*rhodo, red* + *chros, color* + *-ite, mineral*] A vitreous, impure mineral, chiefly manganese carbonate, with a rose-red color. (roh' duh KROH seyet')

rhod/o

rhododendron [*rhodo, red* + *dendr, tree* + *-on*] Any of various evergreen trees and shrubs with pink, white, and purple flowers. (roh' duh DEN drun)

rhodolite [*rhodo, red* + *-lite, mineral*] A rose-red or pink garnet used as a gem. (ROHD l eyet')

rhodonite [*rhodo, red* + *-ite, mineral*] A rose-red mineral, manganese silicate, that is often used as an ornamental stone. (ROHD n eyet')

rhodopsin [*rhod, red* + *ops, eye* + *-in*] A purple pigment in the outer part of the retina that is essential for vision in dim light. Visual purple. See porphyropsin and iodopsin. (roh DOP sin)

rhodora [*rhod, red* + *-or* + *-a*] A shrub of North America that bears rose-colored flowers in the spring before the leaves appear. (roh DOR uh)

rub   red

bilirubin [*bili, bile* + *rub, red* + *-in*] A reddish-yellow pigment of human bile derived from hemoglobin during normal and pathological destruction of erythrocytes. (bil' ih ROO bin)

rubasse [*rub, red*] A variety of quartz stained ruby red by its iron ore content. (roo BAS)

rubefacient [*rub, red* + *fac, to make* + *-ient*] Causing redness of the skin. (roo' buh FAY shent)

rubella [*rub, red*] A mild infectious disease characterized by small red spots on the skin and swollen glands and capable of damaging the fetus when occurring in early pregnancy. German measles. See rubeola (def. 2). (roo BEL uh)

rubellite [*rub, red* + *-lite, stone*] A red variety of tourmaline used as a gemstone. (roo BEL eyet')

rubeola [*rub, red*] 1.Measles. 2.German measles. See rubella. (roo' bee OH luh)

rubescent [*rub, red* + *-escent*] Reddening. Blushing. (roo BES ent)

rubicund [*rub, red* + *-cund*] Having a healthy reddish color. Ruddy. (ROO bih kund')

rubidium [*rub, red* + *-id* + *-ium, chemical element*] A metallic chemical element used in photocells and vacuum tube filaments that reacts violently with water and ignites spontaneously in air. So named from its red spectral lines. (roo BID ee um)

rubiginous [*Ltn > rubigo, rust* + *-ous*] Reddish-brown. Rust-colored. (roo BIJ uh nus)

rubious [*rub, red* + *-ious*] Having the color of a ruby. Red. (ROO bee us)

rubric [*rub, red* + *-ic*] 1.In books and manuscripts, a title, chapter heading, initial letter, etc., appearing in red decorative lettering or otherwise distinguished from the rest of the text. 2.Any rule of conduct or procedure. (ROO brik)

ruby [*rub, red* + *-y*] 1.A deep-red precious stone that is a translucent corundum. 2.A deep-red color. (ROO bee)

esthes, aesthes, esthet, aesthet
feeling, sensation

aesthete [*aesthet, feeling*] A person with a high degree of appreciation for the beauty in art and nature. (ES theet)

aesthetic [*aesthet, feeling* + *-ic*] 1.Pertaining to a sense of the beautiful rather than what is practical or useful. 2.In accordance with accepted notions of good taste. (es THET ik)

aesthetics [*aesthet, feeling* + *-ics, study of*] The branch of philosophy dealing with the study of the qualities perceived in beauty, art, and taste. (es THET iks)

anaesthesia [*an-, without* + *aesthes, feeling* + *-ia*] Total or partial loss of sensibility to pain and other sensations, produced by disease, drugs, hypnosis, etc. Same as anesthesia. (an' es THEE zhuh)

anesthesia [*an-, without* + *esthes, feeling* + *-ia*] Total or partial loss of sensibility to pain and other sensations, produced by disease, drugs, hypnosis, etc. (an' es THEE zhuh)

anesthesiology [*anesthesi(a)* & *-ology, study of*] The branch of medicine dealing with the study and use of anesthesia and anesthetics. See anesthesia. (an' es thee' zee OL uh jee)

esthesia [*esthes, feeling* + *-ia*] The capacity for feeling, sensation, or perception. (es THEE zhuh)

esthesiometer [*esthes, feeling* + *meter, to measure*] An instrument for measuring the degree of tactile sensitivity. (es thee' zee OM et er)

esthete [*esthet, feeling*] A person with a high degree of appreciation for the beauty in art and nature. Same as aesthete. (ES theet)

esthetic [*esthet, feeling* + *-ic*] 1.Pertaining to a sense of the beautiful rather than what is practical or useful. 2.In accordance with accepted notions of good taste. Same as aesthetic. (es THET ik)

esthetics [*esthet, feeling* + *-ics, study of*] The branch of philosophy dealing with the study of the qualities perceived in beauty, art, and taste. Same as aesthetics. (es THET iks)

hyperaesthesia [*hyper-, excessive* + *aesthes, feeling* + *-ia*] Abnormally increased sensitivity to touch, pain, or other stimulation. Same as hyperesthesia. (heye' per es THEE zhuh)

hyperesthesia [*hyper-, excessive* + *esthes, feeling* + *-ia*] Abnormally increased sensitivity to touch, pain, or other stimulation. Opposed to hypesthesia. (heye' per es THEE zhuh)

hypesthesia [*hyp-, less* + *esthes, feeling* + *-ia*] Abnormally decreased sensitivity to touch, pain, or other stimulation. Opposed to hyperesthesia. (hip' es THEE zhuh)

hypoesthesia [*hypo-, less* + *esthes, feeling* + *-ia*] Abnormally decreased sensitivity to touch, pain, or other stimulation. Same as hypesthesia. (heye' poh es THEE zhuh)

kinesthesia [*kine, motion* + *esthes, sensation* + *-ia*] The sensation of body movement perceived through sensory nerve endings in muscles, joints, and tendons. (kin' es THEE zhuh)

synaesthesia [*syn-, together* + *aesthes, sensation* + *-ia*] A sensation produced in one sense by the stimulation of another sense. Same as synesthesia. (sin' es THEE zhuh)

synesthesia [*syn-, together* + *esthes, sensation* + *-ia*] A sensation produced in one sense by the stimulation of another sense. (sin' es THEE zhuh)

telesthesia [*tel, distant* + *esthes, sensation* + *-ia*] The alleged ability to sense things that would normally be beyond the range of the senses. (tel' es THEE zhuh)

path/o, -pathy   disease, feeling

allopathy [*allo, other* + *-pathy, disease*] The practice of treating a disease or condition by using an agent that produces the opposite effect of the disease or condition. Opposed to homeopathy (def. 1).
(uh LOP uh thee)

anthropopathism [*anthropo, human* + *path, feeling* + *-ism*] The ascription of human emotions to a nonhuman object or being. (an' thruh POP uh thiz' um)

antipathy [*anti-, against* + *-pathy, feeling*] A strong feeling of dislike. Repugnance. Aversion. See averse (def. 1). (an TIP uh thee)

apathy [*a-, without* + *-pathy, feeling*] 1.Lack of emotion or feeling. 2.Lack of interest or concern. Indifference. See lethargy. (AP uh thee)

arthropathy [*arthro, joint* + *-pathy, disease*] Any disease of the joints. (ahr THROP uh thee)

cardiomyopathy [*cardio, heart* + *myo, muscle* + *-pathy, disease*] Any disease or disorder of the heart muscle. See cardiopathy. (kahr' dee oh' meye OP uh thee)

cardiopathy [*cardio, heart* + *-pathy, disease*] Any disease, disorder, or condition of the heart. See cardiomyopathy. (kahr' dee OP uh thee)

cytopathic [*cyto, cell* + *path, disease* + *-ic*] Pertaining to or causing pathological disorders or changes in a cell. (seyet' uh PATH ik)

empathy [*em-, intensive* + *-pathy, feeling*] Sensitivity to and understanding of another person's feelings or situation. (EM puh thee)

encephalopathy [*encephalo, brain* + *-pathy, disease*] Any disease or disorder of the brain. (en sef' uh LOP uh thee)

gynecopathy [*gyneco, woman* + *-pathy, disease*] Any of several diseases peculiar to women. (jin' uh KOP uh thee)

histopathology [*histo, tissue* + *path, disease* + *-ology, study of*] The study of changes in diseased tissue. (hist' oh puh THOL uh jee)

homeopathy [*homeo, similar* + *-pathy, disease*] 1.The practice of treating a disease or condition by using a minute quantity of an agent that in much greater doses has a similar effect to that of the disease or condition. Opposed to allopathy. 2.The practice of treating a disease or condition using natural remedies rather than drugs or surgery. See naturopathy. (hoh' mee OP uh thee)

hydropathy [*hydro, water* + *-pathy, disease*] The practice of treating disease with water; particularly, a science that claims to cure all diseases by the internal and external use of water. See hydrotherapy. (heye DROP uh thee)

idiopathy [*idio-, peculiar* + *path, disease* + *-y*] Any disease or condition of unknown cause or origin. See cryptogenic. (id' ee OP uh thee)

myopathy [*myo, muscle* + *-pathy, disease*] Any disease or disorder of the muscles or muscle tissue. (meye OP uh thee)

naturopathy [*natur(e) & -pathy, disease*] A method of treating disease using natural remedies such as special diets, massage, sunlight, etc., rather than drugs or surgery. See homeopathy (def. 2). (nay' chuh ROP uh thee)

neuropathology [*neuro, nerve* + *path, disease* + *-ology, study of*] The branch of medical science dealing with the study of diseases of the nervous system. See neurophysiology and pathology. (noor' oh puh THOL uh jee)

neuropathy [*neuro, nerve* + *-pathy, disease*] A disease or disorder of the nervous system. (noo ROP uh thee)

nonpathogenic [*non-, not* + *patho, disease* + *gen, cause* + *-ic*] Not capable of causing disease. (non' path' uh JEN ik)

osteopathy [*osteo, bone* + *-pathy, disease*] A system of medical treatment and therapy that uses, but is not limited to, techniques of skeletal manipulation for the preservation and restoration of health. (os' tee OP uh thee)

parasympathetic nervous system One of two divisions of the autonomic nervous system, consisting of the cranial and sacral nerves, that works in conjunction with the sympathetic nervous system to control heart, blood vessels, glands, etc. See sympathetic nervous system and autonomic nervous system. (pehr' uh sim' puh THET ik NUR vus SIS tum)

pathetic [*path, feeling* + *-etic*] 1.Arousing pity, sympathy, compassion, etc. 2.Miserably ineffective or inadequate. (puh THET ik)

pathogen [*patho, disease* + *gen, cause*] Any disease-causing agent, especially a microorganism such as a virus or bacterium. (PATH uh jen)

pathogenesis [*patho, disease* + *-genesis, to produce*] The origin and development of a morbid or diseased condition. (path' uh JEN uh sis)

pathognomonic [*patho, disease* + *gnomon, knowledge* + *-ic*] Characteristic or indicative of a particular disease or condition. (puh thog' nuh MON ik)

pathological [*patho, disease* + *-logical*] Pertaining to, involving, or caused by a disease or disorder. (path' uh LOJ ih kul)

pathology [*path, disease* + *-ology, study of*] 1.The branch of medical science dealing with the study of the origin, nature, and development of diseases. 2.The conditions produced by a disease. (puh THOL uh jee)

pathos [*path, feeling* + *-os*] 1.A quality in literature, music, speech, or other forms of expression that arouses feelings of pity, sympathy, compassion, etc. 2.An expression of pity. (PAY thos)

phytopathogen [*phyto, plant* + *patho, disease* + *gen, cause*] An organism that causes a plant disease. (feyet' oh PATH uh jen)

phytopathology [*phyto, plant* + *path, disease* + *-ology, study of*] The branch of botany dealing with the study of plant diseases. Plant pathology. (feyet' oh puh THOL uh jee)

protopathic [*proto-, chief* + *path, feeling* + *-ic*] Pertaining to certain sensory nerves that respond only to rather gross variations in pressure, pain, heat, or cold. Opposed to epicritic. (proht' uh PATH ik)

psychopath [*psycho, mind* + *path, disease*] A person with a severe personality disorder marked by immoral and antisocial behavior. See sociopath. (SEYE kuh path')

psychopathology [*psycho, mind* + *path, disease* + *-ology, study of*] The branch of medical science dealing with the study of disorders and diseases of the mind. (seye' koh puh THOL uh jee)

psychopathy [*psycho, mind* + *-pathy, disease*] Any disease or disorder of the mind. (seye KOP uh thee)

path/o, -pathy

retinopathy [*retin(a) & -pathy, disease*] Any disease or disorder of the retina. (ret' n OP uh thee)

sociopath [*socio, social + path, feeling*] A person with an antisocial behavioral disorder marked by a disregard for moral and social responsibility. See psychopath. (SOH see uh path')

sympathetic nervous system One of two divisions of the autonomic nervous system consisting of the spinal nerves that control the heart, lungs, blood vessels, intestines, and sweat glands. See parasympathetic nervous system and autonomic nervous system. (sim' puh THET ik NUR vus SIS tum)

sympathy [*sym-, same + -pathy, feeling*] 1.Sharing and understanding another person's sorrow or trouble. 2.Mutual agreement. (SIM puh thee)

telepathy [*tele, distant + -pathy, feeling*] The alleged communication between minds by supernatural means, as by extrasensory perception. See precognition and telegnosis. (tuh LEP uh thee)

intra-, intro-   within, inward, inside, into

intraarterial [*intra-, within + arteri, artery + -al*] Occurring or located within an artery. (in' truh ahr TIHR ee ul)

intracardiac [*intra-, within + cardi, heart + -ac*] Occurring or located within the heart. (in' truh KAHR dee ak')

intracellular [*intra-, within & cellular*] Occurring or located within a cell or cells. (in' truh SEL yuh lur)

Intracoastal Waterway [*intra-, within & coastal & waterway*] A mostly inland water route extending 2500 miles along the Atlantic coast from Boston, Mass. to Brownsville, Texas. (in' truh KOH stul WAW ter way')

intracranial [*intra-, within + crani, cranium + -al*] Occurring or located within the cranium. (in' truh KRAY nee ul)

intracutaneous [*intra-, within + Ltn > cutis, skin + -aneous*] Occurring or located within or between the layers of skin. Same as intradermal. (in' truh kyoo TAY nee us)

intradermal [*intra-, within + derm, skin + -al*] Occurring or located within or between the layers of skin. (in' truh DER mul)

intrados [*intra-, inside + French > dos, back*] The inner curve of an arch. See extrados. (IN truh dos')

intragalactic [*intra-, within & galactic*] Occurring or located within the bounds of a single galaxy. (in' truh guh LAK tik)

intramolecular [*intra-, within & molecular*] Occurring or located within a molecule. (in' truh muh LEK yuh lur)

intramural [*intra-, within + Ltn > murus, wall + -al*] 1.Within the walls or boundaries of a city, college, or other institution. 2.Among the members of a single school, college, etc. Opposed to extramural. (in' truh MYOOR ul)

intramuscular [*intra-, within & muscular*] Occurring within or injected into a muscle. (in' truh MUS kyuh lur)

intranuclear [*intra-, within & nuclear*] Occurring or located within the nucleus of a cell. (in' truh NOO klee ur)

intraocular [*intra-, within + ocul, eye + -ar*] Occurring or located within the eyeball. (in' truh OK yuh lur)

intrapersonal [*intra-, within & personal*] Existing within a person's mind. (in' truh PER suh nul)

intrapsychic [*intra-, within + psych, mind + -ic*] Originating or existing within the mind. (in' truh SEYE kik)

intraspecific [*intra-, within + Ltn > specificus, species*] Occurring within or involving members of a single species. (in' truh spih SIF ik)

intrastate [*intra-, within & state*] Occurring or located within the boundaries of a state. See interstate. (in' truh STAYT)

intrauterine [*intra-, within + uter, uterus + -ine*] Occurring or located within the uterus. (in' truh YOOT ur in)

intravascular [*intra-, within & vascular*] Occurring within or administered through a blood vessel. (in' truh VAS kyuh lur)

intravenous [*intra-, within + ven, vein + -ous*] Occurring within or entering through a vein. (in' truh VEE nus)

intrinsic [*intra-, within + Ltn > secus, beside*] 1.Belonging to the essential nature of a thing. Opposed to extrinsic. 2.Belonging entirely to a body part. (in TRIN zik)

introduce [*intro-, inward + duc, to lead*] To present for the first time. (in' truh DOOS)

introgression [*intro-, into + gress, to go + -ion*] The introduction of a gene from the gene pool of one species into the gene pool of another species as a result of hybridization and subsequent backcrossing. (in' truh GRESH un)

introit [*intro-, inward + it, go*] 1.An antiphon recited or sung at the beginning of Mass in the Roman Catholic Church. 2.A psalm or hymn sung at the beginning of a worship service in the Anglican Church. (IN troh' it)

introject [*intro-, inward + ject, to throw*] To unconsciously incorporate another person's attitudes or ideas, or the characteristics of an inanimate object, into one's own personality. (in' truh JEKT)

intromit [*intro-, inward + mit, to send*] 1.To cause or allow to enter. Admit. 2.To insert. (in' truh MIT)

introrse [*intro-, inward + vers, turn*] Turned inward or toward the axis. Opposed to extrorse. (in TRORS)

introspect [*intro-, inward + spect, to look*] To examine one's own thoughts, feelings, and emotions. (in' truh SPEKT)

introvert [*intro-, inward + vert, turn*] A person who directs his interests, thoughts, and feelings primarily upon himself. Opposed to extrovert. See ambivert. (IN truh vurt')

extra-, extro-   outside, beyond

extra [*extra-, beyond*] Beyond what is usual. (EKS truh)

extracellular [*extra-, outside & cellular*] Occurring or located outside a cell. (eks' truh SEL yuh lur)

extracranial [*extra-, outside + crani, cranium + -al*] Occurring or located outside the cranium. (eks' truh KRAY nee ul)

extracurricular [*extra-, outside & curricul(um) & -ar*] Falling outside the regular curriculum. (eks' truh kuh RIK yuh lur)

extrados [*extra-, outside + French > dos, back*] The outer curve of an arch. See intrados. (EKS truh dos')

extragalactic [*extra-, beyond & galactic*] Occurring or located beyond our own galaxy. (eks' truh guh LAK tik)

extrajudicial [*extra-, outside & judicial*] 1.Outside the jurisdiction of a court. 2.Outside the normal due process of law. (eks' truh joo DISH ul)

extralegal [*extra-, outside & legal*] Beyond legal authority or control. (eks' truh LEE gul)

extramarital [*extra-, outside & marital*] Pertaining to sexual relations outside the marriage. (eks' truh MEHR ih tul)

extramundane [*extra-, beyond + Ltn > mundus, world + -ane*] Occurring or existing beyond the physical world. (eks' truh mun' DAYN)

extramural [*extra-, outside + Ltn > murus, wall + -al*] 1.Outside the walls or boundaries of a city, college, or other institution. 2.Among the members of more than one school, college, etc. Opposed to intramural. (eks' truh MYOOR ul)

extraneous [*extra-, outside + -aneous*] 1.Coming from the outside. Not belonging. External. 2.Not pertinent or related to what is being considered. (eks TRAY nee us)

extranuclear [*extra-, outside & nuclear*] Occurring or located outside the nucleus of a cell. (eks' truh NOO klee ur)

extraordinary [*extra-, beyond & ordinary*] Beyond the ordinary. (eks TRORD n ehr' ee)

extrapolate [*extra-, outside & (inter)polate*] 1.To estimate the value of a variable outside its known range. See interpolate (def. 2). 2.To estimate an unknown from something that is known. (eks TRAP uh layt')

extrasensory [*extra-, beyond & sensory*] Occurring beyond the normal function of the senses. (eks' truh SEN suh ree)

extrasystole [*extra-, outside + sys, together + Grk > stellein, to place*] A premature contraction of the heart resulting from any of various stimuli. (eks' truh SIS tuh lee)

extraterrestrial [*extra-, beyond + terr, earth + -ial*] Occurring, existing, or originating beyond the limits of the earth. (eks' truh tuh RES tree ul)

extraterritorial [*extra-, beyond & territor(y) & -ial*] Located or taking place beyond territorial boundaries. (eks' truh tehr' uh TOR ee ul)

extrauterine [*extra-, outside + uter, uterus + -ine*] Occurring or located outside the uterus. (eks' truh YOOT ur in)

extravagant [*extra-, beyond + Ltn > vagari, to wander*] Going beyond reasonable bounds or limits. (eks TRAV uh gunt)

extravasation [*extra-, outside + vas, vessel + -ation*] The leakage of fluid, such as blood, from a vessel into the surrounding tissues. (eks trav' uh SAY shun)

extravascular [*extra-, outside & vascular*] Occurring or located outside the vascular system. (eks' truh VAS kyuh lur)

extravehicular [*extra-, outside & vehicular*] Occurring or performed outside a spacecraft. (eks' truh vee HIK yuh lur)

extravert [*extra-, outside + vert, turn*] A person who directs his interests, thoughts, and feelings primarily outside himself. Same as extrovert. (EKS truh vurt')

extrinsic [*extra-, outside + Ltn > secus, beside*] Not belonging to the essential nature of a thing. Opposed to intrinsic (def. 1). (eks TRIN zik)

extrorse [*extro-, outside + vers, turn*] Turned outward or away from the axis. Opposed to introrse. (eks TRORS)

extrovert [*extro-, outside + vert, turn*] A person who directs his interests, thoughts, and feelings primarily outside himself. Opposed to introvert. See ambivert. (EKS truh vurt')

fid   faith

affidavit [*ad-, to + fid, faith*] A written statement given under oath before an authorized officer. (af' ih DAY vit)

bona fide [*Ltn > bonus, good & fid, faith*] Literally, "in good faith." Performed sincerely without intent to deceive. Genuine. Sincere. Opposed to mala fide. (BOH nuh feyed')

confidant [*con-, together + fid, faith + -ant*] A person with whom private affairs or secrets are shared. (KON fuh dant')

confide [*con-, together + fid, faith*] 1.To reveal with expectations of trust and secrecy. 2.To show faith and confidence. Trust. (kun FEYED)

diffident [*dif-, away + fid, faith + -ent*] Lacking faith and confidence in oneself. Shy. Timid. (DIF uh dent')

fidelity [*fid, faith + -ity*] 1.Faithfulness. 2.Strict adherence to promises, duties, truth, etc. 3.The degree of accuracy that electronic equipment is able to attain in reproducing an audio or video signal. (fih DEL ih tee)

fiduciary [*fid, faith + -ary*] A trustee. (fih DOO shee ehr' ee)

infidel [*in-, without + fid, faith*] 1.One who denies the existence of God. See agnostic and atheist. 2.A non-believer in a particular religion, especially Islam or Christianity. 3.A non-believer in a particular theory, doctrine, principle, etc. (IN fih del')

infidelity [*in-, without + fid, faith + -ity*] 1.Lack of faith in a particular religion. 2.Lack of faithfulness to a spouse. Adultery. (in' fih DEL ih tee)

mala fide [*mal-, bad & fid, faith*] Literally, "in bad faith." Acting in bad faith. Opposed to bona fide. (MAL uh feyed')

perfidy [*per-, through + fid, faith + -y*] Deliberate breach of trust or faith. Treachery. Disloyalty. (PER fih dee)

fus   pour

circumfuse [*circum-, around + fus, pour*] 1.To pour or spread around. 2.To surround, as with a fluid. (sur' kum FYOOZ)

confuse [*con-, together + fus, pour*] To make uncertain or indistinct. Bewilder. Perplex. See perplex (def. 1). (kun FYOOZ)

defuse [*de-, away + fus, pour*] To make less tense, potent, or dangerous. (dee FYOOZ)

diffuse [*dif-, away + fus, pour*] 1.To pour out and allow to spread, as a fluid. (dih FYOOZ {verb}) 2.Using more words than necessary. Wordy. Verbose. See verbose, verbalize (def. 3), and prolix. (dih FYOOS {adjective})

effuse [*ef-, out + fus, pour*] To pour or spread out. Emanate. Exude. (ih FYOOZ)

fuse [*fus, pour*] To liquefy or melt by heating. (fyooz)

infuse [*in-, in + fus, pour*] To put into as if by pouring, as an idea, loyalty, resentment, etc. Instill. Inspire. (in FYOOZ)

interfuse [*inter-, between + fus, pour*] 1.To combine by blending or mixing. 2.To pour upon or pass into or through. (in' ter FYOOZ)

perfuse [*per-, through* + *fus, pour*] To spread over or through with liquid, moisture, light, color, etc. (per FYOOZ)

profuse [*pro-, forth* + *fus, pour*] 1.Very or excessively generous. 2.Given or done freely and abundantly. 3.Plentiful. Abundant. Copious. See prodigal. (pruh FYOOS)

refuse [*re-, back* + *fus, pour*] To decline to accept, give, do, or submit to something. (rih FYOOZ)

suffuse [*sub-, under* + *fus, pour*] 1.To spread from within with liquid, light, color, etc. 2.To overspread with liquid, light, color, etc. (suh FYOOZ)

transfuse [*trans-, across* + *fus, pour*] 1.To cause to flow from one source to another. 2.To transfer blood, blood plasma, etc., into the vessels of a person or animal. (trans FYOOZ)

gam/o, gameto, -gamy
marriage, sexual union, gamete, united

agamete [*a-, without & gamete*] An asexual reproductive cell that progresses directly into an adult, as a spore. (ay GAM eet)

agamic [*a-, without* + *gam, sexual union* + *-ic*] Reproducing without sexual union. Asexual. Opposed to gamic. (ay GAM ik)

agamogenesis [*a-, without* + *gamo, sexual union* + *-genesis, production*] Asexual reproduction by budding, fission, cell division, etc. See monogenesis (def. 2). (ay gam' uh JEN uh sis)

allogamy [*allo, other* + *-gamy, sexual union*] Cross-fertilization in plants and certain animals. Opposed to autogamy. (uh LOG uh mee)

anisogamous [*aniso-, not equal* + *gam, sexual union* + *-ous*] Characterized by the fusion of heterogametes. Same as heterogamous (def. 1). (an' eye SOG uh mus)

anisogamy [*aniso-, not equal* + *-gamy, sexual union*] The union of two dissimilar gametes, as in form, size, or function. See isogamy. (an' eye SOG uh mee)

apogamy [*apo-, away* + *-gamy, sexual union*] A situation in which the sporophyte develops directly from the gametophyte without fertilization, as in pteridophytes. See apospory. (uh POG uh mee)

autogamy [*auto-, self* + *-gamy, sexual union*] 1.Self-fertilization in plants. 2.Self-fertilization in certain fungi and protozoans in which the pronuclei of a divided cell nucleus unite. Opposed to allogamy. (aw TOG uh mee)

bigamy [*bi-, two* + *-gamy, marriage*] The practice of being married to two people at the same time. See monogamy and polygamy. (BIG uh mee)

cleistogamous [*cleisto, closed* + *gam, sexual union* + *-ous*] Pertaining to flowers that produce closed, self-pollinating buds, as the violet. (kleye STOG uh mus)

cryptogam [*crypto, hidden* + *gam, sexual union*] An obsolete term for any plant that does not produce flowers or seeds. So named from the less prominent reproductive organs of the plants in this group. (KRIP tuh gam')

deuterogamy [*deutero, second* + *-gamy, marriage*] A second legal marriage after the divorce or death of the first spouse. Same as digamy. (doot' uh ROG uh mee)

dichogamous [*dicho, apart* + *gam, sexual union* + *-ous*] Pertaining to flowers having stamens and pistils maturing at different times, thus preventing self-pollination and insuring cross-pollination. Opposed to homogamous (def. 2). (deye KOG uh mus)

digamy [*di-, two* + *-gamy, marriage*] A second legal marriage after the divorce or death of the first spouse. (DIG uh mee)

endogamy [*endo-, inside* + *-gamy, marriage*] 1.The custom of marrying within one's clan, tribe, etc. 2.Self-pollination. Opposed to exogamy. (en DOG uh mee)

exogamy [*exo-, outside* + *-gamy, marriage*] 1.The custom of marrying outside one's clan, tribe, etc. 2.Cross-pollination. Opposed to endogamy. (eks OG uh mee)

gamete [*gam, sexual union* + *-ete*] A mature male or female sex cell capable of uniting with another gamete to form a zygote, which develops into a new individual. The male gamete is commonly called a spermatozoon, and the female gamete is commonly called an ovum. See spermatozoon and ovum. (GAM eet)

gametocyte [*gameto, gamete* + *-cyte, cell*] A male or female germ cell that produces gametes through division by meiosis. See spermatocyte and oocyte. (guh MEET uh seyet')

gametogenesis [*gameto, gamete* + *-genesis, formation*] The formation of gametes. (guh meet' oh JEN uh sis)

gametophore [*gameto, gamete* + *-phore, to bear*] A plant structure bearing the gamete-producing organs. (guh MEET uh for')

gametophyte [*gameto, gamete* + *-phyte, plant*] In plants reproducing by alternation of generations, the gamete-producing haploid generation that reproduces sexually by eggs and sperm. This generation produces a zygote which develops into a sporophyte. See sporophyte and alternation of generations. (guh MEET uh feyet')

gamic [*gam, sexual union* + *-ic*] Requiring fertilization in reproduction. Sexual. Opposed to agamic. (GAM ik)

gamogenesis [*gamo, sexual union* + *-genesis, production*] Sexual reproduction by the union of male and female gametes. (gam' uh JEN uh sis)

gamopetalous [*gamo, united & petal & -ous*] Having united or partially united petals. See polypetalous. (gam' uh PET l us)

gamophobia [*gamo, marriage* + *-phobia, fear*] Abnormal fear of marriage. (gam' uh FOH bee uh)

gamosepalous [*gamo, united & sepal & -ous*] Having united or partially united sepals. See polysepalous. (gam' uh SEP uh lus)

heterogamete [*hetero, different & gamete*] A gamete that unites with another of different form, size, or sex chromosome content. See isogamete. (het' uh roh GAM eet)

heterogamous [*hetero, different* + *gam, sexual union* + *-ous*] 1.Characterized by the fusion of heterogametes. 2.Bearing flowers that are sexually different or of different types. Opposed to homogamous (def. 1). (het' uh ROG uh mus)

heterogamy [*hetero, different* + *-gamy, sexual union*] 1.Alternation of generations. See alternation of generations. 2.The union of two dissimilar gametes, as in form, size, or function. Same as anisogamy. See oogamy. (het' uh ROG uh mee)

hologamous [*holo, whole + gam, gamete + -ous*] Pertaining to an organism whose reproductive cells are similar in form and size to its somatic cells. (huh LOG uh mus)

homogamous [*homo, same + gam, sexual union + -ous*] 1.Bearing flowers that are sexually the same. Opposed to heterogamous (def. 2). 2.Pertaining to flowers having stamens and pistils maturing at the same time, thus making self-pollination possible. Opposed to dichogamous. (hoh MOG uh mus)

hypergamy [*hyper-, above + -gamy, marriage*] Marrying a person of a higher social class or status. (heye PER guh mee)

isogamete [*iso-, same & gamete*] A gamete that unites with another of the same form and size. See heterogamete. (eye' soh GAM eet)

isogamy [*iso-, same + -gamy, sexual union*] The union of two similar gametes, as in certain algae. See anisogamy. (eye SOG uh mee)

karyogamy [*karyo, nucleus + -gamy, sexual union*] The fusion of pronuclei during fertilization. See synkaryon. (kehr' ee OG uh mee)

macrogamete [*macro-, large & gamete*] The usually female and larger of two conjugating gametes in a heterogamous organism. See microgamete. (mak' roh GAM eet)

megagametophyte [*mega-, large & gametophyte*] A female gametophyte in heterosporous plants that is produced by a megaspore. See microgametophyte, gametophyte, and megaspore. (meg' uh guh MEET uh feyet')

microgamete [*micro-, small & gamete*] The usually male and smaller of two conjugating gametes in a heterogamous organism. See macrogamete. (meye' kroh GAM eet)

microgametophyte [*micro-, small & gametophyte*] A male gametophyte in heterosporous plants that is produced by a microspore. See megagametophyte, gametophyte, and microspore. (meye' kroh guh MEET uh feyet')

misogamist [*miso, to hate + gam, marriage + -ist*] One who hates marriage. (mih SOG uh mist)

misogamy [*miso, to hate + -gamy, marriage*] Hatred of marriage. (mih SOG uh mee)

monogamy [*mono-, one + -gamy, marriage*] The practice of being married to only one person at a time. See bigamy and polygamy. (muh NOG uh mee)

oogamy [*oo, egg + -gamy, sexual union*] Reproduction characterized by the union of a large nonmotile egg and a small motile sperm. See heterogamy (def. 2). (oh OG uh mee)

polygamy [*poly, many + -gamy, marriage*] The practice of being married to more than one person at the same time. See monogamy and bigamy. (puh LIG uh mee)

syngamy [*syn-, together + -gamy, sexual union*] Fertilization by the union of two gametes. (SIN guh mee)

gastr/o   stomach

epigastrium [*epi-, over + gastr, stomach + -ium*] The uppermost of the three middle regions of the abdomen, between the right hypochondriac region and the left hypochondriac region. See hypogastrium and hypochondrium. (ep' ih GAS tree um)

gastrectomy [*gastr, stomach + ec, out + -tomy, to cut*] Surgical removal of all or part of the stomach. (ga STREK tuh mee)

gastric [*gastr, stomach + -ic*] Pertaining to the stomach. (GAS trik)

gastrin [*gastr, stomach + -in*] A hormone secreted by the pylorus during digestion that stimulates the release of gastric juices. (GAS trin)

gastritis [*gastr, stomach + -itis, inflammation*] Inflammation of the mucous membrane of the stomach. (gas TREYE tis)

gastroenteritis [*gastro, stomach + enter, intestine + -itis, inflammation*] Inflammation of the mucous membrane of the stomach and intestines. (gas' troh ent' uh REYE tis)

gastroenterology [*gastro, stomach + enter, intestine + -ology, study of*] The branch of medical science dealing with the study of the functions and diseases of the stomach and intestines. (gas' troh ent' uh ROL uh jee)

gastrointestinal [*gastro, stomach & intestin(e) & -al*] Pertaining to the stomach and intestines. (gas' troh in TES tuh nul)

gastrolith [*gastro, stomach + lith, stone*] A calculus formed in the stomach. (GAS truh lith')

gastrology [*gastr, stomach + -ology, study of*] The branch of medical science dealing with the study of the functions and diseases of the stomach. (gas TROL uh jee)

gastronomy [*gastro, stomach + -nomy, system of laws*] The art or practice of good eating. (gas TRON uh mee)

gastropod [*gastro, stomach + pod, foot*] Any of a large class of mollusks, including snails, slugs, limpets, etc., that move using a muscular ventral foot. (GAS truh pod')

gastroscope [*gastro, stomach + -scope, to examine*] An endoscope for examining the interior of the stomach. (GAS truh skohp')

gastrotrich [*gastro, stomach + trich, hair*] Any of various minute aquatic animals with a wormlike body that move by means of ventral cilia. (GAS truh trik')

gastrovascular [*gastro, stomach & vascular*] Pertaining to a canal or cavity that performs both digestive and circulatory functions, as in cnidarians. (gas' troh VAS kyuh lur)

gastrula [*gastr, stomach + -ule, small + -a*] An early stage of embryonic development following the blastula stage in which the embryo consists of two germ cell layers, a primitive digestive cavity called the archenteron, and an opening into the archenteron called the blastopore. The outer cell layer is the ectoderm and the inner cell layer later differentiates into the endoderm and mesoderm. See blastula, archenteron, and blastopore. (GAS troo luh)

hypogastrium [*hypo-, below + gastr, stomach + -ium*] The lowest of the three middle regions of the abdomen, between the right inguinal region and the left inguinal region. See epigastrium and hypochondrium. (heye' puh GAS tree um)

gen/o, -gene, -genesis
**production, formation, generation, origin,
cause, birth, kind, race**

abiogenesis [*a-, without* + *bio, living organisms* + *-genesis, generation*] The now discredited theory that living organisms can be spontaneously generated directly from nonliving matter. Opposed to biogenesis. (ay' beye' oh JEN uh sis)

acrogen [*acro, tip* + *gen, origin*] A flowerless plant having a stem with its growing point at the apex, as a moss or fern. (AK ruh jen)

agamogenesis [*a-, without* + *gamo, sexual union* + *-genesis, production*] Asexual reproduction by budding, fission, cell division, etc. See monogenesis (def. 2). (ay gam' uh JEN uh sis)

agenesis [*a-, without* + *-genesis, formation*] Lack of development or absence of an organ or other body part. (ay JEN uh sis)

agglutinogen [*agglutin(in)* & *gen, formation*] An antigen that stimulates the formation of a specific agglutinin. (ag' loo TIN uh jen)

allergen [*aller(gy)* & *gen, cause*] Any substance that causes or is capable of causing an allergy or specific hypersensitivity. (AL ur jen)

alternation of generations The alternation of sexual and asexual reproductive forms in successive generations of the life cycle of an organism. (ahl' ter NAY shun uv jen' uh RAY shuns)

androgen [*andro, male* + *gen, formation*] Any of the steroid hormones that promote male characteristics. (AN druh jen)

androgenous [*andro, male* + *gen, production* + *-ous*] Producing male offspring only. (an DROJ uh nus)

anthropogenesis [*anthropo, man* + *-genesis, origin*] The scientific study of man's origin. (an' thruh puh JEN uh sis)

antigen [*anti(body)* & *gen, production*] Any substance that causes the production of an antibody when introduced into the body. (AN tih jen)

autogenesis [*auto-, self* + *-genesis, generation*] The now discredited theory that living organisms can be spontaneously generated directly from nonliving matter. Same as abiogenesis. (awt' oh JEN uh sis)

autogenous [*auto-, self* + *gen, generation* + *-ous*] 1.Self-generating. 2.Originating within the same organism. See heterogenous, endogenous, and exogenous. (aw TOJ uh nus)

benign [*bene-, good* & *genus (born)*] 1.Having a kind and gentle disposition. 2.Totally or nearly harmless. Not malignant. See malignant. (bih NEYEN)

biogenesis [*bio, living organisms* + *-genesis, production*] The theory that living organisms are only produced from other living organisms. Opposed to abiogenesis. (beye' oh JEN uh sis)

biogenic [*bio, living organisms* + *gen, production* + *-ic*] Essential to or produced by living organisms. (beye' oh JEN ik)

blastogenesis [*blasto, bud* + *-genesis, production*] 1.Reproduction by budding. 2.The theory that hereditary characteristics are carried from parents to offspring by germ plasm. Opposed to pangenesis. (blas' tuh JEN uh sis)

cacogenics [*caco, poor* + *gen, production* + *-ics, study of*] The biological study of the deterioration of hereditary qualities that cause degeneration in offspring. Same as dysgenics. (kak' uh JEN iks)

carcinogen [*carcino, cancer* + *gen, cause*] Any cancer-causing chemical or other agent. (kahr SIN uh jen)

cardiogenic [*cardio, heart* + *gen, origin* + *-ic*] Originating in the heart or resulting from a heart malfunction. (kahr' dee oh JEN ik)

cenogenesis [*ceno, common* + *-genesis, origin*] 1.Common descent from the same ancestral line. See polygenesis. 2.The appearance of new characteristics in response to environmental factors. See palingenesis (def. 3). (see' noh JEN uh sis)

chromogen [*chromo, pigment* + *gen, production*] 1.A substance that can be chemically converted into a dye or pigment. 2.A pigment-producing bacterium. (KROH muh jen)

collagen [*collo, glue* + *gen, production*] A fibrous protein found in bone and connective tissue that yields glue and gelatin when boiled. (KOL uh jen)

congener [*con-, together* + *gen, kind* + *-er*] One of two or more members of the same kind, group, or class, especially an animal or plant belonging to the same genus as another. (KON juh nur)

congenital [*con-, together* + *gen, birth* + *-ital*] 1.Existing at and usually prior to the time of birth, as a disease or defect. 2.Innate. Inherent. (kun JEN ih tul)

cryogen [*cryo, cold* + *gen, to produce*] A liquefied gas used to produce very low temperatures. (KREYE uh jen)

cryogenics [*cryo, cold* + *gen, to produce* + *-ics, science*] The science dealing with the production and effects of very low temperatures. (kreye' oh JEN iks)

cryptogenic [*crypto, hidden* + *gen, origin* + *-ic*] Of uncertain or unknown origin, as a disease. See idiopathy. (krip' tuh JEN ik)

cultigen [*culti(vated)* & *gen, origin*] A cultivated species of plant that has no known wild ancestor. (KUL tuh jen)

cytogenesis [*cyto, cell* + *-genesis, formation*] Cell formation and development. (seyet' oh JEN uh sis)

cytogenetics [*cyto(logy)* & *genetics*] The comparative study of heredity and variation using the principles of cytology and genetics. See cytology and genetics. (seyet' oh juh NET iks)

dermatogen [*dermato, skin* + *gen, to produce*] The outer layer of cells in embryonic plants and growing plant parts that gives rise to the epidermis. (der MAT uh jen)

diagenesis [*dia-, through* + *-genesis, formation*] The chemical and physical changes that occur during the conversion of sediment to sedimentary rock. (deye' uh JEN uh sis)

digenesis [*di-, two* + *-genesis, production*] Reproductive cycles that alternate between asexual in one generation and sexual in the next. (deye JEN uh sis)

dysgenic [*dys-, abnormal* + *gen, production* + *-ic*] Causing deterioration in the hereditary qualities of offspring. See eugenic. (dis JEN ik)

dysgenics [*dys-, abnormal* + *gen, production* + *-ics, study of*] The biological study of the deterioration of hereditary qualities that cause degeneration in offspring. Opposed to eugenics. (dis JEN iks)

ectogenous [*ecto-, outside* + *gen, formation* + *-ous*] Capable of developing and living outside the body of a host, as certain parasitic bacteria. See endobiotic. (ek TOJ uh nus)

embryogenesis [*embryo* & *-genesis, formation*] The process of embryonic formation and development. (em' bree oh JEN uh sis)

endogenous [*endo-, inside* + *gen, origin* + *-ous*] 1.Produced or originating from within. 2.Originating or developing from within the organism. See exogenous, autogenous, and heterogenous. (en DOJ uh nus)

epigene [*epi-, on* + *-gene, formation*] Formed or occurring on or near the surface of the earth. See hypogene. (EP ih jeen')

epigenesis [*epi-, after* + *-genesis, formation*] 1.The theory that the embryo develops by structural elaboration of organs and parts that do not pre-exist in the fertilized egg, rather than by preformation. 2.Alteration of the mineral content of a rock attributed to outside influences. (ep' ih JEN uh sis)

epigenous [*epi-, upon* + *gen, formation* + *-ous*] Developing or growing on the upper surface of a leaf or other plant part, as certain fungi. See hypogenous. (ih PIJ uh nus)

erogenous [*eroto, sexual desire* + *gen, to produce* + *-ous*] Pertaining to certain areas of the body that are particularly responsive to sexual stimulation. (ih ROJ uh nus)

estrogen [*estr(us)* & *gen, to produce*] Any of several natural or synthetic estrus-producing female sex hormones. (ES truh jen)

eugenic [*eu-, good* + *gen, to produce* + *-ic*] Causing improvement in the hereditary qualities of offspring. See dysgenic. (yoo JEN ik)

eugenics [*eu-, good* + *gen, to produce* + *-ics, study of*] The study of the improvement of a species, especially the human species, by genetic control of hereditary factors in breeding. Opposed to dysgenics. See euphenics. (yoo JEN iks)

exogenous [*exo-, outside* + *gen, origin* + *-ous*] 1.Originating or derived externally. 2.Originating or growing outside the organism. See endogenous, autogenous, and heterogenous. (eks OJ uh nus)

fibrinogen [*fibrin* & *gen, formation*] A protein in blood plasma that during blood clotting is converted to fibrin by the action of thrombin. (feye BRIN uh jen)

florigen [*flori, flower* + *gen, to produce*] A plant hormone produced in the leaves that stimulates buds to flower. (FLOR uh jen)

gametogenesis [*gameto, gamete* + *-genesis, formation*] The formation of gametes. (guh meet' oh JEN uh sis)

gamogenesis [*gamo, sexual union* + *-genesis, production*] Sexual reproduction by the union of male and female gametes. (gam' uh JEN uh sis)

gene [*Grk > genos, birth*] The basic functional unit of heredity that is a segment of DNA and is usually located at specific points on the chromosomes of a cell nucleus. See chromosome. (jeen)

genealogy [*Grk > genea, family* + *-logy, study of*] 1.A record of the history or descent of a family, person, group, etc. 2.The study of family histories and pedigrees. 3.A line of descent from an ancestor. Lineage. Pedigree. See pedigree. (jee' nee OL uh jee)

generate [*gen, to produce* + *-er* + *-ate*] To bring into existence. Originate. Produce. (jen' uh rayt')

generatrix [*gen, formation* + *-er* + *-trix, straight line*] A straight line whose motion generates the surface of a geometric figure. (jen' uh RAY triks)

generic [*gen, kind* + *-er* + *-ic*] 1.Pertaining to an entire kind, group, or class. General. 2.Pertaining to a biological genus. 3.Without a brand name or registered trademark. (juh NEHR ik)

genesis [*gen, origin* + *-sis*] 1.The origin or beginning of something. 2.The first book of the Old Testament. (JEN uh sis)

genetics [*gen, birth* + *-ics, study of*] The branch of biology dealing with the study of heredity and variation and the factors controlling them. (juh NET iks)

genocide [*geno, race* + *-cide, to kill*] The deliberate and systematic killing of a racial, cultural, or political group. (JEN uh seyed')

genome [*gen(e)* & *(chromos)ome*] A complete haploid set of chromosomes with its full complement of genes. (JEE nohm)

genotype [*geno, race* & *type*] 1.The genetic composition of an organism. 2.The type species of a genus. (JEN uh teyep')

genre [*gen, kind*] 1.A kind, style, or category of art, literature, etc. 2.The painting style concerned with scenes from everyday life. (ZHON ruh)

genus [*gen, kind* + *-us*] 1.A major category in the classification of organisms that ranks between a family and a species. A family consists of one or more genera, while a genus consists of one or more species. 2.A group or class of individuals or objects having common attributes. (JEE nus)

glycogen [*glyco, sugar* + *gen, formation*] A polysaccharide that is the main carbohydrate reserve in animal tissue, especially in the muscles and liver, and is converted to glucose by the body as needed. (GLEYE kuh jen)

glycogenesis [*glyco, glycogen* + *-genesis, formation*] The conversion of glucose to glycogen. See glycogenolysis and glyconeogenesis. (gleye' koh JEN uh sis)

glycogenolysis [*glyco, glycogen* + *gen, formation* & *(hydr)olysis*] The conversion of glycogen back to glucose by hydrolysis. See glycogenesis and glyconeogenesis. (gleye' koh jen OL uh sis)

glyconeogenesis [*glyco, glycogen* + *neo, new* + *-genesis, formation*] The conversion of noncarbohydrate compounds to glycogen. See glycogenesis and glycogenolysis. (gleye' koh nee' oh JEN uh sis)

hallucinogen [*hallucin(ation)* & *gen, cause*] A substance that causes hallucinations. (huh LOO suh nuh jen)

hematogenesis [*hemato, blood* + *-genesis, production*] The production and development of blood in the body. Same as hematopoiesis. (hih mat' oh JEN uh sis)

hematogenous [*hemato, blood* + *gen, production* + *-ous*] 1.Derived from or produced by the blood. 2.Disseminated through the bloodstream. (hee' muh TOJ uh nus)

hepatogenic [*hepato, liver* + *gen, origin* + *-ic*] Originating in or produced by the liver. (hep' uh toh JEN ik)

heterogeneous [*hetero, different* + *gen, kind* + *-eous*] 1.Differing in kind. 2.Composed of parts of different kinds. Mixed. Opposed to homogeneous. (het' uh roh JEE nee us)

gen/o, -gene, -genesis

heterogenesis [*hetero, other + -genesis, generation*] Alternation of generations. See alternation of generations. (het' uh roh JEN uh sis)

heterogenous [*hetero, different + gen, origin + -ous*] 1.Having a different origin. 2.Originating outside the organism. See autogenous, endogenous, and exogenous. (het' uh ROJ uh nus)

histogen [*histo, tissue + gen, formation*] A zone or region in a plant where tissue develops into specific parts of an organ. (HIST uh jen)

histogenesis [*histo, tissue + -genesis, formation*] Bodily tissue formation and development. (hist' oh JEN uh sis)

homogeneous [*homo, same + gen, kind + -eous*] 1.Of the same kind. 2.Composed of parts of the same kind. Opposed to heterogeneous. (hoh' muh JEE nee us)

homogenize [*homo, same + gen, kind + -ize*] To break up into particles of uniform size and mix evenly throughout a fluid, as the fat globules in homogenized milk. (huh MOJ uh neyez')

homogenous [*homo, similar + gen, origin + -ous*] Having structural similarities due to common origin. Opposed to homoplastic. (huh MOJ uh nus)

hydrogen [*hydro, water + gen, to produce*] A highly flammable, gaseous chemical element that combines with oxygen to form water and is the lightest of the elements. So named from the generation of water during its combustion. (HEYE druh jen)

hypogene [*hypo-, below + -gene, formation*] Formed or occurring below the surface of the earth. See epigene. (HEYE puh jeen')

hypogenous [*hypo-, under + gen, formation + -ous*] Developing or growing beneath or on the lower surface of a leaf or other plant part, as certain fungi. See epigenous. (heye POJ uh nus)

iatrogenic [*iatro, medical treatment + gen, cause + -ic*] 1.Caused by the diagnosis, comments, or medical treatment of a physician or surgeon. 2.Created as a result of medical treatment, as certain antibiotic-resistant microorganisms. (eye at' ruh JEN ik)

immunogenetics [*immuno, immunity & genetics*] The branch of genetics dealing with the study of immunity to disease in relation to heredity. See genetics. (im' yuh noh' juh NET iks)

immunogenic [*immuno, immunity + gen, to produce + -ic*] Capable of producing immunity. (im' yuh noh JEN ik)

indigenous [*Ltn > indu, in + gen, birth + -ous*] 1.Existing naturally or born in a particular environment or region. 2.Innate. Inherent. Intrinsic. (in DIJ uh nus)

isoantigen [*iso-, same & antigen*] An antigen derived from one member of a species that can cause the production of antibodies in other members of the same species, but not in itself. (eye' soh AN tih jen)

isogenous [*iso-, same + gen, origin + -ous*] In biology, of the same or similar origin, as having developed from the same cell or tissue. (eye SOJ uh nus)

ketogenesis [*keto, ketone + -genesis, production*] The metabolic production of ketone bodies. (keet' oh JEN uh sis)

lactogenic [*lacto, milk + gen, to produce + -ic*] Capable of stimulating the secretion of milk. (lak' tuh JEN ik)

malign [*mal-, ill & genus {born}*] To speak ill of. (muh LEYEN)

malignant [*mal-, bad & genus {born} & -ant*] 1.Having a dangerous or evil influence or effect. 2.Very harmful or injurious. Pernicious. See benign. (muh LIG nunt)

malinger [*mal-, ill & genus {born} & -er*] To pretend injury or illness to avoid work. (muh LING ger)

megasporogenesis [*mega-, large + sporo, spore + -genesis, production*] The production and maturation of a megaspore. See megaspore. (meg' uh spor' uh JEN uh sis)

metagenesis [*meta-, between + -genesis, generation*] Alternation of generations. See alternation of generations. (met' uh JEN uh sis)

monogenesis [*mono-, one + -genesis, origin*] 1.The belief that living organisms all originated from a single cell. 2.Asexual reproduction. See agamogenesis. (mon' uh JEN uh sis)

monogenic [*mono-, one + gen, to produce + -ic*] 1.Producing offspring of one sex only. 2.Pertaining to or controlled by a single gene. (mon' uh JEN ik)

monogenism [*mono-, one + gen, origin + -ism*] The theory that all humans have descended from one ancestral line. See polygenism. (muh NOJ uh niz' um)

morphogenesis [*morpho, form + -genesis, to produce*] Differentiation of cells and tissues to form the structure of an organism, organ, or part. (mor' fuh JEN uh sis)

mutagen [*muta(tion) & gen, cause*] A substance or agent capable of causing mutation. (MYOO tuh jen)

myogenic [*myo, muscle + gen, formation + -ic*] 1.Forming muscle tissue. 2.Produced by or originating in muscle tissue. (meye' uh JEN ik)

neogenesis [*neo, new + -genesis, formation*] Tissue regeneration. (nee' oh JEN uh sis)

nephrogenous [*nephro, kidney + gen, origin + -ous*] 1.Originating or arising in the kidney. 2.Developing from kidney tissue. (neh FROJ uh nus)

neurogenic [*neuro, nerve + gen, origin + -ic*] Originating in, caused by, or controlled by the nervous system. (noor' oh JEN ik)

nitrogen [*nitro, niter + gen, to produce*] A gaseous chemical element that makes up about 78 per cent of the volume of the atmosphere and is present in all plant and animal tissue. So named from its discovery during the analysis of nitric acid. (NEYE truh jen)

nonpathogenic [*non-, not + patho, disease + gen, cause + -ic*] Not capable of causing disease. (non' path' uh JEN ik)

ontogeny [*onto, organism + gen, formation + -y*] The origin and development of a single organism. See phylogeny and phytogenesis. (on TOJ uh nee)

oogenesis [*oo, egg + -genesis, formation*] The formation and maturation of the ovum in preparation for fertilization. (oh' uh JEN uh sis)

organogenesis [*organ & -genesis, formation*] The formation and development of bodily organs. (or' guh noh JEN uh sis)

orogeny [*oro, mountain + gen, formation + -y*] The process of mountain formation. (aw ROJ uh nee)

orthogenesis [*ortho, straight + -genesis, generation*] The now discredited theory that evolutionary change progresses in a predetermined direction independent of natural selection and other external factors. (or' thuh JEN uh sis)

oxygen [*oxy, acid + gen, formation*] A gaseous chemical element that makes up 21 per cent of the volume of the atmosphere and is essential to all plant and animal life and to nearly all combustion. So named because it was formerly believed to be the essential element in all acid formation. (OK sih jen)

palingenesis [*Grk > palin, again + -genesis, birth*] 1.Metempsychosis. See metempsychosis. 2.Regeneration. Rebirth. 3.The appearance of ancestral characteristics in successive generations. See cenogenesis (def. 2). (pal' in JEN uh sis)

pangenesis [*pan, all + -genesis, production*] The now discredited theory that hereditary characteristics are carried by very minute particles that come from individual body cells and collect in reproductive cells. Opposed to blastogenesis (def. 2). (pan JEN uh sis)

paragenesis [*para-, beside + -genesis, formation*] The order in which associated minerals crystallize in a rock or vein. (pehr' uh JEN uh sis)

parthenogenesis [*Grk > parthenos, virgin + -genesis, production*] Reproduction in which an egg develops into a new individual without undergoing fertilization or meiosis. See apomixis and amphimixis. (pahr' thuh noh JEN uh sis)

pathogen [*patho, disease + gen, cause*] Any disease-causing agent, especially a microorganism such as a virus or bacterium. (PATH uh jen)

pathogenesis [*patho, disease + -genesis, to produce*] The origin and development of a morbid or diseased condition. (path' uh JEN uh sis)

pedogenesis [*pedo, soil + -genesis, formation*] The formation of soil. (ped' uh JEN uh sis)

pepsinogen [*pepsin & gen, to produce*] The inert precursor of pepsin that is readily converted into pepsin by hydrochloric acid during digestion. (pep SIN uh jen)

pharmacogenetics [*pharmaco, drug & genetics*] The scientific study of the relationship between genetic factors and drug response. (fahr' muh koh' juh NET iks)

philoprogenitive [*philo, love & progenitive*] 1.Loving one's offspring. 2.Producing many offspring. See progenitive and polytocous. (fil' oh proh JEN ih tiv)

photogenic [*photo, light + gen, to produce + -ic*] 1.Having an attractive appearance as a subject for photography. 2.Emitting light, as certain insects or bacteria. Phosphorescent. (foht' oh JEN ik)

phylogeny [*phylo, common ancestry + gen, formation + -y*] The origin and evolutionary development of a species of organisms. See ontogeny and phytogenesis. (feye LOJ uh nee)

phytogenesis [*phyto, plant + -genesis, formation*] The origin and development of plants. See phylogeny and ontogeny. (feyet' oh JEN uh sis)

phytogenic [*phyto, plant + gen, origin + -ic*] Being of plant origin, as coal. (feyet' oh JEN ik)

phytopathogen [*phyto, plant + patho, disease + gen, cause*] An organism that causes a plant disease. (feyet' oh PATH uh jen)

plasmagene [*plasma & -gene, production*] Any structure in cytoplasm thought to determine hereditary characteristics in subsequent generations. (PLAZ muh jeen')

plasminogen [*plasmin & gen, to produce*] An inactive blood protein that is a precursor of plasmin and is found in blood plasma and other body fluids. See plasmin. (plaz MIN uh jen)

polygene [*poly, many & gene*] Any of a set of genes that act together to control a character trait, as height, weight, or skin pigmentation. (POL ee jeen')

polygenesis [*poly, many + -genesis, origin*] Descent from more than one ancestral line. See cenogenesis (def. 1) and polyphyletic. (pol' ee JEN uh sis)

polygenism [*poly, many + gen, origin + -ism*] The theory that humans have descended from more than one ancestral line. See monogenism. (puh LIJ uh niz' um)

primogenitor [*primo, first + gen, birth + -itor*] The earliest ancestor of a people, family, etc. Forefather. (preye' moh JEN ih tur)

primogeniture [*primo, first + gen, birth + -iture*] 1.The condition of being the first-born child. 2.The right of the first-born, especially the first-born son, to inherit the parents' entire estate. (preye' moh JEN ih chur')

progenitive [*pro-, forward + gen, birth + -itive*] Capable of producing offspring. Reproductive. See philoprogenitive (def. 2) and polytocous. (proh JEN ih tiv)

progenitor [*pro-, before + gen, birth + -itor*] 1.A direct ancestor in a line of descent. 2.Predecessor or originator. (proh JEN ih tur)

progeny [*pro-, forward + gen, birth + -y*] Offspring. Descendants. Children. (PROJ uh nee)

psychogenesis [*psycho, mind + -genesis, origin*] The origin and development of personality, behavior, and other mental processes. (seye' koh JEN uh sis)

psychogenic [*psycho, mind + gen, origin + -ic*] Being of mental or emotional origin. (seye' koh JEN ik)

pyogenic [*pyo, pus + gen, to produce + -ic*] Producing pus. (peye' uh JEN ik)

pyrogen [*pyro, fever + gen, cause*] Any substance that causes fever. (PEYE ruh jen)

pyrogenic [*pyro, heat + gen, to produce + -ic*] 1.Inducing or resulting from heat or fever. 2.Produced by heat, as igneous rock. (peye' roh JEN ik)

radiogenic [*radio(activity) & gen, to produce + -ic*] Produced by or resulting from radioactivity. (ray' dee oh JEN ik)

rhizogenic [*rhizo, root + gen, to produce + -ic*] Root-producing. (reye' zoh JEN ik)

saprogenic [*sapro, putrid + gen, to produce + -ic*] Resulting from or producing putrefaction or decay, as some bacteria. (sap' ruh JEN ik)

schizogenesis [*schizo, fission + -genesis, production*] Reproduction by fission. (skiz' oh JEN uh sis)

spermatogenesis [*spermato, sperm + -genesis, formation*] The formation and maturation of spermatozoa. (spur mat' uh JEN uh sis)

spermiogenesis [*spermio, sperm + -genesis, formation*] The formation and maturation of spermatozoa. Same as spermatogenesis. (spur' mee oh JEN uh sis)

sporogenesis [*sporo, spore + -genesis, production*] The formation of or reproduction by spores. (spor' uh JEN uh sis)

sui generis [*Ltn > of his, her, their, or its own kind*] One-of-a-kind. Individual. Unique. (SOO ee JEN ur is)

gen/o, -gene, -genesis

syngenesis [*syn-, together + -genesis, production*] Sexual reproduction by the union of male and female gametes. Same as gamogenesis. (sin JEN uh sis)

telegenic [*tele(vision) & gen, to produce + -ic*] Having an attractive appearance on television. (tel' uh JEN ik)

teratogenic [*terato, monster + gen, formation + -ic*] Causing abnormal fetal development, as a disease, chemical, or other agent. (tehr' uh toh JEN ik)

terrigenous [*terri, earth + gen, production + -ous*] 1.Produced by the earth. 2.Pertaining to oceanic sediment produced from land by erosion. (teh RIJ uh nus)

thermogenesis [*thermo, heat + -genesis, production*] Heat production, especially by oxidation within a human or animal body. (thur' moh JEN uh sis)

toxicogenic [*toxico, poison + gen, to produce + -ic*] Producing poisons. (toks' ih koh JEN ik)

trypsinogen [*trypsin & gen, to produce*] An inactive protein produced by the pancreas that is a precursor of trypsin. (trip SIN uh jen)

xenogenesis [*xeno, foreign + -genesis, production*] The supposed generation of offspring completely different from either parent. (zen' uh JEN uh sis)

zoogenic [*zoo, animal + gen, cause + -ic*] Originating in or caused by animals, as a disease. (zoh' uh JEN ik)

zymogen [*(en)zym(e) & gen, to produce*] A substance from which an enzyme is produced through the action of some activator. (ZEYE muh jen)

gon/o, -gony
reproduction, origination, generation

archegonium [*arche, first + gon, reproduction + -ium*] The female reproductive organ of ferns, mosses, and related plants and of most gymnosperms. See antheridium. (ahr' kuh GOH nee um)

carpogonium [*carpo, fruit + gon, reproduction + -ium*] The female egg-bearing organ in red algae from which a carpospore develops. (kahr' puh GOH nee um)

cosmogony [*cosmo, universe + -gony, origination*] The study or a theory of the origin of the universe. (koz MOG uh nee)

gonad [*gon, reproduction + -ad*] A sex gland that produces gametes. The female gonad is the ovary, and the male gonad is the testis. (GOH nad)

gonococcus [*gono, reproduction + -coccus, bacteria*] The bacterium that causes gonorrhea. (gon' uh KOK us)

gonophore [*gono, reproduction + -phore, to bear*] A stalk bearing male and female reproductive organs or parts. (GON uh for')

gonopore [*gono, reproduction & pore {small opening}*] An external reproductive aperture through which gametes are released, as in earthworms or insects. (GON uh por')

gonorrhea [*gono, reproduction + rrhea, discharge*] A sexually transmitted infectious disease caused by the gonococcus and marked by inflammation of the genital mucous membrane and a discharge of pus. (gon' uh REE uh)

heterogony [*hetero, other + -gony, generation*] Alternation of generations. See alternation of generations. (het' uh ROG uh nee)

oogonium [*oo, egg + gon, reproduction + -ium*] 1.A primitive female germ cell that gives rise to oocytes. (oogonium > oocyte > ovum) See oocyte and ovum. 2.The female reproductive organ in certain algae and fungi, containing one or more oospheres. See oosphere. (oh' uh GOH nee um)

spermatogonium [*spermato, sperm + gon, reproduction + -ium*] A primitive male germ cell that divides and gives rise to spermatocytes. (spermatogonium > spermatocyte > spermatid > spermatozoon) See spermatocyte, spermatid, and spermatozoon. (spur mat' uh GOH nee um)

telegony [*tele, distant + -gony, reproduction*] The supposed genetic influence of one sire on subsequent offspring born by the same mother to other sires. (tuh LEG uh nee)

theogony [*theo, god + -gony, origination*] An account of the origin and genealogy of the gods. (thee OG uh nee)

geo   earth

apogee [*apo-, away + geo, earth*] The point at which the orbit of the moon or a satellite is farthest from the earth. See perigee. (AP uh jee)

astrogeology [*astro, star + geo, earth + -logy, study of*] The scientific study of the origin, history, and structure of celestial bodies in the solar system. (as' troh jee OL uh jee)

biogeography [*bio, life + geo, earth + -graphy, science*] The branch of biology dealing with the study of the geographical distribution of plants and animals. See phytogeography and zoogeography. (beye' oh jee OG ruh fee)

diageotropism [*dia-, through + geo, earth + trop, turning + -ism*] The tendency of certain plants or plant parts to grow or orient themselves at right angles to the direction of the earth's gravitational force. See diatropism. (deye' uh jee OT ruh piz' um)

epigeal [*epi-, on + geo, earth + -al*] Growing on or near the surface of the ground. (ep' ih JEE ul)

geanticline [*geo, earth + anti-, against + -cline, slope*] A massive uplift in the earth's crust comparable in size to a geosyncline. See syncline, anticline, and geosyncline. (jee AN tih kleyen')

geobotany [*geo, earth + Grk > botane, plant + -y*] The branch of biology dealing with the study of the geographical distribution of plants. Same as phytogeography. (jee' oh BOT n ee)

geocentric [*geo, earth + centr, center + -ic*] 1.Pertaining to or calculated from the center of the earth. 2.Having the earth as the center. See heliocentric. (jee' oh SEN trik)

geochemistry [*geo, earth & chemistry*] The branch of geology dealing with the study of the chemical composition of the crust, water, and atmosphere of the earth. (jee' oh KEM ih stree)

geochronology [*geo, earth + chron, time + -ology, study of*] The study of the earth's age, history, developmental stages, etc. See geochronometry. (jee' oh kruh NOL uh jee)

geochronometry [*geo, earth + chrono, time + -metry, science of measuring*] The scientific measurement of geologic time, as from radioactive decay of isotopes. See geochronology. (jee' oh kruh NOM ih tree)

geode [*geo, earth* + *-ode, like*] A geomorphic rock having a hollow cavity lined with crystals. (JEE ohd)

geodesy [*geo, earth* + *Grk > daiein, to divide* + *-y*] The mathematical study of the size and shape of the earth as a whole and the location of points on its surface. (jee OD uh see)

geodynamics [*geo, earth* + *dynam, power* + *-ics, study of*] The branch of geology dealing with the study of forces within the earth. (jee' oh deye NAM iks)

geognosy [*geo, earth* + *gnos, knowledge* + *-y*] The study of the composition and structure of the earth. (jee OG nuh see)

geography [*geo, earth* + *-graphy, writing*] The descriptive study of the features and characteristics of the earth's surface. See geology. (jee OG ruh fee)

geoid [*geo, earth* + *-oid, resembling*] An imaginary view of the earth in which the entire surface is at mean sea level. (JEE oid)

geology [*geo, earth* + *-logy, science*] The science of the origin, history, composition, and structure of the earth. See geography. (jee OL uh jee)

geomagnetism [*geo, earth* & *magnetism*] 1.The earth's magnetism. 2.The scientific study of the earth's magnetism. (jee' oh MAG nuh tiz' um)

geomancy [*geo, earth* + *-mancy, divination*] Divination by means of a figure formed by throwing down a handful of earth or by means of geographical features. (JEE uh man' see)

geometric progression [*geometric* & *pro-, forward* + *gress, to step* + *-ion*] A sequence of terms, as 2, 4, 8, 16, 32 or 1, 1/2, 1/4, 1/8, 1/16, in which any two adjacent terms have the same ratio. (jee' uh MET rik pruh GRESH un)

geometry [*geo, earth* + *-metry, science of measuring*] The branch of mathematics dealing with the study of the relationships and measurement of points, lines, angles, planes, and solids in space. (jee OM ih tree)

geomorphic [*geo, earth* + *morph, form* + *-ic*] Resembling the shape of the earth. (jee' uh MOR fik)

geomorphology [*geo, earth* + *morph, form* + *-ology, study of*] The scientific study of the origin, development, and features of the earth's surface. (jee' oh mor FOL uh jee)

geophagy [*geo, earth* + *phag, to eat* + *-y*] The practice of eating earth, either from a pathological disorder or from lack of food. (jee OF uh jee)

geophone [*geo, earth* + *-phone, sound*] A seismic device for detecting vibrations in the earth. (JEE uh fohn')

geophysics [*geo, earth* & *physics*] The branch of geology dealing with the study of the physics of the earth, including geodesy, oceanography, hydrology, seismology, volcanology, meteorology, climatology, and geomagnetism. (jee' oh FIZ iks)

geophyte [*geo, earth* + *-phyte, plant*] A perennial plant having the buds below the soil surface. (JEE uh feyet')

geopolitics [*geo(graphy)* & *politics*] The study of the relationship between geographical and political factors in a region or country. (jee' oh POL ih tiks)

geoponics [*geo, earth* + *Grk > ponein, to toil* + *-ics, science*] The science of agriculture. See agriculture, aquaculture, and hydroponics. (jee' oh PON iks)

geoscience [*geo, earth* & *science*] The sciences dealing with the earth, such as geology, geophysics, and geochemistry. (jee' oh SEYE ens)

geostationary [*geo, earth* & *stationary*] Pertaining to a satellite whose orbit is approximately 23,000 miles above the earth, resulting in a rate of speed synchronous with the earth's rotation, thus making it seem to remain stationary. Same as geosynchronous. (jee' oh STAY shuh nehr' ee)

geostrophic [*geo, earth* + *Grk > strophe, turning* + *-ic*] Pertaining to the deflective force produced by the earth's rotation. (jee' oh STROF ik)

geosynchronous [*geo, earth* + *syn, same* + *chron, time* + *-ous*] Pertaining to a satellite whose orbit is approximately 23,000 miles above the earth, resulting in a rate of speed synchronous with the earth's rotation, thus making it seem to remain stationary. (jee' oh SING kruh nus)

geosyncline [*geo, earth* + *syn, together* + *-cline, slope*] A massive depression in the earth's crust that varies in form, but is usually linear and consists of volcanic and sedimentary rock. See syncline, anticline, and geanticline. (jee' oh SIN kleyen')

geotaxis [*geo, earth* & *taxis*] The movement of a freely moving organism in response to the earth's gravity. See geotropism. (jee' oh TAK sis)

geotectonic [*geo, earth* + *Grk > tekton, builder* + *-ic*] Pertaining to the structure, composition, and distribution of the rock masses in the earth's crust. See tectonics (def. 2). (jee' oh tek TON ik)

geothermal [*geo, earth* + *therm, heat* + *-al*] Pertaining to heat generated in the interior of the earth. (jee' oh THUR mul)

geotropism [*geo, earth* + *trop, responding to a stimulus* + *-ism*] Any growth or movement of an organism in response to the earth's gravity. See geotaxis. (jee OT ruh piz' um)

hydroponics [*hydro, water* & *(geo)ponics*] The science of growing plants by placing the roots in nutrient-rich solutions rather than soil. See agriculture, aquaculture, and geoponics. (heye' druh PON iks)

hypogeal [*hypo-, below* + *geo, earth* + *-al*] Living, growing, or situated below the surface of the earth. (heye' puh JEE ul)

hypogeum [*hypo-, under* + *geo, earth* + *-um*] 1.An underground vault or chamber, especially in an ancient building. 2.The part of a building below the ground level. (heye' puh JEE um)

paleogeography [*paleo, ancient* + *geo, earth* + *-graphy, science*] The scientific study of the geographic features of the earth as they existed in ancient times. (pay' lee oh' jee OG ruh fee)

perigee [*peri-, around* + *geo, earth*] The point at which the orbit of the moon or a satellite is nearest the earth. See apogee. (PEHR ih jee)

phytogeography [*phyto, plant* + *geo, earth* + *-graphy, science*] The branch of biology dealing with the study of the geographical distribution of plants. See biogeography and zoogeography. (feyet' oh jee OG ruh fee)

zoogeography [*zoo, animal* + *geo, earth* + *-graphy, science*] The branch of biology dealing with the study of the geographical distribution of animals. See biogeography and phytogeography. (zoh' uh jee OG ruh fee)

terr, terra, terri

terr, terra, terri   earth, land

circumterrestrial [*circum-, around* + *terr, earth* + *-ial*] Revolving around or surrounding the earth. See circumsolar and circumlunar. (sur' kum tuh RES tree ul)

extraterrestrial [*extra-, beyond* + *terr, earth* + *-ial*] Occurring, existing, or originating beyond the limits of the earth. (eks' truh tuh RES tree ul)

extraterritorial [*extra-, beyond & territor(y) & -ial*] Located or taking place beyond territorial boundaries. (eks' truh tehr' uh TOR ee ul)

mediterranean [*medi, middle* + *terr, earth* + *-an* + *-ean*] Almost completely surrounded by dry land. (med' ih tuh RAY nee un)

Mediterranean [*medi, middle* + *terr, earth* + *-an* + *-ean*] Pertaining to the Mediterranean Sea or the countries around it. (med' ih tuh RAY nee un)

parterre [*French > par terre, on the ground*] 1.An ornamental flower garden with paths between beds of different shapes and sizes. 2.The part of the main floor of a theater located behind the parquet and under the balcony. Parquet circle. (pahr TEHR)

semiterrestrial [*semi-, partly & terrestrial*] Often found on land, but not entirely terrestrial, as most amphibians. See semiaquatic (def. 2) and amphibian (def. 1). (sem' ee tuh RES tree ul)

subterranean [*sub-, under* + *terr, earth* + *-an* + *-ean*] 1.Existing, situated, or operating beneath the earth's surface. Underground. 2.Existing or operating in secret. (sub' tuh RAY nee un)

terra alba [*terra, earth & Ltn > alba, white*] Any of various white mineral substances, as gypsum, pipeclay, or magnesia. (TEHR uh AL buh)

terra cotta [*terra, earth & Italian > cotta, baked*] 1.A hard, brownish-red, glazed or unglazed earthenware, used for pottery, sculpture, building construction, etc. 2.A brownish-orange color. (TEHR uh KOT uh)

terra firma [*terra, earth & Ltn > firma, solid*] Firm or solid ground. Dry land. (TEHR uh FUR muh)

terra incognita [*terra, land & in-, without + cogn, knowledge*] 1.An unknown land or territory. 2.An unexplored or unknown field of knowledge. (TEHR uh in' kog NEET uh)

terrace [*terra, land*] 1.A level area next to a house, serving as an outdoor living area. 2.A raised piece of land with the top leveled. (TEHR us)

terrain [*terra, land*] A tract of land, especially with regard to its physical features. See topography (def. 2). (tuh RAYN)

terrane [*terra, earth*] 1.A series of related rock formations. 2.An area where a particular rock or group of rocks is prevalent. (tuh RAYN)

terraqueous [*terr, land + aqua, water + -eous*] Composed of both land and water, as the earth. (tehr AY kwee us)

terrarium [*terr, land & (viv)arium*] A place, especially a small glass enclosure, for keeping small land animals and plants. See aquarium and vivarium. (tuh REHR ee um)

terre-verte [*terr, earth + French > verte, green*] Any of several soft green earths used by artists as a pigment. (TEHR vurt)

terrene [*terr, earth + -ene*] Pertaining to the earth. Earthly. Worldly. (tuh REEN)

terreplein [*terr, earth + Ltn > plenus, full*] A level space behind a parapet where heavy guns are mounted. (TEHR uh playn')

terrestrial [*terr, earth + -ial*] 1.Pertaining to the earth or its inhabitants. 2.Pertaining to land, as distinct from water or air. 3.Living, growing, or occurring on land. Not aerial, aquatic, or arboreal. See aerial (def. 2), aquatic, and arboreal (def. 2). (tuh RES tree ul)

terricolous [*terri, earth + -colous, inhabiting*] Living on or in the ground. See terrestrial (def. 3). (teh RIK uh lus)

terrier [*terr, earth + -ier*] Any of various breeds of usually small dogs originally used by hunters to dig for and drive out animals that live underground. (TEHR ee ur)

terrigenous [*terri, earth + gen, production + -ous*] 1.Produced by the earth. 2.Pertaining to oceanic sediment produced from land by erosion. (teh RIJ uh nus)

territory [*terri, land + -ory*] 1.A large tract of land. Region. 2.A geographical area under the jurisdiction of a nation, state, sovereign, etc. (TEHR ih tor' ee)

gon, gonio   angle

agonic [*a-, not + gon, angle + -ic*] Not having or forming an angle. (ay GON ik)

agonic line [*a-, not + gon, angle + -ic & line*] A line on a map connecting points on the earth's surface with zero magnetic declination. See isogonal line and isoclinic line. (ay GON ik leyen)

amblygonite [*Grk > amblys, obtuse + gon, angle + -ite, mineral*] A variously colored crystalline mineral that consists of basic lithium aluminum and produces crystals suitable as gemstones. So named for the obtuse angle at which it cleaves. (am BLIG uh neyet')

decagon [*deca, ten + gon, angle*] A closed plane figure with ten angles and ten sides. (DEK uh gon')

diagonal [*dia-, through + gon, angle + -al*] A straight line going through the vertices of any two nonadjacent angles of a polygon or through any two vertices not in the same face of a polyhedron. (deye AG uh nul)

dodecagon [*dodeca-, twelve + gon, angle*] A closed plane figure with twelve angles and twelve sides. (doh DEK uh gon')

goniometer [*gonio, angle + meter, to measure*] 1.An instrument for measuring angles. 2.An instrument for determining the direction of a radio signal. Automatic direction finder. (goh' nee OM et er)

gonion [*gon, angle + -ion*] The location on the angle of the lower jaw, or mandible, that is at the most inferior, posterior, and lateral point. (GOH nee on')

hendecagon [*hendeca-, eleven + gon, angle*] A closed plane figure with eleven angles and eleven sides. (hen DEK uh gon')

heptagon [*hepta-, seven + gon, angle*] A closed plane figure with seven angles and seven sides. (HEP tuh gon')

hexagon [*hexa-, six + gon, angle*] A closed plane figure with six angles and six sides. (HEKS uh gon')

isogon [*iso-, equal + gon, angle*] A closed plane figure with all angles equal. See equilateral (def. 2). (EYE suh gon')

isogonal line [*iso-, equal + gon, angle + -al & line*] A line on a map connecting points on the earth's surface with equal magnetic declination. See isoclinic line and agonic line. (eye SOG uh nul leyen)

isogonic [*iso-, equal* + *gon, angle* + *-ic*] Having or pertaining to equal angles. (eye' suh GON ik)

nonagon [*Ltn > nonus, ninth* + *gon, angle*] A closed plane figure with nine angles and nine sides. (NON uh gon')

octagon [*octa-, eight* + *gon, angle*] A closed plane figure with eight angles and eight sides. (OK tuh gon')

orthogonal [*ortho, perpendicular* + *gon, angle* + *-al*] Pertaining to or involving right angles. (or THOG uh nul)

pentagon [*penta-, five* + *gon, angle*] A closed plane figure with five angles and five sides. (PENT uh gon')

polygon [*poly, many* + *gon, angle*] A closed plane figure with three or more angles and sides. (POL ee gon')

quindecagon [*quin, five* + *deca, ten* + *gon, angle*] A closed plane figure with fifteen angles and fifteen sides. (kwin DEK uh gon')

tetragon [*tetra-, four* + *gon, angle*] A closed plane figure with four angles and four sides. (TET ruh gon')

trigonal [*tri-, three* + *gon, angle* + *-al*] Triangular. (TRIG uh nul)

trigonometry [*tri-, three* + *gono, angle* + *-metry, science of measuring*] The branch of mathematics dealing with the study of the applications and properties of triangles, especially right triangles. (trig' uh NOM ih tree)

trimetrogon [*tri-, three* + *metro, to measure* + *gon, angle*] A system of aerial topographic mapping and photography using three wide-angle cameras, one pointing downward and the other two pointing at 60 degree angles to it. (treye MET ruh gon')

graph, -graphy
writing, written, recording, drawing, science

aerography [*aero, air* + *-graphy, writing*] The descriptive study of the atmosphere and its phenomena. See aerology. (ehr OG ruh fee)

aerometeorograph [*aero, air* & *meteorograph*] A meteorograph modified for use in an aircraft. (ehr' oh meet' ee OR uh graf')

agrapha [*a-, not* + *graph, written* + *-a*] Sayings attributed to Jesus, but not in the Bible. See logion. (AG ruh fuh)

agraphia [*a-, not* + *graph, writing* + *-ia*] The total or partial loss of the ability to write, usually resulting from a pathological condition. See alexia, dyslexia, and dysgraphia. (ay GRAF ee uh)

allograph [*allo, variation* + *graph, writing*] 1.An alphabetic letter having a particular form or shape. 2.A signature by one person for another, as differentiated from autograph. See autograph. 3.A letter or combination of letters representing a single phoneme. (AL uh graf')

anemograph [*anemo, wind* + *graph, recording*] A device for measuring and recording wind velocity and direction. See anemometer. (uh NEM uh graf')

angiography [*angio, vessel* + *-graphy, recording*] A method of diagnosing heart disease in which x-ray photographs of blood vessels are taken after injection of a radiopaque dye. (an' jee OG ruh fee)

anthropography [*anthropo, man* + *-graphy, writing*] The branch of anthropology dealing with the descriptive study of the distribution of mankind according to physical characteristics, customs, language, etc. See anthropology. (an' thruh POG ruh fee)

arteriography [*arterio, artery* + *-graphy, recording*] X-ray examination of an artery after injection of a radiopaque dye. See venography. (ahr tihr' ee OG ruh fee)

astrophotography [*astro, star* & *photography*] The art or practice of photographing celestial objects. (as' troh fuh TOG ruh fee)

autobiography [*auto-, self* + *bio, life* + *-graphy, written*] The story of one's life written by oneself. See biography. (awt' oh beye OG ruh fee)

autograph [*auto-, self* + *graph, written*] Written or made with one's own hand, as a signature or manuscript. See allograph (def. 2). (AWT uh graf')

autoradiograph [*auto-, same* + *radio, radiation* + *graph, recording*] An x-ray photograph made by laying the film directly on the object, thus revealing the presence of radioactive material. See radiograph. (awt' oh RAY dee uh graf')

bar graph [*bar* & *graph, drawing*] A graph that uses variable length parallel bars to represent quantities of data. (BAHR graf)

barograph [*baro, pressure* + *graph, recording*] An instrument for graphically recording variations in atmospheric pressure. (BEHR uh graf')

bathythermograph [*bathy, deep* + *thermo, heat* + *graph, recording*] An instrument for recording water temperature relative to depth. (bath' uh THUR muh graf')

bibliography [*biblio, book* + *-graphy, writing*] 1.A list of writings by a particular writer, publisher, etc., or on a particular subject. 2.A list of sources used by an author in the production of a text. (bib' lee OG ruh fee)

biogeography [*bio, life* + *geo, earth* + *-graphy, science*] The branch of biology dealing with the study of the geographical distribution of plants and animals. See phytogeography and zoogeography. (beye' oh jee OG ruh fee)

biography [*bio, life* + *-graphy, written*] The story of one's life written by another person. See autobiography. (beye OG ruh fee)

bolograph [*Grk > bole, ray* + *graph, recording*] A graphic recording of the radiant energy variations generated by a bolometer. See bolometer. (BOH luh graf')

cacography [*caco, poor* + *-graphy, writing*] 1.Illegible handwriting. See calligraphy. 2.Incorrect spelling. See orthography. (kuh KOG ruh fee)

calligraphy [*calli, beautiful* + *-graphy, writing*] 1.The art of beautiful handwriting. See cacography (def. 1). 2.Handwriting, or penmanship, in general. See chirography. (kuh LIG ruh fee)

cardiograph [*cardio, heart* + *graph, recording*] An instrument for graphically recording the movements of the heart. (KAHR dee oh graf')

cartography [*French > carte, map* + *-graphy, drawing*] The art of map making. (kahr TOG ruh fee)

chalcography [*chalco, copper* + *-graphy, drawing*] The art or technique of engraving on copper, steel, or brass. (kal KOG ruh fee)

chirography [*chiro, hand* + *-graphy, writing*] The art, style, or skill of handwriting. Penmanship. See calligraphy (def. 2). (keye ROG ruh fee)

graph, -graphy

choreography [*Grk > choreia, dance + -graphy, writing*] 1.The art of composing and arranging techniques and movements for ballets and other dances. 2.The art of dancing. (kor' ee OG ruh fee)

chorography [*Grk > choros, region + -graphy, drawing*] 1.The technique of systematically mapping an area or region. 2.A map or description of a specific area or region. (kuh ROG ruh fee)

chromolithography [*chromo, color + litho, stone + -graphy, recording*] The process of producing colored pictures from a set of stone, aluminum, or zinc plates using lithography. See lithography. (kroh' moh lith OG ruh fee)

chronograph [*chrono, time + graph, recording*] 1.An instrument for measuring and recording brief time intervals, as the duration of the occurrence of an event. 2.An instrument for measuring time intervals. Stopwatch. See chronoscope and chronometer. (KRON uh graf')

cinematography [*kinemato, motion + -graphy, recording*] The art, science, or process of motion picture making. (sin' uh muh TOG ruh fee)

coronagraph [*corona & graph, recording*] An instrument for photographing and observing the sun's corona at times other than during a solar eclipse. (kuh ROH nuh graf')

cosmography [*cosmo, universe + -graphy, science*] 1.The study of the structure and composition of nature, including astronomy, geography, and geology. 2.The descriptive study of the universe. See cosmology. (koz MOG ruh fee)

cryptography [*crypto, secret + -graphy, writing*] The art or science of writing and deciphering secret codes. See cryptanalysis. (krip TOG ruh fee)

crystallography [*crystallo, crystal + -graphy, science*] The science dealing with the structure, form, and classification of crystals. (kris' tuh LOG ruh fee)

dactylography [*dactylo, finger + -graphy, science*] The scientific study of fingerprints for the purpose of identification. (dak' tuh LOG ruh fee)

demographics [*demo, people + graph, recording + -ics, knowledge*] The statistical data of human populations, used to identify age, sex, education, income, etc. (dem' uh GRAF iks)

demography [*demo, people + -graphy, science*] The study of vital statistics, density, growth, etc., of human populations. (dih MOG ruh fee)

diagraph [*dia-, across + graph, drawing*] An instrument for making scaled drawings. (DEYE uh graf')

Dictograph [*dict, speech + graph, recording*] Trademark for a device for reproducing or recording telephone conversations. (DIK tuh graf')

digraph [*di-, two + graph, writing*] 1.A combination of two contiguous letters representing a single speech sound, as the "ph" in *phone*. See trigraph and diphthong. 2.A combination of two overlapping characters having a special sound or meaning. (DEYE graf)

discography [*disco, disk & (biblio)graphy*] 1.The cataloging and analysis of phonograph records. 2.A complete list of the recordings made by a particular artist or composer. (dis KOG ruh fee)

dysgraphia [*dys-, impaired + graph, writing + -ia*] Impairment of the ability to write, usually resulting from a brain lesion. See dyslexia, alexia, and agraphia. (dis GRAF ee uh)

electrocardiograph [*electro, electric + cardio, heart + graph, recording*] An instrument for graphically recording small electric currents originating in the heart. (ih lek' troh KAHR dee uh graf')

electroencephalograph [*electro, electric + encephalo, brain + graph, recording*] An instrument for graphically recording small electric currents in the brain. (ih lek' troh en SEF uh luh graf')

electromyograph [*electro, electric + myo, muscle + graph, recording*] An instrument for graphically recording small electric currents in functioning skeletal muscles, used in diagnosing and treating muscle and nerve disorders. (ih lek' troh MEYE uh graf')

encephalograph [*encephalo, brain + graph, recording*] An x-ray photograph of the brain taken after the cerebrospinal fluid has been removed and replaced with air. (en SEF uh luh graf')

epigraph [*epi-, on + graph, writing*] 1.An inscription on a statue, monument, building, etc. 2.A brief quotation preceding the text of a book, chapter, or other literary work to introduce the theme. (EP ih graf')

epigraphy [*epi-, on + -graphy, writing*] The scientific study and interpretation of inscriptions, especially ancient inscriptions. (ih PIG ruh fee)

ergograph [*ergo, work + graph, recording*] An instrument for measuring and recording a muscle's work capacity while under exertion. (UR guh graf')

ethnography [*ethno, race + -graphy, writing*] The branch of anthropology dealing with the descriptive study of primitive human cultures. See ethnology. (eth NOG ruh fee)

filmography [*film & -graphy, writing*] A list of films classified by director, actor, or subject. (fil MOG ruh fee)

geography [*geo, earth + -graphy, writing*] The descriptive study of the features and characteristics of the earth's surface. See geology. (jee OG ruh fee)

geopolitics [*geo(graphy) & politics*] The study of the relationship between geographical and political factors in a region or country. (jee' oh POL ih tiks)

glossographer [*glosso, language + graph, writing + -er*] A writer and compiler of glossaries. (gluh SOG ruh fer)

glyptograph [*Grk > glyphein, to engrave + graph, drawing*] A design carved or engraved on a precious stone. See glyptics. (GLIP tuh graf')

graph [*graph, drawing*] Any of several diagrams, drawings, or pictures used for displaying numerical relationships. (graf)

grapheme [*graph, writing + -eme, structural unit*] 1.The smallest unit of a writing system, as a letter. 2.One or more letters representing a single phoneme. (GRAF eem)

graphemics [*graphem(e) & -ics, study of*] The branch of linguistics dealing with the study of the relations between the writing system and speech sounds of a language. (gruh FEE miks)

graphic [*graph, written + -ic*] 1.Written, described, or presented in vivid detail. 2.Pertaining to written or pictorial representation. (GRAF ik)

graphics [*graph, drawing + -ics, skill*] The art or practice of making drawings in accordance with mathematical rules, as in engineering, architecture, mathematics, etc. (GRAF iks)

graphite [*graph, writing* + *-ite, mineral*] A common mineral used in lead pencils, electrodes, and as a dry lubricant. (GRAF eyet)

graphology [*graph, writing* + *-ology, study of*] The study and analysis of handwriting, especially for determining the writer's personality and character. (graf OL uh jee)

hagiography [*hagio, holy* + *-graphy, writing*] Biographies written about saints. See hagiology (def. 2). (hag' ee OG ruh fee)

hectograph [*hecto-, hundred* + *graph, recording*] A device that uses a glycerin coated sheet of gelatin to make multiple copies of written or typed material. (HEK tuh graf')

heliograph [*helio, sun* + *graph, writing*] An apparatus for sending coded messages using sunlight reflected intermittently through a mirror by means of a shutter. (HEE lee uh graf')

heterography [*hetero, different* + *-graphy, writing*] 1.Spelling that varies from the current standard. 2.Spelling in which the same letter can represent different sounds when applied to different syllables or words, as the "g" in *give* and *gene*. (het' uh ROG ruh fee)

historiography [*Grk > historia, history* + *-graphy, writing*] The principles, practices, and techniques used in the writing of history. (hist or' ee OG ruh fee)

holograph [*holo, whole* + *graph, written*] A document written exclusively in the author's handwriting. (HOL uh graf')

homograph [*homo, same* + *graph, writing*] One of two or more words that are spelled the same, always differ in meaning, and sometimes differ in pronunciation, as *bar* (unit of pressure) and *bar* (round piece of metal). See homonym and heteronym. (HOM uh graf')

homolographic [*homo, same* + *graph, writing* + *-ic*] Showing parts in the same ratio, as of size or form. (hom' uh luh GRAF ik)

hydrography [*hydro, water* + *-graphy, science*] The scientific study of water on the earth's surface, especially navigable waterways. See hydrology. (heye DROG ruh fee)

hyetography [*hyeto, rain* + *-graphy, science*] The branch of meteorology dealing with the descriptive study of the geographical distribution of rainfall and the graphical representation of rainfall data. See hyetology. (heye' ih TOG ruh fee)

hygrograph [*hygro, moisture* + *graph, recording*] An instrument for graphically recording variations in atmospheric humidity. See hygrometer and hygroscope. (HEYE gruh graf')

hypsography [*hypso, high* + *-graphy, science*] The geographical study of the topography of the earth above sea level. See topography. (hip SOG ruh fee)

iconography [*icono, image* + *-graphy, drawing*] A symbolic representation or illustration using images, pictures, figures, etc. (eye' kuh NOG ruh fee)

ideography [*ideo-, idea* + *-graphy, drawing*] The representation of ideas or objects using graphic symbols. (id' ee OG ruh fee)

idiograph [*idio-, personal* + *graph, writing*] A private mark or signature. Trademark. Logotype. (ID ee uh graf')

isograph [*iso-, equal* + *graph, drawing*] A line on a map that shows regions with common linguistic characteristics. (EYE suh graf')

kymograph [*Grk > kyma, wave* + *graph, recording*] An instrument for measuring and recording fluid pressure and motion variations, as blood pressure, respiratory movements, etc. (KEYE muh graf')

lexicography [*lex, word* + *-ic* + *-graphy, writing*] The branch of linguistics dealing with the writing or compiling of dictionaries. See lexicology. (leks' ih KOG ruh fee)

lithography [*litho, stone* + *-graphy, recording*] The process of printing from a stone, aluminum, or zinc plate by treating the nongraphic areas of the image with an oil-based ink repellent, thus allowing the ink to adhere only to the graphic areas of the image. (lith OG ruh fee)

logography [*logo, word* + *-graphy, recording*] 1.Printing and designing with logotypes. 2.A method of longhand reporting in which several reporters take turns writing down a few words each. (loh GOG ruh fee)

macrograph [*macro-, large* + *graph, drawing*] A representation of an object, as a drawing or photograph, that is as large or larger than the object. (MAK roh graf')

magnetograph [*magneto, magnetic force* + *graph, recording*] An instrument for measuring and recording the strength and direction of a magnetic field. See magnetometer. (mag NEET uh graf')

mammography [*mammo, breast* + *-graphy, recording*] An x-ray examination of the breast that can detect tumors in the early stages of development. (muh MOG ruh fee)

metallography [*metal* & *-graphy, science*] The microscopic study of the structure and properties of metals and alloys. See metallurgy. (met' l OG ruh fee)

meteorograph [*Grk > meteoron, atmospheric phenomenon* + *graph, recording*] An instrument for making simultaneous recordings of several weather conditions such as humidity, temperature, barometric pressure, etc. (meet' ee OR uh graf')

microbarograph [*micro-, small* + *baro, pressure* + *graph, recording*] An instrument for making a continuous recording of minute changes in atmospheric pressure. (meye' kroh BEHR uh graf')

micrograph [*micro-, small* + *graph, writing*] 1.An instrument for writing or engraving minutely. 2.A photograph of a microscopic image. See photomicrograph. (MEYE kroh graf')

microphotograph [*micro-, small* & *photograph*] A small photograph that cannot be viewed without being enlarged. See photomicrograph. (meye' kroh FOH tuh graf')

microradiography [*micro-, small* & *radiograph* & *-y*] A radiographic process that produces an x-ray photograph showing minute details. See radiograph. (meye' kroh ray' dee OG ruh fee)

mimeograph [*mim, to imitate* + *graph, writing*] A printing device for making multiple copies of written, graphic, or typewritten material using an inked stencil attached to the surface of a revolving drum. (MIM ee uh graf')

monograph [*mono-, single* + *graph, writing*] A usually technical or scientific article written on a single subject. (MON uh graf')

myocardiograph [*myo, muscle* + *cardio, heart* + *graph, recording*] An instrument for graphically recording the muscular activity of the heart. (meye' uh KAHR dee uh graf')

graph, -graphy

myograph [*myo, muscle + graph, recording*] An instrument for graphically recording muscular contractions and relaxations. (MEYE uh graf')

mythography [*myth & -graphy, writing*] 1.An anthology of myths. See mythology (def. 2). 2.The use of mythical subjects and ideas in art. (mih THOG ruh fee)

nomography [*nomo, law + -graphy, science*] The art of drafting laws. See nomology (def. 1). (noh MOG ruh fee)

nosography [*noso, disease + -graphy, writing*] The systematic description and classification of diseases. (noh SOG ruh fee)

oceanography [*ocean & -graphy, science*] The scientific study of all aspects of the oceans. (oh' shuh NOG ruh fee)

odograph [*Grk > hodos, journey + graph, recording*] A device for measuring and recording distance traveled. See pedometer and odometer. (OHD uh graf')

organography [*organ & -graphy, science*] The descriptive study of plant and animal organs. See organology. (or' guh NOG ruh fee)

orography [*oro, mountain + -graphy, science*] The branch of geography dealing with the descriptive study of mountains. See orology. (aw ROG ruh fee)

orthography [*ortho, correct + -graphy, writing*] 1.Correct spelling according to established and accepted rules. See cacography (def. 2). 2.The study of spelling. (or THOG ruh fee)

oscillograph [*oscill(ation) & graph, recording*] An instrument for measuring, displaying, and recording electrical oscillations such as alternating current or voltage. See oscilloscope. (uh SIL uh graf')

paleogeography [*paleo, ancient + geo, earth + -graphy, science*] The scientific study of the geographic features of the earth as they existed in ancient times. (pay' lee oh' jee OG ruh fee)

paleography [*paleo, ancient + -graphy, writing*] The scientific study of ancient forms of writing. (pay' lee OG ruh fee)

paleontography [*pale, ancient + onto, organism + -graphy, writing*] The descriptive study of plant and animal fossils. See paleontology. (pay' lee on TOG ruh fee)

pantograph [*panto, all + graph, drawing*] An instrument for producing a map or drawing on any scale. (PANT uh graf')

paragraph [*para-, beside + graph, writing*] A distinct portion of a written document dealing with a specific point that is indented and begins a new line and is used to organize the author's thoughts and ideas and to make the document more readable. (PEHR uh graf')

petrography [*petro, rock + -graphy, writing*] The descriptive study of the classification and composition of rocks. See petrology. (puh TROG ruh fee)

phonocardiograph [*phono, sound + cardio, heart + graph, recording*] An instrument for graphically recording the sounds of the heartbeat. (foh' nuh KAHR dee uh graf')

phonograph [*phono, sound + graph, recording*] A device for reproducing prerecorded sound from a disk that is commonly referred to as a record. (FOH nuh graf')

phonography [*phono, sound + -graphy, written*] A system of speech transcription based on pronunciation. (fuh NOG ruh fee)

photography [*photo, light + -graphy, recording*] The process of recording images by the exposure of sensitized surfaces to light or other forms of radiant energy. (fuh TOG ruh fee)

photolithography [*photo(graph) & litho, stone + -graphy, recording*] A lithographic printing process that uses plates prepared from a photograph. See lithography. (foht' oh lith OG ruh fee)

photomicrograph [*photo, light + micro, small + graph, recording*] A photograph of an image taken through a microscope. See micrograph (def. 2) and microphotograph. (foht' oh MEYE kruh graf')

photozincography [*photo, light & zinc & -graphy, recording*] Photoengraving on sensitized zinc plates. (foht' oh zing KOG ruh fee)

physiography [*physio, physical + -graphy, writing*] The descriptive study of the natural physical features of a celestial body. Physical geography. (fiz' ee OG ruh fee)

phytogeography [*phyto, plant + geo, earth + -graphy, science*] The branch of biology dealing with the study of the geographical distribution of plants. See biogeography and zoogeography. (feyet' oh jee OG ruh fee)

phytography [*phyto, plant + -graphy, writing*] The descriptive study of plants. Descriptive botany. See phytology and zoography. (feye TOG ruh fee)

pictograph [*Ltn > pictus, to paint + graph, writing*] 1.A picture that represents a word, object, or idea. 2.A prehistoric drawing, as a cave drawing. (PIK tuh graf')

planography [*plano, flat + -graphy, recording*] Any printing process done from a plane surface, as lithography. See lithography. (pluh NOG ruh fee)

plethysmograph [*Grk > plethos, quantity + graph, recording*] An instrument for measuring and recording variations in various body functions, as the velocity or volume of blood flow, heart rate, respiratory rate, etc. (pluh THIZ muh graf')

pneumograph [*pneumo, breathing + graph, recording*] An instrument for measuring and recording chest movements resulting from respiration. See spirograph. (NOO muh graf')

polygraph [*poly, many + graph, recording*] An instrument for simultaneously recording changes in various body functions, as respiration, heart rate, blood pressure, etc. Lie detector. (POL ee graf')

pornography [*Grk > porne, prostitute + -graphy, writing*] Writings and pictures intended primarily to arouse sexual excitement. (por NOG ruh fee)

pseudepigraphy [*pseud, false + epi, upon + -graphy, writing*] 1.The false attribution of a novel, poem, etc., to a certain writer. 2.Spurious religious writings professing to be ascribed to Biblical characters. (sood' ih PIG ruh fee)

psychobiography [*psycho, mind & biography*] A biography that psychoanalyzes the subject. (seye' koh beye OG ruh fee)

psychograph [*psycho, mind + graph, writing*] A chart for graphically recording an individual's personality traits. (SEYE kuh graf')

pyrography [*pyro, heat + -graphy, drawing*] The art of making designs with a heated tool, as on wood. (peye ROG ruh fee)

radiograph [*radio, radiation + graph, recording*] An image created on a sensitized surface by x-rays. (RAY dee oh graf')

radiophotography [*radio, by radio & photography*] The transmission of a photograph by radio waves by first converting the image to a matrix of electric impulses and then recreating the image at the reception site. (ray' dee oh' fuh TOG ruh fee)

radiotelegraph [*radio, by radio & telegraph*] A telegraph that uses radio waves instead of wires. See telegraph. (ray' dee oh TEL uh graf')

roentgenography [*roentgen, x-rays + -graphy, recording*] X-ray photography. (rent' guh NOG ruh fee)

scenography [*Grk > skene, scene + -graphy, drawing*] The art of painting or drawing objects in perspective. (see NOG ruh fee)

seismograph [*seismo, earthquake + graph, recording*] An instrument for automatically measuring and recording the magnitude and duration of earthquakes. See seismology and seismometer. (SEYEZ muh graf')

selenography [*seleno, moon + -graphy, science*] The branch of astronomy dealing with the study of the physiography of the moon. See physiography and selenology. (sel' uh NOG ruh fee)

serigraphy [*Ltn > sericum, silk + -graphy, drawing*] The art of printing designs by the silk-screen process. (suh RIG ruh fee)

shadowgraph [*shadow & graph, recording*] A picture created by casting a shadow on a lighted screen. (SHAD oh graf')

spectrograph [*spectro, spectrum + graph, recording*] An instrument for producing, viewing, and photographing spectra. See spectroscope. (SPEK tuh graf')

spectroheliograph [*spectro, spectrum + helio, sun + graph, recording*] An instrument for photographing the sun using light from only one spectral frequency. See spectrohelioscope. (spek' troh HEE lee uh graf')

sphygmograph [*sphygmo, pulse + graph, recording*] An instrument for graphically recording any variations in the pulse, such as strength and rapidity. (SFIG muh graf')

spirograph [*spiro, breathe + graph, recording*] An instrument for graphically recording respiratory movements. See pneumograph. (SPEYE ruh graf')

stenography [*steno, abbreviated + -graphy, writing*] The art or technique of writing in shorthand, as in court reporting, taking dictation, etc. See tachygraphy. (stuh NOG ruh fee)

stereography [*stereo-, three-dimensional + -graphy, drawing*] The art, technique, or process of drawing three-dimensional forms on a plane surface. (stehr' ee OG ruh fee)

stratigraphy [*strat(um) & -graphy, science*] The branch of geology dealing with the study of rock strata. (struh TIG ruh fee)

stylograph [*stylo, style + graph, writing*] A type of fountain pen with a fine tube forming the writing point instead of a nib. (STEYE luh graf')

stylography [*stylo, style + -graphy, writing*] The art or technique of etching or writing with a style. (steye LOG ruh fee)

tachygraphy [*tachy, rapid + -graphy, writing*] The art or technique of rapid writing, especially of the ancient Greeks and Romans. See stenography. (tuh KIG ruh fee)

technography [*techno, art or skill + -graphy, science*] The descriptive study of the arts and sciences with respect to their historical development and geographic distribution. (tek NOG ruh fee)

telegraph [*tele, distant + graph, writing*] A device for sending coded messages to a distant location using electric impulses. (TEL uh graf')

telephotography [*tele, distant & photography*] 1.The art or technique of photographing distant objects with the aid of a telephoto lens. 2.The process of transmitting text or graphics, as by radio waves or telephone lines. Facsimile. (tel' uh fuh TOG ruh fee)

thermograph [*thermo, temperature + graph, recording*] An instrument for graphically recording variations in temperature. (THUR muh graf')

thermography [*thermo, heat + -graphy, writing*] A printing process that produces raised lettering by heating the printed material after dusting it with powder. (thur MOG ruh fee)

tomography [*tomo, to cut + -graphy, recording*] The technique of making x-ray photographs of a single, predetermined plane section of the body or other solid object by eliminating the images produced by other planes. (toh MOG ruh fee)

topography [*Grk > topos, place + -graphy, writing*] 1.The descriptive study of a particular place or region. See topology (def. 1). 2.The surface features of a region or area, including hills, valleys, lakes, streams, bridges, roads, etc. See terrain. 3.The art or technique of drawing the surface features of a place or region on a chart or map. (tuh POG ruh fee)

trigraph [*tri-, three + graph, writing*] A combination of three contiguous letters representing a single speech sound, as the "eau" in *chateau*. See digraph (def. 1) and triphthong. (TREYE graf)

typography [*typo, type + -graphy, writing*] The arrangement, style, and appearance of printed material. (teye POG ruh fee)

uranography [*Grk > ouranos, heaven + -graphy, writing*] The branch of astronomy dealing with the descriptive study and mapping of celestial bodies. (yoor' uh NOG ruh fee)

venography [*ven, vein + -graphy, recording*] X-ray examination of a vein after injection of a radiopaque dye. See arteriography. (vih NOG ruh fee)

xerography [*xero, dry + -graphy, recording*] A dry photocopying process in which areas on a sheet of plain paper corresponding to areas on the original are sensitized by static electricity and sprinkled with colored resin that adheres and is permanently fused to the paper. (zihr OG ruh fee)

xylography [*xylo, wood + graphy, drawing*] The art or technique of engraving on wood. (zeye LOG ruh fee)

zincography [*zinc & -graphy, drawing*] The art or technique of engraving on zinc printing plates. (zing KOG ruh fee)

zoogeography [*zoo, animal + geo, earth + -graphy, science*] The branch of biology dealing with the study of the geographical distribution of animals. See biogeography and phytogeography. (zoh' uh jee OG ruh fee)

zoography [*zoo, animal + -graphy, writing*] The descriptive study of animals. See zoology and phytography. (zoh OG ruh fee)

scrib, script   to write

adscript [*ad-, addition + script, to write*] Written after. (AD skript)

ascribe [*as-, toward + scrib, to write*] To assign or attribute to a specific cause, author, or source. (uh SKREYEB)

circumscribe [*circum-, around + scrib, to write*] 1.To draw a line around. Encircle. 2.To enclose within a boundary. Limit. Restrict. (SUR kum skreyeb')

conscription [*con-, together + script, to write + -ion*] Compulsory enrollment of persons into the armed forces. Draft. (kun SKRIP shun)

describe [*de-, down + scrib, to write*] 1.To give an oral or written account of. 2.To draw an outline of. (dih SKREYEB)

indescribable [*in-, not + de-, down + scrib, to write + -able*] Not able to be described. (in' dih SKREYE buh bul)

inscribe [*in-, on + scrib, to write*] To write, carve, or engrave on a surface such as stone, wood, metal, etc. (in SKREYEB)

lex non scripta [*lex, law & Ltn > non scripta, unwritten*] Unwritten, or common law. See lex scripta. (leks non SKRIP tuh)

lex scripta [*lex, law & Ltn > scripta, written*] Written, or statute law. See lex non scripta. (leks SKRIP tuh)

manuscript [*manu, hand + script, to write*] A book or other composition written by hand, on a typewriter, or on a computer prior to being typeset by a printer or publisher. (MAN yuh skript')

nondescript [*non-, not + de-, down + script, to write*] Difficult to describe or classify due to lack of character or form. (non' dih SKRIPT)

postscript [*post-, after + script, to write*] A paragraph or message appended below the signature in a letter or at the end of a book, document, etc., as an afterthought or to give supplementary information. Abbreviated P.S. (POHST skript)

prescribe [*pre-, before + scrib, to write*] Literally, "to write beforehand." 1.To lay down as a rule or guide. 2.To authorize or order the use of, as a medicine or treatment. (prih SKREYEB)

proscribe [*pro-, before + scrib, to write*] 1.To condemn as harmful or dangerous. Prohibit. 2.To forbid as unlawful. Outlaw. (proh SKREYEB)

rescript [*re-, back + script, to write*] 1.A written answer issued by a Roman emperor or a pope to a question regarding discipline or doctrine. 2.An act or instance of rewriting. 3.An official public order or decree. Edict. (REE skript)

scribble [*scrib, to write + -ble*] 1.To write hastily or illegibly. 2.To make meaningless marks with a pencil or pen. (SKRIB ul)

scribe [*scrib, to write*] 1.A professional manuscript copier, especially in ancient times. 2.An author or writer. 3.A public secretary or clerk, especially in ancient times. See amanuensis. (skreyeb)

script [*script, to write*] 1.Handwriting, as distinguished from printing. 2.The written text of a play, motion picture, or broadcast. 3.A manuscript or document. (skript)

scriptorium [*script, to write + -orium, a place for*] A writing room, especially in a monastery. (skrip TOR ee um)

Scripture [*script, to write + -ure*] 1.A passage from the Bible. 2.Any sacred writing. (SKRIP chur)

scriptwriter [*script & writer*] A writer who does scripts for movies, radio, television, etc. (SKRIPT reye' ter)

subscribe [*sub-, below + scrib, to write*] 1.To write one's name at the end of a document. 2.To agree to contribute or pay a sum of money. 3.To purchase a certain number of, as issues of a periodical, concert tickets, etc. (sub SKREYEB)

subscript [*sub-, below + script, to write*] 1.Written below. 2.A letter, number, or symbol written slightly below and to the right or left of another character. See superscript. (SUB skript)

superscribe [*super-, above + scrib, to write*] To write at or near the top or on the outside of, as an address on a letter. (SOO per skreyeb')

superscript [*super-, above + script, to write*] 1.Written above. 2.A letter, number, or symbol written slightly above and to the right or left of another character. See subscript. (SOO per skript')

transcribe [*trans-, change + scrib, to write*] 1.To write or type a copy of spoken material, as dictation, lectures, court proceedings, etc. 2.To arrange a musical composition for another voice or instrument. 3.To represent speech sounds using phonetic symbols. (tran SKREYEB)

transcript [*trans-, change + script, to write*] 1.A written, typewritten, or printed copy of spoken material. 2.An official copy, as of court proceedings, a student's academic record, etc. (TRAN skript)

typescript [*type & script, to write*] A typewritten copy of something. (TEYEP skript)

unscripted [*un-, not + script, to write + -ed*] Not adhering to a prepared script. (un SKRIP tid)

greg   flock

aggregate [*ag-, toward + greg, flock + -ate*] 1.Sum total. (AG rih git {noun}) 2.Gathered or mixed together so as to constitute a whole. (AG rih git {adjective}) 3.To amount to. Total. (AG rih gayt' {verb})

congregate [*con-, together + greg, flock + -ate*] To gather together into a crowd, group, or assembly. (KONG grih gayt')

desegregate [*de-, remove & segregate*] To eliminate segregation, especially the segregation of races. See segregate. (dee SEG rih gayt')

disaggregate [*dis-, apart & aggregate*] To break up or apart. (dis AG rih git)

egregious [*e-, out + greg, flock + -ious*] 1.Extremely bad. Flagrant. 2.Extraordinary or remarkable in a bad way. (ih GREE jus)

gregarious [*greg, flock + -ar + -ious*] 1.Tending to live in flocks or herds with others of the same kind. 2.Enjoying the company of others. Sociable. See asocial. (grih GEHR ee us)

segregate [*se-, apart + greg, flock + -ate*] To set apart from others or from the main body or group. (SEG rih gayt')

gress, grad, gradi, -grade   to step, to go

aggrade [*ag-, toward + -grade, to go*] To raise the grade of by depositing sediment, as in the bed of a stream. (uh GRAYD)

aggress [*ag-, toward* + *gress, to go*] To initiate a quarrel by committing the first act of hostility. (uh GRES)

aggression [*ag-, toward* + *gress, to go* + *-ion*] The act of committing unprovoked hostilities or invasion. (uh GRESH un)

biodegradable [*bio, living organisms & degradable*] Capable of being decomposed by microorganisms such as bacteria. See biolysis. (beye' oh dih GRAY duh bul)

centigrade [*centi-, hundredth* + *-grade, to step*] A thermometer scale whose markings at 0 and 100 degrees mark the freezing point and boiling point of water. (SENT ih grayd')

congress [*con-, together* + *gress, to go*] The national legislative body of certain nations, as the U.S. Senate and House of Representatives. (KONG gres)

degrade [*de-, down* + *-grade, to go*] 1.To lower in rank, character, or quality. 2.Break down or decompose. (dih GRAYD)

degression [*de-, down* + *gress, to step* + *-ion*] A downward movement by steps or stages. Descent. (dih GRESH un)

digitigrade [*digit & -grade, to step*] Walking on the toes with the heel off the ground, as most quadruped animals. See plantigrade. (DIJ it uh grayd')

digress [*dis-, away* + *gress, to go*] To deviate from the main subject in writing or speaking. (deye GRES)

downgrade [*down & -grade, to go*] 1.A downward slope, as in a road. 2.To lower or minimize the importance of. 3.A decline toward a worse condition. See upgrade. (DOUN grayd)

egress [*e-, out* + *gress, to go*] 1.The act or right of going out or forth. Emergence. See ingress (def. 1) and regress (def. 1). 2.A way or means of going out. Exit. Opposed to ingress. (EE gres)

geometric progression [*geometric & pro-, forward* + *gress, to step* + *-ion*] A sequence of terms, as 2, 4, 8, 16, 32 or 1, 1/2, 1/4, 1/8, 1/16, in which any two adjacent terms have the same ratio. (jee' uh MET rik pruh GRESH un)

gradate [*grad, to step* + *-ate*] To pass imperceptibly by degrees, as from one color, tone, or shade to another. (GRAY dayt)

gradation [*grad, to step* + *-ation*] Any process or change taking place in a series of successive steps or stages. (gray DAY shun)

grade [*grad, to step*] 1.A stage, step, or position in a series, order, or ranking. 2.The degree of a slope. (grayd)

gradient [*gradi, to step* + *-ent*] 1.Rate of inclination or declination. Slope. 2.The rate of change in the value of a physical quantity with respect to distance. (GRAY dee ent)

gradin [*grad, to step* + *-in*] One of a series of steps or seats raised one above another in tiers, as in an amphitheater. (GRAYD n)

gradual [*grad, to step* + *-ual*] 1.Proceeding or progressing by degrees. 2.A book containing the music and words of the liturgy sung by the choir. So named from its being sung on the altar steps. (GRAJ oo ul)

graduate [*grad, to step* + *-ate*] 1.Person who has completed a course of study. (GRAJ oo it {noun}) 2.To complete a course of study. 3.To mark into regular intervals for measuring. (GRAJ oo ayt' {verb})

gressorial [*gress, to step* + *-or* + *-ial*] 1.Adapted for walking, as the feet of some birds. 2.Capable of walking. Ambulatory. (greh SOR ee ul)

ingredient [*in-, in* + *gradi, to go* + *-ent*] A constituent element of a mixture. (in GREE dee ent)

ingress [*in-, in* + *gress, to go*] 1.The act or right of going in or entering. See egress (def. 1) and regress (def. 1). 2.A way or means of entering. Entrance. Opposed to egress. (IN gres)

intergrade [*inter-, between* + *-grade, to step*] To merge gradually into another form or kind through a series of stages. (in' ter GRAYD)

introgression [*intro-, into* + *gress, to go* + *-ion*] The introduction of a gene from the gene pool of one species into the gene pool of another species as a result of hybridization and subsequent backcrossing. (in' truh GRESH un)

orthograde [*ortho, vertical* + *-grade, to step*] Walking or standing with the body in a vertical position, as a biped. See pronograde. (OR thuh grayd')

plantigrade [*Ltn > planta, sole* + *-grade, to step*] Walking on the entire sole of the foot, as humans and bears. See digitigrade. (PLANT ih grayd')

postgraduate [*post-, after & graduate*] Pertaining to advanced study pursued after graduation from college or high school. (pohst' GRAJ oo it)

progress [*pro-, forward* + *gress, to go*] 1.Gradual improvement. (PROG res {noun}) 2.A moving forward toward a specific goal or more advanced stage. (pruh GRES {verb})

progression [*pro-, forward* + *gress, to step* + *-ion*] 1.Forward movement. 2.A sequence of numbers with a constant relation between each number and the one preceding it. (pruh GRESH un)

pronograde [*pron(e) & -grade, to step*] Walking or standing with the body in a horizontal position, as a quadruped. See orthograde. (PROH noh grayd')

regress [*re-, back* + *gress, to go*] 1.The act or right of going back. See ingress (def. 1) and egress (def. 1). (rih GRES {verb}) 2.To go back to an earlier and usually worse condition. See retrogress and retrograde (def. 2). (REE gres {noun})

retrograde [*retro-, backward* + *-grade, to go*] 1.Having a backward direction or motion. 2.Going back to a worse condition. Deteriorating. See regress (def. 2) and retrogress. (RET ruh grayd')

retrogress [*retro-, backward* + *gress, to go*] To go backward, especially to an earlier, inferior, or less advanced condition. See regress (def. 2) and retrograde (def. 2). (RET ruh gres')

tardigrade [*Ltn > tardus, slow* + *-grade, to go*] 1.Any of various microscopic, slow-moving animals living in water or on damp mosses. 2.Slow-moving. (TAHR dih grayd')

transgress [*trans-, beyond* + *gress, to go*] 1.To go beyond, as a boundary, limit, etc. 2.To violate, as the law, a command, etc. (trans GRES)

upgrade [*up & -grade, to go*] 1.An upward slope, as in a road. 2.To raise the importance, quality, or value of. See downgrade. (UP grayd)

heli/o   sun

anthelion [*anti-, opposite* + *heli, sun* + *-on*] A luminous spot occasionally seen on the parhelic circle opposite the sun. See parhelion and parhelic circle. (ant HEE lee un)

heli/o

aphelion [*apo-, away + heli, sun + -on*] The point in a
planet's orbit that is farthest from the sun. See
perihelion. (uh FEE lee un)

heliacal [*heli, sun + -ac + -al*] Pertaining to or occurring
near the sun. (hih LEYE uh kul)

helianthus [*heli, sun + anth, flower + -us*] Any of a genus
of plants including the sunflowers. (hee' lee AN thus)

heliocentric [*helio, sun + centr, center + -ic*] 1.Pertaining
to or calculated from the center of the sun. 2.Having
the sun as the center. See geocentric.
(hee' lee oh SEN trik)

heliograph [*helio, sun + graph, writing*] An apparatus for
sending coded messages using sunlight reflected
intermittently through a mirror by means of a shutter.
(HEE lee uh graf')

heliolatry [*helio, sun + -latry, worship*] Worship of the sun.
(hee' lee OL uh tree)

heliometer [*helio, sun + meter, to measure*] An instrument
originally used for measuring the sun's diameter and
later used for measuring angles between celestial
bodies. (hee' lee OM et er)

Helios [*heli, sun + -os*] In Greek mythology, the sun god.
(HEE lee os')

heliostat [*helio, sun + stat, stationary*] An instrument that
moves a mirror automatically so that it reflects the
sun's rays steadily in one direction. (HEE lee uh stat')

heliotaxis [*helio, sun & taxis*] The movement of a freely
moving organism in response to sunlight. See
heliotropism and phototaxis. (hee' lee oh TAK sis)

heliotherapy [*helio, sun & therapy*] Treatment of disease
by exposure to sunlight. (hee' lee oh THEHR uh pee)

heliotrope [*helio, sun + trop, turning*] 1.A plant with
small, fragrant, white or purple flowers. 2.A plant
whose stem or flowers turn toward the sun. See
helianthus. (HEE lee uh trohp')

heliotropism [*helio, sun + trop, responding to a stimulus + -
ism*] The movement or growth of an organism or part,
especially a plant or plant part, in response to
sunlight. See heliotaxis and phototropism.
(hee' lee OT ruh piz' um)

helium [*heli, sun + -um*] A colorless, odorless,
nonflammable gaseous element, used chiefly for
inflating airships and balloons. So named from its first
being deduced from the solar spectrum. (HEE lee um)

parhelic circle [*para-, beside + heli, sun + -ic & circle*] A
luminous circle passing through the sun in a plane
parallel to the horizon and produced by the sun's rays
reflecting off ice crystals in the atmosphere. See
anthelion and parhelion. (pahr HEE lik SUR kul)

parhelion [*para-, beside + heli, sun + -on*] One of two
luminous spots occasionally appearing on the parhelic
circle on either side of the sun. See anthelion and
parhelic circle. (pahr HEE lee un)

perihelion [*peri-, around + heli, sun + -on*] The point in a
planet's orbit that is nearest the sun. See aphelion.
(pehr' ih HEE lee un)

pyrheliometer [*pyr, heat + helio, sun + meter, to measure*]
An instrument for measuring the intensity of solar
energy. (pihr hee' lee OM et er)

spectroheliograph [*spectro, spectrum + helio, sun + graph,
recording*] An instrument for photographing the sun
using light from only one spectral frequency. See
spectrohelioscope. (spek' troh HEE lee uh graf')

spectrohelioscope [*spectro, spectrum + helio, sun + -scope,
to view*] An instrument for viewing the sun using light
from only one spectral frequency. See
spectroheliograph. (spek' troh HEE lee uh skohp')

sol   sun

circumsolar [*circum-, around + sol, sun + -ar*] Revolving
around or surrounding the sun. See circumlunar and
circumterrestrial. (sur' kum SOH lur)

lunisolar [*luni, moon + sol, sun + -ar*] Pertaining to or
caused by both the moon and the sun. (loo' nih SOH lur)

parasol [*para-, protection from + sol, sun*] A lightweight
umbrella used for protection from the sun.
(PEHR uh sol')

solar [*sol, sun + -ar*] Pertaining to, produced by, or
originating from the sun. (SOH lur)

solar eclipse [*solar & eclipse*] The obstruction of light
from the sun when the moon is positioned between the
sun and a point on the earth. See lunar eclipse.
(SOH lur ih KLIPS)

solarium [*sol, sun + -arium, a place for*] A room or porch
exposed to the sun. (suh LEHR ee um)

hem/o, hemat/o, hema, -emia, -aemia
blood, blood condition

anaemia [*an-, without + -aemia, blood condition*] 1.A
condition in which there is an abnormal decrease in
total blood volume, hemoglobin, or the number of red
blood cells, resulting in pallor of the skin, shortness of
breath, and lethargy. 2.Lack of vitality or vigor. Same
as anemia. (uh NEE mee uh)

anemia [*an-, without + -emia, blood condition*] 1.A
condition in which there is an abnormal decrease in
total blood volume, hemoglobin, or the number of red
blood cells, resulting in pallor of the skin, shortness of
breath, and lethargy. 2.Lack of vitality or vigor.
(uh NEE mee uh)

anoxemia [*an-, without + ox, oxygen + -emia, blood condition*]
An abnormally low level of oxygen in the blood. See
anoxia, hypoxia, and hypoxemia. (an' ok SEE mee uh)

aplastic anemia [*a-, not + plast, forming cells or tissue + -ic
& anemia*] Anemia that results from defective blood-
producing bone marrow. See anemia.
(ay PLAS tik uh NEE mee uh)

azotemia [*azot(e) & -emia, blood condition*] The retention
of urea and other nitrogenous waste products in the
blood due to chronic kidney insufficiency.
(az' oh TEE mee uh)

bacteremia [*bacter(ia) & -emia, blood condition*] The
presence of bacteria in the blood. (bak' tuh REE mee uh)

galactosemia [*galactos(e) & -emia, blood condition*] A
congenital disorder in which the body cannot tolerate
milk. Galactose accumulates in the blood because of
defective galactose metabolism, resulting in liver
damage, cataracts, mental retardation, and often
death in newborn infants. (guh lak' tuh SEE mee uh)

hemachrome [*hema, blood + -chrome, color*] The red
coloring matter in blood. (HEE muh krohm')

hemacytometer [*hema, blood + cyto, cell + meter, to
measure*] An instrument for counting the number of
blood cells in a sample. Same as hemocytometer.
(hee' muh seye TOM et er)

hemagglutination [*hem, blood & agglutination*] The clumping together of red blood cells. (hee' muh gloot' n AY shun)

hemal [*hem, blood + -al*] 1.Pertaining to the blood or blood vessels. 2.Pertaining to or located in the region of the body that contains the heart and major blood vessels. (HEE mul)

hemangioma [*hem, blood + angi, vessel + -oma, tumor*] A common benign tumor composed of blood vessels that occurs most frequently on the skin. (hee man' jee OH muh)

hematic [*hemat, blood + -ic*] Relating to or containing blood. (hih MAT ik)

hematin [*hemat, blood + -in*] A brownish-black powder obtained from hemoglobin. (HEE muh tin)

hematinic [*hemat, blood + -in + -ic*] An agent that increases the number of red blood cells and the amount of hemoglobin in them. Hematinics are often used to treat iron-deficiency anemia. (hee' muh TIN ik)

hematite [*hemat, blood + -ite, mineral*] A very common brick-red mineral, also known as bloodstone, that is the major ore of iron. (HEE muh teyet')

hematoblast [*hemato, blood + blast, immature cell*] An immature blood cell from which other immature blood cells such as lymphoblasts, myeloblasts, and erythroblasts are derived. (hih MAT uh blast')

hematocrit [*hemato, blood + Grk > krinein, to separate*] 1.In whole blood, the ratio of the volume of red blood cells to the total volume. 2.A centrifuge for separating blood cells from plasma. (hih MAT uh krit')

hematogenesis [*hemato, blood + -genesis, production*] The production and development of blood in the body. Same as hematopoiesis. (hih mat' oh JEN uh sis)

hematogenous [*hemato, blood + gen, production + -ous*] 1.Derived from or produced by the blood. 2.Disseminated through the bloodstream. (hee' muh TOJ uh nus)

hematology [*hemat, blood + -ology, study of*] The branch of medical science dealing with the study of blood and blood-forming tissues. (hee' muh TOL uh jee)

hematolysis [*hemato, blood + -lysis, destruction*] Liberation of hemoglobin after the breakdown of red blood cells. Same as hemolysis. (hee' muh TOL uh sis)

hematoma [*hemat, blood + -oma, tumor*] A usually clotted, tumorlike mass of blood, resulting from a break in the wall of a blood vessel. (hee' muh TOH muh)

hematophagous [*hemato, blood + phag, to eat + -ous*] Feeding on blood. (hee' muh TOF uh gus)

hematopoiesis [*hemato, blood + -poiesis, production*] The production and development of blood in the body. (hih mat' oh poi EE sis)

hematosis [*hemat, blood + osis, formation*] The formation of blood. (hee' muh TOH sis)

hematozoon [*hemato, blood + zo, animal + -on*] An animal parasite living in the blood. (hih mat' oh ZOH on)

hematuria [*hemat, blood + -uria, urine*] The presence of blood or red blood cells in the urine. (hee' muh TOOR ee uh)

heme [*hem, blood*] The deep red, nonprotein, iron-containing pigment found in hemoglobin. See hemoglobin. (heem)

hemochromatosis [*hemo, blood + chromat, color + -osis, diseased condition*] A disease of iron metabolism characterized by excess accumulation of iron in the tissues of various organs, especially the skin, pancreas, and liver, causing bronze skin pigmentation, diabetes, and liver enlargement. (hee' muh kroh' muh TOH sis)

hemocyanin [*hemo, blood + cyan, blue + -in*] A blue respiratory pigment similar to hemoglobin, found in the blood of many arthropods and mollusks. See hemoglobin. (hee' muh SEYE uh nin)

hemocyte [*hemo, blood + -cyte, cell*] A mature blood cell. (HEE muh seyet')

hemocytometer [*hemo, blood + cyto, cell + meter, to measure*] An instrument for counting the number of blood cells in a sample. (hee' moh seye TOM et er)

hemodialysis [*hemo, blood & dialysis*] Dialysis of the circulating blood for the purpose of removing impurities and waste. (hee' moh deye AL uh sis)

hemodynamics [*hemo, blood + dynam, power + -ics, study of*] A branch of physiology dealing with the study of blood circulation. (hee' moh deye NAM iks)

hemoflagellate [*hemo, blood & flagellate*] A parasitic flagellate protozoan living in the blood. (hee' muh FLAJ uh layt')

hemoglobin [*hem(e) & globin {protein constituent}*] The respiratory protein pigment in the red blood cells of vertebrates and some invertebrates that carries oxygen to the tissues. Hemoglobin is composed of heme and globin, where heme is the nonprotein constituent and globin is the protein constituent. See heme and myoglobin. (HEE muh gloh' bin)

hemoglobinuria [*hemoglobin & -uria, urine*] The presence of hemoglobin in the urine. (hee' muh gloh' buh NOOR ee uh)

hemolymph [*hemo, blood & lymph*] The fluid in the circulatory systems of invertebrates that acts as blood in arthropods and as blood and lymph in some other invertebrates. (HEE muh limf')

hemolysis [*hemo, blood + -lysis, destruction*] Liberation of hemoglobin after the breakdown of red blood cells. (hih MOL uh sis)

hemophilia [*hemo, blood + phil, affinity for + -ia*] A hereditary blood defect characterized by excessive bleeding due to an abnormal or missing blood-clotting factor. It occurs mainly in males, but can be transmitted in the female line. (hee' muh FIL ee uh)

hemophobia [*hemo, blood + -phobia, fear*] Abnormal fear of blood or of bleeding. (hee' muh FOH bee uh)

hemoptysis [*hemo, blood + ptysis, spitting*] The coughing or spitting up of blood from the bronchial tubes or lungs. (hih MOP tuh sis)

hemorrhage [*hemo, blood + rrhag, excessive flow*] Heavy blood flow, either externally or internally. (HEM ur ij)

hemorrhoid [*hemo, blood + rrhea, flow + -oid*] A varicose vein located within the anus or in the anal wall, causing pain, itching, and often bleeding. (HEM uh roid')

hemorrhoidectomy [*hemorrhoid & ec, out + -tomy, to cut*] Surgical removal of hemorrhoids. (hem' uh roid' EK tuh mee)

hemostasis [*hemo, blood + -stasis, stoppage*] 1.The stoppage of blood flow, either by natural or surgical means. 2.Stopping or slowing blood circulation. (hee' muh STAY sis)

hem/o, hemat/o, hema, -emia, -aemia

hemostat [*hemo, blood + stat, stoppage*] A small surgical clamp used in surgery to reduce or stop bleeding. (HEE muh stat')

hemostatic [*hemo, blood + stat, stoppage + -ic*] Capable of stopping blood flow, as a drug or other agent. (hee' muh STAT ik)

hemotoxin [*hemo, blood & toxin*] A toxin that destroys red blood cells, as cobra venom. See neurotoxin and cytotoxin. (HEE muh tok' sin)

hypercalcemia [*hyper-, excessive + calc, lime + -emia, blood condition*] An abnormally high level of calcium in the blood. Opposed to hypocalcemia. (heye' per kal' SEE mee uh)

hypercholesterolemia [*hyper-, excessive & cholesterol & -emia, blood condition*] The presence of an abnormally high level of cholesterol in the blood. (heye' per kuh les' ter uh LEE mee uh)

hyperemia [*hyper-, excessive + -emia, blood condition*] The presence of excess blood in an organ or other body part. See hypostasis (def. 1). (heye' per EE mee uh)

hyperglycemia [*hyper-, excessive + glyc, sugar + -emia, blood condition*] An abnormally high level of sugar in the blood. Opposed to hypoglycemia. (heye' per gleye SEE mee uh)

hyperlipidemia [*hyper-, excessive & lipid & -emia, blood condition*] An abnormally high level of lipids in the blood. (heye' per lip' ih DEE mee uh)

hyperuricemia [*hyper-, excessive & uric & -emia, blood condition*] An abnormally high level of uric acid in the blood. (heye' per yoor' uh SEE mee uh)

hypocalcemia [*hypo-, below + calc, lime + -emia, blood condition*] An abnormally low level of calcium in the blood. Opposed to hypercalcemia. (heye' poh kal' SEE mee uh)

hypoglycemia [*hypo-, below + glyc, sugar + -emia, blood condition*] An abnormally low level of sugar in the blood. Opposed to hyperglycemia. (heye' poh gleye SEE mee uh)

hypoxemia [*hypo-, below + ox, oxygen + -emia, blood condition*] Abnormal decrease of oxygen in the arterial blood. See anoxia, anoxemia, and hypoxia. (heye' pok SEE mee uh)

ischemia [*Grk > ischein, to hold back + -emia, blood*] A suppression of blood flow due to the functional constriction or actual obstruction of a blood vessel. (is KEE mee uh)

leukemia [*leuk, white + -emia, blood condition*] A disease of the blood forming organs which results in an abnormal increase in the production of white blood cells. See leukopenia. (loo KEE mee uh)

macroglobulinemia [*macroglobulin & -emia, blood condition*] A disorder characterized by the presence of macroglobulins in the blood. (mak' roh glob' yuh luh NEE mee uh)

oxyhemoglobin [*oxy, oxygen & hemoglobin*] A complex of hemoglobin combined with oxygen that is present in arterial blood and is responsible for its bright red color. (ok' see HEE muh gloh' bin)

polycythemia [*poly, many + cyt, cell + -emia, blood condition*] A condition in which there is an abnormal increase in the number of red blood cells. (pol' ee seye THEE mee uh)

pyemia [*py, pus + -emia, blood condition*] Blood poisoning caused by pus-forming microorganisms released into the circulating blood from an abscess, which may result in the development of multiple abscesses in various parts of the body. (peye EE mee uh)

sapremia [*sapr, putrid + -emia, blood condition*] Blood poisoning caused by pathogenic microorganisms or their toxins in the circulating blood. Same as septicemia. (suh PREE mee uh)

septicemia [*Grk > septos, putrid + -ic + -emia, blood condition*] Blood poisoning caused by pathogenic microorganisms or their toxins in the circulating blood. (sep' tuh SEE mee uh)

sickle cell anemia [*sickle cell & anemia*] A hereditary blood disease occurring primarily among blacks that leads to anemia, joint pain, and blood clot formation. It changes normal, round red blood cells to a sickle shape that cannot fit through tiny vessels. See anemia. (SIK ul sel uh NEE mee uh)

thalassemia [*thalass, sea + -emia, blood condition*] An inherited type of anemia marked by abnormal synthesis of hemoglobin, initially occurring among Mediterranean and Southeast Asian peoples. (thal' uh SEE mee uh)

toxemia [*tox, poison + -emia, blood condition*] Blood poisoning caused by bacterial and other toxins in the blood. (toks EE mee uh)

uremia [*ur, urine + -emia, blood condition*] A toxic condition resulting from excess urea and other wastes in the blood, ordinarily eliminated by the kidneys. (yoo REE mee uh)

viremia [*vir(us) & -emia, blood condition*] The presence of one or more viruses in the blood. (veye REE mee uh)

hepat/o   liver

hepatectomy [*hepat, liver + ec, out + -tomy, to cut*] Surgical removal of all or part of the liver. (hep' uh TEK tuh mee)

hepatic [*hepat, liver + -ic*] Pertaining to or affecting the liver. (hih PAT ik)

hepatica [*hepat, liver + -ic + -a*] Any of a genus of plants with three-lobed leaves and delicate bluish, pink, or white flowers. So named for their liver-shaped leaves. (hih PAT ih kuh)

hepatitis [*hepat, liver + -itis, inflammation*] Inflammation of the liver characterized by jaundice, fever, and liver enlargement. (hep' uh TEYE tis)

hepatogenic [*hepato, liver + gen, origin + -ic*] Originating in or produced by the liver. (hep' uh toh JEN ik)

hepatoma [*hepat, liver + -oma, tumor*] A malignant tumor of the liver. (hep' uh TOH muh)

hepatomegaly [*hepato, liver + -megaly, large*] Enlargement of the liver. (hep' uh toh MEG uh lee)

hepatotoxic [*hepato, liver + tox, poison + -ic*] Toxic or damaging to the liver. (hep' uh toh TOK sik)

homo, homoio, homeo   same, similar, equal

anomalous [*an-, not + homo, same + -ous*] Deviating from the normal rule, method, or arrangement. Irregular. Abnormal. (uh NOM uh lus)

anomaly [*an-, not + homo, same + -y*] 1. Deviation from the normal rule, method, or arrangement. 2. The angular distance of an orbiting body, as a planet or satellite, from its previous perihelion or perigee. See perihelion and perigee. (uh NOM uh lee)

homeomorphism [*homeo, similar + morph, form + -ism*] Similarity in crystalline form and structure, but differing in chemical composition. See paramorph. (hoh' mee oh MOR fiz' um)

homeopathy [*homeo, similar + -pathy, disease*] 1. The practice of treating a disease or condition by using a minute quantity of an agent that in much greater doses has a similar effect to that of the disease or condition. Opposed to allopathy. 2. The practice of treating a disease or condition using natural remedies rather than drugs or surgery. See naturopathy. (hoh' mee OP uh thee)

homeostasis [*homeo, equal + -stasis, stable state*] 1. The tendency of a biological system, especially in higher animals, to maintain an internal state of equilibrium through constant monitoring of numerous stimuli. 2. The comfortable weight, or set point, at which the body has learned to function efficiently in the past. (hoh' mee oh STAY sis)

homicide [*homo, same + -cide, to kill*] The killing of another human being. (HOM uh seyed')

homocentric [*homo, same + centr, center + -ic*] Having a common center. See concentric. (hoh' muh SEN trik)

homocercal [*homo, same + cerc, tail + -al*] Characterized by a tail fin having symmetrical upper and lower lobes, as in most adult bony fish. See heterocercal. (hoh' muh SUR kul)

homochromatic [*homo, same + chromat, color + -ic*] Pertaining to or having one color. Same as monochromatic (def. 1). (hoh' moh kroh MAT ik)

homocyclic [*homo, same + cycl, circle + -ic*] Pertaining to a compound having a ring structure composed of only one kind of atom. (hoh' muh SEYE klik)

homoeroticism [*homo, same + eroto, sexual desire + -ic + -ism*] 1. Homosexuality. 2. Sexual desire for another of the same sex. (hoh' moh ih ROT uh siz' um)

homogamous [*homo, same + gam, sexual union + -ous*] 1. Bearing flowers that are sexually the same. Opposed to heterogamous (def. 2). 2. Pertaining to flowers having stamens and pistils maturing at the same time, thus making self-pollination possible. Opposed to dichogamous. (hoh MOG uh mus)

homogeneous [*homo, same + gen, kind + -eous*] 1. Of the same kind. 2. Composed of parts of the same kind. Opposed to heterogeneous. (hoh' muh JEE nee us)

homogenize [*homo, same + gen, kind + -ize*] To break up into particles of uniform size and mix evenly throughout a fluid, as the fat globules in homogenized milk. (huh MOJ uh neyez')

homogenous [*homo, similar + gen, origin + -ous*] Having structural similarities due to common origin. Opposed to homoplastic. (huh MOJ uh nus)

homograft [*homo, same & graft*] Tissue taken from a donor of a species and grafted onto a recipient of the same species. See allograft, heterograft, and autograft. (HOH muh graft')

homograph [*homo, same + graph, writing*] One of two or more words that are spelled the same, always differ in meaning, and sometimes differ in pronunciation, as *bar* (unit of pressure) and *bar* (round piece of metal). See homonym and heteronym. (HOM uh graf')

homoiotherm [*homoio, same + therm, temperature*] A warm-blooded animal, such as a bird or mammal, whose body temperature remains relatively constant. See poikilotherm. (hoh MOI uh thurm')

homoiothermic [*homoio, same + therm, temperature + -ic*] Warm-blooded. See poikilothermic. (hoh moi' uh THUR mik)

Homoiousian [*homoio, similar + Grk > ousia, essence*] An adherent to the 4th century religious belief that the essence of God the Father and God the Son is similar, but not the same. See Homoousian and Heteroousian. (hoh' moi OO zee un)

homolecithal [*homo, equal + Grk > lekithos, egg yolk + -al*] Pertaining to an egg having a small amount of yolk that is equally distributed throughout the cytoplasm. See heterolecithal. (hoh' muh LES uh thul)

homologate [*homo, same + log, discourse + -ate*] 1. To confirm or approve. 2. To confirm or approve officially. (hoh MOL uh gayt')

homologous [*homo, similar + Grk > logos, relationship + -ous*] Similar in structure, position, function, etc. (hoh MOL uh gus)

homolographic [*homo, same + graph, writing + -ic*] Showing parts in the same ratio, as of size or form. (hom' uh luh GRAF ik)

homology [*homo, similar & (ana)logy*] A similarity in structure or arrangement, but not necessarily in function, of organs or parts found in organisms of common origin. Opposed to heterology. (hoh MOL uh jee)

homomorphism [*homo, similar + morph, form + -ism*] 1. Similarity in form, shape, size, etc. See isomorphic and heteromorphic (def. 1). 2. Having perfect flowers of one type only. (hoh' muh MOR fiz' um)

homonym [*homo, same + onym, word*] One of two or more words that are pronounced the same, always differ in meaning, and usually differ in spelling, as *wear* (to carry on the body) and *ware* (articles of merchandise). See heteronym and homograph. (HOM uh nim')

homonymous [*homo, same + onym, name + -ous*] 1. Ambiguous. 2. Having the same name. (hoh MON uh mus)

Homoousian [*homo, same + Grk > ousia, essence*] An adherent to the 4th century religious belief that the essence of God the Father and God the Son is the same. Homoousianism was eventually accepted by the Church. See Homoiousian and Heteroousian. (hoh' moh OO zee un)

homophile [*homo, same + -phile, attracted to*] 1. A homosexual. 2. One who is sensitive to the rights of homosexuals. See homosexual. (HOH muh feyel')

homophobia [*homo, same + -phobia, fear*] Hatred or fear of homosexuals. (hoh' muh FOH bee uh)

homophone [*homo, same + -phone, sound*] One of two or more words that are pronounced the same, always differ in meaning, and usually differ in spelling, as *wear* (to carry on the body) and *ware* (articles of merchandise). Same as homonym. (HOM uh fohn')

homo, homoio, homeo

homophonic [*homo, same + phon, sound + -ic*] 1.Having the same sound. 2.Having one predominate melody with the other instruments or voices serving as accompaniment. See monody (def. 3). (hom' uh FON ik)

homoplastic [*homo, similar + plast, development + -ic*] Having structural similarities due to parallel evolution or evolutionary convergence. Opposed to homogenous. (hoh' muh PLAS tik)

homopterous [*homo, same + pter, wing + -ous*] Pertaining to any of numerous insects belonging to the suborder Homoptera, characterized by membranous forewings that do not differ in thickness from the membranous hindwings. See heteropterous and hemipterous. (hoh MOP ter us)

homosexual [*homo, same & sexual*] A person who is sexually attracted to others of the same sex. See heterosexual and homophile. (hoh' muh SEK shoo ul)

homosporous [*homo, same + spor, spore + -ous*] The production of asexual spores of one kind only. Opposed to heterosporous. (hoh' muh SPOR us)

homotaxis [*homo, similar + tax, arrangement + -is*] Similarity of arrangement or of fossil formations between rock strata located in separate geographical areas. See heterotaxis (def. 2). (hoh' muh TAK sis)

homothallic [*homo, same & thall(us) & -ic*] The condition in algae and fungi of having male and female gametes on the same thallus so that reproduction can occur from the fusion of these gametes or between like strains. See heterothallic. (hoh' muh THAL ik)

homozygote [*homo, same + zyg, pair + -ote*] An organism whose diploid cells contain chromosomes with gene pairs that, at one or more loci, contain identical alleles, thus producing gametes that are all identical. See heterozygote and zygote. (hoh' muh ZEYE goht')

hetero   different, other

heterocercal [*hetero, different + cerc, tail + -al*] Characterized by a tail fin having two unequal lobes, with the upper lobe usually larger than the lower, as in certain sharks. See homocercal. (het' uh roh SUR kul)

heterochromatic [*hetero, different + chromat, color + -ic*] Having several different colors. See monochromatic (def. 1). (het' uh roh' kroh MAT ik)

heterochromatin [*hetero, other & chromatin*] The part of the chromatin in a cell nucleus that is more darkly stained when the nucleus is not in the state of division and is genetically inactive. See chromatin and euchromatin. (het' uh roh KROH muh tin)

heterochromosome [*hetero, different & chromosome*] Either of two chromosomes in the germ cells of humans, animals, and some plants, that together determine an individual's sex. Same as sex chromosome. (het' uh roh KROH muh sohm')

heteroclite [*hetero, different + clin, to lean*] 1.A person or thing that deviates from the norm. Abnormal. 2.A word, especially a noun, that is irregular in inflection. (HET ur uh kleyet')

heterocyclic [*hetero, other + cycl, circle + -ic*] Pertaining to a compound having a ring structure composed of atoms of more than one kind. (het' uh roh SEYE klik)

heterodox [*hetero, different + dox, belief*] Not conforming to established doctrines or beliefs, especially in theology. Unorthodox. Heretical. See orthodox and unorthodox. (HET ur uh doks')

heterodyne [*hetero, different + dyn, power*] Pertaining to the combination of two different radio frequencies to generate an intermediate frequency, which is the difference of the original frequencies. (HET ur uh deyen')

heteroecious [*hetero, different + Grk > oikos, house + -ious*] Pertaining to parasites that spend the stages of their life cycle on two or more different species of hosts, as tapeworms and certain rust fungi. See autoecious. (het' uh REE shus)

heterogamete [*hetero, different & gamete*] A gamete that unites with another of different form, size, or sex chromosome content. See isogamete. (het' uh roh GAM eet)

heterogamous [*hetero, different + gam, sexual union + -ous*] 1.Characterized by the fusion of heterogametes. 2.Bearing flowers that are sexually different or of different types. Opposed to homogamous (def. 1). (het' uh ROG uh mus)

heterogamy [*hetero, different + -gamy, sexual union*] 1.Alternation of generations. See alternation of generations. 2.The union of two dissimilar gametes, as in form, size, or function. Same as anisogamy. See oogamy. (het' uh ROG uh mee)

heterogeneous [*hetero, different + gen, kind + -eous*] 1.Differing in kind. 2.Composed of parts of different kinds. Mixed. Opposed to homogeneous. (het' uh roh JEE nee us)

heterogenesis [*hetero, other + -genesis, generation*] Alternation of generations. See alternation of generations. (het' uh roh JEN uh sis)

heterogenous [*hetero, different + gen, origin + -ous*] 1.Having a different origin. 2.Originating outside the organism. See autogenous, endogenous, and exogenous. (het' uh ROJ uh nus)

heterogony [*hetero, other + -gony, generation*] Alternation of generations. See alternation of generations. (het' uh ROG uh nee)

heterograft [*hetero, different & graft*] Tissue taken from a donor of one species and grafted onto a recipient of a different species. See homograft and autograft. (HET ur uh graft')

heterography [*hetero, different + -graphy, writing*] 1.Spelling that varies from the current standard. 2.Spelling in which the same letter can represent different sounds when applied to different syllables or words, as the "g" in give and gene. (het' uh ROG ruh fee)

heterogynous [*hetero, different + gyn, female + -ous*] Having two forms of female, one nonreproductive and the other reproductive, as bees. (het' uh ROJ uh nus)

heterolecithal [*hetero, different + Grk > lekithos, egg yolk + -al*] Pertaining to an egg whose yolk is unequally distributed throughout the cytoplasm. See homolecithal. (het' uh roh LES uh thul)

heterologous [*hetero, different + Grk > logos, relationship + -ous*] Originating or derived from a different species. (het' uh ROL uh gus)

heterology [*hetero, different & (ana)logy*] A difference in structure or arrangement between apparently similar anatomical organs or parts, resulting from differences in origin. Opposed to homology. (het' uh ROL uh jee)

heterolysis [*hetero, different + -lysis, decomposition*] The decomposition of cells from one species by a lytic agent from another species. (het' uh ROL uh sis)

heteromerous [*hetero, different + mer, part + -ous*] 1.Having an unequal number of elements, or elements that differ in form, size, etc., within the same structure. 2.Pertaining to a flower having one or more whorls with a different number of members than the other whorls. Opposed to isomerous. (het' uh ROM ur us)

heteromorphic [*hetero, different + morph, form + -ic*] 1.Differing in form, shape, size, etc. See isomorphic and homomorphism (def. 1). 2.Having different forms at various stages in the life cycle, as insects. See pleomorphism. (het' uh roh MOR fik)

heteronomous [*hetero, other + nom, law + -ous*] Subject to the laws of another. See autonomous (def. 1) and semiautonomous. (het' uh RON uh mus)

heteronym [*hetero, different + onym, word*] One of two or more words that are spelled the same, but always differ in meaning and pronunciation, as *sow* (to plant seeds) and *sow* (a female pig). See homonym and homograph. (HET ur uh nim')

Heteroousian [*hetero, different + Grk > ousia, essence*] An adherent to the 4th century religious belief that the essence of God the Father and God the Son is different. See Homoousian and Homoiousian. (het' uh roh OO zee un)

heterophyllous [*hetero, different + phyll, leaf + -ous*] Having leaves of different kinds on the same plant. (het' uh roh FIL us)

heterophyte [*hetero, other + -phyte, plant*] A plant that gets its food from other living or dead organisms. See autophyte and saprophyte. (HET ur uh feyet')

heteroplasty [*hetero, other + -plasty, forming cells or tissue*] The surgical grafting of tissue taken from another person or from an individual of another species. See autoplasty and heterograft. (HET ur uh plas' tee)

heteroploid [*hetero, different + -ploid, number of chromosomes*] Pertaining to cells without a full complement of chromosomes and whose chromosomes are therefore not a multiple of the normal haploid number for the species. See euploid and haploid. (HET ur uh ploid')

heteropterous [*hetero, different + pter, wing + -ous*] Pertaining to any of numerous insects belonging to the suborder Heteroptera, characterized by forewings that differ in thickness from the membranous hindwings. See homopterous and hemipterous. (het' uh ROP ter us)

heterosexual [*hetero, other & sexual*] A person who is sexually attracted to persons of the opposite sex. See homosexual. (het' uh roh SEK shoo ul)

heterosis [*hetero, other + -osis, increase*] A marked increase in vigor, size, yield, etc., of plants and animals produced by crossbreeding. Hybrid vigor. (het' uh ROH sis)

heterosporous [*hetero, different + spor, spore + -ous*] Producing spores of two or more different kinds, especially microspores and megaspores in seed plants and ferns. Opposed to homosporous. (het' uh roh SPOR us)

heterotaxis [*hetero, different + tax, arrangement + -is*] 1.An abnormal structural arrangement of body organs or parts. 2.An abnormal structural arrangement of parts, especially of rock strata. See homotaxis. (het' uh roh TAK sis)

heterothallic [*hetero, different & thall(us) & -ic*] The condition in algae and fungi of having different types of thalli so that reproduction can occur only between genetically different strains of the same species. See homothallic. (het' uh roh THAL ik)

heterotroph [*hetero, other + troph, nourishment*] An organism, as all animals, some bacteria, and certain plants, that depends, either directly or indirectly, on other organisms for food due to its inability to manufacture proteins and carbohydrates from inorganic sources. See autotroph. (HET ur uh trof')

heterozygote [*hetero, different + zyg, pair + -ote*] An organism whose diploid cells contain chromosomes with gene pairs that, at one or more loci, contain different alleles, thus producing gametes of two or more different kinds. See homozygote and zygote. (het' uh roh ZEYE goht')

iso-   equal, same

aniseikonia [*aniso-, not equal + icon, image + -ia*] An abnormal visual condition in which the image is not the same size in both eyes. Opposed to iseikonia. (an eye' seye KOH nee uh)

aniso- [*an-, not + iso-, equal*] A word root meaning "not equal." (an EYE soh)

anisogamous [*aniso-, not equal + gam, sexual union + -ous*] Characterized by the fusion of heterogametes. Same as heterogamous (def. 1). (an' eye SOG uh mus)

anisogamy [*aniso-, not equal + -gamy, sexual union*] The union of two dissimilar gametes, as in form, size, or function. See isogamy. (an' eye SOG uh mee)

anisometric [*aniso-, not equal + metr, measure + -ic*] Not having or exhibiting equality in dimensions or measurements. Not isometric. See isometric (def. 1). (an eye' suh MET rik)

anisometropia [*aniso-, not equal + metr, measure + -opia, visual condition*] An abnormal visual condition in which the refractive power is not equal in both eyes. See isometropia. (an eye' soh mih TROH pee uh)

anisotropic [*aniso-, not equal + trop, responding to a stimulus + -ic*] 1.Having unequal responses to external stimuli. 2.Having properties that vary depending on the direction of measurement. See isotropic. (an eye' suh TROP ik)

isallobar [*iso-, equal + allo, variation + bar, pressure*] A line on a map connecting points with equal change of barometric pressure over a given time period. (eye SAL uh bahr')

iseikonia [*iso-, equal + icon, image + -ia*] A visual condition in which the image is the same size in both eyes. Opposed to aniseikonia. (eye' seye KOH nee uh)

isentropic [*iso-, equal & entrop(y) & -ic*] Having constant or equal entropy. See entropy. (eye' sen TROP ik)

isoagglutination [*iso-, same + ag-, to + Ltn > gluten, glue + -ation*] The agglutination of the red blood cells of a member of a species by agglutinins from the blood of a member of the same species. (eye' soh uh gloot' n AY shun)

iso-

isoantibody [*iso-, same & antibody*] An antibody produced by an individual of a species that reacts with antigens of certain other individuals of the same species. (eye' soh AN tih bod' ee)

isoantigen [*iso-, same & antigen*] An antigen derived from one member of a species that can cause the production of antibodies in other members of the same species, but not in itself. (eye' soh AN tih jen)

isobar [*iso-, equal + bar, pressure*] A line on a map connecting points of equal barometric pressure for a specific period or time. (EYE suh bahr')

isobath [*iso-, equal + bath, deep*] A line on a chart connecting points of equal depth below the surface of the earth or in a body of water. (EYE suh bath')

isochromatic [*iso-, equal + chromat, color + -ic*] 1.Of uniform color or tint. 2.Orthochromatic. See orthochromatic. (eye' soh kroh MAT ik)

isochronal [*iso-, equal + chron, time + -al*] Characterized by equal duration or intervals of time. (eye SOK ruh nul)

isochrous [*iso-, equal + chros, color + -ous*] Having identical color or tint throughout. (eye SOK roh us)

isocline [*iso-, same + -cline, slope*] A fold of stratified rock so tightly compressed that both sides have the same downward slope. (EYE suh kleyen')

isoclinic line [*iso-, equal + clin, slope + -ic & line*] A line on a map connecting points on the earth's surface with equal magnetic inclination or dip. See isogonal line and agonic line. (eye' suh KLIN ik leyen)

isocracy [*iso-, equal + -cracy, government*] Government in which all people share equal political power. (eye SOK ruh see)

isocyclic [*iso-, same + cycl, circle + -ic*] Having a ring composed of atoms of the same element. (eye' soh SEYE klik)

isodiametric [*iso-, equal & diamet(e)r & -ic*] Having equal diameters or dimensions in all directions. (eye' soh deye' uh MET rik)

isodynamic [*iso-, equal + dynam, power + -ic*] 1.Having equal force, strength, or intensity. 2.Pertaining to an imaginary line connecting points on the earth's surface with equal magnetic intensity. (eye' soh deye NAM ik)

isoelectric [*iso-, equal & electric*] Exhibiting equal electric potential. (eye' soh ih LEK trik)

isoelectronic [*iso-, equal & electron & -ic*] Pertaining to atoms with an equal number of electrons or an equal number of valence electrons. (eye' soh ih lek' TRON ik)

isoenzyme [*iso-, same & enzyme*] An enzyme that is functionally similar to another enzyme, but has a slightly different composition. (eye' soh EN zeyem)

isogamete [*iso-, same & gamete*] A gamete that unites with another of the same form and size. See heterogamete. (eye' soh GAM eet)

isogamy [*iso-, same + -gamy, sexual union*] The union of two similar gametes, as in certain algae. See anisogamy. (eye SOG uh mee)

isogenous [*iso-, same + gen, origin + -ous*] In biology, of the same or similar origin, as having developed from the same cell or tissue. (eye SOJ uh nus)

isogloss [*iso-, same + gloss, language*] A line on a map that shows regions with different dialects of the same language. (EYE suh glos')

isogon [*iso-, equal + gon, angle*] A closed plane figure with all angles equal. See equilateral (def. 2). (EYE suh gon')

isogonal line [*iso-, equal + gon, angle + -al & line*] A line on a map connecting points on the earth's surface with equal magnetic declination. See isoclinic line and agonic line. (eye SOG uh nul leyen)

isogonic [*iso-, equal + gon, angle + -ic*] Having or pertaining to equal angles. (eye' suh GON ik)

isogram [*iso-, equal + gram, to draw*] A line on a map or chart connecting points of equal or constant value. (EYE suh gram')

isograph [*iso-, equal + graph, drawing*] A line on a map that shows regions with common linguistic characteristics. (EYE suh graf')

isohyet [*iso-, equal + hyet, rain*] A line on a map connecting points receiving equal amounts of rainfall. (eye' soh HEYE it)

isomagnetic [*iso-, equal & magnetic*] Pertaining to an imaginary line connecting points of equal magnetic force. (eye' soh mag NET ik)

isomer [*iso-, same + mer, part*] A chemical compound with the same molecular weight and the same proportions of the same elements as another compound, but different properties due to different molecular structure. (EYE suh mer)

isomerase [*iso-, same + mer, part + -ase, enzyme*] An enzyme that catalyzes the conversion of an organic substance to an isomeric form. (eye SOM uh rayz')

isomerous [*iso-, equal + mer, part + -ous*] 1.Having an equal number of elements, markings, etc. 2.Pertaining to a flower having the same number of members in each whorl. Opposed to heteromerous. (eye SOM ur us)

isometric [*iso-, equal + metr, measure + -ic*] 1.Having or exhibiting equality of measure. See anisometric. 2.Involving the increased contraction of a muscle with little or no increase in length, as in isometric exercises. (eye' suh MET rik)

isometropia [*iso-, equal + metr, measure + -opia, visual condition*] A visual condition in which the refractive power is equal in both eyes. See anisometropia. (eye' soh mih TROH pee uh)

isomorphic [*iso-, same + morph, form + -ic*] Having the same or similar form or structure. See homomorphism (def. 1) and heteromorphic (def. 1). (eye' suh MOR fik)

isomorphism [*iso-, same + morph, form + -ism*] 1.A similarity in form or structure between members of different species. 2.A similarity of crystalline structure between two otherwise different substances. (eye' suh MOR fiz' um)

isonomy [*iso-, equal + -nomy, system of laws*] Equality of laws or civil rights. (eye SON uh mee)

isopiestic [*iso-, equal + Grk > piezein, to press + -ic*] Showing equal pressure. Isobaric. (eye' soh pee ES tik)

isopleth [*iso-, same + Grk > plethos, quantity*] A line on a map or chart connecting points of equal numerical value. (EYE suh pleth')

isopod [*iso-, same + pod, feet*] Any of numerous crustaceans with seven pairs of similar legs, each pair being attached to one of seven thoracic body segments. (EYE suh pod')

isosceles [*iso-, equal + Grk > skelos, leg + -es*] Pertaining to a figure, as an isosceles triangle, with two sides equal. (eye SOS uh leez')

isoseismal [*iso-, equal + seism, earthquake + -al*]
1.Pertaining to or exhibiting equal magnitude of earthquake shock. 2.A line on a map connecting points with equal magnitude of earthquake shock. (eye' soh SEYEZ mul)

isosmotic [*iso-, equal & osmotic*] Pertaining to or exhibiting equal osmotic pressure. See isotonic (def. 2). (eye' soz MOT ik)

isostasy [*iso-, equal + -stasis, stable state + -y*]
1.Equilibrium resulting from equal pressure on all sides. 2.The state of equilibrium of the earth's crust maintained by the force of gravity. (eye SOS tuh see)

isotherm [*iso-, equal + therm, temperature*] A line on a map connecting points with equal average temperature for a given time period or equal temperature at a given time. (EYE suh thurm')

isothermal [*iso-, equal + therm, temperature + -al*] Having equal or constant temperature. (eye' suh THUR mul)

isotonic [*iso-, equal + tono, tension + -ic*] 1.Having equal tension. 2.Having equal osmotic pressure. See hypotonic, hypertonic, and isosmotic. (eye' suh TON ik)

isotope [*iso-, same + Grk > topos, place*] One of two or more forms of an element having the same atomic number, nearly identical chemical properties, and the same place in the periodic table, but different atomic weights and physical properties. (EYE suh tohp')

isotropic [*iso-, equal + trop, turning + -ic*] Having properties that are equal regardless of the direction of measurement. See anisotropic (def. 2). (eye' suh TROP ik)

isozyme [*iso-, same & (en)zyme*] An enzyme that is functionally similar to another enzyme, but has a slightly different composition. Same as isoenzyme. (EYE suh zeyem')

radioisotope [*radio, radiation & isotope*] A usually artificially produced radioactive isotope used in medical and biological research, therapy, etc. (ray' dee oh EYE suh tohp')

stereoisomer [*stereo-, three-dimensional & isomer*] Any of a group of isomers in which the atoms differ in spacial arrangement, but not in kind or order of arrangement. (stehr' ee oh EYE suh mer)

syn-, sym-, syl-, sys-   together, same

asymmetry [*a-, without & symmetry*] Without symmetry. See symmetry. (ay SIM ih tree)

asymptote [*a-, not + sym, together + Grk > ptotos, falling*] A straight line that a curve continually approaches, but never meets, even if the curve is extended to infinity. (AS im toht')

asynchronous [*a-, not + syn, same + chron, time + -ous*]
1.Not occurring at the same time. 2.Not occurring at the same rate. See synchronous. (ay SING kruh nus)

asyndeton [*a-, not + syn, together + Grk > dein, to bind + -on*] The omission of one or more conjunctions between sentence elements for rhetorical effect. See polysyndeton. (uh SIN dih tahn')

biosynthesis [*bio, life + syn, together + the, to put + -sis*] The production of chemical substances by a living organism. (beye' oh SIN thuh sis)

chemosynthesis [*chemo, chemical + syn, together + the, to put + -sis*] The use of energy from chemical reactions to form organic compounds. (kee' moh SIN thuh sis)

decasyllable [*deca, ten & syllable*] A line of verse with ten syllables. (DEK uh sil' uh bul)

dissymmetry [*dis-, lack of & symmetry*] Lack of symmetry. See symmetry. (dih SIM ih tree)

disyllable [*di-, two & syllable*] A word with two syllables. (DEYE sil' uh bul)

dodecasyllable [*dodeca-, twelve & syllable*] A line of verse with twelve syllables. (doh' dek' uh SIL uh bul)

enneasyllable [*ennea, nine & syllable*] A line of verse with nine syllables. (en' ee uh SIL uh bul)

extrasystole [*extra-, outside + sys, together + Grk > stellein, to place*] A premature contraction of the heart resulting from any of various stimuli. (eks' truh SIS tuh lee)

geosynchronous [*geo, earth + syn, same + chron, time + -ous*] Pertaining to a satellite whose orbit is approximately 23,000 miles above the earth, resulting in a rate of speed synchronous with the earth's rotation, thus making it seem to remain stationary. (jee' oh SING kruh nus)

geosyncline [*geo, earth + syn, together + -cline, slope*] A massive depression in the earth's crust that varies in form, but is usually linear and consists of volcanic and sedimentary rock. See syncline, anticline, and geanticline. (jee' oh SIN kleyen')

hendecasyllable [*hendeca-, eleven & syllable*] A line of verse with eleven syllables. (hen' dek' uh SIL uh bul)

hexasyllable [*hexa-, six & syllable*] A line of verse with six syllables. (HEKS uh sil' uh bul)

idiosyncrasy [*idio-, peculiar + syn, together + Grk > krasis, mixture + -y*] A physical or mental characteristic peculiar to a person, as taste, behavior, etc. (id' ee oh SING kruh see)

monosyllable [*mono-, one & syllable*] A word with one syllable. (MON uh sil' uh bul)

nonsyllabic [*non-, not & syllab(le) & -ic*] Pertaining to a speech sound that does not form a syllable. (non' sih LAB ik)

octosyllable [*octo-, eight & syllable*] A line of verse with eight syllables. (OK tuh sil' uh bul)

parasympathetic nervous system One of two divisions of the autonomic nervous system, consisting of the cranial and sacral nerves, that works in conjunction with the sympathetic nervous system to control heart, blood vessels, glands, etc. See sympathetic nervous system and autonomic nervous system. (pehr' uh sim' puh THET ik NUR vus SIS tum)

parasynthesis [*para-, variation + syn, together + the, to put + -sis*] The formation of words by compounding and sometimes adding a suffix. (pehr' uh SIN thuh sis)

pentasyllable [*penta-, five & syllable*] A line of verse with five syllables. (PENT uh sil' uh bul)

photosynthesis [*photo, light + syn, together + the, to put + -sis*] A biological process primarily associated with green plants that forms organic compounds from carbon dioxide and water in the presence of light with simultaneous liberation of oxygen. (foht' oh SIN thuh sis)

polysyllable [*poly, many & syllable*] A word with four or more syllables. (POL ee sil' uh bul)

polysyndeton [*poly, many + syn, together + Grk > dein, to bind + -on*] The repetition of unnecessary conjunctions in close succession for rhetorical effect. See asyndeton. (pol' ee SIN dih tahn')

septisyllable [*sept-, seven & syllable*] A line of verse with seven syllables. (SEP tuh sil' uh bul)

syllabary [*syllab(le) & -ary*] A list of symbols that represent the syllables of a language. (SIL uh behr' ee)

syllabify [*syllab(le) & -ify, to make*] To divide into syllables. (sih LAB uh feye')

syllable [*syl-, together + Grk > lambanein, to take + -le*] A word element consisting of contiguous letters that are pronounced as a single uninterrupted sound. (SIL uh bul)

syllepsis [*syl-, together + Grk > lambanein, to take + -sis*] A grammatical construction in which one word is applied to two or more other words and disagrees with at least one of them in sense, gender, number, etc., as "He lost his job and his mind." (sih LEP sis)

syllogism [*syl-, together + log, discourse + -ism*] A scheme of deductive reasoning with two premises and a conclusion. If both premises are true, then the conclusion is true, as "All people are important; you are a person; therefore, you are important." (SIL uh jiz' um)

symbiosis [*sym-, together + bio, mode of living + -sis*] 1.Two dissimilar species living together in close association, especially if such association is of mutual benefit to each. See antibiosis. 2.Any mutually beneficial relationship between persons, groups, etc. (sim' bee OH sis)

symbol [*sym-, together + Grk > ballein, to throw*] Something that represents something else. (SIM bul)

symbology [*symb(ol) & -ology, study of*] 1.The study of symbols and symbolism. 2.The art of interpreting symbols. (sim BOL uh jee)

symmetry [*sym-, same + -metry, to measure*] Similarity of size, form, or arrangement on either side of a dividing line. (SIM ih tree)

sympathetic nervous system One of two divisions of the autonomic nervous system consisting of the spinal nerves that control the heart, lungs, blood vessels, intestines, and sweat glands. See parasympathetic nervous system and autonomic nervous system. (sim' puh THET ik NUR vus SIS tum)

sympathy [*sym-, same + -pathy, feeling*] 1.Sharing and understanding another person's sorrow or trouble. 2.Mutual agreement. (SIM puh thee)

sympatric [*sym-, same + patr, fatherland + -ic*] Pertaining to species of plants and animals that occur or originate in the same geographical area or region. See allopatric. (sim PAT rik)

sympetalous [*sym-, together & petal & -ous*] Having united or partially united petals. Same as gamopetalous. (sim PET l us)

symphony [*sym-, together + -phony, sound*] 1.Harmony of sounds or colors. 2.An elaborate and usually lengthy musical composition with several movements, one or more of which are in sonata form. 3.A concert by a symphony orchestra. (SIM fuh nee)

symphysis [*sym-, together + Grk > phyein, to grow + -sis*] 1.The joining of two bones either by growing together or by connection with fibrocartilage. 2.The growing together of normally separate parts. See synarthrosis, amphiarthrosis, and diarthrosis. (SIM fuh sis)

symposiarch [*symposi(um) & arch, chief*] 1.The director of a symposium in ancient Greece. 2.A toastmaster. (sim POH zee ahrk')

symposium [*sym-, together + Grk > pinein, to drink + -ium*] 1.A formal meeting for the discussion of a specific topic. 2.A drinking party in ancient Greece that included intellectual discussion. (sim POH zee um)

symptom [*sym-, together + Grk > ptotos, falling*] Evidence regarded as an indication of something. (SIMP tum)

symptomatology [*symptom & -ology, science*] 1.The science of medical symptoms. 2.The combined symptoms of a disease or condition. (simp' tuh muh TOL uh jee)

synaesthesia [*syn-, together + aesthes, sensation + -ia*] A sensation produced in one sense by the stimulation of another sense. Same as synesthesia. (sin' es THEE zhuh)

synagog [*syn-, together + agog, to lead*] 1.A Jewish house of worship and religious study. 2.A Jewish assemblage for worship and religious study. (SIN uh gog')

synagogue [*syn-, together + agog, to lead*] 1.A Jewish house of worship and religious study. 2.A Jewish assemblage for worship and religious study. Same as synagog. (SIN uh gog')

synalepha [*syn-, together + Grk > aleiphein, to smear + -a*] The uniting of two adjacent vowels or syllables into one. See syneresis (def. 1). (sin' l EE fuh)

synapse [*syn-, together + Grk > haptein, to join*] The small gap across which a nerve impulse passes from the axon of one neuron to the dendrites or the cell body of another. (SIN aps)

synapsis [*syn-, together + Grk > haptein, to join + -sis*] The pairing and fusion of homologous paternal and maternal chromosomes in the prophase stage of meiosis. (sih NAP sis)

synarthrosis [*syn-, together + arthr, joint + -osis, action*] Any articulation in which the bones are rigidly joined permitting no motion of the joint. See diarthrosis and amphiarthrosis. (sin' ahr THROH sis)

syncarpous [*syn-, together & carp(el) & -ous*] Pertaining to a flower with the carpels united. See apocarpous. (sin KAHR pus)

synchro- [*syn-, same + chron, time*] A word root meaning "synchronous" or "synchronized." (SING kroh)

synchromesh [*synchro-, synchronous & mesh*] Designating a transmission in which gears are meshed by first synchronizing their speed of rotation. (SING kroh mesh')

synchronic [*syn-, same + chron, time + -ic*] Pertaining to the study of a language during a given time period in its development without concern for historical antecedents. See diachronic. (sin KRON ik)

synchronize [*syn-, same + chron, time + -ize*] To cause to occur at the same time or at the same rate. (SING kruh neyez')

synchronous [*syn-, same + chron, time + -ous*] 1.Occurring at the same time. 2.Occurring at the same rate. See asynchronous. (SING kruh nus)

synchroscope [*synchro-, synchronous + -scope, to observe*] An instrument for determining the degree of synchronism between associated machines, as two or more aircraft engines. (SING kruh skohp')

syncline [*syn-, together + -cline, slope*] A trough-shaped basin of stratified rock with rock beds sloping downward. See anticline, geosyncline, and geanticline. (SIN kleyen)

syncope [*syn-, together* + *Grk > koptein, to cut*] 1.The omission of one or more letters or sounds from the middle of a word. See apheresis and apocope. 2.A brief loss of consciousness due to a temporary loss of adequate blood supply to the brain. (SING kuh pee)

syncretism [*syn-, together & Cret(an) & -ism*] 1.The attempted combination or reconciliation of differing beliefs or principles, as in religion or philosophy. 2.The merging of two or more inflectional forms that were originally different. So named from the supposed manner in which the Cretans formed alliances against a common enemy. (SING krih tiz' um)

syncytium [*syn-, together* + *cyt, cell* + *-ium*] A multinucleate mass of protoplasm without distinct cellular boundaries, as in a muscle fiber. (sin SISH ee um)

syndactyl [*syn-, together* + *dactyl, digit*] Having two or more digits joined together, as by webbing. (sin DAK tul)

syndesmosis [*syn-, together* + *desm, ligament* + *-osis, process*] The joining of bones by ligaments. (sin' dez MOH sis)

syndetic [*syn-, together* + *Grk > dein, to bind* + *-ic*] Serving to connect or join, as a conjunction. (sin DET ik)

syndic [*syn-, same* + *Grk > dike, justice*] 1.A business agent or manager representing a university or corporation. 2.A civil magistrate. (SIN dik)

syndicalism [*syn-, together* + *Grk > dike, justice* + *-al* + *-ism*] A movement, developed mainly during the Industrial Revolution, that sought to give labor unions control of all industrial production and distribution through the use of strikes or violence. (SIN dih kuh liz' um)

syndicate [*syn-, same* + *dic, to speak* + *-ate*] 1.To sell for publication in many newspapers, periodicals, radio stations, or television stations at once. (SIN dih kayt' {verb}) 2.An association of individuals or companies formed to carry out some undertaking usually requiring a large amount of capital. (SIN dih kut {noun})

syndrome [*syn-, together* + *-drome, to run*] A group of symptoms occurring together that collectively indicate a specific disease or disorder. (SIN drohm)

synecdoche [*syn-, together* + *Grk > dechesthai, to receive*] A figure of speech that uses a term describing a part or a portion to represent the whole or vice versa, as *hand* for *worker* or *head* for *livestock*. (sih NEK duh kee)

synecology [*syn-, together* + *eco, environment* + *-logy, study of*] The study of ecology as it relates to plant and animal communities and their environment. See autecology and ecology. (sin' ih KOL uh jee)

syneresis [*syn-, together* + *Grk > hairein, to take* + *-sis*] 1.The uniting of two adjacent vowels or syllables into one, especially to form a diphthong. See dieresis (def. 1), synalepha, and diphthong. 2.The contraction or shrinking of a gel after prolonged standing, as the shrinking of fibrin in a blood clot. (sih NEHR uh sis)

synergism [*syn-, together* + *erg, work* + *-ism*] The combined effect of the cooperative action of separate entities that is greater than the sum of their individual effects, as certain drugs, body parts, etc. (SIN ur jiz' um)

synergy [*syn-, together* + *erg, work* + *-y*] The combined effect of the cooperative action of separate entities that is greater than the sum of their individual effects, as certain drugs, body parts, etc. Same as synergism. (SIN ur jee)

synesis [*syn-, together* + *Grk > hienai, to send*] A grammatical construction that agrees in sense rather than syntax. (SIN uh sis)

synesthesia [*syn-, together* + *esthes, sensation* + *-ia*] A sensation produced in one sense by the stimulation of another sense. (sin' es THEE zhuh)

syngamy [*syn-, together* + *-gamy, sexual union*] Fertilization by the union of two gametes. (SIN guh mee)

syngenesis [*syn-, together* + *-genesis, production*] Sexual reproduction by the union of male and female gametes. Same as gamogenesis. (sin JEN uh sis)

synkaryon [*syn-, together* + *kary, nucleus* + *-on*] The nucleus formed by the fusion of pronuclei during fertilization. See karyogamy. (sin KEHR ee on')

synod [*syn-, together* + *Grk > hodos, way*] 1.A council, convention, or assembly. 2.An ecclesiastical council or assembly. (SIN uhd)

synoecious [*syn-, same* + *Grk > oikos, house* + *-ious*] 1.Having stamens and pistils on the same flower. 2.Having both staminate and pistillate flowers in the same cluster. See monoecious, dioecious, and trioecious. (sih NEE shus)

synonym [*syn-, same* + *onym, name*] A word with a similar meaning in one or more senses to another word in the same language. See antonym. (SIN uh nim')

synonymous [*syn-, same* + *onym, name* + *-ous*] Having a similar meaning. (sih NON uh mus)

synopsis [*syn-, same* + *ops, vision* + *-is*] A brief overview of a subject, book, movie, etc. (sih NOP sis)

synostosis [*syn-, together* + *oste, bone* + *-osis, formation*] The formation of a single bone by the fusion of separate or adjacent bones such as those forming a joint. (sin' os TOH sis)

synsepalous [*syn-, together & sepal & -ous*] Having united or partially united sepals. Same as gamosepalous. (sin SEP uh lus)

syntactics [*syntactic & -ics, study of*] The branch of semiotics dealing with the study of the formal characteristics of signs and symbols, apart from their users. See semantics (def. 2), pragmatics (def. 2), and semiotics. (sin TAK tiks)

syntax [*syn-, together* + *tax, arrangement*] 1.Rules governing the systematic arrangement of words in a grammatical construction according to proper form and relationship. 2.Rules governing the arrangement of components within a system, as in a computer language. (SIN taks)

synthesis [*syn-, together* + *the, to put* + *-sis*] 1.The combination of separate elements or parts to form a whole. 2.The production of a compound from its constituent elements. (SIN thuh sis)

systaltic [*sys-, together* + *Grk > stellein, to place* + *-ic*] Rhythmically contracting and expanding, as the heart. (sis TOL tik)

system [*sys-, together* + *Grk > histanai, to stand*] A group of things that work together to form a whole. (SIS tum)

systematics [*system & -ics, science*] 1.The science of classification. 2.The classification of organisms based on common factors and relationships to each other. Same as taxonomy. (sis' tuh MAT iks)

systole [*sys-, together* + *Grk > stellein, to place*] Rhythmic contraction of the heart after each diastole, causing blood to be pumped through the aorta and pulmonary artery. See diastole. (SIS tuh lee)

syzygy [*syn-, together* + *zyg, pair* + *-y*] 1.Either of two points on a celestial body's orbit at which it is in conjunction with, or in opposition to, the sun. 2.Either of two points on the moon's orbit where the sun, moon, and earth lie in a straight line. (SIZ uh jee)

tetrasyllable [*tetra-, four* & *syllable*] A word with four syllables. (TET ruh sil' uh bul)

trisyllable [*tri-, three* & *syllable*] A word with three syllables. (TREYE sil' uh bul)

hyper-   above, excessive, beyond, over

hyper [*hyper-, excessive*] Excessively excited, nervous, or irritable. (HEYE per)

hyperactive [*hyper-, excessive* & *active*] Excessively active. (heye' per AK tiv)

hyperaesthesia [*hyper-, excessive* + *aesthes, feeling* + *-ia*] Abnormally increased sensitivity to touch, pain, or other stimulation. Same as hyperesthesia. (heye' per es THEE zhuh)

hyperbaric [*hyper-, above* + *bar, pressure* + *-ic*] Pertaining to or occurring at pressures greater than normal atmospheric pressure. (heye' per BEHR ik)

hyperbola [*hyper-, beyond* + *Grk > ballein, to throw* + *-a*] An open plane curve generated by a moving point whose distances from two fixed points in the plane differ by a constant value. (heye PER buh luh)

hyperbole [*hyper-, beyond* + *Grk > ballein, to throw*] A figure of speech that uses an intentional exaggeration for rhetorical effect. (heye PER buh lee)

hyperborean [*hyper-, beyond* + *Grk > boreas, north wind*] Pertaining to the far north. Very cold. Frigid. (heye' per BOR ee un)

Hyperborean [*hyper-, beyond* + *Grk > boreas, north wind*] In Greek mythology, a member of a group of people living beyond the north wind in a land of perpetual sunshine and plenty. (heye' per BOR ee un)

hypercalcemia [*hyper-, excessive* + *calc, lime* + *-emia, blood condition*] An abnormally high level of calcium in the blood. Opposed to hypocalcemia. (heye' per kal' SEE mee uh)

hypercatalectic [*hyper-, over* & *catalectic*] Pertaining to a line of verse with one or more additional syllables after the last complete foot. See acatalectic and catalectic. (heye' per kat' l EK tik)

hypercholesterolemia [*hyper-, excessive* & *cholesterol* & *-emia, blood condition*] The presence of an abnormally high level of cholesterol in the blood. (heye' per kuh les' ter uh LEE mee uh)

hypercorrection [*hyper-, over* & *correction*] An incorrect pronunciation, linguistic form, or grammatical construction, usually resulting from a strong desire to be correct, as in the substitution of *I* for *me* in "He gave the prize to my husband and I." (heye' per kuh REK shun)

hypercritical [*hyper-, excessive* & *critical*] Excessively critical. (heye' per KRIT ih kul)

hyperemia [*hyper-, excessive* + *-emia, blood condition*] The presence of excess blood in an organ or other body part. See hypostasis (def. 1). (heye' per EE mee uh)

hyperesthesia [*hyper-, excessive* + *esthes, feeling* + *-ia*] Abnormally increased sensitivity to touch, pain, or other stimulation. Opposed to hypesthesia. (heye' per es THEE zhuh)

hyperextension [*hyper-, beyond* & *extension*] The extension of a body part, as a knee, elbow, etc., beyond its normal range of motion. (heye' per ik STEN shun)

hypergamy [*hyper-, above* + *-gamy, marriage*] Marrying a person of a higher social class or status. (heye PER guh mee)

hyperglycemia [*hyper-, excessive* + *glyc, sugar* + *-emia, blood condition*] An abnormally high level of sugar in the blood. Opposed to hypoglycemia. (heye' per gleye SEE mee uh)

hypergolic [*hyper-, excessive* + *erg, work* + *-ic*] Igniting spontaneously on contact with an oxidizer, as certain types of rocket fuel. (heye' per GOL ik)

hyperkinesis [*hyper-, excessive* + *kine, motion* + *-sis*] Abnormally excessive muscular movement. (heye' per kih NEE sis)

hyperlipidemia [*hyper-, excessive* & *lipid* & *-emia, blood condition*] An abnormally high level of lipids in the blood. (heye' per lip' ih DEE mee uh)

hypermeter [*hyper-, above* & *meter*] A line of verse with one or more additional syllables after those normal for the meter. See hypercatalectic. (heye PERM et er)

hypermetropia [*hyper-, above* + *metr, measure* + *-opia, visual condition*] A visual condition in which light is focused behind the retina rather than on it, resulting in distant vision being clear and near vision being blurred. Farsightedness. Same as hyperopia. (heye' per mih TROH pee uh)

hypermnesia [*hyper-, excessive* + *mne, memory* + *-ia*] Abnormally vivid or exact memory. (heye' perm NEE zhuh)

hyperon [*hyper-, excessive* + *-on, subatomic particle*] An elementary particle of the baryon group whose mass is greater than that of a proton or neutron. (HEYE per on')

hyperopia [*hyper-, above* + *-opia, visual condition*] A visual condition in which light is focused behind the retina rather than on it, resulting in distant vision being clear and near vision being blurred. Farsightedness. Opposed to myopia (def. 1). (heye' per OH pee uh)

hyperostosis [*hyper-, excessive* + *oste, bone* + *-osis, abnormal condition*] An increase in bulk of bone tissue due to abnormal growth or thickening. (heye' per os TOH sis)

hyperoxia [*hyper-, above* + *ox, oxygen* + *-ia*] An abnormal increase in the amount of oxygen in the blood and body tissues. See hypoxia. (heye' per OK see uh)

hyperphysical [*hyper-, beyond* & *physical*] Beyond the physical. Supernatural. See superphysical. (heye' per FIZ ih kul)

hyperpituitarism [*hyper-, excessive* & *pituitar(y)* & *-ism*] A condition that results from an abnormal increase in the activity of the anterior lobe of the pituitary gland. Opposed to hypopituitarism. (heye' per pih TOO ih tuh riz' um)

hyperplasia [*hyper-, above* + *plas, forming cells or tissue* + *-ia*] An abnormal increase in the number of nonmalignant cells of a tissue, causing a noncancerous enlargement of an organ or part. (heye' per PLAY zhuh)

hyperploid [*hyper-, above + -ploid, number of chromosomes*] Pertaining to cells with a chromosome number that is more than an exact multiple of the normal haploid number. See hypoploid. (HEYE per ploid')

hyperpnea [*hyper-, excessive + -pnea, breathing*] Abnormally deep and rapid breathing. Opposed to hypopnea. (heye PERP nee uh)

hyperpyrexia [*hyper-, above + pyr, fever + -ia*] An abnormally high fever. See pyrexia. (heye' per peye REK see uh)

hypersensitive [*hyper-, excessive & sensitive*] Excessively sensitive. (heye' per SEN sih tiv)

hypersonic [*hyper-, above + son, sound + -ic*] Pertaining to or moving at a speed equal to or greater than five times the speed of sound. (heye' per SON ik)

hypertension [*hyper-, above & tension*] Abnormally high blood pressure. Opposed to hypotension. (heye' per TEN shun)

hyperthermia [*hyper-, above + therm, temperature + -ia*] Abnormally high body temperature, sometimes induced for treatment of illness or disease. See hypothermia. (heye' per THUR mee uh)

hyperthyroidism [*hyper-, above & thyroid & -ism*] An abnormal increase in the activity of the thyroid gland, resulting in an increased metabolic rate. Opposed to hypothyroidism. (heye' per THEYE roid iz' um)

hypertonic [*hyper-, above + tono, tension + -ic*] 1.Having abnormally increased tension or tone, as a muscle. 2.Having the higher osmotic pressure of two fluids under comparison. See hypotonic and isotonic. (heye' per TON ik)

hypertrophy [*hyper-, excessive + -trophy, nourishment*] A usually abnormal enlargement of an organ or body part due to an increase in cell size rather than cell number. (heye PER truh fee)

hyperuricemia [*hyper-, excessive & uric & -emia, blood condition*] An abnormally high level of uric acid in the blood. (heye' per yoor' uh SEE mee uh)

hyperventilation [*hyper-, excessive + Ltn > ventus, wind + -ation*] An excess supply of air in the lungs due to deep and rapid breathing, as from excitement or anxiety. (heye' per vent l AY shun)

hypervitaminosis [*hyper-, above & vitamin & -osis, abnormal condition*] An abnormal condition resulting from taking excessive amounts of one or more vitamins. See avitaminosis. (heye' per veyet' uh mih NOH sis)

hyp-, hypo-   under, below, less

hypabyssal [*hyp-, below & abyss & -al*] Pertaining to igneous rocks, such as dikes and sills, that originated at great depths as molten matter and later rose and solidified as minor intrusions at moderate depths. (hip' uh BIS ul)

hypanthium [*hyp-, under + anth, flower + -ium*] An expanded floral receptacle that bears the sepals, petals, and stamens. (heye PAN thee um)

hypesthesia [*hyp-, less + esthes, feeling + -ia*] Abnormally decreased sensitivity to touch, pain, or other stimulation. Opposed to hyperesthesia. (hip' es THEE zhuh)

hyphen [*hyp-, under + hen, one*] A mark (-) used to join the elements of a compound word, to join two words that function as a modifier, or to divide a word between syllables at the end of a line. (HEYE fun)

hypoblast [*hypo-, below + blast, cell layer*] The inner layer of the three primary germ cell layers of an embryo from which the gastrointestinal tract, most of the respiratory system, and many other organs develop. Same as endoderm. (HEYE puh blast')

hypocalcemia [*hypo-, below + calc, lime + -emia, blood condition*] An abnormally low level of calcium in the blood. Opposed to hypercalcemia. (heye' poh kal' SEE mee uh)

hypocaust [*hypo-, below + caust, to burn*] A space beneath the floor of an ancient Roman building that when filled with hot air provided a central heating system. (HEYE puh kost')

hypocenter [*hypo-, below & center*] The point on the earth's surface directly beneath the center of a nuclear explosion. (HEYE puh sent' ur)

hypochlorous acid [*hypo-, less & chlorous & acid*] A weak and unstable acid used as a disinfectant, bleach, etc. (heye' puh KLOR us AS id)

hypochondria [*hypo-, below + chondr, cartilage + -ia*] Abnormal anxiety regarding one's health, often involving real pain, when illness is neither present nor likely. The seat of the condition supposedly is in the abdomen, which is the soft part of the body lying below the cartilage of the breastbone. (heye' puh KON dree uh)

hypochondrium [*hypo-, below + chondr, cartilage + -ium*] The upper lateral regions of the abdomen that lie on either side of the epigastrium. See hypogastrium and epigastrium. (heye' puh KON dree um)

hypocorism [*hypo-, under + Grk > korizesthai, to caress + -ism*] A pet name or endearing diminutive. (heye POK uh riz' um)

hypocotyl [*hypo-, below & cotyl(edon)*] The portion of an embryonic plant stem located below the cotyledons. See epicotyl. (heye' puh KOT l)

hypocycloid [*hypo-, below + cycl, circle + -oid, resembling*] A curve generated by the motion of a point on the circumference of a circle rolled around the inside of a fixed circle. See cycloid (def. 2) and epicycloid. (heye' puh SEYE kloid')

hypodermic [*hypo-, under + derm, skin + -ic*] 1.Injected under the skin. 2.Relating to parts under the skin. Subcutaneous. (heye' puh DER mik)

hypodermis [*hypo-, under + derm, skin + -is*] 1.The cell layer of a plant that lies immediately below the epidermis. 2.The cell layer in arthropods and certain other organisms that secretes and underlies the cuticle. (heye' puh DER mis)

hypoesthesia [*hypo-, less + esthes, feeling + -ia*] Abnormally decreased sensitivity to touch, pain, or other stimulation. Same as hypesthesia. (heye' poh es THEE zhuh)

hypogastrium [*hypo-, below + gastr, stomach + -ium*] The lowest of the three middle regions of the abdomen, between the right inguinal region and the left inguinal region. See epigastrium and hypochondrium. (heye' puh GAS tree um)

hyp-, hypo-

hypogeal [*hypo-, below + geo, earth + -al*] Living, growing, or situated below the surface of the earth. (heye' puh JEE ul)

hypogene [*hypo-, below + -gene, formation*] Formed or occurring below the surface of the earth. See epigene. (HEYE puh jeen')

hypogenous [*hypo-, under + gen, formation + -ous*] Developing or growing beneath or on the lower surface of a leaf or other plant part, as certain fungi. See epigenous. (heye POJ uh nus)

hypogeum [*hypo-, under + geo, earth + -um*] 1.An underground vault or chamber, especially in an ancient building. 2.The part of a building below the ground level. (heye' puh JEE um)

hypoglossal [*hypo-, under + gloss, tongue + -al*] 1.Located under the tongue. 2.Pertaining to the 12th pair of cranial nerves that innervate the tongue. (heye' puh GLOS ul)

hypoglycemia [*hypo-, below + glyc, sugar + -emia, blood condition*] An abnormally low level of sugar in the blood. Opposed to hyperglycemia. (heye' poh gleye SEE mee uh)

hypogynous [*hypo-, below + gyn, female + -ous*] Having floral parts or organs arranged below and out of contact with the gynoecium, as a buttercup. See epigynous and perigynous. (heye POJ uh nus)

hypolimnion [*hypo-, below + Grk > limne, lake + -ion*] In a stratified lake, the cooler lower layer of water that lies below the thermocline. See epilimnion and thermocline. (heye' poh LIM nee on')

hypomania [*hypo-, less + mania, mental aberration*] A mild form of mania involving slightly abnormal elation and overactivity. (heye' poh MAY nee uh)

hyponasty [*hypo-, below + -nasty, growth in a specific direction*] The condition in which leaves or other plant parts turn upward due to more rapid growth on the lower side. Opposed to epinasty. (HEYE puh nas' tee)

hypophysectomy [*hypophys(is) {pituitary gland} & ec, out + -tomy, to cut*] Surgical removal of the pituitary gland. See hypophysis. (heye pof' uh SEK tuh mee)

hypophysis [*hypo-, under + Grk > phyein, to grow + -sis*] A small endocrine gland located at the base of the brain that influences body growth, stimulates other glands, and regulates numerous other bodily functions. Pituitary gland. (heye POF uh sis)

hypopituitarism [*hypo-, less & pituitar(y) & -ism*] A condition that results from an abnormal decrease in the activity of the anterior lobe of the pituitary gland. Opposed to hyperpituitarism. (heye' poh pih TOO ih tuh riz' um)

hypoplasia [*hypo-, less + plas, development + -ia*] Incomplete or defective development of a bodily organ or part. (heye' poh PLAY zhuh)

hypoploid [*hypo-, less + -ploid, number of chromosomes*] Pertaining to cells with a chromosome number that is less than an exact multiple of the normal haploid number. See hyperploid. (HEYE poh ploid')

hypopnea [*hypo-, less + -pnea, breathing*] Abnormally shallow and slow breathing. Opposed to hyperpnea. (heye POP nee uh)

hypostasis [*hypo-, below + -stasis, stationary*] 1.An accumulation of blood or other fluid in the lower portion of an organ or body part due to poor circulation. See hyperemia. 2.The underlying nature or essence of a thing. (heye POS tuh sis)

hypotaxis [*hypo-, less + tax, arrangement + -is*] The arrangement of clauses in a subordinate relationship, as by conjunctions. See parataxis. (heye' poh TAK sis)

hypotension [*hypo-, below & tension*] Abnormally low blood pressure. Opposed to hypertension. (heye' poh TEN shun)

hypotenuse [*hypo-, under + Grk > teinein, to stretch*] In a right triangle, the side located opposite the right angle formed by the other two sides. (heye POT n oos')

hypothalamus [*hypo-, below & thalamus*] The portion of the brain lying just below the thalamus, that controls many body functions including the endocrine system and the autonomic nervous system. (heye' puh THAL uh mus)

hypothermia [*hypo-, below + therm, temperature + -ia*] Abnormally low body temperature. See hyperthermia. (heye' puh THUR mee uh)

hypothesis [*hypo-, under + the, to put + -sis*] A theory that is unproved, but assumed to be true for argumentative or investigative purposes. (heye POTH uh sis)

hypothetical [*hypo-, under + the, to put + -ical*] Assumed for the purpose of argument or investigation, but not proved. (heye' puh THET ih kul)

hypothyroidism [*hypo-, less & thyroid & -ism*] An abnormal decrease in the activity of the thyroid gland, resulting in a decreased metabolic rate. Opposed to hyperthyroidism. (heye' puh THEYE roid iz' um)

hypotonic [*hypo-, less + tono, tension + -ic*] 1.Having abnormally decreased tension or tone, as a muscle. 2.Having the lower osmotic pressure of two fluids under comparison. See isotonic and hypertonic. (heye' puh TON ik)

hypoxemia [*hypo-, below + ox, oxygen + -emia, blood condition*] Abnormal decrease of oxygen in the arterial blood. See anoxia, anoxemia, and hypoxia. (heye' pok SEE mee uh)

hypoxia [*hypo-, less + ox, oxygen + -ia*] An abnormal decrease in the amount of oxygen supplied to body tissues. See anoxia, anoxemia, and hypoxemia. (heye POK see uh)

iatr/o   healing, medical treatment

bariatrics [*bar, weight + iatr, healing + -ics, study of*] The branch of medicine dealing with the study and treatment of obesity. (behr' ee AT riks)

geriatrics [*Grk > geras, old age + iatr, healing + -ics, study of*] The branch of medicine dealing with the study and treatment of diseases and disorders associated with old age and aging persons. See gerontology. (jehr' ee AT riks)

gyniatrics [*gyn, woman + iatr, healing + -ics, study of*] The branch of medical science dealing with the study and treatment of diseases peculiar to women. See gynecology. (jin' ee AT riks)

iatrogenic [*iatro, medical treatment + gen, cause + -ic*] 1.Caused by the diagnosis, comments, or medical treatment of a physician or surgeon. 2.Created as a result of medical treatment, as certain antibiotic-resistant microorganisms. (eye at' ruh JEN ik)

neuropsychiatry [*neuro, nerve + psych, mind + iatr, healing + -y*] The branch of medical science dealing with the study and treatment of diseases and disorders of the mind and nervous system. (noor' oh seye KEYE uh tree)

orthopsychiatry [*ortho, correct + psych, mind + iatr, healing + -y*] The branch of medical science dealing with the study and treatment of emotional and behavioral disorders, especially in children. (or' thoh seye KEYE uh tree)

pediatrics [*ped, child + iatr, healing + -ics, study of*] The branch of medicine dealing with the study and treatment of diseases and disorders of infants and children. (pee' dee AT riks)

physiatrics [*physi, physical + iatr, healing + -ics, study of*] The study of physical therapy. (fiz' ee AT riks)

podiatry [*pod, foot + iatr, healing + -y*] The branch of medicine dealing with the study and treatment of disorders of the feet. See chiropody. (puh DEYE uh tree)

psychiatry [*psych, mind + iatr, healing + -y*] The branch of medicine dealing with the study and treatment of mental disorders. See psychology. (seye KEYE uh tree)

icon/o   image

aniseikonia [*aniso-, not equal + icon, image + -ia*] An abnormal visual condition in which the image is not the same size in both eyes. Opposed to iseikonia. (an eye' seye KOH nee uh)

icon [*icon, image*] 1.An image. 2.A conventional religious image of some sacred Christian personage which itself is regarded as sacred, especially in the tradition of Eastern Orthodox Churches. (EYE kon)

iconoclast [*icono, image + Grk > klastes, breaker*] 1.A person who destroys religious images. 2.A person who attacks and seeks to destroy established beliefs or institutions. (eye KON uh klast')

iconography [*icono, image + -graphy, drawing*] A symbolic representation or illustration using images, pictures, figures, etc. (eye' kuh NOG ruh fee)

iconolatry [*icono, image + -latry, worship*] Worship of icons or images. (eye' kuh NOL uh tree)

iconology [*icon, image + -ology, science*] The science of symbols and icons. (eye' kuh NOL uh jee)

iconostasis [*icono, image + -stasis, stationary*] A screen decorated with icons that separates the sanctuary from the main body in an Eastern Orthodox Church. (eye' kuh NOS tuh sis)

iseikonia [*iso-, equal + icon, image + -ia*] A visual condition in which the image is the same size in both eyes. Opposed to aniseikonia. (eye' seye KOH nee uh)

idio-   peculiar, personal, distinct

idioblast [*idio-, distinct + blast, cell*] A plant cell that differs markedly from surrounding cells within the same tissue. (ID ee uh blast')

idiogram [*idio-, personal + gram, to write*] A written symbol that represents an idea or object. (ID ee uh gram')

idiograph [*idio-, personal + graph, writing*] A private mark or signature. Trademark. Logotype. (ID ee uh graf')

idiolect [*idio-, personal & (dia)lect*] The speech pattern of an individual, considered to be unique among users of the same dialect or language. (ID ee uh lekt')

idiom [*idio-, peculiar*] 1.An expression in a language that is peculiar to itself and cannot be understood from the meanings of its constituent elements, as *kick the bucket* meaning "to die." 2.The language peculiar to a certain area or group of people. (ID ee um)

idiomatic [*idio-, peculiar + -tic*] Characteristic of or peculiar to a particular language. (id' ee uh MAT ik)

idiomorphic [*idio-, peculiar + morph, form + -ic*] 1.Possessing its own distinct form or shape. 2.Pertaining to minerals with unaltered crystalline growth. (id' ee uh MOR fik)

idiopathy [*idio-, peculiar + path, disease + -y*] Any disease or condition of unknown cause or origin. See cryptogenic. (id' ee OP uh thee)

idiosyncrasy [*idio-, peculiar + syn, together + Grk > krasis, mixture + -y*] A physical or mental characteristic peculiar to a person, as taste, behavior, etc. (id' ee oh SING kruh see)

idiot [*idio-, personal*] 1.A person deficient in ordinary mental capabilities. 2.A person who is very foolish or stupid. (ID ee ut)

inter-   between, among

extrapolate [*extra-, outside & (inter)polate*] 1.To estimate the value of a variable outside its known range. See interpolate (def. 2). 2.To estimate an unknown from something that is known. (eks TRAP uh layt')

inter alia [*inter-, among & Ltn > alius, other*] Among other things. (IN ter AY lee uh)

inter vivos [*inter-, between & viv, living*] Taking place between living persons, as a gift or trust. (IN ter VEE vohs)

intercalate [*inter-, between + Ltn > calare, to proclaim + -ate*] 1.To insert in the calendar, as an extra day or month. 2.To insert, interpose, or interpolate between existing elements. See interpose (def. 1) and interpolate (def. 3). (in TER kuh layt')

intercede [*inter-, between + cede, to go*] 1.To act as a go-between in a disagreement. Mediate. 2.To plead in behalf of another. See intervene, mediate, and intermediary. (in' ter SEED)

intercept [*inter-, between + cept, to take*] 1.To stop the progress of. 2.To take or seize between the starting point and destination. (in' ter SEPT)

interdental [*inter-, between + dent, teeth + -al*] 1.Located between the teeth. 2.Articulated with the tip of the tongue between the upper and lower front teeth. See dental and labiodental. (in' ter DENT l)

interdict [*inter-, between + dict, to speak*] 1.To prohibit or forbid, usually in an official manner. (in' ter DIKT {verb}) 2.A disciplinary action in the Roman Catholic Church prohibiting certain privileges and functions. (IN ter dikt' {noun})

interfere [*inter-, between + Ltn > ferire, to strike*] To come into opposition between, especially with the effect of hindering. Impede. See impede. (in' ter FIHR)

interferometer [*interfer(e) & meter, to measure*] Any of several instruments that use the interference phenomena of light, sound, or radio waves for measuring wave length, minute distances, and indices of refraction. (in' ter fuh ROM et er)

interferon [*interfer(e) & -on*] A cellular protein that is produced in response to a viral infection and inhibits reproduction and spread of the virus. (in' ter FIHR on')

interfuse [*inter-, between + fus, pour*] 1.To combine by blending or mixing. 2.To pour upon or pass into or through. (in' ter FYOOZ)

intergalactic [*inter-, between & galactic*] Occurring or existing between galaxies. (in' ter guh LAK tik)

intergrade [*inter-, between + -grade, to step*] To merge gradually into another form or kind through a series of stages. (in' ter GRAYD)

interim [*inter-, between + -im*] The period of time between one event, process, or period and another. Meantime. Interval. See interval. (IN ter im)

interject [*inter-, between + ject, to throw*] 1.To insert between other elements. 2.To introduce abruptly, as a statement or remark. (in' ter JEKT)

interlace [*inter-, between & lace*] To unite by lacing or weaving together. (in' ter LAYS)

interleave [*inter-, between & lea(f)*] To insert a page or pages between the existing pages of a book, document, etc. (in' ter LEEV)

interlinear [*inter-, between + Ltn > linea, line + -ar*] 1.Printed or written between the lines of a text. 2.Having the same text printed on alternate lines in different languages. (in' ter LIN ee ur)

Interlingua [*inter-, between + lingu, language + -a*] An artificial language, largely derived from Latin-based languages, used for communication especially between nations of the scientific community. (in' ter LING gwuh)

interlocution [*inter-, between + locu, to speak + -tion*] Dialogue or conversation between two or more people. (in' ter loh KYOO shun)

interlocutor [*inter-, between + locu, to speak + -tor*] One who takes part in a conversation or dialogue. (in' ter LOK yuh tur)

interloper [*inter-, between + Ltn > lopen, to run*] 1.A person who violates the legal rights of others, as in trade. 2.A person who interferes wrongly in the affairs of others. Intruder. (IN ter lohp' ur)

interlude [*inter-, between + lud, to play*] 1.Any episode, period, performance, etc., that takes place between two things. 2.Entertainment between the acts of a play. 3.Music played between parts of a composition. See prelude and postlude. (IN ter lood')

interlunar [*inter-, between + lun, moon + -ar*] Pertaining to the period of time each month between the old moon and the new moon during which the moon is not visible from the earth. (in' ter LOO nur)

intermediary [*inter-, between + medi, middle + -ary*] 1.One who acts as an agent between parties. 2.Intermediate. See mediate, intercede, and intervene. (in' ter MEE dee ehr' ee)

intermediate [*inter-, between + medi, middle + -ate*] Occurring or positioned between two things in time or order. (in' ter MEE dee it)

intermittent [*inter-, between + mit, to send + -ent*] Occurring at intervals. Periodic. Not continuous. (in' ter MIT nt)

intermolecular [*inter-, between & molecular*] Existing or acting between or among molecules. (in' ter muh LEK yuh lur)

internet [*inter-, between & net(work)*] A huge computer network among government agencies, universities, corporations, and individuals. (IN ter net')

interneuron [*inter-, between + neur, nerve + -on*] Neurons that link sensory and motor neurons in the brain and spinal cord. (in' ter NOOR on')

interpellate [*inter-, between + pel, to drive + -ate*] To formally question a government official about policy or personal behavior. (in' ter PEL ayt')

interpolate [*inter-, between + Ltn > polire, to polish + -ate*] 1.To make insertions or additions to refurbish text, especially deceptively or without authorization. 2.To estimate a value between two known values. See extrapolate (def. 1). 3.To insert between other elements. See interpose (def. 1) and intercalate (def. 2). (in TER puh layt')

interpose [*inter-, between + pos, place*] 1.To place or introduce between. Insert. See interpolate (def. 3) and intercalate (def. 2). 2.To act as an intermediary. Intervene. See intervene and intermediary. (in' ter POHZ)

interracial [*inter-, between & rac(e) & -ial*] Between persons of different races. (in' ter RAY shul)

interrogate [*inter-, between + rog, to ask + -ate*] To question formally and thoroughly. (in TEHR uh gayt')

interrupt [*inter-, between + rupt, to break*] 1.To hinder or stop by breaking in upon, as a person speaking, work, rest, etc. 2.A signal to a computer to stop executing the current program in order to execute a higher priority program. (in' tuh RUPT)

intersect [*inter-, between + sect, to cut*] 1.To divide by cutting through or across. 2.To cross each other at a point. (in' ter SEKT)

intersperse [*inter-, among + Ltn > spargere, to scatter*] To scatter or place at intervals among other things. (in' ter SPURS)

interstate [*inter-, between & state*] Occurring or located between two or more states. See intrastate. (in' ter STAYT)

interval [*inter-, between + Ltn > vallum, wall*] A gap of space or time between two things. See interim. (IN ter vul)

intervene [*inter-, between + ven, to come*] 1.To come between. 2.To act as an intermediary. See intercede, mediate, and intermediary. (in' ter VEEN)

intervocalic [*inter-, between + voc, voice + -al + -ic*] Pertaining to a consonant or other linguistic element that occurs between two vowels. See vocalic, prevocalic, and postvocalic. (in' ter voh KAL ik)

-itis   inflammation

adenitis [*aden, gland + -itis, inflammation*] Inflammation of a gland or lymph node. (ad' n EYE tis)

appendicitis [*appendi(x) & -itis, inflammation*] Inflammation of the vermiform appendix. (uh pen' duh SEYE tis)

arteritis [*arter(y) & -itis, inflammation*] Inflammation of an artery. (ahr' tuh REYE tis)

arthritis [*arthr, joint* + *-itis, inflammation*] Inflammation of a joint, as in gout or rheumatoid arthritis. (ahr THREYE tis)

blepharitis [*blephar, eyelid* + *-itis, inflammation*] Inflammation of the eyelid. (blef' uh REYE tis)

bronchitis [*bronch, bronchial tube* + *-itis, inflammation*] Inflammation of the mucous membrane of the bronchial tubes. (brong KEYE tis)

bursitis [*burs(a)* & *-itis, inflammation*] Inflammation of a bursa, especially of the shoulder, hip, elbow, or knee joint. (bur SEYE tis)

carditis [*cardi, heart* + *-itis, inflammation*] Inflammation of the heart. (kahr DEYE tis)

cholecystitis [*chole, gall* + *cyst, bladder* + *-itis, inflammation*] Inflammation of the gallbladder. (koh' luh sih STEYE tis)

colitis [*col, colon* + *-itis, inflammation*] Inflammation of the colon. (koh LEYE tis)

conjunctivitis [*conjunctiv(a)* & *-itis, inflammation*] Inflammation of the conjunctiva. (kun jungk' tuh VEYE tis)

dermatitis [*dermat, skin* + *-itis, inflammation*] Inflammation of the skin. (der' muh TEYE tis)

encephalitis [*encephal, brain* + *-itis, inflammation*] Inflammation of the brain. (en sef' uh LEYE tis)

encephalomyelitis [*encephalo, brain* + *myel, spinal cord* + *-itis, inflammation*] Any of various viral diseases resulting in acute inflammation of the brain and spinal cord. (en sef' uh loh meye' uh LEYE tis)

endocarditis [*endo-, inside* + *cardi, heart* + *-itis, inflammation*] Inflammation of the endocardium. (en' doh kahr DEYE tis)

enteritis [*enter, intestine* + *-itis, inflammation*] Inflammation of the intestinal tract, especially the small intestine. (ent' uh REYE tis)

gastritis [*gastr, stomach* + *-itis, inflammation*] Inflammation of the mucous membrane of the stomach. (gas TREYE tis)

gastroenteritis [*gastro, stomach* + *enter, intestine* + *-itis, inflammation*] Inflammation of the mucous membrane of the stomach and intestines. (gas' troh ent' uh REYE tis)

gingivitis [*gingiv, gum* + *-itis, inflammation*] Inflammation of the gums, marked by redness, swelling, and occasional bleeding, that may progress to periodontitis and usually results from poor oral hygiene. See pyorrhea and periodontitis. (jin' jih VEYE tis)

glomerulonephritis [*glomerul(us)* & *nephr, kidney* + *-itis, inflammation*] A type of nephritis marked by inflammation of the capillaries of the renal glomeruli. (gloh mehr' yuh loh' neh FREYE tis)

hepatitis [*hepat, liver* + *-itis, inflammation*] Inflammation of the liver characterized by jaundice, fever, and liver enlargement. (hep' uh TEYE tis)

ileitis [*ile(um)* & *-itis, inflammation*] Inflammation of the ileum. (il' ee EYE tis)

iritis [*ir(is)* & *-itis, inflammation*] Inflammation of the iris of the eye. (eye REYE tis)

keratitis [*kerat, cornea* + *-itis, inflammation*] Inflammation of the cornea. (kehr' uh TEYE tis)

laryngitis [*laryng, larynx* + *-itis, inflammation*] Inflammation of the larynx, often accompanied by sore throat and temporary loss of voice. (lehr' un JEYE tis)

lymphadenitis [*lymph, lymph* + *aden, gland* + *-itis, inflammation*] Inflammation of the lymph nodes. (lim fad' n EYE tis)

mastitis [*mast, breast* + *-itis, inflammation*] Inflammation of the breast or udder. (mas TEYE tis)

mastoiditis [*mastoid* & *-itis, inflammation*] Inflammation of the mastoid process. (mas' toid' EYE tis)

meningitis [*mening, meninges* + *-itis, inflammation*] Inflammation of the meninges, especially as the result of bacterial infection. (men' in JEYE tis)

metritis [*metr, uterus* + *-itis, inflammation*] Inflammation of the uterus. (mih TREYE tis)

myelitis [*myel, spinal cord or marrow* + *-itis, inflammation*] 1. Inflammation of the spinal cord. 2. Inflammation of the bone marrow. (meye' uh LEYE tis)

myocarditis [*myo, muscle* + *cardi, heart* + *-itis, inflammation*] Inflammation of the myocardium. (meye' oh kahr DEYE tis)

nephritis [*nephr, kidney* + *-itis, inflammation*] Acute or chronic inflammation of the kidneys. (neh FREYE tis)

neuritis [*neur, nerve* + *-itis, inflammation*] Inflammation of a nerve, resulting in pain, sensory disturbances, and muscular atrophy. (noo REYE tis)

oophoritis [*oophor-, ovary* + *-itis, inflammation*] Inflammation of an ovary. (oh' uh fuh REYE tis)

osteitis [*oste, bone* + *-itis, inflammation*] Inflammation of a bone. (os' tee EYE tis)

osteoarthritis [*osteo, bone* + *arthr, joint* + *-itis, inflammation*] Inflammation caused by a slowly progressive disease marked by degeneration of the cartilage in joints. (os' tee oh' ahr THREYE tis)

osteomyelitis [*osteo, bone* + *myel, marrow* + *-itis, inflammation*] Inflammation of a bone or bone marrow, normally caused by a bacterium or other pathogenic microorganism. (os' tee oh meye' uh LEYE tis)

otitis [*ot, ear* + *-itis, inflammation*] Inflammation of the ear. (oh TEYE tis)

ovaritis [*ovar(y)* & *-itis, inflammation*] Inflammation of an ovary. Same as oophoritis. (oh' vuh REYE tis)

pancreatitis [*pancreat, pancreas* + *-itis, inflammation*] Inflammation of the pancreas. (pan' kree uh TEYE tis)

parotitis [*para-, beside* + *ot, ear* + *-itis, inflammation*] Inflammation and swelling of the parotid glands, as with mumps. (pehr' oh TEYE tis)

pericarditis [*peri-, around* + *cardi, heart* + *-itis, inflammation*] Inflammation of the pericardium. (pehr' ih kahr DEYE tis)

periodontitis [*peri-, around* + *odont, tooth* + *-itis, inflammation*] Inflammation of the tissues surrounding a tooth, which may result in pus-filled abscesses forming in the gums and spreading into the tooth socket, causing eventual tooth loss. See gingivitis and pyorrhea. (pehr' ee oh don TEYE tis)

periostitis [*peri-, around* + *oste, bone* + *-itis, inflammation*] Inflammation of the periosteum. (pehr' ee os TEYE tis)

peritonitis [*periton(eum)* & *-itis, inflammation*] Inflammation of the peritoneum. (pehr' ih tuh NEYE tis)

pharyngitis [*pharyng, pharynx* + *-itis, inflammation*] Inflammation of the mucous membrane of the pharynx. Sore throat. (fehr' in JEYE tis)

phlebitis [*phleb, vein* + *-itis, inflammation*] Inflammation of a vein. (flih BEYE tis)

poliomyelitis [*Grk > polios, gray + myel, spinal cord + -itis, inflammation*] An acute, infectious viral disease caused by inflammation of the gray matter of the spinal cord and resulting in paralysis, muscular atrophy, and often permanent deformities. Polio. (poh' lee oh meye' uh LEYE tis)

polyneuritis [*poly, many + neur, nerve + -itis, inflammation*] Inflammation of two or more peripheral nerves. (pol' ee noo REYE tis)

prostatitis [*prostat, prostate gland + -itis, inflammation*] Inflammation of the prostate gland. (pros' tuh TEYE tis)

pyelitis [*pyel, renal pelvis + -itis, inflammation*] Inflammation of both the kidney and the lining of its pelvis. Same as pyelonephritis. (peye' uh LEYE tis)

pyelonephritis [*pyelo, renal pelvis + nephr, kidney + -itis, inflammation*] Inflammation of both the kidney and the lining of its pelvis. (peye' uh loh' neh FREYE tis)

retinitis [*retin(a) & -itis, inflammation*] Inflammation of the retina. (ret' n EYE tis)

rheumatoid arthritis [*rheumat(ism) & arthr, joint + -itis, inflammation*] A chronic disease marked by stiffness, pain, swelling, inflammation, and often deformity of joints. (ROO muh toid' ahr THREYE tis)

rhinitis [*rhin, nose + -itis, inflammation*] Inflammation of the mucous membrane of the nose. (reye NEYE tis)

rhinopharyngitis [*rhino, nose + pharyng, pharynx + -itis, inflammation*] Inflammation of the mucous membrane of the nose and pharynx. (reye' noh fehr' in JEYE tis)

salpingitis [*salping, fallopian tube + -itis, inflammation*] Inflammation of the fallopian tube or eustachian tube. (sal' pin JEYE tis)

scleritis [*scler(a) & -itis, inflammation*] Inflammation of the sclera. (skluh REYE tis)

sialadenitis [*sial, saliva + aden, gland + -itis, inflammation*] Inflammation of a salivary gland. (seye' uh lad' n EYE tis)

sinusitis [*sinus & -itis, inflammation*] Inflammation of a sinus or sinuses. (seye' nyuh SEYE tis)

spondylitis [*spondyl, vertebrae + -itis, inflammation*] Inflammation of the vertebrae. (spon' duh LEYE tis)

stomatitis [*stomat, mouth + -itis, inflammation*] Inflammation of the mucous membrane of the mouth. (stoh' muh TEYE tis)

tendinitis [*tend(on) & -itis, inflammation*] Inflammation of a tendon. (ten' duh NEYE tis)

thrombophlebitis [*thrombo, blood clot + phleb, vein + -itis, inflammation*] Inflammation of the inner lining of a vein associated with the formation of a blood clot. (throm' boh flih BEYE tis)

thyroiditis [*thyroid & -itis, inflammation*] Inflammation of the thyroid gland. (theye' roid' EYE tis)

tonsillitis [*tonsil & -itis, inflammation*] Inflammation of the tonsils. (ton' suh LEYE tis)

tracheitis [*trache, trachea + -itis, inflammation*] Inflammation of the trachea. (tray' kee EYE tis)

urethritis [*urethr, urethra + -itis, inflammation*] Inflammation of the urethra. (yoor' uh THREYE tis)

uveitis [*uve(a) & -itis, inflammation*] Inflammation of the uvea of the eye. (yoo' vee EYE tis)

uvulitis [*uvul(a) & -itis, inflammation*] Inflammation of the uvula. (yoo' vuh LEYE tis)

vaginitis [*vagin(a) & -itis, inflammation*] Inflammation of the vagina. (vaj' uh NEYE tis)

vulvitis [*vulv(a) & -itis, inflammation*] Inflammation of the vulva. (vul VEYE tis)

vulvovaginitis [*vulv(a) & vagin(a) & -itis, inflammation*] Inflammation of the vulva and vagina. (vul' voh vaj' uh NEYE tis)

ject   to throw

abject [*ab-, down + ject, to throw*] 1.Utterly hopeless and miserable. 2.Despicable. Contemptible. (AB jekt)

adjective [*ad-, toward + ject, to throw + -ive*] A word that modifies a noun or pronoun to indicate quality, quantity, extent, etc. (AJ ik tiv)

conjecture [*con-, together + ject, to throw + -ure*] A statement, opinion, or conclusion based on inconclusive or incomplete evidence. (kun JEK chur)

deject [*de-, down + ject, to throw*] To lower in spirit. Depress. Dishearten. (dih JEKT)

eject [*e-, out + ject, to throw*] 1.To throw out forcefully. Discharge. 2.To dismiss, as from competition, occupancy, office, etc. (ih JEKT)

inject [*in-, in + ject, to throw*] 1.To throw, force, or drive into something. 2.To introduce a fluid into, especially for medical purposes. 3.To introduce a suggestion, remark, etc., into a conversation. (in JEKT)

interject [*inter-, between + ject, to throw*] 1.To insert between other elements. 2.To introduce abruptly, as a statement or remark. (in' ter JEKT)

introject [*intro-, inward + ject, to throw*] To unconsciously incorporate another person's attitudes or ideas, or the characteristics of an inanimate object, into one's own personality. (in' truh JEKT)

object [*ob-, against + ject, to throw*] 1.To argue in opposition to. 2. To show disapproval or dislike. (ub JEKT)

project [*pro-, forward + ject, to throw*] To throw or impel forward, outward, or upward. See protrude and protuberant. (pruh JEKT)

projectile [*pro-, forward + ject, to throw + -ile*] An object, such as a bullet, that is fired, thrown, or otherwise projected forward. (pruh JEKT ul)

reject [*re-, back + ject, to throw*] To refuse to accept, recognize, or consider. (rih JEKT)

subject [*sub-, under + ject, to throw*] 1.To bring under control. 2.To cause to undergo. (sub JEKT)

traject [*trans-, across + ject, to throw*] To transmit. (truh JEKT)

trajectory [*trans-, across + ject, to throw + -ory*] The path of a moving projectile, rocket, particle, etc. (truh JEKT uh ree)

junct   to join

adjunct [*ad-, addition + junct, to join*] 1.Something joined or added to something else without being a necessary part of it. 2.A word or phrase that modifies, qualifies, or clarifies another word or phrase. 3.A person acting as an assistant to another person of higher rank, authority, etc. (AJ ungkt)

conjunct [*con-, together + junct, to join*] Joined together. Combined. United. (kun JUNGKT)

conjunction [*con-, together + junct, to join + -ion*] 1.A joining together. Union. 2.A word that connects sentences, clauses, phrases, or other words. 3.Simultaneous occurrence. Concurrence. Combination. (kun JUNGK shun)

conjunctiva [*con-, together + junct, to join + -ive + -a*] The mucous membrane that lines the inner surface of the eyelid and covers the exposed surface of the eyeball. (kon' jungk TEYE vuh)

conjunctivitis [*conjunctiv(a) & -itis, inflammation*] Inflammation of the conjunctiva. (kun jungk' tuh VEYE tis)

disjunct [*dis-, apart + junct, to join*] Disjoined. Separated. (dis JUNGKT)

injunction [*in-, in + junct, to join + -ion*] 1.The act of enjoining. 2.A court order commanding or prohibiting the doing of a specified act. 3.Command. Directive. Order. (in JUNGK shun)

junction [*junct, to join + -ion*] 1.The act of joining. 2.The point or place where two or more things meet. (JUNGK shun)

juncture [*junct, to join + -ure*] A critical point in time or convergence of events. (JUNGK chur)

subjunctive [*sub-, beneath + junct, to join + -ive*] 1.Pertaining to a verb form used to represent contingent or hypothetical action rather than actual fact. 2.The subjunctive mood. (sub JUNGK tiv)

thermojunction [*thermo, heat & junction*] The junction between the two dissimilar metal conductors of a thermocouple. (thur' moh JUNGK shun)

kilo-   thousand (10³)

kilo [*kilo-, thousand*] Short for kilogram or kilometer. (KEE loh)

kilobar [*kilo-, thousand + bar, pressure*] A metric unit of pressure equal to 1,000 bars. (KIL uh bahr')

kilobit [*kilo-, thousand & bit*] One thousand twenty four (2¹⁰) binary digits. (KIL uh bit')

kilobyte [*kilo-, thousand & byte*] One thousand twenty four (2¹⁰) bytes. (KIL uh beyet')

kilocycle [*kilo-, thousand & cycle*] One thousand cycles per second. Kilohertz. (KIL uh seye' kul)

kilogram [*kilo-, thousand & gram*] A metric unit of weight equal to 1,000 grams. (KIL uh gram')

kilogrammeter [*kilogram & meter*] A metric unit of work equal to the energy needed to raise one kilogram to a vertical distance of one meter. (kil' uh gram MEE ter)

kilohertz [*kilo-, thousand & hertz*] One thousand cycles per second. Kilocycle. (KIL uh hurts')

kiloliter [*kilo-, thousand & liter*] A metric unit of volume equal to 1,000 liters. (KIL uh lee' ter)

kilometer [*kilo-, thousand & meter*] A metric unit of length equal to 1,000 meters. (kih LOM et er)

kiloton [*kilo-, thousand & ton*] 1.One thousand tons. 2.An explosive force equal to one thousand tons of TNT. (KIL uh tun')

kilovolt [*kilo-, thousand & volt*] One thousand volts. (KIL uh vohlt')

kilowatt [*kilo-, thousand & watt*] One thousand watts. (KIL uh wot')

kilowatt-hour [*kilowatt & hour*] A unit of electrical energy equal to the power supplied by one kilowatt for one hour. (KIL uh wot our')

meter-kilogram-second Pertaining to a system of measurement that uses the meter, kilogram, and second as the basic units corresponding to length, mass, and time. (MEE ter KIL uh gram' SEK und)

mill   thousand (10³)
milli-   thousandth (10⁻³)

cinquecento [*mill, thousand + quinque, five + cent, hundred*] Short for millecinquecento. The 16th century (1500-1599) period of Italian art and literature. See trecento, quattrocento, and seicento. (ching' kwih CHEN toh)

micromillimeter [*micro-, millionth & millimeter*] A metric unit of length equal to one millionth of a millimeter. (meye' kroh MIL uh mee' ter)

milfoil [*mill, thousand + foli, leaf*] An aromatic composite plant with finely divided fernlike leaves and white or pink flower clusters. Yarrow. (MIL foil)

millenarian [*mill, thousand + enn, years + -arian*] 1.Pertaining to one thousand, especially one thousand years. 2.Pertaining to belief in the millennium. (mil' uh NEHR ee un)

millennium [*mill, thousand + enn, years + -ium*] 1.A period of one thousand years. 2.The period of one thousand years mentioned in the Bible during which Christ will rule on earth. (mih LEN ee um)

millepede [*mill, thousand + -pede, feet*] Any of numerous elongated, cylindrical, herbivorous arthropods of the class Diplopoda with numerous body segments each having two pairs of legs and no poisonous fangs. Same as millipede. (MIL uh peed')

millesimal [*milli-, thousandth + -imal*] 1.Thousandth. 2.Divided into thousandths. (mih LES uh mul)

milliammeter [*milliam(pere) & meter, to measure*] An instrument for measuring small electric currents that is calibrated to indicate values in milliamperes. (mil' ee AM mee' ter)

milliampere [*milli-, thousandth & ampere*] A metric unit of electric current equal to one thousandth of an ampere. (mil' ee AM pihr)

milliard [*mill, thousand + -ard*] One thousand million. Billion. (MIL yurd)

milliary [*mill, thousand + -ary*] Pertaining to an ancient Roman mile which equaled one thousand paces. (MIL ee ehr' ee)

millibar [*milli-, thousandth + bar, pressure*] A metric unit of pressure equal to one thousandth of a bar, or 1,000 dynes per square centimeter. (MIL uh bahr')

millicurie [*milli-, thousandth & curie*] A metric unit of radioactivity equal to one thousandth of a curie. (MIL uh kyoor' ee)

millieme [*milli-, thousandth + -eme*] A monetary unit of Egypt and Libya equal to one thousandth of a pound. (meel YEM)

millifarad [*milli-, thousandth & farad*] A metric unit of capacitance equal to one thousandth of a farad. (MIL uh fehr' uhd)

milligal [*milli-, thousandth & gal*] A metric unit of acceleration equal to one thousandth of a gal. (MIL uh gal')

mill, milli-

milligram [*milli-, thousandth & gram*] A metric unit of weight equal to one thousandth of a gram. (MIL uh gram')

millihenry [*milli-, thousandth & henry*] A metric unit of inductance equal to one thousandth of a henry. (MIL uh hen' ree)

milliliter [*milli-, thousandth & liter*] A metric unit of volume equal to one thousandth of a liter. (MIL uh lee' ter)

millimeter [*milli-, thousandth & meter*] A metric unit of length equal to one thousandth of a meter. (MIL uh mee' ter)

millimicron [*milli-, thousandth & micron*] A metric unit of length equal to one thousandth of a micron. (mil' uh MEYE kron)

millipede [*mill, thousand + -pede, feet*] Any of numerous elongated, cylindrical, herbivorous arthropods of the class Diplopoda with numerous body segments each having two pairs of legs and no poisonous fangs. See centipede and myriapod. (MIL uh peed')

millirem [*milli-, thousandth & rem*] A metric unit of radiation equal to one thousandth of a rem. (MIL uh rem')

millisecond [*milli-, thousandth & second*] A metric unit of time equal to one thousandth of a second. (MIL uh sek' und)

millivolt [*milli-, thousandth & volt*] A metric unit of electric potential equal to one thousandth of a volt. (MIL uh vohlt')

milliwatt [*milli-, thousandth & watt*] A metric unit of power equal to one thousandth of a watt. (MIL uh wot')

postmillennial [*post-, after + mill, thousand + enn, years + -ial*] Occurring or existing after the millennium. See premillennial. (pohst' mih LEN ee ul)

premillennial [*pre-, before + mill, thousand + enn, years + -ial*] Occurring or existing before the millennium. See postmillennial. (pree' mih LEN ee ul)

quattrocento [*mill, thousand + quattro, four + cent, hundred*] Short for millequattrocento. The 15th century (1400-1499) period of Italian art and literature. See trecento, cinquecento, and seicento. (kwot' roh CHEN toh)

seicento [*mill, thousand + sex, six + cent, hundred*] Short for milleseicento. The 17th century (1600-1699) period of Italian art and literature. See trecento, quattrocento, and cinquecento. (say CHEN toh)

trecento [*mill, thousand + Ltn > tres, three + cent, hundred*] Short for milletrecento. The 14th century (1300-1399) period of Italian art and literature. See quattrocento, cinquecento, and seicento. (tray CHEN toh)

million [*mill, thousand + -ion*] A number expressed as 1 followed by 6 zeros, which is 1 group of three zeros after 1,000. (MIL yun)

billion [*bi-, two + (m)ill, thousand + -ion*] A number expressed as 1 followed by 9 zeros, which is 2 groups of three zeros after 1,000. (BIL yun)

trillion [*tri-, three + (m)ill, thousand + -ion*] A number expressed as 1 followed by 12 zeros, which is 3 groups of three zeros after 1,000. (TRIL yun)

quadrillion [*quadr, four + (m)ill, thousand + -ion*] A number expressed as 1 followed by 15 zeros, which is 4 groups of three zeros after 1,000. (kwah DRIL yun)

quintillion [*quint, five + (m)ill, thousand + -ion*] A number expressed as 1 followed by 18 zeros, which is 5 groups of three zeros after 1,000. (kwin TIL yun)

sextillion [*sex-, six + (m)ill, thousand + -ion*] A number expressed as 1 followed by 21 zeros, which is 6 groups of three zeros after 1,000. (seks TIL yun)

septillion [*sept-, seven + (m)ill, thousand + -ion*] A number expressed as 1 followed by 24 zeros, which is 7 groups of three zeros after 1,000. (sep TIL yun)

octillion [*oct-, eight + (m)ill, thousand + -ion*] A number expressed as 1 followed by 27 zeros, which is 8 groups of three zeros after 1,000. (ok TIL yun)

nonillion [*Ltn > nonus, ninth + (m)ill, thousand + -ion*] A number expressed as 1 followed by 30 zeros, which is 9 groups of three zeros after 1,000. (noh NIL yun)

decillion [*dec, ten + (m)ill, thousand + -ion*] A number expressed as 1 followed by 33 zeros, which is 10 groups of three zeros after 1,000. (dih SIL yun)

undecillion [*uni-, one + dec, ten + (m)ill, thousand + -ion*] A number expressed as 1 followed by 36 zeros, which is 11 groups of three zeros after 1,000. (un' dih SIL yun)

duodecillion [*duodec-, twelve + (m)ill, thousand + -ion*] A number expressed as 1 followed by 39 zeros, which is 12 groups of three zeros after 1,000. (doo' oh dih SIL yun)

tredecillion [*Ltn > tres, three + dec, ten + (m)ill, thousand + -ion*] A number expressed as 1 followed by 42 zeros, which is 13 groups of three zeros after 1,000. (tree' dih SIL yun)

quattuordecillion [*quattr, four + dec, ten + (m)ill, thousand + -ion*] A number expressed as 1 followed by 45 zeros, which is 14 groups of three zeros after 1,000. (kwot' oo or' dih SIL yun)

quindecillion [*quin, five + dec, ten + (m)ill, thousand + -ion*] A number expressed as 1 followed by 48 zeros, which is 15 groups of three zeros after 1,000. (kwin' dih SIL yun)

sexdecillion [*sex-, six + dec, ten + (m)ill, thousand + -ion*] A number expressed as 1 followed by 51 zeros, which is 16 groups of three zeros after 1,000. (seks' dih SIL yun)

septendecillion [*sept-, seven + dec, ten + (m)ill, thousand + -ion*] A number expressed as 1 followed by 54 zeros, which is 17 groups of three zeros after 1,000. (sep' ten' dih SIL yun)

octodecillion [*octo-, eight + dec, ten + (m)ill, thousand + -ion*] A number expressed as 1 followed by 57 zeros, which is 18 groups of three zeros after 1,000. (ok' toh dih SIL yun)

novemdecillion [*Ltn > novem, nine + dec, ten + (m)ill, thousand + -ion*] A number expressed as 1 followed by 60 zeros, which is 19 groups of three zeros after 1,000. (noh' vem' dih SIL yun)

vigintillion [*Ltn > viginti, twenty + (m)ill, thousand + -ion*] A number expressed as 1 followed by 63 zeros, which is 20 groups of three zeros after 1,000. (vih' jin TIL yun)

centillion [*cent, hundred + (m)ill, thousand + -ion*] A number expressed as 1 followed by 303 zeros, which is 100 groups of three zeros after 1,000. (sen TIL yun)

kine, kinet, kinemat   motion, division

cinematography [*kinemato, motion + -graphy, recording*] The art, science, or process of motion picture making. (sin' uh muh TOG ruh fee)

cytokinesis [*cyto, cell* + *kine, division* + *-sis*] The changes that occur in the cytoplasm during cell division after the division of the nucleus. See cytoplasm and karyokinesis. (seyet' oh kih NEE sis)

diakinesis [*dia-, through* + *kine, motion* + *-sis*] The last stage of the prophase in meiosis, characterized by the homologous chromosomes repelling each other and the disappearance of the nucleolus. (deye' uh kih NEE sis)

dyskinesia [*dys-, impaired* + *kine, motion* + *-ia*] Impairment of voluntary muscular movements. (dis' kih NEE zhuh)

electrokinetics [*electro, electricity* + *kinet, motion* + *-ics, study of*] The branch of physics dealing with the study of electricity in motion. See electrostatics. (ih lek' troh kih NET iks)

hydrokinetics [*hydro, liquid* + *kinet, motion* + *-ics, science*] The branch of hydrodynamics dealing with the study of liquids in motion. See hydrodynamics. (heye' droh kih NET iks)

hyperkinesis [*hyper-, excessive* + *kine, motion* + *-sis*] Abnormally excessive muscular movement. (heye' per kih NEE sis)

karyokinesis [*karyo, nucleus* + *kine, division* + *-sis*] The changes that occur in the nucleus during cell division. See cytokinesis. (kehr' ee oh' kih NEE sis)

kinematics [*kinemat, motion* + *-ics, study of*] The branch of mechanics dealing with the study of pure motion without reference to force or mass. See dynamics and kinetics. (kin' uh MAT iks)

kinesics [*kine, motion* + *-ics, study of*] The study of body movements, facial expressions, and gestures that aid in communication. Body language. (kih NEE siks)

kinesiology [*kine, motion* + *-ology, study of*] The study of human body movement and the muscles involved. (kih nee' see OL uh jee)

kinesthesia [*kine, motion* + *esthes, sensation* + *-ia*] The sensation of body movement perceived through sensory nerve endings in muscles, joints, and tendons. (kin' es THEE zhuh)

kinetic [*kinet, motion* + *-ic*] Pertaining to, resulting from, or produced by motion. (kih NET ik)

kinetics [*kinet, motion* + *-ics, study of*] The branch of mechanics dealing with the study of the effects of forces on the motion of material bodies. See dynamics and kinematics. (kih NET iks)

kinetin [*kinet, division* + *-in*] A plant substance that regulates growth by promoting cell division. (KEYE nuh tin)

optokinetic [*opto, eye* + *kinet, motion* + *-ic*] Pertaining to or involving eye movements. (op' toh kih NET ik)

pharmacokinetics [*pharmaco, drug* + *kinet, motion* + *-ics, study of*] The branch of pharmacology dealing with the study of the rate of absorption, excretion, etc., of drugs. (fahr' muh koh' kih NET iks)

photokinesis [*photo, light* + *kine, motion* + *-sis*] Movement or activity in response to light. See phototaxis and phototropism. (foht' oh kih NEE sis)

psychokinesis [*psycho, mind* + *kine, motion* + *-sis*] The alleged ability to move physical objects with the powers of the mind. See telekinesis. (seye' koh kih NEE sis)

telekinesis [*tele, distant* + *kine, motion* + *-sis*] The alleged ability to cause movement of an object without the use of physical force, as by psychic forces. See psychokinesis. (tel' uh kih NEE sis)

-latry   worship

bibliolatry [*biblio, book* + *-latry, worship*] 1.Excessive adherence to a literal interpretation of the Bible. 2.Excessive devotion to or dependence on books. (bib' lee OL uh tree)

demonolatry [*demon & -latry, worship*] Worship of demons. (dee' muh NOL uh tree)

heliolatry [*helio, sun* + *-latry, worship*] Worship of the sun. (hee' lee OL uh tree)

iconolatry [*icono, image* + *-latry, worship*] Worship of icons or images. (eye' kuh NOL uh tree)

idolatry [*ido(l) & -latry, worship*] 1.Worship of idols. 2.Excessive devotion to a person or thing. (eye DOL uh tree)

Mariolatry [*Mar(y) & -latry, worship*] Worship of the Virgin Mary to an excessive degree. (mehr' ee OL uh tree)

necrolatry [*necro, dead* + *-latry, worship*] Worship of the dead. (nuh KROL uh tree)

zoolatry [*zoo, animal* + *-latry, worship*] Worship of animals. (zoh OL uh tree)

leuk/o, leuc/o   white, colorless

leucine [*leuc, white* + *-ine*] A white, crystalline amino acid essential to digestion that results from the hydrolysis of protein by pancreatic enzymes. (LOO seen)

leucite [*leuc, white* + *-ite, mineral*] A mineral, potassium-aluminum silicate, that is whitish or grayish in color and found in igneous rocks. (LOO seyet)

leucoplast [*leuco, colorless & plast(id)*] A colorless plastid found in plant cells, where starch is often formed and stored. See chromoplast and chloroplast. (LOO kuh plast')

leukemia [*leuk, white* + *-emia, blood condition*] A disease of the blood forming organs which results in an abnormal increase in the production of white blood cells. See leukopenia. (loo KEE mee uh)

leukocyte [*leuko, white* + *-cyte, cell*] A mature white blood cell. Leukocytes are divided into granulocytes (neutrophils, eosinophils, and basophiles) and agranulocytes (monocytes and lymphocytes). See erythrocyte, granulocyte, and agranulocyte. (LOO kuh seyet')

leukocytosis [*leuko, white* + *cyt, cell* + *-osis, increase*] An abnormal increase in the number of white blood cells in the blood, resulting from various conditions or diseases, as infection or leukemia. (loo' koh seye TOH sis)

leukoderma [*leuko, white* + *derma, skin*] Partial or total absence of skin pigmentation. See achromic (def. 2). (loo' kuh DER muh)

leukoma [*leuk, white* + *-oma, tumor*] A dense, white, opaque spot on the cornea of the eye. (loo KOH muh)

leukopenia [*leuko, white* + *-penia, lacking*] An abnormal decrease in the number of white blood cells in the circulating blood. See leukemia. (loo' kuh PEE nee uh)

leuk/o, leuc/o

leukoplakia [*leuko, white* + *Grk* > *plax, plate* + *-ia*] An abnormal condition of the mouth and genitals characterized by thick white patches on mucous membranes. (loo' koh PLAY kee uh)

leukopoiesis [*leuko, white* + *-poiesis, production*] The production and development of white blood cells. See erythropoiesis. (loo' koh poi EE sis)

leukorrhea [*leuko, white* + *rrhea, discharge*] A whitish discharge from the vagina that is usually normal, but in large amounts may be the result of infection or inflammation. (loo' kuh REE uh)

lingu   language, tongue

bilingual [*bi-, two* + *lingu, language* + *-al*] 1.Able to use two languages with nearly equal fluency. 2.Expressed in or involving two languages. (beye LING gwul)

cunnilingus [*Ltn* > *cunnus, vulva* + *lingu, tongue*] Sexual activity that involves oral stimulation of the vulva or clitoris. (kun' uh LING gus)

Interlingua [*inter-, between* + *lingu, language* + *-a*] An artificial language, largely derived from Latin-based languages, used for communication especially between nations of the scientific community. (in' ter LING gwuh)

lingua [*lingu, tongue* + *-a*] A tongue or anatomic structure resembling a tongue. (LING gwuh)

lingua franca [*lingua & franca*] Literally, "Frankish tongue." 1.A hybrid language spoken in various Mediterranean ports, consisting of Italian mixed with French, Greek, Spanish, Arabic, and Turkish. 2.Any language widely used for communication among peoples of different languages. (LING gwuh FRANG kuh)

lingual [*lingu, tongue* + *-al*] 1.Pertaining to the tongue. 2.Articulated with the tip of the tongue and the front teeth or the alveolar process. 3.Pertaining to language. Linguistic. (LING gwul)

linguine [*lingu, tongue* + *-ine*] Long, thin, flat pasta. So named for its tongued shape. (ling GWEE nee)

linguist [*lingu, language* + *-ist*] 1.A linguistics expert. 2.A person who is able to use several languages. See polyglot and multilingual. (LING gwist)

linguistic [*lingu, language* + *-istic*] Pertaining to language or linguistics. (ling GWIS tik)

linguistics [*lingu, language* + *-ist* + *-ics, study of*] The study of the nature, structure, and use of language, including phonology, morphology, syntax, and semantics. (ling GWIS tiks)

lingulate [*lingu, tongue* + *-ule* + *-ate*] Tongue-shaped. (LING gyuh layt')

metalinguistics [*meta-, between* + *lingu, language* + *-ist* + *-ics, study of*] The branch of linguistics dealing with the study of the relations between language and other cultural factors. (met' uh ling GWIS tiks)

monolingual [*mono-, one* + *lingu, language* + *-al*] 1.Able to use only one language. 2.Expressed in or involving only one language. (mon' uh LING gwul)

multilingual [*multi-, many* + *lingu, language* + *-al*] 1.Able to use several languages with nearly equal fluency. 2.Expressed in or involving several languages. See linguist and polyglot. (mul' tih LING gwul)

psycholinguistics [*psycho, mind* + *lingu, language* + *-ist* + *-ics, study of*] The study of the relationship between psychological behavior and the understanding and use of language. (seye' koh ling GWIS tiks)

sociolinguistics [*socio, social* + *lingu, language* + *-ist* + *-ics, study of*] The study of social and cultural factors and their effects on language usage. (soh' see oh' ling GWIS tiks)

sublingual [*sub-, under* + *lingu, tongue* + *-al*] Situated or occurring under the tongue or on the underside of the tongue. (sub' LING gwul)

trilingual [*tri-, three* + *lingu, language* + *-al*] 1.Able to use three languages with nearly equal fluency. 2.Expressed in or involving three languages. (treye LING gwul)

unilingual [*uni-, one* + *lingu, language* + *-al*] 1.Able to use only one language. 2.Expressed in or involving only one language. Same as monolingual. (yoo' nuh LING gwul)

lip/o   fat

hyperlipidemia [*hyper-, excessive & lipid & -emia, blood condition*] An abnormally high level of lipids in the blood. (heye' per lip' ih DEE mee uh)

lipase [*lip, fat* + *-ase, enzyme*] Any of a class of enzymes found in blood, gastric juices, and tissues that break down fats into glycerol and fatty acids. See lipolysis. (LEYEP ayz)

lipid [*lip, fat* + *-id*] Any of various fats or fatlike materials that together with carbohydrates and proteins constitute the main structural components of a living cell. (LIP id)

lipoid [*lip, fat* + *-oid, resembling*] 1.Resembling fat. 2.A lipid. (LIP oid)

lipolysis [*lipo, fat* + *-lysis, decomposition*] The chemical decomposition of fat, as in digestion. See lipase. (lih POL uh sis)

lipoma [*lip, fat* + *-oma, tumor*] A benign tumor composed of fatty tissue. (lih POH muh)

lipophilic [*lipo, fat* + *phil, affinity for* + *-ic*] Having a strong affinity for fats. (lip' uh FIL ik)

lipoprotein [*lipo, fat & protein*] Any of a large group of proteins consisting of a simple protein combined with a lipid. (lip' oh PROH teen')

lipotropic [*lipo, fat* + *trop, changing* + *-ic*] Preventing or correcting the accumulation of excess fat in the liver. (lip' oh TROP ik)

-lite, -ite   mineral, rock, stone, fossil

aerolite [*aero, air* + *-lite, stone*] A stony meteorite. See chondrite. (EHR uh leyet')

alexandrite [*Alexand(e)r & -ite, stone*] A green variety of chrysoberyl that appears deep red under artificial light and is used as a gem. Named after Alexander I, Russian Czar. (al' ig ZAN dreyet')

almandite [*Alabanda & -ite, mineral*] A deep red garnet with a violet tint. Named after Alabanda, an ancient city in Asia Minor. (AL mun deyet')

alunite [*Ltn* > *alumen, alum* + *-ite, mineral*] A mineral consisting of hydrated sulfate of potassium and aluminum and used mainly in making alum and fertilizer. (AL yuh neyet')

amblygonite [*Grk > amblys, obtuse + gon, angle + -ite, mineral*] A variously colored crystalline mineral that consists of basic lithium aluminum and produces crystals suitable as gemstones. So named for the obtuse angle at which it cleaves. (am BLIG uh neyet')

ammonite [*Ltn > cornu Ammonis, horn of Ammon + -ite, fossil*] Any of various flat, spiraled fossil shells with interior chambers from extinct cephalopod mollusks of the Mesozoic era. So named for their resemblance to the ram's horns in Jupiter Ammon's statues. (AM uh neyet')

amphibolite [*amphibol(e) & -ite, rock*] A metamorphic rock consisting mainly of amphibole. (am FIB uh leyet')

analcite [*an-, not + Grk > alkimos, strong + -ite, mineral*] A white or light-colored zeolite mineral. So named for its weak electric power when rubbed. (uh NAL seyet')

andalusite [*Andalus(ia) & -ite, mineral*] A mineral that usually occurs in orthorhombic prisms of various colors and shows green when viewed from one direction and brownish-red from another. Named after Andalusia, Spain, where it was discovered. (an' duh LOO seyet')

andesite [*Andes & -ite, rock*] A dark-gray volcanic rock consisting essentially of plagioclase feldspar. Named after the Andes Mountains in South America, where it was discovered. (AN duh zeyet')

andradite [*Andrad(a) & -ite, mineral*] A common variety of garnet containing iron and calcium and varying in color from light-green and yellow to black. Named after J.B. de Andrada, Brazilian geologist. (AN druh deyet')

anglesite [*Angles(ey) & -ite, mineral*] A lead sulfate mineral formed by oxidation with galena and occurring in colorless or slightly tinted orthorhombic crystals. Named after Anglesey, Wales, where it was discovered. (ANG gul seyet')

anhydrite [*an-, without + hydr, water + -ite, mineral*] A usually white to gray mineral composed of anhydrous calcium sulfate that is similar to gypsum, but does not contain water. (an HEYE dreyet')

ankerite [*Anker & -ite, mineral*] A translucent mineral similar to dolomite, but with iron partially replacing the magnesium. Named after M.J. Anker, Austrian mineralogist. (ANG kuh reyet')

anorthite [*an-, not + ortho, straight + -ite, rock*] A white, gray, or pink plagioclase feldspar found in many igneous rocks. So named for its oblique crystals. (an OR theyet')

anorthosite [*an-, not + ortho, straight + -ite, rock*] A plutonic igneous rock, chiefly plagioclase feldspar. So named for its oblique crystals. (an OR thuh seyet')

anthracite [*Grk > anthrax, coal + -ite, mineral*] A hard mineral coal that burns with much heat and little smoke or flame and has an extremely high content of carbon and a low proportion of volatile matter. (AN thruh seyet')

apatite [*Grk > apate, deceit + -ite, mineral*] Any of a group of common minerals, occurring in various forms and colors, that are calcium phosphates usually with some fluorine. So named because their varied forms and colors often caused them to be mistaken by early mineralogists for other minerals. (AP uh teyet')

aphanite [*a-, not + Grk > phainein, to show + -ite, rock*] A fine-grained rock with constituents so small they cannot be seen with the naked eye. (AF uh neyet')

apophyllite [*apo-, off + phyll, leaf + -ite, mineral*] A white, pale-pink, or pale-green crystalline mineral usually occurring in square transparent prisms or in white or grayish masses. So named from its tendency to flake off under intense heat. (uh POF uh leyet')

aragonite [*Aragon & -ite, mineral*] An orthorhombic mineral that is chemically the same as calcite, but is slightly harder and heavier. Synthetic coral, pearls, and the mother-of-pearl lining of sea shells are all aragonite. Named after Aragon in Spain. (uh RAG uh neyet')

argentite [*argent, silver + -ite, mineral*] A dark-gray silver sulfide mineral that is the major ore of silver. (AHR jen teyet')

augite [*Grk > auge, brightness + -ite, mineral*] A green to black silicate mineral with a vitreous luster that is a variety of pyroxene. (AW jeyet')

autunite [*Autun & -ite, mineral*] A yellow to green uranium mineral that occurs as crusts, aggregates, and grains. Named after Autun, France, near the main source of supply. (AWT n eyet')

barite [*bar, weight + -ite, mineral*] A usually white mineral with a high specific gravity, consisting mainly of barium sulfate. (BEHR eyet)

bauxite [*Les Baux & -ite, rock*] A rock consisting of hydrous aluminum oxide and iron oxides that is the major ore of aluminum. Named after the town of Les Baux, France. (BOKS eyet)

biotite [*Biot & -ite, mineral*] A dark-colored mineral of the mica group found in both igneous and metamorphic rocks. Named after Jean B. Biot, French mineralogist. (BEYE uh teyet')

boehmite [*Bohm & -ite, mineral*] A mineral, hydrous aluminum oxide, that is found in bauxite. Named after J. Bohm, 20th century German scientist. (BAY meyet)

bornite [*Born & -ite, mineral*] A common, brownish-bronze mineral that is an important ore of copper and is commonly referred to as "peacock ore" in reference to its shiny purple tarnish. Named after Ignaz von Born, Austrian mineralogist. (BOR neyet)

calamite [*Ltn > calamus, reed + -ite, fossil*] Any of various extinct paleozoic fossil plants related to, but much larger than modern horsetails. (KAL uh meyet')

calcite [*Ltn > calx, lime + -ite, mineral*] A very common carbonate mineral found in many forms, including limestone, marble, and chalk. (KAL seyet)

carnallite [*Carnall & -ite, mineral*] A white, reddish, or colorless mineral used to make potash salts. Named after Rudolf von Carnall, German mining official. (KAHRN l eyet')

carnotite [*Carnot & -ite, mineral*] A complex yellow mineral that is an ore of uranium. Named after M.A. Carnot, French mine inspector. (KAHR nuh teyet')

cassiterite [*Grk > kassiteros, tin + -ite, mineral*] A very heavy, black or brown mineral, tin oxide, that is the major ore of tin. (kuh SIT uh reyet')

celestite [*celest(ial) & -ite, mineral*] A usually colorless or milky white mineral, strontium sulfate, that is the major ore of strontium. So named for the lovely pale-blue color sometimes displayed by this mineral. (SEL uh steyet')

cerussite [*cerus(e) & -ite, mineral*] A usually colorless mineral, lead carbonate, that is an important ore of lead. (suh RUS eyet')

chalcocite [*chalco, copper* + *-ite, mineral*] A dark metallic mineral, copper sulfide, that is an important ore of copper. See chalcopyrite. (KAL kuh seyet')

chalcopyrite [*chalco, copper & pyrite*] A very common mineral, copper-iron sulfide, that is an important ore of copper. See chalcocite. (kal' kuh PEYE reyet')

chiastolite [*Grk > chiastos, crossed* + *-lite, mineral*] A mineral variety of andalusite, often worn as an amulet, that occurs as long prisms which make a cross when cut and polished. (keye AS tuh leyet')

chlorite [*chlor, green* + *-ite, mineral*] A group of minerals that are usually green, are hydrous silicates of magnesium, aluminum, and iron, and resemble the micas. (KLOR eyet)

chondrite [*chondr(ule) & -ite, stone*] A stony meteorite that contains chondrules. See aerolite. (KON dreyet)

chromite [*chrom, chromium* + *-ite, mineral*] A metallic black or brownish-black mineral, ferrous chromate, that is an important ore of chromium. (KROH meyet)

chrysolite [*chryso, yellow* + *-lite, mineral*] A yellowish-green transparent olivine used as a gem. (KRIS uh leyet')

coprolite [*copro, excrement* + *-lite, fossil*] Fossilized animal excrement. (KOP ruh leyet')

cordierite [*Cordier & -ite, mineral*] An often intensely pleochroic blue mineral composed of a silicate of aluminum, magnesium, and iron. Named after Pierre Cordier, French geologist. (KOR dee uh reyet')

cryolite [*cryo, cold* + *-lite, mineral*] A vitreous mineral, sodium aluminum fluoride, that is found in Greenland and used in the production of aluminum. So named for its clear, icy appearance. (KREYE uh leyet')

cuprite [*cupr, copper* + *-ite, mineral*] A reddish-brown mineral that is an ore of copper. (KYOO preyet)

cyanite [*cyan, blue* + *-ite, mineral*] A mineral, aluminum silicate, sometimes used as a gemstone and usually blue in color. (SEYE uh neyet')

dendrite [*dendr, tree* + *-ite, mineral*] 1.A mineral or rock with branching, treelike markings. 2.One of the branching, treelike processes of a nerve cell that carries impulses toward the cell body. See axon and neuron. (DEN dreyet)

diorite [*dia-, apart* + *Grk > horizein, to separate* + *-ite, rock*] A basic igneous rock consisting mainly of plagioclase feldspar and hornblende. (DEYE uh reyet')

dolomite [*Dolom(ieu) & -ite, mineral*] A common mineral, calcium magnesium carbonate, that forms in hydrothermal veins and magnesian limestones. Named after Deodat de Dolomieu, French mineralogist. (DOH luh meyet')

elaterite [*elater (elasticity) & -ite, mineral*] A dark-brown, elastic mineral resin. (ih LAT uh reyet')

erythrite [*erythr, red* + *-ite, mineral*] A mineral, hydrous cobalt arsenate, usually rose-colored and used for coloring glass. (EHR uh threyet')

euxenite [*eu-, good* + *xen, foreign* + *-ite, mineral*] A lustrous, brownish-black mineral consisting primarily of cerium, erbium, columbium, titanium, uranium, and yttrium. So named for the rare elements it contains. (YOOK suh neyet')

evaporite [*evapor(ate) & -ite, rock*] A sedimentary rock that is created by the evaporation of seawater from an enclosed reservoir. (ih VAP uh reyet')

felsite [*fel(d)s(par) & -ite, rock*] A fine-grained igneous rock consisting mostly of feldspar and quartz. (FEL seyet)

fluorite [*fluor, fluorine* + *-ite, mineral*] A common mineral, calcium fluoride, occurring in a great variety of colors and used in making glass, high test gasoline, freon, etc. It is the major source of fluorine. (FLOOR eyet)

gadolinite [*Gadolin & -ite, mineral*] A black to greenish-black or brown silicate mineral composed of several rare-earth metals in combination with iron. Named after John Gadolin, Finnish chemist. (GAD l uh neyet')

gahnite [*Gahn & -ite, mineral*] A usually dark-green mineral, zinc aluminate. Named after J.J. Gahn, Swedish chemist. (GON eyet)

garnierite [*Garnier & -ite, mineral*] A brilliant green mineral, hydrous nickel magnesium silicate, that is an important ore of nickel. Named after Jules Garnier, French geologist. (GAHR nee uh reyet')

geyserite [*geyser & -ite, mineral*] A siliceous sinter in the form of opal that is deposited around the edges of geysers and hot springs. (GEYE zuh reyet')

glauconite [*glauco, bluish-green* + *-ite, mineral*] A mineral, usually dull green in color, consisting of iron potassium silicate and occurring abundantly in greensand. (GLAW kuh neyet')

goethite [*Goeth(e) & -ite, mineral*] A blackish-brown mineral, formed by the oxidation of iron rich deposits, that is an ore of iron. Named after J.W. von Goethe, German scholar and writer. (GOH theyet)

granite [*Italian > granito, grained* + *-ite, rock*] A hard, granular igneous rock consisting of feldspar, quartz, and other minerals and used in monuments and buildings. (GRAN it)

granulite [*granul(ar) & -ite, rock*] A granular metamorphic rock composed mainly of feldspar and quartz. (GRAN yuh leyet')

graphite [*graph, writing* + *-ite, mineral*] A common mineral used in lead pencils, electrodes, and as a dry lubricant. (GRAF eyet)

grossularite [*Ltn > grossularia, gooseberry* + *-ite, mineral*] A variously colored garnet named from the color of a gooseberry green variety in Siberia. (GROS yuh luh reyet')

halite [*hal, salt* + *-ite, mineral*] A colorless or white mineral, sodium chloride, known as rock salt. (HAL eyet)

hematite [*hemat, blood* + *-ite, mineral*] A very common brick-red mineral, also known as bloodstone, that is the major ore of iron. (HEE muh teyet')

hyalite [*hyal, glass* + *-ite, mineral*] A translucent, colorless variety of opal. (HEYE uh leyet')

ilmenite [*Ilmen & -ite, mineral*] A metallic, black mineral, iron titanate, that is the major ore of titanium. Named after Ilmen, a range in the Ural Mountains in Russia, where it was discovered. (IL muh neyet')

kernite [*Kern & -ite, mineral*] An often colorless mineral, chemically similar to borax, that is an important ore of boron. Named after Kern County, California. (KUR neyet)

labradorite [*Labrador & -ite, mineral*] A mineral of the plagioclase feldspar series that shows a rich play of colors on cleavage surfaces. Named after the Labrador peninsula in Canada, where it was discovered. (LAB ruh dor' eyet')

lepidolite [*lepido, scale + -lite, mineral*] A mineral of the mica family, occurring as scaly aggregates and cleavable masses, that is an important ore of lithium. (lih PID l eyet')

leucite [*leuc, white + -ite, mineral*] A mineral, potassium-aluminum silicate, that is whitish or grayish in color and found in igneous rocks. (LOO seyet)

lignite [*lign, wood + -ite, mineral*] A brown-colored coal with a carbon content between peat and bituminous coal, in which the texture of the original wood is often visible. (LIG neyet)

limonite [*Grk > leimon, meadow + -ite, mineral*] A common, yellow or brownish-yellow mineral that is an important ore of iron and sometimes occurs by precipitation in the sea, in fresh water, or in marshes. (LEYE muh neyet')

magnesite [*magnes(ia) & -ite, mineral*] A usually dull white mineral, magnesium carbonate, occurring in massive and granular habits. (MAG nuh seyet')

magnetite [*magnet & -ite, mineral*] A common black mineral that is highly magnetic and is an important ore of iron. (MAG nuh teyet')

malachite [*Grk > malache, mallow + -ite, mineral*] A rich green mineral, carbonate of copper, that is an ore of copper and is used for gems and ornaments. Named from the color of the leaves of the mallow plant. (MAL uh keyet')

manganite [*mangan, manganese + -ite, mineral*] A dark-gray to black mineral, hydrous manganese oxide, that is an ore of manganese. (MANG guh neyet')

melanite [*melan, black + -ite, mineral*] A deep black variety of garnet. (MEL uh neyet')

millerite [*Miller & -ite, mineral*] A brass-yellow mineral usually occurring in very thin crystals. Named after William Miller, English mineralogist. (MIL uh reyet')

molybdenite [*molybden(um) & -ite, mineral*] A soft, metallic mineral that is the major ore of molybdenum. (muh LIB duh neyet')

natrolite [*natro(n) & -lite, mineral*] A colorless to yellow or white zeolite mineral that is a hydrous sodium aluminum silicate. (NAY truh leyet')

nephelinite [*nephelin(e) & -ite, rock*] A dark, fine-grained igneous rock consisting mainly of nepheline. (NEF uh luh neyet')

nephelite [*nephel, cloudy + -ite, mineral*] A mineral occurring in igneous rocks that is used in manufacturing ceramics and enamels. So named for its cloudy appearance when immersed in acid. (NEF uh leyet')

nephrite [*nephr, kidney + -ite, stone*] An often translucent, white to dark-green type of jade that is a less precious jade. So named from the former belief that it could be worn as a remedy for kidney disorders. (NEF reyet')

novaculite [*Ltn > novacula, razor + -ite, stone*] A hard, fine-grained siliceous rock used for whetstones. (noh VAK yuh leyet')

oolite [*oo, egg + -lite, rock*] A rock consisting of small round grains of calcium carbonate cemented together like fish eggs. (OH uh leyet')

ozocerite [*ozo, smell + cero, wax + -ite, mineral*] A brown to black or green mineral wax used in making lubricants, candles, insulation, etc., and often having an unpleasant odor. (oh' zoh SIHR eyet')

pegmatite [*Grk > pegia, to bind + -ite, rock*] A coarse-grained vein or dike rock, usually granite, composed of feldspar, quartz, and mica and sometimes rich in rare minerals. (PEG muh teyet')

perlite [*French > perle, pearl + -ite, rock*] A glassy volcanic rock with a pearly luster that when expanded by heat forms a lightweight aggregate. Used in concrete. (PER leyet)

phonolite [*phono, sound + -lite, rock*] A light-gray to light-green igneous rock that produces a ringing sound when struck. (FOHN l eyet')

phyllite [*phyll, leaf + -ite, rock*] A gray or green foliated rock similar to slate. The foliation results from the alignment of mica and chlorite under low or moderate pressure. (FIL eyet)

phytolite [*phyto, plant + -lite, fossil*] A fossil plant. (FEYET l eyet')

pisolite [*Grk > pisos, pea + -lite, stone*] A small limestone mass composed of pea-shaped pebbles. (PEYE suh leyet')

pyrargyrite [*pyr, fire + argyr, silver + -ite, mineral*] A dark-red to black mineral that is an important ore of silver. (peye RAHR juh reyet')

pyrite [*pyr, fire + -ite, mineral*] A common, pale-yellow mineral with a metallic luster that is often mistaken for gold and therefore nicknamed "fool's gold." It is the main source of sulfur in the manufacture of sulfuric acid. So named because it emits sparks when struck. (PEYE reyet)

pyrolusite [*pyro, fire + Grk > lousis, washing + -ite, mineral*] A black to dark-gray mineral with a metallic luster that is sometimes heated and used for removing color from glass. (peye' roh LOO seyet)

pyroxenite [*pyroxen(e) & -ite, rock*] An igneous rock consisting mainly of pyroxene. (peye ROK suh neyet')

pyrrhotite [*Grk > pyrrhotes, redness + -ite, mineral*] A common mineral, iron sulfide, with a bronze color, a metallic luster, and weak magnetic properties. (PIHR uh teyet')

quartzite [*quartz & -ite, rock*] A granular metamorphic rock that has recrystallized to form very hard quartz sandstone that breaks through the quartz grains instead of through the cement. (KWORT seyet)

rhodochrosite [*rhodo, red + chros, color + -ite, mineral*] A vitreous, impure mineral, chiefly manganese carbonate, with a rose-red color. (roh' duh KROH seyet)

rhodolite [*rhodo, red + -lite, mineral*] A rose-red or pink garnet used as a gem. (ROHD l eyet')

rhodonite [*rhodo, red + -ite, mineral*] A rose-red mineral, manganese silicate, that is often used as an ornamental stone. (ROHD n eyet')

rhyolite [*Grk > rhein, to flow + -lite, rock*] A fine-grained volcanic rock resembling granite and usually exhibiting flow lines. (REYE uh leyet')

rubellite [*rub, red + -lite, stone*] A red variety of tourmaline used as a gemstone. (roo BEL eyet')

samarskite [*Samarski & -ite, mineral*] A black or brownish mineral containing thorium, uranium, and a number of other rare-earth metals. Named after Col. von Samarski, Russian mine inspector. (suh MAHR skeyet')

saprolite [*sapro, decomposed + -lite, rock*] Rock that is decomposed and remains in its original place. (SAP ruh leyet')

scapolite [*Grk > scapus, stalk + -lite, mineral*] Any of a group of minerals that are complex silicates of aluminum, calcium, and sodium, some of which are used as semiprecious stones. So named for the shape of their prismatic crystals. (SKAP uh leyet')

scheelite [*Scheel(e) & -ite, mineral*] A variously colored, glassy mineral, calcium tungstate, that is an important ore of tungsten. Named after Carl W. Scheele, Swedish chemist. (SHAY leyet)

scolecite [*Grk > skolex, worm + -ite, mineral*] A zeolite mineral, a hydrous calcium aluminum silicate, that occurs in needle-shaped prismatic crystals or radiating fibrous masses. So named in reference to certain forms that curl up like a worm when heated. See vermiculite. (SKOL uh seyet')

selenite [*selen, moon + -ite, mineral*] A very soft, colorless variety of gypsum occurring in crystals. So named because its brightness was believed to wax and wane with the moon. (SEL uh neyet')

siderite [*sider, iron + -ite, mineral*] A pale-yellow, gray, or brown mineral, iron carbonate, that is an important ore of iron. (SID uh reyet')

siderolite [*sidero, iron + -lite, stone*] A stony iron meteorite. (SID ur uh leyet')

sodalite [*soda & -lite, rock*] A vitreous silicate of soda and aluminum found in various igneous rocks. (SOH duh leyet')

sperrylite [*Sperry & -lite, mineral*] A bluish-white mineral, platinum arsenide, that is found near Sudbury, Ontario. Named after F.L. Sperry, Canadian mineralogist. (SPEHR ih leyet')

sphalerite [*Grk > sphaleros, deceptive + -ite, mineral*] A yellow, brown, or black mineral, zinc sulfide, that is the major ore of zinc. So named because it is often mistaken for galena, but contains no lead. (SFAL uh reyet')

spherulite [*spher(e) & -ule, small + -ite, mineral*] A small and usually spherical aggregate of radiating crystals found in obsidian and other vitreous volcanic rocks. (SFIHR yoo leyet')

stalactite [*Grk > stalaktos, dripping + -ite, rock*] A long, slender, cylindrical structure of calcium carbonate hanging from the roof of a cavern, that is the result of mineral-rich water seeping through fractures in the roof and dripping from the roof to the floor of the cavern. See stalagmite. (stuh LAK teyet')

stalagmite [*Grk > stalagmos, dripping + -ite, rock*] A long, slender, cylindrical structure of calcium carbonate resembling an inverted stalactite, that is the result of mineral-rich water seeping through fractures in the roof and dripping from the roof to the floor of the cavern. See stalactite. (stuh LAG meyet')

stannite [*Ltn > stannum, tin + -ite, mineral*] A black or gray mineral with a metallic luster that is a sulfide of tin, copper, and iron. (STAN eyet)

staurolite [*Grk > stauros, cross + -lite, mineral*] A dark-colored mineral, occasionally used as a gem, whose crystals are often paired to resemble a cross. (STOR uh leyet')

steatite [*steat, fat + -ite, mineral*] A massive talc, a soft-green to gray mineral, used in making sinks, table tops, etc., and commonly known as soapstone. (STEE uh teyet')

stibnite [*Ltn > stibium, antimony + -ite, mineral*] A steel-gray mineral, antimony sulfide, that is the major ore of antimony. (STIB neyet)

stromatolite [*Grk > stromat, bed + -lite, rock*] A laminated sedimentary rock structure formed from layers of marine algae. (stroh MAT l eyet')

strontianite [*stronti(um) & -ite, mineral*] A variously colored mineral, strontium carbonate, with a vitreous to resinous luster that is an ore of strontium. (STRON chee uh neyet')

sylvanite [*(Tran)sylvan(ia) & -ite, mineral*] An opaque mineral with a metallic luster that often occurs in crystals whose arrangement resembles written characters. Named after Transylvania, a region in Romania, where it was discovered. (SIL vuh neyet')

tachylite [*tachy, rapid + -lite, rock*] A black, glassy, basaltic volcanic rock that is readily fusible. (TAK uh leyet')

taconite [*Tacon(ic) & -ite, rock*] A very hard sedimentary rock used as a low-grade iron ore. Named after the Taconic Mountains in the eastern U.S. (TAK uh neyet')

tantalite [*tantal(um) & -ite, mineral*] A heavy, black to reddish-brown mineral, the major ore of tantalum. (TANT l eyet')

tektite [*Grk > tektos, molten + -ite, rock*] Any of several silica-rich glassy objects originally thought to be of meteoric origin, but whose exact origin is unknown. (TEK teyet)

tetrahedrite [*tetra-, four + -hedron, surface + -ite, mineral*] A grayish-black mineral occurring in tetrahedral crystals, used as an ore of copper or silver and often containing other elements. (tet' ruh HEE dreyet')

thorite [*thor(ium) & -ite, mineral*] A rare, brown to black mineral, thorium silicate, that is an ore of thorium. (THOR eyet)

tremolite [*Tremol(a) & -ite, mineral*] A white, gray, or colorless mineral that is a silicate of calcium and magnesium and usually occurs as distinct crystals or fibrous aggregates. Named after the Tremola valley in Switzerland where it is found. (TREM uh leyet')

trichite [*trich, hair + -ite, mineral*] Any of several small, hairlike mineral bodies occurring in some vitreous rocks. (TRIK eyet)

troilite [*Troili & -ite, mineral*] A sparsely distributed variety of pyrrhotite that is found on earth, in meteorites, and in lunar soil samples. Named after Domenico Troili, 18th century Italian scientist. (TROH uh leyet')

troostite [*Troost & -ite, mineral*] A reddish mineral, occurring in hexagonal crystals, in which zinc is partially replaced by manganese. Named after Gerard Troost, American mineralogist. (TROO steyet)

tungstite [*tungst(en) & -ite, mineral*] A yellow to yellowish-green mineral, tungsten trioxide, usually occurring in powdery form. (TUNG steyet)

uraninite [*urani(um) & -ite, mineral*] A highly radioactive, black, opaque mineral, uranium oxide, that contains various metals, and sometimes gases, and is the major ore of uranium. (yoo RAY nuh neyet')

uvarovite [*Uvarov & -ite, mineral*] A garnet with a bright green color that is due to the presence of chromium. Named after Count Uvarov, Russian statesman. (yoo VAHR uh veyet') vanadinite [*vanadi(um) & -ite, mineral*] A bright red, brown, or yellow mineral that is an ore of vanadium and lead. (vuh NAYD n eyet')

vermiculite [*vermi, worm + -cule, small + -ite, mineral*] Any of various silicate minerals that expand when heated and break up with a vermicular motion, like a mass of worms; used for light-weight aggregates, heat insulation, etc. See scolecite. (vur MIK yuh leyet')

vesuvianite [*vesuvian {Mount Vesuvius} & -ite, mineral*] A vitreous, brown to green or yellow mineral that is mainly a hydrous silicate of aluminum and calcium. Named after Mount Vesuvius in Italy, where it was discovered. (vuh SOO vee uh neyet')

willemite [*Willem & -ite, mineral*] A variously colored mineral, a silicate of zinc, that is often fluorescent and is a minor ore of zinc. Named after King William I of the Netherlands. (WIL uh meyet')

zeolite [*Grk > zein, to boil + -lite, mineral*] Any of various widely distributed silicate minerals that, with the addition of water, are chemically related to the feldspars. So named from their boiling and swelling when heated. (ZEE uh leyet')

lith/o   stone, rock

aerolith [*aero, air + lith, stone*] A stony meteorite. Same as aerolite. (EHR uh lith')

batholith [*batho, deep + lith, rock*] A large body of igneous rock deep in the earth's crust that has melted and intruded into surrounding strata. (BATH uh lith')

chromolithography [*chromo, color + litho, stone + -graphy, recording*] The process of producing colored pictures from a set of stone, aluminum, or zinc plates using lithography. See lithography. (kroh' moh lith OG ruh fee)

Eolithic [*eo-, early + lith, stone + -ic*] Pertaining to the earliest period of the Stone Age, beginning with the use of very crudely chipped flint. (ee' uh LITH ik)

gastrolith [*gastro, stomach + lith, stone*] A calculus formed in the stomach. (GAS truh lith')

granolith [*grano, granite + lith, stone*] An artificial paving stone composed of crushed granite and cement. (GRAN uh lith')

laccolith [*Grk > lakkos, cistern + lith, rock*] An intrusive mass of igneous rock forced between layers of sedimentary rock, causing an upward bulge. (LAK uh lith')

lithiasis [*lith, stone + -iasis*] The formation of calculi and concretions in the body. (lith EYE uh sis)

lithic [*lith, stone + -ic*] 1.Pertaining to or made of stone. 2.Pertaining to lithium. (LITH ik)

lithography [*litho, stone + -graphy, recording*] The process of printing from a stone, aluminum, or zinc plate by treating the nongraphic areas of the image with an oil-based ink repellent, thus allowing the ink to adhere only to the graphic areas of the image. (lith OG ruh fee)

lithoid [*lith, stone + -oid, resembling*] Resembling stone. (LITH oid)

lithology [*lith, stone + -ology, study of*] The scientific study of the structure and composition of rocks and minerals. (lith OL uh jee)

lithophyte [*litho, stone + -phyte, plant*] A plant that grows on the surface of rocks. (LITH uh feyet')

lithosphere [*litho, stone & sphere*] The solid outer part of the earth, not including the hydrosphere or atmosphere. See hydrosphere and atmosphere (def. 1). (LITH uh sfihr')

lithotomy [*litho, stone + -tomy, to cut*] Surgical incision of a duct or organ, especially of the urinary bladder to remove a stone. (lith OT uh mee)

megalith [*mega-, large + lith, stone*] A large stone used in prehistoric monuments or architecture. (MEG uh lith')

Mesolithic [*meso-, middle + lith, stone + -ic*] Pertaining to the transitional period of the Stone Age, between the Paleolithic and Neolithic periods, marked by the appearance of small flint cutting tools mounted in bone or wood. (mez' uh LITH ik)

microlith [*micro-, small + lith, stone*] A small flint tool mounted in wood or bone and used especially in the Mesolithic period. (MEYE kroh lith')

monolith [*mono-, single + lith, stone*] 1.A large single piece of stone. 2.A large unified organization that acts as a whole. (MON uh lith')

monolithic [*mono-, single + lith, stone + -ic*] Characterized by solidity, uniformity, and intractability. (mon' uh LITH ik)

Neolithic [*neo, new + lith, stone + -ic*] Pertaining to the latest period of the Stone Age, characterized by the use of advanced stone tools and weapons and the introduction of farming. (nee' oh LITH ik)

otolith [*oto, ear + lith, stone*] A stonelike particle or structure found in the inner ear of vertebrates and in the statocyst of various invertebrates. (OHT l ith')

Paleolithic [*paleo, ancient + lith, stone + -ic*] Pertaining to the second period of the Stone Age, beginning with the use of crudely chipped stone tools. (pay' lee uh LITH ik)

photolithography [*photo(graph) & litho, stone + -graphy, recording*] A lithographic printing process that uses plates prepared from a photograph. See lithography. (foht' oh lith OG ruh fee)

phytolith [*phyto, plant + lith, stone*] A fossil plant. Same as phytolite. (FEYET l ith')

protolithic [*proto-, first + lith, stone + -ic*] Early name for the Eolithic period. See Eolithic. (proht' uh LITH ik)

regolith [*Grk > rhegos, blanket + lith, rock*] The layer of the earth's crust consisting of loose rock and soil lying just above bedrock. (REG uh lith')

statolith [*stato, stationary + lith, stone*] Any of the stonelike granules found in a statocyst. (STAT l ith')

urolith [*uro, urine + lith, stone*] A calculus in the urinary tract. (YOOR uh lith')

xenolith [*xeno, foreign + lith, stone*] A fragment of rock foreign to the igneous rock in which it is enclosed. (ZEN l ith')

-ology, -logy   study of, science

acarology [*acar(id) & -ology, study of*] The scientific study of ticks and mites. (ak' uh ROL uh jee)

aerobiology [*aero, air + bio, life + -logy, study of*] The study of the dispersion of air-borne biological materials such as microbes, pollen, and pollutants. (ehr' oh beye OL uh jee)

aerology [*aero, air* + *-logy, study of*] The branch of meteorology dealing with the study of air in the atmosphere, especially in the upper levels. See aerography. (ehr OL uh jee)

agriology [*Grk > agrios, wild* + *-ology, study of*] The branch of ethnology dealing with the study of the cultures and customs of primitive peoples. (ag' ree OL uh jee)

agrobiology [*agro, crop production* + *bio, life* + *-logy, science*] The quantitative science of plant growth and nutrition, as related to soil control and crop yield. (ag' roh beye OL uh jee)

agrology [*agr, crop production* + *-ology, science*] The science of soils dealing especially with crop production. (uh GROL uh jee)

agrostology [*Grk > agrostis, grass* + *-ology, study of*] The branch of botany dealing with the study of grasses. (ag' ruh STOL uh jee)

algology [*alg(ae)* & *-ology, study of*] The branch of botany dealing with the study of algae. (al GOL uh jee)

anemology [*anem, wind* + *-ology, study of*] The branch of meteorology dealing with the study of winds. (an' uh MOL uh jee)

anesthesiology [*anesthesi(a)* & *-ology, study of*] The branch of medicine dealing with the study and use of anesthesia and anesthetics. See anesthesia. (an' es thee' zee OL uh jee)

angiology [*angi, vessel* + *-ology, study of*] The branch of anatomy dealing with the study of blood and lymph vessels. (an' jee OL uh jee)

anthropology [*anthrop, man* + *-ology, study of*] The study of the origin, distribution, and development of man. See anthropography. (an' thruh POL uh jee)

archaeology [*archae, ancient* + *-ology, study of*] The study of the life and history of ancient peoples. (ahr' kee OL uh jee)

archeology [*arche, ancient* + *-ology, study of*] The study of the life and history of ancient peoples. Same as archaeology. (ahr' kee OL uh jee)

Assyriology [*Assyri(a)* & *-ology, study of*] The study of the history, language, and civilization of the ancient Assyrians. (uh sihr' ee OL uh jee)

astrobiology [*astro, star* + *bio, living organisms* + *-logy, study of*] The branch of biology dealing with the search for and study of extraterrestrial living organisms. Same as exobiology. (as' troh beye OL uh jee)

astrogeology [*astro, star* + *geo, earth* + *-logy, study of*] The scientific study of the origin, history, and structure of celestial bodies in the solar system. (as' troh jee OL uh jee)

astrology [*astro, star* + *-logy, study of*] The mathematical study of the supposed connection between the positions and aspects of heavenly bodies and the course of human affairs. See astronomy. (uh STROL uh jee)

audiology [*audi, hearing* + *-ology, study of*] The scientific study of hearing disorders and their treatment. (awd' ee OL uh jee)

autecology [*auto-, same* + *eco, environment* + *-logy, study of*] The study of ecology as it relates to an individual organism and its environment or to a species and its environment. See synecology and ecology. (awt' ih KOL uh jee)

axiology [*Grk > axios, worth* + *-ology, study of*] The branch of philosophy dealing with the theory or study of the nature of values and value judgments, as those of ethics or religion. (ak' see OL uh jee)

bacteriology [*bacteri, bacteria* + *-ology, study of*] The scientific study of bacteria as applied to medicine, industry, etc. (bak tihr' ee OL uh jee)

balneology [*Ltn > balneum, bath* + *-ology, science*] The science of treating disease and disorders by bathing, as in hot mineral water. (bal' nee OL uh jee)

bioclimatology [*bio, living organisms* + *climat, climate* + *-ology, study of*] The scientific study of the impact of climate on living organisms. (beye' oh kleye' muh TOL uh jee)

bioecology [*bio, living organisms* + *eco, environment* + *-logy, science*] The science dealing with the interrelations between living organisms and their environment. (beye' oh ih KOL uh jee)

biology [*bio, life* + *-logy, study of*] The scientific study of the origin, history, habits, etc., of living organisms and life processes, including both botany and zoology. (beye OL uh jee)

biometeorology [*bio, living organisms* + *Grk > meteoron, atmospheric phenomenon* + *-ology, study of*] The study of the impact of natural or artificial atmospheric conditions on living organisms. (beye' oh meet' ee uh ROL uh jee)

biotechnology [*bio, living organisms* + *techn, skill* + *-ology, science*] The science of using living organisms to make or improve products or to improve other living organisms. (beye' oh tek NOL uh jee)

bryology [*bryo, moss* + *-ology, study of*] The branch of botany dealing with the study of mosses and liverworts. (breye OL uh jee)

campanology [*Ltn > campana, bell* + *-ology, science*] The art of bell ringing and bell casting. (kam' puh NOL uh jee)

cardiology [*cardi, heart* + *-ology, study of*] The study of the functions and diseases of the heart. (kahr' dee OL uh jee)

carpology [*carp, fruit* + *-ology, study of*] The branch of botany dealing with the study of fruits and seeds. (kahr POL uh jee)

cetology [*Ltn > cetus, whale* + *-ology, study of*] The branch of zoology dealing with the study of whales. (see TOL uh jee)

chronobiology [*chrono, time* + *bio, life* + *-logy, study of*] The study of how time affects life, as in various biological rhythms. (kron' oh beye OL uh jee)

chronology [*chron, time* + *-ology, science*] 1.The science of measuring time and arranging events in time. See horology. 2.An order of events from earliest to latest. (kruh NOL uh jee)

climatology [*climat, climate* + *-ology, study of*] The branch of meteorology dealing with the study of climates and climatic conditions. (kleye' muh TOL uh jee)

conchology [*conch, shell* + *-ology, study of*] The branch of zoology dealing with the study of shells and mollusks. (kong KOL uh jee)

cosmetology [*Grk > kosmetikos, adornment* + *-ology, study of*] The study of cosmetics and their application. (koz' muh TOL uh jee)

cosmology [*cosm, universe* + *-ology, science*] The science of the origin, structure, and development of the universe. See cosmography. (koz MOL uh jee)

craniology [*crani, skull* + *-ology, study of*] The branch of anatomy dealing with the study of skull characteristics, especially human skulls. (kray' nee OL uh jee)

criminology [*Ltn > crimen, crime* + *-ology, study of*] The scientific study of crime and the behavior and punishment of criminals. See penology. (krim' uh NOL uh jee)

cryobiology [*cryo, cold* + *bio, living organisms* + *-logy, study of*] The scientific study of the effects of below-normal temperatures on living organisms. (kreye' oh beye OL uh jee)

cytology [*cyt, cell* + *-ology, study of*] The branch of biology dealing with the study of the origin, structure, function, and pathology of cells. (seye TOL uh jee)

demonology [*demon* & *-ology, study of*] The study of demons and evil spirits. (dee' muh NOL uh jee)

dendrochronology [*dendro, tree* + *chron, time* + *-ology, study of*] The study of the annular growth rings in trees for the purpose of dating and determining past events and climatic changes. (den' droh kruh NOL uh jee)

dendrology [*dendr, tree* + *-ology, study of*] The botanical study of trees and shrubs. (den DROL uh jee)

deontology [*Grk > deontos, obligation* + *-ology, study of*] The branch of ethics dealing with the study of moral obligation. (dee' on TOL uh jee)

dermatology [*dermat, skin* + *-ology, study of*] The branch of medical science dealing with the study of the functions and diseases of the skin. (der' muh TOL uh jee)

dialectology [*dialect* & *-ology, study of*] The branch of linguistics dealing with the study of dialects. (deye' uh lek' TOL uh jee)

ecclesiology [*ecclesi, church* + *-ology, study of*] 1.The study of the nature and structure of the Church. 2.The study of church architecture and decoration. (ik lee' zee OL uh jee)

ecology [*eco, environment* + *-logy, study of*] The branch of biology dealing with the study of the interrelations between organisms and their environment. (ih KOL uh jee)

Egyptology [*Egypt* & *-ology, study of*] The study of the civilization of ancient Egypt. (ee' jip TOL uh jee)

embryology [*embryo* & *-logy, study of*] The branch of biology dealing with the study of the formation, structure, and development of embryos. (em' bree OL uh jee)

endocrinology [*endocrin(e)* & *-ology, study of*] The branch of medical science dealing with the study of the endocrine system. See endocrine. (en' doh krih NOL uh jee)

enology [*Grk > oinos, wine* + *-ology, science*] The science of wine and winemaking. Same as oenology. (ee NOL uh jee)

entomology [*entom, insect* + *-ology, study of*] The branch of zoology dealing with the study of insects. (ent' uh MOL uh jee)

enzymology [*enzym(e)* & *-ology, study of*] The branch of biochemistry dealing with the study of the structure and functions of enzymes. See zymology. (en' zeye MOL uh jee)

epidemiology [*epi-, among* + *demi, people* + *-ology, study of*] The study of the causes, prevention, and control of epidemic diseases among people. See epizootiology. (ep' ih dee' mee OL uh jee)

epistemology [*Grk > episteme, knowledge* + *-ology, study of*] The study of human knowledge and its limitations. (ih pis' tuh MOL uh jee)

epizootiology [*epi-, among* + *zo, animal* + *-ology, study of*] The study of the causes, prevention, and control of epidemic diseases among animals. See epidemiology. (ep' ih zoh ot' ee OL uh jee)

escapology [*escap(e)* & *-ology, science*] The art of escaping from confinement, especially on stage for the purpose of entertainment. (is kay' POL uh jee)

eschatology [*Grk > eskhatos, last* + *-ology, study of*] The branch of theology dealing with the study of last and future things, as death and the afterlife. (es' kuh TOL uh jee)

ethnology [*ethn, race* + *-ology, study of*] The branch of anthropology dealing with the study of the origin, development, and characteristics of the races of mankind. See ethnography. (eth NOL uh jee)

ethnomusicology [*ethno, race* & *music* & *-ology, study of*] The comparative study of the music of two or more cultures, especially non-European cultures. See musicology. (eth' noh myoo' zih KOL uh jee)

ethology [*Grk > ethos, character* + *-ology, study of*] 1.The study of animal behavior, particularly in their natural habitat. 2.The study of human character formation. (ee THOL uh jee)

etiology [*etio, cause* + *-logy, study of*] The study of causes, especially of diseases. (eet' ee OL uh jee)

etymology [*Grk > etymos, true meaning* + *-ology, study of*] The study of the true meaning, derivation, and history of a word, phrase, etc. (et' uh MOL uh jee)

exobiology [*exo-, outside* + *bio, living organisms* + *-logy, study of*] The branch of biology dealing with the search for and study of extraterrestrial living organisms. (eks' oh beye OL uh jee)

fetology [*feto, fetus* + *-logy, study of*] The branch of medical science dealing with the study of the fetus in the uterus, including the diagnosis and treatment of disorders and diseases. (fee TOL uh jee)

gastroenterology [*gastro, stomach* + *enter, intestine* + *-ology, study of*] The branch of medical science dealing with the study of the functions and diseases of the stomach and intestines. (gas' troh ent' uh ROL uh jee)

gastrology [*gastr, stomach* + *-ology, study of*] The branch of medical science dealing with the study of the functions and diseases of the stomach. (gas TROL uh jee)

gemmology [*gem* & *-ology, study of*] The scientific study of gemstones. Same as gemology. (jem OL uh jee)

gemology [*gem* & *-ology, study of*] The scientific study of gemstones. (jem OL uh jee)

genealogy [*Grk > genea, family* + *-logy, study of*] 1.A record of the history or descent of a family, person, group, etc. 2.The study of family histories and pedigrees. 3.A line of descent from an ancestor. Lineage. Pedigree. See pedigree. (jee' nee OL uh jee)

geochronology [*geo, earth* + *chron, time* + *-ology, study of*] The study of the earth's age, history, developmental stages, etc. See geochronometry. (jee' oh kruh NOL uh jee)

geology [*geo, earth* + *-logy, science*] The science of the origin, history, composition, and structure of the earth. See geography. (jee OL uh jee)

geomorphology [*geo, earth* + *morph, form* + *-ology, study of*] The scientific study of the origin, development, and features of the earth's surface. (jee' oh mor FOL uh jee)

gerontology [*geront, old age* + *-ology, science*] The science dealing with the problems and effects of the aging process. See geriatrics. (jehr' un TOL uh jee)

glaciology [*glaci(er)* & *-ology, study of*] The branch of geology dealing with the study of glaciers. (glay' shee OL uh jee)

glottochronology [*glotto, language* + *chron, time* + *-ology, study of*] The comparative study of two or more related languages to determine the time of their divergence from the parent language. See lexicostatistics. (glot' oh kruh NOL uh jee)

graphology [*graph, writing* + *-ology, study of*] The study and analysis of handwriting, especially for determining the writer's personality and character. (graf OL uh jee)

gynecology [*gynec, woman* + *-ology, study of*] The branch of medical science dealing with the study of disorders and diseases peculiar to women, especially those of the reproductive system. See gyniatrics. (geye' nuh KOL uh jee)

helminthology [*Grk > helminthos, worm* + *-ology, study of*] The branch of zoology dealing with the study of worms, especially intestinal parasitic worms. (hel' min THOL uh jee)

hematology [*hemat, blood* + *-ology, study of*] The branch of medical science dealing with the study of blood and blood-forming tissues. (hee' muh TOL uh jee)

herpetology [*Grk > herpeton, reptile* + *-ology, study of*] The branch of zoology dealing with the study of reptiles and amphibians. (hur' pih TOL uh jee)

histology [*hist, tissue* + *-ology, study of*] The branch of biology dealing with the study of plant and animal tissue structure. (hist OL uh jee)

histopathology [*histo, tissue* + *path, disease* + *-ology, study of*] The study of changes in diseased tissue. (hist' oh puh THOL uh jee)

histophysiology [*histo, tissue* + *physi, physical* + *-ology, study of*] The branch of physiology dealing with the study of the functions and activities of tissue. (hist' oh fiz' ee OL uh jee)

horology [*Grk > hora, hour* + *-ology, science*] The science of designing and making instruments for measuring time. See chronology (def. 1). (huh ROL uh jee)

hydrology [*hydr, water* + *-ology, study of*] The study of the distribution, effects, and properties of water on and beneath the earth's surface and in the atmosphere. See hydrography. (heye DROL uh jee)

hydrometeorology [*hydro, water* + *Grk > meteoron, atmospheric phenomenon* + *-ology, study of*] The branch of meteorology dealing with the study of water in the atmosphere. (heye' droh meet' ee uh ROL uh jee)

hyetology [*hyet, rain* + *-ology, study of*] The branch of meteorology dealing with the study of rainfall. See hyetography. (heye' ih TOL uh jee)

hymnology [*hymn* & *-ology, study of*] The study of the history, classification, and utilization of hymns. (him NOL uh jee)

hypnology [*hypn, sleep* + *-ology, study of*] The scientific study of sleep and hypnotism. (hip NOL uh jee)

ichthyology [*ichthy, fish* + *-ology, study of*] The branch of zoology dealing with the study of fishes. (ik' thee OL uh jee)

iconology [*icon, image* + *-ology, science*] The science of symbols and icons. (eye' kuh NOL uh jee)

ideology [*ideo-, idea* + *-logy, study of*] 1.The doctrines and philosophy of an individual, group, movement, etc. 2.The study of the origin and nature of ideas. (eye' dee OL uh jee)

immunology [*immuno, immunity* + *-logy, study of*] The branch of medical science dealing with the study of immunity to infection and disease. (im' yuh NOL uh jee)

kinesiology [*kine, motion* + *-ology, study of*] The study of human body movement and the muscles involved. (kih nee' see OL uh jee)

Kremlinology [*Kremlin* & *-ology, study of*] The study of Russian government, policies, practices, etc. (krem' lih NOL uh jee)

laryngology [*laryng, larynx* + *-ology, study of*] The branch of medical science dealing with the study of the functions and diseases of the larynx. (lehr' un GOL uh jee)

lepidopterology [*lepido, scale* + *pter, wing* + *-ology, study of*] The branch of zoology dealing with the study of lepidopterans. See lepidopteran. (lep' ih dop' tuh ROL uh jee)

lexicology [*lex, word* + *-ic* + *-ology, study of*] The branch of linguistics dealing with the study of the history and meanings of words. See lexicography. (leks' ih KOL uh jee)

limnology [*Grk > limne, lake* + *-ology, study of*] The scientific study of the geographical, physical, and biological phenomena of fresh water lakes, ponds, and streams. (lim NOL uh jee)

lithology [*lith, stone* + *-ology, study of*] The scientific study of the structure and composition of rocks and minerals. (lith OL uh jee)

macroclimatology [*macro-, large* + *climat, climate* + *-ology, study of*] The study of the climate over a large geographical area. See microclimatology. (mak' roh kleye' muh TOL uh jee)

malacology [*malac, mollusks* + *-ology, study of*] The branch of zoology dealing with the study of mollusks. (mal' uh KOL uh jee)

mammalogy [*mamma(l)* & *-logy, study of*] The branch of zoology dealing with the study of mammals. (muh MAL uh jee)

metapsychology [*meta-, beyond* + *psych, mind* + *-ology, science*] A term applied to theories about the origin, structure, and functions of the mind that extend beyond the empirical laws of psychology. (met' uh seye KOL uh jee)

meteorology [*Grk > meteoron, atmospheric phenomenon* + *-ology, study of*] The study of atmospheric phenomena, especially those related to weather and weather forecasting. (meet' ee uh ROL uh jee)

methodology [*method* & *-ology, science*] The science of methods; specifically, the system of principles and procedures applied to a particular field of knowledge. (meth' uh DOL uh jee)

metrology [*metr, measure* + *-ology, study of*] The scientific study of weights and measures. (mih TROL uh jee)

microbiology [*micro-, small + bio, life + -logy, study of*] The study of microscopic forms of life, as viruses, bacteria, protozoans, and other microorganisms. (meye' kroh beye OL uh jee)

microclimatology [*micro-, small + climat, climate + -ology, study of*] The study of the climate in a small area or habitat. See macroclimatology. (meye' kroh kleye' muh TOL uh jee)

micrometeorology [*micro-, small + Grk > meteoron, atmospheric phenomenon + -ology, study of*] The branch of meteorology dealing with the study of small-scale atmospheric phenomena. (meye' kroh meet' ee uh ROL uh jee)

micropaleontology [*micro-, small + pale, ancient + ont, being + -ology, study of*] The branch of paleontology dealing with the study of microscopic plant and animal fossils. See paleontology. (meye' kroh pay' lee on TOL uh jee)

mineralogy [*minera(l) & -logy, study of*] The study of minerals, including their characteristics, classification, and distribution. (min' uh ROL uh jee)

mixology [*mix & -ology, science*] The art of preparing cocktails. (mik SOL uh jee)

molecular biology [*molecular & biology*] The branch of biology dealing with the study of the molecular structure of biological systems. (muh LEK yuh lur beye OL uh jee)

morphology [*morph, form + -ology, study of*] 1.The branch of biology dealing with the study of the form and structure of plants and animals. 2.The study of word formation in a particular language. (mor FOL uh jee)

musicology [*music & -ology, study of*] The historical and scientific study of all aspects of music. See ethnomusicology. (myoo' zih KOL uh jee)

mycology [*myc, fungus + -ology, study of*] The branch of botany dealing with the study of fungi. (meye KOL uh jee)

myology [*myo, muscle + -logy, study of*] The branch of anatomy dealing with the study of the functions and diseases of the muscles. (meye OL uh jee)

myrmecology [*myrmec, ant + -ology, study of*] The branch of entomology dealing with the study of ants. (mur' mih KOL uh jee)

mythology [*myth & -ology, study of*] 1.The study of myths. 2.An anthology of myths about the origin and history of a specific people. See mythography (def. 1). (mih THOL uh jee)

nanotechnology [*nano-, billionth (10⁻⁹) + techn, skill + -ology, science*] The manufacture of structures and materials measuring up to 100 nanometers. See nanometer. (nan' oh tek NOL uh jee)

neonatology [*neo, new + nat, born + -ology, study of*] The branch of medicine dealing with the study of the care, development, and treatment of newborn children. (nee' oh nay TOL uh jee)

nephology [*neph, cloud + -ology, study of*] The branch of meteorology dealing with the study of clouds. (neh FOL uh jee)

nephrology [*nephr, kidney + -ology, study of*] The branch of medical science dealing with the study of the functions and diseases of the kidneys. (neh FROL uh jee)

neurology [*neur, nerve + -ology, study of*] The branch of medical science dealing with the study of the structure, functions, and diseases of the nervous system. (noo ROL uh jee)

neuropathology [*neuro, nerve + path, disease + -ology, study of*] The branch of medical science dealing with the study of diseases of the nervous system. See neurophysiology and pathology. (noor' oh puh THOL uh jee)

neurophysiology [*neuro, nerve + physi, physical + -ology, study of*] The branch of medical science dealing with the study of the functions and activities of the nervous system. See neuropathology and physiology. (noor' oh fiz' ee OL uh jee)

nomology [*nom, law + -ology, science*] 1.The science of law and lawmaking. See nomography. 2.The laws that govern the phenomena of a science. (noh MOL uh jee)

numerology [*numer, number + -ology, study of*] The study of numbers as related to occultism or as a means of predicting the future. (noo' muh ROL uh jee)

oceanology [*ocean & -ology, study of*] The scientific study of all aspects of the oceans. Same as oceanography. (oh' shuh NOL uh jee)

odontology [*odont, teeth + -ology, science*] The branch of medical science dealing with the diagnosis, prevention, and treatment of diseases and disorders of the teeth and associated structures. Same as dentistry. (oh' don TOL uh jee)

oenology [*Grk > oinos, wine + -ology, science*] The science of wine and winemaking. (ee NOL uh jee)

oncology [*onco, tumor + -logy, study of*] The branch of medical science dealing with the study of tumors. (on KOL uh jee)

onomatology [*onomat, name + -ology, study of*] The study of the origin, evolution, and use of proper names. Same as onomastics. (on' uh muh TOL uh jee)

ontology [*ont, being + -ology, study of*] The branch of metaphysics dealing with the study of the nature of being or reality. See phenomenology (def. 1). (on TOL uh jee)

oology [*oo, egg + -logy, study of*] The branch of ornithology dealing with the study of birds' eggs. (oh OL uh jee)

ophiology [*ophi, snake + -ology, study of*] The branch of herpetology dealing with the study of snakes. (ahf' ee OL uh jee)

ophthalmology [*ophthalm, eye + -ology, study of*] The branch of medical science dealing with the study of the functions and diseases of the eye. See optometry. (ahf' thul MOL uh jee)

organology [*organ & -ology, study of*] The branch of biology dealing with the study of the structure, development, and functions of plant and animal organs. See organography. (or' guh NOL uh jee)

ornithology [*ornith, bird + -ology, study of*] The branch of zoology dealing with the study of birds. (or' nuh THOL uh jee)

orology [*oro, mountain + -logy, study of*] The branch of geology dealing with the study of mountains. See orography. (aw ROL uh jee)

osteology [*oste, bone + -ology, study of*] The branch of anatomy dealing with the study of the structure and function of bones. (os' tee OL uh jee)

otolaryngology [*oto, ear + laryng, larynx + -ology, study of*] The branch of medical science dealing with the study and treatment of diseases and disorders of the ear, nose, and throat. Same as otorhinolaryngology. (oh' toh lehr' un GOL uh jee)

otology [*ot, ear + -ology, study of*] The branch of medical science dealing with the study of the functions and diseases of the ear. (oh TOL uh jee)

otorhinolaryngology [*oto, ear + rhino, nose + laryng, larynx + -ology, study of*] The branch of medical science dealing with the study and treatment of diseases and disorders of the ear, nose, and throat. (ot' oh reye' noh lehr' un GOL uh jee)

paleethnology [*pale, ancient + ethn, race + -ology, study of*] The branch of ethnology dealing with the study of early races of mankind. (pay' lee eth NOL uh jee)

paleoanthropology [*paleo, ancient + anthrop, man + -ology, study of*] The branch of anthropology dealing with the study of prehistoric man prior to homo sapiens. (pay' lee oh an' thruh POL uh jee)

paleoecology [*paleo, ancient + eco, environment + -logy, study of*] The branch of ecology dealing with the study of the interrelations between ancient plants and animals and their environment. (pay' lee oh' ih KOL uh jee)

paleontology [*pale, ancient + ont, being + -ology, study of*] The science dealing with the study of ancient plant and animal life through the study of fossil remains. See paleobotany and paleozoology. (pay' lee on TOL uh jee)

paleozoology [*paleo, ancient + zo, animal + -ology, study of*] The branch of paleontology dealing with the study of ancient animal life through the study of fossil remains. See paleobotany and paleontology. (pay' lee oh' zoh OL uh jee)

palynology [*Grk > palynein, to sprinkle + -ology, study of*] The study of pollen and other spores. (pal' uh NOL uh jee)

parapsychology [*para-, beyond + psych, mind + -ology, study of*] The branch of psychology dealing with the study of psychic phenomena, such as extrasensory perception, clairvoyance, and telepathy, that appear to fall beyond the scope of physical law. (pehr' uh seye KOL uh jee)

parasitology [*parasit(e) & -ology, study of*] The branch of biology dealing with the study of parasites. (pehr' uh seye TOL uh jee)

pathology [*path, disease + -ology, study of*] 1.The branch of medical science dealing with the study of the origin, nature, and development of diseases. 2.The conditions produced by a disease. (puh THOL uh jee)

pedology¹ [*ped, child + -ology, study of*] The study of the behavior and development of children. (pih DOL uh jee)

pedology² [*ped, soil + -ology, study of*] The science dealing with the study of the properties of soils. (pih DOL uh jee)

penology [*Grk > poine, penalty + -ology, study of*] The study of the punishment and rehabilitation of criminals. See criminology. (pee NOL uh jee)

petrology [*petr, rock + -ology, study of*] The study of the origin, composition, and classification of rocks. See petrography. (puh TROL uh jee)

pharmacology [*pharmac, drug + -ology, study of*] The study of the preparation, administration, and effects of drugs. See pharmaceutics. (fahr' muh KOL uh jee)

phenology [*phen(omenon) & -ology, study of*] The study of recurring natural phenomena, as bird migration, blooming, etc., and their relation to climate. (fih NOL uh jee)

phenomenology [*phenomen(on) & -ology, study of*] 1.The scientific study of phenomena, as distinct from ontology. See ontology. 2.The philosophical doctrine of phenomena. (fih nom' uh NOL uh jee)

phlebology [*phleb, vein + -ology, study of*] The branch of medical science dealing with the study of the functions and diseases of veins. (flih BOL uh jee)

phonology [*phon, sound + -ology, study of*] The study of the elements and principles that determine the overall sound pattern of a language, including phonetics and phonemics. See phonemics and phonetics. (fuh NOL uh jee)

phrenology [*phren, mind + -ology, study of*] The study of the shape of the skull as being indicative of mental faculties and character. (frih NOL uh jee)

phycology [*phyc, algae + -ology, study of*] The branch of botany dealing with the study of algae. Same as algology. (fih KOL uh jee)

physiology [*physi, physical + -ology, study of*] 1.The biological study of the functions and activities of organisms or their parts, including all physical and chemical processes. 2.The functions and vital processes of an organism or any of its parts. (fiz' ee OL uh jee)

phytology [*phyt, plant + -ology, study of*] The branch of biology dealing with the study of plants. Botany. See phytography. (feye TOL uh jee)

phytopathology [*phyto, plant + path, disease + -ology, study of*] The branch of botany dealing with the study of plant diseases. Plant pathology. (feyet' oh puh THOL uh jee)

phytosociology [*phyto, plant + socio, social + -logy, study of*] The branch of ecology dealing with the study of the interrelations between plant communities and their environment. (feyet' oh soh' see OL uh jee)

pneumatology [*pneumat, spirit + -ology, science*] 1.The science of spiritual beings and spiritual phenomena. 2.The Christian doctrine of the Holy Spirit. (noo' muh TOL uh jee)

pomology [*Ltn > pomum, fruit + -ology, study of*] The science dealing with the study of fruit growing. (poh MOL uh jee)

primatology [*primat(e) & -ology, study of*] The branch of zoology dealing with the study of the origin and evolution of primates. (preye' muh TOL uh jee)

proctology [*proct, rectum + -ology, study of*] The branch of medical science dealing with the study of disorders and diseases of the anus and rectum. (prok TOL uh jee)

protozoology [*protozo(a) & -ology, study of*] The branch of zoology dealing with the study of protozoans. (proht' oh zoh OL uh jee)

psephology [*Grk > psephos, ballot + -ology, study of*] The study and statistical analysis of political elections. (see FOL uh jee)

psychobiology [*psycho, mind + bio, life + -logy, study of*] 1.The scientific study of the integration of mind and body. 2.The scientific study of the biology of the mind. (seye' koh beye OL uh jee)

psychology [*psych, mind* + *-ology, science*] The science of the mind, including emotional and behavioral processes and characteristics. See psychiatry. (seye KOL uh jee)

psychopathology [*psycho, mind* + *path, disease* + *-ology, study of*] The branch of medical science dealing with the study of disorders and diseases of the mind. (seye' koh puh THOL uh jee)

psychopharmacology [*psycho, mind* + *pharmac, drug* + *-ology, study of*] The branch of medical science dealing with the study of the relationships between drugs and mental and emotional behavior. (seye' koh fahr' muh KOL uh jee)

psychophysiology [*psycho, mind* + *physi, physical* + *-ology, study of*] The branch of medical science dealing with the study of the interrelations between mental and physical processes. (seye' koh fiz' ee OL uh jee)

pteridology [*pterid, fern* + *-ology, study of*] The branch of botany dealing with the study of ferns. (tehr' ih DOL uh jee)

radiobiology [*radio, radiation* + *bio, living organisms* + *-logy, study of*] The branch of biology dealing with the study of the effects of radiation on living organisms. (ray' dee oh' beye OL uh jee)

radiology [*radio, radiation* + *-logy, study of*] The study of x-rays and other forms of radiation, especially as applied to the medical diagnosis and treatment of disease. See roentgenology. (ray' dee OL uh jee)

reflexology [*re-, back* + *flex, to bend* + *-ology, study of*] 1.The study of behavior in terms of reflexes. 2.The practice of foot and hand massage in the treatment of bodily disorders and ailments. (ree' flek SOL uh jee)

rheology [*rheo, flow* + *-logy, study of*] The science dealing with the study of the deformation and flow of matter. (ree OL uh jee)

rheumatology [*rheumat(ism)* & *-ology, study of*] The branch of medical science dealing with the study of rheumatic diseases. (roo' muh TOL uh jee)

rhinology [*rhin, nose* + *-ology, study of*] The branch of medical science dealing with the study of the functions and diseases of the nose. (reye NOL uh jee)

roentgenology [*roentgen, x-rays* + *-ology, study of*] The branch of medical science dealing with the study of x-rays for the diagnosis and treatment of disease. See radiology. (rent' guh NOL uh jee)

scatology [*scat, excrement* + *-ology, study of*] The medical and biological study of excrement. (skuh TOL uh jee)

seismology [*seism, earthquake* + *-ology, study of*] The science dealing with the study of earthquakes. See seismometer and seismograph. (seyez MOL uh jee)

selenology [*selen, moon* + *-ology, study of*] The branch of astronomy dealing with study of the moon. See selenography. (sel' uh NOL uh jee)

semasiology [*Grk > sema, sign* + *-ology, study of*] The branch of semiotics dealing with the study of the relationships between signs and symbols and their representations. Same as semantics (def. 2). (sih may' see OL uh jee)

semeiology [*Grk > sema, sign* + *-ology, study of*] The study of signs, symbols, and sign language. Same as semiology. (see' mee OL uh jee)

semiology [*Grk > sema, sign* + *-ology, study of*] The study of signs, symbols, and sign language. (see' mee OL uh jee)

serology [*sero, serum* + *-logy, study of*] The branch of medical science dealing with the study of the actions of serums, especially blood serum. (sih ROL uh jee)

sexology [*sex* & *-ology, study of*] The scientific study of human sexuality and sexual behavior. (seks OL uh jee)

Sinology [*Sino, Chinese* + *-logy, study of*] The study of the language, history, and culture of China. (seye NOL uh jee)

sitology [*sito, food* + *-logy, study of*] The study of food, nutrition, and diet. See dietetics. (seye TOL uh jee)

sociobiology [*socio, social* + *bio, life* + *-logy, study of*] The biological study of social organization and behavior in humans and animals. See sociology. (soh' see oh' beye OL uh jee)

sociology [*socio, social* + *-logy, study of*] The scientific study of human social behavior, especially the origin, development, and organization of social groups and institutions. See sociobiology. (soh' see OL uh jee)

somatology [*somat, body* + *-ology, study of*] The branch of anthropology dealing with the study of the physical characteristics of the body. (soh' muh TOL uh jee)

speleology [*Ltn > speleum, cave* + *-ology, study of*] The science dealing with the exploration and study of the physical and geological features of caves. (spee' lee OL uh jee)

stomatology [*stomat, mouth* + *-ology, study of*] The branch of medical science dealing with the study of diseases and disorders of the mouth. (stoh' muh TOL uh jee)

suicidology [*suicid(e)* & *-ology, study of*] The study of the causes and prevention of suicide. (soo' uh seye DOL uh jee)

symbology [*symb(ol)* & *-ology, study of*] 1.The study of symbols and symbolism. 2.The art of interpreting symbols. (sim BOL uh jee)

symptomatology [*symptom* & *-ology, science*] 1.The science of medical symptoms. 2.The combined symptoms of a disease or condition. (simp' tuh muh TOL uh jee)

synecology [*syn-, together* + *eco, environment* + *-logy, study of*] The study of ecology as it relates to plant and animal communities and their environment. See autecology and ecology. (sin' ih KOL uh jee)

syphilology [*syphil(is)* & *-ology, study of*] The branch of medical science dealing with the study of the cause, prevention, and treatment of syphilis. (sif' uh LOL uh jee)

technology [*techn, art or skill* + *-ology, study of*] 1.The study of the industrial arts, applied sciences, etc. 2.The practical application of science to industry, the arts, etc. (tek NOL uh jee)

teleology [*tele, end* + *-ology, study of*] 1.The branch of cosmology dealing with the study of final causes. 2.The doctrine that attributes purpose or design to natural phenomena in the material world. See dysteleology. (tel' ee OL uh jee)

teratology [*terat, monster* + *-ology, study of*] The biological study of malformations in plants or animals. (tehr' uh TOL uh jee)

thanatology [*thanat, death* + *-ology, study of*] The study of the phenomena of death and dying and of ways of coping with them. (than' uh TOL uh jee)

thaumatology [*thaumat, miracle* + *-ology, study of*] The study of miracles. (thaw' muh TOL uh jee)

theology [*the, God + -ology, study of*] The study and interpretation of religion, especially Christianity. (thee OL uh jee)

thremmatology [*Grk > thremma, nursling + -ology, study of*] The scientific study of animal and plant breeding. (threm' uh TOL uh jee)

tocology [*toco, birth + -logy, science*] The branch of medical science dealing with the care and treatment of women before, after, and during childbirth. Same as obstetrics. (toh KOL uh jee)

topology [*Grk > topos, place + -ology, study of*] 1.The topographical study of a specific place. See topography (def. 1). 2.The anatomy of a specific region of the body. (tuh POL uh jee)

toxicology [*toxico, poison + -ology, study of*] The study of poisons and their antidotes, effects, etc. (toks' ih KOL uh jee)

tribology [*trib, friction + -ology, study of*] The scientific study of friction and ways of reducing it. (treye BOL uh jee)

typology [*typo, type + -logy, study of*] The scientific study of systematic classification based on types. (teye POL uh jee)

urbanology [*Ltn > urbanus, city + -ology, study of*] The study of problems peculiar to urban areas. (ur' buh NOL uh jee)

urology [*ur, urine + -ology, study of*] The branch of medical science dealing with the study of the urinary tract in both sexes and the genital tract in males. (yoo ROL uh jee)

venereology [*venere(al) & -ology, study of*] The branch of medical science dealing with the study of venereal diseases. (vuh nihr' ee OL uh jee)

virology [*vir(us) & -ology, study of*] The branch of medical science dealing with the study of viruses and viral diseases. (veye ROL uh jee)

volcanology [*Ltn > Volcanus, Roman god of fire + -ology, study of*] The branch of science dealing with the study of volcanoes. (vol' kuh NOL uh jee)

vulcanology [*Ltn > Volcanus, Roman god of fire + -ology, study of*] The branch of science dealing with the study of volcanoes. Same as volcanology. (vul' kuh NOL uh jee)

zoology [*zo, animal + -ology, study of*] 1.The branch of biology dealing with the study of animals. See zoography. 2.The animals of a particular region. Fauna. (zoh OL uh jee)

zymology [*zym, fermentation + -ology, study of*] The branch of science dealing with the study of fermentation and enzyme action. See enzymology and zymurgy. (zeye MOL uh jee)

-ics   study of, science, skill, practice, knowledge

acoustics [*Grk > akouein, to hear + -ics, study of*] The branch of physics dealing with the study of sound and hearing. (uh KOO stiks)

acoustooptics [*acoust(ics) & optics*] The branch of physics dealing with the study of the interaction between sound waves and light waves. (uh koo' stoh OP tiks)

acrobatics [*acro, high + Grk > bainein, to walk + -ics, skill*] 1.The skill of performing gymnastic feats. 2.An impressive display of agility. (ak' ruh BAT iks)

aeroballistics [*aero(dynamics) & ballistics*] The combined science of aerodynamics and ballistics that deals with the flight of missiles, bombs, and other projectiles in the atmosphere. See aerodynamics and ballistics. (ehr' oh buh LIS tiks)

aerobatics [*aero, air & (acro)batics*] The skill of performing difficult aerial maneuvers in an aircraft. See acrobatics. (ehr' uh BAT iks)

aerobics [*aero, air + bio, life + -ics, practice*] A system of vigorous exercises designed to improve the body's ability to take in and utilize oxygen. (ehr OH biks)

aerodynamics [*aero, air + dynam, power + -ics, study of*] The branch of dynamics dealing with the study of the forces exerted by the motion of air and other gases. See aeromechanics and aerostatics. (ehr' oh deye NAM iks)

aeromechanics [*aero, air & mechanics*] The science dealing with the motion and equilibrium of air and other gases, including aerodynamics and aerostatics. See aerodynamics and aerostatics. (ehr' oh muh KAN iks)

aeronautics [*aero, air + naut, sailor + -ics, science*] The science dealing with the design, construction, performance, and flight characteristics of aircraft. (ehr' uh NOT iks)

aerostatics [*aero, air + stat, stationary + -ics, study of*] The branch of statics dealing with the study of the equilibrium of air and other gases and the equilibrium of solid bodies immersed in them. See aeromechanics and aerodynamics. (ehr' oh STAT iks)

aerothermodynamics [*aero, air + thermo, heat + dynam, energy + -ics, study of*] The branch of dynamics dealing with the study of the relationship between heat and mechanical energy in air and other gases. See thermodynamics. (ehr' oh thur' moh deye NAM iks)

aesthetics [*aesthet, feeling + -ics, study of*] The branch of philosophy dealing with the study of the qualities perceived in beauty, art, and taste. (es THET iks)

agronomics [*agro, crop production + nom, system of laws + -ics, science*] The science of soil management and crop production. Same as agronomy. (ag' ruh NOM iks)

analytics [*analy(sis) & -ics, science*] The branch of science dealing with logical analysis. (an' l IT iks)

apologetics [*apo-, from + log, discourse + -ics, study of*] The branch of theology dealing with the defense or proof of Christianity. (uh pol' uh JET iks)

architectonics [*architect(ure) & -ics, study of*] 1.The scientific study of architecture. See tectonics (def. 1). 2.The scientific study of the systematization of knowledge. (ahr' kih tek TON iks)

astrodynamics [*astro, star + dynam, power + -ics, science*] The science dealing with the dynamics of space vehicles and celestial bodies. (as' troh deye NAM iks)

astronautics [*astro, star + naut, sailor + -ics, science*] The science dealing with spacecraft and space flight. (as' truh NOT iks)

astrophysics [*astro, star & physics*] The branch of astronomy dealing with the study of the physical properties and characteristics of stars, planets, and other celestial bodies. (as' troh FIZ iks)

athletics [*Grk > athlon, contest + -ics, skill*] Athletic sports, games, events, etc., requiring skill and strength. (ath LET iks)

atmospherics [*atmospher(e) & -ics, knowledge*] Natural electromagnetic disturbances in the atmosphere that cause interference in the reception of radio waves. Static. (at' muh SFIHR iks)

atomics [*atom & -ics, study of*] The branch of physics dealing with the study of atoms, especially when involving atomic energy. (uh TOM iks)

autonetics [*auto-, self & (cyber)netics*] The study of automatic control systems. See cybernetics. (awt' oh NET iks)

avionics [*avi(ation) & (electr)onics*] The science and technology dealing with the use of electronics in aviation. (ay' vee ON iks)

ballistics [*Grk > ballein, to throw + -ist + -ics, study of*] 1.The scientific study of the dynamics and characteristics of projectiles in flight. 2.The study of the functionality and effects of firearms and ammunition. (buh LIS tiks)

bariatrics [*bar, weight + iatr, healing + -ics, study of*] The branch of medicine dealing with the study and treatment of obesity. (behr' ee AT riks)

bibliotics [*biblio, book + -ics, knowledge*] The analysis of handwriting and written documents to determine origin or authenticity. (bib' lee OT iks)

bioastronautics [*bio, life + astro, star + naut, sailor + -ics, science*] The branch of science dealing with the medical and biological effects of space travel on living things. (beye' oh as' truh NOT iks)

biocybernetics [*bio, life & cybernetics*] The study of biological control and communication systems. See cybernetics. (beye' oh seye' ber NET iks)

bioenergetics [*bio, living organisms & energetics*] The branch of biology dealing with the study of the conversion of sunlight, food, etc., into energy by living organisms. See energetics. (beye' oh en' ur JET iks)

bioethics [*bio, life & ethics*] The study of the moral and ethical ramifications of biological and medical research. See ethics. (beye' oh ETH iks)

biomathematics [*bio, life & mathematics*] The application of mathematical principles to the study of medicine and biology. (beye' oh math' uh MAT iks)

biomechanics [*bio, life & mechanics*] The application of mechanical principles to the study of medicine and biology. (beye' oh muh KAN iks)

biometrics [*bio, life + metr, to measure + -ics, study of*] The branch of biology dealing with the statistical and mathematical study of biological data. (beye' oh MET riks)

bionics [*bio, life & (electr)onics*] The application of biological principles to the study of engineering, especially electrical engineering. (beye ON iks)

bionomics [*bio, life + nom, law + -ics, study of*] Ecology. (beye' uh NOM iks)

biophysics [*bio, life & physics*] The application of the techniques and principles of physics to the study of medicine and biology. (beye' oh FIZ iks)

biostatistics [*bio, life & statistics*] The application of statistical principles and processes to the study of medicine and biology. (beye' oh stuh TIS tiks)

cacogenics [*caco, poor + gen, production + -ics, study of*] The biological study of the deterioration of hereditary qualities that cause degeneration in offspring. Same as dysgenics. (kak' uh JEN iks)

calisthenics [*calli, beautiful + sthen, strength + -ics, practice*] 1.Systematic, rhythmic exercises designed to improve muscle tone and cardiovascular fitness. 2.The art or practice of such exercise. (kal' is THEN iks)

chromatics [*chromat, color + -ics, study of*] The study of colors. (kroh MAT iks)

chromodynamics [*chromo, color + dynam, energy + -ics, knowledge*] The theory dealing with the strong interactive forces that bind quarks together. These forces are characterized by three seemingly distinct, nonelectrical charges known as colors that are completely unrelated to real, visible colors. (kroh' moh deye NAM iks)

civics [*Ltn > civis, citizen + -ics, science*] The science, art, or practice of civil government. (SIV iks)

cliometrics [*Clio {Muse of history} & metr, to measure + -ics, science*] The application of statistical and mathematical methods to the study of history. (kleye' uh MET riks)

cryogenics [*cryo, cold + gen, to produce + -ics, science*] The science dealing with the production and effects of very low temperatures. (kreye' oh JEN iks)

cryonics [*cryo, cold & (bio)nics*] The practice of freezing the body of a recently deceased person to preserve it for possible revival by future medical cures. See bionics. (kreye ON iks)

cybernetics [*Grk > kybernan, to steer + -ics, study of*] The science dealing with the study of electronic, mechanical, and biological control systems. See autonetics and biocybernetics. (seye' ber NET iks)

cyberphobia [*cyber(netics) & -phobia, fear*] Abnormal fear of computers. See technophobia (def. 2). (seye' ber FOH bee uh)

cytogenetics [*cyto(logy) & genetics*] The comparative study of heredity and variation using the principles of cytology and genetics. See cytology and genetics. (seyet' oh juh NET iks)

demographics [*demo, people + graph, recording + -ics, knowledge*] The statistical data of human populations, used to identify age, sex, education, income, etc. (dem' uh GRAF iks)

diagnostics [*diagnos(is) & -ics, science*] The science or practice of diagnosis. (deye' ig NOS tiks)

didactics [*Grk > didaktikos, skillful at teaching + -ics, science*] The art or science of teaching or systematic instruction. Pedagogy. See pedagogy and pedagogics. (deye DAK tiks)

dietetics [*diet & -ics, study of*] The study of nutrition in the diet. See sitology. (deye' uh TET iks)

dioptrics [*dia-, through + opt, sight + -ics, study of*] The branch of optics dealing with the study of refracted light. See optics. (deye OP triks)

dogmatics [*dogma & -ics, study of*] The study of religious dogmas, especially those taught by the Christian Church. (dog MAT iks)

dramatics [*drama & -ics, skill*] 1.The art of producing and performing dramas, especially by amateurs. 2.Dramatic or overemotional behavior. (druh MAT iks)

dynamics [*dynam, power + -ics, study of*] The branch of mechanics dealing with the study of force, mass, and motion. See statics, kinetics, and kinematics. (deye NAM iks)

dysgenics [*dys-, abnormal + gen, production + -ics, study of*] The biological study of the deterioration of hereditary qualities that cause degeneration in offspring. Opposed to eugenics. (dis JEN iks)

econometrics [*econo(mics) & metr, measure + -ics, knowledge*] The application of statistical and mathematical analysis to economics to solve problems and verify theories. (ih kon' uh MET riks)

economics [*Grk > oikos, house + nom, management + -ics, study of*] The scientific study of the production and distribution of wealth. (ek' uh NOM iks)

ekistics [*Grk > oikos, house + -ist + -ics, study of*] The science dealing with the study of human settlements, including city and area planning designed to meet the needs of the individual and the community. (ih KIS tiks)

electroacoustics [*electro, electric + Grk > akouein, to hear + -ics, science*] The science dealing with the transformation of sound into electricity and vice versa. (ih lek' troh uh KOO stiks)

electrodynamics [*electro, electric + dynam, power + -ics, study of*] The branch of physics dealing with the study of the relationships between electric currents and associated magnetic forces. (ih lek' troh deye NAM iks)

electrokinetics [*electro, electricity + kinet, motion + -ics, study of*] The branch of physics dealing with the study of electricity in motion. See electrostatics. (ih lek' troh kih NET iks)

electronics [*electron & -ics, science*] The science and technology dealing with the behavior, control, and effects of electrons. (ih lek' TRON iks)

electrostatics [*electro, electricity + stat, stationary + -ics, study of*] The branch of physics dealing with the study of static electricity. See electrokinetics. (ih lek' troh STAT iks)

endodontics [*endo-, inside + dont, tooth + -ics, practice*] The branch of dentistry dealing with the prevention and treatment of diseases and disorders of the tooth pulp. (en' doh DONT iks)

energetics [*en-, at + erg, work + -ics, science*] The science dealing with the laws that govern all forms of energy and the transformation from one form to another. (en' ur JET iks)

ergonomics [*erg, work & (ec)onomics*] The study of the relationship between people and their working environment. (ur' guh NOM iks)

esthetics [*esthet, feeling + -ics, study of*] The branch of philosophy dealing with the study of the qualities perceived in beauty, art, and taste. Same as aesthetics. (es THET iks)

ethics [*Grk > ethos, character + -ics, study of*] 1.The branch of philosophy dealing with the study of the rules of conduct and moral principles. 2.A code of moral conduct governing a person, profession, etc. (ETH iks)

eugenics [*eu-, good + gen, to produce + -ics, study of*] The study of the improvement of a species, especially the human species, by genetic control of hereditary factors in breeding. Opposed to dysgenics. See euphenics. (yoo JEN iks)

euphenics [*eu-, good & phen(otype) & -ics, study of*] The study of biological improvement of humans either before or after birth, as through prenatal manipulation of genes. See eugenics. (yoo FEN iks)

eurhythmics [*eu-, good & rhythm & -ics, skill*] The art of performing rhythmical body movements, usually in response to music. Same as eurythmics. (yoo RITH miks)

eurythmics [*eu-, good & r(h)ythm & -ics, skill*] The art of performing rhythmical body movements, usually in response to music. (yoo RITH miks)

euthenics [*Grk > euthenein, to prosper + -ics, study of*] The study of the improvement of human well-being by improvement of living conditions. (yoo THEN iks)

exodontics [*exo-, out + dont, tooth + -ics, practice*] The branch of dentistry dealing with the extraction of teeth. (eks' oh DONT iks)

floristics [*flor, flower + -ist + -ics, study of*] The branch of botany dealing with the study of the number and species of plants in a particular region. See flora. (flor IS tiks)

fluid mechanics [*fluid {liquids and gases} & mechanics*] The branch of mechanics dealing with the basic principles of liquids and gases. (FLOO id muh KAN iks)

fluidics [*fluid {liquids and gases} + -ics, science*] The science or technology dealing with the control of fluids, especially for use in various devices for sensing, amplifying, controlling, computing, etc. (floo ID iks)

forensics [*Ltn > forensis, of the forum + -ics, study of*] The practice or study of formal debate and argumentation. (fuh REN siks)

general semantics [*general & semantics*] The educational principle that attempts to improve human behavior by a careful and exact evaluation of the use of symbols and words. See semantics. (JEN ur ul sih MAN tiks)

genetics [*gen, birth + -ics, study of*] The branch of biology dealing with the study of heredity and variation and the factors controlling them. (juh NET iks)

geodynamics [*geo, earth + dynam, power + -ics, study of*] The branch of geology dealing with the study of forces within the earth. (jee' oh deye NAM iks)

geophysics [*geo, earth & physics*] The branch of geology dealing with the study of the physics of the earth, including geodesy, oceanography, hydrology, seismology, volcanology, meteorology, climatology, and geomagnetism. (jee' oh FIZ iks)

geopolitics [*geo(graphy) & politics*] The study of the relationship between geographical and political factors in a region or country. (jee' oh POL ih tiks)

geoponics [*geo, earth + Grk > ponein, to toil + -ics, science*] The science of agriculture. See agriculture, aquaculture, and hydroponics. (jee' oh PON iks)

geriatrics [*Grk > geras, old age + iatr, healing + -ics, study of*] The branch of medicine dealing with the study and treatment of diseases and disorders associated with old age and aging persons. See gerontology. (jehr' ee AT riks)

glyptics [*Grk > glyphein, to engrave + -ics, skill*] The art of carving or engraving on precious stones. See glyptograph. (GLIP tiks)

gnotobiotics [*gnos, knowledge + bio, living organisms + -ics, study of*] The science dealing with the study of organisms living in an environment free from germs or other microorganisms, except those known to be present. (noht' oh beye OT iks)

graphemics [*graphem(e) & -ics, study of*] The branch of linguistics dealing with the study of the relations between the writing system and speech sounds of a language. (gruh FEE miks)

graphics [*graph, drawing + -ics, skill*] The art or practice of making drawings in accordance with mathematical rules, as in engineering, architecture, mathematics, etc. (GRAF iks)

gymnastics [*gymnast & -ics, skill*] The art or practice of developing and exhibiting body strength and control, especially as performed in a gymnasium with special equipment. (jim NAS tiks)

gyniatrics [*gyn, woman + iatr, healing + -ics, study of*] The branch of medical science dealing with the study and treatment of diseases peculiar to women. See gynecology. (jin' ee AT riks)

harmonics [*harmon(y) & -ics, science*] The doctrine or science dealing with the physical properties of musical sounds. (hahr MON iks)

hemodynamics [*hemo, blood + dynam, power + -ics, study of*] A branch of physiology dealing with the study of blood circulation. (hee' moh deye NAM iks)

hermeneutics [*Grk > hermeneus, interpreter + -ics, science*] The science of the interpretation of literature, especially of the Bible. (hur' muh NOOT iks)

histrionics [*Ltn > histrio, actor + -ics, skill*] 1.Theatrical arts and performances. Acting. 2.Intentional display of emotional behavior or speech done for effect. See theatrics. (his' tree ON iks)

homiletics [*Grk > homiletikos, of conversation + -ics, skill*] The art of preaching. (hom' uh LET iks)

hydraulics [*hydr, liquid + Grk > aulos, pipe + -ics, science*] The science dealing with the laws governing the motion of water and other liquids. (heye DRAW liks)

hydrodynamics [*hydro, liquid + dynam, power + -ics, science*] The branch of hydromechanics dealing with the study of fluids in motion and of solid bodies immersed in them. See hydromechanics and hydrostatics. (heye' droh deye NAM iks)

hydrokinetics [*hydro, liquid + kinet, motion + -ics, science*] The branch of hydrodynamics dealing with the study of liquids in motion. See hydrodynamics. (heye' droh kih NET iks)

hydromagnetics [*hydro, liquid & magnetics*] Magnetohydrodynamics. (heye' droh mag NET iks)

hydromechanics [*hydro, liquid & mechanics*] The science dealing with the motion and equilibrium of fluids and of solid bodies immersed in them, including hydrodynamics and hydrostatics. See hydrodynamics and hydrostatics. (heye' droh muh KAN iks)

hydroponics [*hydro, water & (geo)ponics*] The science of growing plants by placing the roots in nutrient-rich solutions rather than soil. See agriculture, aquaculture, and geoponics. (heye' druh PON iks)

hydrostatics [*hydro, liquid + stat, stationary + -ics, science*] The branch of hydromechanics dealing with the study of fluids at rest or in equilibrium, especially the pressure and equilibrium of liquids. See hydromechanics and hydrodynamics. (heye' druh STAT iks)

hydrotherapeutics [*hydro, water & therapeutics*] Hydrotherapy. See hydrotherapy. (heye' droh thehr' uh PYOO tiks)

hygienics [*Grk > hygies, healthy + -ics, science*] The scientific study of health maintenance and disease prevention. (heye' jee EN iks)

immunogenetics [*immuno, immunity & genetics*] The branch of genetics dealing with the study of immunity to disease in relation to heredity. See genetics. (im' yuh noh' juh NET iks)

kinematics [*kinemat, motion + -ics, study of*] The branch of mechanics dealing with the study of pure motion without reference to force or mass. See dynamics and kinetics. (kin' uh MAT iks)

kinesics [*kine, motion + -ics, study of*] The study of body movements, facial expressions, and gestures that aid in communication. Body language. (kih NEE siks)

kinetics [*kinet, motion + -ics, study of*] The branch of mechanics dealing with the study of the effects of forces on the motion of material bodies. See dynamics and kinematics. (kih NET iks)

lexicostatistics [*lex, word + -ic & statistics*] The statistical study of the vocabulary of languages to determine when the languages under study separated. See glottochronology. (leks' ih koh' stuh TIS tiks)

linguistics [*lingu, language + -ist + -ics, study of*] The study of the nature, structure, and use of language, including phonology, morphology, syntax, and semantics. (ling GWIS tiks)

liturgics [*Grk > leos, people + erg, work + -ics, study of*] The study of prescribed forms of formal public worship. (lih TUR jiks)

logistics [*Grk > logistikos, of calculation + -ics, science*] The military science dealing with the procurement, maintenance, and distribution of personnel and equipment. (loh JIS tiks)

macrobiotics [*macro-, long + bio, life + -ics, study of*] The science of extending longevity, as through nutritious diets, stress reduction, etc. (mak' roh beye OT iks)

macroeconomics [*macro-, large & economics*] A branch of economics dealing with the study of the overall forces at work in an economy. See microeconomics. (mak' roh ek' uh NOM iks)

magnetohydrodynamics [*magneto, magnetic force & hydrodynamics*] The science dealing with the motion of water and other electrically conductive fluids in magnetic fields. See hydrodynamics. (mag NEET oh heye' droh deye NAM iks)

mathematics [*Grk > mathematikos, mathematical + -ics, study of*] The study of the relations between numbers, quantities, measurements, etc. (math' uh MAT iks)

mechanics [*mechan(ic) & -ics, science*] The science dealing with the action of energy and forces and their effect on matter or material systems, including dynamics, kinetics, kinematics, and statics. (muh KAN iks)

metaethics [*meta-, beyond & ethics*] The branch of philosophy dealing with the study of ethical terms, arguments, and judgments. See ethics. (met' uh ETH iks)

metalinguistics [*meta-, between + lingu, language + -ist + -ics, study of*] The branch of linguistics dealing with the study of the relations between language and other cultural factors. (met' uh ling GWIS tiks)

metamathematics [*meta-, beyond & mathematics*] The study of the fundamental concepts of logical systems, especially mathematical systems. See mathematics. (met' uh math' uh MAT iks)

metaphysics [*meta-, after & physics*] The area of philosophy dealing with the study of the nature and structure of reality. So named from the reference to Aristotle's writings that came after his studies in physics. (met' uh FIZ iks)

metrics [*metr, measure + -ics, science*] The art or science of writing in meter. (MET riks)

microeconomics [*micro-, small & economics*] A branch of economics dealing with the study of certain specific factors at work in an economy. See macroeconomics. (meye' kroh ek' uh NOM iks)

microelectronics [*micro-, small & electronics*] The science dealing with the design, manufacture, and application of miniaturized electronic circuits and components. (meye' kroh ih lek' TRON iks)

microphysics [*micro-, small & physics*] The branch of physics dealing with the study of objects that are too small to be observed directly, such as atoms, molecules, and other elementary particles. (meye' kroh FIZ iks)

mnemonics [*mne, memory + -ics, practice*] A system or technique of improving or developing the memory. (nih MON iks)

morphemics [*morphem(e) & -ics, study of*] 1.The branch of linguistics dealing with the study of the morphemes of a language. 2.Language structure in terms of the description and classification of morphemes. See morpheme. (mor FEE miks)

nucleonics [*nucleo, nucleus + -ics, science*] The branch of science dealing with atomic nuclei and nucleons and especially with practical applications of nuclear power. (noo' klee ON iks)

numismatics [*Ltn > numisma, coin + -ics, study of*] The study or collection of coins, medals, etc. (noo' miz MAT iks)

obstetrics [*Ltn > obstetrix, midwife + -ics, science*] The branch of medical science dealing with the care and treatment of women before, after, and during childbirth. (ob STET riks)

onomastics [*onomas, name + -ics, study of*] The study of the origin, evolution, and use of proper names. (on' uh MAS tiks)

optics [*opt, vision + -ics, study of*] The scientific study of vision and the properties of light. (OP tiks)

orthodontics [*ortho, straight + dont, teeth + -ics, practice*] The branch of dentistry dealing with the straightening of abnormally aligned or positioned teeth. (or' thuh DONT iks)

orthopaedics [*ortho, correct + ped, child + -ics, practice*] The branch of medicine dealing with the treatment of disorders and diseases of the musculoskeletal system, which includes bones, joints, muscles, tendons, and ligaments. Same as orthopedics. (or' thuh PEED iks)

orthopedics [*ortho, correct + ped, child + -ics, practice*] The branch of medicine dealing with the treatment of disorders and diseases of the musculoskeletal system, which includes bones, joints, muscles, tendons, and ligaments. (or' thuh PEED iks)

orthotics [*ortho, correct + -ics, science*] The branch of medical science dealing with the making and fitting of specialized orthopedic devices for the support of weakened joints or limbs. (or THOT iks)

pedagogics [*ped, child + agog, leader + -ics, science*] The science, art, or profession of teaching. Same as pedagogy. (ped' uh GOJ iks)

pediatrics [*ped, child + iatr, healing + -ics, study of*] The branch of medicine dealing with the study and treatment of diseases and disorders of infants and children. (pee' dee AT riks)

periodontics [*peri-, around + odont, teeth + -ics, practice*] The branch of dentistry dealing with diseases of the bone and tissue surrounding and supporting the teeth. (pehr' ee oh DONT iks)

pharmaceutics [*pharmac, drug + -ics, science*] The science or practice of preparing and dispensing drugs. See pharmacology. (fahr' muh SOO tiks)

pharmacodynamics [*pharmaco, drug + dynam, strength + -ics, study of*] The branch of pharmacology dealing with the study of the effects and actions of drugs on living organisms. (fahr' muh koh' deye NAM iks)

pharmacogenetics [*pharmaco, drug & genetics*] The scientific study of the relationship between genetic factors and drug response. (fahr' muh koh' juh NET iks)

pharmacokinetics [*pharmaco, drug + kinet, motion + -ics, study of*] The branch of pharmacology dealing with the study of the rate of absorption, excretion, etc., of drugs. (fahr' muh koh' kih NET iks)

phonemics [*phonem(e) & -ics, study of*] The branch of linguistics dealing with the study of the phonemes of a language. See phonology, phonetics, and phoneme. (fuh NEE miks)

phonetics [*phon, sound + -ics, study of*] 1.The branch of linguistics dealing with the study of the production, analysis, and written representation of speech sounds. 2.The speech sounds of a particular language. See phonology and phonemics. (fuh NET iks)

phonics [*phon, sound + -ics, study of*] 1.The study of sound. 2.A method of teaching reading to beginners by associating letters and syllables with sounds. (FON iks)

photodynamics [*photo, light + dynam, power + -ics, study of*] The study of the effects of light on plants and animals. (foht' oh deye NAM iks)

physiatrics [*physi, physical + iatr, healing + -ics, study of*] The study of physical therapy. (fiz' ee AT riks)

physics [*physi, nature + -ics, science*] The science dealing with the interactions between nonliving matter and energy, excluding the phenomena of chemical change. (FIZ iks)

pneumatics [*pneumat, air + -ics, study of*] The branch of physics dealing with the study of the properties of air and other gases. (noo MAT iks)

poetics [*poet(ry) & -ics, skill*] 1.The art of writing poetry. 2.A treatise on poetic theory or structure. 3.The study of poetry. (poh ET iks)

politics [*Grk > polites, citizen + -ics, science*] The science, art, or practice of political government. (POL ih tiks)

pragmatics [*pragmat(ic) & -ics, study of*] 1.The branch of linguistics dealing with the study of meanings in context. See semantics (def. 1). 2.The branch of semiotics dealing with the study of signs and symbols and their relationships to their users. See syntactics, semantics (def. 2), and semiotics. (prag MAT iks)

prosthetics [*Grk > prosthetos, to add to* + *-ics, science*] The art or science of making and fitting artificial parts of the body. (pros THET iks)

prosthodontics [*prosth(esis)* & *odont, teeth* + *-ics, practice*] The branch of dentistry dealing with the replacement of teeth with synthetic substitutes. (pros' thuh DONT iks)

proxemics [*prox(imity)* & *-ics, study of*] The study of the patterns of spacial separation among individuals in human and animal populations. (prok SEE miks)

psychodynamics [*psycho, mental process* + *dynam, power* + *-ics, study of*] The study of mental or emotional processes or forces and their relation to human behavior and metal states. (seye' koh deye NAM iks)

psycholinguistics [*psycho, mind* + *lingu, language* + *-ist* + *-ics, study of*] The study of the relationship between psychological behavior and the understanding and use of language. (seye' koh ling GWIS tiks)

psychometrics [*psycho, mental process* + *metr, to measure* + *-ics, science*] The science of measuring mental capabilities, functions, processes, traits, etc. (seye' kuh MET riks)

psychophysics [*psycho, mental process* + *physi, physical* + *-ics, study of*] The branch of psychology dealing with the study of the effects of physical stimuli on mental processes. (seye' koh FIZ iks)

pyrotechnics [*pyro, fire* + *techn, art* + *-ics, skill*] The art of making and displaying fireworks. (peye' roh TEK niks)

rhythmics [*rhythm* & *-ics, science*] The science of rhythms. (RITH miks)

robotics [*robot* & *-ics, science*] The science and technology of the design, production, and application of robots. (roh BOT iks)

semantics [*Grk > semantikos, having meaning* + *-ics, study of*] 1.The branch of linguistics dealing with the study of the structure and developmental changes of meanings in a language. See pragmatics (def. 1). 2.The branch of semiotics dealing with the study of the relationships between signs and symbols and their representations. See syntactics, pragmatics (def. 2), and semiotics. (sih MAN tiks)

semiotics [*Grk > sema, sign* + *-ics, study of*] The study of signs and symbols in a language, usually including syntactics, semantics, and pragmatics. See syntactics, semantics (def. 2), and pragmatics (def. 2). (see' mee OT iks)

sferics [*(atmo)s(ph)erics*] Short for atmospherics. See atmospherics. (SFIHR iks)

sociolinguistics [*socio, social* + *lingu, language* + *-ist* + *-ics, study of*] The study of social and cultural factors and their effects on language usage. (soh' see oh' ling GWIS tiks)

spherics [*(atmo)spherics*] Short for atmospherics. Same as sferics. See atmospherics. (SFIHR iks)

statics [*stat, stationary* + *-ics, study of*] The branch of mechanics dealing with the study of the interaction between forces and matter in equilibrium. See dynamics. (STAT iks)

statistics [*stat(e)* & *-ist* + *-ics, science*] The science dealing with the collection, organization, presentation, and interpretation of numerical data. (stuh TIS tiks)

stylistics [*styl(e)* & *-ist* + *-ics, study of*] The study of style as a method of analyzing literary works. (steye LIS tiks)

supersonics [*super-, above* + *son, sound* + *-ics, study of*] The study of the aerodynamics of a body moving through a medium at speeds greater than the speed of sound. (soo' per SON iks)

syntactics [*syntactic* & *-ics, study of*] The branch of semiotics dealing with the study of the formal characteristics of signs and symbols, apart from their users. See semantics (def. 2), pragmatics (def. 2), and semiotics. (sin TAK tiks)

systematics [*system* & *-ics, science*] 1.The science of classification. 2.The classification of organisms based on common factors and relationships to each other. Same as taxonomy. (sis' tuh MAT iks)

tactics [*Grk > taktos, to arrange* + *-ics, science*] 1.The art or science of deploying and maneuvering combat forces. 2.The art or skill of using available means for gaining success or advantage. (TAK tiks)

tectonics [*Grk > tekton, builder* + *-ics, science*] 1.The art or science of construction, especially buildings that are aesthetically pleasing and practical. See architectonics (def. 1). 2.The branch of geology dealing with the study of the formation, history, and changes in the structure of the earth's crust. See geotectonic. (tek TON iks)

theatrics [*theatr(e)* & *-ics, skill*] 1.The art of the theater. 2.Theatrical effects, actions, mannerisms, etc. See histrionics. (thee AT riks)

therapeutics [*Grk > therapeutikos, to treat medically* + *-ics, science*] The art or science of treating and curing disease through the use of remedies. (thehr' uh PYOO tiks)

thermionics [*thermion* & *-ics, study of*] The scientific study of thermionic phenomena. See thermion. (thur' meye ON iks)

thermodynamics [*thermo, heat* + *dynam, energy* + *-ics, study of*] The branch of physics dealing with the study of the relationships between heat and other forms of energy. See aerothermodynamics. (thur' moh deye NAM iks)

tonetics [*tone* & *-ics, study of*] The study of linguistic tones in a language. (toh NET iks)

toreutics [*Grk > toreutikos, to work in relief* + *-ics, skill*] The art and process of engraving, embossing, or chasing metal or other materials. (tuh ROOT iks)

ultrasonics [*ultra-, beyond* + *son, sound* + *-ics, science*] The science dealing with the characteristics and phenomena of ultrasonic sound. (ul' truh SON iks)

vitrics [*vitri, glass* + *-ics, skill*] The art of glassmaking. (VIT riks)

zootechnics [*zoo, animal* + *techn, skill* + *-ics, science*] The science and technology of breeding, rearing, and utilizing animals. (zoh' uh TEK niks)

lud, lus   to play

allude [*al-, near* + *lud, to play*] To refer to indirectly or casually. (uh LOOD)

collude [*col-, together* + *lud, to play*] To act together secretly for a fraudulent purpose. Conspire. Plot. (kuh LOOD)

delude [*de-, away* + *lud, to play*] To mislead the mind or judgment of. Deceive. (dih LOOD)

disillusion [*dis-, away* & *illusion*] To free from illusion. Disenchant. See illusion. (dis' uh LOO zhun)

lud, lus

elude [*e-, out* + *lud, to play*] To escape from or avoid skillfully, cleverly, etc. See evade and circumvent (def. 2). (ee LOOD)

illusion [*il-, at* + *lus, to play* + *-ion*] 1.A false or misleading optical image. Also called an optical illusion. 2.A general impression not based on actual fact or reality. (ih LOO zhun)

interlude [*inter-, between* + *lud, to play*] 1.Any episode, period, performance, etc., that takes place between two things. 2.Entertainment between the acts of a play. 3.Music played between parts of a composition. See prelude and postlude. (IN ter lood')

postlude [*post-, after* + *lud, to play*] 1.A concluding piece of music, especially an organ voluntary at the end of a church service. 2.A closing phase. See prelude and interlude. (POHST lood)

prelude [*pre-, before* + *lud, to play*] 1.Something that serves as an introduction to a major performance, event, action, etc. 2.A musical movement that serves as an introduction to another more important movement. See interlude and postlude. (PREL yood)

prolusion [*pro-, before* + *lus, to play* + *-ion*] 1.An introductory essay or article. 2.A preliminary exercise or attempt. (proh LOO zhun)

lun, luni   moon

apolune [*apo-, away* + *lun, moon*] The point in a satellite's lunar orbit that is farthest from the moon. See perilune. (AP uh loon')

circumlunar [*circum-, around* + *lun, moon* + *-ar*] Revolving around or surrounding the moon. See circumsolar and circumterrestrial. (sur' kum LOO nur)

cislunar [*cis, on the near side* + *lun, moon* + *-ar*] Lying between the earth and the moon. (sis LOO nur)

interlunar [*inter-, between* + *lun, moon* + *-ar*] Pertaining to the period of time each month between the old moon and the new moon during which the moon is not visible from the earth. (in' ter LOO nur)

lunacy [*lun, moon* + *-acy*] 1.Intermittent insanity. So named from the former belief that insanity fluctuated with the phases of the moon. 2.Extreme or wild foolishness. (LOO nuh see)

lunar [*lun, moon* + *-ar*] 1.Pertaining to the moon. 2.Measured by the revolutions of the moon. (LOO nur)

lunar eclipse [*lun, moon* + *-ar & eclipse*] The obstruction of light from the moon when the earth is positioned between the moon and the sun. See solar eclipse. (LOO nur ih KLIPS)

lunar month [*lun, moon* + *-ar & month*] The period of time of one revolution of the moon around the earth, which is the interval between two successive new moons, or about 29.5 days. See lunation. (LOO nur munth)

lunate [*lun, moon* + *-ate*] Crescent-shaped. (LOO nayt)

lunatic [*lun, moon* + *-tic*] 1.A person affected with lunacy. 2.An extremely reckless or foolish person. (LOO nuh tik)

lunation [*lun, moon* + *-ation*] The interval between two successive new moons, about 29.5 days. Lunar month. See lunar month. (loo NAY shun)

lune [*lun, moon*] A crescent-shaped figure that is formed on a plane or spherical surface by the intersecting arcs of two circles. (loon)

lunette [*lun, moon* + *-ette, diminutive*] Any of various figures or objects shaped like a half-moon or a crescent. (loo NET)

lunisolar [*luni, moon* + *sol, sun* + *-ar*] Pertaining to or caused by both the moon and the sun. (loo' nih SOH lur)

lunitidal [*luni, moon & tidal*] Pertaining to tidal movements caused by the attraction of the moon. (loo' nih TEYED l)

lunule [*lun, moon* + *-ule, small*] A crescent-shaped marking or structure, as the whitish area at the base of a fingernail. (LOON yool)

perilune [*peri-, around* + *lun, moon*] The point in a satellite's lunar orbit that is nearest the moon. See apolune. (PEHR ih loon')

semilunar [*semi-, half* + *lun, moon* + *-ar*] Having the shape of a half-moon or crescent. (sem' ee LOO nur)

sublunary [*sub-, beneath* + *lun, moon* + *-ary*] 1.Situated between the earth and the moon or beneath the moon. 2.Terrestrial. Earthly. Worldly. (sub' LOO nuh ree)

superlunary [*super-, beyond* + *lun, moon* + *-ary*] Situated beyond the moon. Celestial. (soo' per LOO nuh ree)

macro-   large, long

amphimacer [*amphi-, on both sides* + *macro, long* + *-er*] A trisyllabic metrical foot consisting of a short syllable between two long syllables in quantitative meter, and an unstressed syllable between two stressed syllables in accentual meter. See amphibrach. (am FIM uh sur)

macro [*macro-, long*] A single computer instruction representing two or more instructions in a given sequence. (MAK roh)

macrobiotics [*macro-, long* + *bio, life* + *-ics, study of*] The science of extending longevity, as through nutritious diets, stress reduction, etc. (mak' roh beye OT iks)

macrocephaly [*macro-, large* + *cephal, head* + *-y*] A condition characterized by an abnormally large head. See microcephaly. (mak' roh SEF uh lee)

macroclimate [*macro-, large* + *climat, climate*] The general climate over a large area. Opposed to microclimate. (MAK roh kleye' mit)

macroclimatology [*macro-, large* + *climat, climate* + *-ology, study of*] The study of the climate over a large geographical area. See microclimatology. (mak' roh kleye' muh TOL uh jee)

macrocosm [*macro-, large* + *cosm, universe*] The entire universe. See microcosm. (MAK roh koz' um)

macrocyte [*macro-, large* + *-cyte, cell*] An abnormally large red blood cell occurring in certain anemias and associated with folic acid deficiency. See microcyte. (MAK roh seyet')

macroeconomics [*macro-, large & economics*] A branch of economics dealing with the study of the overall forces at work in an economy. See microeconomics. (mak' roh ek' uh NOM iks)

macroevolution [*macro-, large & evolution*] Large-scale and long-range evolution of organisms, resulting in relatively large and complex changes. See evolve and microevolution. (mak' roh ev' uh LOO shun)

macrogamete [*macro-, large & gamete*] The usually female and larger of two conjugating gametes in a heterogamous organism. See microgamete. (mak' roh GAM eet)

macroglobulinemia [*macroglobulin & -emia, blood condition*] A disorder characterized by the presence of macroglobulins in the blood.
(mak' roh glob' yuh luh NEE mee uh)

macrograph [*macro-, large + graph, drawing*] A representation of an object, as a drawing or photograph, that is as large or larger than the object.
(MAK roh graf')

macroinstruction [*macro-, large & instruction*] A single computer instruction representing two or more instructions in a given sequence. Same as macro.
(mak' roh in STRUK shun)

macromolecule [*macro-, large & molecule*] A large molecule, as that of a polymer or protein.
(mak' roh MOL ih kyool')

macron [*macro-, long + -on*] A mark placed above a vowel to indicate a long sound or to indicate a long or stressed syllable in a metrical foot. See circumflex (def. 1). (MAY kron)

macronucleus [*macro-, large & nucleus*] Of the two nuclei found in ciliate protozoans, the larger nucleus that controls cell metabolism. See micronucleus.
(mak' roh NOO klee us)

macronutrient [*macro-, large & nutrient*] Any element, as carbon, nitrogen, or potassium, required in relatively large amounts for plant growth and development. See micronutrient. (mak' roh NOO tree ent)

macrophage [*macro-, large + -phage, to eat*] A large phagocyte found in blood, lymph, and connective tissue that ingests and destroys cell debris, microorganisms, and other harmful foreign material. See phagocyte and microphage. (MAK roh fayj')

macrophyte [*macro-, large + -phyte, plant*] A plant that is large enough to be visible to the naked eye, especially one in an aquatic environment. See macroscopic and microphyte. (MAK roh feyet')

macropterous [*macro-, large + pter, wing + -ous*] Pertaining to birds, insects, or fish with unusually large wings or fins. (muh KROP ter us)

macroscopic [*macro-, large + scop, to view + -ic*] Visible to the naked eye. Opposed to microscopic.
(mak' roh SKOP ik)

macrosporangium [*macro-, large & sporangium*] In heterosporous plants, a sporangium that produces only megaspores and is borne on a megasporophyll. Same as megasporangium. (mak' roh spuh RAN jee um)

macrospore [*macro-, large & spore*] The usually larger of two kinds of spores in heterosporous plants that gives rise to a female gametophyte. Same as megaspore.
(MAK roh spor')

micro-   small, millionth (10^{-6})

electron microscope [*electron & microscope*] A powerful microscope that focuses a beam of electrons instead of visible light to produce an enlarged image of a minute object on a fluorescent screen.
(ih LEK tron' MEYE kruh skohp')

microampere [*micro-, millionth & ampere*] One millionth of an ampere. (meye' kroh AM pihr)

microbar [*micro-, millionth + bar, pressure*] A metric unit of pressure equal to one millionth of a bar or one dyne per square centimeter. (MEYE kroh bahr')

microbarograph [*micro-, small + baro, pressure + graph, recording*] An instrument for making a continuous recording of minute changes in atmospheric pressure.
(meye' kroh BEHR uh graf')

microbe [*micro-, small + bio, life*] A microorganism; especially a virus, bacterium, protozoan, etc., that causes disease. Germ. (MEYE krohb)

microbicide [*microb(e) & -cide, to kill*] An agent for killing microbes. (meye KROH buh seyed')

microbiology [*micro-, small + bio, life + -logy, study of*] The study of microscopic forms of life, as viruses, bacteria, protozoans, and other microorganisms.
(meye' kroh beye OL uh jee)

microcephaly [*micro-, small + cephal, head + -y*] A condition characterized by an abnormally small head. See macrocephaly. (meye' kroh SEF uh lee)

microclimate [*micro-, small + climat, climate*] The climate of a small specific area, as a greenhouse, building, mountain, etc. Opposed to macroclimate.
(MEYE kroh kleye' mit)

microclimatology [*micro-, small + climat, climate + -ology, study of*] The study of the climate in a small area or habitat. See macroclimatology.
(meye' kroh kleye' muh TOL uh jee)

micrococcus [*micro-, small + -coccus, bacteria*] Small spherical bacteria that usually occur in irregular masses. (meye' kroh KOK us)

microcosm [*micro-, small + cosm, world*] 1.A miniature world or system sometimes representative of a larger system. 2.Something viewed as the epitome of the world or universe. See macrocosm. (MEYE kroh koz' um)

microcyte [*micro-, small + -cyte, cell*] An abnormally small mature red blood cell, occurring mainly in anemias, that is five microns or less in diameter. See macrocyte.
(MEYE kroh seyet')

microdont [*micro-, small + dont, teeth*] Having small teeth. (MEYE kroh dont')

microeconomics [*micro-, small & economics*] A branch of economics dealing with the study of certain specific factors at work in an economy. See macroeconomics.
(meye' kroh ek' uh NOM iks)

microelectronics [*micro-, small & electronics*] The science dealing with the design, manufacture, and application of miniaturized electronic circuits and components.
(meye' kroh ih lek' TRON iks)

microevolution [*micro-, small & evolution*] Small-scale and short-range evolution of organisms. See evolve and macroevolution. (meye' kroh ev' uh LOO shun)

microfarad [*micro-, millionth & farad*] One millionth of a farad. (MEYE kroh fehr' uhd)

microfiche [*micro-, small + French > fiche, card*] A small sheet of microfilm containing microphotographs of the pages of books, magazines, newspapers, and other documents. (MEYE kroh fish')

microfilm [*micro-, small & film*] A length of film containing microphotographs of the pages of books, magazines, newspapers, and other documents.
(MEYE kroh film')

microgamete [*micro-, small & gamete*] The usually male and smaller of two conjugating gametes in a heterogamous organism. See macrogamete.
(meye' kroh GAM eet)

micro-

microgametophyte [*micro-, small & gametophyte*] A male gametophyte in heterosporous plants that is produced by a microspore. See megagametophyte, gametophyte, and microspore. (meye' kroh guh MEET uh feyet')

microgram [*micro-, millionth & gram*] One millionth of a gram. (MEYE kroh gram')

micrograph [*micro-, small + graph, writing*] 1.An instrument for writing or engraving minutely. 2.A photograph of a microscopic image. See photomicrograph. (MEYE kroh graf')

microlith [*micro-, small + lith, stone*] A small flint tool mounted in wood or bone and used especially in the Mesolithic period. (MEYE kroh lith')

micrometeorite [*micro-, small & meteorite*] A very small particle of meteoric dust. (meye' kroh MEET ee uh reyet')

micrometeorology [*micro-, small + Grk > meteoron, atmospheric phenomenon + -ology, study of*] The branch of meteorology dealing with the study of small-scale atmospheric phenomena. (meye' kroh meet' ee uh ROL uh jee)

micrometer[1] [*micro-, small + meter, to measure*] An instrument for measuring minute distances, thicknesses, angles, etc. (meye KROM et er)

micrometer[2] [*micro-, millionth & meter*] A metric unit of length equal to one millionth of a meter. Same as micron. (meye KROM et er)

micromillimeter [*micro-, millionth & millimeter*] A metric unit of length equal to one millionth of a millimeter. (meye' kroh MIL uh mee' ter)

microminiature [*micro-, small & miniature*] Pertaining to a device or component built on a very small scale. (meye' kroh MIN ee uh chur')

micron [*micro-, millionth*] A metric unit of length equal to one millionth of a meter. (MEYE kron)

micronucleus [*micro-, small & nucleus*] Of the two nuclei found in ciliate protozoans, the smaller nucleus. See macronucleus. (meye' kroh NOO klee us)

micronutrient [*micro-, small & nutrient*] Any trace element required only in small amounts by an organism. See macronutrient. (meye' kroh NOO tree ent)

microorganism [*micro-, small & organism*] Any microscopic organism, as bacteria, protozoans, viruses, algae, etc. (meye' kroh OR guh niz' um)

micropaleontology [*micro-, small + pale, ancient + ont, being + -ology, study of*] The branch of paleontology dealing with the study of microscopic plant and animal fossils. See paleontology. (meye' kroh pay' lee on TOL uh jee)

microphage [*micro-, small + -phage, to eat*] A small phagocyte that ingests and destroys bacteria and other microorganisms. See phagocyte and macrophage. (MEYE kroh fayj')

microphobia [*micro(organism) & -phobia, fear*] Abnormal fear of microbes. (meye' kroh FOH bee uh)

microphone [*micro-, small + -phone, sound*] An instrument that converts sound waves into a small electric current that is fed into an amplifier, transmitter, recorder, etc. (MEYE kruh fohn')

microphotograph [*micro-, small & photograph*] A small photograph that cannot be viewed without being enlarged. See photomicrograph. (meye' kroh FOH tuh graf')

microphotometer [*micro-, small + photo, light + meter, to measure*] An instrument for measuring the light intensity of minute objects. See photometer. (meye' kroh foh TOM et er)

microphysics [*micro-, small & physics*] The branch of physics dealing with the study of objects that are too small to be observed directly, such as atoms, molecules, and other elementary particles. (meye' kroh FIZ iks)

microphyte [*micro-, small + -phyte, plant*] A plant that is not large enough to be visible to the naked eye. See microscopic and macrophyte. (MEYE kroh feyet')

microplankton [*micro-, small + Grk > planktos, wandering*] Minute floating aquatic organisms of animal or plant life that can only be seen through a microscope. See phytoplankton and zooplankton. (meye' kroh PLANK tun)

microprocessor [*micro-, small & processor*] A central processing unit for a computer that resides on a single chip. (meye' kroh PRAH ses ur)

micropyle [*micro-, small + Grk > pyle, gate*] A small opening in the ovule of a seed plant for the entrance of the pollen tube. (MEYE kroh peyel')

micropyrometer [*micro-, small + pyro, temperature + meter, to measure*] An optical instrument for measuring the temperature of minute glowing bodies. (meye' kroh peye ROM et er)

microradiography [*micro-, small & radiograph & -y*] A radiographic process that produces an x-ray photograph showing minute details. See radiograph. (meye' kroh ray' dee OG ruh fee)

microscope [*micro-, small + -scope, to view*] An optical instrument for making enlarged images of minute objects by means of a magnifying lens or combination of lenses. (MEYE kruh skohp')

microscopic [*micro-, small + scop, to view + -ic*] Able to be seen through a microscope, but not visible to the naked eye. Opposed to macroscopic. (meye' kroh SKOP ik)

microsecond [*micro-, millionth & second*] One millionth of a second. (MEYE kroh sek' und)

microseism [*micro-, small + seism, earthquake*] A small tremor or vibration of the earth's crust. (MEYE kroh seyez' um)

microsome [*micro-, small + -some, body*] A minute granule of endoplasm in the cytoplasm of a cell. (MEYE kroh sohm')

microsphere [*micro-, small & sphere*] A minute sphere. (MEYE kroh sfihr')

microsporangium [*micro-, small & sporangium*] In heterosporous plants, a sporangium that produces only microspores and is borne on a microsporophyll. See megasporangium and microsporophyll. (meye' kroh spuh RAN jee um)

microspore [*micro-, small & spore*] The usually smaller of two kinds of spores in heterosporous plants that gives rise to a male gametophyte. See megaspore. (MEYE kroh spor')

microsporophyll [*micro-, small + sporo, spore + phyll, leaf*] A leaf or modified leaf that produces only microsporangia. See megasporophyll and microsporangium. (meye' kroh SPOR uh fil')

microsurgery [*micro-, small & surgery*] Surgery using a microscope and very small instruments to repair or attach body parts. (meye' kroh SUR jer ee)

microtome [*micro-, small + -tome, to cut*] A precise instrument for cutting thin sections of organic tissue or other material for microscopic examination. (MEYE kroh tohm')

microtubule [*micro-, small & tubule*] Any of numerous minute, tubular structures found in the cytoplasm of most living cells. (meye' kroh TOO byool)

microvillus [*micro-, small & villus*] A minute hairlike projection on the surface of an epithelial cell. (meye' kroh VIL us)

microwave [*micro-, small & wave*] A very short radio wave, between one millimeter and fifty centimeters in length, used in communications, radar, and microwave ovens. (MEYE kroh wayv')

millimicron [*milli-, thousandth & micron*] A metric unit of length equal to one thousandth of a micron. (mil' uh MEYE kron)

photomicrograph [*photo, light + micro, small + graph, recording*] A photograph of an image taken through a microscope. See micrograph (def. 2) and microphotograph. (foht' oh MEYE kruh graf')

photomicroscope [*photo(graph) & microscope*] A microscope for taking photomicrographs. See photomicrograph. (foht' oh MEYE kruh skohp')

pneumonoultramicroscopicsilicovolcanoconiosis [*pneumono, lung & ultramicroscopic & silico, silica & volcano & coni, dust + -osis, diseased condition*] A lung disease caused by prolonged breathing of extremely fine siliceous dust. Sometimes cited as one of the longest words in the English language. (NOO muh noh ul' truh meye' kruh skop' ik SIL uh koh' vol kay' noh koh' nee oh' sis)

stereomicroscope [*stereo-, three-dimensional & microscope*] A microscope equipped with a set of optics for each eye to make objects appear three-dimensional. (stehr' ee oh MEYE kruh skohp')

submicroscopic [*sub-, under & microscopic*] Too small for viewing through an optical microscope. (sub' meye' kruh SKOP ik)

ultramicroscope [*ultra-, beyond & microscope*] A microscope used to study very minute objects by picking up the reflections of light rays dispersed by them. (ul' truh MEYE kruh skohp')

ultramicrotome [*ultra-, beyond + micro, small + -tome, to cut*] A precise instrument for cutting very thin sections of organic tissue or other material for microscopic examination. (ul' truh MEYE kruh tohm')

mega-, megal/o, -megaly
large, great, million (10^6)

acromegaly [*acro, extremity + -megaly, large*] A chronic disease caused by a disorder of the pituitary gland and marked by progressive enlargement of bones in the head, hands, and feet. (ak' roh MEG uh lee)

cardiomegaly [*cardio, heart + megal, large + -y*] Enlargement of the heart. (kahr' dee oh MEG uh lee)

cytomegalic [*cyto, cell + megal, large + -ic*] Characterized by an abnormal enlargement of cells. (seyet' oh mih GAL ik)

cytomegalovirus [*cyto, cell + megalo, large & virus*] Any of various herpesviruses that cause enlargement of cells in various organs, and in humans, cause cytomegalic inclusion disease. (seyet' uh meg' uh loh VEYE rus)

hepatomegaly [*hepato, liver + -megaly, large*] Enlargement of the liver. (hep' uh toh MEG uh lee)

megabit [*mega-, million & bit*] In computer science, a unit of storage containing 1,048,576 (2^{20}) bits. (MEG uh bit')

megabyte [*mega-, million & byte*] In computer science, a unit of storage containing 1,048,576 (2^{20}) bytes. (MEG uh beyet')

megacity [*mega-, large & city*] A very large city usually containing at least 20 million inhabitants. See megalopolis. (MEG uh sih' tee)

megacycle [*mega-, million & cycle*] One million cycles per second. Megahertz. (MEG uh seye' kul)

megadeath [*mega-, million & death*] A unit used to represent one million deaths, usually in reference to lives lost in a nuclear explosion or a nuclear war. (MEG uh deth')

megadose [*mega-, large & dose*] An unusually large dose, as of a vitamin or drug. (MEG uh dohs')

megagametophyte [*mega-, large & gametophyte*] A female gametophyte in heterosporous plants that is produced by a megaspore. See microgametophyte, gametophyte, and megaspore. (meg' uh guh MEET uh feyet')

megahertz [*mega-, million & hertz*] One million cycles per second. Megacycle. (MEG uh hurts')

megakaryocyte [*mega-, large + karyo, nucleus + -cyte, cell*] A large platelet-producing cell in the bone marrow with a highly lobulated nucleus. See thrombocyte. (meg' uh KEHR ee oh seyet')

megalith [*mega-, large + lith, stone*] A large stone used in prehistoric monuments or architecture. (MEG uh lith')

megaloblast [*megalo, large + blast, cell*] An abnormally large, dysfunctional erythroblast present in the blood, especially in cases of pernicious anemia and folic acid deficiency. (MEG uh loh blast')

megalocardia [*megalo, large + cardi, heart + -a*] Enlargement of the heart. Same as cardiomegaly. (meg' uh loh KAHR dee uh)

megalomania [*megalo, great + mania, mental aberration*] A mental disorder characterized by unfounded belief in one's omnipotence, grandeur, wealth, etc. (meg' uh loh MAY nee uh)

megalopolis [*megalo, large + -polis, city*] A densely populated region consisting of one or more large cities and the surrounding area. See megacity. (meg' uh LOP uh lis)

megalosaur [*megalo, large + saur, lizard*] A very large carnivorous dinosaur of the Jurassic period. (MEG uh luh sor')

megameter [*mega-, million & meter*] A metric unit of length equal to 1,000,000 meters. (MEG uh mee' ter)

megaphone [*mega-, large + -phone, voice*] A cone-shaped device designed to amplify and direct the voice. (MEG uh fohn')

megapode [*mega-, large + -pode, foot*] Any of a family of large-footed birds found in Australia and many South Pacific islands, that incubate their eggs by burying them in mounds of earth. (MEG uh pohd')

mega-, megal/o, -megaly

megasporangium [*mega-, large & sporangium*] In heterosporous plants, a sporangium that produces only megaspores and is borne on a megasporophyll. See microsporangium and megasporophyll. (meg' uh spuh RAN jee um)

megaspore [*mega-, large & spore*] The usually larger of two kinds of spores in heterosporous plants that gives rise to a female gametophyte. See microspore. (MEG uh spor')

megasporogenesis [*mega-, large + sporo, spore + -genesis, production*] The production and maturation of a megaspore. See megaspore. (meg' uh spor' uh JEN uh sis)

megasporophyll [*mega-, large + sporo, spore + phyll, leaf*] A leaf or modified leaf that produces only megasporangia. See microsporophyll and megasporangium. (meg' uh SPOR uh fil')

megaton [*mega-, million & ton*] A unit of explosive force equal to one million tons of TNT. (MEG uh tun')

megavolt [*mega-, million & volt*] A unit of electrical potential equal to one million volts. (MEG uh vohlt')

megawatt [*mega-, million & watt*] A unit of electrical power equal to one million watts. (MEG uh wot')

megohm [*mega-, million & ohm*] A unit of electrical resistance equal to one million ohms. (MEG ohm)

splenomegaly [*spleno, spleen + -megaly, large*] Enlargement of the spleen. (splee' noh MEG uh lee)

magn, magna, magni   great, large

Magna Carta [*magna, great & Ltn > charta, charter*] The great charter signed by King John at Runnymeade in June 1215, granting English political and civil liberties. (MAG nuh KAHR tuh)

magna cum laude [*magna, great & Ltn > cum, with & Ltn > laude, praise*] Literally, "with great praise." Used in diplomas to grant the 2nd highest of three special honors for above-average academic standing from a college or university. See cum laude and summa cum laude. (MOG nuh koom LOWD uh)

magnanimous [*magn, great + anim, spirit + -ous*] 1.Showing a courageous spirit, especially in forgiving insult or injury. 2.Not showing meanness or pettiness in feelings or conduct. Not selfish. (mag NAN uh mus)

magnate [*magn, great + -ate*] An important, powerful, or influential person in a field or activity, especially in business or industry. (MAG nayt)

magnificent [*magni, great + fic, to make + -ent*] 1.Beautiful in a splendid and majestic way. 2.Noble in thought or action. (mag NIF uh sent)

magnify [*magni, great + -fy, to make*] 1.Enlarge. 2.Exaggerate. (MAG nuh feye')

magniloquent [*magni, great + loqu, to speak + -ent*] Grandiose, lofty, or pompous speech. See grandiloquence. (mag NIL uh kwent)

magnitude [*magni, great + -tude*] Greatness in size, importance, or position. (MAG nuh tood')

magnum [*magn, large + -um*] 1.A large bottle of wine or spirits holding about two fifths of a gallon. 2.A firearm that uses a cartridge with more explosive power than an ordinary cartridge of the same caliber. (MAG num)

magnum opus [*magn, great + -um & Ltn > opus, work*] 1.A great work, especially of an artist or writer. 2.The greatest and most important work of an artist, writer, etc. Masterpiece. (MAG num OH pus)

-mancy   divination

bibliomancy [*biblio, book + -mancy, divination*] Divination by means of a book, especially a randomly chosen Bible verse or literary passage. (BIB lee uh man' see)

chiromancy [*chiro, hand + -mancy, divination*] Divination by analysis of the palm of the hand. Palmistry. (KEYE ruh man' see)

geomancy [*geo, earth + -mancy, divination*] Divination by means of a figure formed by throwing down a handful of earth or by means of geographical features. (JEE uh man' see)

hydromancy [*hydro, water + -mancy, divination*] Divination by observing the motion of water. (HEYE druh man' see)

necromancy [*necro, dead + -mancy, divination*] Divination through communication with the dead. (NEK ruh man' see)

oneiromancy [*Grk > oneiros, dream + -mancy, divination*] Divination through the analysis of dreams. (oh NEYE ruh man' see)

pyromancy [*pyro, fire + -mancy, divination*] Divination by fire. (PEYE roh man' see)

rhabdomancy [*rhabdo, rod + -mancy, divination*] Divination by means of a rod or wand, used especially in the search for underground water or ores. (RAB duh man' see)

mania   excessive desire, mental aberration

bibliomania [*biblio, book + mania, excessive desire*] An excessive fondness for collecting books, especially rare ones. (bib' lee uh MAY nee uh)

decalcomania [*de-, from + French > calquer, to trace + mania, excessive desire*] The art or process of transferring decorative pictures or designs from treated paper to glass, metal, or other materials. So named from its popularity in France during the 19th century. (dih kal' kuh MAY nee uh)

dipsomania [*Grk > dipsa, thirst + mania, excessive desire*] An irresistible craving for alcoholic liquors. (dip' suh MAY nee uh)

egomania [*ego, self + -mania, excessive desire*] Abnormally excessive preoccupation with oneself. See egocentric. (ee' goh MAY nee uh)

erotomania [*eroto, sexual desire + mania, excessive desire*] Abnormally excessive sexual desire. (ih rot' uh MAY nee uh)

hypomania [*hypo-, less + mania, mental aberration*] A mild form of mania involving slightly abnormal elation and overactivity. (heye' poh MAY nee uh)

kleptomania [*klepto, to steal + mania, mental aberration*] An irresistible impulse to steal, not attributed to economic necessity. (klep' tuh MAY nee uh)

mania [*mania, mental aberration*] 1.A mental disorder characterized by great excitement and, in its acute stage, by violence. 2.Unusual or excessive fondness or enthusiasm for something. (MAY nee uh)

maniac [*mania, mental aberration + -ac*] 1.A raving or violent person in an acute stage of mania. 2.A person with an excessive amount of desire or enthusiasm for something. (MAY nee ak')

manic-depressive [*manic & depressive*] Characterized by alternating extremes of mania and depression. (MAN ik dih PRES iv)

megalomania [*megalo, great + mania, mental aberration*] A mental disorder characterized by unfounded belief in one's omnipotence, grandeur, wealth, etc. (meg' uh loh MAY nee uh)

monomania [*mono-, one + mania, excessive desire*] A pathological condition characterized by excessive enthusiasm or desire for one thing. (mon' uh MAY nee uh)

mythomania [*myth & mania, mental aberration*] An abnormal compulsion to lie or exaggerate. (mith' uh MAY nee uh)

nymphomania [*nymph & mania, excessive desire*] Abnormally excessive sexual desire in a female. (nim' fuh MAY nee uh)

pyromania [*pyro, fire + mania, mental aberration*] An irresistible impulse to start fires. (peye' roh MAY nee uh)

man, mani, manu   hand

amanuensis [*Ltn > servus a manu, servant at handwriting*] A person who takes dictation or copies manuscript. Secretary. See scribe. (uh man' yoo EN sis)

bimanual [*bi-, two + manu, hand + -al*] Requiring the use of or involving both hands. (beye MAN yoo ul)

emancipate [*e-, out + manu, hand + Ltn > capere, to take + -ate*] 1.To release from slavery or bondage. Liberate. See manumit. 2.To free from control or restraint. (ih MAN suh payt')

manacle [*man, hand + -cle, small*] 1.Either of a connected pair of devices for shackling the hands. Handcuff. 2.Any restraint. (MAN uh kul)

manage [*man, hand + -age*] 1. To take charge of and make decisions about. 2.To succeed in accomplishing. 3.To control the behavior, use, or movement of. (MAN ij)

maneuver [*man, hand + Ltn > operare, to work*] 1.A planned military movement. 2.Skillful action, management, or procedure. (muh NOO vur)

manicure [*mani, hand + Ltn > cura, care*] Professional care of the hands and fingernails. See pedicure. (MAN ih kyoor')

manifest [*Ltn > manifestus, struck by the hand*] Clearly apparent to the senses or the mind. Obvious. Evident. See evident and perspicuous. (MAN uh fest')

manifest destiny [*manifest (obvious) & destiny*] The 19th century belief that the U.S. was destined to expand to the Pacific Ocean. (MAN uh fest' DES tuh nee)

manipulate [*mani, hand + -ate*] 1.To treat or operate with skillful use of the hands. 2.To adapt or change for personal gain. 3.To manage cleverly and often unfairly. (muh NIP yuh layt')

manual [*manu, hand + -al*] Pertaining to, involving, or done with the hands. (MAN yoo ul)

manubrium [*manu, hand*] An anatomical structure or part resembling a handle, as the upper end of the sternum. (muh NOO bree um)

manufacture [*manu, hand + fact, to make + -ure*] To make something from raw materials by hand or with machinery. (man' yuh FAK chur)

manumit [*manu, hand + Ltn > mittere, to release*] To release from slavery or bondage. Liberate. Emancipate. See emancipate (def. 1). (man' yuh MIT)

manuscript [*manu, hand + script, to write*] A book or other composition written by hand, on a typewriter, or on a computer prior to being typeset by a printer or publisher. (MAN yuh skript')

mortmain [*mort, dead + manu, hand*] Ownership of real estate by an institution such as a church, school, etc., who cannot sell it. (MORT mayn)

quadrumanous [*quadru, four + man, hand + -ous*] Having four feet that resemble and function as hands, as primates other than humans. Four-handed. (kwah DROO muh nus)

mar, mari   sea

aquamarine [*aqua, water + mar, sea + -ine*] 1.A transparent bluish-green variety of beryl. 2.A bluish-green color. (ak' wuh muh REEN)

mal de mer [*mal-, ill & French > mer, sea*] Seasickness. (mal' duh MEHR)

mare clausum [*mar, sea & Ltn > clausum, closed*] A body of navigable water, as a sea, under the jurisdiction of one nation and not open to all other nations. See mare liberum and mare nostrum (def. 1). (MAHR ay KLAW sum)

mare liberum [*mar, sea & Ltn > liber, free + -um*] A body of navigable water, as a sea, open to all nations. See mare clausum and mare nostrum (def. 1). (MAHR ay LEEB ur um)

mare nostrum [*mar, sea & Ltn > noster, our + -um*] 1.A body of navigable water, as a sea, under the jurisdiction of one nation or shared by two or more nations. See mare clausum and mare liberum. 2.The Roman name for the Mediterranean Sea. (MAHR ay NOH strum)

mariculture [*mari, sea & culture*] The cultivation of marine animals and plants in their natural environment. Marine aquaculture. See aquaculture. (MEHR ih kul' chur)

marina [*mar, sea + -ina*] A small harbor that has docks, moorings, and supplies for boats and yachts. (muh REE nuh)

marine [*mar, sea + -ine*] 1.Pertaining to, occurring on, or existing in the sea. 2.A member of a body of troops trained for service at sea and on land, specifically the U.S. Marine Corps. (muh REEN)

mariner [*mar, sea + -in + -er*] A seaman. Sailor. (MEHR uh nur)

maritime [*mari, sea*] 1.Pertaining to or characteristic of the sea. 2.Existing or occurring on or near the sea. Nautical. (MEHR ih teyem')

submarine [*sub-, under + mar, sea + -ine*] 1.Beneath the surface of the water, especially the sea. 2.A ship that can be operated under water. (SUB muh reen')

transmarine [*trans-, across + mar, sea + -ine*] 1.Crossing over the sea. 2.Coming from or going across the sea. (trans' muh REEN)

mar, mari

ultramarine [*ultra-, beyond* + *mar, sea* + *-ine*] 1.A deep-blue color. 2.Situated beyond the sea. (ul' truh muh REEN)

matr, matri, mater   mother

alma mater [*Ltn > alma, nourishing* & *mater, mother*] A school or college that one has attended and usually graduated from. (AL muh MAH ter)

dura mater [*Ltn > dura, hard* & *mater, mother*] The tough fibrous membrane, lying over the arachnoid and the pia mater, that forms the outermost of the three coverings of the brain and spinal cord. See arachnoid (def. 1) and pia mater. (DUR uh MAYT ur)

mater [*mater, mother*] Mother. (MAYT ur)

materfamilias [*mater, mother* + *Ltn > familia, family*] The mother of a family or female head of household. See paterfamilias. (mayt' ur fuh MIL ee us)

maternal [*mater, mother* + *-al*] 1.Pertaining to or characteristic of a mother or motherhood. Motherly. 2.Related through the mother's side of the family. See paternal. (muh TURN l)

maternity [*mater, mother* + *-ity*] 1.The state of being a mother. Motherhood. 2.The qualities of a mother. Motherliness. See paternity. (muh TUR nih tee)

matriarch [*matri, mother* + *arch, rule*] 1.The mother and ruler of a family, clan, etc. 2.A well-respected elderly woman. See patriarch. (MAY tree ahrk')

matricide [*matri, mother* + *-cide, to kill*] The killing of one's own mother. (MAT ruh seyed')

matriclinous [*matri, mother* + *clin, to lean* + *-ous*] Characterized by predominantly maternal hereditary traits. See patriclinous. (mat' ruh KLEYE nus)

matriculate [*matri(x) {womb}* & *-ule* + *-ate*] To enroll, especially at a college or university. (muh TRIK yuh layt')

matrilineal [*matri, mother* + *Ltn > linea, line* + *-al*] Pertaining to descent or derivation through the female line. See patrilineal. (mat' ruh LIN ee ul)

matrilocal [*matri, mother* & *local*] Pertaining to a living arrangement in which a married couple lives with or near the wife's parents. See patrilocal. (mat' ruh LOH kul)

matrimony [*matri, mother* + *-mony*] Marriage. (MAT ruh moh' nee)

matrix [*mater, mother*] 1.Originally, the womb. 2.Mold in which something is shaped or cast. (MAY triks)

matron [*matr, mother* + *-on*] 1.A married woman or widow, especially one with a mature appearance and manner. 2.A woman who manages the domestic affairs of an institution such as a school, hospital, dormitory, etc. (MAY trun)

matron of honor The principal married woman attending the bride at a wedding. See maid of honor. (MAY trun uv ON ur)

matronymic [*matr, mother* + *onym, name* + *-ic*] Pertaining to a name derived from the name of the mother or other female ancestor. See patronymic. (mat' ruh NIM ik)

pia mater [*Ltn > pia, tender* & *mater, mother*] The fine vascular membrane, lying under the arachnoid and the dura mater, that forms the innermost of the three coverings of the brain and spinal cord. See arachnoid (def. 1) and dura mater. (PEYE uh MAYT ur)

patr, patri, pater   father, fatherland

allopatric [*allo, other* + *patr, fatherland* + *-ic*] Pertaining to a plant or animal species that occurs or originates in separate geological areas or regions. See sympatric. (al' uh PAT rik)

eupatrid [*eu-, good* + *patr, father* + *-id*] Pertaining to the hereditary aristocracy who formed the ruling class of ancient Athens. (yoo PAT rid)

expatriate [*ex-, out* + *patri, fatherland* + *-ate*] 1.To remove a person from his or her native land. Banish. Exile. (eks PAY tree ayt' {verb}) 2.A person who gives up allegiance to his or her native land. See repatriate. (eks PAY tree ut {noun})

paterfamilias [*pater, father* + *Ltn > familia, family*] The father of a family or male head of household. See materfamilias. (pat' ur fuh MIL ee us)

paternal [*pater, father* + *-al*] 1.Pertaining to or characteristic of a father. Fatherly. 2.Related through the father's side of the family. See maternal. (puh TURN l)

paternalism [*pater, father* + *-al* + *-ism*] The practice of managing or governing in a fatherly manner. (puh TURN l iz' um)

paternity [*pater, father* + *-ity*] 1.The state of being a father. Fatherhood. 2.Origin from a father. See maternity. (puh TUR nih tee)

paternoster [*pater, father* + *Ltn > noster, our*] 1.The Lord's prayer, especially in Latin. 2.One of the large beads on a rosary on which the Lord's prayer is said. (paht' ur NOS ter)

patriarch [*patri, father* + *arch, rule*] 1.The father and ruler of a family, clan, etc. 2.A well-respected elderly man. See matriarch. (PAY tree ahrk')

patrician [*patr, father* + *-ician*] 1.A member of the ancient Roman nobility. 2.A person of noble birth or rank. Aristocrat. (puh TRISH un)

patricide [*patri, father* + *-cide, to kill*] The killing of one's own father. (PAT ruh seyed')

patriclinous [*patri, father* + *clin, to lean* + *-ous*] Characterized by predominantly paternal hereditary traits. See matriclinous. (pat' ruh KLEYE nus)

patrilineal [*patri, father* + *Ltn > linea, line* + *-al*] Pertaining to descent or derivation through the male line. See matrilineal. (pat' ruh LIN ee ul)

patrilocal [*patri, father* & *local*] Pertaining to a living arrangement in which a married couple lives with or near the husband's parents. See matrilocal. (pat' ruh LOH kul)

patrimony [*patri, father* + *-mony*] 1.Property inherited from one's father or other ancestor. 2.The endowment of a church or other institution. 3.Any inheritance. (PAT ruh moh' nee)

patriotism [*patri, fatherland* + *-tism*] Love, support, and defense of one's own country. (PAY tree uh tiz' um)

patristic [*patr, father* + *-istic*] Pertaining to the fathers of the early Christian Church or their writings. (puh TRIS tik)

patron [*patr, father* + *-on*] 1.A person who supports, protects, or champions someone or some activity. See patroness. 2.A regular customer. (PAY trun)

patron saint [*patron & saint*] A saint who is considered to be the special guardian of a person, place, church, etc. (PAY trun saynt)

patroness [*patron & -ess, feminine*] A female patron who supports, protects, or champions someone or some activity. See patron (def. 1). (PAY truh nes)

patronymic [*patr, father + onym, name + -ic*] Pertaining to a name derived from the name of the father or other male ancestor. See matronymic. (pat' ruh NIM ik)

repatriate [*re-, back + patri, fatherland + -ate*] To return a person to his or her native land, especially a prisoner of war, refugee, etc. See expatriate (def. 1). (ree PAY tree ayt')

sympatric [*sym-, same + patr, fatherland + -ic*] Pertaining to species of plants and animals that occur or originate in the same geographical area or region. See allopatric. (sim PAT rik)

medi   middle

immediate [*im-, without + medi, middle + -ate*] 1.Without delay. 2.Without intervention. Direct. 3.Next in line or order. (ih MEE dee it)

intermediary [*inter-, between + medi, middle + -ary*] 1.One who acts as an agent between parties. 2.Intermediate. See mediate, intercede, and intervene. (in' ter MEE dee ehr' ee)

intermediate [*inter-, between + medi, middle + -ate*] Occurring or positioned between two things in time or order. (in' ter MEE dee it)

mediaeval [*medi, middle + ev, age + -al*] Pertaining or belonging to the Middle Ages. Same as medieval. (mid EE vul)

medial [*medi, middle + -al*] Pertaining to or situated in or near the middle. (MEE dee ul)

median [*medi, middle + -an*] 1.Situated in or passing through the middle. 2.Pertaining to a plane that divides something into two equal parts. (MEE dee un)

mediant [*medi, middle + -ant*] The third tone or note of a diatonic musical scale. (MEE dee unt)

mediastinum [*medi, middle + -um*] A median partition, formed of the opposing walls of the pleura, that separates the right and left chest cavities and contains all the thoracic viscera except the lungs. (mee' dee uh STEYE num)

mediate [*medi, middle + -ate*] To act as an intermediary between two or more conflicting parties. See intermediary, intercede, and intervene. (MEE dee ayt')

medieval [*medi, middle + ev, age + -al*] Pertaining or belonging to the Middle Ages. (mid EE vul)

mediocre [*medi, middle + Ltn > ocris, peak*] Of moderate to below average quality. Ordinary. (mee' dee OH kur)

mediterranean [*medi, middle + terr, earth + -an + -ean*] Almost completely surrounded by dry land. (med' ih tuh RAY nee un)

Mediterranean [*medi, middle + terr, earth + -an + -ean*] Pertaining to the Mediterranean Sea or the countries around it. (med' ih tuh RAY nee un)

medium [*medi, middle + -um*] 1.A middle state, condition, or degree. Mean. 2.A surrounding substance in which something moves, exists, or is produced. 3.A person allegedly able to communicate with the dead. (MEE dee um)

meso-   middle

mesencephalon [*meso-, middle + encephal, brain + -on*] 1.The embryonic midbrain from which the corpora quadrigemina, the cerebral peduncles, and the aqueduct of Sylvius develop. 2.Midbrain. See prosencephalon and rhombencephalon. (mez' en SEF uh lon')

mesenchyme [*meso-, middle + -enchyma, type of cell tissue*] The embryonic connective tissue in the embryonic mesoderm from which the body's connective tissue, skeletal tissue, blood, blood vessels, and lymphatic system are derived. (MEZ en keyem')

mesentery [*meso-, middle + enter, intestine + -y*] A fold of the peritoneum that connects most of the small intestine to the dorsal abdominal wall. (MEZ en tehr' ee)

mesic [*meso-, middle + -ic*] 1.Characterized by or requiring a moderate amount of moisture. 2.Pertaining or adapted to a moderately moist climate. See hydric (def. 2) and xeric. (MEZ ik)

mesoblast [*meso-, middle + blast, cell layer*] 1.Undifferentiated embryonic mesoderm. 2.Mesoderm. See mesoderm, endoblast, and ectoblast. (MEZ uh blast')

mesocarp [*meso-, middle + carp, fruit*] The middle layer of the pericarp of a fruit, as the meat of a cherry. See endocarp, epicarp, and pericarp. (MEZ uh kahrp')

mesocephalic [*meso-, middle + cephal, head + -ic*] Having a head of average length with a cephalic index between 76 and 80. See cephalic index, brachycephalic, and dolichocephalic. (mez' oh suh FAL ik)

mesoderm [*meso-, middle + derm, skin*] The middle layer of the three primary germ cell layers of an embryo, lying between the ectoderm and the endoderm, from which bones, connective tissue, muscles, and the vascular and urogenital systems develop. See mesoblast, endoderm, and ectoderm. (MEZ uh derm')

mesoglea [*meso-, middle + Grk > glia, glue*] A jellylike layer of material lying between the ectoderm and the endoderm in cnidarians. (mez' uh GLEE uh)

mesogloea [*meso-, middle + Grk > glia, glue*] A jellylike layer of material lying between the ectoderm and the endoderm in cnidarians. Same as mesoglea. (mez' uh GLEE uh)

Mesolithic [*meso-, middle + lith, stone + -ic*] Pertaining to the transitional period of the Stone Age, between the Paleolithic and Neolithic periods, marked by the appearance of small flint cutting tools mounted in bone or wood. (mez' uh LITH ik)

mesomorphic [*meso-, middle + morph, form + -ic*] Having a muscular body build characterized by the prominence of structures derived from the embryonic mesoderm. See endomorphic and ectomorphic. (mez' uh MOR fik)

meson [*meso-, middle + -on, subatomic particle*] Any of a group of elementary particles with a mass between that of an electron and a proton. (MEZ on)

mesonephros [*meso-, middle + nephr, kidney + -os*] One of the three embryonic excretory organs of vertebrates that functions as the embryonic kidney in higher vertebrates and becomes the adult kidney in fishes and amphibians. See pronephros and metanephros. (mez' uh NEF ros)

meso-

mesopause [*meso(sphere) & pause*] The outermost boundary of the mesosphere. See tropopause and stratopause. (MEZ uh poz')

mesophyll [*meso-, middle + phyll, leaf*] The specialized tissue of a leaf, between the lower and upper epidermis, that is usually photosynthetic. (MEZ uh fil')

mesophyte [*meso-, middle + -phyte, plant*] A plant that grows well in moderately moist soil. See hydrophyte and xerophyte. (MEZ uh feyet')

Mesopotamia [*meso-, middle + Grk > potamos, river + -ia*] An ancient Asian country, now a part of Iraq, between the lower Tigris and Euphrates rivers. (mes' uh puh TAY mee uh)

mesosphere [*meso-, middle & sphere*] An atmospheric zone, 30 to 50 miles above the earth between the stratosphere and the thermosphere, characterized by decreasing temperature with increasing altitude. (MEZ uh sfihr')

mesothelioma [*mesotheli(um) & -oma, tumor*] A malignant tumor composed of mesothelial tissue, as that lining the pleura, peritoneum, or pericardium. See epithelioma. (mez' uh thee' lee OH muh)

mesothelium [*meso-, middle & (epi)thelium*] The layer of cells that forms the epithelium and is derived from the mesoderm. See epithelium. (mez' uh THEE lee um)

mesothorax [*meso-, middle & thorax*] The middle segment of the three thoracic segments of an insect, bearing the first pair of wings and the second pair of legs. See prothorax and metathorax. (mez' uh THOR aks')

Mesozoic [*meso-, middle + zo, animal + -ic*] Designating the fourth geological era, between the Paleozoic and the Cenozoic eras, occurring between 230,000,000 and 70,000,000 years ago and characterized by the development of birds and mammals. See Cenozoic. (mez' uh ZOH ik)

melan/o   black

melancholia [*melan, black + chol, bile + -ia*] A mental disorder characterized by feelings of extreme depression, sadness, and anxiety. See melancholy. (mel' un KOH lee uh)

melancholy [*melan, black + chol, bile + -y*] Sadness, dejection, or depression. So named from the medieval belief that it resulted from too much black bile. (MEL un kol' ee)

Melanesian [*melan, black + -ian*] Any of the native people of Melanesia. So named for their dark skin. (mel' uh NEE zhun)

melanin [*melan, black + -in*] A dark-brown or black plant or animal pigment that in humans accounts for dark skin, dark hair, etc. (MEL uh nin)

melanism [*melan, black + -ism*] Abnormally dark pigmentation of the skin, hair, eyes, feathers, etc. (MEL uh niz' um)

melanite [*melan, black + -ite, mineral*] A deep black variety of garnet. (MEL uh neyet')

melanoblast [*melano, black + blast, immature cell*] An immature cell that is the precursor to a melanophore or melanocyte. See melanophore and melanocyte. (muh LAN uh blast')

melanocyte [*melano, black + -cyte, cell*] A melanin-producing epidermal cell responsible for skin color variations. (muh LAN uh seyet')

melanoid [*melan, black + -oid, resembling*] 1.Pertaining to or resembling melanin. 2.Characterized by or resembling melanosis. (MEL uh noid')

melanoma [*melan, black + -oma, tumor*] A usually malignant tumor of the skin containing dark pigment. (mel' uh NOH muh)

melanophore [*melano, black + -phore, to produce*] A melanin-containing chromatophore. (muh LAN uh for')

melanosis [*melan, black + -osis, abnormal condition*] Abnormal deposits of dark-brown or black pigmentation in the skin or other tissues. (mel' uh NOH sis)

melanous [*melan, black + -ous*] Having dark-brown or black skin and hair. (MEL uh nus)

melaphyre [*melan, black & (por)phyr(y)*] Any of various dark-colored, porphyritic igneous rocks embedded with feldspar crystals. (MEL uh fihr')

meta-   change, between, after, beyond

anabolism [*ana-, up & (meta)bolism*] The constructive metabolic process in organisms by which food is changed into complex body substance. Opposed to catabolism. See metabolism. (uh NAB uh liz' um)

catabolism [*cata-, down & (meta)bolism*] The destructive metabolic process in organisms by which complex body substance is changed into energy and waste products of a simpler composition. Opposed to anabolism. See metabolism. (kuh TAB uh liz' um)

hemimetabolic [*hemi-, half & metabolic*] Experiencing incomplete metamorphosis, as certain insects. See holometabolic. (hem' ih met' uh BOL ik)

holometabolic [*holo, whole & metabolic*] Experiencing complete metamorphosis, as most insects. See hemimetabolic. (hol' oh met' uh BOL ik)

metabolism [*meta-, change + Grk > ballein, to throw + -ism*] The sum of the physical and chemical processes necessary for the maintenance of life, consisting of anabolism and catabolism. See anabolism and catabolism. (muh TAB uh liz' um)

metacarpus [*meta-, between + carp, wrist + -us*] 1.The part of the hand that includes the five bones between the wrist, or carpus, and the fingers. 2.The part of the forefoot in four-legged animals that includes the five bones between the carpus and the phalanges. See metatarsus. (met' uh KAHR pus)

metacenter [*meta-, between & center*] The point of intersection in a floating body of two vertical lines that are drawn through the center of buoyancy when the body is upright and when it is tilted. (MET uh sent' ur)

metachromatism [*meta-, change + chromat, color + -ism*] A color change, especially as the result of a temperature change. (met' uh KROH muh tiz' um)

metaethics [*meta-, beyond & ethics*] The branch of philosophy dealing with the study of ethical terms, arguments, and judgments. See ethics. (met' uh ETH iks)

metagalaxy [*meta-, between & galaxy*] The entire material universe including the Milky Way and all other galaxies. (met' uh GAL uk see)

metagenesis [*meta-, between + -genesis, generation*] Alternation of generations. See alternation of generations. (met' uh JEN uh sis)

metagnathous [*meta-, change + gnath, jaw + -ous*]
1.Having biting mouth-parts in the larval stage and
sucking mouth-parts in the adult stage, as certain
insects. 2.Having the tips of the beaks crossed, as in
the crossbills. (muh TAG nuh thus)

metalinguistics [*meta-, between + lingu, language + -ist + -
ics, study of*] The branch of linguistics dealing with the
study of the relations between language and other
cultural factors. (met' uh ling GWIS tiks)

metamathematics [*meta-, beyond & mathematics*] The
study of the fundamental concepts of logical systems,
especially mathematical systems. See mathematics.
(met' uh math' uh MAT iks)

metamere [*meta-, after + -mere, part*] One of a linear
series of body segments, as in earthworms, lobsters,
etc. (MET uh mihr')

metamorphosis [*meta-, change + morph, form + -osis,
process*] A complete change of form, appearance,
structure, or function. (met' uh MOR fuh sis)

metanephros [*meta-, after + nephr, kidney + -os*] One of
the three embryonic excretory organs of higher
vertebrates that becomes the adult kidney in
mammals, reptiles, and birds. See pronephros and
mesonephros. (met' uh NEF ros)

metaphase [*meta-, after & phase*] In mitosis, the phase
after the prophase and before the anaphase, during
which the chromosomes become aligned along the
equator of the spindle. See prophase, anaphase, and
telophase. (MET uh fayz')

metaphor [*meta-, beyond + phor, to carry*] A figure of
speech with an implied comparison between a word or
phrase and an object or concept it does not ordinarily
represent, as "a mountain of debt." See simile and
metonymy. (MET uh for')

metaphysics [*meta-, after & physics*] The area of
philosophy dealing with the study of the nature and
structure of reality. So named from the reference to
Aristotle's writings that came after his studies in
physics. (met' uh FIZ iks)

metaplasia [*meta-, change + plas, forming cells or tissue + -ia*]
The conversion of a particular type of tissue to an
abnormal type for that tissue, as the ossification of
muscular tissue. (met' uh PLAY zhuh)

metaplasm [*meta-, change + plasm, form*] 1.The changing
of the form of a word by removing, adding, or
transposing letters or syllables. 2.The nonliving
material in the protoplasm of a cell, as carbohydrates,
pigments, or fat. (MET uh plaz' um)

metaprotein [*meta-, beyond & protein*] A protein
derivative that is insoluble in water, but soluble in
weak acids or alkalies, and is obtained from the
reaction between acids or alkalies and a protein.
(met' uh PROH teen')

metapsychology [*meta-, beyond + psych, mind + -ology,
science*] A term applied to theories about the origin,
structure, and functions of the mind that extend
beyond the empirical laws of psychology.
(met' uh seye KOL uh jee)

metastable [*meta-, change & stab(ility) & -le*] Showing a
state of pseudoequilibrium, but marked by only a
small margin of stability due to slow passage between
states. (met' uh STAY bul)

metastasis [*meta-, change + -stasis, stable state*] The
transmission of disease, microorganisms, etc., from the
original site to other parts of the body, as the transfer
of cancer cells through the bloodstream.
(muh TAS tuh sis)

metatarsus [*meta-, between & tarsus*] 1.The part of the
foot that includes the five bones between the ankle
and the toes, forming the instep. 2.The part of the
hind foot in four-legged animals that includes the
bones between the tarsus and the phalanges. See
metacarpus. (met' uh TAHR sus)

metathesis [*meta-, change + the, to put + -sis*] The
transposition of letters, syllables, or sounds within a
word, as *aks* for *ask*. (muh TATH uh sis)

metathorax [*meta-, after & thorax*] The hindmost
segment of the three thoracic segments of an insect,
bearing the second pair of wings and the third pair of
legs. See prothorax and mesothorax.
(met' uh THOR aks')

Metazoa [*meta-, after + zo, animal + -a*] A large zoological
division that includes all multicellular animals whose
cells are organized into tissues and organs.
(met' uh ZOH uh)

metempsychosis [*meta-, beyond + en-, into + psych, soul + -
osis, action*] The belief that after death the soul passes
into another human or animal body.
(met' em seye' KOH sis)

metencephalon [*meta-, after + encephal, brain + -on*] The
anterior portion of the rhombencephalon from which
the cerebellum and pons develop. See myelencephalon
and rhombencephalon. (met' en SEF uh lon')

metonymy [*meta-, change + onym, name + -y*] A figure of
speech having the name of one object or concept
replaced by the name of another related object or
concept usually associated with it, as "Capitol Hill"
for "the Congress." See metaphor. (muh TON uh mee)

metopic [*meta-, between + op, eye + -ic*] Relating to the
forehead. (mih TOP ik)

meter, metr, -metry
measure, to measure, science of measuring

accelerometer [*acceler(ation) & meter, to measure*] An
instrument for measuring acceleration, especially of
an aircraft, spacecraft, or rocket. (ak sel' uh ROM et er)

acetometer [*aceto, acetic acid + meter, to measure*] A device
for measuring the quantity of acetic acid in a mixture
or solution. (as' ih TOM et er)

acidimeter [*acid & meter, to measure*] A device for
measuring the quantity of acid in a mixture or
solution. (as' ih DIM et er)

actinometer [*actino, ray + meter, to measure*] 1.An
instrument for measuring the heat intensity of the
sun's rays. 2.An instrument for measuring radiation
intensity. (ak' tuh NOM et er)

aerometer [*aero, air + meter, to measure*] An instrument
for measuring the weight and estimating the density
of air and other gases. (ehr OM et er)

alcoholometer [*alcohol & meter, to measure*] A device for
measuring the quantity of alcohol in a liquid.
(al' kuh hol OM et er)

meter, metr, -metry

algometer [*algo, pain + meter, to measure*] An instrument for measuring the degree of sensitivity to pain resulting from a stimulus such as pressure. (al GOM et er)

alkalimeter [*alkali & meter, to measure*] A device for measuring the quantity of alkali in a solution or substance. (al' kuh LIM et er)

allometry [*allo, other + -metry, science of measuring*] The scientific study of the measurement and comparison of the growth of one part of an organism in relation to the rest of the organism or to a standard. (uh LOM ih tree)

altimeter [*alti, high + meter, to measure*] An instrument for measuring altitude above sea level, especially one that uses atmospheric pressure, as in an aneroid barometer. (al TIM et er)

ametropia [*a-, not + metr, measure + -opia, visual condition*] Any visual condition resulting from abnormal refraction of the eye, such as astigmatism, nearsightedness, or farsightedness. (am' ih TROH pee uh)

ammeter [*am(pere) & meter, to measure*] An instrument for measuring current in amperes. See voltmeter and wattmeter. (AM mee' ter)

anemometer [*anemo, wind + meter, to measure*] A device for measuring wind velocity and direction. See anemograph. (an' uh MOM et er)

aneroid barometer [*a-, without + Grk > neros, fluid + -oid & barometer*] A barometer that measures atmospheric pressure by measuring the movement of a thin metal disk rather than the movement of a column of fluid. (AN uh roid' buh ROM et er)

anisometric [*aniso-, not equal + metr, measure + -ic*] Not having or exhibiting equality in dimensions or measurements. Not isometric. See isometric (def. 1). (an eye' suh MET rik)

anisometropia [*aniso-, not equal + metr, measure + -opia, visual condition*] An abnormal visual condition in which the refractive power is not equal in both eyes. See isometropia. (an eye' soh mih TROH pee uh)

anthropometry [*anthropo, human + -metry, science of measuring*] The scientific study of human anatomical and physiological measurements for the purpose of analysis, comparison, and classification. (an' thruh POM ih tree)

astrometry [*astro, star + -metry, science of measuring*] The scientific study of the measurement of the relative brightness, motions, distances, and positions of celestial bodies. (uh STROM ih tree)

asymmetry [*a-, without & symmetry*] Without symmetry. See symmetry. (ay SIM ih tree)

atmometer [*atmo, vapor + meter, to measure*] An instrument for measuring the evaporation of water into the atmosphere at various times or under various conditions. (at MOM et er)

audiometer [*audio, hearing + meter, to measure*] An instrument for measuring hearing acuteness using controlled audio frequencies and volume. (awd' ee OM et er)

barometer [*baro, pressure + meter, to measure*] 1.An instrument for measuring atmospheric pressure. 2.Something that monitors changes. An indicator. (buh ROM et er)

bathometer [*batho, deep + meter, to measure*] An instrument for measuring the depth of water. (buh THOM et er)

bathymetry [*bathy, deep + -metry, science of measuring*] The scientific study of the depth measurement of large bodies of water. (buh THIM ih tree)

biometrics [*bio, life + metr, to measure + -ics, study of*] The branch of biology dealing with the statistical and mathematical study of biological data. (beye' oh MET riks)

biometry [*bio, life + -metry, science of measuring*] The scientific study of the measurement of the probable life span of humans. (beye OM ih tree)

biotelemetry [*bio, life & telemetry*] The remote monitoring of the physical activities, conditions, or functions of a human or animal. See telemetry. (beye' oh tuh LEM ih tree)

bolometer [*Grk > bole, ray + meter, to measure*] An instrument for measuring very small amounts of radiant energy. See bolograph. (boh LOM et er)

calorimeter [*calori, heat + meter, to measure*] An instrument for measuring the amount of heat absorbed or generated by an organism, combustion, friction, chemical change, etc. (kal' uh RIM et er)

ceilometer [*ceil(ing) & meter, to measure*] A photoelectric device that uses the principles of triangulation for measuring the distance from the earth to the cloud ceiling. (see LOM et er)

centimeter [*centi-, hundredth & meter*] A metric unit of length equal to one hundredth of a meter. (SENT ih mee' ter)

centimetre [*centi-, hundredth & metre*] A metric unit of length equal to one hundredth of a meter. Same as centimeter. (SENT ih mee' ter)

cephalometer [*cephalo, head + meter, to measure*] An instrument for measuring the dimensions of the head. See craniometer. (sef' uh LOM et er)

cephalometry [*cephalo, head + -metry, science of measuring*] The scientific measurement of the dimensions of the head. See craniometry. (sef' uh LOM ih tree)

chronometer [*chrono, time + meter, to measure*] An instrument for measuring extremely accurate time, as for science or navigation. See chronograph and chronoscope. (kruh NOM et er)

clinometer [*clino, slope + meter, to measure*] An instrument for measuring slopes and other angles of inclination. (kleye NOM et er)

cliometrics [*Clio {Muse of history} & metr, to measure + -ics, science*] The application of statistical and mathematical methods to the study of history. (kleye' uh MET riks)

colorimeter [*color & meter, to measure*] An instrument for measuring, analyzing, and comparing colors. (kul' uh RIM et er)

craniometer [*cranio, skull + meter, to measure*] An instrument for measuring the dimensions of skulls. See cephalometer. (kray' nee OM et er)

craniometry [*cranio, skull + -metry, science of measuring*] The scientific measurement of the dimensions of skulls. See cephalometry. (kray' nee OM ih tree)

cryometer [*cryo, cold + meter, to measure*] A thermometer for measuring very low temperatures, usually using alcohol in place of mercury. (kreye OM et er)

cyclometer [*cyclo, circle + meter, to measure*] 1.An instrument for measuring circular arcs. 2.An instrument for measuring distance traveled by recording the revolutions of a wheel. (seye KLOM et er)

cytophotometry [*cyto, cell & photometry*] The scientific study of cells using photometry. See photometry. (seyet' oh foh TOM ih tree)

decameter [*deca, ten & meter*] A metric unit of length equal to 10 meters. Same as dekameter. (DEK uh mee' ter)

decimeter [*deci-, tenth & meter*] A metric unit of length equal to one tenth of a meter. (DES uh mee' ter)

dekameter [*deka, ten & meter*] A metric unit of length equal to 10 meters. (DEK uh mee' ter)

densimeter [*Ltn > densus, dense + meter, to measure*] An instrument for measuring the density or specific gravity of a liquid, solid, or gas. See hydrometer. (den SIM et er)

densitometer [*densit(y) & meter, to measure*] An instrument for measuring the optical density of a material such as a photograph negative, using photometry. See photometry and densimeter. (den' sih TOM et er)

diameter [*dia-, through + meter, to measure*] A straight line that measures the distance through the center of a circle, sphere, etc. (deye AM et er)

dilatometer [*dilat(e) & meter, to measure*] An instrument for measuring thermal expansion of a substance caused by temperature changes in the substance. (dil' uh TOM et er)

dimeter [*di-, two & meter*] A line of verse consisting of two metrical feet. (DIM et er)

dioptometer [*dia-, through + opto, eye + meter, to measure*] An optical instrument for measuring and testing the refraction and accommodation of the eye. (deye' op TOM et er)

dissymmetry [*dis-, lack of & symmetry*] Lack of symmetry. See symmetry. (dih SIM ih tree)

dosimeter [*Grk > dosis, dose + meter, to measure*] An instrument for measuring the dosage received from x-rays or other radiation. (doh SIM et er)

dosimetry [*Grk > dosis, dose + -metry, science of measuring*] The scientific measurement of doses, as of radiation, medicine, etc. (doh SIM ih tree)

drunkometer [*drunk & meter, to measure*] A device for measuring the quantity of alcohol in the blood by analyzing the breath. (drunk OM et er)

dynameter [*dyna, power + meter, to measure*] An instrument for measuring the power of a telescope. (deye NAM et er)

dynamometer [*dynamo, power + meter, to measure*] An instrument for measuring mechanical power or force. (deye' nuh MOM et er)

econometrics [*econo(mics) & metr, measure + -ics, knowledge*] The application of statistical and mathematical analysis to economics to solve problems and verify theories. (ih kon' uh MET riks)

electrodynamometer [*electro, electricity + dynamo, power + meter, to measure*] An instrument for measuring current by using the interaction between the magnetic fields of fixed and movable sets of coils to move an indicator. (ih lek' troh deye' nuh MOM et er)

electrometer [*electro, electricity + meter, to measure*] An instrument for measuring voltage by measuring the electrostatic force between two charged bodies. (ih lek' TROM et er)

emmetropia [*en-, in + metr, to measure + -opia, visual condition*] The visual condition of normal refraction in the eye in which light is focused exactly on the retina, resulting in perfect vision. See myopia (def. 1) and hyperopia. (em' ih TROH pee uh)

ergometer [*ergo, work + meter, to measure*] An apparatus for measuring the work done by a muscle or muscle group over a given period of time. (ur GOM et er)

erythrocytometer [*erythro, red + cyto, cell + meter, to measure*] An instrument for counting red blood cells. (ih rith' roh seye TOM et er)

esthesiometer [*esthes, feeling + meter, to measure*] An instrument for measuring the degree of tactile sensitivity. (es thee' zee OM et er)

extensometer [*extens(ion) & meter, to measure*] An instrument for measuring minute amounts of deformation or expansion in a test specimen, as a metal bar. (eks' ten SOM et er)

femtometer [*femto-, quadrillionth (10⁻¹⁵) & meter*] A metric unit of length equal to one quadrillionth of a meter. (fem TOM et er)

fluorometer [*fluoro, fluorescence + meter, to measure*] An instrument for measuring the intensity of fluorescence and other forms of radiation. (floo ROM et er)

galvanometer [*Italian > galvanismo, galvanism + meter, to measure*] An instrument for measuring small electric currents. Galvanism, or direct-current electricity produced by chemical action, was named for the Italian physician Luigi Galvani (1797), after his achievements in animal electricity, which led Alessandro Volta to the discovery of current electricity. See galvanoscope. (gal' vuh NOM et er)

gasometer [*gas & meter, to measure*] A laboratory apparatus for measuring and holding gas. (gas OM et er)

geochronometry [*geo, earth + chrono, time + -metry, science of measuring*] The scientific measurement of geologic time, as from radioactive decay of isotopes. See geochronology. (jee' oh kruh NOM ih tree)

geometric progression [*geometric & pro-, forward + gress, to step + -ion*] A sequence of terms, as 2, 4, 8, 16, 32 or 1, 1/2, 1/4, 1/8, 1/16, in which any two adjacent terms have the same ratio. (jee' uh MET rik pruh GRESH un)

geometry [*geo, earth + -metry, science of measuring*] The branch of mathematics dealing with the study of the relationships and measurement of points, lines, angles, planes, and solids in space. (jee OM ih tree)

goniometer [*gonio, angle + meter, to measure*] 1.An instrument for measuring angles. 2.An instrument for determining the direction of a radio signal. Automatic direction finder. (goh' nee OM et er)

gravimeter [*gravi(ty) & meter, to measure*] 1.An instrument for measuring gravitational forces of the earth. 2.An instrument for measuring specific gravity. (gra VIM et er)

hectometer [*hecto-, hundred & meter*] A metric unit of length equal to 100 meters. (HEK tuh mee' ter)

heliometer [*helio, sun + meter, to measure*] An instrument originally used for measuring the sun's diameter and later used for measuring angles between celestial bodies. (hee' lee OM et er)

hemacytometer [*hema, blood* + *cyto, cell* + *meter, to measure*] An instrument for counting the number of blood cells in a sample. Same as hemocytometer. (hee' muh seye TOM et er)

hemocytometer [*hemo, blood* + *cyto, cell* + *meter, to measure*] An instrument for counting the number of blood cells in a sample. (hee' moh seye TOM et er)

heptameter [*hepta-, seven* & *meter*] A line of verse consisting of seven metrical feet. (hep TAM et er)

hexameter [*hexa-, six* & *meter*] A line of verse consisting of six metrical feet; specifically, a six-foot dactylic line consisting of five dactyls and a spondee or trochee. (heks AM et er)

hydrometer [*hydro, water* + *meter, to measure*] A floating instrument for measuring the density or specific gravity of liquids. See densimeter. (heye DROM et er)

hygrometer [*hygro, moisture* + *meter, to measure*] An instrument for measuring relative or absolute atmospheric humidity. See hygroscope and hygrograph. (heye GROM et er)

hypermeter [*hyper-, above* & *meter*] A line of verse with one or more additional syllables after those normal for the meter. See hypercatalectic. (heye PERM et er)

hypermetropia [*hyper-, above* + *metr, measure* + *-opia, visual condition*] A visual condition in which light is focused behind the retina rather than on it, resulting in distant vision being clear and near vision being blurred. Farsightedness. Same as hyperopia. (heye' per mih TROH pee uh)

hypsometer [*hypso, high* + *meter, to measure*] An instrument that uses the boiling point of water, which is dependent on altitude, for measuring elevation above sea level. (hip SOM et er)

inclinometer [*inclin(e)* & *meter, to measure*] 1.An instrument for measuring the inclination of an aircraft or ship with reference to the horizontal. 2.An instrument for measuring the inclination of the earth's magnetic force. (in' kluh NOM et er)

interferometer [*interfer(e)* & *meter, to measure*] Any of several instruments that use the interference phenomena of light, sound, or radio waves for measuring wave length, minute distances, and indices of refraction. (in' ter fuh ROM et er)

isodiametric [*iso-, equal* & *diamet(e)r* & *-ic*] Having equal diameters or dimensions in all directions. (eye' soh deye' uh MET rik)

isometric [*iso-, equal* + *metr, measure* + *-ic*] 1.Having or exhibiting equality of measure. See anisometric. 2.Involving the increased contraction of a muscle with little or no increase in length, as in isometric exercises. (eye' suh MET rik)

isometropia [*iso-, equal* + *metr, measure* + *-opia, visual condition*] A visual condition in which the refractive power is equal in both eyes. See anisometropia. (eye' soh mih TROH pee uh)

kilogrammeter [*kilogram* & *meter*] A metric unit of work equal to the energy needed to raise one kilogram to a vertical distance of one meter. (kil' uh gram MEE ter)

kilometer [*kilo-, thousand* & *meter*] A metric unit of length equal to 1,000 meters. (kih LOM et er)

lysimeter [*lysi, dissolving* + *meter, to measure*] An instrument for measuring the solubility of a substance. (leye SIM et er)

magnetometer [*magneto, magnetic force* + *meter, to measure*] An instrument for measuring the strength and direction of a magnetic field. See magnetograph. (mag' nuh TOM et er)

manometer [*Grk > manos, sparse* + *meter, to measure*] An instrument for measuring the pressure of fluids. See tensimeter and piezometer. (muh NOM et er)

megameter [*mega-, million* & *meter*] A metric unit of length equal to 1,000,000 meters. (MEG uh mee' ter)

meter [*meter, to measure*] 1.The basic unit of metric length measurement equal to 39.37 inches. 2.A specific rhythmic pattern in music and verse. (MEE ter)

meter-kilogram-second Pertaining to a system of measurement that uses the meter, kilogram, and second as the basic units corresponding to length, mass, and time. (MEE ter KIL uh gram' SEK und)

metrics [*metr, measure* + *-ics, science*] The art or science of writing in meter. (MET riks)

metrology [*metr, measure* + *-ology, study of*] The scientific study of weights and measures. (mih TROL uh jee)

metronome [*metr, measure* + *nom, rule*] An instrument for marking exact musical time in preselected intervals. (MET ruh nohm')

micrometer[1] [*micro-, small* + *meter, to measure*] An instrument for measuring minute distances, thicknesses, angles, etc. (meye KROM et er)

micrometer[2] [*micro-, millionth* & *meter*] A metric unit of length equal to one millionth of a meter. Same as micron. (meye KROM et er)

micromillimeter [*micro-, millionth* & *millimeter*] A metric unit of length equal to one millionth of a millimeter. (meye' kroh MIL uh mee' ter)

microphotometer [*micro-, small* + *photo, light* + *meter, to measure*] An instrument for measuring the light intensity of minute objects. See photometer. (meye' kroh foh TOM et er)

micropyrometer [*micro-, small* + *pyro, temperature* + *meter, to measure*] An optical instrument for measuring the temperature of minute glowing bodies. (meye' kroh peye ROM et er)

milliammeter [*milliam(pere)* & *meter, to measure*] An instrument for measuring small electric currents that is calibrated to indicate values in milliamperes. (mil' ee AM mee' ter)

millimeter [*milli-, thousandth* & *meter*] A metric unit of length equal to one thousandth of a meter. (MIL uh mee' ter)

monometer [*mono-, one* & *meter*] A line of verse consisting of one metrical foot. (muh NOM et er)

nanometer [*nano-, billionth (10⁻⁹)* & *meter*] A metric unit of length equal to one billionth of a meter. (NAN uh mee' ter)

nephelometer [*nephelo, cloudy* + *meter, to measure*] An instrument for measuring the density of particles suspended in a liquid or other medium by analyzing the scattering of a light beam transmitted through it. (nef' uh LOM et er)

octameter [*octa-, eight* & *meter*] A line of verse consisting of eight metrical feet. (ok TAM et er)

odometer [*Grk > hodos, journey* + *meter, to measure*] A device for measuring distance traveled in a vehicle. See pedometer and odograph. (oh DOM et er)

ohmmeter [*ohm & meter, to measure*] An instrument for directly measuring the resistance of an electrical conductor in ohms. (OHM mee' ter)

optometry [*opto, eye + -metry, science of measuring*] The science of measuring and diagnosing visual defects and disorders with treatment limited to glasses and exercises and not including drugs or surgery. See ophthalmology. (op TOM ih tree)

osmometer [*osmo(sis) & meter, to measure*] An instrument for measuring the pressure resulting from osmosis. (oz MOM et er)

parameter [*para-, variation + meter, to measure*] A quantity whose value depends on the particular circumstances of its application. (puh RAM et er)

pedometer [*pedo, foot + meter, to measure*] A device for measuring distance traveled on foot by recording the number of steps. See odometer and odograph. (pih DOM et er)

penetrometer [*penetr(ate) & meter, to measure*] 1.An instrument for measuring the penetrating ability of x-rays and other forms of radiation. 2.An instrument for measuring the penetrability of a substance by comparing the depth to which a needle can be inserted into the substance with that of other substances under the same conditions. (pen' ih TROM et er)

pentameter [*penta-, five & meter*] A line of verse consisting of five metrical feet. (pen TAM et er)

perimeter [*peri-, around + meter, to measure*] 1.The outer boundary of an area. 2.The length of the outer boundary of a closed plane figure. (puh RIM et er)

photogrammetry [*photogram & -metry, science of measuring*] The art or process of making accurate measurements for maps and surveys using aerial photography. (foht' oh GRAM ih tree)

photometer [*photo, light + meter, to measure*] An instrument for measuring light intensity. See microphotometer. (foh TOM et er)

photometry [*photo, light + -metry, science of measuring*] The scientific measurement of light intensity. (foh TOM ih tree)

picometer [*pico-, trillionth (10^{-12}) + meter, to measure*] A metric unit of length equal to one trillionth of a meter. (PEYE koh mee' ter)

piezometer [*piezo, pressure + meter, to measure*] An instrument for measuring pressure or compressibility of fluids. See manometer and tensimeter. (peye' uh ZOM et er)

planimeter [*plani, flat + meter, to measure*] An instrument for measuring the area of a figure on a plane surface by tracing its perimeter. (pluh NIM et er)

pluviometer [*pluvio, rain + meter, to measure*] An instrument for measuring rainfall amounts. (ploo' vee OM et er)

polarimeter [*polari(ze) & meter, to measure*] An instrument for measuring the angular rotation of linearly polarized light passing through a substance. (poh' luh RIM et er)

potentiometer [*potenti(al) & meter, to measure*] A device for measuring or controlling an electric potential by comparing it with a standard voltage. (puh ten' shee OM et er)

psychometrics [*psycho, mental process + metr, to measure + -ics, science*] The science of measuring mental capabilities, functions, processes, traits, etc. (seye' kuh MET riks)

psychometry [*psycho, mental process + -metry, to measure*] The alleged divination of knowledge concerning an object or a person associated with it through proximity to or physical contact with the object. (seye KOM ih tree)

psychrometer [*psychro, cold + meter, to measure*] An instrument for measuring atmospheric humidity using the temperature difference between a wet bulb thermometer cooled by evaporation and a dry bulb thermometer. (seye KROM et er)

pulsimeter [*puls(e) & meter, to measure*] An instrument for measuring the strength and rapidity of the pulse. (pul SIM et er)

pycnometer [*pycno, dense + meter, to measure*] A standard container for measuring the density of liquids or solids. (pik NOM et er)

pyrheliometer [*pyr, heat + helio, sun + meter, to measure*] An instrument for measuring the intensity of solar energy. (pihr hee' lee OM et er)

pyrometer [*pyro, heat + meter, to measure*] An electrical thermometer for measuring high temperatures. See pyrophotometer. (peye ROM et er)

pyrophotometer [*pyro, heat + photo, light + meter, to measure*] An optical thermometer for measuring very high temperatures. See pyrometer. (peye' roh foh TOM et er)

radiometer [*radio, radiation + meter, to measure*] An instrument for measuring the intensity of radiant energy. (ray' dee OM et er)

refractometer [*Ltn > refractus, to break up + meter, to measure*] Any instrument for measuring the index of refraction of a substance. (ree' frak TOM et er)

rheometer [*rheo, flow + meter, to measure*] An instrument for measuring the velocity of a flowing liquid, as circulating blood. (ree OM et er)

saccharimeter [*sacchari, sugar + meter, to measure*] An instrument, especially a form of polarimeter, for measuring the quantity of sugar in a solution. See saccharometer. (sak' uh RIM et er)

saccharometer [*saccharo, sugar + meter, to measure*] An instrument, especially a form of hydrometer, for measuring the quantity of sugar in a solution. See saccharimeter. (sak' uh ROM et er)

salimeter [*sali, salt + meter, to measure*] An instrument, such as a hydrometer, for measuring the quantity of salt in a solution. Same as salinometer. (suh LIM et er)

salinometer [*salin(e) & meter, to measure*] An instrument, such as a hydrometer, for measuring the quantity of salt in a solution. (sal' uh NOM et er)

sclerometer [*sclero, hard + meter, to measure*] An instrument for measuring the hardness of a material by determining the pressure required to scratch its surface using a diamond point. (skluh ROM et er)

seismometer [*seismo, earthquake + meter, to measure*] An instrument for detecting and measuring actual ground movement. See seismology and seismograph. (seyez MOM et er)

meter, metr, -metry

semidiameter [*semi-, half & diameter*] 1.Half of a diameter. Radius. 2.The perceived radius of a spherical celestial body observed from the earth. (sem' ee deye AM et er)

sensitometer [*sensit(ivity) & meter, to measure*] An instrument for measuring the light sensitivity of photographic film. (sen' sih TOM et er)

sociometry [*socio, social + -metry, science of measuring*] The science of measuring the interrelationships of individuals within a group. (soh' see OM ih tree)

spectrometer [*spectro, spectrum + meter, to measure*] An optical instrument for measuring wavelengths of spectra and indices of refraction. See spectrophotometer. (spek TROM et er)

spectrophotometer [*spectro, spectrum + photo, light + meter, to measure*] An instrument for measuring wavelengths in light spectra for accurate analysis of color and the comparison of luminous intensity. See spectrometer. (spek' troh foh TOM et er)

speedometer [*speed & meter, to measure*] An instrument for measuring the speed of a vehicle, that is often combined with an odometer for measuring distance traveled. See odometer. (spih DOM et er)

spherometer [*spher(e) & meter, to measure*] An instrument for measuring the curvature of a sphere, cylinder, lens, or other curved surface. (sfihr OM et er)

sphygmomanometer [*sphygmo, pulse & manometer*] An instrument for indirectly measuring arterial blood pressure. See manometer. (sfig' moh muh NOM et er)

spirometer [*spiro, breathe + meter, to measure*] An instrument for measuring the breathing rate and capacity of the lungs. (speye ROM et er)

stichometry [*stich {line of verse} & -metry, to measure*] The practice of writing prose using line lengths determined by sense or natural rhythms. (stih KOM ih tree)

stoichiometry [*Grk > stoicheion, element + -metry, science of measuring*] The methodology for determining the proportions in which chemical elements combine or are produced in a chemical reaction. (stoi' kee OM ih tree)

symmetry [*sym-, same + -metry, to measure*] Similarity of size, form, or arrangement on either side of a dividing line. (SIM ih tree)

tachometer [*tacho, rapid + meter, to measure*] An instrument for measuring the speed of rotation of an engine, shaft, etc. (tak OM et er)

tachymeter [*tachy, rapid + meter, to measure*] A surveying instrument for quickly measuring distance, direction, and elevation. (tuh KIM et er)

taximeter [*taxi & meter, to measure*] A device for measuring the fare and distance traveled in a taxicab. (TAKS ee mee' ter)

telemetry [*tele, distant + -metry, science of measuring*] The scientific measurement and transmission of data from a remote source to a receiving station for recording and analysis. (tuh LEM ih tree)

tensimeter [*tensi(on) & meter, to measure*] An instrument that uses a manometer for measuring the differences in vapor pressure of two liquids. See manometer and piezometer. (ten SIM et er)

tensiometer [*tensio(n) & meter, to measure*] An instrument for measuring tension in wires, fabric, etc. (ten' see OM et er)

tetrameter [*tetra-, four & meter*] A line of verse consisting of four metrical feet. (teh TRAM et er)

thermometer [*thermo, heat + meter, to measure*] An instrument for measuring temperature. (thur MOM et er)

tiltmeter [*tilt & meter, to measure*] An instrument for measuring small changes in the tilt of the earth's surface. (TILT mee' ter)

tonometer [*Grk > tonos, tone + meter, to measure*] 1.An instrument for measuring tonal frequency. 2.An instrument for measuring pressure within the eyeball. (toh NOM et er)

trigonometry [*tri-, three + gono, angle + -metry, science of measuring*] The branch of mathematics dealing with the study of the applications and properties of triangles, especially right triangles. (trig' uh NOM ih tree)

trimeter [*tri-, three & meter*] A line of verse consisting of three metrical feet. (TRIM et er)

trimetrogon [*tri-, three + metro, to measure + gon, angle*] A system of aerial topographic mapping and photography using three wide-angle cameras, one pointing downward and the other two pointing at 60 degree angles to it. (treye MET ruh gon')

turbidimeter [*turbidi(ty) & meter, to measure*] An instrument for measuring the turbidity of a liquid. (tur' bih DIM et er)

urinometer [*urino, urine + meter, to measure*] An instrument, such as a form of hydrometer, for measuring the specific gravity of urine. (yoor' uh NOM et er)

variometer [*vario, variation + meter, to measure*] 1.An instrument for measuring the inductance in an electronic circuit. 2.An instrument for measuring variations in the earth's magnetic field. (vehr' ee OM et er)

velocimeter [*veloci(ty) & meter, to measure*] An instrument for measuring the velocity of sound in water. (vee' loh SIM et er)

viscometer [*visco(sity) & meter, to measure*] An instrument for measuring viscosity. (vis KOM et er)

viscosimeter [*viscosi(ty) & meter, to measure*] An instrument for measuring viscosity. Same as viscometer. (vis' kuh SIM et er)

voltameter [*volta(ic) & meter, to measure*] A device for measuring the electric charge flowing through a conductor by measuring the electrically produced chemical change. (vohl TAM et er)

voltammeter [*volt & am(pere) & meter, to measure*] An instrument for measuring either voltage or current. See voltmeter and ammeter. (vohlt' AM mee' ter)

voltmeter [*volt & meter, to measure*] An instrument for measuring voltage in volts. See ammeter and wattmeter. (VOHLT mee' ter)

volumeter [*volu(me) & meter, to measure*] An instrument for measuring the volume of liquids, gases, or solids. (VOL yoo mee' ter)

wattmeter [*watt & meter, to measure*] An instrument for measuring electrical power in watts. See voltmeter and ammeter. (WOT mee' ter)

mis/o   to hate

misandry [*mis, to hate + andr, man + -y*] Hatred of, or animosity toward, men. See misogyny. (MIS an' dree)

misanthrope [*mis, to hate + anthrop, man*] One who hates or distrusts mankind. (MIS un throhp')

misanthropy [*mis, to hate + anthrop, man + -y*] Hatred or distrust of mankind. (mis AN thruh pee)

misogamist [*miso, to hate + gam, marriage + -ist*] One who hates marriage. (mih SOG uh mist)

misogamy [*miso, to hate + -gamy, marriage*] Hatred of marriage. (mih SOG uh mee)

misogynist [*miso, to hate + gyn, woman + -ist*] One who hates women. (mih SOJ uh nist)

misogyny [*miso, to hate + gyn, woman + -y*] Hatred of, or animosity toward, women. See misandry and philogyny. (mih SOJ uh nee)

misology [*miso, to hate + log, discourse + -y*] Hatred or distrust of argument, reasoning, or enlightenment. (mih SOL uh jee)

misoneism [*miso, to hate + neo, new + -ism*] Hatred, intolerance, or fear of change, innovation, or anything new or unfamiliar. (mis' oh NEE iz' um)

mono-, mon-   one, single, alone

monad [*mon-, one + -ad, group*] 1.A simple and indivisible unit. 2.A simple single-celled microorganism, especially a flagellated protozoan. (MOH nad)

monandry [*mon-, one + andr, man + -y*] The custom or practice of having only one husband at a time. See monogyny, polygyny, and polyandry. (muh NAN dree)

monanthous [*mon-, one + anth, flower + -ous*] Bearing only one flower, as certain plants. (muh NAN thus)

monarch [*mon-, one + arch, rule*] The sole ruler of a nation or state. (MON ahrk)

monarchy [*mon-, one + arch, rule + -y*] Government by one ruler. (MON ahr' kee)

monastery [*mon-, alone + Grk > terion, a place + -y*] A residence for monks or others living apart from the rest of the world under religious vows. (MON uh stehr' ee)

monaural [*mon-, one + aur, ear + -al*] 1.Involving the use of one ear only. 2.Pertaining to a system of sound reproduction that uses only one source of sound. See binaural (def. 2). (mon OR ul)

monaxial [*mon-, one + ax, axis + -ial*] Having only one axis, as a plant or crystal. Same as uniaxial. (mon AK see ul)

monocarpellary [*mono-, single & carpel & -ary*] Having one carpel only. (mon' uh KAHR puh lehr' ee)

monocarpic [*mono-, one + carp, fruit + -ic*] Capable of flowering or fruiting only once, as annual and biennial plants. See polycarpic. (mon' uh KAHR pik)

monochord [*mono-, one & chord (string)*] An acoustical instrument consisting of a wooden sounding box with one string and a movable bridge, used for mathematically determining musical intervals. (MON uh kord')

monochromatic [*mono-, one + chromat, color + -ic*] 1.Pertaining to or having one color. See heterochromatic. 2.Pertaining to light or other radiation that consists of a very narrow range of wavelengths or of a single wavelength. (mon' oh kroh MAT ik)

monochromatism [*mono-, one + chromat, color + -ism*] Complete color blindness in which all objects and colors appear as various shades of gray. (mon' uh KROH muh tiz' um)

monochrome [*mono-, one + -chrome, color*] A photograph, painting, or drawing done in various shades of a single color. (MON uh krohm')

monocle [*mon-, one + ocul, eye*] An eyeglass for use with one eye only. (MON uh kul)

monocline [*mono-, one + -cline, slope*] A rock formation in which all strata have the same oblique inclination. (MON uh kleyen')

monoclinous [*mono-, one + Grk > kline, bed + -ous*] Having stamens and pistils on the same flower. Same as synoecious (def. 1). (mon' uh KLEYE nus)

monocracy [*mono-, one + -cracy, government*] Government by one person possessing absolute power. Same as autocracy (def. 1). (muh NOK ruh see)

monocular [*mon-, one + ocul, eye + -ar*] Pertaining to or used by one eye only. See binocular. (muh NOK yuh lur)

monoculture [*mono-, one & culture*] Using the land for raising only one crop. (MON uh kul' chur)

monocyclic [*mono-, one + cycl, circle + -ic*] 1.Forming only one cycle or circle. 2.Having one ring of atoms in a molecule. See polycyclic. (mon' uh SEYE klik)

monocyte [*mono-, one + -cyte, cell*] A nongranular white blood cell with a single nucleus. See lymphocyte, agranulocyte, and leukocyte. (MON uh seyet')

monodrama [*mono-, one & drama*] A drama performed by only one person. (MON uh drah' muh)

monody [*mon-, single & od(e) & -y*] 1.In ancient Greece, an ode sung by a single voice, as in a tragedy. 2.A poem mourning someone's death. 3.A style of musical composition with one predominating part or melody. See homophonic (def. 2). (MON uh dee)

monoecious [*mono-, one + Grk > oikos, house + -ious*] 1.Having both staminate and pistillate flowers on the same plant. 2.Having both male and female reproductive organs in the same individual. See dioecious, trioecious, and synoecious. (muh NEE shus)

monogamy [*mono-, one + -gamy, marriage*] The practice of being married to only one person at a time. See bigamy and polygamy. (muh NOG uh mee)

monogenesis [*mono-, one + -genesis, origin*] 1.The belief that living organisms all originated from a single cell. 2.Asexual reproduction. See agamogenesis. (mon' uh JEN uh sis)

monogenic [*mono-, one + gen, to produce + -ic*] 1.Producing offspring of one sex only. 2.Pertaining to or controlled by a single gene. (mon' uh JEN ik)

monogenism [*mono-, one + gen, origin + -ism*] The theory that all humans have descended from one ancestral line. See polygenism. (muh NOJ uh niz' um)

monoglot [*mono-, one + glot, language*] 1.A person who is able to use only one language. 2.Able to use only one language. Same as monolingual (def. 1). (MON uh glot')

mono-, mon-

monogram [*mono-, single + gram, to write*] A character or symbol consisting of two or more letters combined into one design. (MON uh gram')

monograph [*mono-, single + graph, writing*] A usually technical or scientific article written on a single subject. (MON uh graf')

monogyny [*mono-, one + gyn, woman + -y*] The custom or practice of having only one wife at a time. See monandry, polygyny, and polyandry. (muh NOJ uh nee)

monolingual [*mono-, one + lingu, language + -al*] 1.Able to use only one language. 2.Expressed in or involving only one language. (mon' uh LING gwul)

monolith [*mono-, single + lith, stone*] 1.A large single piece of stone. 2.A large unified organization that acts as a whole. (MON uh lith')

monolithic [*mono-, single + lith, stone + -ic*] Characterized by solidity, uniformity, and intractability. (mon' uh LITH ik)

monologue [*mono-, one + log, discourse*] A long speech by one speaker. (MON uh log')

monomania [*mono-, one + mania, excessive desire*] A pathological condition characterized by excessive enthusiasm or desire for one thing. (mon' uh MAY nee uh)

monomer [*mono-, single + mer, part*] A simple molecule that can combine with other identical or similar molecules to form a polymer. See dimer, trimer, and polymer. (MON uh mer)

monometer [*mono-, one & meter*] A line of verse consisting of one metrical foot. (muh NOM et er)

monomial [*mon-, one + nom, name + -ial*] 1.A mathematical expression consisting of only one term. 2.A taxonomic name consisting of one word. See binomial, trinomial, and polynomial. (muh NOH mee ul)

monomorphemic [*mono-, one & morphem(e) & -ic*] Consisting of only one morpheme, as the word *talk*. (mon' oh mor FEE mik)

monomorphic [*mono-, one + morph, form + -ic*] Having only one form, shape, or size. (mon' oh MOR fik)

mononuclear [*mono-, one & nuclear*] Having a single nucleus. (mon' oh NOO klee ur)

mononucleosis [*mono-, single & nucle(us) & -osis, increase*] An abnormal increase in the number of mononuclear leukocytes in the blood. (mon' oh noo' klee OH sis)

monopetalous [*mono-, one & petal & -ous*] Having united or partially united petals. Same as gamopetalous. (mon' uh PET l us)

monophagous [*mono-, one + phag, to eat + -ous*] Feeding on one kind of food only. (muh NOF uh gus)

monophobia [*mono-, alone + -phobia, fear*] Abnormal fear of being alone. (mon' uh FOH bee uh)

monophony [*mono-, single + -phony, sound*] Music performed by a single voice or instrument without accompaniment. (muh NOF uh nee)

monophthong [*mono-, single + phthong, sound*] A single vowel sound, as the "oa" in *coat*. See diphthong and triphthong. (MON uhf thong')

monophyletic [*mono-, single + phyl, common ancestry + -etic*] Derived from one ancestral form. See polyphyletic. (mon' oh feye LET ik)

monoplane [*mono-, one & plane*] An airplane with one main pair of wings. See biplane and triplane. (MON uh playn')

monoplegia [*mono-, single + -plegia, paralysis*] Paralysis of a single limb or muscle group. (mon' uh PLEE jee uh)

monoploid [*mono-, one + -ploid, number of chromosomes*] Pertaining to cells with a chromosome number equal to the basic haploid number. Haploid. See haploid. (MON uh ploid')

monopode [*mono-, one + -pode, foot*] Anything supported by only one foot. (MON uh pohd')

monopody [*mono-, one + pod, foot + -y*] A prosodic measure consisting of one foot. (muh NOP uh dee)

monopoly [*mono-, one + Grk > polein, to sell + -y*] 1.Ownership or control of a commodity or service by only one seller. See duopoly. 2.Exclusive possession or control by one party. (muh NOP uh lee)

monopsony [*mono-, one + Grk > opsonia, purchase + -y*] The market condition that exists when there is only one buyer whose actions can impact price. See oligopsony and oligopoly. (muh NOP suh nee)

monorhyme [*mono-, one & rhyme*] A poem with the same end rhyme in all lines. (MON uh reyem')

monosaccharide [*mono-, one & saccharide*] A simple sugar that cannot be further decomposed by hydrolysis, as fructose, or glucose. See saccharide. (mon' uh SAK uh reyed')

monosepalous [*mono-, one & sepal & -ous*] Having united or partially united sepals. Same as gamosepalous. (mon' uh SEP uh lus)

monosome [*mono-, one & (chromo)some*] 1.An unpaired sex chromosome. 2.An unpaired X chromosome. (MON uh sohm')

monostich [*mono-, one & stich {line of verse}*] A stanza or epigram consisting of one line. (MON uh stik')

monosyllable [*mono-, one & syllable*] A word with one syllable. (MON uh sil' uh bul)

monotheism [*mono-, one + the, God + -ism*] The belief in only one God. (MON uh thee iz' um)

monotone [*mono-, one & tone*] Successive words or sounds in one unvarying tone. (MON uh tohn')

monotonous [*mono-, one & ton(e) & -ous*] Being dull because of little or no variation or variety. (muh NOT n us)

monotreme [*mono-, single + Grk > trema, hole*] Any of an order of the most primitive mammals, including the platypus and the echidnas, with a single opening for the digestive tract and the urinary and genital organs. (MON uh treem')

monotypic [*mono-, one & typ(e) & -ic*] Being the only member of its group, as a single species that constitutes and genus. (mon' uh TIP ik)

monovalent [*mono-, one + -valent, having a specified valence*] Having a valence of one. Same as univalent. (mon' uh VAY lent)

monoxide [*mon-, one + ox, oxygen + -ide*] An oxide containing one oxygen atom per molecule. (muh NOK seyed')

monozygotic [*mono-, one + zyg, pair + -otic*] Derived from one fertilized egg, as identical twins. See dizygotic, zygote, and polyembryony. (mon' oh zeye GOT ik)

uni-   one

disunion [*dis-, lack of & union*] Lack of unity or agreement. Separation. Dissension. (dis YOON yun)

reunion [*re-, again & union*] 1.The act of uniting again. 2.A social gathering of friends, classmates, relatives, etc., after separation. (ree YOON yun)

triune [*tri-, three + uni, one*] Consisting of three in one, especially with reference to the Trinity. (TREYE yoon)

undecillion [*uni-, one + dec, ten + (m)ill, thousand + -ion*] A number expressed as 1 followed by 36 zeros, which is 11 groups of three zeros after 1,000. (un' dih SIL yun)

uniaxial [*uni-, one + ax, axis + -ial*] Having only one axis, as a plant or crystal. (yoo' nee AK see ul)

unicameral [*uni-, one & cameral*] Composed of only one legislative chamber. See bicameral and tricameral. (yoo' nih KAM ur ul)

unicellular [*uni-, one & cellular*] Consisting of a single cell. (yoo' nih SEL yuh lur)

unicorn [*uni-, one + corn, horn*] A mythical animal resembling a horse with a single horn on the center of its forehead. (YOO nih korn)

unicycle [*uni-, one + cycl, wheel*] A vehicle with one wheel, usually propelled by the rider pushing pedals. (YOO nih seye' kul)

unidirectional [*uni-, one & directional*] Involving, functioning, or moving in one direction only. See bidirectional and omnidirectional. (yoo' nih duh REK shuh nul)

unifoliate [*uni-, one + foli, leaf + -ate*] Having only one leaf. (yoo' nuh FOH lee it)

unifoliolate [*uni-, one + foli, leaf + -ate*] Compound in structure, but bearing only one leaflet. (yoo' nuh FOH lee uh layt')

uniform [*uni-, one & form*] 1.Having the same form, size, or design. 2.Without variation, fluctuation, or change. (YOO nuh form')

unify [*uni-, one + -fy, to make*] To make into a single unit. Consolidate. Merge. (YOO nuh feye')

unilateral [*uni-, one + Ltn > latus, side + -al*] 1.Pertaining to, occurring on, or affecting one side only. 2.Pertaining to or affecting one party, country, etc., and not another or others. See bilateral and multilateral. (yoo' nuh LAT ur ul)

unilinear [*uni-, one + Ltn > linea, line + -ar*] Following a single path of evolution or development. (yoo' nuh LIN ee ur)

unilingual [*uni-, one + lingu, language + -al*] 1.Able to use only one language. 2.Expressed in or involving only one language. Same as monolingual. (yoo' nuh LING gwul)

uninucleate [*uni-, one & nucle(us) & -ate*] Having a single nucleus. Same as mononuclear. (yoo' nuh NOO klee it)

union [*uni-, one + -on*] 1.Being combined, joined, or grouped into one. 2.A group of people, states, etc., united for a common purpose. (YOON yun)

uniparous [*uni-, one + -parous, to produce*] 1.Producing only one offspring at a time. 2.Not having previously given birth. See multiparous. (yoo NIP ur us)

unipolar [*uni-, one & polar*] Pertaining to or having only one magnetic or electric pole. See bipolar (def. 1). (yoo' nuh POH lur)

unique [*uni-, one + -ic*] 1.Existing as one of a kind. Having no equal. 2.Very unusual. Remarkable. (yoo NEEK)

unisexual [*uni-, one & sexual*] 1.Pertaining to one sex only. 2.Having the reproductive organs of either male or female in one individual. (yoo' nuh SEK shoo ul)

unison [*uni-, one + son, sound*] 1.Identity in pitch of two or more tones, voices, etc. 2.Complete and harmonious agreement. (YOO nih sun)

unit [*uni-, one + -it*] A single quantity regarded as part of a more complex whole. (YOO nit)

unite [*uni-, one + -ite*] To combine or join into one. (yoo NEYET)

univalent [*uni-, one + -valent, having a specified valence*] Having a valence of one. (yoo' nuh VAY lent)

universe [*uni-, one + vers, turn*] 1.The totality of all things observed or postulated. 2.The world or sphere in which something exists. (YOO nuh vurs')

university [*univers(e) & -ity*] An institution of higher learning that offers degrees in specialized fields as well as the arts and sciences. (yoo' nuh VUR sih tee)

univocal [*uni-, one + voc, voice + -al*] 1.Having only one meaning. Unambiguous. Unequivocal. See ambiguous (def. 1), equivocal, and unequivocal. 2.A word or term with only one proper meaning. (yoo NIV uh kul)

bi-, bin-   two, twice

biannual [*bi-, two + ann, year + -ual*] Occurring twice a year. See biennial (def. 1). (beye AN yoo ul)

biathlon [*bi-, two + Grk > athlon, contest*] An athletic contest that includes both rifle shooting and cross-country skiing. See triathlon, pentathlon, and decathlon. (beye ATH lon)

biaxial [*bi-, two + ax, axis + -ial*] Having two axes, as certain crystals. (beye AK see ul)

bicameral [*bi-, two & cameral*] Composed of two legislative chambers. See unicameral and tricameral. (beye KAM ur ul)

bicentennial [*bi-, two + cent, hundred + enn, years + -ial*] Occurring once every two hundred years. See semicentennial. (beye' sen TEN ee ul)

bicephalous [*bi-, two + cephal, head + -ous*] Having two heads. (beye SEF uh lus)

biceps [*bi-, two + Ltn > caput, head*] A muscle with two heads, especially the large flexor muscle of the upper arm. See triceps and quadriceps. (BEYE seps)

bichloride [*bi-, two & chloride*] A chloride containing two atoms of chlorine per molecule. (beye KLOR eyed')

bichromate [*bi-, two + chrom, chromium + -ate*] An orange to red chemical compound containing two chromium atoms. Same as dichromate. (beye KROH mayt')

biconcave [*bi-, two & concave*] Concave on both sides. See biconvex. (beye' kon KAYV)

biconvex [*bi-, two & convex*] Convex on both sides. See biconcave. (beye' kon VEKS)

bicuspid [*bi-, two + Ltn > cuspis, point + -id*] Any of eight adult human teeth with double-pointed crowns for tearing and grinding food. See tricuspid. (beye KUS pid)

bicycle [*bi-, two + cycl, wheel*] A vehicle with two large wire-spoked wheels in tandem, usually propelled by the rider pushing pedals. (BEYE sih' kul)

bidentate [*bi-, two + dent, teeth + -ate*] Having two teeth or toothlike processes. (beye DEN tayt')

bidialectal [*bi-, two & dialect & -al*] Having the ability to use two dialects of the same language. (beye' deye uh LEK tul)

bi-, bin-

bidirectional [*bi-, two & directional*] Involving, functioning, or moving in two, usually opposite, directions. See unidirectional and omnidirectional. (beye' duh REK shuh nul)

biennial [*bi-, two + enn, years + -ial*] 1.Occurring once every two years. See biannual. 2.Lasting or living for two years. (beye EN ee ul)

biennium [*bi-, two + enn, years + -ium*] A period of two years. (beye EN ee um)

bifid [*bi-, two + fid, split*] Divided into two parts or lobes by a cleft. (BEYE fid)

bifocal [*bi-, two & focal*] Having two focal lengths. See trifocal. (beye FOH kul)

bifoliate [*bi-, two + foli, leaf + -ate*] Having two leaves or leaflike parts. (beye FOH lee it)

bifurcate [*bi-, two + Ltn > furca, fork + -ate*] Having two branches or forks. See trifurcate. (BEYE fur kayt')

bigamy [*bi-, two + -gamy, marriage*] The practice of being married to two people at the same time. See monogamy and polygamy. (BIG uh mee)

bilabial [*bi-, two + labio, lip + -al*] Articulated with the lips touching or close together, as "b," "m," and "p." (beye LAY bee ul)

bilateral [*bi-, two + Ltn > latus, side + -al*] 1.Pertaining to or having two sides. 2.Having two symmetrical sides. 3.Binding, affecting, or taking place between two parties, countries, etc., as a treaty or agreement. See unilateral and multilateral. (beye LAT ur ul)

bilingual [*bi-, two + lingu, language + -al*] 1.Able to use two languages with nearly equal fluency. 2.Expressed in or involving two languages. (beye LING gwul)

billion [*bi-, two + (m)ill, thousand + -ion*] A number expressed as 1 followed by 9 zeros, which is 2 groups of three zeros after 1,000. (BIL yun)

bilobate [*bi-, two + lob, lobe + -ate*] Divided into two lobes. (beye LOH bayt')

bimanual [*bi-, two + manu, hand + -al*] Requiring the use of or involving both hands. (beye MAN yoo ul)

bimonthly [*bi-, two & month & -ly*] Occurring once every two months. See semimonthly. (beye MUNTH lee)

bimorphemic [*bi-, two & morphem(e) & -ic*] Having two morphemes. (beye' mor FEE mik)

binary [*bin-, two + -ary*] 1.Pertaining to a number system of base two. 2.Consisting of or involving two parts or things. (BEYE nehr' ee)

binaural [*bin-, two + aur, ear + -al*] 1.Involving the use of both ears. 2.Pertaining to a system of sound reproduction that uses two sources of sound to create a stereophonic effect. See monaural (def. 2) and stereophonic. (beye NOR ul)

binocular [*bin-, two + ocul, eye + -ar*] Pertaining to or used by both eyes. See monocular. (buh NOK yuh lur)

binomial [*bi-, two + nom, name + -ial*] 1.A mathematical expression consisting of two terms. 2.In taxonomy, a two-part name designating the genus and the species of an organism. See monomial, trinomial, and polynomial. (beye NOH mee ul)

bipartisan [*bi-, two & partisan*] Pertaining to or supported by two parties. (beye PAHR tih zun)

bipartite [*bi-, two & partite*] 1.Consisting of two parts. 2.Shared by or involving two parties. (beye PAHR teyet')

biped [*bi-, two + ped, feet*] A two-footed animal. (BEYE ped)

bipinnate [*bi-, twice & pinnate*] Pertaining to a leaf with pinnate primary and secondary divisions. (beye PIN ayt')

biplane [*bi-, two & plane*] An airplane with two main pairs of wings arranged one above the other. See monoplane and triplane. (BEYE playn)

bipod [*bi-, two + pod, feet*] Any two-legged support, as for the barrel of a rifle. (BEYE pod)

bipolar [*bi-, two & polar*] 1.Pertaining to or having two magnetic or electric poles. See unipolar. 2.Characterized by two opposing opinions, views, etc. (beye POH lur)

biquarterly [*bi-, two & quarter & -ly*] Occurring twice in a three month period. (beye KWORT ur lee)

biramous [*bi-, two + ram, branch + -ous*] Having two branches, as the forked appendage of a crustacean. (beye RAY mus)

bisect [*bi-, two + sect, to cut*] To divide or cut into two equal parts. See dissect. (beye SEKT)

bisexual [*bi-, two & sexual*] 1.Pertaining to or involving both sexes. 2.Sexually attracted to both sexes. 3.Having both male and female sex organs in the same individual, as certain plants and animals. Hermaphroditic. (beye SEK shoo ul)

bivalent [*bi-, two + -valent, having a specified valence*] Having a valence of two. (beye VAY lent)

biweekly [*bi-, two & week & -ly*] Occurring once every two weeks. See semiweekly. (beye WEEK lee)

biyearly [*bi-, two & year & -ly*] Occurring once every two years. Same as biennial (def. 1). See semiyearly. (beye YIHR lee)

di-, diplo   two, double

anadiplosis [*ana-, again + diplo, double + -sis*] Rhetorical repetition of the last word or words of one clause, phrase, etc., at the beginning of the next, as "She gave her time; time was all she had to give." (an' uh dih PLOH sis)

diandrous [*di-, two + andr, stamen + -ous*] Having two stamens. (deye AN drus)

diarchy [*di-, two + arch, rule + -y*] Government by two rulers or authorities. (DEYE ahr' kee)

dicentric [*di-, two + centr, center + -ic*] Having two centromeres. (deye SEN trik)

dicephalous [*di-, two + cephal, head + -ous*] Having two heads. Same as bicephalous. (deye SEF uh lus)

dichloride [*di-, two & chloride*] A chloride containing two atoms of chlorine per molecule. Same as bichloride. (deye KLOR eyed')

dichroism [*di-, two + chros, color + -ism*] 1.The property of some crystals to display two different colors when viewed from two different directions. See trichroism and pleochroism. 2.The property of a substance to reflect light in one color and transmit light in another color. (DEYE kroh iz' um)

dichromate [*di-, two + chrom, chromium + -ate*] An orange to red chemical compound containing two chromium atoms. (deye KROH mayt')

dichromatic [*di-, two + chromat, color + -ic*] 1.Having or displaying two colors. 2.Displaying two distinct adult color phases that are unrelated to sex or age, as certain insects or birds. 3.Capable of distinguishing only two of the three primary colors. Red, green, and blue are the three primary colors. (deye' kroh MAT ik)

dichroscope [*di-, two + chros, color + -scope, to view*] An instrument for viewing the dichroism of crystals. See dichroism (def. 1). (DEYE kruh skohp')

didymium [*Grk > didymos, twin + -ium*] A metallic mixture of neodymium and praseodymium, once thought to be an element. See neodymium. (deye DIM ee um)

didymous [*Grk > didymos, twin + -ous*] Occurring or growing in pairs. Twin. (DID uh mus)

diencephalon [*di-, two + encephal, brain + -on*] The posterior portion of the prosencephalon, including the epithalamus, thalamus, metathalamus, and hypothalamus. See telencephalon and prosencephalon. (deye' en SEF uh lon')

digamma [*di-, two & gamma*] The sixth letter of the early Greek alphabet, which had a pronunciation similar to English "w" and was later disused. (deye GAM uh)

digamy [*di-, two + -gamy, marriage*] A second legal marriage after the divorce or death of the first spouse. (DIG uh mee)

digenesis [*di-, two + -genesis, production*] Reproductive cycles that alternate between asexual in one generation and sexual in the next. (deye JEN uh sis)

digraph [*di-, two + graph, writing*] 1.A combination of two contiguous letters representing a single speech sound, as the "ph" in *phone*. See trigraph and diphthong. 2.A combination of two overlapping characters having a special sound or meaning. (DEYE graf)

dihedral [*di-, two + -hedral, surface*] The figure formed by two intersecting plane surfaces. See trihedron. (deye HEE drul)

dilemma [*di-, two + Grk > lemma, premise*] A situation necessitating a choice between two equally undesirable or unfavorable alternatives. (dih LEM uh)

dimer [*di-, two + mer, part*] A compound consisting of two identical molecules linked together. See monomer, trimer, and polymer. (DEYE mer)

dimeter [*di-, two & meter*] A line of verse consisting of two metrical feet. (DIM et er)

dimorphic [*di-, two + morph, form + -ic*] Occurring in two distinct forms. (deye MOR fik)

dimorphism [*di-, two + morph, form + -ism*] 1.The occurrence of two distinct types of plant parts on the same plant or on plants of the same species. 2.The occurrence of different form, color, etc., between two distinct types of animals of the same species. 3.The property of a substance of crystallizing in two chemically identical forms. See polymorphism. (deye MOR fiz' um)

dimorphous [*di-, two + morph, form + -ous*] Pertaining to an element or compound that crystallizes in two distinct forms. (deye MOR fus)

dioecious [*di-, two + Grk > oikos, house + -ious*] 1.Pertaining to a species having staminate and pistillate flowers on different plants. 2.Having male and female reproductive organs in separate individuals. See monoecious, trioecious, and synoecious. (deye EE shus)

diopside [*di-, double + Grk > opsis, appearance + -ide*] A monoclinic pyroxene mineral that is green to almost black in color and often occurs in well-formed crystals. (deye OP seyed')

dioxide [*di-, two + ox, oxygen + -ide*] An oxide containing two oxygen atoms per molecule. (deye OK seyed')

diphthong [*di-, two + phthong, sound*] A combination of two vowel sounds in one syllable, as the "ou" in *house* or *louse*. See monophthong, triphthong, and digraph (def. 1). (DIF thong)

diphyllous [*di-, two + phyll, leaf + -ous*] Having two leaves. (deye FIL us)

diphyodont [*di-, two + Grk > phyein, to grow + odont, teeth*] Developing two sets of teeth, the first set deciduous and the second set permanent, as in humans. (DIF ee oh dont')

diplegia [*di-, two + -plegia, paralysis*] Paralysis of corresponding parts on both sides of the body. (deye PLEE jee uh)

diplex [*di-, two + -plex, fold*] Capable of simultaneous communication in opposite directions using a common link. Same as duplex (def. 2). (DEYE pleks)

diploblastic [*diplo, double + blast, cell layer + -ic*] 1.Pertaining to animals whose body wall consists of two cell layers: the endoderm and ectoderm. Includes only the cnidarians. See triploblastic. 2.Having two germ layers. (dip' loh BLAS tik)

diplococcus [*diplo, double + -coccus, bacteria*] Any of various spherical bacteria occurring in pairs. (dip' loh KOK us)

diploe [*diplo, double*] The spongy tissue between the internal and external layers of the cranium. (DIP loh ee')

diploid [*di-, two + -ploid, number of chromosomes*] 1.Double. 2.Pertaining to cells with two complete sets of chromosomes, which is twice the haploid number. In humans, most body cells are diploid and contain 46 chromosomes, while male and female sex cells are haploid, each containing 23 chromosomes. See haploid. (DIP loid)

diploma [*Grk > diploma, letter folded double*] 1.A certificate given to a student upon graduation from a school, college, or university. 2.Any certificate bestowing privileges, honors, etc. (dih PLOH muh)

diplopia [*diplo, double + -opia, visual condition*] A visual condition in which objects appear double. Double vision. See haplopia. (dip LOH pee uh)

diplopod [*diplo, double + pod, feet*] Millipede. See millipede. (DIP luh pod')

dipody [*di-, two + pod, feet + -y*] A prosodic measure consisting of two feet. (DIP uh dee)

dipole [*di-, two & pole*] Any system or object with two equal but opposite magnetic poles or electrical charges separated by a small specified distance, as in a molecule. (DEYE pohl)

dipterous [*di-, two + pter, wing + -ous*] Any of a large order of insects with two wings or winglike appendages. (DIP ter us)

disaccharide [*di-, two & saccharide*] Any of a class of sugars that yield two monosaccharides on hydrolysis, as sucrose or lactose. (deye SAK uh reyed')

distich [*di-, two & stich {line of verse}*] A stanza consisting of two lines. (DIS tik)

disyllable [*di-, two & syllable*] A word with two syllables. (DEYE sil' uh bul)

divalent [*di-, two + -valent, having a specified valence*] Having a valence of two. Same as bivalent. (deye VAY lent)

dizygotic [*di-, two + zyg, pair + -otic*] Derived from two eggs fertilized at the same time, as fraternal twins. See monozygotic, zygote, and polyembryony. (deye' zeye GOT ik)

hydrocortisone [*dihydro-, addition of two hydrogen atoms & cortisone*] A steroid hormone, $C_{21}H_{30}O_5$, produced by the adrenal cortex that has applications and effects similar to cortisone, $C_{21}H_{28}O_5$. So named because it contains two more hydrogen atoms than cortisone. (heye' druh KORT uh zohn')

neodymium [*neo, new & (di)dymium*] A rare-earth metallic element used in certain alloys, in lasers, and for coloring glass. So named because it is split from didymium. See didymium. (nee' oh DIM ee um)

du-, duo-   two

dodeca- [*duo-, two + deca, ten*] A word root meaning "twelve." (doh DEK uh)

dodecagon [*dodeca-, twelve + gon, angle*] A closed plane figure with twelve angles and twelve sides. (doh DEK uh gon')

dodecahedron [*dodeca-, twelve + -hedron, surface*] A solid figure with twelve plane surfaces. (doh' dek' uh HEE drun)

dodecaphonic [*dodeca-, twelve + phon, sound + -ic*] Pertaining to a system of music based on all twelve tones of the chromatic scale. (doh' dek' uh FON ik)

dodecasyllable [*dodeca-, twelve & syllable*] A line of verse with twelve syllables. (doh' dek' uh SIL uh bul)

duad [*du-, two + -ad, group*] A group of two units or objects. Pair. (DOO ad)

dual [*du-, two + -al*] 1.Consisting of two similar elements or parts. 2.Having a double nature or character. (DOO ul)

duet [*du-, two + -et*] A musical composition or performance involving two voices or instruments. See trio (def. 1). (doo ET)

duo [*duo-, two*] 1.A musical composition or performance involving two voices or instruments. Same as duet. 2.A pair of persons or things normally thought of as being together. See trio (def. 2). (DOO oh)

duodec- [*duo-, two + dec, ten*] A word root meaning "twelve." (DOO oh des')

duodecillion [*duodec-, twelve + (m)ill, thousand + -ion*] A number expressed as 1 followed by 39 zeros, which is 12 groups of three zeros after 1,000. (doo' oh dih SIL yun)

duodecimal [*duodec-, twelve + -imal*] 1.Pertaining to a number system of base twelve. 2.Pertaining to the number *12* or to twelfths. (doo' oh DES uh mul)

duodecimo [*Ltn > duodecimo, twelfth*] 1.A page size equal to one twelfth of a printer's sheet. 2.A book size in which each page is one twelfth of a printer's sheet. (doo' oh DES ih moh')

duodenum [*duodec-, twelve + -um*] The first portion of the small intestine between the lower end of the stomach and the jejunum. So named for its length, which is about the width of twelve fingers. (doo' oh DEE num)

duologue [*duo-, two + log, discourse*] A conversation between two people. See dialogue (def. 1) and trialogue. (DOO uh log')

duopoly [*duo-, two + Grk > polein, to sell + -y*] Ownership or control of a commodity or service by only two sellers. See monopoly (def. 1). (doo OP uh lee)

duple [*du-, two + -ple, times*] 1.Twofold. Double. Same as duplex (def. 1). 2.In music, having two, or a multiple of two, beats to the measure. See quadruple and sextuple. (DOO pul)

duplex [*du-, two + -plex, fold*] 1.Twofold. Double. 2.Capable of simultaneous communication in opposite directions using a common link. (DOO pleks)

duplicate [*du-, two + plic, fold + -ate*] 1.To multiply by two. (DOO plih kayt' {verb}) 2.A set of two identical copies. (DOO plih kut {noun})

duplicity [*du-, two + plic, fold + -ity*] Deliberate deception in speech or conduct. Double-dealing. (doo PLIS ih tee)

tri-   three

triad [*tri-, three + -ad, group*] 1.A group of three persons, things, etc. 2.A basic musical chord of three tones, consisting of a fundamental tone with its major or minor third and a perfect fifth. (TREYE ad)

trialogue [*tri-, three & (di)alogue*] A conversation between three people or three groups of people. See duologue and dialogue (def. 1). (TREYE uh log')

triangle [*tri-, three & angle*] A closed plane figure with three angles and three sides. (TREYE ang' gul)

triarchy [*tri-, three + arch, rule + -y*] Government by three rulers. Triumvirate. See triumvirate. (TREYE ahr' kee)

triathlon [*tri-, three + Grk > athlon, contest*] An athletic contest that includes swimming, bicycling, and running. See biathlon, pentathlon, and decathlon. (treye ATH lon)

triaxial [*tri-, three + ax, axis + -ial*] Having three axes, as certain crystals. (treye AK see ul)

tribrach [*tri-, three + brachy, short*] A metrical foot consisting of three short syllables. See dactyl (def. 2) and anapest. (TREYE brak)

tricameral [*tri-, three & cameral*] Composed of three legislative chambers. See unicameral and bicameral. (treye KAM ur ul)

tricentennial [*tri-, three + cent, hundred + enn, years + -ial*] Occurring once every three hundred years. (treye' sen TEN ee ul)

triceps [*tri-, three + Ltn > caput, head*] A muscle with three heads, especially the large muscle at the back of the upper arm. See biceps and quadriceps. (TREYE seps)

trichloride [*tri-, three & chloride*] A chloride containing three atoms of chlorine per molecule. (treye KLOR eyed')

trichotomy [*tri-, three & (di)chotomy*] 1.Division into three parts, branches, kinds, etc. See dichotomy and polychotomy. 2.The division of man into body, soul, and spirit. (treye KOT uh mee)

trichroism [*tri-, three* + *chros, color* + *-ism*] The property of some crystals to display three different colors when viewed from three different directions. See dichroism (def. 1) and pleochroism. (TREYE kroh iz' um)

trichromatic [*tri-, three* + *chromat, color* + *-ic*] 1.Having or displaying three colors, as in color photography and printing. 2.Capable of distinguishing all three primary colors, as in normal vision. The three primary colors are red, green, and blue. (treye' kroh MAT ik)

triclinic [*tri-, three* + *clin, slope* + *-ic*] Pertaining to a crystal whose structure is characterized by three unequal axes intersecting at oblique angles. See orthorhombic. (treye KLIN ik)

tricorn [*tri-, three* + *corn, horn*] 1.Having three horns or hornlike projections. 2.A hat with the brim turned up on three sides. (TREYE korn)

tricuspid [*tri-, three* + *Ltn > cuspis, point* + *-id*] Any of twelve adult human teeth with triple-pointed crowns for grinding food. See bicuspid. (treye KUS pid)

tricycle [*tri-, three* + *cycl, wheel*] A vehicle with three wheels, usually propelled by the rider pushing pedals. (TREYE sik' ul)

tridentate [*tri-, three* + *dent, teeth* + *-ate*] Having three teeth or toothlike processes. (treye DEN tayt')

triennial [*tri-, three* + *enn, years* + *-ial*] 1.Occurring once every three years. 2.Lasting or continuing for three years. (treye EN ee ul)

triennium [*tri-, three* + *enn, years* + *-ium*] A period of three years. (treye EN ee um)

trierarch [*tri-, three* + *Grk > eres, to row* + *arch, chief*] The commander of a trireme. See trireme. (TREYE uh rahrk')

trifecta [*tri-, three* & *(per)fecta*] A form of gambling, especially on horse races, in which the bettor must pick the first three winners in the correct sequence. See perfecta. (treye FEK tuh)

trifid [*tri-, three* + *fid, split*] Divided into three parts or lobes by clefts. (TREYE fid)

trifocal [*tri-, three* & *focal*] Having three focal lengths. See bifocal. (treye FOH kul)

trifoliate [*tri-, three* + *foli, leaf* + *-ate*] Having three leaves or leaflike parts. (treye FOH lee it)

trifurcate [*tri-, three* + *Ltn > furca, fork* + *-ate*] Having three branches or forks. See bifurcate. (treye FUR kayt')

trigeminal [*tri-, three* + *Ltn > geminus, double* + *-al*] Pertaining to either of the fifth and largest pair of cranial nerves, each of which divides into three branches having motor and sensory functions in the head and face. (treye JEM uh nul)

trigonal [*tri-, three* + *gon, angle* + *-al*] Triangular. (TRIG uh nul)

trigonometry [*tri-, three* + *gono, angle* + *-metry, science of measuring*] The branch of mathematics dealing with the study of the applications and properties of triangles, especially right triangles. (trig' uh NOM ih tree)

trigraph [*tri-, three* + *graph, writing*] A combination of three contiguous letters representing a single speech sound, as the "eau" in *chateau*. See digraph (def. 1) and triphthong. (TREYE graf)

trihedron [*tri-, three* + *-hedron, surface*] The figure formed by three intersecting plane surfaces. See dihedral. (treye HEE drun)

trilateral [*tri-, three* + *Ltn > latus, side* + *-al*] Having three sides. (treye LAT ur ul)

trilingual [*tri-, three* + *lingu, language* + *-al*] 1.Able to use three languages with nearly equal fluency. 2.Expressed in or involving three languages. (treye LING gwul)

triliteral [*tri-, three* + *liter, letter* + *-al*] Consisting of three letters, especially of three consonants, as most roots of Semitic languages. (treye LIT ur ul)

trillion [*tri-, three* + *(m)ill, thousand* + *-ion*] A number expressed as 1 followed by 12 zeros, which is 3 groups of three zeros after 1,000. (TRIL yun)

trilobate [*tri-, three* + *lob, lobe* + *-ate*] Divided into three lobes. (treye LOH bayt')

trilobite [*tri-, three* + *lob, lobe* + *-ite*] Any of a large group of extinct marine arthropods having a segmented body divided into three vertical lobes. (TREYE luh beyet')

trilogy [*tri-, three* + *log, discourse* + *y*] A series of three related plays, novels, or other literary works. See tetralogy. (TRIL uh jee)

trimaran [*tri-, three* & *(cata)maran*] A boat with three separate hulls side by side. (TREYE muh ran')

trimer [*tri-, three* + *mer, part*] A compound consisting of three identical molecules linked together. See monomer, dimer, and polymer. (TREYE mer)

trimester [*tri-, three* + *men, month* + *-er*] 1.A period of three months. 2.One of the three terms into which some colleges and universities divide the academic year. (treye MES ter)

trimeter [*tri-, three* & *meter*] A line of verse consisting of three metrical feet. (TRIM et er)

trimetrogon [*tri-, three* + *metro, to measure* + *gon, angle*] A system of aerial topographic mapping and photography using three wide-angle cameras, one pointing downward and the other two pointing at 60 degree angles to it. (treye MET ruh gon')

trimonthly [*tri-, three* & *month* & *-ly*] Occurring once every three months. (treye MUNTH lee)

trimorph [*tri-, three* + *morph, form*] A substance occurring in three structurally distinct forms. (TREYE morf)

trinomial [*tri-, three* + *nom, name* + *-ial*] 1.A mathematical expression consisting of three terms. 2.In taxonomy, a three-part name designating the genus, species, and subspecies of an organism. See monomial, binomial, and polynomial. (treye NOH mee ul)

trio [*tri-, three*] 1.A musical composition or performance involving three voices or instruments. See duet. 2.A group of three persons or things normally thought of as being together. See duo (def. 2). (TREE oh)

trioecious [*tri-, three* + *Grk > oikos, house* + *-ious*] Pertaining to a species having male, female, and bisexual flowers occurring on separate plants. See monoecious, dioecious, and synoecious. (treye EE shus)

triose [*tri-, three* + *-ose, carbohydrate*] A monosaccharide with three carbon atoms per molecule. See monosaccharide. (TREYE ohs)

trioxide [*tri-, three* + *ox, oxygen* + *-ide*] An oxide containing three oxygen atoms per molecule. (treye OK seyed')

tripartite [*tri-, three* & *partite*] 1.Consisting of three parts. 2.Shared by or involving three parties. (treye PAHR teyet')

tri-

triphibian [*tri-, three & (am)phibian*] Able to operate or function in water, on land, or in the air. See amphibian. (treye FIB ee un)

triphthong [*tri-, three + phthong, sound*] 1.Three contiguous vowels representing a single vowel sound, as the "eau" in *beau*. 2.A combination of three vowel sounds in one syllable. See monophthong, diphthong, and trigraph. (TRIF thong)

triplane [*tri-, three & plane*] An early type of airplane with three main pairs of wings arranged one above the other. See monoplane and biplane. (TREYE playn)

triple [*tri-, three + -ple, times*] 1.Threefold. Consisting of three parts. 2.Three times as great. (TRIP ul)

triplet [*tri-, three + -ple, times + -et*] 1.Each of three offspring born at a single birth. 2.Any group or combination of three. 3.Three successive lines of verse, usually rhyming and of the same length. (TRIP lit)

triplicate [*tri-, three + plic, fold + -ate*] 1.To multiply by three. (TRIP lih kayt' {verb}) 2.A set of three identical copies. (TRIP lih kut {noun})

triploblastic [*tripl(e) & blast, cell layer + -ic*] Pertaining to animals, including humans, whose embryo consists of three germ cell layers: the endoderm, mesoderm, and ectoderm. Includes all animals except cnidarians, sponges, and mesozoans. See diploblastic (def. 1). (trip' loh BLAS tik)

triploid [*tri-, three + -ploid, number of chromosomes*] Pertaining to cells with a chromosome number three times the basic haploid number. (TRIP loid)

tripod [*tri-, three + pod, feet*] Any three-legged support, as for a camera, transit, etc. (TREYE pod)

tripody [*tri-, three + pod, feet + -y*] A prosodic measure consisting of three feet. (TRIP uh dee)

trireme [*tri-, three + Ltn > remus, oar*] An ancient Greek or Roman ship with three rows of oars, one above the other, on each side. See trierarch. (TREYE reem)

trisaccharide [*tri-, three & saccharide*] Any of a class of sugars that yield three monosaccharides on hydrolysis, as raffinose. (treye SAK uh reyed')

trisect [*tri-, three + sect, to cut*] To divide or cut into three equal parts. (TREYE sekt)

triskaidekaphobia [*tri-, three + kai, and + deka, ten + -phobia, fear*] Fear of the number 13. (tris' keye dek' uh FOH bee uh)

trisoctahedron [*Grk > tris, three times + octa, eight + -hedron, surface*] A solid figure with twenty-four plane surfaces that correspond in groups of three to the faces of an octahedron. See octahedron. (tris ok' tuh HEE drun)

trisomic [*tri-, three + some, chromosome + -ic*] Pertaining to a cell or individual having one set of chromosomes that contains an extra chromosome in addition to the normal two. (treye SOH mik)

tristich [*tri-, three & stich {line of verse}*] A stanza or poem consisting of three lines. (TRIS tik)

trisyllable [*tri-, three & syllable*] A word with three syllables. (TREYE sil' uh bul)

tritanopia [*Grk > tritos, third + an-, without + -opia, visual condition*] A visual defect in which the retina fails to respond to the color blue. So named from the blindness to blue, which is regarded as the third primary color. See protanopia and deuteranopia. (treye' tuh NOH pee uh)

tritheism [*tri-, three + the, god + -ism*] Belief in three gods; specifically, the belief that the Father, Son, and Holy Ghost are three separate and distinct gods. (TREYE thee iz' um)

tritone [*tri-, three & tone*] A musical interval containing three whole tones. (TREYE tohn)

triumvirate [*tri-, three + Ltn > vir, men + -ate*] 1.Government by three persons. 2.An association of three persons who share authority. See triarchy. (treye UM vur it)

triune [*tri-, three + uni, one*] Consisting of three in one, especially with reference to the Trinity. (TREYE yoon)

trivalent [*tri-, three + -valent, having a specified valence*] Having a valence of three. (treye VAY lent)

triweekly [*tri-, three & week & -ly*] Occurring once every three weeks. (treye WEEK lee)

quadr, quadri, quadru, quadra   four

quadragenarian [*Ltn > quadragenarius, containing forty*] A person between 40 and 49 years of age. (kwod' ruh juh NEHR ee un)

Quadragesima [*Ltn > quadraginta, forty*] The 1st Sunday of Lent. So named for its date of occurrence which is approximately 40 days before Easter. See Quinquagesima, Sexagesima, and Septuagesima. (kwod' ruh JES ih muh)

quadrangle [*quadr, four & angle*] 1.A closed plane figure with four angles and four sides. Same as quadrilateral (def. 2). 2.A rectangular area surrounded by buildings on all four sides. (KWOD rang' gul)

quadrant [*quadr, four + -ant*] 1.An arc of 90 degrees, which is one fourth of the circumference of a circle. See sextant (def. 1) and octant (def. 1). 2.Any of the four areas into which a plane is divided by rectangular, coordinate axes. (KWOD runt)

quadraphonic [*quadra, four + phon, sound + -ic*] Using four channels for sound reproduction, each from a separate source. See stereophonic. (kwod' ruh FON ik)

quadratic [*quadra, four + -tic*] 1.Square. 2.In algebra, pertaining to or involving quantities that are raised to the second power. (kwah DRAT ik)

quadrennial [*quadr, four + enn, years + -ial*] 1.Occurring once every four years. 2.Lasting or continuing for four years. (kwah DREN ee ul)

quadrennium [*quadr, four + enn, years + -ium*] A period of four years. (kwah DREN ee um)

quadricentennial [*quadri, four + cent, hundred + enn, years + -ial*] Occurring once every four hundred years. (kwod' ruh sen TEN ee ul)

quadriceps [*quadri, four + Ltn > caput, head*] A muscle with four heads, especially the large muscle at the front of the thigh. See biceps and triceps. (KWOD ruh seps')

quadrifid [*quadri, four + fid, split*] Divided into four parts or lobes by clefts. (KWOD ruh fid')

quadrilateral [*quadri, four + Ltn > latus, side + -al*] 1.Having four sides. 2.A closed plane figure with four angles and four sides. (kwod' ruh LAT ur ul)

quadrille [*quadr, four*] A square dance consisting of five parts or figures and performed by four couples. (kwah DRIL)

quadrillion [*quadr, four* + *(m)ill, thousand* + *-ion*] A number expressed as 1 followed by 15 zeros, which is 4 groups of three zeros after 1,000. (kwah DRIL yun)

quadripartite [*quadri, four & partite*] 1.Consisting of four parts. 2.Shared by or involving four parties. (kwod' ruh PAHR teyet')

quadriplegia [*quadri, four* + *-plegia, paralysis*] Paralysis affecting all four extremities of the body. See paraplegia. (kwod' ruh PLEE jee uh)

quadrisect [*quadri, four* + *sect, to cut*] To divide or cut into four equal parts. (KWOD ruh sekt')

quadrivalent [*quadri, four* + *-valent, having a specified valence*] Having a valence of four. Same as tetravalent. (kwod' ruh VAY lent)

quadrivium [*quadri, four* + *via, road* + *-um*] The courses in arithmetic, geometry, astronomy, and music which were considered to be the more advanced of the seven liberal arts in medieval universities. (kwah DRIV ee um)

quadrumanous [*quadru, four* + *man, hand* + *-ous*] Having four feet that resemble and function as hands, as primates other than humans. Four-handed. (kwah DROO muh nus)

quadruped [*quadru, four* + *ped, feet*] An animal with four feet. (KWOD ruh ped')

quadruple [*quadru, four* + *-ple, times*] 1.Fourfold. Consisting of four parts. 2.Four times as great. 3.In music, having four beats to the measure with the first and third being accented. See duple and sextuple. (kwah DROO pul)

quadruplet [*quadru, four* + *-ple, times* + *-et*] 1.Each of four offspring born at a single birth. 2.Any group or combination of four. (kwah DROOP lit)

quadruplicate [*quadru, four* + *plic, fold* + *-ate*] 1.To multiply by four. (kwah DROO plih kayt' {verb}) 2.A set of four identical copies. (kwah DROO plih kut {noun})

quart   fourth

biquarterly [*bi-, two & quarter & -ly*] Occurring twice in a three month period. (beye KWORT ur lee)

forequarter [*fore-, before & quarter*] The front half of half a carcass, as of beef, lamb, etc. See hindquarter. (FOR kwort' ur)

hindquarter [*hind & quarter*] The back half of half a carcass, as of beef, lamb, etc. See forequarter. (HEYEND kwort' ur)

quart [*quart, fourth*] A unit of volume equal to one-fourth of a gallon or two pints. (kwort)

quartan [*quart, fourth* + *-an*] Occurring every fourth day, as a fever. (KWORT n)

quarter [*quart, fourth* + *-er*] 1.A one-fourth part of something. 2.To divide into four equal or nearly equal parts. (KWORT ur)

quarter horse [*quarter & horse*] A lean, strong saddle horse capable of reaching high speed in a short distance. So named from the quarter-mile tracks on which it was raced. (KWORT ur hors)

quarterly [*quarter & -ly*] Occurring or done at the end of a three month period. (KWORT ur lee)

quartern [*quart, fourth* + *-ern*] A one-fourth part of something. Quarter. (KWORT urn)

quartet [*quart, fourth* + *-et*] 1.A musical composition or performance involving four voices or instruments. 2.A group of four persons or things. (kwor TET)

quartette [*quart, fourth* + *-ette*] 1.A musical composition or performance involving four voices or instruments. 2.A group of four persons or things. Same as quartet. (kwor TET)

quartic [*quart, fourth* + *-ic*] Pertaining to the fourth degree. (KWORT ik)

quartile [*quart, fourth* + *-ile*] Any of the three values that divide a statistical frequency distribution into four equal parts. See quintile (def. 2), decile, and percentile. (KWOR teyel)

quarto [*quart, fourth*] 1.A page size equal to one fourth of a printer's sheet. 2.A book size in which each page is one fourth of a printer's sheet. (KWOR toh)

tetra-   four

tetrachloride [*tetra-, four & chloride*] A chloride containing four atoms of chlorine per molecule. (tet' ruh KLOR eyed')

tetrachord [*tetra-, four & chord {tone}*] In music, a diatonic series of four consecutive tones. Half an octave. See octave. (TET ruh kord')

tetrad [*tetra-, four* + *-ad, group*] 1.A group of four. 2.A group of four chromatids formed during meiosis by the longitudinal division of a homologous pair of chromosomes. (TET rad)

tetradynamous [*tetra-, four* + *dynam, strength* + *-ous*] Having four long stamens and two somewhat shorter stamens. (tet' ruh DEYE nuh mus)

tetragon [*tetra-, four* + *gon, angle*] A closed plane figure with four angles and four sides. (TET ruh gon')

tetragrammaton [*tetra-, four* + *gramma, letter* + *-on*] The four consonants of the ancient Hebrew name for God, usually transliterated as YHWH or JHVH. (tet' ruh GRAM uh tahn')

tetrahedrite [*tetra-, four* + *-hedron, surface* + *-ite, mineral*] A grayish-black mineral occurring in tetrahedral crystals, used as an ore of copper or silver and often containing other elements. (tet' ruh HEE dreyet')

tetrahedron [*tetra-, four* + *-hedron, surface*] A solid figure with four plane surfaces. A triangular pyramid. (tet' ruh HEE drun)

tetralogy [*tetra-, four* + *log, discourse* + *-y*] A series of four related plays, novels, or other literary works. See trilogy. (teh TROL uh jee)

tetrameter [*tetra-, four & meter*] A line of verse consisting of four metrical feet. (tch TRAM et er)

tetraploid [*tetra-, four* + *-ploid, number of chromosomes*] Pertaining to cells with a chromosome number four times the basic haploid number. (TET ruh ploid')

tetrapod [*tetra-, four* + *pod, feet*] Any vertebrate with four limbs, including mammals, birds, amphibians, and reptiles. (TET ruh pod')

tetrapody [*tetra-, four* + *pod, feet* + *-y*] A prosodic measure consisting of four feet. (teh TRAP uh dee)

tetrapterous [*tetra-, four* + *pter, wing* + *-ous*] Having four wings or winglike appendages, as many insects. (teh TRAP ter us)

tetrarch [*tetra-, four* + *arch, rule*] 1.The ruler of one of four provinces in the ancient Roman Empire. 2.A subordinate governor, ruler, etc. (TET rahrk)

tetrarchy [*tetra-, four* + *arch, rule* + *-y*] 1.Government by four rulers. 2.The territory under the jurisdiction of a tetrarch. (TET rahr' kee)

tetra-

tetraspore [*tetra-, four & spore*] One of a group of four haploid, asexual spores produced in red algae. (TET ruh spor')

tetrastich [*tetra-, four & stich {line of verse}*] A stanza or poem consisting of four lines. (TET ruh stik')

tetrasyllable [*tetra-, four & syllable*] A word with four syllables. (TET ruh sil' uh bul)

tetravalent [*tetra-, four + -valent, having a specified valence*] Having a valence of four. (tet' ruh VAY lent)

tetrose [*tetra-, four + -ose, carbohydrate*] A monosaccharide with four carbon atoms per molecule. See monosaccharide. (TET rohs)

tetroxide [*tetra-, four + ox, oxygen + -ide*] An oxide containing four oxygen atoms per molecule. (teh TROK seyed')

penta-, pent-　five

pentacle [*penta-, five + -cle*] A five-pointed star previously used as a symbolic figure in magic and formed by connecting five straight lines of equal length so that they form a pentagon in the center. Same as pentagram. (PENT uh kul)

pentad [*pent-, five + -ad, group*] A group or series of five. (PEN tad)

pentadactyl [*penta-, five + dactyl, finger*] Having five fingers or toes on each hand or foot. (pent' uh DAK tul)

pentagon [*penta-, five + gon, angle*] A closed plane figure with five angles and five sides. (PENT uh gon')

pentagram [*penta-, five + gram, to draw*] A five-pointed star previously used as a symbolic figure in magic and formed by connecting five straight lines of equal length so that they form a pentagon in the center. See hexagram. (PENT uh gram')

pentahedron [*penta-, five + -hedron, surface*] A solid figure with five plane surfaces. (pent' uh HEE drun)

pentameter [*penta-, five & meter*] A line of verse consisting of five metrical feet. (pen TAM et er)

pentaploid [*penta-, five + -ploid, number of chromosomes*] Pertaining to cells with a chromosome number five times the basic haploid number. (PENT uh ploid')

pentapody [*penta-, five + pod, feet + -y*] A prosodic measure consisting of five feet. (pen TAP uh dee)

pentarchy [*pent-, five + arch, rule + -y*] 1.Government by five rulers. 2.A group of five states, each having its own ruler. (PEN tahr' kee)

pentastich [*penta-, five & stich {line of verse}*] A stanza or poem consisting of five lines. (PENT uh stik')

pentasyllable [*penta-, five & syllable*] A line of verse with five syllables. (PENT uh sil' uh bul)

Pentateuch [*penta-, five + Grk > teuchos, book*] The first five books of the Old Testament, consisting of Genesis, Exodus, Leviticus, Numbers, and Deuteronomy. (PENT uh took')

pentathlon [*pent-, five + Grk > athlon, contest*] An athletic contest that includes five separate events, all five of which are performed by each participant. See biathlon, triathlon, and decathlon. (pen TATH lon)

pentavalent [*penta-, five + -valent, having a specified valence*] Having a valence of five. (pent' uh VAY lent)

pentose [*pent-, five + -ose, carbohydrate*] A monosaccharide with five carbon atoms per molecule. See monosaccharide. (PEN tohs)

pentoxide [*pent-, five + ox, oxygen + -ide*] An oxide containing five oxygen atoms per molecule. (pent OK seyed')

quin, quint, quintu, quinque　five, fifth

cinquecento [*mill, thousand + quinque, five + cent, hundred*] Short for millecinquecento. The 16th century (1500-1599) period of Italian art and literature. See trecento, quattrocento, and seicento. (ching' kwih CHEN toh)

quincentennial [*quin, five + cent, hundred + enn, years + -ial*] Occurring once every five hundred years. (kwin' sen TEN ee ul)

quindecagon [*quin, five + deca, ten + gon, angle*] A closed plane figure with fifteen angles and fifteen sides. (kwin DEK uh gon')

quindecennial [*quin, five + dec, ten + enn, years + -ial*] 1.Occurring once every fifteen years. 2.Lasting or continuing for fifteen years. (kwin' dih SEN ee ul)

quindecillion [*quin, five + dec, ten + (m)ill, thousand + -ion*] A number expressed as 1 followed by 48 zeros, which is 15 groups of three zeros after 1,000. (kwin' dih SIL yun)

quinquagenarian [*Ltn > quinquagenarius, containing fifty*] A person between 50 and 59 years of age. (kwin' kwuh juh NEHR ee un)

Quinquagesima [*Ltn > quinquaginta, fifty*] The 1st Sunday before Lent. Shrove Sunday. So named for its date of occurrence which is approximately 50 days before Easter. See Quadragesima, Sexagesima and Septuagesima. (kwin' kwuh JES ih muh)

quinquennial [*quinque, five + enn, years + -ial*] 1.Occurring once every five years. 2.Lasting or continuing for five years. (kwin KWEN ee ul)

quinquennium [*quinque, five + enn, years + -ium*] A period of five years. (kwin KWEN ee um)

quinquevalent [*quinque, five + -valent, having a specified valence*] Having a valence of five. Same as pentavalent. (kwin' kwuh VAY lent)

quintessence [*quint, fifth & essence*] 1.The purest or most essential part of some quality or substance. Pure essence. 2.The most perfect example of something. See epitome (def. 1). 3.In ancient and medieval philosophy, a fifth element in addition to the four elements of earth, air, fire, and water, that composed the heavenly bodies and pervaded all things. (kwin TES ens)

quintet [*quint, five + -et*] 1.A musical composition or performance involving five voices or instruments. 2.A group of five persons or things. (kwin TET)

quintette [*quint, five + -ette*] 1.A musical composition or performance involving five voices or instruments. 2.A group of five persons or things. Same as quintet. (kwin TET)

quintile [*quint, five + -ile*] 1.In astrology, the aspect of two celestial bodies that are 72 degrees, or one fifth of a circle, apart. See sextile. 2.Any of the four values that divide a statistical frequency distribution into five equal parts. See quartile, decile, and percentile. (KWIN teyel)

quintillion [*quint, five + (m)ill, thousand + -ion*] A number expressed as 1 followed by 18 zeros, which is 5 groups of three zeros after 1,000. (kwin TIL yun) quintuple [*quintu, five* + *-ple, times*] 1.Fivefold. Consisting of five parts. 2.Five times as great. (kwin TOO pul)

quintuplet [*quintu, five* + *-ple, times* + *-et*] 1.Each of five offspring born at a single birth. 2.Any group or combination of five. (kwin TUP lit)

quintuplicate [*quintu, five* + *plic, fold* + *-ate*] 1.To multiply by five. (kwin TOO plih kayt' {verb}) 2.A set of five identical copies. (kwin TOO plih kut {noun})

hexa-, hex-   six

hexachord [*hexa-, six* & *chord {tone}*] In medieval music, a diatonic series of six consecutive tones with a semitone between the third and fourth tones only. (HEKS uh kord')

hexad [*hex-, six* + *-ad, group*] A group or series of six. (HEKS ad)

hexadecimal [*hexa-, six* + *dec, ten* + *-imal*] Pertaining to a number system of base sixteen. (heks' uh DES uh mul)

hexagon [*hexa-, six* + *gon, angle*] A closed plane figure with six angles and six sides. (HEKS uh gon')

hexagram [*hexa-, six* + *gram, to draw*] A six-pointed star formed by connecting six straight lines of equal length so that they form a hexagon in the center. See pentagram. (HEKS uh gram')

hexahedron [*hexa-, six* + *-hedron, surface*] A solid figure with six plane surfaces, as a cube. (heks' uh HEE drun)

hexameter [*hexa-, six* & *meter*] A line of verse consisting of six metrical feet; specifically, a six-foot dactylic line consisting of five dactyls and a spondee or trochee. (heks AM et er)

hexaploid [*hexa-, six* + *-ploid, number of chromosomes*] Pertaining to cells with a chromosome number six times the basic haploid number. (HEKS uh ploid')

hexapod [*hexa-, six* + *pod, feet*] Any of a large class of arthropods with three pairs of legs, three body segments, and usually capable of flight. Insect. (HEKS uh pod')

hexapody [*hexa-, six* + *pod, feet* + *-y*] A prosodic measure consisting of six feet. (heks AP uh dee)

hexastich [*hexa-, six* & *stich {line of verse}*] A stanza or poem consisting of six lines. (HEKS uh stik')

hexasyllable [*hexa-, six* & *syllable*] A line of verse with six syllables. (HEKS uh sil' uh bul)

Hexateuch [*hexa-, six* + *Grk* > *teuchos, book*] The first six books of the Old Testament. (HEKS uh took')

hexavalent [*hexa-, six* + *-valent, having a specified valence*] Having a valence of six. (heks' uh VAY lent)

hexose [*hex-, six* + *-ose, carbohydrate*] A monosaccharide with six carbon atoms per molecule. See monosaccharide. (HEKS ohs)

sex-   six

seicento [*mill, thousand* + *sex, six* + *cent, hundred*] Short for milleseicento. The 17th century (1600-1699) period of Italian art and literature. See trecento, quattrocento, and cinquecento. (say CHEN toh)

sexagenarian [*Ltn* > *sexagenarius, containing sixty*] A person between 60 and 69 years of age. (seks' uh juh NEHR ee un)

Sexagesima [*Ltn* > *sexaginta, sixty*] The 2nd Sunday before Lent. So named for its date of occurrence which is approximately 60 days before Easter. See Quadragesima, Quinquagesima and Septuagesima. (seks' uh JES ih muh)

sexcentenary [*sex-, six* + *cent, hundred* + *enn, years* + *-ary*] Occurring once every six hundred years. (seks' sen TEN uh ree)

sexdecillion [*sex-, six* + *dec, ten* + *(m)ill, thousand* + *-ion*] A number expressed as 1 followed by 51 zeros, which is 16 groups of three zeros after 1,000. (seks' dih SIL yun)

sexennial [*sex-, six* + *enn, years* + *-ial*] 1.Occurring once every six years. 2.Lasting or continuing for six years. (seks EN ee ul)

sext [*sex-, six*] The fourth of the seven canonical hours originally observed at noon, which was the sixth hour of the day counting from 6 A.M. (sekst)

sextant [*sex-, six* + *-ant*] 1.An arc of 60 degrees, which is one sixth of the circumference of a circle. See quadrant (def. 1) and octant (def. 1). 2.A navigational instrument for determining latitude by measuring the altitudes of celestial bodies. See astrolabe and octant (def. 2). (SEKS tunt)

sextet [*sex-, six* + *-et*] 1.A musical composition or performance involving six voices or instruments. 2.A group of six persons or things. (seks TET)

sextette [*sex-, six* + *-ette*] 1.A musical composition or performance involving six voices or instruments. 2.A group of six persons or things. Same as sextet. (seks TET)

sextile [*Ltn* > *sextus, sixth* + *-ile*] In astrology, the aspect of two celestial bodies that are 60 degrees, or one sixth of a circle, apart. See quintile (def. 1). (SEKS teyel)

sextillion [*sex-, six* + *(m)ill, thousand* + *-ion*] A number expressed as 1 followed by 21 zeros, which is 6 groups of three zeros after 1,000. (seks TIL yun)

sextodecimo [*Ltn* > *sextodecimo, sixteenth*] 1.A page size equal to one sixteenth of a printer's sheet. 2.A book size in which each page is one sixteenth of a printer's sheet. (seks' toh DES ih moh')

sextuple [*sex-, six* + *-ple, times*] 1.Sixfold. Consisting of six parts. 2.Six times as great. 3.In music, having six beats to the measure. See duple and quadruple. (seks TOO pul)

sextuplet [*sex-, six* + *-ple, times* + *-et*] 1.Each of six offspring born at a single birth. 2.Any group or combination of six. (seks TUP lit)

hepta-, hept-   seven

heptad [*hept-, seven* + *-ad, group*] A group or series of seven. (HEP tad)

heptagon [*hepta-, seven* + *gon, angle*] A closed plane figure with seven angles and seven sides. (HEP tuh gon')

heptahedron [*hepta-, seven* + *-hedron, surface*] A solid figure with seven plane surfaces. (hep' tuh HEE drun)

heptameter [*hepta-, seven* & *meter*] A line of verse consisting of seven metrical feet. (hep TAM et er)

heptaploid [*hepta-, seven* + *-ploid, number of chromosomes*] Pertaining to cells with a chromosome number seven times the basic haploid number. (HEP tuh ploid')

heptapody [*hepta-, seven* + *pod, feet* + *-y*] A prosodic measure consisting of seven feet. (hep TAP uh dee)

heptarchy [*hept-, seven* + *arch, rule* + *-y*] 1.Government by seven rulers. 2.The supposed seven Anglo-Saxon kingdoms existing in England during the 7th and 8th centuries. (HEP tahr' kee)

heptastich [*hepta-, seven* & *stich {line of verse}*] A stanza or poem consisting of seven lines. (HEP tuh stik')

Heptateuch [*hepta-, seven* + *Grk > teuchos, book*] The first seven books of the Old Testament. (HEP tuh took')

heptavalent [*hepta-, seven* + *-valent, having a specified valence*] Having a valence of seven. (hep' tuh VAY lent)

heptose [*hept-, seven* + *-ose, carbohydrate*] A monosaccharide with seven carbon atoms per molecule. See monosaccharide. (HEP tohs)

sept- seven

September [*Ltn > septem, seven* + *-ber*] The 9th month of the year. So named from the 7th month of the early Roman calendar, which began with March. See October, November, and December. (sep TEM ber)

septendecillion [*sept-, seven* + *dec, ten* + *(m)ill, thousand* + *-ion*] A number expressed as 1 followed by 54 zeros, which is 17 groups of three zeros after 1,000. (sep' ten' dih SIL yun)

septennial [*sept-, seven* + *enn, years* + *-ial*] 1.Occurring once every seven years. 2.Lasting or continuing for seven years. (sep TEN ee ul)

septet [*sept-, seven* + *-et*] 1.A musical composition or performance involving seven voices or instruments. 2.A group of seven persons or things. (sep TET)

septette [*sept-, seven* + *-ette*] 1.A musical composition or performance involving seven voices or instruments. 2.A group of seven persons or things. Same as septet. (sep TET)

septillion [*sept-, seven* + *(m)ill, thousand* + *-ion*] A number expressed as 1 followed by 24 zeros, which is 7 groups of three zeros after 1,000. (sep TIL yun)

septisyllable [*sept-, seven* & *syllable*] A line of verse with seven syllables. (SEP tuh sil' uh bul)

septuagenarian [*Ltn > septuagenarius, containing seventy*] A person between 70 and 79 years of age. (sep' too' uh juh NEHR ee un)

Septuagesima [*Ltn > septuaginta, seventy*] The 3rd Sunday before Lent. So named for its date of occurrence which is approximately 70 days before Easter. See Quadragesima, Quinquagesima and Sexagesima. (sep' too' uh JES ih muh)

Septuagint [*Ltn > septuaginta, seventy*] The pre-Christian Greek translation of the Old Testament. So named because it was supposedly done by seventy Jewish scholars. (sep TOO uh jint')

septuple [*sept-, seven* + *-ple, times*] 1.Sevenfold. Consisting of seven parts. 2.Seven times as great. (sep TOO pul)

octa-, oct-, octo- eight

octad [*oct-, eight* + *-ad, group*] A group or series of eight. (OK tad)

octagon [*octa-, eight* + *gon, angle*] A closed plane figure with eight angles and eight sides. (OK tuh gon')

octahedron [*octa-, eight* + *-hedron, surface*] A solid figure with eight plane surfaces. (ok' tuh HEE drun)

octal [*oct-, eight* + *-al*] Pertaining to a number system of base eight. (OK tul)

octameter [*octa-, eight* & *meter*] A line of verse consisting of eight metrical feet. (ok TAM et er)

octant [*oct-, eight* + *-ant*] 1.An arc of 45 degrees, which is one eighth of the circumference of a circle. See quadrant (def. 1) and sextant (def. 1). 2.A navigational instrument, similar to a sextant, with an arc of 45 degrees. See sextant (def. 2). (OK tunt)

octavalent [*octa-, eight* + *-valent, having a specified valence*] Having a valence of eight. (ok' tuh VAY lent)

octave [*Ltn > octavus, eighth*] 1.A space of eight degrees between musical tones. 2.A tone or note that is eight whole tones above or below a given tone. See tetrachord. (OK tiv)

octavo [*Ltn > octavus, eighth*] 1.A page size equal to one eighth of a printer's sheet. 2.A book size in which each page is one eighth of a printer's sheet. (ok TAY voh)

octennial [*oct-, eight* + *enn, years* + *-ial*] 1.Occurring once every eight years. 2.Lasting or continuing for eight years. (ok TEN ee ul)

octet [*oct-, eight* + *-et*] 1.A musical composition or performance involving eight voices or instruments. 2.A group of eight persons or things. (ok TET)

octette [*oct-, eight* + *-ette*] 1.A musical composition or performance involving eight voices or instruments. 2.A group of eight persons or things. Same as octet. (ok TET)

octillion [*oct-, eight* + *(m)ill, thousand* + *-ion*] A number expressed as 1 followed by 27 zeros, which is 8 groups of three zeros after 1,000. (ok TIL yun)

October [*octo-, eight* + *-ber*] The 10th month of the year. So named from the 8th month of the early Roman calendar, which began with March. See September, November, and December. (ok TOH ber)

octodecillion [*octo-, eight* + *dec, ten* + *(m)ill, thousand* + *-ion*] A number expressed as 1 followed by 57 zeros, which is 18 groups of three zeros after 1,000. (ok' toh dih SIL yun)

octodecimo [*Ltn > octodecimo, eighteenth*] 1.A page size equal to one eighteenth of a printer's sheet. 2.A book size in which each page is one eighteenth of a printer's sheet. (ok' tuh DES ih moh')

octogenarian [*Ltn > octogenarius, containing eighty*] A person between 80 and 89 years of age. (ok' toh juh NEHR ee un)

octoploid [*octo-, eight* + *-ploid, number of chromosomes*] Pertaining to cells with a chromosome number eight times the basic haploid number. (OK tuh ploid')

octopod [*octo-, eight* + *pod, feet*] Any of an order of cephalopod mollusks with eight arms, as an octopus. (OK tuh pod')

octopus [*octo-, eight* + *Grk > pous, foot*] Any of a genus of marine animals with a rounded saclike body, a large distinct head, and eight arms, each with two rows of suckers. (OK tuh pus)

octosyllable [*octo-, eight* & *syllable*] A line of verse with eight syllables. (OK tuh sil' uh bul)

octuple [*oct-, eight* + *-ple, times*] 1.Eightfold. Consisting of eight parts. 2.Eight times as great. (ok TOO pul)

trisoctahedron [*Grk > tris, three times + octa, eight + -hedron, surface*] A solid figure with twenty-four plane surfaces that correspond in groups of three to the faces of an octahedron. See octahedron. (tris ok' tuh HEE drun)

deca, dec, deka   ten
deci-   tenth

decade [*dec, ten + -ad, group*] 1.A period of ten years. 2.A group or series of ten. (DEK ayd)

decagon [*deca, ten + gon, angle*] A closed plane figure with ten angles and ten sides. (DEK uh gon')

decagram [*deca, ten & gram*] A metric unit of weight equal to 10 grams. Same as dekagram. (DEK uh gram')

decahedron [*deca, ten + -hedron, surface*] A solid figure with ten plane surfaces. (dek' uh HEE drun)

decaliter [*deca, ten & liter*] A metric unit of volume equal to 10 liters. Same as dekaliter. (DEK uh lee' ter)

Decalog [*deca, ten + log, discourse*] The Ten Commandments. Same as Decalogue. (DEK uh log')

Decalogue [*deca, ten + log, discourse*] The Ten Commandments. (DEK uh log')

decameter [*deca, ten & meter*] A metric unit of length equal to 10 meters. Same as dekameter. (DEK uh mee' ter)

decapod [*deca, ten + pod, feet*] 1.Any of an order of crustaceans, including shrimps, lobsters, crabs, and pawns, with five pairs of walking legs, the first two pairs often bearing pincers. 2.Any cephalopod mollusk of the order Decapoda, including the squids and cuttlefishes, with five pairs of armlike tentacles, one pair being longer than the remaining four pairs. (DEK uh pod')

decare [*dec, ten & are {100 square meters}*] A metric unit of area equal to 10 ares, 0.2471 acres, or 1,000 square meters. (DEK ehr)

decasyllable [*deca, ten & syllable*] A line of verse with ten syllables. (DEK uh sil' uh bul)

decathlon [*dec, ten + Grk > athlon, contest*] An athletic contest that includes ten separate events, all ten of which are performed by each participant. See biathlon, triathlon, and pentathlon. (dih KATH lon)

December [*Ltn > decem, ten + -ber*] The 12th month of the year. So named from the 10th month of the early Roman calendar, which began with March. See September, October, and November. (dih SEM ber)

decemvir [*Ltn > decem, ten + Ltn > vir, men*] 1.Any of the ten magistrates of ancient Rome appointed in 451 B.C. to draft a code of laws. 2.A member of any body or council of ten persons. (dih SEM vir)

decennial [*dec, ten + enn, years + -ial*] 1.Occurring once every ten years. 2.Lasting or continuing for ten years. (dih SEN ee ul)

decennium [*dec, ten + enn, years + -ium*] A period of ten years. Decade. (dih SEN ee um)

decibar [*deci-, tenth + bar, pressure*] A metric unit of pressure equal to one tenth of a bar, or 100,000 dynes per square centimeter. (DES uh bahr')

decibel [*deci-, tenth & bel*] A unit for measuring relative sound volume, equal to one tenth of a bel. The bel is named after Alexander Graham Bell. See phon. (DES uh bel')

decigram [*deci-, tenth & gram*] A metric unit of weight equal to one tenth of a gram. (DES uh gram')

decile [*dec, ten + -ile*] Any of the nine values that divide a statistical frequency distribution into ten equal parts. See quartile, quintile (def. 2), and percentile. (DES eyel)

deciliter [*deci-, tenth & liter*] A metric unit of volume equal to one tenth of a liter. (DES uh lee' ter)

decillion [*dec, ten + (m)ill, thousand + -ion*] A number expressed as 1 followed by 33 zeros, which is 10 groups of three zeros after 1,000. (dih SIL yun)

decimal [*dec, ten + -imal*] 1.Pertaining to a number system of base ten. 2.Pertaining the number 10 or to tenths. (DES uh mul)

decimeter [*deci-, tenth & meter*] A metric unit of length equal to one tenth of a meter. (DES uh mee' ter)

decuple [*dec, ten + -ple, times*] 1.Tenfold. Consisting of ten parts. 2.Ten times as great. (DEK yoo pul)

dekagram [*deka, ten & gram*] A metric unit of weight equal to 10 grams. (DEK uh gram')

dekaliter [*deka, ten & liter*] A metric unit of volume equal to 10 liters. (DEK uh lee' ter)

dekameter [*deka, ten & meter*] A metric unit of length equal to 10 meters. (DEK uh mee' ter)

dodeca- [*duo-, two + deca, ten*] A word root meaning "twelve." (doh DEK uh)

dodecagon [*dodeca-, twelve + gon, angle*] A closed plane figure with twelve angles and twelve sides. (doh DEK uh gon')

dodecahedron [*dodeca-, twelve + -hedron, surface*] A solid figure with twelve plane surfaces. (doh' dek' uh HEE drun)

dodecaphonic [*dodeca-, twelve + phon, sound + -ic*] Pertaining to a system of music based on all twelve tones of the chromatic scale. (doh' dek' uh FON ik)

dodecasyllable [*dodeca-, twelve & syllable*] A line of verse with twelve syllables. (doh' dek' uh SIL uh bul)

duodec- [*duo-, two + dec, ten*] A word root meaning "twelve." (DOO oh des')

duodecillion [*duodec-, twelve + (m)ill, thousand + -ion*] A number expressed as 1 followed by 39 zeros, which is 12 groups of three zeros after 1,000. (doo' oh dih SIL yun)

duodecimal [*duodec-, twelve + -imal*] 1.Pertaining to a number system of base twelve. 2.Pertaining to the number *12* or to twelfths. (doo' oh DES uh mul)

duodecimo [*Ltn > duodecimo, twelfth*] 1.A page size equal to one twelfth of a printer's sheet. 2.A book size in which each page is one twelfth of a printer's sheet. (doo' oh DES ih moh')

duodenum [*duodec-, twelve + -um*] The first portion of the small intestine between the lower end of the stomach and the jejunum. So named for its length, which is about the width of twelve fingers. (doo' oh DEE num)

hendeca- [*hen, one + deca, ten*] A word root meaning "eleven." (hen DEK uh)

hendecagon [*hendeca-, eleven + gon, angle*] A closed plane figure with eleven angles and eleven sides. (hen DEK uh gon')

hendecahedron [*hendeca-, eleven + -hedron, surface*] A solid figure with eleven plane surfaces. (hen' dek' uh HEE drun)

hendecasyllable [*hendeca-, eleven & syllable*] A line of verse with eleven syllables. (hen' dek' uh SIL uh bul)

hexadecimal [*hexa-, six + dec, ten + -imal*] Pertaining to a number system of base sixteen. (heks' uh DES uh mul)

novemdecillion [*Ltn > novem, nine + dec, ten + (m)ill, thousand + -ion*] A number expressed as 1 followed by 60 zeros, which is 19 groups of three zeros after 1,000. (noh' vem' dih SIL yun)

octodecillion [*octo-, eight + dec, ten + (m)ill, thousand + -ion*] A number expressed as 1 followed by 57 zeros, which is 18 groups of three zeros after 1,000. (ok' toh dih SIL yun)

octodecimo [*Ltn > octodecimo, eighteenth*] 1.A page size equal to one eighteenth of a printer's sheet. 2.A book size in which each page is one eighteenth of a printer's sheet. (ok' tuh DES ih moh')

quattuordecillion [*quattr, four + dec, ten + (m)ill, thousand + -ion*] A number expressed as 1 followed by 45 zeros, which is 14 groups of three zeros after 1,000. (kwot' oo or' dih SIL yun)

quindecagon [*quin, five + deca, ten + gon, angle*] A closed plane figure with fifteen angles and fifteen sides. (kwin DEK uh gon')

quindecennial [*quin, five + dec, ten + enn, years + -ial*] 1.Occurring once every fifteen years. 2.Lasting or continuing for fifteen years. (kwin' dih SEN ee ul)

quindecillion [*quin, five + dec, ten + (m)ill, thousand + -ion*] A number expressed as 1 followed by 48 zeros, which is 15 groups of three zeros after 1,000. (kwin' dih SIL yun)

septendecillion [*sept-, seven + dec, ten + (m)ill, thousand + -ion*] A number expressed as 1 followed by 54 zeros, which is 17 groups of three zeros after 1,000. (sep' ten' dih SIL yun)

sexdecillion [*sex-, six + dec, ten + (m)ill, thousand + -ion*] A number expressed as 1 followed by 51 zeros, which is 16 groups of three zeros after 1,000. (seks' dih SIL yun)

sextodecimo [*Ltn > sextodecimo, sixteenth*] 1.A page size equal to one sixteenth of a printer's sheet. 2.A book size in which each page is one sixteenth of a printer's sheet. (seks' toh DES ih moh')

tredecillion [*Ltn > tres, three + dec, ten + (m)ill, thousand + -ion*] A number expressed as 1 followed by 42 zeros, which is 13 groups of three zeros after 1,000. (tree' dih SIL yun)

triskaidekaphobia [*tri-, three + kai, and + deka, ten + -phobia, fear*] Fear of the number 13. (tris' keye dek' uh FOH bee uh)

undecillion [*uni-, one + dec, ten + (m)ill, thousand + -ion*] A number expressed as 1 followed by 36 zeros, which is 11 groups of three zeros after 1,000. (un' dih SIL yun)

poly   many

polyandry [*poly, many + andr, man + -y*] 1.The custom or practice of having more than one husband at a time. 2.Having many stamens in one flower. See polygyny, monogyny, and monandry. (POL ee an' dree)

polyanthus [*poly, many + anth, flower + -us*] 1.Any of a variety of primroses bearing multi-flowered umbels. 2.A narcissus bearing clusters of fragrant yellow or white flowers. (pol' ee AN thus)

polycarpellary [*poly, many & carpel & -ary*] Having many carpels. (pol' ee KAHR puh lehr' ee)

polycarpic [*poly, many + carp, fruit + -ic*] Capable of flowering or fruiting many times, as perennial plants. See monocarpic. (pol' ee KAHR pik)

polycentrism [*poly, many + centr, center + -ism*] The existence of two or more centers of power or authority within a political system, especially in the Communist world. (pol' ee SEN triz' um)

polychotomy [*poly, many & (di)chotomy*] Division into many parts, branches, kinds, etc. See dichotomy and trichotomy (def. 1). (pol' ee KOT uh mee)

polychromatic [*poly, many + chromat, color + -ic*] Having or displaying many colors. (pol' ee kroh MAT ik)

polychrome [*poly, many + -chrome, color*] Done or decorated in many colors. (POL ee krohm')

polychromy [*poly, many + chrom, color + -y*] The art of painting or decorating in many colors. (POL ee kroh' mee)

polyclinic [*poly, many & clinic*] A clinic or hospital able to diagnose and treat many different diseases and injuries. (pol' ee KLIN ik)

polycyclic [*poly, many + cycl, circle + -ic*] Having more than one ring of atoms in a molecule. See monocyclic (def. 2). (pol' ee SEYE klik)

polycythemia [*poly, many + cyt, cell + -emia, blood condition*] A condition in which there is an abnormal increase in the number of red blood cells. (pol' ee seye THEE mee uh)

polydactyl [*poly, many + dactyl, finger*] Having more than the normal number of fingers or toes. (pol' ee DAK tul)

polydipsia [*poly, many + Grk > dipsa, thirst*] Abnormal or excessive thirst. (pol' ee DIP see uh)

polyembryony [*poly, many & embryo & -y*] The development of two or more embryos from a single fertilized ovum. See monozygotic and dizygotic. (pol' ee EM bree uh nee)

polygamy [*poly, many + -gamy, marriage*] The practice of being married to more than one person at the same time. See monogamy and bigamy. (puh LIG uh mee)

polygene [*poly, many & gene*] Any of a set of genes that act together to control a character trait, as height, weight, or skin pigmentation. (POL ee jeen')

polygenesis [*poly, many + -genesis, origin*] Descent from more than one ancestral line. See cenogenesis (def. 1) and polyphyletic. (pol' ee JEN uh sis)

polygenism [*poly, many + gen, origin + -ism*] The theory that humans have descended from more than one ancestral line. See monogenism. (puh LIJ uh niz' um)

polyglot [*poly, many + glot, language*] 1.A person who is able to use several languages. 2.Speaking or writing several languages. 3.A confusion or mixture of languages. See linguist and multilingual. (POL ee glot')

polygon [*poly, many + gon, angle*] A closed plane figure with three or more angles and sides. (POL ee gon')

polygraph [*poly, many + graph, recording*] An instrument for simultaneously recording changes in various body functions, as respiration, heart rate, blood pressure, etc. Lie detector. (POL ee graf')

polygyny [*poly, many + gyn, woman + -y*] 1.The custom or practice of having more than one wife at a time. 2.Having many pistils in one flower. See polyandry, monogyny, and monandry. (puh LIJ uh nee)

polyhedron [*poly, many + -hedron, surface*] A solid figure with four or more plane surfaces. (pol' ee HEE drun)

polymath [*poly, many* + *Grk > mathanein, learn*] A person of extensive and varied learning. (POL ee math')

polymer [*poly, many* + *mer, part*] A compound consisting of large molecules that are composed of simple molecules linked together in chains or rings. The number of structural units forming a polymer may vary from a few to millions. See monomer, dimer, and trimer. (POL uh mer)

polymorphic [*poly, many* + *morph, form* + *-ic*] Exhibiting various forms, stages, or styles. (pol' ee MOR fik)

polymorphism [*poly, many* + *morph, form* + *-ism*] 1.The occurrence of significant numbers of different types of individuals within the same plant or animal species. 2.The property of a substance of crystallizing in two or more distinct forms. See dimorphism. (pol ee MOR fiz' um)

polymorphonuclear [*poly, many* + *morpho, form* & *nuclear*] Having a multi-lobed nucleus, as some leukocytes. (pol' ee mor' fuh NOO klee ur)

polyneuritis [*poly, many* + *neur, nerve* + *-itis, inflammation*] Inflammation of two or more peripheral nerves. (pol' ee noo REYE tis)

polynomial [*poly, many* + *nom, name* + *-ial*] A mathematical expression consisting of two or more terms. See monomial, binomial, and trinomial. (pol' uh NOH mee ul)

polynuclear [*poly, many* & *nuclear*] Having many nuclei. (pol' ee NOO klee ur)

polypeptide [*poly, many* & *peptide*] A compound that contains two or more amino acids chained together. (pol' ee PEP teyed')

polypetalous [*poly, many* & *petal* & *-ous*] Having separate petals. See gamopetalous. (pol' ee PET l us)

polyphagous [*poly, many* + *phag, to eat* + *-ous*] 1.Having an excessive desire for food. 2.Feeding on a wide variety of food. See euryphagous. (puh LIF uh gus)

polyphase [*poly, many* & *phase*] Pertaining to an alternating electric current having two or more phases. (POL ee fayz')

polyphony [*poly, many* + *-phony, sound*] Music combining two or more independent melodies in harmony. (puh LIF uh nee)

polyphyletic [*poly, many* + *phyl, common ancestry* + *-etic*] Descended from more than one ancestral line. See monophyletic and polygenesis. (pol' ee feye LET ik)

polyploid [*poly, many* + *-ploid, number of chromosomes*] Pertaining to cells with a chromosome number three or more times the basic haploid number. (POL ee ploid')

polypnea [*poly, many* + *-pnea, breathing*] Abnormally deep and rapid breathing. Same as hyperpnea. (pol IP nee uh)

polypody [*poly, many* + *pod, feet* + *-y*] Any of various ferns with compound fronds and creeping rhizomes. (POL ee poh' dee)

polyrhythm [*poly, many* & *rhythm*] The simultaneous combination of contrasting musical rhythms. (POL ee rith' um)

polysaccharide [*poly, many* & *saccharide*] Any of a class of sugars that yield more than three monosaccharides on hydrolysis, as starch or cellulose. (pol' ee SAK uh reyed')

polysaprobic [*poly, many* + *sapro, decomposed* + *bio, life* + *-ic*] Pertaining to a body of water containing rapidly decomposing organic matter and little or no free oxygen. (pol' ee suh PROH bik)

polysemy [*poly, many* + *Grk > sema, sign* + *-y*] Having many meanings, as a word, sign, etc. (POL ee see' mee)

polysepalous [*poly, many* & *sepal* & *-ous*] Having separate sepals. See gamosepalous. (pol' ee SEP uh lus)

polysyllable [*poly, many* & *syllable*] A word with four or more syllables. (POL ee sil' uh bul)

polysyndeton [*poly, many* + *syn, together* + *Grk > dein, to bind* + *-on*] The repetition of unnecessary conjunctions in close succession for rhetorical effect. See asyndeton. (pol' ee SIN dih tahn')

polytechnic [*poly, many* + *techn, skill* + *-ic*] Offering instruction in many technical and scientific subjects. (pol' ee TEK nik)

polytheism [*poly, many* + *the, god* + *-ism*] The belief in more than one god. (POL ee thee iz' um)

polytocous [*poly, many* + *toco, birth* + *-ous*] Producing many offspring at a single birth. See philoprogenitive (def. 2) and progenitive. (puh LIT uh kus)

polytonality [*poly, many* & *ton(e)* & *-ality*] The simultaneous use of two or more keys in a musical composition. (pol' ee toh NAL ih tee)

polytrophic [*poly, many* + *troph, nourishment* + *-ic*] Obtaining nourishment from a variety of organic material, as certain bacteria. (pol' ee TROF ik)

polytypic [*poly, many* & *typ(e)* & *-ic*] Existing in many forms or types. (pol' ee TIP ik)

polyunsaturated [*poly, many* & *unsaturated*] Containing many unsaturated chemical bonds, as certain animal and vegetable fats and oils. (pol' ee un SACH uh ray' tid)

polyuria [*poly, many* + *-uria, urine*] Excessive secretion of urine, as in some diseases. (pol' ee YOOR ee uh)

polyvalent [*poly, many* + *-valent, having a specified valence*] Having a valence of three or more. Same as multivalent. (pol' ee VAY lent)

polyzoan [*poly, many* + *zo, animal* + *-an*] Any of the minute aquatic invertebrates of the phylum Bryozoa that form mosslike colonies and are known as moss animals. Same as bryozoan. (pol' ee ZOH un)

polyzoarium [*polyzo(an)* & *-arium, a place for*] The skeletal system of a polyzoan colony. (pol' ee zoh EHR ee um)

olig/o   few, deficiency

oligarchy [*olig, few* + *arch, rule* + *-y*] Government by a few rulers. (OL uh gahr' kee)

oligoclase [*oligo, few* + *Grk > klasis, breaking*] A mineral of the feldspar group occurring commonly in white crystals and characterized by cleavages that differ slightly from 90 degrees. See orthoclase. (OL ih goh klayz')

oligophagous [*oligo, few* + *phag, to eat* + *-ous*] Feeding on a limited variety of food. Same as stenophagous. (ol' uh GOF uh gus)

oligopoly [*oligo, few* + *Grk > polein, to sell* + *-y*] The market condition that exists when there are so few sellers that the actions of any one of them can impact price. See oligopsony and monopsony. (ol' uh GOP uh lee)

oligopsony [*olig, few* + *Grk* > *opsonia, purchase* + *-y*] The market condition that exists when there are so few buyers that the actions of any one of them can impact price. See monopsony and oligopoly. (ol' uh GOP suh nee)

oligosaccharide [*oligo, few* & *saccharide*] Any of a class of sugars that yield a relatively small number of monosaccharides on hydrolysis. (ol' ih goh SAK uh reyed')

oligotrophic [*oligo, deficiency* + *troph, nourishment* + *-ic*] Pertaining to a body of water deficient in nutrients for supporting plant life, but rich in oxygen for supporting animal life. See eutrophic. (ol' ih goh TROF ik)

morph/o   form

allomorph [*allo, variation* + *morph, form*] 1.A mineral formed by a change in the crystalline form and structure of a compound with no change in chemical composition. Same as paramorph. 2.Any of the variant forms of a morpheme. (AL uh morf')

amorphous [*a-, without* + *morph, form* + *-ous*] 1.Without distinct form or shape. Shapeless. 2.Not belonging to a particular type or pattern. Anomalous. 3.Without crystalline form or structure. (uh MOR fus)

anamorphic [*ana-, again* + *morph, form* + *-ic*] Producing optical magnification that is different from each of two perpendicular directions. (an' uh MOR fik)

anthropomorphism [*anthropo, human* + *morph, form* + *-ism*] The ascription of human form or characteristics to nonhuman things such as gods or animals. (an' thruh puh MOR fiz' um)

bimorphemic [*bi-, two* & *morphem(e)* & *-ic*] Having two morphemes. (beye' mor FEE mik)

dimorphic [*di-, two* + *morph, form* + *-ic*] Occurring in two distinct forms. (deye MOR fik)

dimorphism [*di-, two* + *morph, form* + *-ism*] 1.The occurrence of two distinct types of plant parts on the same plant or on plants of the same species. 2.The occurrence of different form, color, etc., between two distinct types of animals of the same species. 3.The property of a substance of crystallizing in two chemically identical forms. See polymorphism. (deye MOR fiz' um)

dimorphous [*di-, two* + *morph, form* + *-ous*] Pertaining to an element or compound that crystallizes in two distinct forms. (deye MOR fus)

ectomorphic [*ecto, outside* + *morph, form* + *-ic*] Having a lean and slightly muscular body build characterized by the prominence of structures derived from the embryonic ectoderm. See endomorphic and mesomorphic. (ek' toh MOR fik)

enantiomorph [*en-, in* + *anti-, opposite* + *morph, form*] Either of two crystals, isomers, chemical compounds, etc., that are mirror images of each other. (en AN tee uh morf')

endomorph [*endo-, inside* + *morph, form*] A mineral enclosed inside another mineral. See perimorph. (EN duh morf')

endomorphic [*endo-, inside* + *morph, form* + *-ic*] Having a generally round and soft body build characterized by the prominence of structures derived from the embryonic endoderm. See mesomorphic and ectomorphic. (en' doh MOR fik)

endorphins [*endo-, inside* & *(m)orphin(e)*] Chemical substances produced in the brain that have a pain-relieving effect similar to morphine. See morphine. (en DOR fins)

geomorphic [*geo, earth* + *morph, form* + *-ic*] Resembling the shape of the earth. (jee' uh MOR fik)

geomorphology [*geo, earth* + *morph, form* + *-ology, study of*] The scientific study of the origin, development, and features of the earth's surface. (jee' oh mor FOL uh jee)

gynandromorph [*gyn, female* + *andro, male* + *morph, form*] An abnormal individual exhibiting a mixture of male and female characteristics. (jih NAN druh morf')

hemimorphic [*hemi-, half* + *morph, form* + *-ic*] Pertaining to a crystal that is not symmetric at opposite axial ends. (hem' ih MOR fik)

heteromorphic [*hetero, different* + *morph, form* + *-ic*] 1.Differing in form, shape, size, etc. See isomorphic and homomorphism (def. 1). 2.Having different forms at various stages in the life cycle, as insects. See pleomorphism. (het' uh roh MOR fik)

homeomorphism [*homeo, similar* + *morph, form* + *-ism*] Similarity in crystalline form and structure, but differing in chemical composition. See paramorph. (hoh' mee oh MOR fiz' um)

homomorphism [*homo, similar* + *morph, form* + *-ism*] 1.Similarity in form, shape, size, etc. See isomorphic and heteromorphic (def. 1). 2.Having perfect flowers of one type only. (hoh' muh MOR fiz' um)

hydromorphic [*hydro, water* + *morph, form* + *-ic*] Being structurally adapted to an aquatic environment, as water plants. (heye' druh MOR fik)

idiomorphic [*idio-, peculiar* + *morph, form* + *-ic*] 1.Possessing its own distinct form or shape. 2.Pertaining to minerals with unaltered crystalline growth. (id' ee uh MOR fik)

isomorphic [*iso-, same* + *morph, form* + *-ic*] Having the same or similar form or structure. See homomorphism (def. 1) and heteromorphic (def. 1). (eye' suh MOR fik)

isomorphism [*iso-, same* + *morph, form* + *-ism*] 1.A similarity in form or structure between members of different species. 2.A similarity of crystalline structure between two otherwise different substances. (eye' suh MOR fiz' um)

lagomorph [*lago, hare* + *morph, form*] Any of an order of gnawing mammals, including rabbits, hares, and pikas, that resemble rodents, but have two pairs of upper incisors and a short tail. (LAG uh morf')

mesomorphic [*meso-, middle* + *morph, form* + *-ic*] Having a muscular body build characterized by the prominence of structures derived from the embryonic mesoderm. See endomorphic and ectomorphic. (mez' uh MOR fik)

metamorphosis [*meta-, change* + *morph, form* + *-osis, process*] A complete change of form, appearance, structure, or function. (met' uh MOR fuh sis)

monomorphemic [*mono-, one* & *morphem(e)* & *-ic*] Consisting of only one morpheme, as the word *talk*. (mon' oh mor FEE mik)

monomorphic [*mono-, one* + *morph, form* + *-ic*] Having only one form, shape, or size. (mon' oh MOR fik)

morphallaxis [*morph, form* + *Grk* > *allaxis, exchange*] The regeneration of a body part by transformation and reorganization of remaining or adjacent tissue with little cell proliferation, as in certain crustaceans. (mor' fuh LAK sis)

morpheme [*morph, form + -eme, structural unit*] The smallest meaningful linguistic unit of a language that cannot be further divided, as an affix, word root, or a word such as *walk*. (MOR feem)

morphemics [*morphem(e) & -ics, study of*] 1.The branch of linguistics dealing with the study of the morphemes of a language. 2.Language structure in terms of the description and classification of morphemes. See morpheme. (mor FEE miks)

morphine [*Morph(eus) & -ine*] A white, bitter crystalline compound derived from opium and used as a sedative, to dull pain, and to induce sleep. So named from Morpheus, the god of dreams, alluding to its sleep inducing properties. (MOR feen)

morphogenesis [*morpho, form + -genesis, to produce*] Differentiation of cells and tissues to form the structure of an organism, organ, or part. (mor' fuh JEN uh sis)

morphology [*morph, form + -ology, study of*] 1.The branch of biology dealing with the study of the form and structure of plants and animals. 2.The study of word formation in a particular language. (mor FOL uh jee)

paramorph [*para-, variation + morph, form*] A mineral formed by a change in the crystalline form and structure of a compound with no change in chemical composition. See homeomorphism. (PEHR uh morf')

perimorph [*peri-, around + morph, form*] A mineral enclosing a different kind of mineral. See endomorph. (PEHR ih morph')

pleomorphism [*pleo, more + morph, form + -ism*] The occurrence of two or more distinct forms during the life cycle, as in certain plants or other organisms. See heteromorphic (def. 2). (plee' uh MOR fiz' um)

polymorphic [*poly, many + morph, form + -ic*] Exhibiting various forms, stages, or styles. (pol' ee MOR fik)

polymorphism [*poly, many + morph, form + -ism*] 1.The occurrence of significant numbers of different types of individuals within the same plant or animal species. 2.The property of a substance of crystallizing in two or more distinct forms. See dimorphism. (pol' ee MOR fiz' um)

polymorphonuclear [*poly, many + morpho, form & nuclear*] Having a multi-lobed nucleus, as some leukocytes. (pol' ee mor' fuh NOO klee ur)

pseudomorph [*pseudo, false + morph, form*] 1.An irregular or false form. 2.An altered mineral exhibiting the crystalline form of another mineral. (SOOD uh morf')

rhizomorphous [*rhizo, root + morph, form + -ous*] Having the shape or form of a root. (reye' zoh MOR fus)

theomorphic [*theo, God + morph, form + -ic*] Having the form or appearance of a god or of God. (thee' oh MOR fik)

theriomorphic [*Grk > therion, beast + morph, form + -ic*] Exhibiting the form of a beast. (thihr' ee uh MOR fik)

trimorph [*tri-, three + morph, form*] A substance occurring in three structurally distinct forms. (TREYE morf)

zoomorphic [*zoo, animal + morph, form + -ic*] Having or representing the form of an animal. (zoh' uh MOR fik)

zoomorphism [*zoo, animal + morph, form + -ism*] The use of animal forms in art or symbolism. (zoh' uh MOR fiz' um)

zygomorphic [*zygo, pair + morph, form + -ic*] Pertaining to organisms or parts that can be divided into symmetrical halves along one axis only. Bilaterally symmetrical. (zeye' guh MOR fik)

plas, plast, plasm, -plasty
to form, forming cells or tissue, protoplasm, development

achondroplasia [*a-, without + chondro, cartilage + plas, development + -ia*] A congenital bone disorder caused by abnormal conversion of cartilage into bone, resulting in deformities and dwarfism. (ay kon' druh PLAY zhuh)

anaplasia [*ana-, back + plas, forming cells or tissue + -ia*] The reversion of mature cells to a less differentiated form, as in most malignant tissue. See cataplasia. (an' uh PLAY zhuh)

angioplasty [*angio, vessel + -plasty, to form*] Any of various methods for surgically reconstructing or replacing blood vessels. (AN jee uh plas' tee)

antineoplastic [*anti-, against + neo, new + plast, forming cells or tissue + -ic*] Inhibiting or preventing the formation, growth, or proliferation of malignant cells. See neoplasm. (an' tee nee' oh PLAS tik)

aplastic anemia [*a-, not + plast, forming cells or tissue + -ic & anemia*] Anemia that results from defective blood-producing bone marrow. See anemia. (ay PLAS tik uh NEE mee uh)

autoplasty [*auto-, self + -plasty, forming cells or tissue*] The surgical grafting of tissue taken from another part of the same body. See heteroplasty and autograft. (AWT uh plas' tee)

blepharoplasty [*blepharo, eyelid + -plasty, to form*] The surgical restructuring of an eyelid to remove fat deposits, sagging tissue, or to repair injury. Eye lift. See rhytidectomy. (BLEF uh roh plas' tee)

cataplasia [*cata-, down + plas, forming cells or tissue + -ia*] The degenerative reversion of cells or tissue to an earlier, more embryonic stage. See anaplasia. (kat' uh PLAY zhuh)

chloroplast [*chloro(phyll) & plast(id)*] A plastid containing chlorophyll found in the cytoplasm of photosynthetic plant cells. See chromoplast and leucoplast. (KLOR uh plast')

chromoplast [*chromo, color & plast(id)*] A colored, pigment-containing plastid that contains either the green pigment chlorophyll or variously colored carotenoid pigments. See chloroplast and leucoplast. (KROH muh plast')

cytoplasm [*cyto, cell + plasm, protoplasm*] The protoplasm of a cell outside the nucleus. See nucleoplasm and protoplasm. (SEYET uh plaz' um)

dermatoplasty [*dermato, skin + -plasty, to form*] Skin grafting in plastic surgery operations. (der MAT uh plas' tee)

dysplasia [*dys-, abnormal + plas, forming cells or tissue + -ia*] Abnormal growth or development of various cells or tissues. (dis PLAY zhuh)

ectoplasm [*ecto-, outside + plasm, protoplasm*] The outer, more rigid portion of the cytoplasm of a cell. See endoplasm. (EK tuh plaz' um)

plas, plast, plasm, -plasty

endoplasm [*endo-, inside* + *plasm, protoplasm*] The inner, more fluid portion of the cytoplasm of a cell. See ectoplasm. (EN duh plaz' um)

esemplastic [*Grk* > *es-, into* + *hen, one* + *plast, to form* + *-ic*] Forming different concepts and thoughts into a unified whole. (es' em PLAS tik)

euplastic [*eu-, well* + *plast, forming cells or tissue* + *-ic*] Healing readily and well, as a wound. (yoo PLAS tik)

heteroplasty [*hetero, other* + *-plasty, forming cells or tissue*] The surgical grafting of tissue taken from another person or from an individual of another species. See autoplasty and heterograft. (HET ur uh plas' tee)

homoplastic [*homo, similar* + *plast, development* + *-ic*] Having structural similarities due to parallel evolution or evolutionary convergence. Opposed to homogenous. (hoh' muh PLAS tik)

hyaloplasm [*hyalo, transparent* + *plasm, protoplasm*] The clear, fluid portion of the protoplasm of a cell. (heye AL uh plaz' um)

hyperplasia [*hyper-, above* + *plas, forming cells or tissue* + *-ia*] An abnormal increase in the number of nonmalignant cells of a tissue, causing a noncancerous enlargement of an organ or part. (heye' per PLAY zhuh)

hypoplasia [*hypo-, less* + *plas, development* + *-ia*] Incomplete or defective development of a bodily organ or part. (heye' poh PLAY zhuh)

karyoplasm [*karyo, nucleus* + *plasm, protoplasm*] The protoplasm of a cell inside the nucleus. Same as nucleoplasm. (KEHR ee uh plaz' um)

leucoplast [*leuco, colorless* & *plast(id)*] A colorless plastid found in plant cells, where starch is often formed and stored. See chromoplast and chloroplast. (LOO kuh plast')

metaplasia [*meta-, change* + *plas, forming cells or tissue* + *-ia*] The conversion of a particular type of tissue to an abnormal type for that tissue, as the ossification of muscular tissue. (met' uh PLAY zhuh)

metaplasm [*meta-, change* + *plasm, form*] 1.The changing of the form of a word by removing, adding, or transposing letters or syllables. 2.The nonliving material in the protoplasm of a cell, as carbohydrates, pigments, or fat. (MET uh plaz' um)

neoplasm [*neo, new* + *plasm, forming cells or tissue*] Any abnormal new growth of tissue. Tumor. (NEE uh plaz' um)

nucleoplasm [*nucleo, nucleus* + *plasm, protoplasm*] The protoplasm of a cell inside the nucleus. See cytoplasm and protoplasm. (NOO klee uh plaz' um)

osteoplasty [*osteo, bone* + *-plasty, to form*] The surgical restructuring, repairing, or replacement of bone. (OS tee uh plas' tee)

plasma [*plasm, to form* + *-a*] 1.The clear, fluid part of blood and lymph in which the material elements are suspended. 2.Protoplasm. (PLAZ muh)

plasmagel [*plasma* & *gel*] The more firm and jellylike state of cytoplasm. See plasmasol. (PLAZ muh jel')

plasmagene [*plasma* & *-gene, production*] Any structure in cytoplasm thought to determine hereditary characteristics in subsequent generations. (PLAZ muh jeen')

plasmapheresis [*plasm(a)* & *apo, away* + *Grk* > *hairein, to take* + *-sis*] A medical process in which blood is drawn from a donor, the plasma removed, and the blood cells returned to the circulatory system of the donor. (plaz' muh FEHR uh sis)

plasmasol [*plasma* & *(hydro)sol*] The fluid state of cytoplasm that is more liquid than plasmagel. See plasmagel. (PLAZ muh sol')

plasmid [*plasm, protoplasm* + *-id*] A genetic element in some bacterial cells that can replicate independently of the chromosomes and carries genes for certain functions not necessary to cell growth. See episome. (PLAZ mid)

plasmin [*plasm(a)* & *-in*] A proteolytic enzyme that dissolves the fibrin of blood clots and is derived from plasminogen. See thromboplastin and plasminogen. (PLAZ min)

plasminogen [*plasmin* & *gen, to produce*] An inactive blood protein that is a precursor of plasmin and is found in blood plasma and other body fluids. See plasmin. (plaz MIN uh jen)

plasmodium [*plasm, protoplasm* + *-ode, like* + *-ium*] 1.A multinucleate mass of protoplasm with no definite size or shape. 2.A parasitic protozoan that causes malaria. (plaz MOH dee um)

plasmolysis [*plasmo, protoplasm* + *-lysis, loosening*] Shrinking of the cytoplasm in a living cell caused by loss of water through the cell wall by osmosis. (plaz MOL uh sis)

plaster [*plast, to form* + *-er*] A mixture of lime, sand, and water that forms a smooth solid and is used as a hard covering for walls and ceilings. (PLAS ter)

plastic [*plast, to form* + *-ic*] 1.Any of various synthetic or natural materials that can be molded when soft and then hardened. 2.Able to be molded, shaped, or formed. (PLAS tik)

plastid [*plast, protoplasm* + *-id*] Any of several organelles in the cytoplasm of plant cells that perform photosynthetic or storage functions, as chloroplasts or leucoplasts. (PLAS tid)

protoplasm [*proto-, primitive* + *plasm, forming cells or tissue*] A complex, jellylike colloidal substance conceived of as forming the essential living matter of all plant and animal cells. The protoplasm surrounding the nucleus is the cytoplasm and that composing the nucleus is the nucleoplasm. See nucleoplasm and cytoplasm. (PROHT uh plaz' um)

protoplast [*proto-, first* + *plast, form*] 1.A being or thing that is the first made or formed. 2.The living portion of a plant or bacterial cell, including the cytoplasm, nucleus, and plasma membrane, but not the cell wall. (PROHT uh plast')

rhinoplasty [*rhino, nose* + *-plasty, to form*] Plastic surgery of the nose. (REYE noh plas' tee)

sarcoplasm [*sarco, flesh* + *plasm, protoplasm*] The nonfibrillar cytoplasm of striated muscle fiber cells. (SAHR kuh plaz' um)

somatoplasm [*somato, body* + *plasm, protoplasm*] The protoplasm of the body cells collectively, as distinguished from the germ plasm. (soh MAT uh plaz' um)

thermoplastic [*thermo, heat* + *plast, to form* + *-ic*] Pertaining to substances that become hard when cooled and soft and pliable when heated. (thur' moh PLAS tik)

thromboplastin [*thrombo, blood clot* + *plast, to form* + *-in*] An enzyme in blood platelets and tissue that aids in blood clotting. See plasmin. (throm' boh PLAS tin)

tonoplast [*tono, tension* + *plast, protoplasm*] The membrane surrounding the vacuole in the cytoplasm of a plant cell. (TOH nuh plast')

zooplasty [*zoo, animal* + *-plasty, forming cells or tissue*] The surgical grafting of tissue from an animal to a human. (ZOH uh plas' tee)

mort   dead, death

amortize [*ad-, to* + *mort, death* + *-ize*] To liquidate by paying at intervals, as a mortgage, debt, or other obligation. (AM ur teyez')

antemortem [*ante-, before* + *mort, death* + *-em*] Occurring before death. See postmortem (def. 1). (an' tee MORT um)

immortal [*im-, not* + *mort, dead* + *-al*] 1.Not subject to death. 2.Living or lasting forever. 3.Having everlasting fame. (ih MORT l)

moribund [*mort, death* + *-bund*] Near death or extinction. Dying. (MOR uh bund')

mortal [*mort, death* + *-al*] 1.Subject to death. 2.Pertaining to mankind. Human. 3.Causing or capable of causing death. Fatal. (MORT l)

mortician [*mort, death* + *-ician*] A person who prepares the dead for burial and arranges funerals. Undertaker. Funeral director. (mor TISH un)

mortify [*mort, dead* + *-ify, to make*] 1.To humiliate, shame, etc. 2.To become gangrenous or necrotic. 3.To discipline bodily desires and feelings with austerities. (MORT uh feye')

mortmain [*mort, dead* + *manu, hand*] Ownership of real estate by an institution such as a church, school, etc., who cannot sell it. (MORT mayn)

mortuary [*mort, dead* + *-ary, a place for*] A place for keeping dead bodies prior to burial. (MOR choo ehr' ee)

postmortem [*post-, after* + *mort, death* + *-em*] 1.Occurring after death. See antemortem. 2.Autopsy. 3.Occurring after an event, as a game or political election. (pohst MORT um)

rigor mortis [*Ltn* > *rigor, stiffness* & *mort, death* + *-is*] Muscular stiffening that occurs several hours after death. (RIG ur MORT is)

necr/o   dead, death

necrobiosis [*necro, death* + *bio, living tissue* + *-sis*] The natural process of death or decay of cells and tissues not due to disease or injury. See necrosis. (nek' roh beye OH sis)

necrolatry [*necro, dead* + *-latry, worship*] Worship of the dead. (nuh KROL uh tree)

necrology [*necro, dead* + *log, discourse* + *-y*] A list of persons who have recently died. Obituary. (nuh KROL uh jee)

necromancy [*necro, dead* + *-mancy, divination*] Divination through communication with the dead. (NEK ruh man' see)

necrophagous [*necro, dead* + *phag, to eat* + *-ous*] Feeding on dead or decaying flesh. See carrion (def. 3). (nuh KROF uh gus)

necrophilia [*necro, death* + *phil, attracted to* + *-ia*] An obsessive and especially erotic interest in death and corpses. (nek' ruh FIL ee uh)

necrophobia [*necro, death* + *-phobia, fear*] Abnormal fear of death or dead bodies. (nek' ruh FOH bee uh)

necropolis [*necro, dead* + *-polis, city*] A cemetery, especially a large one belonging to an ancient city. (nuh KROP uh lis)

necropsy [*necr, dead* + *-opsy, inspection*] The examination of a dead body. Autopsy. (NEK rop' see)

necrosis [*necr, death* + *-osis, diseased condition*] The death or decay of localized cells or tissues due to disease or injury. See necrobiosis. (nuh KROH sis)

necrotomy [*necro, dead* + *-tomy, to cut*] 1.The dissection of a dead body. 2.The surgical removal of dead bone or tissue. (nuh KROT uh mee)

my/o   muscle

actomyosin [*act(in)* & *myosin*] A combination of the proteins actin and myosin, that is a major component of muscle fiber and together with ATP is responsible for muscular contraction. See myosin. (ak' tuh MEYE uh sin)

amyotonia [*a-, without* + *myo, muscle* + *Grk* > *tonos, tone* + *-ia*] Lacking muscle tone. (ay' meye uh TOH nee uh)

cardiomyopathy [*cardio, heart* + *myo, muscle* + *-pathy, disease*] Any disease or disorder of the heart muscle. See cardiopathy. (kahr' dee oh' meye OP uh thee)

electromyograph [*electro, electric* + *myo, muscle* + *graph, recording*] An instrument for graphically recording small electric currents in functioning skeletal muscles, used in diagnosing and treating muscle and nerve disorders. (ih lek' troh MEYE uh graf')

endomysium [*endo-, inside* + *my, muscle* + *-ium*] The sheath of connective tissue surrounding each muscle fiber. See perimysium and epimysium. (en' doh MIZ ee um)

epimysium [*epi-, outside* + *my, muscle* + *-ium*] The sheath of connective tissue surrounding each individual muscle. See endomysium and perimysium. (ep' ih MIZ ee um)

myalgia [*my, muscle* + *alg, pain* + *-ia*] Pain in a muscle. (meye AL juh)

myasthenia [*my, muscle* + *a-, without* + *sthen, strength* + *-ia*] Abnormal muscle fatigue or weakness. (meye' us THEE nee uh)

myocardiograph [*myo, muscle* + *cardio, heart* + *graph, recording*] An instrument for graphically recording the muscular activity of the heart. (meye' uh KAHR dee uh graf')

myocarditis [*myo, muscle* + *cardi, heart* + *-itis, inflammation*] Inflammation of the myocardium. (meye' oh kahr DEYE tis)

myocardium [*myo, muscle* + *cardi, heart* + *-um*] The middle layer of muscle in the walls of the heart. (meye' uh KAHR dee um)

myoclonus [*myo, muscle* & *clonus {spasm}*] Involuntary muscle spasm or twitching. (meye OK luh nus)

my/o

myogenic [*myo, muscle* + *gen, formation* + *-ic*] 1.Forming muscle tissue. 2.Produced by or originating in muscle tissue. (meye' uh JEN ik)

myoglobin [*myo, muscle & globin {protein constituent}*] A respiratory protein pigment in muscle fibers similar to hemoglobin in red blood cells, but with a higher affinity for oxygen. See hemoglobin. (meye' uh GLOH bin)

myograph [*myo, muscle* + *graph, recording*] An instrument for graphically recording muscular contractions and relaxations. (MEYE uh graf')

myology [*myo, muscle* + *-logy, study of*] The branch of anatomy dealing with the study of the functions and diseases of the muscles. (meye OL uh jee)

myoma [*my, muscle* + *-oma, tumor*] A tumor composed of muscle tissue. (meye OH muh)

myoneural [*myo, muscle* + *neur, nerve* + *-al*] Having to do with both muscle and nerve, especially the nerve endings in muscle tissue. See neuromuscular. (meye' uh NOOR ul)

myopathy [*myo, muscle* + *-pathy, disease*] Any disease or disorder of the muscles or muscle tissue. (meye OP uh thee)

myosin [*myo, muscle* + *-in*] The most common protein in muscle tissue that, along with actin, forms actomyosin. See actomyosin. (MEYE uh sin)

myotome [*myo, muscle* + *-tome, to cut*] 1.A knife for cutting muscle. 2.The portion of an embryonic somite from which skeletal muscle is derived. (MEYE uh tohm')

myotonia [*myo, muscle & ton(ic) & -ia*] A sustained muscle spasm following a strong muscle contraction. (meye' uh TOH nee uh)

perimysium [*peri-, around* + *my, muscle* + *-ium*] The sheath of connective tissue surrounding each primary bundle of muscle fibers. See endomysium and epimysium. (pehr' ih MIZ ee um)

rhabdomyoma [*rhabdo, rod* + *my, muscle* + *-oma, tumor*] A benign tumor composed of striated muscle tissue. See rhabdomyosarcoma. (rab' doh meye OH muh)

rhabdomyosarcoma [*rhabdo, rod* + *myo, muscle* + *-sarcoma, malignant tumor*] An extremely malignant tumor composed of striated muscle tissue. See rhabdomyoma. (rab' doh meye' oh sahr KOH muh)

nat   birth, born

antenatal [*ante-, before* + *nat, birth* + *-al*] Existing or occurring before birth. Same as prenatal. (an' tee NAYT l)

innate [*in-, in* + *nat, born*] Existing in a person since birth. Inborn. Natural. (in AYT)

native [*nat, birth* + *-ive*] 1.Born in a particular place or country. 2.Belonging to a person because of the place, time, or circumstances of birth. 3.Natural. Inherent. Innate. (NAYT iv)

nativity [*nat, birth* + *-ive* + *-ity*] Birth, especially the place, time, or circumstances of a person's birth. (nuh TIV ih tee)

Nativity [*nat, birth* + *-ive* + *-ity*] 1.The birth of Christ. 2.A picture or representation of the birth of Christ. 3.Christmas. (nuh TIV ih tee)

neonatal [*neo, new* + *nat, born* + *-al*] Pertaining to a newborn child, especially during the first month after birth. See prenatal, postnatal, and perinatal. (nee' oh NAYT l)

neonatology [*neo, new* + *nat, born* + *-ology, study of*] The branch of medicine dealing with the study of the care, development, and treatment of newborn children. (nee' oh nay TOL uh jee)

perinatal [*peri-, around* + *nat, birth* + *-al*] Existing or occurring during the period near the time of birth; specifically, the period from the 28th week after gestation through the 7th week after birth. See prenatal, postnatal, and neonatal. (pehr' ih NAYT l)

postnatal [*post-, after* + *nat, birth* + *-al*] Existing or occurring after birth. See prenatal, neonatal, and perinatal. (pohst NAYT l)

prenatal [*pre-, before* + *nat, birth* + *-al*] Existing or occurring before birth. See postnatal, neonatal, and perinatal. (pree NAYT l)

neo   new, recent

antineoplastic [*anti-, against* + *neo, new* + *plast, forming cells or tissue* + *-ic*] Inhibiting or preventing the formation, growth, or proliferation of malignant cells. See neoplasm. (an' tee nee' oh PLAS tik)

glyconeogenesis [*glyco, glycogen* + *neo, new* + *-genesis, formation*] The conversion of noncarbohydrate compounds to glycogen. See glycogenesis and glycogenolysis. (gleye' koh nee' oh JEN uh sis)

misoneism [*miso, to hate* + *neo, new* + *-ism*] Hatred, intolerance, or fear of change, innovation, or anything new or unfamiliar. (mis' oh NEE iz' um)

Neo-Scholasticism [*neo, new & scholasticism*] A movement that attempts to redefine medieval Scholasticism by incorporating new elements such as scientific discoveries and modern intellectual concepts. (nee' oh skuh LAS tih siz' um)

neoclassic [*neo, recent & classic*] Pertaining to a revival of classic form and style in art, music, literature, and architecture. (nee' oh KLAS ik)

neocolonialism [*neo, recent & colonialism*] The indirect economical and political control of a country or region by a more powerful or influential foreign power. (nee' oh kuh LOH nee ul iz' um)

neocortex [*neo, recent & cortex*] The outermost layer of the cerebral cortex that is the most recently developed part of the brain and is normally associated with higher intelligence. (nee' oh KOR teks')

neodymium [*neo, new & (di)dymium*] A rare-earth metallic element used in certain alloys, in lasers, and for coloring glass. So named because it is split from didymium. See didymium. (nee' oh DIM ee um)

neogenesis [*neo, new* + *-genesis, formation*] Tissue regeneration. (nee' oh JEN uh sis)

neoimpressionism [*neo, recent & impressionism*] A French theory and technique of painting in the late 19th century that sought to make impressionism more formal and precise. (nee' oh im PRESH uh niz' um)

Neolithic [*neo, new* + *lith, stone* + *-ic*] Pertaining to the latest period of the Stone Age, characterized by the use of advanced stone tools and weapons and the introduction of farming. (nee' oh LITH ik)

neologism [*neo, new + log, word + -ism*] 1.A new word, phrase, or expression. 2.An established word used in a new sense. (nee OL uh jiz' um)

neonatal [*neo, new + nat, born + -al*] Pertaining to a newborn child, especially during the first month after birth. See prenatal, postnatal, and perinatal. (nee' oh NAYT l)

neonatology [*neo, new + nat, born + -ology, study of*] The branch of medicine dealing with the study of the care, development, and treatment of newborn children. (nee' oh nay TOL uh jee)

neoorthodoxy [*neo, new + ortho, correct + dox, belief + -y*] A 20th century movement in Protestant theology that opposes liberalism and adheres to certain doctrines of the Reformation. (nee' oh OR thuh dok' see)

neophobia [*neo, new + -phobia, fear*] Abnormal fear of novelty or the unknown. (nee' oh FOH bee uh)

neophyte [*neo, new + -phyte, to grow*] 1.A beginner. Novice. 2.A person recently converted to a belief, especially in a religious faith. (NEE uh feyet')

neoplasm [*neo, new + plasm, forming cells or tissue*] Any abnormal new growth of tissue. Tumor. (NEE uh plaz' um)

neoteny [*neo, recent + Grk > teinein, to stretch + -y*] 1.The retention by the adult of some of the immature characteristics of youth. 2.Attainment of sexual maturity while still in the larval stage. (nee OT n ee)

neoteric [*neo, recent + Grk > terikos*] Modern. Recently invented. (nee' oh TEHR ik)

nephr/o   kidney

glomerulonephritis [*glomerul(us) & nephr, kidney + -itis, inflammation*] A type of nephritis marked by inflammation of the capillaries of the renal glomeruli. (gloh mehr' yuh loh' neh FREYE tis)

mesonephros [*meso-, middle + nephr, kidney + -os*] One of the three embryonic excretory organs of vertebrates that functions as the embryonic kidney in higher vertebrates and becomes the adult kidney in fishes and amphibians. See pronephros and metanephros. (mez' uh NEF ros)

metanephros [*meta-, after + nephr, kidney + -os*] One of the three embryonic excretory organs of higher vertebrates that becomes the adult kidney in mammals, reptiles, and birds. See pronephros and mesonephros. (met' uh NEF ros)

nephralgia [*nephr, kidney + alg, pain + -ia*] Pain in the kidneys. (neh FRAL juh)

nephrectomy [*nephr, kidney + ec, out + -tomy, to cut*] Surgical removal of a kidney. (neh FREK tuh mee)

nephrite [*nephr, kidney + -ite, stone*] An often translucent, white to dark-green type of jade that is a less precious jade. So named from the former belief that it could be worn as a remedy for kidney disorders. (NEF reyet)

nephritis [*nephr, kidney + -itis, inflammation*] Acute or chronic inflammation of the kidneys. (neh FREYE tis)

nephrogenous [*nephro, kidney + gen, origin + -ous*] 1.Originating or arising in the kidney. 2.Developing from kidney tissue. (neh FROJ uh nus)

nephrology [*nephr, kidney + -ology, study of*] The branch of medical science dealing with the study of the functions and diseases of the kidneys. (neh FROL uh jee)

nephron [*nephr, kidney + -on*] A single excretory unit in the vertebrate kidney that filters urea and other waste materials from the blood. (NEF ron)

nephrosis [*nephr, kidney + -osis, diseased condition*] A degenerative, noninflammatory disease of the kidneys. (neh FROH sis)

nephrotomy [*nephro, kidney + -tomy, to cut*] Surgical incision of a kidney. (neh FROT uh mee)

perinephrium [*peri-, around + nephr, kidney + -ium*] The fatty and connective tissue surrounding a kidney. (pehr' ih NEF ree um)

pronephros [*pro-, before + nephr, kidney + -os*] One of the three embryonic excretory organs of vertebrates that disappears during the embryonic development of higher vertebrates and becomes the adult kidney in certain lower fishes. See mesonephros and metanephros. (proh NEF ros)

pyelonephritis [*pyelo, renal pelvis + nephr, kidney + -itis, inflammation*] Inflammation of both the kidney and the lining of its pelvis. (peye' uh loh' neh FREYE tis)

neur/o   nerve

aeroneurosis [*aero, air + neur, nerve + -osis, abnormal condition*] A neurosis in aircraft pilots characterized by insomnia, mild depression, and various physical symptoms. (ehr' oh noo ROH sis)

endoneurium [*endo-, inside + neur, nerve + -ium*] The protective covering of connective tissue surrounding each individual nerve fiber in a peripheral nerve. See perineurium and epineurium. (en' doh NOOR ee um)

epineurium [*epi-, outside + neur, nerve + -ium*] The protective covering of connective tissue surrounding a peripheral nerve. See endoneurium and perineurium. (ep' ih NOOR ee um)

interneuron [*inter-, between + neur, nerve + -on*] Neurons that link sensory and motor neurons in the brain and spinal cord. (in' ter NOOR on')

myoneural [*myo, muscle + neur, nerve + -al*] Having to do with both muscle and nerve, especially the nerve endings in muscle tissue. See neuromuscular. (meye' uh NOOR ul)

neural [*neur, nerve + -al*] Pertaining to the nervous system or to a nerve. (NOOR ul)

neuralgia [*neur, nerve + alg, pain + -ia*] Intense pain along the course of one or more nerves. (noo RAL juh)

neurasthenia [*neur, nerve + a-, without + sthen, strength + -ia*] A disorder originally thought to result from neural exhaustion, including such symptoms as chronic fatigue, weakness, and irritability. (noor' us THEE nee uh)

neurectomy [*neur, nerve + ec, out + -tomy, to cut*] Surgical removal of all or part of a nerve. (noo REK tuh mee)

neurilemma [*neur, nerve + Grk > eilema, covering*] A thin membranous sheath surrounding a nerve fiber. (noor' uh LEM uh)

neuritis [*neur, nerve + -itis, inflammation*] Inflammation of a nerve, resulting in pain, sensory disturbances, and muscular atrophy. (noo REYE tis)

neuroanatomy [*neuro, nerve & anatomy*] The branch of neurology dealing with the study of the anatomy of the nervous system. (noor' oh uh NAT uh mee)

neur/o

neuroblast [*neuro, nerve* + *blast, immature cell*] An immature nerve cell that develops into a neuron. (NOOR uh blast')

neuroblastoma [*neuro, nerve* + *blast, cell* + *-oma, tumor*] A malignant tumor composed of neuroblasts, most often affecting the adrenal medulla of infants and children. See neuroblast. (noor' oh blas TOH muh)

neurochemistry [*neuro, nerve* & *chemistry*] The branch of medical science dealing with the study of the chemical structure and activities of the nervous system. (noor' oh KEM ih stree)

neurofibril [*neuro, nerve* & *fibril (small fiber)*] Any of numerous tiny filaments of a nerve cell body that also extend into the axon and dendrites. (noor' oh FIB rul)

neurogenic [*neuro, nerve* + *gen, origin* + *-ic*] Originating in, caused by, or controlled by the nervous system. (noor' oh JEN ik)

neuroglia [*neuro, nerve* + *Grk* > *glia, glue*] Cells, other than neurons, that form the supporting tissue of the brain and spinal cord. (noo ROG lee uh)

neurology [*neur, nerve* + *-ology, study of*] The branch of medical science dealing with the study of the structure, functions, and diseases of the nervous system. (noo ROL uh jee)

neuroma [*neur, nerve* + *-oma, tumor*] A tumor composed of nerve tissue. (noo ROH muh)

neuromuscular [*neuro, nerve* & *muscular*] Pertaining to or involving nerves and muscles. See myoneural. (noor' oh MUS kyuh lur)

neuron [*neur, nerve* + *-on*] The basic functional and structural unit of the nervous system composed of the cell body, the axon, and one or more dendrites. See axon and dendrite (def. 2). (NOOR on)

neuropathology [*neuro, nerve* + *path, disease* + *-ology, study of*] The branch of medical science dealing with the study of diseases of the nervous system. See neurophysiology and pathology. (noor' oh puh THOL uh jee)

neuropathy [*neuro, nerve* + *-pathy, disease*] A disease or disorder of the nervous system. (noo ROP uh thee)

neurophysiology [*neuro, nerve* + *physi, physical* + *-ology, study of*] The branch of medical science dealing with the study of the functions and activities of the nervous system. See neuropathology and physiology. (noor' oh fiz' ee OL uh jee)

neuropsychiatry [*neuro, nerve* + *psych, mind* + *iatr, healing* + *-y*] The branch of medical science dealing with the study and treatment of diseases and disorders of the mind and nervous system. (noor' oh seye KEYE uh tree)

neuropterous [*neuro, nerve* + *pter, wing* + *-ous*] Pertaining to carnivorous insects with four membranous wings and biting mouth parts. (noo ROP ter us)

neurosis [*neur, nerve* + *-osis, abnormal condition*] Any of various mental or emotional disorders, including anxiety, phobias, and obsessions, that usually do not include an impaired perception of reality. See psychosis. (noo ROH sis)

neurosurgery [*neuro, nerve* & *surgery*] Any surgery involving the nervous system. (noor' oh SUR jer ee)

neurotomy [*neuro, nerve* + *-tomy, to cut*] The surgical cutting of a nerve, usually to relieve pain or cause loss of sensation. (noo ROT uh mee)

neurotoxin [*neuro, nerve* & *toxin*] A toxin that destroys nerve tissue, as rattlesnake venom. See hemotoxin and cytotoxin. (NOOR oh tok' sin)

neurotransmitter [*neuro, nerve* & *transmitter*] A chemical substance that transmits impulses between two nerve cells. (noor' oh TRANS mit ur)

neurotropic [*neuro, nerve* + *trop, turning* + *-ic*] Having a natural attraction to nerve tissue, as certain toxins or viruses. See neurotoxin. (noor' oh TROP ik)

perineurium [*peri-, around* + *neur, nerve* + *-ium*] The protective covering of connective tissue surrounding each bundle of nerve fibers in a peripheral nerve. See endoneurium and epineurium. (pehr' ih NOOR ee um)

polyneuritis [*poly, many* + *neur, nerve* + *-itis, inflammation*] Inflammation of two or more peripheral nerves. (pol' ee noo REYE tis)

psychoneurosis [*psycho, mind* + *neur, nerve* + *-osis, abnormal condition*] Any of various mental or emotional disorders, including anxiety, phobias, and obsessions, that usually do not include an impaired perception of reality. Same as neurosis. (seye' koh noo ROH sis)

nom/o, -nomy
law, system of laws, management, rule

aeronomy [*aero, air* + *-nomy, system of laws*] The science dealing with the study of the physics and chemistry of the upper atmosphere. (ehr ON uh mee)

agronomics [*agro, crop production* + *nom, system of laws* + *-ics, science*] The science of soil management and crop production. Same as agronomy. (ag' ruh NOM iks)

agronomy [*agro, crop production* + *-nomy, system of laws*] The science of soil management and crop production. (uh GRON uh mee)

anomie [*a-, without* + *nom, system of laws* + *-ie*] A lack of standards and values, resulting in social or personal instability. (AN uh mee)

anomy [*a-, without* + *-nomy, system of laws*] A lack of standards and values, resulting in social or personal instability. Same as anomie. (AN uh mee)

antinomian [*anti-, against* + *nom, law* + *-ian*] A person who believes that by the virtue of grace Christians are free from the obligations of moral law. (an' tih NOH mee un)

antinomy [*anti-, against* + *-nomy, law*] 1.A contradiction between laws, statements, or principles that seem equally reasonable and necessary. 2.Opposition between laws, principles, rules, etc. (an TIN uh mee)

astronomical [*astronom(y)* & *-ical*] 1.Having to do with astronomy. 2.Extremely large, as the values used in astronomy. See enormous and cosmic (def. 2). (as' truh NOM ih kul)

astronomical unit [*astronomical* & *unit*] A unit of length, approximately 93 million miles, equal to the average distance from the earth to the sun, used to express astronomical distances. (as' truh NOM ih kul YOO nit)

astronomy [*astro, star* + *-nomy, system of laws*] The scientific study of the universe. See astrology. (uh STRON uh mee)

autonomic [*auto-, self* + *nom, management* + *-ic*] Functioning or occurring involuntarily. See autonomic nervous system. (awt' uh NOM ik)

autonomic nervous system The part of the nervous system that controls the activity of involuntary body functions, including cardiac, respiratory, glandular, and other automatic functions. See sympathetic nervous system and parasympathetic nervous system. (awt' uh NOM ik NUR vus SIS tum)

autonomous [*auto-, self* + *nom, law* + *-ous*] 1.Self-governing. Independent. See heteronomous and semiautonomous. 2.Functioning or developing independently. 3.Existing as an independent organism. (aw TON uh mus)

autonomy [*auto-, self* + *-nomy, law*] The right of self-government. Independence. (aw TON uh mee)

bionomics [*bio, life* + *nom, law* + *-ics, study of*] Ecology. (beye' uh NOM iks)

chemotaxonomy [*chemo, chemical* + *taxo, arrangement* + *-nomy, system of laws*] The classification of organisms based on biochemical criteria. See taxonomy. (kee' moh taks ON uh mee)

cytotaxonomy [*cyto, cell* + *taxo, arrangement* + *-nomy, system of laws*] The classification of organisms based on chromosome characteristics and cellular structure. See taxonomy. (seyet' oh taks ON uh mee)

Deuteronomy [*deutero, second* + *-nomy, law*] The fifth book of the Old Testament in which the law of Moses is stated for the second time. (doot' uh RON uh mee)

econometrics [*econo(mics)* & *metr, measure* + *-ics, knowledge*] The application of statistical and mathematical analysis to economics to solve problems and verify theories. (ih kon' uh MET riks)

economics [*Grk* > *oikos, house* + *nom, management* + *-ics, study of*] The scientific study of the production and distribution of wealth. (ek' uh NOM iks)

economy [*Grk* > *oikos, house* + *-nomy, management*] The management of the income, expenditures, and affairs of a household, business, community, or government. (ih KON uh mee)

ergonomics [*erg, work* & *(ec)onomics*] The study of the relationship between people and their working environment. (ur' guh NOM iks)

gastronomy [*gastro, stomach* + *-nomy, system of laws*] The art or practice of good eating. (gas TRON uh mee)

heteronomous [*hetero, other* + *nom, law* + *-ous*] Subject to the laws of another. See autonomous (def. 1) and semiautonomous. (het' uh RON uh mus)

isonomy [*iso-, equal* + *-nomy, system of laws*] Equality of laws or civil rights. (eye SON uh mee)

macroeconomics [*macro-, large* & *economics*] A branch of economics dealing with the study of the overall forces at work in an economy. See microeconomics. (mak' roh ek' uh NOM iks)

metronome [*metr, measure* + *nom, rule*] An instrument for marking exact musical time in preselected intervals. (MET ruh nohm')

microeconomics [*micro-, small* & *economics*] A branch of economics dealing with the study of certain specific factors at work in an economy. See macroeconomics. (meye' kroh ek' uh NOM iks)

nomography [*nomo, law* + *-graphy, science*] The art of drafting laws. See nomology (def. 1). (noh MOG ruh fee)

nomology [*nom, law* + *-ology, science*] 1.The science of law and lawmaking. See nomography. 2.The laws that govern the phenomena of a science. (noh MOL uh jee)

nom, nomin, nomen, onomas, onomat

nomothetic [*nomo, law* + *the, to put* + *-ic*] 1.Enacting laws. 2.Pertaining to a science of abstract, universal, or general laws. (nom' uh THET ik)

semiautonomous [*semi-, partly* & *autonomous*] Self-governing only with regard to certain affairs. See autonomous (def. 1) and heteronomous. (sem' ee aw TON uh mus)

socioeconomic [*socio, social* & *economic*] Pertaining to the interaction between social and economic factors. (soh' see oh ek' uh NOM ik)

taxonomy [*taxo, arrangement* + *-nomy, system of laws*] 1.The science of classification. 2.The classification of organisms based on common factors and relationships to each other. (taks ON uh mee)

theonomous [*theo, God* + *nom, system of laws* + *-ous*] Governed or controlled by God. (thee ON uh mus)

nom, nomin, nomen, onomas, onomat
name, noun

agnomen [*ag-, addition to* + *nomen, name*] 1.In ancient Rome, an additional name given to a Roman citizen in honor of some achievement. 2.Nickname. (ag NOH mun)

antonomasia [*anti-, instead of* + *onomas, name* + *-ia*] 1.The use of a title or epithet in place of a proper name, such as referring to a judge as "your honor." 2.The use of a proper name to designate a person or class that it is typical of, such as referring to a philanderer as "Casanova" or "Don Juan." (an' tuh noh MAY zhuh)

binomial [*bi-, two* + *nom, name* + *-ial*] 1.A mathematical expression consisting of two terms. 2.In taxonomy, a two-part name designating the genus and the species of an organism. See monomial, trinomial, and polynomial. (beye NOH mee ul)

cognomen [*co-, together* + *nomen, name*] 1.Any family name. 2.The third name of an ancient Roman citizen. 3.Any name or nickname. (kog NOH mun)

denominate [*de-, derived from* + *nomin, name* + *-ate*] To give a name to. Designate. (dih NOM uh nayt')

denomination [*de-, derived from* + *nomin, name* + *-ation*] 1.The name of a class or group of things. 2.A religious body or sect. (dih nom' uh NAY shun)

ignominy [*ig-, without* + *nomin, name* + *-y*] 1.Loss of one's good name and reputation. 2.Great personal shame and dishonor. (IG nuh min' ee)

innominate [*in-, without* + *nomin, name* + *-ate*] Without a name. Anonymous. See anonymous (def. 1). (ih NOM uh nit)

misnomer [*mis-, bad* + *nom, name* + *-er*] 1.An erroneous name of a person, place, or thing. 2.A misapplied name of a person, place, or thing. (mis NOH mer)

monomial [*mon-, one* + *nom, name* + *-ial*] 1.A mathematical expression consisting of only one term. 2.A taxonomic name consisting of one word. See binomial, trinomial, and polynomial. (muh NOH mee ul)

nom de guerre [*French* > *nom de querre, war name*] Pseudonym. See pseudonym, nom de plume, and anonym. (nom' duh GEHR)

nom de plume [*French* > *nom de plume, pen name*] Pen name. See pseudonym, nom de guerre, and allonym. (nom' duh PLOOM)

nom, nomin, nomen, onomas, onomat

nomenclator [*nomen, name* + *Ltn > calare, to call* + *-ator*] A person who invents and assigns names, as in scientific classification. (NOH mun klay' tur)

nomenclature [*nomen, name* + *Ltn > calare, to call* + *-ature*] A system of names used in a particular branch of art or science. (NOH mun klay' chur)

nominal [*nomin, name* + *-al*] 1.Pertaining to or consisting of a name or names. 2.Pertaining to, functioning as, or being a noun. 3.Being something in name only. Insignificantly small. (NOM uh nul)

nominate [*nomin, name* + *-ate*] 1.To name as a candidate for election to public office. 2.To appoint to an office or duty. 3.To name as a possible recipient of an award or honor. (NOM uh nayt')

onomastic [*onomas, name* + *-tic*] Pertaining to or consisting of a name or names. (on' uh MAS tik)

onomasticon [*onomas, name* + *-ic* + *-on*] A book or list of proper names. (on' uh MAS tih kon')

onomastics [*onomas, name* + *-ics, study of*] The study of the origin, evolution, and use of proper names. (on' uh MAS tiks)

onomatology [*onomat, name* + *-ology, study of*] The study of the origin, evolution, and use of proper names. Same as onomastics. (on' uh muh TOL uh jee)

onomatopoeia [*onomat, name* + *Grk > poiein, to make* + *-ia*] The naming of something by a vocal imitation of its sound, as buzz, hum, etc. (on' uh mat' uh PEE uh)

paronomasia [*para-, variation* + *onomas, name* + *-ia*] A play on words. Pun. (pehr' uh noh MAY zhuh)

polynomial [*poly, many* + *nom, name* + *-ial*] A mathematical expression consisting of two or more terms. See monomial, binomial, and trinomial. (pol' uh NOH mee ul)

trinomial [*tri-, three* + *nom, name* + *-ial*] 1.A mathematical expression consisting of three terms. 2.In taxonomy, a three-part name designating the genus, species, and subspecies of an organism. See monomial, binomial, and polynomial. (treye NOH mee ul)

onym   name, word

acronym [*acro, high* + *onym, name*] A word formed from the first letter or group of letters from each word of a series of words, such as *radar* from (ra)dio (d)etecting (a)nd (r)anging. (AK ruh nim')

allonym [*all, other* + *onym, name*] Another person's name assumed by a writer as a pen name. See pseudonym and nom de plume. (AL uh nim')

anonym [*an-, without* + *onym, name*] 1.An anonymous person. 2.Pseudonym. See pseudonym and nom de guerre. (AN uh nim')

anonymous [*an-, without* + *onym, name* + *-ous*] 1.Without a known or acknowledged name. 2.Of unknown source or origin. 3.Without individuality or distinct characteristics. (uh NON uh mus)

antonym [*anti-, opposite* + *onym, word*] A word with the opposite meaning of another word in the same language. (AN tuh nim')

eponym [*ep-, upon* + *onym, name*] A real or mythical person after whom something, such as a place, period, theory, discovery, etc., is named. (EP uh nim')

heteronym [*hetero, different* + *onym, word*] One of two or more words that are spelled the same, but always differ in meaning and pronunciation, as *sow* (to plant seeds) and *sow* (a female pig). See homonym and homograph. (HET ur uh nim')

homonym [*homo, same* + *onym, word*] One of two or more words that are pronounced the same, always differ in meaning, and usually differ in spelling, as *wear* (to carry on the body) and *ware* (articles of merchandise). See heteronym and homograph. (HOM uh nim')

homonymous [*homo, same* + *onym, name* + *-ous*] 1.Ambiguous. 2.Having the same name. (hoh MON uh mus)

matronymic [*matr, mother* + *onym, name* + *-ic*] Pertaining to a name derived from the name of the mother or other female ancestor. See patronymic. (mat' ruh NIM ik)

metonymy [*meta-, change* + *onym, name* + *-y*] A figure of speech having the name of one object or concept replaced by the name of another related object or concept usually associated with it, as "Capitol Hill" for "the Congress." See metaphor. (muh TON uh mee)

metronymic [*Grk > meter, mother* + *onym, name* + *-ic*] Pertaining to a name derived from the name of the mother or other female ancestor. Same as matronymic. (mee' truh NIM ik)

paronym [*para-, beside* + *onym, word*] A word derived from the same root as another, as *heal* and *health*. Cognate. (PEHR uh nim')

patronymic [*patr, father* + *onym, name* + *-ic*] Pertaining to a name derived from the name of the father or other male ancestor. See matronymic. (pat' ruh NIM ik)

pseudonym [*pseud, false* + *onym, name*] A fictitious name, as one assumed by a writer. Pen name. See allonym, nom de plume, and nom de guerre. (SOOD n im')

retronym [*retro-, back* + *onym, name*] A term used to distinguish ideas or objects from innovations replacing or improving them, as *night baseball* or *skim milk*. (RET ruh nim')

synonym [*syn-, same* + *onym, name*] A word with a similar meaning in one or more senses to another word in the same language. See antonym. (SIN uh nim')

synonymous [*syn-, same* + *onym, name* + *-ous*] Having a similar meaning. (sih NON uh mus)

tautonym [*taut, same* + *onym, name*] A scientific name, commonly used in zoology, but forbidden in botany, in which the genus and the species are given the same name. (TAW tuh nim')

toponym [*Grk > topos, place* + *onym, name*] The name of a place or region. (TOP uh nim')

toponymy [*Grk > topos, place* + *onym, name* + *-y*] The etymological study of the place names of a language or region. (tuh PON uh mee)

ocul   eye

binocular [*bin-, two* + *ocul, eye* + *-ar*] Pertaining to or used by both eyes. See monocular. (buh NOK yuh lur)

intraocular [*intra-, within* + *ocul, eye* + *-ar*] Occurring or located within the eyeball. (in' truh OK yuh lur)

monocle [*mon-, one* + *ocul, eye*] An eyeglass for use with one eye only. (MON uh kul)

monocular [*mon-, one* + *ocul, eye* + *-ar*] Pertaining to or used by one eye only. See binocular. (muh NOK yuh lur)

ocular [*ocul, eye + -ar*] 1.Pertaining to the eye or vision. See optic and ophthalmic. 2.The eyepiece of an optical instrument. (OK yuh lur)

oculist [*ocul, eye + -ist*] An obsolete term for ophthalmologist or optometrist. (OK yuh list)

oculomotor [*ocul, eye & motor*] 1.Pertaining to eyeball movements. 2.Pertaining to the oculomotor nerve. (ok' yuh loh MOHT ur)

retroocular [*retro-, behind + ocul, eye + -ar*] Located behind the eyeball. (ret' roh OK yuh lur)

op, ops, opt/o, ophthalm/o, -opia, -opsy
eye, visual condition, vision, sight, inspection

acoustooptics [*acoust(ics) & optics*] The branch of physics dealing with the study of the interaction between sound waves and light waves. (uh koo' stoh OP tiks)

amblyopia [*Grk > amblys, dim + -opia, visual condition*] Impairment of vision without apparent injury or disease of the eye. (am' blee OH pee uh)

ametropia [*a-, not + metr, measure + -opia, visual condition*] Any visual condition resulting from abnormal refraction of the eye, such as astigmatism, nearsightedness, or farsightedness. (am' ih TROH pee uh)

anisometropia [*aniso-, not equal + metr, measure + -opia, visual condition*] An abnormal visual condition in which the refractive power is not equal in both eyes. See isometropia. (an eye' soh mih TROH pee uh)

asthenopia [*a-, without + sthen, strength + -opia, visual condition*] Eye weakness or strain, often causing headache, ocular discomfort, etc. (as thuh NOH pee uh)

autopsy [*auto-, self + -opsy, inspection*] The examination of a dead body, including the internal organs and structures, to determine the cause of death or the nature of pathological conditions. See necropsy. (AW top see)

biopsy [*bio, living tissue + -opsy, inspection*] The removal of a small sample of living tissue for examination and diagnosis. (BEYE op' see)

coreopsis [*Grk > koris, bug + Grk > opsis, appearance*] Any of various composite plants with rayed, yellow or reddish flowers. So named from the shape of the seed. (kor' ee OP sis)

cyclops [*cycl, circle + ops, eye*] In Greek mythology, any of the giants with a single eye located in the middle of the forehead. (SEYE klops)

deuteranopia [*deuter, second + an-, without + -opia, visual condition*] A visual defect in which the retina fails to respond to the color green. So named from the blindness to green, which is regarded as the second primary color. See protanopia and tritanopia. (doot' uh ruh NOH pee uh)

diopside [*di-, double + Grk > opsis, appearance + -ide*] A monoclinic pyroxene mineral that is green to almost black in color and often occurs in well-formed crystals. (deye OP seyed')

diopter [*dia-, through + opt, sight + -er*] A unit of measure of the refractive power of a lens equal to the reciprocal of its focal length expressed in meters. (deye OP ter)

op, ops, opt/o, ophthalm/o, -opia, -opsy

dioptometer [*dia-, through + opto, eye + meter, to measure*] An optical instrument for measuring and testing the refraction and accommodation of the eye. (deye' op TOM et er)

dioptrics [*dia-, through + opt, sight + -ics, study of*] The branch of optics dealing with the study of refracted light. See optics. (deye OP triks)

diplopia [*diplo, double + -opia, visual condition*] A visual condition in which objects appear double. Double vision. See haplopia. (dip LOH pee uh)

emmetropia [*en-, in + metr, to measure + -opia, visual condition*] The visual condition of normal refraction in the eye in which light is focused exactly on the retina, resulting in perfect vision. See myopia (def. 1) and hyperopia. (em' ih TROH pee uh)

exophthalmos [*ex-, out + ophthalm, eye + -os*] Abnormal protrusion of the eyeball. (eks' ahf THAL mus)

exophthalmus [*ex-, out + ophthalm, eye + -us*] Abnormal protrusion of the eyeball. Same as exophthalmos. (eks' ahf THAL mus)

haplopia [*haplo-, single + -opia, visual condition*] Normal vision. See diplopia. (hap LOH pee uh)

hemeralopia [*hemer, day + -opia, visual condition*] A visual condition characterized by the inability to see as well in bright light as in dim light. See nyctalopia. (hem' ur uh LOH pee uh)

hypermetropia [*hyper-, above + metr, measure + -opia, visual condition*] A visual condition in which light is focused behind the retina rather than on it, resulting in distant vision being clear and near vision being blurred. Farsightedness. Same as hyperopia. (heye' per mih TROH pee uh)

hyperopia [*hyper-, above + -opia, visual condition*] A visual condition in which light is focused behind the retina rather than on it, resulting in distant vision being clear and near vision being blurred. Farsightedness. Opposed to myopia (def. 1). (heye' per OH pee uh)

iodopsin [*Grk > iodes, violet + ops, eye + -in*] A light-sensitive violet pigment found in the cones of the retina and important for color vision. Visual violet. See rhodopsin and porphyropsin. (eye' uh DOP sin)

isometropia [*iso-, equal + metr, measure + -opia, visual condition*] A visual condition in which the refractive power is equal in both eyes. See anisometropia. (eye' soh mih TROH pee uh)

metopic [*meta-, between + op, eye + -ic*] Relating to the forehead. (mih TOP ik)

myopia [*Grk > myein, to shut + -opia, eye*] 1.A visual condition in which light is focused in front of the retina rather than on it because of increased strength in refractive power, resulting in distant vision being blurred and near vision being clear. Nearsightedness. Opposed to hyperopia. 2.Lack of foresight in thinking or planning. (meye OH pee uh)

necropsy [*necr, dead + -opsy, inspection*] The examination of a dead body. Autopsy. (NEK rop' see)

nyctalopia [*nyct, night + Grk > alaos, blindness + -opia, visual condition*] A visual condition characterized by the inability to see well in dim light. Night blindness. See hemeralopia. (nik' tuh LOH pee uh)

ommatidium [*Grk > ommat, eye + -idium*] One of the radial elements that make up the compound eye of an insect or other arthropod. (om' uh TID ee um)

op, ops, opt/o, ophthalm/o, -opia, -opsy

ophthalmia [*ophthalm, eye* + *-ia*] Severe inflammation of the eye. (ahf THAL mee uh)

ophthalmic [*ophthalm, eye* + *-ic*] Pertaining to the eye. See ocular (def. 1) and optic. (ahf THAL mik)

ophthalmology [*ophthalm, eye* + *-ology, study of*] The branch of medical science dealing with the study of the functions and diseases of the eye. See optometry. (ahf' thul MOL uh jee)

ophthalmoscope [*ophthalmo, eye* + *-scope, to examine*] An instrument for examining the interior of the eye. (ahf THAL muh skohp')

optic [*opt, eye* + *-ic*] Pertaining to the eye or vision. See ocular (def. 1) and ophthalmic. (OP tik)

optical [*opt, sight* + *-ical*] Pertaining to vision. Visual. (OP tih kul)

optician [*opt, eye* + *-ician*] A maker or seller of eyeglasses, lenses, or other optical instruments. (op TISH un)

optics [*opt, vision* + *-ics, study of*] The scientific study of vision and the properties of light. (OP tiks)

optokinetic [*opto, eye* + *kinet, motion* + *-ic*] Pertaining to or involving eye movements. (op' toh kih NET ik)

optometry [*opto, eye* + *-metry, science of measuring*] The science of measuring and diagnosing visual defects and disorders with treatment limited to glasses and exercises and not including drugs or surgery. See ophthalmology. (op TOM ih tree)

panoptic [*pan, all* + *opt, vision* + *-ic*] Having everything visible included in one view. (pan OP tik)

photopia [*phot, light* + *-opia, vision*] Adaptation of the eyes to bright light. Opposed to scotopia. (foh TOH pee uh)

porphyropsin [*porphyr, violet* + *ops, eye* + *-in*] A purple pigment found in the retinal rods of freshwater fishes that closely resembles rhodopsin. See rhodopsin and iodopsin. (por' fuh ROP sin)

presbyopia [*presby, old* + *-opia, visual condition*] Farsightedness that occurs with advancing age as the crystalline lens of the eye loses elasticity. (prez' bee OH pee uh)

protanopia [*prot-, first* + *an-, without* + *-opia, visual condition*] A visual defect in which the retina fails to respond to the color red. So named from the blindness to red, which is regarded as the first primary color. See deuteranopia and tritanopia. (proht' n OH pee uh)

rhodopsin [*rhod, red* + *ops, eye* + *-in*] A purple pigment in the outer part of the retina that is essential for vision in dim light. Visual purple. See porphyropsin and iodopsin. (roh DOP sin)

scotopia [*Grk > skotos, darkness* + *-opia, vision*] Adaptation of the eyes to dim light. Opposed to photopia. (skuh TOH pee uh)

stereopsis [*stereo-, three-dimensional* + *ops, vision* + *-is*] Three-dimensional vision. (stehr' ee OP sis)

synopsis [*syn-, same* + *ops, vision* + *-is*] A brief overview of a subject, book, movie, etc. (sih NOP sis)

thanatopsis [*thanat, death* + *ops, vision* + *-is*] A contemplation or vision of death. (than' uh TOP sis)

tritanopia [*Grk > tritos, third* + *an-, without* + *-opia, visual condition*] A visual defect in which the retina fails to respond to the color blue. So named from the blindness to blue, which is regarded as the third primary color. See protanopia and deuteranopia. (treye' tuh NOH pee uh)

xerophthalmia [*xer, dry* + *ophthalm, eye* + *-ia*] Abnormal dryness of the conjunctiva and cornea of the eyeball due to vitamin A deficiency. (zihr' ahf THAL mee uh)

omni-   all

omnibus [*omni, all & bus*] 1.A vehicle designed to carry a large number of passengers. 2.A volume of written works by a single author or on a single subject. 3.Including or covering numerous items or cases at once, as a law. (OM nih bus')

omnidirectional [*omni-, all & directional*] Able to transmit and receive signals in all directions, as certain antennas. See unidirectional and bidirectional. (om' nee duh REK shuh nul)

omnifarious [*omni-, all* + *Ltn > farius, fold*] Of all kinds, forms, or varieties. (om' nih FEHR ee us)

omnificent [*omni-, all* + *fic, to make* + *-ent*] Having all-creative powers. (om NIF uh sent)

omnipotent [*omni-, all & potent*] Having unlimited power or influence. All-powerful. (om NIP uh tent)

omnipresent [*omni-, all & present*] 1.Present everywhere at the same time. 2.Widely or often encountered. Ubiquitous. (om' nih PREZ unt)

omnirange [*omni-, all & range*] A radio navigation system that sends signals in all directions, thus providing complete bearing information for aircraft. (OM nih raynj')

omniscient [*omni-, all* + *Ltn > scientia, knowledge*] Having unlimited knowledge. All-knowing. (om NISH ent)

omnium-gatherum [*omni-, all* + *-um & gather* + *-um*] A miscellaneous collection. (OM nee um GATH ur um)

omnivorous [*omni-, all* + *vor, to eat* + *-ous*] 1.Feeding on both animal and vegetable food. 2.Avidly taking in everything available, as with the mind. (om NIV ur us)

pan, panto   all

cyclorama [*cycl, circle* & *(pan)orama*] A pictorial representation consisting of large pictures or projections on the inside wall of a circular room, creating a natural perspective for an observer standing in or near the center. See panorama. (seye' kluh RAM uh)

panacea [*pan, all* + *Grk > akos, cure* + *-a*] A presumed cure for all ills, evils, or difficulties. (pan' uh SEE uh)

panchromatic [*pan, all* + *chromat, color* + *-ic*] Pertaining to films or plates that correctly represent all visible colors in the spectrum. See orthochromatic (def. 2). (pan' kroh MAT ik)

pancreas [*pan, all* + *Grk > kreas, flesh*] An elongated gland situated near the stomach that functions both as an exocrine and an endocrine gland, secreting pancreatic juice into the small intestine through the pancreatic duct and secreting the hormones insulin and glucagon into the blood stream. (PAN kree us)

pandect [*pan, all* + *Grk > dektes, to receive*] A complete body of laws. (PAN dekt)

pandemic [*pan, all* + *dem, people* + *-ic*] A disease that is prevalent over a very large area, a continent, or the entire world. See epidemic. (pan DEM ik)

pandemonium [*pan, all & demon* & *-ium*] 1.Wild uproar and confusion. 2.The home of all demons. Hell. (pan' duh MOH nee um)

Pandora's box [*pan, all + Grk > doron, gift & box*] A source of unforseen problems. So named from the myth that the first woman, out of curiosity, opened a box given to her by the gods, thereby releasing all that is evil on mankind. (pan DOR uhz boks)

panegyric [*pan, all + Grk > agyris, assembly + -ic*] 1.A formal speech or writing giving high praise to someone or something. 2.Elaborate or extravagant praise. See eulogy. (pan' uh JIHR ik)

pangenesis [*pan, all + -genesis, production*] The now discredited theory that hereditary characteristics are carried by very minute particles that come from individual body cells and collect in reproductive cells. Opposed to blastogenesis (def. 2). (pan JEN uh sis)

panhuman [*pan, all & human*] Pertaining to all humanity. (pan HYOO mun)

panophobia [*pano, all + -phobia, fear*] Fear of everything. (pan' uh FOH bee uh)

panoply [*pan, all + Grk > hopla, armor + -y*] 1.A full suit of armor. 2.A protective covering. (PAN uh plee)

panoptic [*pan, all + opt, vision + -ic*] Having everything visible included in one view. (pan OP tik)

panorama [*pan, all + orama, view*] 1.A complete and unobstructed view of a wide area. 2.A series of pictures presented one at a time so as to appear as a continuous scene. (pan' uh RAM uh)

pansophy [*pan, all + -sophy, wisdom*] Universal wisdom or knowledge. (PAN suh fee)

pantheism [*pan, all + the, God + -ism*] 1.The doctrine that identifies God with the laws and forces of nature. 2.Toleration and worship of all the gods. (PAN thee iz' um)

pantheon [*pan, all + the, god + -on*] 1.A temple built in Rome in 27 B.C. for all the gods. 2.A temple for all the gods. 3.A building containing memorials or tombs of a nation's celebrated dead. (PAN thee on')

pantograph [*panto, all + graph, drawing*] An instrument for producing a map or drawing on any scale. (PANT uh graf')

pantomime [*panto, all + mim, to imitate*] 1.A dance or drama in which performers express themselves without dialog. 2.Conveyance of meaning using gestures and facial expressions. (PANT uh meyem')

ortho   straight, correct, vertical, perpendicular

anorthite [*an-, not + ortho, straight + -ite, rock*] A white, gray, or pink plagioclase feldspar found in many igneous rocks. So named for its oblique crystals. (an OR theyet')

anorthosite [*an-, not + ortho, straight + -ite, rock*] A plutonic igneous rock, chiefly plagioclase feldspar. So named for its oblique crystals. (an OR thuh seyet')

neoorthodoxy [*neo, new + ortho, correct + dox, belief + -y*] A 20th century movement in Protestant theology that opposes liberalism and adheres to certain doctrines of the Reformation. (nee' oh OR thuh dok' see)

orthocenter [*ortho, perpendicular & center*] The point where the three altitudes of a triangle intersect. (OR thuh sent' ur)

orthocephalous [*ortho, correct + cephal, head + -ous*] Having a normally proportioned head. (or' thuh SEF uh lus)

orthochromatic [*ortho, correct + chromat, color + -ic*] 1.Correctly representing the relative intensity of colors. 2.Pertaining to films and plates treated to correctly represent all colors except red. See panchromatic. (or' thoh kroh MAT ik)

orthoclase [*ortho, straight + Grk > klasis, breaking*] A common mineral of the feldspar group characterized by perpendicular cleavages, causing it to always break straight. See oligoclase. (OR thuh klayz')

orthodontics [*ortho, straight + dont, teeth + -ics, practice*] The branch of dentistry dealing with the straightening of abnormally aligned or positioned teeth. (or' thuh DONT iks)

orthodox [*ortho, correct + dox, belief*] Conforming to established doctrines or beliefs. See unorthodox and heterodox. (OR thuh doks')

orthoepy [*ortho, correct + Grk > epos, word + -y*] The study of correct word pronunciation. (or THOH uh pee)

orthogenesis [*ortho, straight + -genesis, generation*] The now discredited theory that evolutionary change progresses in a predetermined direction independent of natural selection and other external factors. (or' thuh JEN uh sis)

orthognathous [*ortho, straight + gnath, jaw + -ous*] Having the lower and upper jaws aligned. See prognathous. (or THOG nuh thus)

orthogonal [*ortho, perpendicular + gon, angle + -al*] Pertaining to or involving right angles. (or THOG uh nul)

orthograde [*ortho, vertical + -grade, to step*] Walking or standing with the body in a vertical position, as a biped. See pronograde. (OR thuh grayd')

orthography [*ortho, correct + -graphy, writing*] 1.Correct spelling according to established and accepted rules. See cacography (def. 2). 2.The study of spelling. (or THOG ruh fee)

orthopaedics [*ortho, correct + ped, child + -ics, practice*] The branch of medicine dealing with the treatment of disorders and diseases of the musculoskeletal system, which includes bones, joints, muscles, tendons, and ligaments. Same as orthopedics. (or' thuh PEED iks)

orthopedics [*ortho, correct + ped, child + -ics, practice*] The branch of medicine dealing with the treatment of disorders and diseases of the musculoskeletal system, which includes bones, joints, muscles, tendons, and ligaments. (or' thuh PEED iks)

orthopsychiatry [*ortho, correct + psych, mind + iatr, healing + -y*] The branch of medical science dealing with the study and treatment of emotional and behavioral disorders, especially in children. (or' thoh seye KEYE uh tree)

orthopteran [*ortho, straight + pter, wing + -an*] Any of an order of insects, including locusts, crickets, and grasshoppers, that have, when present, a pair of straight and thickened forewings and a pair of membranous hindwings. (or THOP ter un)

orthorhombic [*ortho, perpendicular & rhomb(us) & -ic*] Pertaining to a crystal whose structure is characterized by three unequal axes intersecting at right angles. See triclinic. (or' thuh ROM bik)

orthoscope [*ortho, correct + -scope, to examine*] An instrument for examining the interior of the eye through a layer of water that corrects distortion due to corneal refraction. (OR thuh skohp')

DICTIONARY

orthostatic [*ortho, vertical* + *stat, standing* + *-ic*] Caused by standing in an upright position. (or' thuh STAT ik)

orthostichous [*ortho, vertical* + *-stichous, having rows*] Characterized by an arrangement of parallel rows on a vertical axis, as leaves on a stem. (or THOS tih kus)

orthotics [*ortho, correct* + *-ics, science*] The branch of medical science dealing with the making and fitting of specialized orthopedic devices for the support of weakened joints or limbs. (or THOT iks)

orthotropic [*ortho, vertical* + *trop, turning* + *-ic*] Exhibiting vertical growth, as some plants and plant parts. (or' thuh TROP ik)

orthotropous [*ortho, vertical* + *trop, turning* + *-ous*] In the ovary of an angiosperm, having the ovule vertical so that the micropyle lies in a straight line with and directly opposite the stalk. See campylotropous and anatropous. (or THOT ruh pus)

unorthodox [*un-, not* + *ortho, correct* + *dox, belief*] Not conforming to established doctrines or beliefs. See orthodox and heterodox. (un' OR thuh doks')

oste/o   bone

endosteum [*endo-, inside* + *oste, bone* + *-um*] A layer of connective tissue lining the inner surface of the medullary cavity of a bone. (en DOS tee um)

exostosis [*exo-, outside* + *oste, bone* + *-osis, abnormal condition*] A bony outgrowth formed on the surface of a bone or tooth. (eks' os TOH sis)

hyperostosis [*hyper-, excessive* + *oste, bone* + *-osis, abnormal condition*] An increase in bulk of bone tissue due to abnormal growth or thickening. (heye' per os TOH sis)

osteitis [*oste, bone* + *-itis, inflammation*] Inflammation of a bone. (os' tee EYE tis)

osteoarthritis [*osteo, bone* + *arthr, joint* + *-itis, inflammation*] Inflammation caused by a slowly progressive disease marked by degeneration of the cartilage in joints. (os' tee oh' ahr THREYE tis)

osteoblast [*osteo, bone* + *blast, cell*] A bone-forming cell arising from a fibroblast. (OS tee uh blast')

osteoclasis [*osteo, bone* + *Grk > klasis, breaking*] 1.The surgical fracturing or refracturing of a bone for the purpose of correcting a deformity. 2.The decomposition and absorption of bony tissue. (os' tee OK luh sis)

osteoclast [*osteo, bone* + *Grk > klastes, breaker*] A large multinucleate cell found in the marrow of developing bone that is involved in the decomposition, absorption, and removal of bony tissue. (OS tee uh klast')

osteocyte [*osteo, bone* + *-cyte, cell*] A mature bone cell embedded within the bone matrix. (OS tee uh seyet')

osteoid [*oste, bone* + *-oid, resembling*] Resembling bone. (OS tee oid')

osteology [*oste, bone* + *-ology, study of*] The branch of anatomy dealing with the study of the structure and function of bones. (os' tee OL uh jee)

osteoma [*oste, bone* + *-oma, tumor*] A benign tumor composed of bony tissue. (os' tee OH muh)

osteomalacia [*osteo, bone* + *malac, soft* + *-ia*] A disease resulting in a gradual softening of the bones due to a deficiency of calcium and vitamin D. (os' tee oh' muh LAY shuh)

osteomyelitis [*osteo, bone* + *myel, marrow* + *-itis, inflammation*] Inflammation of a bone or bone marrow, normally caused by a bacterium or other pathogenic microorganism. (os' tee oh meye' uh LEYE tis)

osteopathy [*osteo, bone* + *-pathy, disease*] A system of medical treatment and therapy that uses, but is not limited to, techniques of skeletal manipulation for the preservation and restoration of health. (os' tee OP uh thee)

osteophyte [*osteo, bone* + *-phyte, to grow*] An abnormal bony outgrowth or bone enlargement. (OS tee uh feyet')

osteoplasty [*osteo, bone* + *-plasty, to form*] The surgical restructuring, repairing, or replacement of bone. (OS tee uh plas' tee)

osteoporosis [*osteo, bone* + *Grk > porosis, porous*] A bone condition, mainly in women who have passed menopause, in which the bone becomes increasingly porous, leading to fractures from minimal trauma. (os' tee oh' puh ROH sis)

osteosarcoma [*osteo, bone* + *-sarcoma, malignant tumor*] A malignant tumor of a bone. (os' tee oh' sahr KOH muh)

osteotomy [*osteo, bone* + *-tomy, to cut*] The surgical cutting of a bone or excision of a piece of bone. (os' tee OT uh mee)

periosteum [*peri-, around* + *oste, bone* + *-um*] The fibrous membrane of connective tissue covering every bone in the body, but not covering the joint surfaces. (pehr' ee OS tee um)

periostitis [*peri-, around* + *oste, bone* + *-itis, inflammation*] Inflammation of the periosteum. (pehr' ee os TEYE tis)

synostosis [*syn-, together* + *oste, bone* + *-osis, formation*] The formation of a single bone by the fusion of separate or adjacent bones such as those forming a joint. (sin' os TOH sis)

teleost [*tele, complete* + *oste, bone*] Any of a group of mostly modern fishes with consolidated internal bony skeletons. (TEL ee ost')

para-¹   beside, beyond, abnormal, variation, assistant
para-²   protection from

parabiosis [*para-, beside* + *bio, life* + *-sis*] The joining of two individuals, as Siamese twins or as laboratory animals by surgical operation. (pehr' uh beye OH sis)

parable [*para-, beside* + *Grk > ballein, to throw*] A short allegorical story used to teach some moral or spiritual truth. See apologue. (PEHR uh bul)

parabola [*para-, beside* + *Grk > ballein, to throw* + *-a*] An open plane curve generated by a moving point whose distances from a fixed point and a fixed straight line are equal. (puh RAB uh luh)

parachute [*para-, protection from* + *French > chute, a fall*] A folding umbrella-shaped apparatus made of light fabric and used to slow the falling speed of a person or object dropped from an aircraft. (PEHR uh shoot')

paradigm [*para-, beside* + *Grk > deiknynai, to show*] 1.An example, model, or pattern. 2.A list of all the inflected forms of a word. (PEHR uh deyem')

paradox [*para-, beyond* + *dox, belief*] 1.A statement that is true, but seems unbelievable, contradictory, or absurd, as "Water water everywhere, but not a drop to drink." 2.A statement that is self-contradictory and false. (PEHR uh doks')

paragenesis [*para-, beside + -genesis, formation*] The order in which associated minerals crystallize in a rock or vein. (pehr' uh JEN uh sis)

paragon [*para-, beside + Grk > akone, whetstone*] A model of excellence or perfection. (PEHR uh gon')

paragraph [*para-, beside + graph, writing*] A distinct portion of a written document dealing with a specific point that is indented and begins a new line and is used to organize the author's thoughts and ideas and to make the document more readable. (PEHR uh graf')

paralanguage [*para-, beside & language*] Elements of verbal communication, as tone and volume of voice, gesture, etc., that are not part of the language system, but help to communicate meaning. (PEHR uh lang' gwij)

paralegal [*para-, assistant & legal*] An assistant to an attorney. (pehr' uh LEE gul)

parallax [*para-, beside + Grk > allassein, change*] The apparent difference in position of an object when viewed from two different points. (PEHR uh laks')

parallel [*para-, beside + allo, other*] Extending alongside in the same direction and always an equal distance apart, as lines or planes. (PEHR uh lel')

parallelism [*parallel & -ism*] 1.Close resemblance. Similarity. Correspondence. 2.Parallel grammatical structure in writing. (PEHR uh lel' iz' um)

parallelogram [*parallel & gram, to write*] A four-sided plane figure with opposite sides parallel and equal. (pehr' uh LEL uh gram')

paralysis [*para-, abnormal + -lysis, loosening*] 1.Total or partial loss of the function of a body part. 2.A state of powerlessness or helplessness. (puh RAL uh sis)

paramedic [*para-, assistant & medic(al)*] An assistant to a physician, who is also trained to give emergency medical treatment in the absence of a physician. (pehr' uh MED ik)

parameter [*para-, variation + meter, to measure*] A quantity whose value depends on the particular circumstances of its application. (puh RAM et er)

paramilitary [*para-, beyond & military*] Organized militarily, but not necessarily a part of the armed forces of a nation. (pehr' uh MIL ih tehr' ee)

paramnesia [*para-, beyond & amnesia*] A mental disorder characterized by confusion of fact and fantasy. (pehr' am' NEE zhuh)

paramorph [*para-, variation + morph, form*] A mineral formed by a change in the crystalline form and structure of a compound with no change in chemical composition. See homeomorphism. (PEHR uh morf')

paranoia [*para-, abnormal + Grk > noos, mind + -ia*] 1.A mental disorder characterized by continuing feelings of grandeur and persecution. 2.An irrational and excessive distrust of others. (pehr' uh NOI uh)

paranormal [*para-, beyond & normal*] Beyond the scope of normal science or reason. (pehr' uh NOR mul)

parapet [*para-, protection from + Ltn > petto, chest*] 1.A protective wall or railing along the outside edge of a roof, balcony, bridge, or other structure. 2.A low wall or mound of earth or stone to conceal and protect soldiers. Rampart. (PEHR uh pet')

paraphernalia [*para-, beyond + Grk > pherne, dowry + -al + -ia*] 1.Personal belongings. 2.A collection of articles, equipment, etc., used in a particular activity. Originally, it referred to the personal property that a bride was allowed to keep, not including her dowry, which went to her husband. (pehr' uh fur NAYL yuh)

paraphrase [*para-, beside & phrase*] To express the meaning of a passage in other words. (PEHR uh frayz')

paraplegia [*para-, beside + -plegia, paralysis*] Paralysis affecting the lower extremities of the body. See quadriplegia. (pehr' uh PLEE jee uh)

parapodium [*para-, beside + pod, foot + -ium*] Either of the paired, lateral appendages on most segments of polychaete worms, used in locomotion and respiration. (pehr' uh POHD ee um)

paraprofessional [*para-, assistant & professional*] A trained assistant to a licensed professional, as in teaching, law, medicine, etc. (pehr' uh pruh FESH uh nul)

parapsychology [*para-, beyond + psych, mind + -ology, study of*] The branch of psychology dealing with the study of psychic phenomena, such as extrasensory perception, clairvoyance, and telepathy, that appear to fall beyond the scope of physical law. (pehr' uh seye KOL uh jee)

paraselene [*para-, beside + selen, moon*] A luminous spot occasionally appearing on a lunar halo. (pehr' uh suh LEE nee)

parasite [*para-, beside + Grk > sitos, food*] 1.An organism that lives on or within the body of another organism from which it obtains most of its nourishment. 2.A person who lives at the expense of others while making no contribution in return. (PEHR uh seyet')

parasol [*para-, protection from + sol, sun*] A lightweight umbrella used for protection from the sun. (PEHR uh sol')

parasympathetic nervous system One of two divisions of the autonomic nervous system, consisting of the cranial and sacral nerves, that works in conjunction with the sympathetic nervous system to control heart, blood vessels, glands, etc. See sympathetic nervous system and autonomic nervous system. (pehr' uh sim' puh THET ik NUR vus SIS tum)

parasynthesis [*para-, variation + syn, together + the, to put + -sis*] The formation of words by compounding and sometimes adding a suffix. (pehr' uh SIN thuh sis)

parataxis [*para-, beside + tax, arrangement + -is*] The arrangement of clauses, phrases, etc., without the use of conjunctions to indicate subordination, as "I came, I saw, I conquered." See hypotaxis. (pchr' uh TAK sis)

parathyroid gland [*para-, beside & thyroid & gland*] One of usually four small endocrine glands located near the thyroid gland that produces a hormone used to regulate the body's metabolism of calcium and phosphorus. (pehr' uh THEYE roid' gland)

parathyroidectomy [*para-, beside & thyroid & ec, out + -tomy, to cut*] Surgical removal of the parathyroid glands. (pehr' uh theye' roid' EK tuh mee)

paratrooper [*para(chute) & trooper*] A soldier trained to jump from an aircraft into a target area using a parachute. (PEHR uh troo' per)

parenchyma [*para-, beside + -enchyma, type of cell tissue*] 1.Fundamental plant tissue composed of soft, thin-walled cells. See sclerenchyma. 2.The functional tissue of a body organ, as distinguished from its supporting or connective tissue. (puh RENG kuh muh)

parenthesis [*para-, beside + en-, in + the, to put + -sis*] 1.A word, phrase, etc., inserted into a passage as a comment or explanation. 2.Either of a pair of marks () used to enclose a comment or explanation within a sentence or to group mathematical symbols and values. (puh REN thuh sis)

parenthetical [*para-, beside + en-, in + the, to put + -ical*] 1.Serving to qualify or explain. 2.Enclosed in parentheses. (pehr' en THET ih kul)

paresis [*para-, beside + Grk > hienai, to send*] Partial paralysis characterized by impaired movement, but normal sensation. (puh REE sis)

parhelic circle [*para-, beside + heli, sun + -ic & circle*] A luminous circle passing through the sun in a plane parallel to the horizon and produced by the sun's rays reflecting off ice crystals in the atmosphere. See anthelion and parhelion. (pahr HEE lik SUR kul)

parhelion [*para-, beside + heli, sun + -on*] One of two luminous spots occasionally appearing on the parhelic circle on either side of the sun. See anthelion and parhelic circle. (pahr HEE lee un)

parody [*para-, abnormal & od(e) & -y*] 1.A satirical or humorous imitation of a serious literary or musical work. 2.A poor imitation. (PEHR uh dee)

paronomasia [*para-, variation + onomas, name + -ia*] A play on words. Pun. (pehr' uh noh MAY zhuh)

paronym [*para-, beside + onym, word*] A word derived from the same root as another, as *heal* and *health*. Cognate. (PEHR uh nim')

parotid [*para-, beside + ot, ear + -id*] 1.Located near the ear. 2.Pertaining to either of two salivary glands located below and in front of each external ear. (puh ROT id)

parotitis [*para-, beside + ot, ear + -itis, inflammation*] Inflammation and swelling of the parotid glands, as with mumps. (pehr' oh TEYE tis)

ped/o   child

orthopaedics [*ortho, correct + ped, child + -ics, practice*] The branch of medicine dealing with the treatment of disorders and diseases of the musculoskeletal system, which includes bones, joints, muscles, tendons, and ligaments. Same as orthopedics. (or' thuh PEED iks)

orthopedics [*ortho, correct + ped, child + -ics, practice*] The branch of medicine dealing with the treatment of disorders and diseases of the musculoskeletal system, which includes bones, joints, muscles, tendons, and ligaments. (or' thuh PEED iks)

pedagog [*ped, child + agog, leader*] A schoolteacher, especially one who instructs in a pedantic, dogmatic, and formal manner. Same as pedagogue. (PED uh gog')

pedagogics [*ped, child + agog, leader + -ics, science*] The science, art, or profession of teaching. Same as pedagogy. (ped' uh GOJ iks)

pedagogue [*ped, child + agog, leader*] A schoolteacher, especially one who instructs in a pedantic, dogmatic, and formal manner. (PED uh gog')

pedagogy [*ped, child + agog, leader + -y*] The science, art, or profession of teaching. See didactics and pedagogics. (PED uh goh' jee)

pederasty [*ped, child + Grk > erasthai, to love + -y*] Sexual relations between a man and a boy. (PED uh ras' tee)

pediatrics [*ped, child + iatr, healing + -ics, study of*] The branch of medicine dealing with the study and treatment of diseases and disorders of infants and children. (pee' dee AT riks)

pedology[1] [*ped, child + -ology, study of*] The study of the behavior and development of children. (pih DOL uh jee)

pedophile [*pedo, child + -phile, attracted to*] An adult who is sexually attracted to children. (PEED uh feyel')

pedophilia [*pedo, child + phil, attracted to + -ia*] The engagement by an adult in sexual activity with a child. (pee' duh FIL ee uh)

ped, pedi, -pede   foot, feet

biped [*bi-, two + ped, feet*] A two-footed animal. (BEYE ped)

centipede [*cent, hundred + -pede, feet*] Any of numerous elongated, flattened, predaceous arthropods of the class Chilopoda with numerous body segments each having one pair of legs, the front pair being modified into poisonous biting organs. See millipede and myriapod. (SENT ih peed')

cirriped [*Ltn > cirrus, curl + ped, foot*] Any of various crustaceans, including barnacles and similar organisms, that have threadlike appendages and, in the adult stage, are either parasitic or become permanently attached to objects. (SIHR uh ped')

expedient [*Ltn > expedire, set free + -ent*] 1.Suitable to a particular purpose. 2.Concerned with immediate advantage rather than principle. (eks PEE dee ent)

expedite [*Ltn > expedire, set free*] To accelerate the progress of. See impede. (EKS pih deyet')

impedance [*Ltn > impedire, to entangle + -ance*] The total opposition to alternating current flow in an electrical circuit. (im PEED ns)

impede [*Ltn > impedire, to entangle*] To slow the progress of. See expedite. (im PEED)

maxilliped [*maxill(ae) & ped, foot*] Any of the three pairs of head appendages situated immediately behind the maxillae of a crustacean. (mak SIL uh ped')

millepede [*mill, thousand + -pede, feet*] Any of numerous elongated, cylindrical, herbivorous arthropods of the class Diplopoda with numerous body segments each having two pairs of legs and no poisonous fangs. Same as millipede. (MIL uh peed')

millipede [*mill, thousand + -pede, feet*] Any of numerous elongated, cylindrical, herbivorous arthropods of the class Diplopoda with numerous body segments each having two pairs of legs and no poisonous fangs. See centipede and myriapod. (MIL uh peed')

pedal [*ped, foot + -al*] A foot-operated lever used to supply power for certain mechanisms or devices. (PED l)

pedestal [*ped, foot + Italian > stallo, stall*] A supporting base for a statue, vase, column, etc. (PED uh stul)

pedestrian [*ped, foot + -ian*] 1.A person traveling on foot. 2.Without imagination or excitement. Dull. (puh DES tree un)

pedicab [*pedi, foot & cab*] A three-wheeled vehicle operated by pedals and capable of carrying two passengers. (PED ih kab')

pedicure [*pedi, foot + Ltn > cura, care*] Professional care of the feet and toenails. See manicure. (PED ih kyoor')

pedigree [*French > pie de grue, foot of a crane*] 1.Ancestral line. Lineage. Descent. 2.A record of ancestry, especially of animals. 3.The derivation, origin, or history of something. So named from the resemblance of a crane's foot to the lines of a genealogical chart. See genealogy. (PED ih gree')

pedipalp [*pedi, foot & palp(us)*] Either of the second pair of leglike appendages of an arachnid, often modified for various functions such as locomotion, fertilization, grasping, etc. (PED ih palp')

pedometer [*pedo, foot + meter, to measure*] A device for measuring distance traveled on foot by recording the number of steps. See odometer and odograph. (pih DOM et er)

peduncle [*ped, foot + -cle*] 1.A flower stalk supporting a flower, flower cluster, or fructification. 2.A stalklike part or structure. 3.A stemlike connecting part, especially a collection of nerve fibers connecting different regions of the central nervous system. (pih DUNG kul)

quadruped [*quadru, four + ped, feet*] An animal with four feet. (KWOD ruh ped')

sesquipedalian [*sesqui-, one and a half + ped, foot + -al + -ian*] 1.Very long; said of very long words because they seem a foot and a half long. 2.A foot and a half long. 3.Characterized by or given to the use of very long words. (ses' kwih pih DAYL yun)

velocipede [*Ltn > velox, swift + -pede, foot*] 1.An early form of bicycle or tricycle. 2.A light vehicle used on railroad tracks and propelled by hands or feet. (vuh LOS uh peed')

pod, -pode   foot, feet

amphipod [*amphi-, both + pod, feet*] Any of a large order of crustaceans with legs for walking and legs for swimming, as beach fleas and sand hoppers. (AM fuh pod')

apodal [*a-, without + pod, feet + -al*] Without feet or legs. (AP uh dul)

arbovirus [*ar(thropod) & bo(rne) & virus*] Any of a group of arthropod-borne viruses, including the causative agents of yellow fever and encephalitis, that are transmitted to humans primarily by mosquitoes and ticks. (ahr' buh VEYE rus)

arthropod [*arthro, joint + pod, foot*] Any of the largest phylum of invertebrate animals, including crustaceans, arachnids, and insects, with jointed legs, an exoskeleton, and a segmented body. (AHR thruh pod')

bipod [*bi-, two + pod, feet*] Any two-legged support, as for the barrel of a rifle. (BEYE pod)

brachiopod [*brachio, arm + pod, foot*] Any of a small phylum of marine invertebrate animals with bivalve shells and a pair of tentacle-bearing arms. (BRAY kee uh pod')

branchiopod [*branchio, gill + pod, foot*] Any of various, mostly freshwater crustaceans with numerous leaflike appendages used for locomotion and respiration. (BRANG kee uh pod')

cephalopod [*cephalo, head + pod, foot*] Any of various marine mollusks that have a large, distinct head with tentacles around the mouth and well-developed eyes, as the octopus or squid. (SEF uh luh pod')

chiropody [*chiro, hand + pod, foot + -y*] An obsolete term originally defined as the study and treatment of disorders of the hands and feet. See podiatry. (keye ROP uh dee)

decapod [*deca, ten + pod, feet*] 1.Any of an order of crustaceans, including shrimps, lobsters, crabs, and pawns, with five pairs of walking legs, the first two pairs often bearing pincers. 2.Any cephalopod mollusk of the order Decapoda, including the squids and cuttlefishes, with five pairs of armlike tentacles, one pair being longer than the remaining four pairs. (DEK uh pod')

diplopod [*diplo, double + pod, feet*] Millipede. See millipede. (DIP luh pod')

dipody [*di-, two + pod, feet + -y*] A prosodic measure consisting of two feet. (DIP uh dee)

gastropod [*gastro, stomach + pod, foot*] Any of a large class of mollusks, including snails, slugs, limpets, etc., that move using a muscular ventral foot. (GAS truh pod')

heptapody [*hepta-, seven + pod, feet + -y*] A prosodic measure consisting of seven feet. (hep TAP uh dee)

hexapod [*hexa-, six + pod, feet*] Any of a large class of arthropods with three pairs of legs, three body segments, and usually capable of flight. Insect. (HEKS uh pod')

hexapody [*hexa-, six + pod, feet + -y*] A prosodic measure consisting of six feet. (heks AP uh dee)

isopod [*iso-, same + pod, feet*] Any of numerous crustaceans with seven pairs of similar legs, each pair being attached to one of seven thoracic body segments. (EYE suh pod')

megapode [*mega-, large + -pode, foot*] Any of a family of large-footed birds found in Australia and many South Pacific islands, that incubate their eggs by burying them in mounds of earth. (MEG uh pohd')

monopode [*mono-, one + -pode, foot*] Anything supported by only one foot. (MON uh pohd')

monopody [*mono-, one + pod, foot + -y*] A prosodic measure consisting of one foot. (muh NOP uh dee)

myriapod [*myria, many + pod, feet*] Any of a group of terrestrial arthropods, including the centipedes and millipedes, with numerous body segments and many legs. See centipede and millipede. (MIHR ee uh pod')

octopod [*octo-, eight + pod, feet*] Any of an order of cephalopod mollusks with eight arms, as an octopus. (OK tuh pod')

ornithopod [*ornitho, bird + pod, feet*] Any herbivorous dinosaur of the suborder Ornithopoda and the order Ornithischia that walked upright on the hind feet. See ornithischian. (OR nuh thuh pod')

parapodium [*para-, beside + pod, foot + -ium*] Either of the paired, lateral appendages on most segments of polychaete worms, used in locomotion and respiration. (pehr' uh POHD ee um)

pentapody [*penta-, five + pod, feet + -y*] A prosodic measure consisting of five feet. (pen TAP uh dee)

pleopod [*Grk > plein, swim + pod, foot*] A biramous abdominal appendage of certain crustaceans that is used for swimming. Swimmeret. (PLEE uh pod')

podagra [*pod, foot + Grk > agra, seizure*] Acute pain in the big toe resulting from gout. (puh DAG ruh)

podiatry [*pod, foot + iatr, healing + -y*] The branch of medicine dealing with the study and treatment of disorders of the feet. See chiropody. (puh DEYE uh tree)

pod, -pode

podite [*pod, foot + -ite*] An arthropod appendage. (POD eyet)

podium [*pod, foot + -ium*] 1.An elevated platform used by a public speaker, orchestra conductor, etc. 2.A foot or any structure resembling or functioning as a foot. (POHD ee um)

polypody [*poly, many + pod, feet + -y*] Any of various ferns with compound fronds and creeping rhizomes. (POL ee poh' dee)

pseudopodium [*pseudo, false + pod, foot + -ium*] A temporary protrusion of the cytoplasm of certain protozoans or amebocytes that functions in locomotion and in the intake of food or foreign particles. See rhizopod. (sood' uh POHD ee um)

pteropod [*ptero, wing + pod, feet*] Any of various small gastropod mollusks, commonly called sea butterflies, with a winglike structure in the foot used for swimming. (TEHR uh pod')

rhizopod [*rhizo, root + pod, foot*] Any of numerous one-celled protozoans with rootlike pseudopodia. See pseudopodium. (REYE zuh pod')

sauropod [*sauro, lizard + pod, foot*] Any of a class of large plant-eating dinosaurs with four feet, a small head, and a long neck. (SOR uh pod')

schizopod [*schizo, split + pod, foot*] Any of certain shrimplike crustaceans with appendages split into inner and outer branches. (SKIZ uh pod')

tetrapod [*tetra-, four + pod, feet*] Any vertebrate with four limbs, including mammals, birds, amphibians, and reptiles. (TET ruh pod')

tetrapody [*tetra-, four + pod, feet + -y*] A prosodic measure consisting of four feet. (teh TRAP uh dee)

tripod [*tri-, three + pod, feet*] Any three-legged support, as for a camera, transit, etc. (TREYE pod)

tripody [*tri-, three + pod, feet + -y*] A prosodic measure consisting of three feet. (TRIP uh dee)

uropod [*uro, tail + pod, feet*] Either of the appendages on the posterior abdominal segment of various crustaceans, as a shrimp or lobster. (YOOR uh pod')

pel   to drive

compel [*com-, together + pel, to drive*] To drive or urge irresistibly. Force. (kum PEL)

dispel [*dis-, away + pel, to drive*] 1.To drive away in various directions. Disperse. Dissipate. 2.To cause to vanish. (dis PEL)

expel [*ex-, out + pel, to drive*] 1.To drive or force out. 2.To dismiss permanently. See exclude (def. 2). (ek SPEL)

impel [*im-, in + pel, to drive*] 1.To drive or urge into action. 2.To cause to move forward or onward. Propel. See propel. (im PEL)

interpellate [*inter-, between + pel, to drive + -ate*] To formally question a government official about policy or personal behavior. (in' ter PEL ayt')

propel [*pro-, forward + pel, to drive*] To cause to move forward or onward. (pruh PEL)

repel [*re-, back + pel, to drive*] 1.To drive back. 2.To force away or apart. 3.To keep out. (rih PEL)

pept, peps   digestion

dyspepsia [*dys-, abnormal + peps, digestion + -ia*] Abnormal digestion. Indigestion. See eupepsia. (dis PEP shuh)

eupepsia [*eu-, good + peps, digestion + -ia*] Normal digestion. See dyspepsia. (yoo PEP shuh)

pepsin [*peps, digestion + -in*] A digestive enzyme present in gastric juice that begins protein digestion by breaking them down into proteoses and peptones. (PEP sin)

pepsinogen [*pepsin & gen, to produce*] The inert precursor of pepsin that is readily converted into pepsin by hydrochloric acid during digestion. (pep SIN uh jen)

peptic [*pept, digestion + -ic*] 1.Pertaining to or aiding digestion. 2.Pertaining to pepsin. (PEP tik)

peptidase [*pept, digestion + -ide + -ase, enzyme*] Any enzyme that converts peptides into amino acids. (PEP tih dayz')

peptide [*pept, digestion + -ide*] Any of a group of compounds that yield two or more amino acids on hydrolysis. (PEP teyed)

peptize [*pept, digestion + -ize*] To convert into a sol from a gel. (PEP teyez)

peptone [*pept, digestion + -one*] Any of a group of protein derivatives into which natural protein is converted by acid or enzyme hydrolysis. (PEP tohn)

polypeptide [*poly, many & peptide*] A compound that contains two or more amino acids chained together. (pol' ee PEP teyed')

per-   through, thoroughly, wrong

impermeable [*im-, not & perme(ate) & -able*] 1.Not able to be penetrated. 2.Not permitting the passage of fluid. See permeate. (im PER mee uh bul)

imperturbable [*im-, not + per, through + turb, agitate + -able*] Not capable of being disturbed or upset. Calm. See equanimity and equable (def. 2). (im' per TUR buh bul)

impervious [*im-, not + per, through + via, way + -ous*] 1.Not capable of being penetrated. Impenetrable. Impermeable. 2.Not disturbed or affected by. See pervious. (im PER vee us)

parvenu [*per-, through + ven, to come*] A person who has recently risen above his or her social or economic class without the background or qualifications associated with it. (PAHR vuh noo')

perambulate [*per-, through & ambulate {walk}*] 1.To walk through, around, or over, especially to inspect, survey, or examine. 2.To walk or stroll about. See circumambulate. (per AM byuh layt')

percolate [*per-, through + Ltn > colare, to filter + -ate*] To pass gradually through a porous substance. Filter. (PER kuh layt')

percutaneous [*per-, through + Ltn > cutis, skin + -aneous*] Administered or effected through the skin, as medication, injections, etc. (per' kyoo TAY nee us)

perennate [*per-, through + enn, years + -ate*] To last from year to year or for many years. (PEHR uh nayt')

perennial [*per-, through + enn, years + -ial*] Lasting or continuing through the year or through many years. (puh REN ee ul)

perfect [*per-, thoroughly + fac, to do*] Without fault or defect. (PER fikt)

perfecta [*Spanish > perfecta, perfect*] A form of gambling, especially on horse races, in which the bettor must pick the first two winners in the correct sequence. Exacta. See trifecta. (per FEK tuh)

perfidy [*per-, through + fid, faith + -y*] Deliberate breach of trust or faith. Treachery. Disloyalty. (PER fih dee)

perfoliate [*per-, through + foli, leaf + -ate*] Designating a leaf with its base surrounding the stem so that the stem appears to pass through the leaf. (per FOH lee it)

perforate [*per-, through + Ltn > forare, to bore + -ate*] To make holes through by boring, piercing, punching, etc. (PER fuh rayt')

perfunctory [*per-, through + Ltn > fungi, to perform + -ory*] Done in a routine manner without interest, care, or enthusiasm. (per FUNGK tuh ree)

perfuse [*per-, through + fus, pour*] To spread over or through with liquid, moisture, light, color, etc. (per FYOOZ)

perjury [*per-, through + Ltn > jurare, swear + -y*] The act of knowingly giving false, misleading, or incomplete information under oath. (PER juh ree)

permeate [*per-, through + Ltn > meare, to pass + -ate*] 1.To pass through the pores, openings, interstices, etc., of. 2.To spread throughout. Pervade. See pervade. (PER mee ayt')

permit [*per-, through + mit, to send*] To allow or give consent to. Tolerate. (per MIT)

permute [*per-, thoroughly + mut, change*] To change the arrangement or order of. (per MYOOT)

pernicious [*per-, thoroughly + nic, deadly + -ious*] 1.Very harmful, destructive, or injurious. 2.Deadly. Fatal. (per NISH us)

peroral [*per-, through & oral {mouth}*] Administered or occurring through the mouth. (per OR ul)

perorate [*per-, through + Ltn > orare, to speak + -ate*] 1.To conclude or sum up a speech. 2.To give a lengthy speech. (PEHR uh rayt')

perpetual [*per-, through + Ltn > petere, to seek + -al*] 1.Enduring or continuing forever. 2.Continuing without interruption. 3.Blooming throughout the growing season. (per PECH oo ul)

perplex [*per-, thoroughly + Ltn > plectere, twist*] 1.To make uncertain or doubtful. Confuse. See confuse. 2.To make intricate or complicated. (per PLEKS)

persecute [*per-, through + secut, follow*] 1.To harass in an injurious or harmful manner, especially because of religious or political beliefs. 2.To annoy or harass constantly. (PER sih kyoot')

persevere [*per-, thoroughly + Ltn > severus, strict*] To continue resolutely in spite of difficulties, setbacks, obstacles, etc. See persist (def. 1). (per' suh VIHR)

persist [*per-, through + Ltn > stare, to stand*] 1.To continue resolutely in spite of difficulties, setbacks, obstacles, etc. See persevere. 2.To continue to exist. Endure. (per SIST)

perspective [*per-, through + spect, to see + -ive*] 1.The art or technique of representing three-dimensional objects on a flat surface. 2.The ability to see things in their true relationship to each other. (per SPEK tiv)

perspicacious [*per-, through + spic, to see + -acious*] Having or showing keen judgment or understanding. Shrewd. (per' spih KAY shus)

perspicuous [*per-, through + spic, to see + -ous*] Easily understood. Clear. Lucid. See inscrutable, evident, and manifest. (per SPIK yoo us)

perspire [*per-, through + spir, breathe*] To secrete sweat through the pores of the skin. (per SPEYER)

persuade [*per-, thoroughly + Ltn > suadere, to advise*] To induce to some belief or action. Convince. (per SWAYD)

pertinacious [*per-, thoroughly + Ltn > tenax, tenacious + -ious*] 1.Holding tenaciously to some purpose, opinion, or action. Persistent. 2.Stubbornly persistent. Obstinate. (pert' n AY shus)

perturb [*per-, thoroughly + Ltn > tubare, to disturb*] To disturb greatly. Agitate. Disquiet. (per TURB)

peruse [*per-, thoroughly & use*] 1.To read thoroughly and carefully. 2.To examine something in detail. Scrutinize. (puh ROOZ)

pervade [*per-, through + vas, to go*] To spread or diffuse throughout. Permeate. See permeate (def. 2). (per VAYD)

perverse [*per-, wrong + vers, turn*] 1.Turned against what is right or sensible. 2.Persistent or obstinate in error. Stubborn. 3.Morally wrong or bad. Corrupt. Wicked. (per VURS)

pervert [*per-, wrong + vert, turn*] A person affected with perversion, especially sexual perversion. (PER vurt)

pervious [*per-, through + via, way + -ous*] 1.Permitting passage or entrance. Permeable. 2.Open-minded to argument, reason, change, etc. See impervious. (PER vee us)

semipermeable [*semi-, partly & permeable*] Partially permeable, as a membrane that allows only smaller molecules to pass through. See permeate. (sem' ee PUR mee uh bul)

phag, -phage   to eat

aerophagia [*aero, air + phag, to eat + -ia*] Abnormal swallowing of air. (ehr' uh FAY juh)

anthropophagy [*anthropo, human + phag, to eat + -y*] Cannibalism. (an' thruh POF uh jee)

bacteriophage [*bacterio, bacteria + -phage, to eat*] A virus that infects and destroys bacteria. (bak TIHR ee uh fayj')

carpophagous [*carpo, fruit + phag, to eat + -ous*] Feeding on fruit. Same as frugivorous. (kahr POF uh gus)

coprophagous [*copro, dung + phag, to eat + -ous*] Feeding on dung. (kuh PROF uh gus)

dysphagia [*dys-, difficult + phag, to eat + -ia*] Difficulty in swallowing. (dis FAY juh)

entomophagous [*entomo, insect + phag, to eat + -ous*] Feeding on insects, as many animals and certain plants. Same as insectivorous. (ent' uh MOF uh gus)

esophagus [*Grk > oisein, to carry + phag, to eat + -us*] The muscular tube that carries food from the pharynx to the stomach. (ih SOF uh gus)

euryphagous [*eury, wide + phag, to eat + -ous*] Feeding on a wide variety of foods. Opposed to stenophagous. See polyphagous (def. 2). (yoo RIF uh gus)

geophagy [*geo, earth + phag, to eat + -y*] The practice of eating earth, either from a pathological disorder or from lack of food. (jee OF uh jee)

hematophagous [*hemato, blood + phag, to eat + -ous*] Feeding on blood. (hee' muh TOF uh gus)

phag, -phage

macrophage [*macro-, large* + *-phage, to eat*] A large phagocyte found in blood, lymph, and connective tissue that ingests and destroys cell debris, microorganisms, and other harmful foreign material. See phagocyte and microphage. (MAK roh fayj')

microphage [*micro-, small* + *-phage, to eat*] A small phagocyte that ingests and destroys bacteria and other microorganisms. See phagocyte and macrophage. (MEYE kroh fayj')

monophagous [*mono-, one* + *phag, to eat* + *-ous*] Feeding on one kind of food only. (muh NOF uh gus)

myrmecophagous [*myrmeco, ant* + *phag, to eat* + *-ous*] Feeding on ants. (mur' mih KOF uh gus)

necrophagous [*necro, dead* + *phag, to eat* + *-ous*] Feeding on dead or decaying flesh. See carrion (def. 3). (nuh KROF uh gus)

oesophagus [*Grk > oisein, to carry* + *phag, to eat* + *-us*] The muscular tube that carries food from the pharynx to the stomach. Same as esophagus. (ih SOF uh gus)

oligophagous [*oligo, few* + *phag, to eat* + *-ous*] Feeding on a limited variety of food. Same as stenophagous. (ol' uh GOF uh gus)

phagocyte [*phago, to eat* + *-cyte, cell*] A white blood cell that protects the body against infection and disease by ingesting and destroying harmful foreign material such as cell debris, microorganisms, etc. See macrophage and microphage. (FAG uh seyet')

phagocytosis [*phagocyt(e)* & *-osis, action*] The ingestion and destruction of cells, microorganisms, and other foreign matter by phagocytes. See phagocyte. (fag' uh seye TOH sis)

phyllophagous [*phyllo, leaf* + *phag, to eat* + *-ous*] Feeding on leaves. (fih LOF uh gus)

phytophagous [*phyto, plant* + *phag, to eat* + *-ous*] Feeding on plants. Same as herbivorous. (feye TOF uh gus)

polyphagous [*poly, many* + *phag, to eat* + *-ous*] 1.Having an excessive desire for food. 2.Feeding on a wide variety of food. See euryphagous. (puh LIF uh gus)

rhizophagous [*rhizo, root* + *phag, to eat* + *-ous*] Feeding on roots. (reye ZOF uh gus)

saprophagous [*sapro, decaying* + *phag, to eat* + *-ous*] Feeding on dead or decaying organic matter. See saprozoic and saprophyte. (suh PROF uh gus)

sarcophagous [*sarco, flesh* + *phag, to eat* + *-ous*] Feeding on flesh. Same as carnivorous (def. 1). (sahr KOF uh gus)

stenophagous [*steno, narrow* + *phag, to eat* + *-ous*] Feeding on a limited variety of food. Opposed to euryphagous. (stuh NOF uh gus)

xylophagous [*xylo, wood* + *phag, to eat* + *-ous*] Feeding on wood, as certain insects, fungi, or crustaceans. (zeye LOF uh gus)

zoophagous [*zoo, animal* + *phag, to eat* + *-ous*] Feeding on animal tissue. See carnivorous (def. 1). (zoh OF uh gus)

vor   to eat

apivorous [*api, bee* + *vor, to eat* + *-ous*] Feeding on bees. (ay PIV ur us)

carnivore [*carni, flesh* + *vor, to eat*] 1.Any of an order of flesh-eating mammals. 2.A plant that feeds on insects. (KAHR nuh vor')

carnivorous [*carni, flesh* + *vor, to eat* + *-ous*] 1.Feeding on flesh. See zoophagous. 2.Feeding on insects, as certain plants. See insectivorous. (kahr NIV ur us)

formicivorous [*Ltn > formica, ant* + *vor, to eat* + *-ous*] Feeding on ants. (for' mih SIV ur us)

frugivorous [*Ltn > frugi, fruit* + *vor, to eat* + *-ous*] Feeding on fruit. (froo JIV ur us)

graminivorous [*Ltn > gramen, grass* + *vor, to eat* + *-ous*] Feeding on grasses. (gram' ih NIV ur us)

granivorous [*grani, grain* + *vor, to eat* + *-ous*] Feeding on grain or seeds. (gruh NIV ur us)

herbivore [*herb* & *vor, to eat*] A plant-eating animal. (HUR buh vor')

herbivorous [*herb* & *vor, to eat* + *-ous*] Feeding on plants. (hur BIV ur us)

insectivore [*insect* & *vor, to eat*] 1.Any of various animals, and certain plants, that feed mainly on insects. 2.Any of certain small mammals, as hedgehogs, moles, and shrews, that feed mainly on insects. See carnivore. (in SEK tuh vor')

insectivorous [*insect* & *vor, to eat* + *-ous*] Feeding on insects, as many animals and certain plants. See carnivorous (def. 2). (in' sek' TIV ur us)

omnivorous [*omni-, all* + *vor, to eat* + *-ous*] 1.Feeding on both animal and vegetable food. 2.Avidly taking in everything available, as with the mind. (om NIV ur us)

piscivorous [*pisci, fish* + *vor, to eat* + *-ous*] Feeding on fish. (pih SIV ur us)

voracious [*vor, to eat* + *-acious*] 1.Consuming or craving large amounts of food. Ravenous. 2.Excessively eager in the desire for or pursuit of something. Insatiable. (vuh RAY shus)

phil/o, -phile
love, attracted to, affinity for,
a natural liking

acidophilus milk [*acid* & *phil, a natural liking* + *-us* & *milk*] Milk containing added bacteria that grow vigorously in dilute acid, often used to treat intestinal disorders by modifying intestinal bacteria. (as' ih DOF uh lus milk)

ailurophile [*Grk > ailouros, cat* + *-phile, love*] A lover of cats. (eye LOOR uh feyel')

anemophilous [*anemo, wind* + *phil, affinity for* + *-ous*] Pertaining to plants pollinated by wind-borne pollen. See entomophilous and zoophilous. (an' uh MOF uh lus)

Anglophile [*Anglo, English* + *-phile, love*] An admirer of England and English customs, institutions, etc. (ANG gluh feyel')

audiophile [*audio, hearing* + *-phile, love*] A lover of high-fidelity music reproduction. (AWD ee uh feyel')

basophil [*bas(ic)* & *phil, affinity for*] A granular white blood cell that is easily stained with basic dyes. See granulocyte, neutrophil, and eosinophil. (BAY suh fil')

bibliophile [*biblio, book* + *-phile, love*] A lover or collector of books. (BIB lee uh feyel')

chromophil [*chromo, color* + *phil, affinity for*] Capable of being readily stained with dyes. (KROH muh fil')

coprophilia [*copro, dung* + *phil, attracted to* + *-ia*] An abnormal interest in excrement or filth. (kop' ruh FIL ee uh)

coprophilous [*copro, dung* + *phil, a natural liking* + *-ous*] Growing or living in dung, as certain fungi. (kuh PROF uh lus)

cryophilic [*cryo, cold* + *phil, a natural liking* + *-ic*] Existing or thriving at low temperatures. See psychrophilic. (kreye' uh FIL ik)

discophile [*disco, disk* + *-phile, love*] An experienced and knowledgeable collector of phonograph records. (DIS kuh feyel')

drosophila [*Grk* > *drosos, dew* + *phil, a natural liking* + *-a*] Any of a genus of fruit flies; specifically, the species Drosophila melanogaster which is used in the study of genetics and heredity because of its large chromosomes, prolific reproduction, and frequent mutations. So named from the inability of certain light-colored mutants to survive well in dry air. (droh SOF uh luh)

entomophilous [*entomo, insect* + *phil, affinity for* + *-ous*] Pertaining to plants pollinated by insects. See anemophilous and zoophilous. (ent' uh MOF uh lus)

eosinophil [*eosin & phil, affinity for*] A granular white blood cell that is easily stained with eosin dyes. See granulocyte, neutrophil, and basophil. (ee' uh SIN uh fil')

Germanophile [*Germano, German* + *-phile, love*] An admirer of Germany and German customs, institutions, etc. (jur MAN uh feyel')

gypsophila [*Grk* > *gypsos, chalk* + *phil, love* + *-a*] Any of various plants of the pink family bearing numerous small white or pink flowers on branching stalks with sparse foliage. Baby's breath. (jip SOF uh luh)

halophilic [*halo, salt* + *phil, a natural liking* + *-ic*] Thriving in a salty environment. (hal' uh FIL ik)

hemophilia [*hemo, blood* + *phil, affinity for* + *-ia*] A hereditary blood defect characterized by excessive bleeding due to an abnormal or missing blood-clotting factor. It occurs mainly in males, but can be transmitted in the female line. (hee' muh FIL ee uh)

homophile [*homo, same* + *-phile, attracted to*] 1.A homosexual. 2.One who is sensitive to the rights of homosexuals. See homosexual. (HOH muh feyel')

hydrophilic [*hydro, water* + *phil, affinity for* + *-ic*] Capable of absorbing or dissolving in water or having an affinity for water. (heye' druh FIL ik)

hygrophilous [*hygro, moisture* + *phil, a natural liking* + *-ous*] Thriving in a moist environment. (heye GROF uh lus)

lipophilic [*lipo, fat* + *phil, affinity for* + *-ic*] Having a strong affinity for fats. (lip' uh FIL ik)

logophile [*logo, word* + *-phile, love*] A lover of words. (LOG uh feyel')

necrophilia [*necro, death* + *phil, attracted to* + *-ia*] An obsessive and especially erotic interest in death and corpses. (nek' ruh FIL ee uh)

Negrophile [*Negro & -phile, love*] One who is sensitive to the rights of blacks. (NEE groh feyel')

neutrophil [*neutro, neutral* + *phil, affinity for*] A granular white blood cell that is easily stained with neutral dyes. See granulocyte, eosinophil, and basophil. (NOO truh fil')

oenophile [*Grk* > *oinos, wine* + *-phile, love*] A connoisseur of wine. A lover of wine. (EE nuh feyel')

pedophile [*pedo, child* + *-phile, attracted to*] An adult who is sexually attracted to children. (PEED uh feyel')

pedophilia [*pedo, child* + *phil, attracted to* + *-ia*] The engagement by an adult in sexual activity with a child. (pee' duh FIL ee uh)

Philadelphia [*phil, love* + *adelph, brother* + *-ia*] A city in southeastern Pennsylvania known as the city of brotherly love. (fil' uh DEL fee uh)

philander [*phil, love* + *andr, man* + *-er*] (of a man) To engage in a love affair with no intention of marriage. (fih LAN der)

philanthropist [*phil, love* + *anthrop, man* + *-ist*] A lover of mankind and active promoter of goodwill. (fih LAN thruh pist)

philanthropy [*phil, love* + *anthrop, man* + *-y*] A love of and desire to help mankind, especially by doing good deeds. (fih LAN thruh pee)

philately [*phil, love* + *Grk* > *ateleia, exemption from charges* + *-y*] The collection and study of postage stamps, postmarks, postal cards, etc. So named from the fact that the recipient pays no delivery charges by virtue of the stamp affixed to the letter by the sender. (fih LAT l ee)

philharmonic [*phil, love & harmonic {musical harmony}*] Loving music. (fil' hahr MON ik)

Philharmonic [*phil, love & harmonic {musical harmony}*] Pertaining to a symphony orchestra or other musical society. (fil' hahr MON ik)

philhellene [*phil, love & Hellene {a Greek}*] An admirer and supporter of Greece and the Greeks. (fil HEL een')

philodendron [*philo, love* + *dendr, tree* + *-on*] Any of a genus of tree-climbing plants indigenous to tropical America and often grown as ornamental house plants. Literally means "loving trees," in reference to its climbing habit. (fil' uh DEN drun)

philogyny [*philo, love* + *gyn, woman* + *-y*] Love and admiration of women. See misogyny. (fih LOJ uh nee)

philology [*philo, love* + *log, discourse* + *-y*] 1.An early name for linguistics, especially historical and comparative linguistics. 2.Love of literature and learning. 3.The scientific study of written records to determine meaning, authenticity, etc. (fih LOL uh jee)

philoprogenitive [*philo, love & progenitive*] 1.Loving one's offspring. 2.Producing many offspring. See progenitive and polytocous. (fil' oh proh JEN ih tiv)

philosophe [*philo, love* + *soph, wisdom*] Any of the popular French intellectuals and writers of the 18th century. (fee' luh ZOF)

philosophy [*philo, love* + *-sophy, wisdom*] Love of wisdom as obtained through intellectual knowledge and reasoning. (fih LOS uh fee)

philter [*phil, love* + *-er*] 1.A love potion thought to have the power to arouse sexual passion. 2.Any magic potion. (FIL ter)

philtre [*phil, love* + *-er*] 1.A love potion thought to have the power to arouse sexual passion. 2.Any magic potion. Same as philter. (FIL ter)

photophilous [*photo, light* + *phil, a natural liking* + *-ous*] Thriving in the presence of light or exhibiting positive phototropism, as a plant. (foh TOF uh lus)

psychrophilic [*psychro, cold* + *phil, a natural liking* + *-ic*] Thriving best at relatively low temperatures. See cryophilic. (seye' kroh FIL ik)

Russophile [*Russo, Russian* + *-phile, love*] An admirer of Russia and Russian customs, institutions, etc. (RUS uh feyel')

thermophile [*thermo, heat* + *-phile, a natural liking*] An organism requiring high temperatures for normal development. (THUR muh feyel')

phil/o, -phile

toxophilite [*Grk > toxon, bow + phil, love + -ite*] A lover of or expert in archery. (toks OF uh leyet')

tropophilous [*tropo, changing + phil, a natural liking + -ous*] Thriving in a region marked by extreme seasonal climatic changes, as certain plants. See tropophyte. (troh POF uh lus)

xenophile [*xeno, foreign + -phile, attracted to*] One who is attracted to foreigners or foreign things. (ZEN uh feyel')

xerophilous [*xero, dry + phil, a natural liking + -ous*] Thriving in an environment having only a small amount of moisture. (zihr OF uh lus)

zoophile [*zoo, animal + -phile, love*] A lover of animals; specifically, one who objects to the use of vivisection in study or research. See vivisection. (ZOH uh feyel')

zoophilia [*zoo, animal + phil, love + -ia*] The engagement in sexual activity with an animal. (zoh' uh FIL ee uh)

zoophilous [*zoo, animal + phil, affinity for + -ous*] Pertaining to plants that can be pollinated by animals other than insects. See anemophilous and entomophilous. (zoh OF uh lus)

-phobia   fear

acrophobia [*acro, high + -phobia, fear*] Abnormal fear of heights. (ak' ruh FOH bee uh)

aerophobia [*aero, air + -phobia, fear*] Abnormal fear of air, especially of drafts. (ehr' uh FOH bee uh)

agoraphobia [*agora {marketplace} & -phobia, fear*] Abnormal fear of being in open or public places. (ag' uh ruh FOH bee uh)

ailurophobia [*Grk > ailouros, cat + -phobia, fear*] Abnormal fear of cats. (eye loor' uh FOH bee uh)

algophobia [*algo, pain + -phobia, fear*] Abnormal fear of pain. (al' guh FOH bee uh)

amaxophobia [*Grk > amaxa, carriage + -phobia, fear*] Abnormal fear of riding in a vehicle. (uh mak' suh FOH bee uh)

androphobia [*andro, man + -phobia, fear*] Abnormal fear of men. (an' druh FOH bee uh)

Anglophobia [*Anglo, English + -phobia, fear*] Hatred or fear of England or anything English. (ang' gluh FOH bee uh)

arachnephobia [*Grk > arachne, spider + -phobia, fear*] Abnormal fear of spiders. (uh rak' nuh FOH bee uh)

astraphobia [*Grk > astrape, the heavens + -phobia, fear*] Abnormal fear of thunder and lightning. (as' truh FOH bee uh)

automysophobia [*auto-, self + Grk > mysos, filth + -phobia, fear*] Abnormal fear of personal uncleanliness. (awt' oh meye' suh FOH bee uh)

bibliophobia [*biblio, book + -phobia, fear*] Abnormal fear of or distaste for books. (bib' lee uh FOH bee uh)

cancerphobia [*cancer & -phobia, fear*] Abnormal fear of getting cancer. (kan' ser FOH bee uh)

cardiophobia [*cardio, heart + -phobia, fear*] Abnormal fear of heart disease. (kahr' dee oh FOH bee uh)

claustrophobia [*Ltn > claudere, to close + -phobia, fear*] Abnormal fear of closed or narrow places. (klos' truh FOH bee uh)

coitophobia [*coit(us) {sexual intercourse} & -phobia, fear*] Abnormal fear of sexual intercourse. (koh it' uh FOH bee uh)

cyberphobia [*cyber(netics) & -phobia, fear*] Abnormal fear of computers. See technophobia (def. 2). (seye' ber FOH bee uh)

cynophobia [*cyno, dog + -phobia, fear*] Abnormal fear of dogs. (seye' nuh FOH bee uh)

entomophobia [*entomo, insect + -phobia, fear*] Abnormal fear of insects. (ent' uh moh' FOH bee uh)

ergophobia [*ergo, work + -phobia, fear*] Abnormal fear of work. (ur' guh FOH bee uh)

erythrophobia [*erythro, red + -phobia, fear*] Abnormal fear of anything red, or of blushing. (ih rith' roh FOH bee uh)

gamophobia [*gamo, marriage + -phobia, fear*] Abnormal fear of marriage. (gam' uh FOH bee uh)

gephyrophobia [*Grk > gephyra, bridge + -phobia, fear*] Abnormal fear of crossing a bridge. (jef' uh roh FOH bee uh)

Germanophobia [*Germano, German + -phobia, fear*] Hatred or fear of Germany or anything German. (jer man' uh FOH bee uh)

gymnophobia [*gymno, naked + -phobia, fear*] Abnormal fear or dread of viewing a naked body. (jim' nuh FOH bee uh)

gynephobia [*gyne, woman + -phobia, fear*] Abnormal fear of women. (jin' uh FOH bee uh)

haphephobia [*Grk > haphe, touch + -phobia, fear*] Abnormal fear of being touched by another person. (haf' uh FOH bee uh)

hemophobia [*hemo, blood + -phobia, fear*] Abnormal fear of blood or of bleeding. (hee' muh FOH bee uh)

hodophobia [*Grk > hodos, journey + -phobia, fear*] Abnormal fear of traveling. (hoh' duh FOH bee uh)

homophobia [*homo, same + -phobia, fear*] Hatred or fear of homosexuals. (hoh' muh FOH bee uh)

hydrophobia [*hydro, water + -phobia, fear*] 1.Abnormal fear of water. 2.Rabies. So named from the victim's inability to swallow liquids in spite of extreme thirst. (heye' druh FOH bee uh)

lalophobia [*lalo, talk + -phobia, fear*] Abnormal fear of speaking due to fear of committing errors or stammering. (lal' uh FOH bee uh)

lexophobia [*lexo, reading + -phobia, fear*] Hatred or fear of reading. (leks' uh FOH bee uh)

microphobia [*micro(organism) & -phobia, fear*] Abnormal fear of microbes. (meye' kroh FOH bee uh)

monophobia [*mono-, alone + -phobia, fear*] Abnormal fear of being alone. (mon' uh FOH bee uh)

mysophobia [*Grk > mysos, filth + -phobia, fear*] Abnormal fear of dirt or contamination. (meye' suh FOH bee uh)

necrophobia [*necro, death + -phobia, fear*] Abnormal fear of death or dead bodies. (nek' ruh FOH bee uh)

Negrophobia [*Negro & -phobia, fear*] Hatred or fear of blacks. (nee' gruh FOH bee uh)

neophobia [*neo, new + -phobia, fear*] Abnormal fear of novelty or the unknown. (nee' oh FOH bee uh)

nosophobia [*noso, disease + -phobia, fear*] Abnormal fear of sickness or disease. (nos' uh FOH bee uh)

nostophobia [*Grk > nostos, return home + -phobia, fear*] Abnormal fear of returning home. (nos' tuh FOH bee uh)

nyctophobia [*nycto, night + -phobia, fear*] Abnormal fear of darkness or night. (nik' tuh FOH bee uh)

ochlophobia [*Grk > ochlos, crowd + -phobia, fear*] Abnormal fear of crowds. (ok' luh FOH bee uh)

ophidiophobia [*ophi, snake* + *-phobia, fear*] Abnormal fear of snakes. (oh fid' ee uh FOH bee uh)

panophobia [*pano, all* + *-phobia, fear*] Fear of everything. (pan' uh FOH bee uh)

peniaphobia [*Grk > penia, poverty* + *-phobia, fear*] Abnormal fear of poverty. (pee' nee uh FOH bee uh)

phasmophobia [*Grk > phasma, apparition* + *-phobia, fear*] Abnormal fear of ghosts. (fas' moh FOH bee uh)

photophobia [*photo, light* + *-phobia, fear*] Abnormal fear or intolerance of light. (foht' oh FOH bee uh)

pnigophobia [*Grk > pnigos, choking* + *-phobia, fear*] Abnormal fear of choking. (nig' uh FOH bee uh)

psychrophobia [*psychro, cold* + *-phobia, fear*] Abnormal fear of, or sensitivity to, cold. (seye' kroh FOH bee uh)

pyrophobia [*pyro, fire* + *-phobia, fear*] Abnormal fear of fire. (peye' roh FOH bee uh)

Russophobia [*Russo, Russian* + *-phobia, fear*] Hatred or fear of Russia or Russian things. (rus' uh FOH bee uh)

taphephobia [*Grk > taphos, tomb* + *-phobia, fear*] Abnormal fear of being buried alive. (taf' uh FOH bee uh)

technophobia [*techno(logy)* & *-phobia, fear*] 1.Abnormal fear of new technology. 2.Abnormal fear of computers. See cyberphobia. (tek' nuh FOH bee uh)

thanatophobia [*thanato, death* + *-phobia, fear*] Abnormal fear of death. (than' uh tuh FOH bee uh)

theophobia [*theo, God* + *-phobia, fear*] Abnormal fear of the wrath of God. (thee' oh FOH bee uh)

tocophobia [*toco, birth* + *-phobia, fear*] Abnormal fear of childbirth. (toh' koh FOH bee uh)

triskaidekaphobia [*tri-, three* + *kai, and* + *deka, ten* + *-phobia, fear*] Fear of the number 13. (tris' keye dek' uh FOH bee uh)

venereophobia [*venere(al)* & *-phobia, fear*] Abnormal fear of venereal disease. (vuh nihr' ee oh FOH bee uh)

xenophobia [*xeno, foreign* + *-phobia, fear*] Abnormal fear of foreigners or strangers. (zen' uh FOH bee uh)

zoophobia [*zoo, animal* + *-phobia, fear*] Abnormal fear of animals. (zoh' uh FOH bee uh)

phon/o, -phone, -phony   sound, voice

allophone [*allo, variation* + *-phone, sound*] Any of the variant forms of the same phoneme. See phoneme and phone. (AL uh fohn')

antiphon [*anti-, opposite* + *phon, voice*] A psalm, prayer, or hymn sung or recited by two alternating groups. (AN tih fahn')

aphonia [*a-, without* + *phon, voice* + *-ia*] Loss of voice due to disease, injury, or structural abnormality. (ay FOH nee uh)

cacophony [*caco, harsh* + *-phony, sound*] Harsh or disagreeable sounds. Discord. Dissonance. See euphonious. (kuh KOF uh nee)

Dictaphone [*dict, to speak* + *-phone, sound*] Trademark for a device for recording dictation so it may be transcribed later. (DIK tuh fohn')

dodecaphonic [*dodeca-, twelve* + *phon, sound* + *-ic*] Pertaining to a system of music based on all twelve tones of the chromatic scale. (doh' dek' uh FON ik)

dysphonia [*dys-, difficult* + *phon, sound* + *-ia*] Difficulty in producing articulate speech sounds. (dis FOH nee uh)

euphonious [*eu-, good* + *phon, sound* + *-ious*] Having a pleasant or agreeable sound. Harmonious. See cacophony. (yoo FOH nee us)

geophone [*geo, earth* + *-phone, sound*] A seismic device for detecting vibrations in the earth. (JEE uh fohn')

homophone [*homo, same* + *-phone, sound*] One of two or more words that are pronounced the same, always differ in meaning, and usually differ in spelling, as *wear* (to carry on the body) and *ware* (articles of merchandise). Same as homonym. (HOM uh fohn')

homophonic [*homo, same* + *phon, sound* + *-ic*] 1.Having the same sound. 2.Having one predominate melody with the other instruments or voices serving as accompaniment. See monody (def. 3). (hom' uh FON ik)

hydrophone [*hydro, water* + *-phone, sound*] A device for monitoring underwater sounds, as from a submarine. (HEYE druh fohn')

megaphone [*mega-, large* + *-phone, voice*] A cone-shaped device designed to amplify and direct the voice. (MEG uh fohn')

microphone [*micro-, small* + *-phone, sound*] An instrument that converts sound waves into a small electric current that is fed into an amplifier, transmitter, recorder, etc. (MEYE kruh fohn')

monophony [*mono-, single* + *-phony, sound*] Music performed by a single voice or instrument without accompaniment. (muh NOF uh nee)

phon [*phon, sound*] A unit of sound volume measured in decibels by comparing a given sound with a 1,000 hertz reference tone. See decibel. (fahn)

phonate [*phon, sound* + *-ate*] To generate articulate speech sounds. (FOH nayt)

phone [*phon, sound*] A distinct speech sound. See allophone and phoneme. (fohn)

phoneme [*phon, sound* + *-eme, structural unit*] The smallest unit of speech sound in a language. See allophone, phone, and toneme. (FOH neem)

phonemics [*phonem(e)* & *-ics, study of*] The branch of linguistics dealing with the study of the phonemes of a language. See phonology, phonetics, and phoneme. (fuh NEE miks)

phonetic [*phon, sound* + *-etic*] Pertaining to speech sounds or spoken language. (fuh NET ik)

phonetic alphabet [*phonetic* & *alphabet*] A set of symbols each representing a distinct speech sound, used for phonetic transcription. (fuh NET ik AL fuh bet')

phonetics [*phon, sound* + *-ics, study of*] 1.The branch of linguistics dealing with the study of the production, analysis, and written representation of speech sounds. 2.The speech sounds of a particular language. See phonology and phonemics. (fuh NET iks)

phonic [*phon, sound* + *-ic*] Pertaining to or producing sound. (FON ik)

phonics [*phon, sound* + *-ics, study of*] 1.The study of sound. 2.A method of teaching reading to beginners by associating letters and syllables with sounds. (FON iks)

phonocardiograph [*phono, sound* + *cardio, heart* + *graph, recording*] An instrument for graphically recording the sounds of the heartbeat. (foh' nuh KAHR dee uh graf')

phonogram [*phono, sound* + *gram, to write*] A graphic symbol representing a speech sound, as in shorthand. See phonotype. (FOH nuh gram')

phon/o, -phone, -phony

phonograph [*phono, sound + graph, recording*] A device for reproducing prerecorded sound from a disk that is commonly referred to as a record. (FOH nuh graf')

phonography [*phono, sound + -graphy, written*] A system of speech transcription based on pronunciation. (fuh NOG ruh fee)

phonolite [*phono, sound + -lite, rock*] A light-gray to light-green igneous rock that produces a ringing sound when struck. (FOHN l eyet')

phonology [*phon, sound + -ology, study of*] The study of the elements and principles that determine the overall sound pattern of a language, including phonetics and phonemics. See phonemics and phonetics. (fuh NOL uh jee)

phonon [*phon, sound + -on*] The basic unit of sound energy. (FOH non)

phonoscope [*phono, sound + -scope, to view*] An instrument for viewing the properties of sounding bodies, especially musical strings. (FOH nuh skohp')

phonotype [*phono, sound & type*] A graphic symbol representing a speech sound, as in printing. See phonogram. (FOH nuh teyep')

polyphony [*poly, many + -phony, sound*] Music combining two or more independent melodies in harmony. (puh LIF uh nee)

quadraphonic [*quadra, four + phon, sound + -ic*] Using four channels for sound reproduction, each from a separate source. See stereophonic. (kwod' ruh FON ik)

stereophonic [*stereo-, three-dimensional + phon, sound + -ic*] Pertaining to a three-dimensional effect of sound reproduction using two or more channels, each from a separate source. See quadraphonic. (stehr' ee oh FON ik)

symphony [*sym-, together + -phony, sound*] 1.Harmony of sounds or colors. 2.An elaborate and usually lengthy musical composition with several movements, one or more of which are in sonata form. 3.A concert by a symphony orchestra. (SIM fuh nee)

telephone [*tele, distant + -phone, voice*] A device for transmitting and receiving speech sounds or other data from a distant location. (TEL uh fohn')

xylophone [*xylo, wood + -phone, sound*] A musical instrument played with two wooden mallets that consists of a set of wooden bars each of which corresponds to a note of the chromatic scale. (ZEYE luh fohn')

voc, vok   to call, voice

advocate [*ad-, to + voc, to call + -ate*] 1.To speak or write in favor of something. (AD vuh kayt' {verb}) 2.A person who speaks or writes in favor of something. See proponent (def. 1). (AD vuh kut {noun})

convocation [*con-, together + voc, to call + -ation*] A meeting or assembly. (kon' vuh KAY shun)

convoke [*con-, together + vok, to call*] To call together for a meeting or assembly. (kun VOHK)

devocalize [*de-, remove + voc, voice + -al + -ize*] To enunciate without using the vocal cords. (dee VOH kuh leyez')

equivocal [*equi, equal + voc, voice + -al*] Having more than one meaning and often intended to deceive or mislead. Ambiguous. See ambiguous (def. 1), unequivocal, and univocal (def. 1). (ih KWIV uh kul)

equivocate [*equi, equal + voc, voice + -ate*] To use ambiguous or unclear expressions, usually to mislead, deceive, or to avoid giving a direct answer. Quibble. See tergiversate (def. 1). (ih KWIV uh kayt')

equivoke [*equi, equal + vok, voice*] An ambiguous word, phrase, or expression. (EK wuh vohk')

evocative [*e-, out + voc, to call + -ative*] Tending to evoke. (ih VOK uh tiv)

evoke [*e-, out + vok, to call*] To bring out or call forth, as feelings, memories, etc. See educe (def. 1) and elicit. (ih VOHK)

intervocalic [*inter-, between + voc, voice + -al + -ic*] Pertaining to a consonant or other linguistic element that occurs between two vowels. See vocalic, prevocalic, and postvocalic. (in' ter voh KAL ik)

invocation [*in-, on + voc, to call + -ation*] 1.The act of calling upon God or a deity for inspiration, support, or other assistance. 2.A formal prayer at the beginning of a religious service. (in' vuh KAY shun)

invoke [*in-, on + vok, to call*] 1.To call on or appeal to for support, assistance, etc. 2.To initiate or put into use. (in VOHK)

irrevocable [*ir-, not + re-, back + voc, to call + -able*] Not able to be called back or undone, as a decision. Unalterable. Final. (ihr REV uh kuh bul)

postvocalic [*post-, after + voc, voice + -al + -ic*] Pertaining to a consonant or other linguistic element that occurs immediately after a vowel. See vocalic, prevocalic, and intervocalic. (pohst' voh KAL ik)

prevocalic [*pre-, before + voc, voice + -al + -ic*] Pertaining to a consonant or other linguistic element that occurs immediately before a vowel. See vocalic, intervocalic, and postvocalic. (pree' voh KAL ik)

provoke [*pro-, forth + vok, to call*] To incite to some action, feeling, or desire. Excite. Cause. (pruh VOHK)

revoke [*re-, back + vok, to call*] To take back or cancel, as a license, permit, etc. See retract (def. 2). (rih VOHK)

unequivocal [*un-, not + equi, equal + voc, voice + -al*] Not ambiguous. Unmistakable. Clear. See ambiguous (def. 1), equivocal, and univocal (def. 1). (un' ih KWIV uh kul)

univocal [*uni-, one + voc, voice + -al*] 1.Having only one meaning. Unambiguous. Unequivocal. See ambiguous (def. 1), equivocal, and unequivocal. 2.A word or term with only one proper meaning. (yoo NIV uh kul)

viva voce [*viv, living & voc, voice*] 1.By word of mouth. Orally. 2.An oral examination in British universities. (VEYE vuh VOH see)

vocable [*voc, voice + -able*] A word composed of a sequence of letters or sounds without regard to its meaning. (VOH kuh bul)

vocabulary [*Ltn > vocabulum, word + -ary*] 1.A list of all the words of a language. 2.All the words known or used by an individual, group, profession, etc. (voh KAB yuh lehr' ee)

vocal [*voc, voice + -al*] 1.Pertaining to or produced by the voice. 2.Outspoken. (VOH kul)

vocalic [*voc, voice + -al + -ic*] 1.Pertaining to or functioning as a vowel. 2.Consisting of vowels. See prevocalic, intervocalic, and postvocalic. (voh KAL ik)

vocalist [*voc, voice + -al + -ist*] A singer. (VOH kuh list)

vocation [*voc, to call + -ation*] 1.A call or strong inclination to enter a certain profession, career, trade, etc. 2.A profession, career, trade, etc. (voh KAY shun)

vociferous [*voc, voice* + *fer, to carry* + *-ous*] Making a loud or vehement outcry. Noisy. Clamorous. (voh SIF ur us)

vocoder [*voc, voice* & *(c)oder*] An electronic device for coding, transmitting, and decoding speech. (VOH koh' der)

phor, -phore to bear, to produce, to carry, state

aerophore [*aero, air* + *-phore, to carry*] A device, used by firemen, pilots, etc., for carrying air to the lungs in case of oxygen shortage or on newborn infants to stimulate breathing. (EHR uh for')

amphora [*amphi-, on both sides* + *phor, to carry* + *-a*] A jar with a handle on each side and a narrow neck, used by the ancient Greeks to carry oil or wine. (AM fur uh)

anaphora [*ana-, again* + *phor, to produce* + *-a*] 1.The deliberate repetition of a word or words at the beginning of successive phrases, clauses, sentences, or verses. See epistrophe. 2.The use of a word or words to avoid repetition of a word or words used previously in the same sentence, as "I know it and *so do you*" vs. "I know it and *you know it too*." (uh NAF uh ruh)

anthophore [*antho, flower* + *-phore, to bear*] A stalk between the calyx and corolla of certain flowers that supports the floral parts. (AN thuh for')

carpophore [*carp(el)* & *-phore, to bear*] The extended receptacle that attaches to the carpels in certain flowering plants. (KAHR puh for')

chromatophore [*chromato, pigment* + *-phore, to produce*] A pigment-containing dermal cell found mostly in lower animals that causes skin color changes by contracting or expanding. (kroh MAT uh for')

chromophore [*chromo, color* + *-phore, to produce*] A group of atoms in an organic compound whose arrangement gives rise to color. (KROH muh for')

ctenophore [*cteno, comb* + *-phore, to bear*] Marine animals resembling jellyfish that bear eight rows of comblike cilia used for swimming. (TEN uh for')

diaphoresis [*dia-, through* + *phor, to produce* + *-esis*] Copious perspiration. (deye' uh fuh REE sis)

dysphoria [*dys-, bad* + *phor, state* + *-ia*] A general feeling of ill-being. Opposed to euphoria. (dis FOR ee uh)

euphoria [*eu-, good* + *phor, state* + *-ia*] A feeling of well-being. Opposed to dysphoria. (yoo FOR ee uh)

gametophore [*gameto, gamete* + *-phore, to bear*] A plant structure bearing the gamete-producing organs. (guh MEET uh for')

gonophore [*gono, reproduction* + *-phore, to bear*] A stalk bearing male and female reproductive organs or parts. (GON uh for')

gynophore [*gyno, female* + *-phore, to bear*] The floral stalk that bears the gynoecium. (JIN uh for')

melanophore [*melano, black* + *-phore, to produce*] A melanin-containing chromatophore. (muh LAN uh for')

metaphor [*meta-, beyond* + *phor, to carry*] A figure of speech with an implied comparison between a word or phrase and an object or concept it does not ordinarily represent, as "a mountain of debt." See simile and metonymy. (MET uh for')

odontophore [*odonto, teeth* + *-phore, to bear*] A structure at the base of the mouth of most mollusks that supports the radula, which is drawn back and forth to break up food. (oh DONT uh for')

oophor- [*oo, egg* + *phor, to bear*] A word root meaning "ovary." (OH uh for')

oophorectomy [*oophor-, ovary* + *ec, out* + *-tomy, to cut*] Surgical removal of an ovary. Same as ovariectomy. (oh' uh fuh REK tuh mee)

oophoritis [*oophor-, ovary* + *-itis, inflammation*] Inflammation of an ovary. (oh' uh fuh REYE tis)

phosphorescence [*phos, light* + *phor, to produce* + *-escence*] The property of a substance of emitting light after exposure to x-rays or other radiant energy. (fos' fuh RES ens)

phosphorus [*phos, light* + *phor, to produce* + *-us*] A solid, nonmetallic element existing in one form that is yellow, poisonous, flammable, and luminous in the dark and in another form that is red, less poisonous, and less flammable. (FOS fur us)

photophore [*photo, light* + *-phore, to produce*] A light-producing organ of certain deep-sea fishes, cephalopods, and crustaceans. (FOHT uh for')

pneumatophore [*pneumato, breathing* + *-phore, to carry*] A root of certain aquatic plants, often serving as a specialized respiratory organ. (noo MAT uh for')

pyrophoric [*pyro, fire* + *phor, state* + *-ic*] 1.Pertaining to materials that ignite spontaneously. 2.Emitting sparks when struck or scratched. (peye' roh FOR ik)

spermatophore [*spermato, sperm* + *-phore, to produce*] A capsule containing spermatozoa produced by the male of certain invertebrates and a few primitive vertebrates. (spur MAT uh for')

sporangiophore [*sporangi(a)* & *-phore, to bear*] A stalk or filament bearing one or more sporangia. (spuh RAN jee uh for')

sporophore [*sporo, spore* + *-phore, to bear*] A spore-bearing structure or organ in various fungi. (SPOR uh for')

phot/o light

aphotic [*a-, without* + *phot, light* + *-ic*] Without light; specifically, the lower part of the ocean that does not receive enough light for photosynthesis. (ay FOHT ik)

astrophotography [*astro, star* & *photography*] The art or practice of photographing celestial objects. (as' troh fuh TOG ruh fee)

cytophotometry [*cyto, cell* & *photometry*] The scientific study of cells using photometry. See photometry. (seyet' oh foh TOM ih tree)

euphotic [*eu-, good* + *phot, light* + *-ic*] Pertaining to the uppermost zone in a body of water through which sunlight penetrates in sufficient amounts for photosynthesis to occur. (yoo FOHT ik)

microphotograph [*micro-, small* & *photograph*] A small photograph that cannot be viewed without being enlarged. See photomicrograph. (meye' kroh FOH tuh graf')

microphotometer [*micro-, small* + *photo, light* + *meter, to measure*] An instrument for measuring the light intensity of minute objects. See photometer. (meye' kroh foh TOM et er)

phot [*phot, light*] A unit of illumination equal to one lumen per square centimeter. (foht)

phot/o

photoautotrophic [*photo, light & autotrophic*] Pertaining to an organism that produces its own food using inorganic materials and photosynthesis, as most plants. See chemoautotrophic and autotroph. (foht' oh ot' uh TROF ik)

photochromic [*photo, light + chrom, color + -ic*] Pertaining to materials that change color when exposed to light or other radiant energy and in some cases return to their original color upon removal of the radiation source. (foht' oh KROH mik)

photodynamic [*photo, light + dynam, energy + -ic*] Pertaining to, operated by, or reacting to the energy of light. (foht' oh deye NAM ik)

photodynamics [*photo, light + dynam, power + -ics, study of*] The study of the effects of light on plants and animals. (foht' oh deye NAM iks)

photoelectric [*photo, light & electric*] Pertaining to a substance or device that emits electrons when exposed to light. (foht' oh ih LEK trik)

photogenic [*photo, light + gen, to produce + -ic*] 1.Having an attractive appearance as a subject for photography. 2.Emitting light, as certain insects or bacteria. Phosphorescent. (foht' oh JEN ik)

photogrammetry [*photogram & -metry, science of measuring*] The art or process of making accurate measurements for maps and surveys using aerial photography. (foht' oh GRAM ih tree)

photography [*photo, light + -graphy, recording*] The process of recording images by the exposure of sensitized surfaces to light or other forms of radiant energy. (fuh TOG ruh fee)

photokinesis [*photo, light + kine, motion + -sis*] Movement or activity in response to light. See phototaxis and phototropism. (foht' oh kih NEE sis)

photolithography [*photo(graph) & litho, stone + -graphy, recording*] A lithographic printing process that uses plates prepared from a photograph. See lithography. (foht' oh lith OG ruh fee)

photolysis [*photo, light + -lysis, decomposition*] Chemical decomposition of a substance caused by the action of light. (foh TOL uh sis)

photometer [*photo, light + meter, to measure*] An instrument for measuring light intensity. See microphotometer. (foh TOM et er)

photometry [*photo, light + -metry, science of measuring*] The scientific measurement of light intensity. (foh TOM ih tree)

photomicrograph [*photo, light + micro, small + graph, recording*] A photograph of an image taken through a microscope. See micrograph (def. 2) and microphotograph. (foht' oh MEYE kruh graf')

photomicroscope [*photo(graph) & microscope*] A microscope for taking photomicrographs. See photomicrograph. (foht' oh MEYE kruh skohp')

photon [*phot, light + -on*] The basic unit of electromagnetic energy. (FOH tahn)

photophilous [*photo, light + phil, a natural liking + -ous*] Thriving in the presence of light or exhibiting positive phototropism, as a plant. (foh TOF uh lus)

photophobia [*photo, light + -phobia, fear*] Abnormal fear or intolerance of light. (foht' oh FOH bee uh)

photophore [*photo, light + -phore, to produce*] A light-producing organ of certain deep-sea fishes, cephalopods, and crustaceans. (FOHT uh for')

photopia [*phot, light + -opia, vision*] Adaptation of the eyes to bright light. Opposed to scotopia. (foh TOH pee uh)

photoreceptor [*photo, light & receptor*] A cell, nerve ending, or organ that responds to light stimuli. (foht' oh rih SEP tur)

photosensitive [*photo, light & sensitive*] Sensitive to light or other radiant energy. (foht' oh SEN sih tiv)

photosphere [*photo, light & sphere*] The luminous, visible surface of the sun or other stars. See chromosphere. (FOHT uh sfihr')

photosynthesis [*photo, light + syn, together + the, to put + -sis*] A biological process primarily associated with green plants that forms organic compounds from carbon dioxide and water in the presence of light with simultaneous liberation of oxygen. (foht' oh SIN thuh sis)

phototaxis [*photo, light & taxis*] The movement of a freely moving organism in response to light. See phototropism, heliotaxis, and photokinesis. (foht' oh TAK sis)

phototropism [*photo, light + trop, responding to a stimulus + -ism*] The movement or growth of an organism or part in response to light. See phototaxis, heliotropism, and photokinesis. (foh TOT ruh piz' um)

photovoltaic [*photo, light & voltaic*] Producing an electric current when exposed to light or other radiant energy. (foht' oh vol TAY ik)

photozincography [*photo, light & zinc & -graphy, recording*] Photoengraving on sensitized zinc plates. (foht' oh zing KOG ruh fee)

pyrophotometer [*pyro, heat + photo, light + meter, to measure*] An optical thermometer for measuring very high temperatures. See pyrometer. (peye' roh foh TOM et er)

radiophotography [*radio, by radio & photography*] The transmission of a photograph by radio waves by first converting the image to a matrix of electric impulses and then recreating the image at the reception site. (ray' dee oh' fuh TOG ruh fee)

spectrophotometer [*spectro, spectrum + photo, light + meter, to measure*] An instrument for measuring wavelengths in light spectra for accurate analysis of color and the comparison of luminous intensity. See spectrometer. (spek' troh foh TOM et er)

telephoto [*tele, distant & photo(graphy)*] Pertaining to a camera lens that produces a magnified image of a distant object. (tel' uh FOHT oh)

telephotography [*tele, distant & photography*] 1.The art or technique of photographing distant objects with the aid of a telephoto lens. 2.The process of transmitting text or graphics, as by radio waves or telephone lines. Facsimile. (tel' uh fuh TOG ruh fee)

phyt/o, -phyte   plant, to grow

autophyte [*auto-, self + -phyte, plant*] A plant that produces its own food by using inorganic matter and photosynthesis. See heterophyte and saprophyte. (AWT uh feyet')

bryophyte [*bryo, moss + -phyte, plant*] Any of a division of simple plants comprising the mosses and liverworts. (BREYE uh feyet')

chrysophyte [*chryso, yellow + -phyte, plant*] Any of a large group of golden-brown and yellowish-green algae with xanthophyll and carotene pigments in addition to chlorophyll pigments. (KRIS uh feyet')

cryophyte [*cryo, cold + -phyte, plant*] A plant that grows on snow or ice, as mosses, algae, fungi, or bacteria. (KREYE uh feyet')

dermatophyte [*dermato, skin + -phyte, plant*] Any parasitic fungus of the skin, hair, or nails, such as athlete's foot or ringworm. (der MAT uh feyet')

endophyte [*endo-, inside + -phyte, plant*] A parasitic or symbiotic plant growing within another plant. See epiphyte. (EN duh feyet')

epiphyte [*epi-, upon + -phyte, plant*] A plant growing independently on the surface of another plant on which it is dependent for support only. See endophyte. (EP ih feyet')

gametophyte [*gameto, gamete + -phyte, plant*] In plants reproducing by alternation of generations, the gamete-producing haploid generation that reproduces sexually by eggs and sperm. This generation produces a zygote which develops into a sporophyte. See sporophyte and alternation of generations. (guh MEET uh feyet')

geophyte [*geo, earth + -phyte, plant*] A perennial plant having the buds below the soil surface. (JEE uh feyet')

halophyte [*halo, salt + -phyte, plant*] A plant that grows well in salty soil. (HAL uh feyet')

heterophyte [*hetero, other + -phyte, plant*] A plant that gets its food from other living or dead organisms. See autophyte and saprophyte. (HET ur uh feyet')

hydrophyte [*hydro, water + -phyte, plant*] A plant that grows only in water or extremely wet soil. See mesophyte and xerophyte. (HEYE druh feyet')

hygrophyte [*hygro, moisture + -phyte, plant*] A plant that grows only in water or extremely wet soil. Same as hydrophyte. (HEYE gruh feyet')

lithophyte [*litho, stone + -phyte, plant*] A plant that grows on the surface of rocks. (LITH uh feyet')

macrophyte [*macro-, large + -phyte, plant*] A plant that is large enough to be visible to the naked eye, especially one in an aquatic environment. See macroscopic and microphyte. (MAK roh feyet')

megagametophyte [*mega-, large & gametophyte*] A female gametophyte in heterosporous plants that is produced by a megaspore. See microgametophyte, gametophyte, and megaspore. (meg' uh guh MEET uh feyet')

mesophyte [*meso-, middle + -phyte, plant*] A plant that grows well in moderately moist soil. See hydrophyte and xerophyte. (MEZ uh feyet')

microgametophyte [*micro-, small & gametophyte*] A male gametophyte in heterosporous plants that is produced by a microspore. See megagametophyte, gametophyte, and microspore. (meye' kroh guh MEET uh feyet')

microphyte [*micro-, small + -phyte, plant*] A plant that is not large enough to be visible to the naked eye. See microscopic and macrophyte. (MEYE kroh feyet')

neophyte [*neo, new + -phyte, to grow*] 1.A beginner. Novice. 2.A person recently converted to a belief, especially in a religious faith. (NEE uh feyet')

osteophyte [*osteo, bone + -phyte, to grow*] An abnormal bony outgrowth or bone enlargement. (OS tee uh feyet')

periphyton [*peri-, around + phyt, plant + -on*] Organisms that spend their life cycle attached to aquatic plants and other underwater surfaces, as snails and algae. (puh RIF ih tahn')

phytoalexin [*phyto, plant + Grk > alexein, to defend*] An antibiotic produced by higher plants in response to a pathogen such as a fungus. (feyet' oh uh LEK sin)

phytochrome [*phyto, plant + -chrome, pigment*] A protein pigment in plants that regulates growth and other physiological processes by responding to variations of red light. (FEYET uh krohm')

phytogenesis [*phyto, plant + -genesis, formation*] The origin and development of plants. See phylogeny and ontogeny. (feyet' oh JEN uh sis)

phytogenic [*phyto, plant + gen, origin + -ic*] Being of plant origin, as coal. (feyet' oh JEN ik)

phytogeography [*phyto, plant + geo, earth + -graphy, science*] The branch of biology dealing with the study of the geographical distribution of plants. See biogeography and zoogeography. (feyet' oh jee OG ruh fee)

phytography [*phyto, plant + -graphy, writing*] The descriptive study of plants. Descriptive botany. See phytology and zoography. (feye TOG ruh fee)

phytolite [*phyto, plant + -lite, fossil*] A fossil plant. (FEYET l eyet')

phytolith [*phyto, plant + lith, stone*] A fossil plant. Same as phytolite. (FEYET l ith')

phytology [*phyt, plant + -ology, study of*] The branch of biology dealing with the study of plants. Botany. See phytography. (feye TOL uh jee)

phyton [*phyt, plant + -on*] The smallest plant part that when removed is able to grow into a new plant. (FEYE tahn)

phytopathogen [*phyto, plant + patho, disease + gen, cause*] An organism that causes a plant disease. (feyet' oh PATH uh jen)

phytopathology [*phyto, plant + path, disease + -ology, study of*] The branch of botany dealing with the study of plant diseases. Plant pathology. (feyet' oh puh THOL uh jee)

phytophagous [*phyto, plant + phag, to eat + -ous*] Feeding on plants. Same as herbivorous. (feye TOF uh gus)

phytoplankton [*phyto, plant + Grk > planktos, wandering*] Minute floating aquatic plants or plantlike organisms. See zooplankton and microplankton. (feyet' oh PLANK tun)

phytosociology [*phyto, plant + socio, social + -logy, study of*] The branch of ecology dealing with the study of the interrelations between plant communities and their environment. (feyet' oh soh' see OL uh jee)

phytosterol [*phyto, plant & sterol*] Any of various sterols derived from plants. See zoosterol. (feye TOS tuh rol')

phytotoxic [*phyto, plant + tox, poison + -ic*] 1.Pertaining to toxic substances of plant origin. 2.Poisonous to plants. (feyet' oh TOK sik)

pteridophyte [*pterido, fern + -phyte, plant*] A mostly outdated classification of various vascular plants, including the ferns, club mosses, and horsetails, that have roots, stems, and leaves, but no flowers or seeds. (tuh RID uh feyet')

saprophyte [*sapro, decaying + -phyte, plant*] A plant or other organism that gets its food from decaying organic matter. See autophyte and heterophyte. (SAP ruh feyet')

phyt/o, -phyte

spermatophyte [*spermato, seed* + *-phyte, plant*] Any plant that produces seeds, including the angiosperms and gymnosperms. (spur MAT uh feyet')

sporophyte [*sporo, spore* + *-phyte, plant*] In plants reproducing by alternation of generations, the spore-producing diploid generation that reproduces asexually by spores. This generation produces a gametophyte. See gametophyte and alternation of generations. (SPOR uh feyet')

thallophyte [*thallo, young shoot* + *-phyte, plant*] A mostly outdated division of the plant kingdom comprising plants without differentiated leaves, stems, and roots, including fungi, lichens, algae, and bacteria. (THAL uh feyet')

tracheophyte [*tracheo, trachea* + *-phyte, plant*] Any of numerous plants with a differentiated vascular system. (TRAY kee uh feyet')

tropophyte [*tropo, changing* + *-phyte, plant*] A plant capable of adapting to changing climatic conditions such as temperature or moisture. See tropophilous. (TROP uh feyet')

xerophyte [*xero, dry* + *-phyte, plant*] A plant that grows only in a dry climate. See hydrophyte and mesophyte. (ZIHR uh feyet')

zoophyte [*zoo, animal* + *-phyte, plant*] Any of various animals that resemble plants, as a sea anemone or coral. (ZOH uh feyet')

phyll/o   leaf

aphyllous [*a-, without* + *phyll, leaf* + *-ous*] Without leaves. (ay FIL us)

apophyllite [*apo-, off* + *phyll, leaf* + *-ite, mineral*] A white, pale-pink, or pale-green crystalline mineral usually occurring in square transparent prisms or in white or grayish masses. So named from its tendency to flake off under intense heat. (uh POF uh leyet')

chlorophyll [*chloro, green* + *phyll, leaf*] A group of green pigments found in the chloroplasts of plants, which absorb the light energy required in photosynthesis. (KLOR uh fil')

chloroplast [*chloro(phyll)* & *plast(id)*] A plastid containing chlorophyll found in the cytoplasm of photosynthetic plant cells. See chromoplast and leucoplast. (KLOR uh plast')

cladophyll [*clado, branch* + *phyll, leaf*] A flattened stem that resembles and functions as a leaf. Cladode. (KLAD uh fil')

diphyllous [*di-, two* + *phyll, leaf* + *-ous*] Having two leaves. (deye FIL us)

heterophyllous [*hetero, different* + *phyll, leaf* + *-ous*] Having leaves of different kinds on the same plant. (het' uh roh FIL us)

megasporophyll [*mega-, large* + *sporo, spore* + *phyll, leaf*] A leaf or modified leaf that produces only megasporangia. See microsporophyll and megasporangium. (meg' uh SPOR uh fil')

mesophyll [*meso, middle* + *phyll, leaf*] The specialized tissue of a leaf, between the lower and upper epidermis, that is usually photosynthetic. (MEZ uh fil')

microsporophyll [*micro-, small* + *sporo, spore* + *phyll, leaf*] A leaf or modified leaf that produces only microsporangia. See megasporophyll and microsporangium. (meye' kroh SPOR uh fil')

phyllite [*phyll, leaf* + *-ite, rock*] A gray or green foliated rock similar to slate. The foliation results from the alignment of mica and chlorite under low or moderate pressure. (FIL eyet)

phylloclade [*phyllo, leaf* + *clad, branch*] A flattened stem that resembles and functions as a leaf. Same as cladophyll. (FIL uh klayd')

phyllode [*phyll, leaf* + *-ode, like*] A flattened stem that resembles and functions as the missing leaf blade that it replaces. (FIL ohd)

phylloid [*phyll, leaf* + *-oid, resembling*] Resembling a leaf. (FIL oid)

phyllophagous [*phyllo, leaf* + *phag, to eat* + *-ous*] Feeding on leaves. (fih LOF uh gus)

phyllotaxis [*phyllo, leaf* + *tax, arrangement* + *-is*] The arrangement of leaves on a stem. (fil' uh TAK sis)

phylloxera [*phyllo, leaf* + *xer, dry* + *-a*] Any of various small insects that attack the roots and leaves of certain plants, especially the grapevine. (fil' ok SIHR uh)

sporophyll [*sporo, spore* + *phyll, leaf*] A leaf or modified leaf that produces sporangia. See microsporophyll and megasporophyll. (SPOR uh fil')

theophylline [*Ltn* > *thea, tea* + *phyll, leaf* + *-ine*] A drug extracted from tea leaves and used in medicine as a vasodilator and muscle relaxant. (thee OF uh lin)

xanthophyll [*xantho, yellow* + *phyll, leaf*] Any of a group of carotenoid pigments in certain green plants that is responsible for the yellow to orange coloration in some autumn leaves. (ZAN thuh fil')

physi/o   nature, physical

astrophysics [*astro, star* & *physics*] The branch of astronomy dealing with the study of the physical properties and characteristics of stars, planets, and other celestial bodies. (as' troh FIZ iks)

biophysics [*bio, life* & *physics*] The application of the techniques and principles of physics to the study of medicine and biology. (beye' oh FIZ iks)

geophysics [*geo, earth* & *physics*] The branch of geology dealing with the study of the physics of the earth, including geodesy, oceanography, hydrology, seismology, volcanology, meteorology, climatology, and geomagnetism. (jee' oh FIZ iks)

histophysiology [*histo, tissue* + *physi, physical* + *-ology, study of*] The branch of physiology dealing with the study of the functions and activities of tissue. (hist' oh fiz' ee OL uh jee)

hyperphysical [*hyper-, beyond* & *physical*] Beyond the physical. Supernatural. See superphysical. (heye' per FIZ ih kul)

metaphysics [*meta-, after* & *physics*] The area of philosophy dealing with the study of the nature and structure of reality. So named from the reference to Aristotle's writings that came after his studies in physics. (met' uh FIZ iks)

microphysics [*micro-, small* & *physics*] The branch of physics dealing with the study of objects that are too small to be observed directly, such as atoms, molecules, and other elementary particles. (meye' kroh FIZ iks)

neurophysiology [*neuro, nerve* + *physi, physical* + *-ology, study of*] The branch of medical science dealing with the study of the functions and activities of the nervous system. See neuropathology and physiology. (noor' oh fiz' ee OL uh jee)

physiatrics [*physi, physical* + *iatr, healing* + *-ics, study of*] The study of physical therapy. (fiz' ee AT riks)

physic [*physi, nature* + *-ic*] 1.A medicine, especially a strong laxative or purgative. See purgative. 2.An obsolete term for the art of medicine. (FIZ ik)

physical [*physi, nature* + *-ical*] 1.Pertaining to nature or natural science. 2.Pertaining to that which is material rather than spiritual, imaginary, or mental. (FIZ ih kul)

physical therapy [*physical & therapy*] The health profession dedicated to the rehabilitation or prevention of disability, injury, and disease specifically related to the movement and function of the neuromuscular, musculoskeletal, cardiopulmonary, and integumentary systems of the human body. (FIZ ih kul THEHR uh pee)

physician [*physi, physical* + *-ician*] A doctor of medicine, as distinguished from a surgeon. (fih ZISH un)

physicist [*physic(s) & -ist*] A scientist specializing in physics. (FIZ ih sist)

physicochemical [*physic(al) & chemical*] Pertaining to or having both physical and chemical properties. (fiz' ih koh KEM ih kul)

physics [*physi, nature* + *-ics, science*] The science dealing with the interactions between nonliving matter and energy, excluding the phenomena of chemical change. (FIZ iks)

physiocracy [*physio, nature* + *-cracy, government*] A school of political thought characterized by the belief that government policy should not interfere with natural economic laws. (fiz' ee OK ruh see)

physiognomy [*physio, nature* + *gnom, knowledge* + *-y*] 1.The art or practice of judging character from body form or facial features. 2.Facial features, especially when taken as a sign of character. (fiz' ee OG nuh mee)

physiography [*physio, physical* + *-graphy, writing*] The descriptive study of the natural physical features of a celestial body. Physical geography. (fiz' ee OG ruh fee)

physiology [*physi, physical* + *-ology, study of*] 1.The biological study of the functions and activities of organisms or their parts, including all physical and chemical processes. 2.The functions and vital processes of an organism or any of its parts. (fiz' ee OL uh jee)

physiotherapy [*physio, physical & therapy*] Physical therapy. (fiz' ee oh THEHR uh pee)

physique [*physi, nature* + *-ic*] The physical structure and appearance of the body. (fih ZEEK)

psychophysics [*psycho, mental process* + *physi, physical* + *-ics, study of*] The branch of psychology dealing with the study of the effects of physical stimuli on mental processes. (seye' koh FIZ iks)

psychophysiology [*psycho, mind* + *physi, physical* + *-ology, study of*] The branch of medical science dealing with the study of the interrelations between mental and physical processes. (seye' koh fiz' ee OL uh jee)

superphysical [*super-, beyond & physical*] Beyond the physical. Unexplainable by the laws of physics. See hyperphysical. (soo' per FIZ ih kul)

pneum/o, pneumon/o, pneumat/o, -pnea, -pnoea

pneum/o, pneumon/o, pneumat/o, -pnea, -pnoea
breathing, lung, air, spirit

apnea [*a-, not* + *-pnea, breathing*] Temporary cessation of breathing. See dyspnea and eupnea. (AP nee uh)

apnoea [*a-, not* + *-pnoea, breathing*] Temporary cessation of breathing. Same as apnea. (AP nee uh)

bronchopneumonia [*broncho, bronchial tube & pneumonia*] A form of pneumonia resulting in inflammation of the lungs and bronchial tubes. (brong' koh noo MOHN yuh)

dyspnea [*dys-, difficult* + *-pnea, breathing*] Difficult breathing, often resulting from lung or heart disease. See apnea and eupnea. (DISP nee uh)

eupnea [*eu-, good* + *-pnea, breathing*] Normal breathing. See apnea and dyspnea. (yoop NEE uh)

hyperpnea [*hyper-, excessive* + *-pnea, breathing*] Abnormally deep and rapid breathing. Opposed to hypopnea. (heye PERP nee uh)

hypopnea [*hypo-, less* + *-pnea, breathing*] Abnormally shallow and slow breathing. Opposed to hyperpnea. (heye POP nee uh)

pleuropneumonia [*pleur(isy) & pneumonia*] Combined pleurisy and pneumonia. (ploor' oh noo MOHN yuh)

pneuma [*pneum, spirit* + *-a*] The spirit or soul. (NOO muh)

pneumatic [*pneumat, air* + *-ic*] 1.Pertaining to air or other gases. 2.Operated by compressed air. (noo MAT ik)

pneumatics [*pneumat, air* + *-ics, study of*] The branch of physics dealing with the study of the properties of air and other gases. (noo MAT iks)

pneumatology [*pneumat, spirit* + *-ology, science*] 1.The science of spiritual beings and spiritual phenomena. 2.The Christian doctrine of the Holy Spirit. (noo' muh TOL uh jee)

pneumatolysis [*pneumato, air* + *-lysis, decomposition*] The process of mineral and ore formation through the action of gases emitted by solidifying rock magmas. (noo' muh TOL uh sis)

pneumatophore [*pneumato, breathing* + *-phore, to carry*] A root of certain aquatic plants, often serving as a specialized respiratory organ. (noo MAT uh for')

pneumobacillus [*pneumo, lung & bacillus*] A bacterium associated with respiratory infections, especially pneumonia. (noo' moh buh SIL us)

pneumococcus [*pneumo, lung* + *-coccus, bacteria*] A bacterium that causes pneumonia and certain other diseases such as meningitis. (noo' muh KOK us)

pneumoconiosis [*pneumo, lung* + *coni, dust* + *-osis, diseased condition*] A lung disease characterized by fibrosis and caused by prolonged breathing of mineral or metallic dust. (noo' moh koh' nee OH sis)

pneumograph [*pneumo, breathing* + *graph, recording*] An instrument for measuring and recording chest movements resulting from respiration. See spirograph. (NOO muh graf')

pneumonectomy [*pneumon, lung* + *ec, out* + *-tomy, to cut*] Surgical removal of all or part of a lung. (noo' muh NEK tuh mee)

pneum/o, pneumon/o, pneumat/o, -pnea, -pnoea

pneumonia [*pneumon, lung* + *-ia*] A chronic disease marked by inflammation and congestion of the lungs and caused by any of numerous microorganisms such as bacteria or viruses or by chemical irritants. (noo MOHN yuh)

pneumonic [*pneumon, lung* + *-ic*] 1.Pertaining to the lungs. 2.Pertaining to or affected with pneumonia. (noo MON ik)

pneumonoultramicroscopicsilicovolcanoconiosis [*pneumono, lung & ultramicroscopic & silico, silica & volcano & coni, dust* + *-osis, diseased condition*] A lung disease caused by prolonged breathing of extremely fine siliceous dust. Sometimes cited as one of the longest words in the English language. (NOO muh noh ul' truh meye' kruh skop' ik SIL uh koh' vol kay' noh koh' nee oh' sis)

pneumothorax [*pneumo, air & thorax*] The presence of air or gas in the pleural cavity, either induced deliberately or as the result of injury or disease. (noo' muh THOR aks')

polypnea [*poly, many* + *-pnea, breathing*] Abnormally deep and rapid breathing. Same as hyperpnea. (pol IP nee uh)

spir/o   breathe

aspirate [*as-, on* + *spir, breathe* + *-ate*] 1.To pronounce the beginning of a word or syllable using a puff of breath, as in "hot" or "when." 2.To remove by suction, as fluid from a body cavity. (AS puh rayt')

aspire [*as-, on* + *spir, breathe*] To strive to attain something, especially something great or of high value. (uh SPEYER)

cardiorespiratory [*cardio, heart & respiratory*] Pertaining to or involving the heart and respiratory system. (kahr' dee oh RES per uh tor' ee)

conspire [*con-, together* + *spir, breathe*] 1.To plan together secretly to commit an unlawful or wrongful act. 2.To work or act together. See collogue. (kun SPEYER)

inspire [*in-, in* + *spir, breathe*] 1.To stimulate or arouse to activity, as confidence, creativity, motivation, etc. 2.To have an animating, enlivening, or exalting effect on. 3.To inhale. (in SPEYER)

inspirit [*in-, in & spirit*] To instill courage, life, or energy into. Animate. (in SPIHR it)

perspire [*per-, through* + *spir, breathe*] To secrete sweat through the pores of the skin. (per SPEYER)

respire [*re-, again* + *spir, breathe*] 1.To breathe in and out. 2.To recover and breathe freely again, as from anxiety, exertion, etc. (rih SPEYER)

spiracle [*spir, breathe* + *-cle, small*] 1.Air hole. 2.A breathing aperture in certain insects, fishes, cetaceans, etc. 3.A small volcanic vent formed on the surface of a stream of lava. (SPIHR uh kul)

spirit [*spir, breathe* + *-it*] 1.The vital force within a human being that is believed to give the body life, energy, and power. Soul. 2.An invisible supernatural being. Ghost. (SPIHR it)

spirograph [*spiro, breathe* + *graph, recording*] An instrument for graphically recording respiratory movements. See pneumograph. (SPEYE ruh graf')

spirometer [*spiro, breathe* + *meter, to measure*] An instrument for measuring the breathing rate and capacity of the lungs. (speye ROM et er)

suspire [*sub-, up* + *spir, breathe*] 1.To take a deep breath. Sigh. 2.To breathe. (suh SPEYER)

transpire [*trans-, through* + *spir, breathe*] 1.To take place or occur. Happen. 2.To become known. 3.To give off vapor containing waste products through a membrane or pores, as from the human body or from leaves. See transude. (tran SPEYER)

port   to carry

comportment [*com-, together* + *port, to carry* + *-ment*] Behavior. Manner of carrying or conducting oneself. See deportment. (kum PORT ment)

deport [*de-, away* + *port, to carry*] To remove, as an alien or criminal, from a country by force. Exile. Banish. (dih PORT)

deportment [*de-, away* + *port, to carry* + *-ment*] Behavior according to a set of rules or ethics. See comportment. (dih PORT ment)

disport [*dis-, apart* + *port, to carry*] To occupy oneself with amusement or diversion. (dis PORT)

export [*ex-, out* + *port, to carry*] To send or carry commodities out of the country, especially for sale or trade. See import. (eks PORT)

import [*im-, in* + *port, to carry*] To bring or carry commodities into the country, especially for sale or trade. See export. (im PORT)

portable [*port, to carry* + *-able*] Easily carried or moved. (PORT uh bul)

portage [*port, to carry* + *-age*] The act of transporting or carrying. (PORT ij)

portamento [*port, to carry* + *-ment*] In music, a smooth, continuous gliding from one note to another. (port' uh MEN toh)

porter [*port, to carry* + *-er*] A person employed to carry baggage. (PORT ur)

portfolio [*port, to carry* + *foli, leaf*] 1.An itemized list of investments owned by a person or company. 2.A portable case for carrying loose papers, etc. (port FOH lee oh')

portmanteau [*port, to carry* + *Ltn > mantellum, cloak*] A large leather traveling bag that opens into two halves. (port MAN toh)

portmanteau word [*port, to carry* + *Ltn > mantellum, cloak & word*] A word formed by combining some or all of the letters of two other words, as the combination of trans(mitter) and (re)ceiver to form the word *transceiver.* (port MAN toh wurd)

rapport [*re-, back* + *port, to carry*] Harmonious and agreeable relationship between people. (ruh POR)

report [*re-, back* + *port, to carry*] To carry back and repeat information or give an account of something seen, done, etc. (rih PORT)

support [*sub-, under* + *port, to carry*] 1.To carry or bear the weight of, especially from below. 2.To give assistance, comfort, etc., to. (suh PORT)

transport [*trans-, across* + *port, to carry*] To carry, move, or convey from one place to another, especially over long distances. (trans PORT)

pseud/o   false

pseudepigraphy [*pseud, false* + *epi, upon* + *-graphy, writing*] 1.The false attribution of a novel, poem, etc., to a certain writer. 2.Spurious religious writings professing to be ascribed to Biblical characters. (sood' ih PIG ruh fee)

pseudocarp [*pseudo, false* + *carp, fruit*] A fruit produced from other parts in addition to the ovary, as an apple. False fruit. Also referred to as accessory fruit. (SOOD uh kahrp')

pseudocyesis [*pseudo, false* & *cyesis {pregnancy}*] A false pregnancy, usually resulting from emotional disturbances, in which nearly all the normal signs of pregnancy exist. (sood' oh seye EE sis)

pseudomorph [*pseudo, false* + *morph, form*] 1.An irregular or false form. 2.An altered mineral exhibiting the crystalline form of another mineral. (SOOD uh morf')

pseudonym [*pseud, false* + *onym, name*] A fictitious name, as one assumed by a writer. Pen name. See allonym, nom de plume, and nom de guerre. (SOOD n im')

pseudopodium [*pseudo, false* + *pod, foot* + *-ium*] A temporary protrusion of the cytoplasm of certain protozoans or amebocytes that functions in locomotion and in the intake of food or foreign particles. See rhizopod. (sood' uh POHD ee um)

pseudopregnancy [*pseudo, false* & *pregnancy*] 1.A physiological state occurring in some lower mammals that resembles pregnancy and usually follows sterile copulation. 2.A false pregnancy, usually resulting from emotional disturbances, in which nearly all the normal signs of pregnancy exist. Same as pseudocyesis. (sood' oh PREG nun see)

pseudoscience [*pseudo, false* & *science*] Methods or theories presumed, but not shown to have a scientific basis. (sood' oh SEYE ens)

psych/o   mind, soul, mental process

antipsychotic [*anti-, against* + *psych, mind* + *-otic*] Pertaining to effective methods of treating psychosis, as certain drugs. (an' tee seye KOT ik)

intrapsychic [*intra-, within* + *psych, mind* + *-ic*] Originating or existing within the mind. (in' truh SEYE kik)

metapsychology [*meta-, beyond* + *psych, mind* + *-ology, science*] A term applied to theories about the origin, structure, and functions of the mind that extend beyond the empirical laws of psychology. (met' uh seye KOL uh jee)

metempsychosis [*meta-, beyond* + *en-, into* + *psych, soul* + *-osis, action*] The belief that after death the soul passes into another human or animal body. (met' em seye' KOH sis)

neuropsychiatry [*neuro, nerve* + *psych, mind* + *iatr, healing* + *-y*] The branch of medical science dealing with the study and treatment of diseases and disorders of the mind and nervous system. (noor' oh seye KEYE uh tree)

orthopsychiatry [*ortho, correct* + *psych, mind* + *iatr, healing* + *-y*] The branch of medical science dealing with the study and treatment of emotional and behavioral disorders, especially in children. (or' thoh seye KEYE uh tree)

parapsychology [*para-, beyond* + *psych, mind* + *-ology, study of*] The branch of psychology dealing with the study of psychic phenomena, such as extrasensory perception, clairvoyance, and telepathy, that appear to fall beyond the scope of physical law. (pehr' uh seye KOL uh jee)

psyche [*psych, soul*] 1.The human spirit considered separately from the body. 2.All the conscious and unconscious functions of the mind. (SEYE kee)

psychedelic [*psych, mind* + *Grk > deloun, to reveal* + *-ic*] Pertaining to or producing drastic changes in the mental state, as hallucinations, distorted perceptions, etc. (seye' kuh DEL ik)

psychiatry [*psych, mind* + *iatr, healing* + *-y*] The branch of medicine dealing with the study and treatment of mental disorders. See psychology. (seye KEYE uh tree)

psychic [*psych, mind* + *-ic*] 1.Pertaining to or originating in the mind. 2.One who possesses supernatural mental abilities. (SEYE kik)

psychoactive [*psycho, mind* & *active*] Affecting mental behavior, as a drug, chemical, or other substance. (seye' koh AK tiv)

psychoanalysis [*psycho, mental process* & *analysis*] A method of analyzing mental processes and treating mental disorders. (seye' koh uh NAL uh sis)

psychobiography [*psycho, mind* & *biography*] A biography that psychoanalyzes the subject. (seye' koh beye OG ruh fee)

psychobiology [*psycho, mind* + *bio, life* + *-logy, study of*] 1.The scientific study of the integration of mind and body. 2.The scientific study of the biology of the mind. (seye' koh beye OL uh jee)

psychodynamics [*psycho, mental process* + *dynam, power* + *-ics, study of*] The study of mental or emotional processes or forces and their relation to human behavior and metal states. (seye' koh deye NAM iks)

psychogenesis [*psycho, mind* + *-genesis, origin*] The origin and development of personality, behavior, and other mental processes. (seye' koh JEN uh sis)

psychogenic [*psycho, mind* + *gen, origin* + *-ic*] Being of mental or emotional origin. (seye' koh JEN ik)

psychograph [*psycho, mind* + *graph, writing*] A chart for graphically recording an individual's personality traits. (SEYE kuh graf')

psychohistory [*psycho, mind* & *history*] The study of people or events in history through the use of psychology. (seye' koh HIS tree)

psychokinesis [*psycho, mind* + *kine, motion* + *-sis*] The alleged ability to move physical objects with the powers of the mind. See telekinesis. (seye' koh kih NEE sis)

psycholinguistics [*psycho, mind* + *lingu, language* + *-ist* + *-ics, study of*] The study of the relationship between psychological behavior and the understanding and use of language. (seye' koh ling GWIS tiks)

psychological [*psycho, mind* + *-logical*] 1.Pertaining to psychology. 2.Pertaining to, origination in, or affecting the mind. (seye' kuh LOJ ih kul)

psychology [*psych, mind* + *-ology, science*] The science of the mind, including emotional and behavioral processes and characteristics. See psychiatry. (seye KOL uh jee)

psych/o

psychometrics [*psycho, mental process + metr, to measure + -ics, science*] The science of measuring mental capabilities, functions, processes, traits, etc. (seye' kuh MET riks)

psychometry [*psycho, mental process + -metry, to measure*] The alleged divination of knowledge concerning an object or a person associated with it through proximity to or physical contact with the object. (seye KOM ih tree)

psychomotor [*psycho, mind & motor*] Pertaining to mental processes affecting muscular activity. (seye' koh MOHT ur)

psychoneurosis [*psycho, mind + neur, nerve + -osis, abnormal condition*] Any of various mental or emotional disorders, including anxiety, phobias, and obsessions, that usually do not include an impaired perception of reality. Same as neurosis. (seye' koh noo ROH sis)

psychopath [*psycho, mind + path, disease*] A person with a severe personality disorder marked by immoral and antisocial behavior. See sociopath. (SEYE kuh path')

psychopathology [*psycho, mind + path, disease + -ology, study of*] The branch of medical science dealing with the study of disorders and diseases of the mind. (seye' koh puh THOL uh jee)

psychopathy [*psycho, mind + -pathy, disease*] Any disease or disorder of the mind. (seye KOP uh thee)

psychopharmacology [*psycho, mind + pharmac, drug + -ology, study of*] The branch of medical science dealing with the study of the relationships between drugs and mental and emotional behavior. (seye' koh fahr' muh KOL uh jee)

psychophysics [*psycho, mental process + physi, physical + -ics, study of*] The branch of psychology dealing with the study of the effects of physical stimuli on mental processes. (seye' koh FIZ iks)

psychophysiology [*psycho, mind + physi, physical + -ology, study of*] The branch of medical science dealing with the study of the interrelations between mental and physical processes. (seye' koh fiz' ee OL uh jee)

psychosexual [*psycho, mind & sexual*] Pertaining to or involving the mental and emotional aspects of sexuality. (seye' koh SEK shoo ul)

psychosis [*psych, mind + -osis, abnormal condition*] A severe mental disorder marked by delusions, regressive behavior, impaired thinking, etc., and usually including an impaired perception of reality. See neurosis. (seye KOH sis)

psychosocial [*psycho, mind & social*] Pertaining to both psychological and social aspects of behavior. (seye' koh SOH shul)

psychosomatic [*psycho, mind + somat, body + -ic*] Pertaining to diseases, disorders, or conditions of the body created or influenced by the mind. (seye' koh suh MAT ik)

psychosurgery [*psycho, mind & surgery*] Surgery of the brain to treat severe mental disorders. (seye' koh SUR jer ee)

psychotherapy [*psycho, mind & therapy*] The use of psychological techniques for treating mental, behavioral, and emotional disorders. (seye' koh THEHR uh pee)

psychotropic [*psycho, mind + trop, changing + -ic*] Capable of affecting the mind, as certain drugs used to treat mental disorders. (seye' koh TROP ik)

pter/o, pteryg, pteryx   wing, fin

acanthopterygian [*acantho, spine + pteryg, fin + -ian*] Any of numerous teleost fishes with spiny fins, as perch or bass. See teleost. (ak' un thop' tuh RIJ ee un)

apteral [*a-, without + pter, wing + -al*] Pertaining to a structure with columns on each end, but none along the sides. See peripteral. (AP ter ul)

apterous [*a-, without + pter, wing + -ous*] Without wings or winglike appendages. (AP ter us)

apteryx [*a-, without + pteryx, wing*] A New Zealand bird with undeveloped wings and no tail. Kiwi. (AP ter iks')

archaeopteryx [*archaeo, first + pteryx, wing*] An extinct reptilelike bird, often called the first bird, that had feathers and well-developed wings. (ahr' kee OP ter iks)

brachypterous [*brachy, short + pter, wing + -ous*] Having underdeveloped or very short wings, as certain insects. (bra KIP ter us)

chiropter [*chiro, hand + pter, wing*] An order of placental mammals, including bats and flying foxes, with the forelimbs modified for flight. (keye ROP ter)

Coleoptera [*coleo, sheath + pter, wing + -a*] Any of a large order of insects with an outer pair of wings that when at rest encase and protect an inner pair of wings, as the weevils and beetles. (koh' lee OP ter uh)

dipterous [*di-, two + pter, wing + -ous*] Any of a large order of insects with two wings or winglike appendages. (DIP ter us)

eurypterid [*eury, wide + pter, wing + -id*] Any of various extinct aquatic arthropods with wide winglike appendages. (yoo RIP ter id')

helicopter [*helico, circular + pter, wing*] An aircraft with a horizontal rotating wing that provides both lift and propulsion. See autogiro and gyroplane. (HEL ih kop' ter)

hemipterous [*hemi-, half + pter, wing + -ous*] Any of a large number of insects belonging to the order Hemiptera that are commonly referred to as the true bugs. The order Hemiptera is composed of the suborders Homoptera and Heteroptera. See homopterous and heteropterous. (hih MIP ter us)

heteropterous [*hetero, different + pter, wing + -ous*] Pertaining to any of numerous insects belonging to the suborder Heteroptera, characterized by forewings that differ in thickness from the membranous hindwings. See homopterous and hemipterous. (het' uh ROP ter us)

homopterous [*homo, same + pter, wing + -ous*] Pertaining to any of numerous insects belonging to the suborder Homoptera, characterized by membranous forewings that do not differ in thickness from the membranous hindwings. See heteropterous and hemipterous. (hoh MOP ter us)

hymenopterous [*hymeno, membrane + pter, wing + -ous*] Pertaining to any of a large order of insects, including ants, bees, wasps, and termites, that have two pairs of membranous wings coupled together to provide more stable flight. (heye' muh NOP ter us)

lepidopteran [*lepido, scale + pter, wing + -an*] Any of a large order of insects, including butterflies, moths, and skippers, the adults of which have two pairs of membranous wings covered with often brightly colored scales. (lep' ih DOP ter un)

lepidopterology [*lepido, scale + pter, wing + -ology, study of*] The branch of zoology dealing with the study of lepidopterans. See lepidopteran. (lep' ih dop' tuh ROL uh jee)

macropterous [*macro-, large + pter, wing + -ous*] Pertaining to birds, insects, or fish with unusually large wings or fins. (muh KROP ter us)

neuropterous [*neuro, nerve + pter, wing + -ous*] Pertaining to carnivorous insects with four membranous wings and biting mouth parts. (noo ROP ter us)

ornithopter [*ornitho, bird + pter, wing*] An early experimental aircraft designed to be lifted and propelled by flapping wings. (OR nuh thop' ter)

orthopteran [*ortho, straight + pter, wing + -an*] Any of an order of insects, including locusts, crickets, and grasshoppers, that have, when present, a pair of straight and thickened forewings and a pair of membranous hindwings. (or THOP ter un)

peripteral [*peri-, around + pter, wing + -al*] Pertaining to a structure with a row of columns on every side. See apteral. (puh RIP ter ul)

pterodactyl [*ptero, wing + dactyl, finger*] Any of an order of extinct flying reptiles with featherless wings of skin extending from the elongated fourth digit, along the forelimb to the back of the body. See pterosaur. (tehr' uh DAK tul)

pteropod [*ptero, wing + pod, feet*] Any of various small gastropod mollusks, commonly called sea butterflies, with a winglike structure in the foot used for swimming. (TEHR uh pod')

pterosaur [*ptero, wing + saur, lizard*] Extinct flying reptiles commonly referred to as pterodactyls. See pterodactyl. (TEHR uh sor')

pterygoid [*pteryg, wing + -oid, resembling*] Wing-shaped. (TEHR uh goid')

tetrapterous [*tetra-, four + pter, wing + -ous*] Having four wings or winglike appendages, as many insects. (teh TRAP ter us)

trichopteran [*tricho, hair + pter, wing + -an*] Any of an order of insects, commonly called caddis flies, the adults of which have two pairs of hairy membranous wings. (trih KOP ter un)

purg   clean

compurgation [*com-, together + purg, clean + -ation*] The former practice of acquitting a person of a charge through the oaths of several others testifying to the innocence of the accused. (kom' pur GAY shun)

expurgate [*ex-, out + purg, clean + -ate*] To remove objectionable, obscene, or erroneous passages from a book or other publication. (EKS pur gayt')

purgative [*purg, clean + -ative*] A strong laxative. See physic (def. 1). (PUR guh tiv)

purgatory [*purg, clean + -atory*] According to Roman Catholics and others, a place in which the souls of those who have died in the grace of God must make atonement for their sins. (PUR guh tor' ee)

purge [*purg, clean*] To remove anything undesirable, as unused elements, impurities, sin, etc. (purj)

pyr/o   fire, heat, fever

antipyretic [*anti-, against + pyr, fever + -etic*] 1. Reducing fever. 2. A medicine or other agent that reduces fever. (an' tee peye RET ik)

chalcopyrite [*chalco, copper & pyrite*] A very common mineral, copper-iron sulfide, that is an important ore of copper. See chalcocite. (kal' kuh PEYE reyet')

empyrean [*em-, intensive + pyr, fire + -ean*] 1. The highest heaven, believed by ancient cosmologists to be a sphere of pure fire or light. 2. The sky. (em' peye REE un)

hyperpyrexia [*hyper-, above + pyr, fever + -ia*] An abnormally high fever. See pyrexia. (heye' per peye REK see uh)

micropyrometer [*micro-, small + pyro, temperature + meter, to measure*] An optical instrument for measuring the temperature of minute glowing bodies. (meye' kroh peye ROM et er)

pyracantha [*pyr, fire + acanth, thorn + -a*] A small shrub commonly referred to as the fire thorn. (peye' ruh KAN thuh)

pyralid [*Grk > pyralis, insect believed to live in fire*] Any of various moths of the family Pyralidae, once believed to live in fire. (PIHR uh lid)

pyrargyrite [*pyr, fire + argyr, silver + -ite, mineral*] A dark-red to black mineral that is an important ore of silver. (peye RAHR juh reyet')

pyre [*pyr, fire*] A pile of wood or other combustibles used to burn a dead body as a funeral rite. (peyer)

pyretic [*pyr, fever + -etic*] Pertaining to or producing fever. (peye RET ik)

Pyrex [*pyr, fire + ex-, out*] A trade name for a type of heat-resistant glassware. (PEYE reks)

pyrexia [*pyr, fever + -ia*] Fever. See hyperpyrexia. (peye REK see uh)

pyrheliometer [*pyr, heat + helio, sun + meter, to measure*] An instrument for measuring the intensity of solar energy. (pihr hee' lee OM et er)

pyrite [*pyr, fire + -ite, mineral*] A common, pale-yellow mineral with a metallic luster that is often mistaken for gold and therefore nicknamed "fool's gold." It is the main source of sulfur in the manufacture of sulfuric acid. So named because it emits sparks when struck. (PEYE reyet)

pyrochemical [*pyro, heat & chemical*] Producing or affected by chemical action at high temperatures. (peye' roh KEM ih kul)

pyroclastic [*pyro, fire + Grk > klastes, breaker + -ic*] Formed by rock fragmentation through volcanic action. (peye' roh KLAS tik)

pyroelectricity [*pyro, heat & electricity*] An electrical charge generated in certain crystals by temperature changes. (peye' roh ih lek' TRIS ih tee)

pyrogen [*pyro, fever + gen, cause*] Any substance that causes fever. (PEYE ruh jen)

pyrogenic [*pyro, heat + gen, to produce + -ic*] 1. Inducing or resulting from heat or fever. 2. Produced by heat, as igneous rock. (peye' roh JEN ik)

pyrognostics [*pyro, fire + gnos, knowledge + -tic*] The properties exhibited by a mineral when heated. (peye' rog NOS tiks)

pyr/o

pyrography [*pyro, heat + -graphy, drawing*] The art of making designs with a heated tool, as on wood. (peye ROG ruh fee)

pyrolusite [*pyro, fire + Grk > lousis, washing + -ite, mineral*] A black to dark-gray mineral with a metallic luster that is sometimes heated and used for removing color from glass. (peye' roh LOO seyet')

pyrolysis [*pyro, heat + -lysis, decomposition*] Chemical decomposition of a substance caused by the action of heat. See thermolysis (def. 1). (peye ROL uh sis)

pyromancy [*pyro, fire + -mancy, divination*] Divination by fire. (PEYE roh man' see)

pyromania [*pyro, fire + mania, mental aberration*] An irresistible impulse to start fires. (peye' roh MAY nee uh)

pyrometallurgy [*pyro, heat & metallurgy*] The process of extracting metals from their ores using high temperatures. (peye' roh MET l ur jee)

pyrometer [*pyro, heat + meter, to measure*] An electrical thermometer for measuring high temperatures. See pyrophotometer. (peye ROM et er)

pyrope [*Grk > pyropos, fiery*] A variety of garnet with a fiery-red color, often used as a gem. (PEYE rohp)

pyrophobia [*pyro, fire + -phobia, fear*] Abnormal fear of fire. (peye' roh FOH bee uh)

pyrophoric [*pyro, fire + phor, state + -ic*] 1.Pertaining to materials that ignite spontaneously. 2.Emitting sparks when struck or scratched. (peye' roh FOR ik)

pyrophotometer [*pyro, heat + photo, light + meter, to measure*] An optical thermometer for measuring very high temperatures. See pyrometer. (peye' roh foh TOM et er)

pyrosis [*pyr, fire + -osis, abnormal condition*] Heartburn. (peye ROH sis)

pyrostat [*pyro, heat + stat, stationary*] A thermostat for regulating high temperatures. (PEYE ruh stat')

pyrotechnics [*pyro, fire + techn, art + -ics, skill*] The art of making and displaying fireworks. (peye' roh TEK niks)

pyroxene [*pyro, fire + xen, foreign*] Any of a group of crystalline mineral silicates that do not contain the hydroxyl radical and are important constituents of igneous and some metamorphic rocks. So named from its being foreign to igneous rocks. (peye ROK seen')

pyroxenite [*pyroxen(e) & -ite, rock*] An igneous rock consisting mainly of pyroxene. (peye ROK suh neyet')

pyroxylin [*pyro, fire + xyl, wood + -in*] A flammable mixture of cellulose nitrates used in the manufacture of plastics, lacquers, and some explosives. (peye ROK suh lin)

radic, radix   root

eradicate [*e-, out + radic, root + -ate*] 1.To get rid of completely. Exterminate. 2.To pull out by, or as if by, the roots. Uproot. See ineradicable. (ih RAD ih kayt')

ineradicable [*in-, not + e-, out + radic, root + -able*] Impossible to completely get rid of. Not eradicable. See eradicate. (in' ih RAD ih kuh bul)

irradicable [*ir-, not + radic, root + -able*] Impossible to completely get rid of. Not eradicable. Same as ineradicable. (ihr RAD ih kul bul)

radical [*radic, root + -al*] 1.Of or from the roots. Fundamental. 2.In favor of fundamental or drastic political, economic, or social change. (RAD ih kul)

radical sign [*radic, root + -al & sign*] In mathematics, a sign placed before a quantity indicating that the specified root indicated by an imposed index number is to be extracted. (RAD ih kul seyen)

radicand [*radic, root*] The quantity under a radical sign. (RAD ih kand')

radicle [*radic, root + -cle, small*] 1.The part of a plant embryo that develops into the primary root. 2.A small rootlike structure, as the beginning of a nerve, vein, etc. (RAD ih kul)

radish [*radic, root*] A red or white edible root of the mustard family. (RAD ish)

radix [*radix, root*] 1.A number taken as the base of a number system or of logarithms. 2.An origin or source. (RAY diks)

ram, rami   branch

biramous [*bi-, two + ram, branch + -ous*] Having two branches, as the forked appendage of a crustacean. (beye RAY mus)

ramate [*ram, branch + -ate*] Having branches. Branched. (RAY mayt)

ramification [*rami, branch + fic, to make + -ation*] 1.The act or process of branching out, as a nerve or plant. 2.The result or consequence of a decision, act, or statement. (ram' uh fih KAY shun)

ramiform [*rami, branch & form*] Having the shape of a branch. Branchlike. (RAM uh form')

ramify [*rami, branch + -fy, to make*] To spread or branch out. (RAM uh feye')

ramose [*ram, branch + -ose*] Having many branches. Branching. (RAY mohs)

ramous [*ram, branch + -ous*] 1.Resembling branches. 2.Ramose. (RAY mus)

ramulose [*ram, branch + -ule, small + -ose*] Bearing numerous small branches. (RAM yuh lohs')

ramus [*ram, branch + -us*] A branchlike part or process, as of a nerve, plant, etc. (RAY mus)

retro-   back, backward, behind

retroactive [*retro-, back & active*] Applying to a date prior to enactment, as a law or pay increase. See ex post facto. (ret' roh AK tiv)

retrocede [*retro-, back + cede, to go*] 1.To go back. Recede. See recede. 2.To give back. See cede. (ret' roh SEED)

retrofit [*retro-, back & fit*] To modify equipment already in service in order to incorporate changes or improvements. (RET roh fit')

retroflex [*retro-, backward + flex, to bend*] 1.Turned backward. 2.Articulated with the tip of the tongue raised and bent backward toward the roof of the mouth. (RET ruh fleks')

retrograde [*retro-, backward + -grade, to go*] 1.Having a backward direction or motion. 2.Going back to a worse condition. Deteriorating. See regress (def. 2) and retrogress. (RET ruh grayd')

retrogress [*retro-, backward + gress, to go*] To go backward, especially to an earlier, inferior, or less advanced condition. See regress (def. 2) and retrograde (def. 2). (RET ruh gres')

retronym [*retro-, back + onym, name*] A term used to distinguish ideas or objects from innovations replacing or improving them, as *night baseball* or *skim milk*. (RET ruh nim')

retroocular [*retro-, behind + ocul, eye + -ar*] Located behind the eyeball. (ret' roh OK yuh lur)

retrorocket [*retro-, back & rocket*] An auxiliary rocket engine used to retard or reverse the motion of a larger rocket, spacecraft, or other vehicle. (RET roh rok' it)

retrorse [*retro-, backward + vers, turn*] Turned or directed backward or downward. (rih TRORS)

retrospect [*retro-, back + spect, to look*] A looking back on conditions or events of the past. (RET ruh spekt')

retroversion [*retro-, backward + vers, turn + -ion*] 1.A tilting or turning backward. 2.The tilting or turning of an organ, especially the uterus. (ret' roh VUR zhun)

rhin/o   nose

catarrhine [*cata-, down + rhin, nose*] Having a nose with nostrils close together and directed downward, as in Old World monkeys, higher apes, and man. See platyrrhine. (KAT uh reyen')

otorhinolaryngology [*oto, ear + rhino, nose + laryng, larynx + -ology, study of*] The branch of medical science dealing with the study and treatment of diseases and disorders of the ear, nose, and throat. (ot' oh reye' noh lehr' un GOL uh jee)

platyrrhine [*platy, flat + rhin, nose*] Having a broad, flat nose with the nostrils far apart and directed to the side, as in New World monkeys. See catarrhine. (PLAT ih reyen')

rhinal [*rhin, nose + -al*] Pertaining to the nose. Nasal. (REYE nul)

rhinitis [*rhin, nose + -itis, inflammation*] Inflammation of the mucous membrane of the nose. (reye NEYE tis)

rhinoceros [*rhino, nose + cerat, horn + -os*] Any of several large, thick-skinned, plant-eating mammals of Asia and Africa with one or two upright horns on the snout. (reye NOS ur us)

rhinology [*rhin, nose + -ology, study of*] The branch of medical science dealing with the study of the functions and diseases of the nose. (reye NOL uh jee)

rhinopharyngitis [*rhino, nose + pharyng, pharynx + -itis, inflammation*] Inflammation of the mucous membrane of the nose and pharynx. (reye' noh fehr' in JEYE tis)

rhinoplasty [*rhino, nose + -plasty, to form*] Plastic surgery of the nose. (REYE noh plas' tee)

rhinovirus [*rhino, nose & virus*] Any of numerous small RNA viruses that arc responsible for the common cold and many other respiratory diseases. (reye' noh VEYE rus)

rrhea, rrhoea, rrhag
flow, excessive flow, discharge

amenorrhea [*a-, without + meno, menstruation + rrhea, flow*] Abnormal absence or suppression of menstruation. (ay men' uh REE uh)

catarrh [*cata-, down + rrhea, excessive flow*] Inflammation of a mucous membrane, especially of the nose and throat, accompanied by increased discharge of mucous. (kuh TAHR)

diarrhea [*dia-, through + rrhea, excessive flow*] Abnormally excessive and frequent fluid bowl movements, often a symptom of a gastrointestinal disorder. (deye' uh REE uh)

diarrhoea [*dia-, through + rrhoea, excessive flow*] Abnormally excessive and frequent fluid bowl movements, often a symptom of a gastrointestinal disorder. Same as diarrhea. (deye' uh REE uh)

dysmenorrhea [*dys-, difficult + meno, menstruation + rrhea, flow*] Painful menstruation. (dis' men' uh REE uh)

galactorrhea [*galacto, milk + rrhea, excessive flow*] Spontaneous or excessive flow of milk from the breasts. (guh lak' tuh REE uh)

gonorrhea [*gono, reproduction + rrhea, discharge*] A sexually transmitted infectious disease caused by the gonococcus and marked by inflammation of the genital mucous membrane and a discharge of pus. (gon' uh REE uh)

hemorrhage [*hemo, blood + rrhag, excessive flow*] Heavy blood flow, either externally or internally. (HEM ur ij)

hemorrhoid [*hemo, blood + rrhea, flow + -oid*] A varicose vein located within the anus or in the anal wall, causing pain, itching, and often bleeding. (HEM uh roid')

hemorrhoidectomy [*hemorrhoid & ec, out + -tomy, to cut*] Surgical removal of hemorrhoids. (hem' uh roid' EK tuh mee)

leukorrhea [*leuko, white + rrhea, discharge*] A whitish discharge from the vagina that is usually normal, but in large amounts may be the result of infection or inflammation. (loo' kuh REE uh)

logorrhea [*logo, discourse + rrhea, excessive flow*] Pathologically excessive, repetitious, and often incoherent speech. (log' uh REE uh)

menorrhagia [*meno, menstruation + rrhag, excessive flow + -ia*] Abnormally excessive or prolonged menstrual flow. (men' uh RAY jee uh)

metrorrhagia [*metro, uterus + rrhag, flow + -ia*] Abnormal bleeding from the uterus, especially between menstrual cycles. (mee' truh RAY jee uh)

pyorrhea [*pyo, pus + rrhea, discharge*] 1.A discharge of pus. 2.Periodontitis. See gingivitis and periodontitis. (peye' uh REE uh)

pyorrhoea [*pyo, pus + rrhoea, discharge*] 1.A discharge of pus. 2.Periodontitis. Same as pyorrhea. (peye' uh REE uh)

seborrhea [*sebo, fat + rrhea, excessive flow*] Excessive discharge of sebum from the sebaceous glands, resulting in abnormally oily skin. (seb' uh REE uh)

spermatorrhea [*spermato, sperm + rrhea, discharge*] Abnormally frequent involuntary discharge of semen without sexual excitement or orgasm. (spur mat' uh REE uh)

rupt   to break, burst

abrupt [*ab-, off + rupt, to break*] 1.Sudden or unexpected. 2.Rising or falling sharply. Steep. 3.Lacking continuity in speech or manner. (uh BRUPT)

bankrupt [*bank & rupt, to break*] 1.Declared legally unable to repay one's debts. Insolvent. 2.Completely failed or depleted. Destitute. (BANGK rupt)

corrupt [*cor-, with + rupt, to break*] Changed from good to bad by immorality or perversion. (kuh RUPT)

rupt

disrupt [*dis-, apart + rupt, to break*] 1.To break apart. 2.To bring disorder to. Disturb. (dis RUPT)

erupt [*e-, out + rupt, burst*] To burst or break out violently from limits or restraint. (ih RUPT)

incorrupt [*in-, not & corrupt*] 1.Not corrupt. 2.Not subject to decay or contamination. 3.Error-free. (in' kuh RUPT)

interrupt [*inter-, between + rupt, to break*] 1.To hinder or stop by breaking in upon, as a person speaking, work, rest, etc. 2.A signal to a computer to stop executing the current program in order to execute a higher priority program. (in' tuh RUPT)

irrupt [*ir-, within + rupt, burst*] 1.To break or burst in suddenly or violently. Invade. 2.To increase abruptly in number, as a population. (ih RUPT)

rupture [*rupt, burst + -ure*] 1.The act or process of breaking apart or bursting. 2.A break in friendly relations, as between countries or individuals. (RUP chur)

scler/o   hard

arteriosclerosis [*arterio, artery + scler, hard + -osis, diseased condition*] A chronic disease often present in old age and marked by abnormal thickening and hardening of arterial walls. See atherosclerosis. (ahr tihr' ee oh' skluh ROH sis)

atherosclerosis [*athero, fatty degeneration + scler, hard + -osis, diseased condition*] An extremely common form of arteriosclerosis in which the innermost lining of the artery becomes thickened with fatty deposits that increase in size and harden, thus impeding the flow of blood through the artery. See arteriosclerosis. (ath' uh roh' skluh ROH sis)

multiple sclerosis [*multiple & scler, hard + -osis, diseased condition*] A chronic disease of the central nervous system, occurring chiefly in young adults, in which hardening of tissue occurs in the brain and spinal cord, resulting in speech defects, weakness, loss of muscle coordination, etc. (MUL tuh pul skluh ROH sis)

sclera [*scler, hard + -a*] The tough, white fibrous membrane that, except for the cornea, covers the entire eyeball. (SKLEHR uh)

sclerenchyma [*scler, hard + -enchyma, type of cell tissue*] Supporting plant tissue composed of lignified cells with thick walls. See parenchyma (def. 1). (skluh RENG kuh muh)

sclerite [*scler, hard + -ite*] One of the hard outer plates forming the exoskeleton of an arthropod. (SKLEHR eyet)

scleritis [*scler(a) & -itis, inflammation*] Inflammation of the sclera. (skluh REYE tis)

scleroderma [*sclero, hard + derma, skin*] A disease marked by chronic thickening and hardening of the skin, caused by abnormal growth or swelling of fibrous tissues. (sklehr' uh DER muh)

sclerodermatous [*sclero, hard + dermat, skin + -ous*] Having a hard outer covering consisting of horny or bony tissue. (sklehr' uh DER muh tus)

scleroid [*scler, hard + -oid, resembling*] Hardened. (SKLEHR oid)

scleroma [*scler, hard + -oma, tumor*] A hardened, tumorlike area of granulation tissue in the skin or mucous membrane. (skluh ROH muh)

sclerometer [*sclero, hard + meter, to measure*] An instrument for measuring the hardness of a material by determining the pressure required to scratch its surface using a diamond point. (skluh ROM et er)

scleroprotein [*sclero, hard & protein*] Any of a large class of fibrous animal proteins found in skeletal and connective tissue, hair, nails, animal horns, etc. (sklehr' oh PROH teen')

sclerosis [*scler, hard + -osis, abnormal condition*] An abnormal hardening of tissue or a body part as a result of conditions such as chronic inflammation, excessive fibrous tissue growth, mineral deposits, etc. (skluh ROH sis)

sclerotium [*sclero, hard + -ium*] A hardened mass of mycelium in certain fungi in which food is stored until favorable conditions for growth occur. (skluh ROH shee um)

sclerotomy [*scler(a) & -tomy, to cut*] Surgical incision of the sclera. (skluh ROT uh mee)

sclerous [*scler, hard + -ous*] Hard, calloused, or bony. (SKLEHR us)

scop, -scope, -scopy
to view, to examine, to observe

arthroscope [*arthro, joint + -scope, to examine*] An endoscope for examining or performing surgery on the interior of a joint, as the knee. (AHR thruh skohp')

bronchoscope [*broncho, bronchial tube + -scope, to examine*] An endoscope for examining the interior of the trachea and bronchial tubes. (BRONG kuh skohp')

chronoscope [*chrono, time + -scope, to view*] An optical instrument for measuring brief time intervals. See chronograph and chronometer. (KRON uh skohp')

colposcope [*Grk > kolpos, vagina + -scope, to examine*] An endoscope for magnifying and examining the tissues of the vagina and cervix. (KOL puh skohp')

cryoscope [*cryo, cold + -scope, to observe*] An instrument for measuring the freezing points of liquids and solutions. (KREYE uh skohp')

cryoscopy [*cryo, cold + -scopy, to observe*] The scientific study of the freezing points of liquids and solutions. (kreye OS kuh pee)

cystoscope [*cysto, bladder + -scope, to examine*] An endoscope for examining the interior of the ureter and urinary bladder. (SIS tuh skohp')

dichroscope [*di-, two + chros, color + -scope, to view*] An instrument for viewing the dichroism of crystals. See dichroism (def. 1). (DEYE kruh skohp')

electron microscope [*electron & microscope*] A powerful microscope that focuses a beam of electrons instead of visible light to produce an enlarged image of a minute object on a fluorescent screen. (ih LEK tron' MEYE kruh skohp')

electroscope [*electro, electric + -scope, to observe*] An instrument for detecting the presence and polarity of an electric charge on a body by the mutual repulsion or attraction of electrically charged strips of gold leaf. (ih LEK truh skohp')

endoscope [*endo-, inside + -scope, to examine*] A tubular optical instrument for examining the interior of a cavity, organ, or other body part. (EN duh skohp')

epidiascope [*epi-, on + dia, through + -scope, to view*] A projector for displaying a magnified image of a transparency or an opaque object on a screen. (ep' ih DEYE uh skohp')

fetoscope [*feto, fetus + -scope, to examine*] An endoscope for examining the fetus in the uterus. (FEET uh skohp')

fluoroscope [*fluoro, fluorescence + -scope, to view*] An instrument for examining the internal structures of objects by viewing the shadows of x-rays on a fluorescent screen. (FLOOR uh skohp')

galvanoscope [*Italian > galvanismo, galvanism + -scope, to observe*] A galvanometer for detecting the presence and determining the direction of an electric current. Galvanism, or direct-current electricity produced by chemical action, was named for the Italian physician Luigi Galvani (1797), after his achievements in animal electricity, which led Alessandro Volta to the discovery of current electricity. See galvanometer. (gal VAN uh skohp')

gastroscope [*gastro, stomach + -scope, to examine*] An endoscope for examining the interior of the stomach. (GAS truh skohp')

gyrocompass [*gyro(scope) & compass*] A navigational device containing a gyroscope with a rotating axis parallel to the earth's axis and thus pointing to true north instead of magnetic north. (JEYE roh kum' pus)

gyroscope [*gyro, circle & scope*] An apparatus with a wheel mounted so that its axis of rotation is able to turn freely in any direction and when spun rapidly keeps its original direction irrespective of the position of the mountings. (JEYE ruh skohp')

horoscope [*Grk > hora, hour + -scope, to observe*] 1.A diagram of the stars and planets showing their relative positions at a certain time, as at the time of a person's birth; used in astrology for calculating events in a person's life. 2.Predictions and advice based on the aspects of such a diagram. (HOR uh skohp')

hydroscope [*hydro, water + -scope, to view*] An optical instrument for viewing objects at considerable depths underwater. (HEYE druh skohp')

hygroscope [*hygro, moisture + -scope, to observe*] An instrument for approximating atmospheric humidity. See hygrometer and hygrograph. (HEYE gruh skohp')

kaleidoscope [*Grk > kalos, beautiful + Grk > eidos, form + -scope, to view*] A tube-shaped optical device in which bits of colored glass at one end of the tube are viewed in continually changing symmetrical patterns by reflections in mirrors set at angles to each other. (kuh LEYE duh skohp')

laparoscope [*laparo, abdominal wall + -scope, to examine*] An endoscope that is surgically inserted through the abdominal wall for examining and performing surgery on the interior of the abdominal cavity. (LAP uh ruh skohp')

laryngoscope [*laryngo, larynx + -scope, to examine*] An endoscope for examining and performing surgery on the interior of the larynx. (luh RING guh skohp')

macroscopic [*macro-, large + scop, to view + -ic*] Visible to the naked eye. Opposed to microscopic. (mak' roh SKOP ik)

microscope [*micro-, small + -scope, to view*] An optical instrument for making enlarged images of minute objects by means of a magnifying lens or combination of lenses. (MEYE kruh skohp')

microscopic [*micro-, small + scop, to view + -ic*] Able to be seen through a microscope, but not visible to the naked eye. Opposed to macroscopic. (meye' kroh SKOP ik)

nephoscope [*nepho, cloud + -scope, to observe*] An instrument for measuring the velocity and direction of cloud movement. (NEF uh skohp')

ophthalmoscope [*ophthalmo, eye + -scope, to examine*] An instrument for examining the interior of the eye. (ahf THAL muh skohp')

orthoscope [*ortho, correct + -scope, to examine*] An instrument for examining the interior of the eye through a layer of water that corrects distortion due to corneal refraction. (OR thuh skohp')

oscilloscope [*oscill(ation) & -scope, to view*] An instrument for viewing electrical oscillations such as alternating current or voltage. See oscillograph. (uh SIL uh skohp')

otoscope [*oto, ear + -scope, to examine*] An endoscope for examining the interior of the ear. (OHT uh skohp')

periscope [*peri-, around + -scope, to view*] A tubular optical instrument for viewing objects that are not in the direct line of sight, as on a submerged submarine. (PEHR ih skohp')

phonoscope [*phono, sound + -scope, to view*] An instrument for viewing the properties of sounding bodies, especially musical strings. (FOH nuh skohp')

photomicroscope [*photo(graph) & microscope*] A microscope for taking photomicrographs. See photomicrograph. (foht' oh MEYE kruh skohp')

pneumonoultramicroscopicsilicovolcanoconiosis [*pneumono, lung & ultramicroscopic & silico, silica & volcano & coni, dust + -osis, diseased condition*] A lung disease caused by prolonged breathing of extremely fine siliceous dust. Sometimes cited as one of the longest words in the English language. (NOO muh noh ul' truh meye' kruh skop' ik SIL uh koh' vol kay' noh koh' nee oh' sis)

polariscope [*polari(ze) & -scope, to view*] An instrument for determining and viewing the properties of polarized light. (poh LEHR ih skohp')

radarscope [*radar & -scope, to view*] The cathode-ray tube in a radar receiver that displays the reflected radio signals. (RAY dahr skohp')

radio telescope [*radio & tele, distant + -scope, to observe*] A radio antenna system designed to detect and analyze radio waves from celestial bodies. (RAY dee oh' TEL uh skohp')

radioscopy [*radio, radiation + -scopy, to examine*] The examination of the interior of opaque bodies by x-rays or other forms of radiation. (ray' dee OS kuh pee)

retinoscope [*retin(a) & -scope, to view*] An optical instrument for viewing and diagnosing refractive errors in the eye. (RET n uh skohp')

sniperscope [*sniper & -scope, to view*] A snooperscope that can be attached to a rifle or carbine. (SNEYE per skohp')

snooperscope [*snooper & -scope, to view*] An optical instrument that uses reflected infrared rays for viewing objects in the dark. (SNOO per skohp')

spectrohelioscope [*spectro, spectrum + helio, sun + -scope, to view*] An instrument for viewing the sun using light from only one spectral frequency. See spectroheliograph. (spek' troh HEE lee uh skohp')

scop, -scope, -scopy

spectroscope [*spectro, spectrum* + *-scope, to view*] An optical instrument for producing and viewing spectra. See spectrograph. (SPEK truh skohp')

spectroscopy [*spectro, spectrum* + *-scopy, to observe*] The scientific study of spectra using a spectroscope or spectrograph. See spectroscope and spectrograph. (spek TROS kuh pee)

spinthariscope [*Grk > spintharis, spark* + *-scope, to observe*] An instrument for observing radioactivity by showing scintillations produced by alpha particles as flashes on a fluorescent screen. (spin THEHR uh skohp')

statoscope [*stato, stationary* + *-scope, to observe*] 1.A very sensitive aneroid barometer for measuring and recording minute changes in atmospheric pressure. 2.An instrument for determining small changes in an aircraft's altitude. (STAT uh skohp')

stereomicroscope [*stereo-, three-dimensional & microscope*] A microscope equipped with a set of optics for each eye to make objects appear three-dimensional. (stehr' ee oh MEYE kruh skohp')

stereoscope [*stereo-, three-dimensional* + *-scope, to view*] An optical instrument for viewing two pictures made from slightly different points of view, but of the same object, thus producing an image that appears three-dimensional. (STEHR ee uh skohp')

stethoscope [*stetho, chest* + *-scope, to observe*] An instrument for listening to sounds within the chest or other parts of the body. (STETH uh skohp')

stroboscope [*Grk > strobos, a whirling* + *-scope, to view*] An instrument for viewing, calibrating, or balancing a rotating or vibrating object by intermittently illuminating it so that it appears to slow down or stop. (STROH buh skohp')

submicroscopic [*sub-, under & microscopic*] Too small for viewing through an optical microscope. (sub' meye' kruh SKOP ik)

synchroscope [*synchro-, synchronous* + *-scope, to observe*] An instrument for determining the degree of synchronism between associated machines, as two or more aircraft engines. (SING kruh skohp')

tachistoscope [*tachisto, rapid* + *-scope, to view*] An apparatus that uses a brief exposure of words or images to aid in learning and to test for visual perception. (tuh KIS tuh skohp')

telescope [*tele, distant* + *-scope, to view*] An optical instrument for viewing celestial bodies and other objects at great distances. (TEL uh skohp')

thermoscope [*thermo, temperature* + *-scope, to observe*] An instrument for detecting temperature changes in a substance by observing corresponding volume changes. (THUR muh skohp')

ultramicroscope [*ultra-, beyond & microscope*] A microscope used to study very minute objects by picking up the reflections of light rays dispersed by them. (ul' truh MEYE kruh skohp')

urethroscope [*urethro, urethra* + *-scope, to examine*] An endoscope for examining the interior of the urethra. (yoo REE thruh skohp')

sect   to cut

bisect [*bi-, two* + *sect, to cut*] To divide or cut into two equal parts. See dissect. (beye SEKT)

dissect [*dis-, apart* + *sect, to cut*] 1.To cut apart, as a plant, animal, body, etc., for examination or medical research. 2.To examine or analyze thoroughly. See bisect. (dih SEKT)

intersect [*inter-, between* + *sect, to cut*] 1.To divide by cutting through or across. 2.To cross each other at a point. (in' ter SEKT)

midsection [*mid-, middle & section*] The middle section of something, especially the middle portion of the human body. (MID sek' shun)

prosector [*pro-, before* + *sect, to cut* + *-or*] A person who dissects cadavers in preparation for anatomical demonstrations. (proh SEK tur)

quadrisect [*quadri, four* + *sect, to cut*] To divide or cut into four equal parts. (KWOD ruh sekt')

resection [*re-, back* + *sect, to cut* + *-ion*] The surgical removal of part of an organ, bone, or other structure. (rih SEK shun)

sectile [*sect, to cut* + *-ile*] Capable of being cut or severed smoothly with a knife. (SEK tul)

section [*sect, to cut* + *-ion*] One of several subdivisions of something. Portion. (SEK shun)

sector [*sect, to cut* + *-or*] 1.The part of a circle bounded by two radii and the included arc of the circle. 2.A distinctive part, especially of an economy or society. (SEK tur)

transect [*trans-, across* + *sect, to cut*] To divide by cutting across. (tran SEKT)

trisect [*tri-, three* + *sect, to cut*] To divide or cut into three equal parts. (TREYE sekt)

venesection [*ven, vein* + *sect, to cut* + *-ion*] The surgical opening of a vein to draw blood as a therapeutic measure. Same as phlebotomy. (VEN uh sek' shun)

vivisection [*vivi, living* + *sect, to cut* + *-ion*] The practice of cutting into the body of a living animal, especially for scientific research. (viv' uh SEK shun)

tom, -tome, -tomy, -stomy   to cut

anatomy [*ana-, up* + *-tomy, to cut*] 1.The structural makeup of a plant or animal or any of its parts. 2.Dissection of all or part of a plant or animal to study its parts. 3.The science dealing with the structure of plants and animals. (uh NAT uh mee)

appendectomy [*append(ix) & ec, out* + *-tomy, to cut*] Surgical removal of the vermiform appendix. (ap' un DEK tuh mee)

atom [*a-, not* + *tom, to cut*] 1.Anything considered to be an irreducible constituent of a specified system. 2.The smallest component of an element having all the properties of the element, with protons and neutrons at its positively charged nucleus surrounded by a complex arrangement of revolving electrons. (AT um)

atomics [*atom & -ics, study of*] The branch of physics dealing with the study of atoms, especially when involving atomic energy. (uh TOM iks)

autotomy [*auto-, self* + *-tomy, to cut*] The self-amputation and later regeneration of a lost or damaged appendage such as a lizard's tail or a crab's leg. (aw TOT uh mee)

cholecystectomy [*chole, gall* + *cyst, bladder* + *ec, out* + *-tomy, to cut*] Surgical removal of the gallbladder. (koh' luh sih STEK tuh mee)

colostomy [*colo, colon* + *-stomy, to cut*] The surgical creation of an excretory opening into the colon. See ostomy. (kuh LOS tuh mee)

craniotomy [*cranio, skull* + *-tomy, to cut*] Surgical cutting into the skull, as for brain surgery. (kray' nee OT uh mee)

dermatome [*derma, skin* + *-tome, to cut*] 1.A surgical instrument for cutting thin slices of skin, as for grafting. 2.An area of the skin innervated by nerves from a single spinal nerve root. 3.The lateral portion of an embryonic somite from which the skin is derived. (DER muh tohm')

diatom [*dia-, through* + *tom, to cut*] Unicellular, aquatic algae with a two-part, overlapping, symmetrical cell wall containing silica. (DEYE uh tom')

dichotomy [*dicho, apart* + *-tomy, to cut*] Division into two usually contradictory or opposing parts, branches, kinds, etc. See trichotomy (def. 1) and polychotomy. (deye KOT uh mee)

episiotomy [*Grk > epision, pubic region* + *-tomy, to cut*] Surgical incision of the vulva during childbirth to allow sufficient clearance for delivery. (ih piz' ee OT uh mee)

epitome [*epi-, upon* + *-tome, to cut*] 1.A person or thing that is typical or a perfect example of something. See quintessence (def. 2). 2.A brief summary of a literary work. (ih PIT uh mee)

gastrectomy [*gastr, stomach* + *ec, out* + *-tomy, to cut*] Surgical removal of all or part of the stomach. (ga STREK tuh mee)

hemorrhoidectomy [*hemorrhoid* & *ec, out* + *-tomy, to cut*] Surgical removal of hemorrhoids. (hem' uh roid' EK tuh mee)

hepatectomy [*hepat, liver* + *ec, out* + *-tomy, to cut*] Surgical removal of all or part of the liver. (hep' uh TEK tuh mee)

hypophysectomy [*hypophys(is) {pituitary gland}* & *ec, out* + *-tomy, to cut*] Surgical removal of the pituitary gland. See hypophysis. (heye pof' uh SEK tuh mee)

hysterectomy [*hyster, womb* + *ec, out* + *-tomy, to cut*] Surgical removal of all or part of the uterus. (his' tuh REK tuh mee)

hysterotomy [*hystero, womb* + *-tomy, to cut*] 1.Surgical incision of the uterus. 2.Cesarean section. (his' tuh ROT uh mee)

ileostomy [*ile(um)* & *-stomy, to cut*] The surgical creation of an opening into the ileum. (il ee OS tuh mee)

laminectomy [*lamin(a)* & *ec, out* + *-tomy, to cut*] Surgical removal of all or part of a vertebral lamina. (lam' ih NEK tuh mee)

laparotomy [*laparo, abdominal wall* + *-tomy, to cut*] Surgical incision into the abdominal wall. (lap' uh ROT uh mee)

laryngectomy [*laryng, larynx* + *ec, out* + *tomy, to cut*] Surgical removal of all or part of the larynx. (lehr' un JEK tuh mee)

lithotomy [*litho, stone* + *-tomy, to cut*] Surgical incision of a duct or organ, especially of the urinary bladder to remove a stone. (lith OT uh mee)

lobectomy [*lob, lobe* + *ec, out* + *-tomy, to cut*] Surgical removal of a lobe, as of a lung or gland. (loh BEK tuh mee)

lobotomy [*lobo, lobe* + *-tomy, to cut*] Surgical incision into or across a lobe of the brain, usually the frontal lobe of the cerebrum, for the relief of certain mental disorders. (loh BOT uh mee)

mastectomy [*mast, breast* + *ec, out* + *-tomy, to cut*] Surgical removal of a breast. (mas TEK tuh mee)

mastoidectomy [*mastoid* & *ec, out* + *-tomy, to cut*] Surgical removal of all or part of a mastoid. (mas' toid' EK tuh mee)

microtome [*micro-, small* + *-tome, to cut*] A precise instrument for cutting thin sections of organic tissue or other material for microscopic examination. (MEYE kroh tohm')

myotome [*myo, muscle* + *-tome, to cut*] 1.A knife for cutting muscle. 2.The portion of an embryonic somite from which skeletal muscle is derived. (MEYE uh tohm')

necrotomy [*necro, dead* + *-tomy, to cut*] 1.The dissection of a dead body. 2.The surgical removal of dead bone or tissue. (nuh KROT uh mee)

nephrectomy [*nephr, kidney* + *ec, out* + *-tomy, to cut*] Surgical removal of a kidney. (neh FREK tuh mee)

nephrotomy [*nephro, kidney* + *-tomy, to cut*] Surgical incision of a kidney. (neh FROT uh mee)

neurectomy [*neur, nerve* + *ec, out* + *-tomy, to cut*] Surgical removal of all or part of a nerve. (noo REK tuh mee)

neuroanatomy [*neuro, nerve* & *anatomy*] The branch of neurology dealing with the study of the anatomy of the nervous system. (noor' oh uh NAT uh mee)

neurotomy [*neuro, nerve* + *-tomy, to cut*] The surgical cutting of a nerve, usually to relieve pain or cause loss of sensation. (noo ROT uh mee)

oophorectomy [*oophor-, ovary* + *ec, out* + *-tomy, to cut*] Surgical removal of an ovary. Same as ovariectomy. (oh' uh fuh REK tuh mee)

osteotomy [*osteo, bone* + *-tomy, to cut*] The surgical cutting of a bone or excision of a piece of bone. (os' tee OT uh mee)

ostomy [*(col)ostomy*] Any surgical creation of an opening for an artificial excretory passage, as a colostomy. See colostomy. (OS tuh mee)

ovariectomy [*ovar(y)* & *ec, out* + *-tomy, to cut*] Surgical removal of an ovary. (oh vehr' ee EK tuh mee)

ovariotomy [*ovar(y)* & *-tomy, to cut*] Surgical incision of an ovary. (oh vehr' ee OT uh mee)

parathyroidectomy [*para-, beside* & *thyroid* & *ec, out* + *-tomy, to cut*] Surgical removal of the parathyroid glands. (pehr' uh theye' roid' EK tuh mee)

phlebotomy [*phlebo, vein* + *-tomy, to cut*] The surgical opening of a vein to draw blood as a therapeutic measure. (flih BOT uh mee)

pneumonectomy [*pneumon, lung* + *ec, out* + *-tomy, to cut*] Surgical removal of all or part of a lung. (noo' muh NEK tuh mee)

polychotomy [*poly, many* & *(di)chotomy*] Division into many parts, branches, kinds, etc. See dichotomy and trichotomy (def. 1). (pol' ee KOT uh mee)

prostatectomy [*prostat, prostate gland* + *ec, out* + *-tomy, to cut*] Surgical removal of all or part of the prostate gland. (pros' tuh TEK tuh mee)

rhizotomy [*rhizo, root* + *-tomy, to cut*] Surgical cutting of a spinal nerve root to relieve pain. (reye ZOT uh mee)

rhytidectomy [*Grk > rhytis, wrinkle* + *ec, out* + *-tomy, to cut*] Surgical removal of skin from the face to eliminate wrinkles, sagging skin, etc. Face lift. See blepharoplasty. (rit' ih DEK tuh mee)

salpingectomy [*salping, fallopian tube* + *ec, out* + *-tomy, to cut*] Surgical removal of the fallopian tube. (sal' pin JEK tuh mee)

tom, -tome, -tomy, -stomy

sclerotomy [*scler(a) & -tomy, to cut*] Surgical incision of the sclera. (skluh ROT uh mee)

splenectomy [*splen, spleen + ec, out + -tomy, to cut*] Surgical removal of the spleen. (splih NEK tuh mee)

thoracotomy [*thoraco, chest + -tomy, to cut*] Surgical incision into the chest wall. (thor' uh KOT uh mee)

thyroidectomy [*thyroid & ec, out + -tomy, to cut*] Surgical removal of all or part of the thyroid gland. (theye' roid' EK tuh mee)

tome [*tom, to cut > Grk > tomos, volume*] 1.Any of the books in a series of several volumes. 2.A book, especially one that is large or scholarly. (tohm)

tomography [*tomo, to cut + -graphy, recording*] The technique of making x-ray photographs of a single, predetermined plane section of the body or other solid object by eliminating the images produced by other planes. (toh MOG ruh fee)

tonsillectomy [*tonsil & ec, out + -tomy, to cut*] Surgical removal of the tonsils. (ton' suh LEK tuh mee)

tonsillotomy [*tonsil & -tomy, to cut*] Surgical incision of a tonsil. (ton' suh LOT uh mee)

tracheotomy [*tracheo, trachea + -tomy, to cut*] Surgical incision into the trachea through the neck, as for creating an artificial breathing hole. (tray' kee OT uh mee)

trichotomy [*tri-, three & (di)chotomy*] 1.Division into three parts, branches, kinds, etc. See dichotomy and polychotomy. 2.The division of man into body, soul, and spirit. (treye KOT uh mee)

ultramicrotome [*ultra-, beyond + micro, small + -tome, to cut*] A precise instrument for cutting very thin sections of organic tissue or other material for microscopic examination. (ul' truh MEYE kruh tohm')

vaginectomy [*vagin(a) & ec, out + -tomy, to cut*] Surgical removal of all or part of the vagina. (vaj' uh NEK tuh mee)

vagotomy [*vag(us) & -tomy, to cut*] Surgical cutting of the vagus nerve. (vay GOT uh mee)

varicotomy [*varico, varicose vein + -tomy, to cut*] Surgical removal of a varix or a varicose vein. (vehr' ih KOT uh mee)

vasectomy [*vas, vessel + ec, out + -tomy, to cut*] Surgical removal of all or part of the vas deferens as a means of birth control. (va SEK tuh mee)

vitrectomy [*vitr(eous humor) & ec, out + -tomy, to cut*] Surgical removal of all or part of the vitreous humor. (vih TREK tuh mee)

xylotomy [*xylo, wood + -tomy, to cut*] The preparation of thin sections of wood for microscopic examination. (zeye LOT uh mee)

zootomy [*zoo, animal + -tomy, to cut*] 1.The dissection of animals. 2.The anatomy of animals. (zoh OT uh mee)

soph, -sophy   wise, wisdom

anthroposophy [*anthropo, man + -sophy, wisdom*] A religious philosophy, established by Rudolf Steiner, that emphasizes the study of the nature of man and is similar to theosophy. (an' thruh POS uh fee)

gymnosophist [*gymno, naked + soph, wisdom + -ist*] A member of an ancient sect of naked Hindu ascetic philosophers. (jim NOS uh fist)

pansophy [*pan, all + -sophy, wisdom*] Universal wisdom or knowledge. (PAN suh fee)

philosophe [*philo, love + soph, wisdom*] Any of the popular French intellectuals and writers of the 18th century. (fee' luh ZOF)

philosophy [*philo, love + -sophy, wisdom*] Love of wisdom as obtained through intellectual knowledge and reasoning. (fih LOS uh fee)

sophism [*soph, wise + -ism*] A clever, but misleading argument for deceiving or defeating someone. (SOF iz' um)

sophist [*soph, wise + -ist*] 1.Any of a group of teachers, politicians, etc., of ancient Greece, some of whom were notorious for their clever and often misleading argumentation. 2.A person who practices clever, but misleading reasoning. (SOF ist)

sophistic [*soph, wise + -istic*] Being subtle and clever, but based on a false notion. (suh FIS tik)

sophisticated [*soph, wise + -ist + -icate + -ed*] 1.Altered by education, experience, etc., so as to have acquired refinement or worldly knowledge. 2.Very complicated or complex. (suh FIS tih kay' tid)

sophistry [*soph, wise + -ist + -ry*] A clever and plausible argument that is usually false. (SOF ih stree)

sophomore [*sopho, wise + Grk > moros, foolish*] A high school or college student in the second year. See sophomoric (def. 2). (SOF uh mor')

sophomoric [*sopho, wise + Grk > moros, foolish + -ic*] 1.Characteristic of a sophomore. 2.Self-assured, but immature and overconfident of knowledge. (sof' uh MOR ik)

theosophy [*theo, God + -sophy, wisdom*] 1.A religious philosophy claiming mystical insight into the divine nature. 2.The philosophy and beliefs of the Theosophical Society, which adhere chiefly to Buddhist and Hindu philosophies and were introduced into the United States in 1875. (thee OS uh fee)

spect, spec, spic   to look, to see
spectro   spectrum

aspect [*as-, toward + spect, to look*] 1.A particular facial expression. Look. 2.The way in which something appears to the mind. 3.The way in which something appears to the eye. (AS pekt)

auspices [*avi, bird + spic, to see + -es*] 1.Kindly patronage and support. 2.A usually favorable omen, especially when observed in the actions of birds. 3.Divination, especially from the actions of birds. (AW spuh siz')

auspicious [*avi, bird + spic, to see + -ious*] 1.Marked by success. Fortunate. 2.Of good omen. Favorable. See auspices. (aw SPISH us)

circumspect [*circum-, around + spect, to look*] Careful to consider all possible consequences before judging, acting, etc. Prudent. Cautious. (SUR kum spekt')

conspectus [*con-, together + spect, to see + -us*] 1.A comprehensive or general view of a subject. 2.A summary or digest. Synopsis. (kun SPEK tus)

conspicuous [*con-, completely + spic, to see + -ous*] 1.Easily noticed. Obvious. See prominent (def. 2). 2.Attracting special attention. Remarkable. See inconspicuous. (kun SPIK yoo us)

despicable [*de-, down + spic, to look + -able*] Deserving to be scorned or despised. Contemptible. (dih SPIK uh bul)

despise [*de-, down* + *spic, to look*] 1.To look down on with scorn or contempt. 2.To regard with extreme dislike. Loathe. (dih SPEYEZ)

inauspicious [*in-, not & auspicious*] Unfavorable. Unlucky. Not auspicious. See auspicious. (in' aw SPISH us)

inconspicuous [*in-, not & conspicuous*] 1.Not easily noticed. 2.Attracting little or no attention. See conspicuous. (in' kun SPIK yoo us)

inspect [*in-, in* + *spect, to look*] 1.To examine closely and carefully. 2.To examine officially or formally. (in SPEKT)

introspect [*intro-, inward* + *spect, to look*] To examine one's own thoughts, feelings, and emotions. (in' truh SPEKT)

irrespective [*ir-, without & respect & -ive*] Without consideration for or regard to. Regardless. (ihr' rih SPEK tiv)

perspective [*per-, through* + *spect, to see* + *-ive*] 1.The art or technique of representing three-dimensional objects on a flat surface. 2.The ability to see things in their true relationship to each other. (per SPEK tiv)

perspicacious [*per-, through* + *spic, to see* + *-acious*] Having or showing keen judgment or understanding. Shrewd. (per' spih KAY shus)

perspicuous [*per-, through* + *spic, to see* + *-ous*] Easily understood. Clear. Lucid. See inscrutable, evident, and manifest. (per SPIK yoo us)

prospect [*pro-, forward* + *spect, to look*] 1.The act of looking forward. Anticipation. 2.A possible candidate or customer. 3.To explore, as for gold or other mineral deposits. (PROS pekt)

prospective [*pro-, forward* + *spect, to look* + *-ive*] 1.Pertaining to or in the future. 2.Likely to occur or become. Potential. Expected. (pruh SPEK tiv)

prospectus [*pro-, forward* + *spect, to look* + *-us*] A formal document describing a proposed commercial enterprise, literary work, or other project. (pruh SPEK tus)

respect [*re-, back* + *spect, to look*] 1.To feel or show high regard for. 2.A feeling of high regard. Esteem. (rih SPEKT)

respective [*re-, back* + *spect, to look* + *-ive*] Pertaining separately to each of several persons or things under consideration. Separate. Individual. Particular. (rih SPEK tiv)

retrospect [*retro-, back* + *spect, to look*] A looking back on conditions or events of the past. (RET ruh spekt')

specimen [*Ltn > specere, to look at* + *-men*] 1.An individual part typical or representative of a whole. Sample. 2.A sample of urine, tissue, etc., taken for medical examination and analysis. (SPES uh mun)

specious [*Ltn > specere, to look at* + *-ious*] 1.Seeming to be reasonable, desirable, or probable, but lacking real merit. 2.Attractive, but deceptive. (SPEE shus)

spectacle [*spect, to look* + *-cle*] 1.An object of interest, especially something large-scale or impressive. 2.A regrettable object of public display. 3.A public display, performance, or exhibition. (SPEK tuh kul)

spectacular [*spectac(le) & -ar*] Impressive. Striking. Sensational. (spek' TAK yuh lur)

spectator [*spect(acle) & -ator*] One who observes without taking part. (SPEK tayt' ur)

specter [*spect, to see* + *-er*] 1.A ghost. An apparition. 2.A haunting or threatening possibility. (SPEK ter)

spectre [*spect, to see* + *-er*] 1.A ghost. An apparition. 2.A haunting or threatening possibility. Same as specter. (SPEK ter)

spectrograph [*spectro, spectrum* + *graph, recording*] An instrument for producing, viewing, and photographing spectra. See spectroscope. (SPEK tuh graf')

spectroheliograph [*spectro, spectrum* + *helio, sun* + *graph, recording*] An instrument for photographing the sun using light from only one spectral frequency. See spectrohelioscope. (spek' troh HEE lee uh graf')

spectrohelioscope [*spectro, spectrum* + *helio, sun* + *-scope, to view*] An instrument for viewing the sun using light from only one spectral frequency. See spectroheliograph. (spek' troh HEE lee uh skohp')

spectrometer [*spectro, spectrum* + *meter, to measure*] An optical instrument for measuring wavelengths of spectra and indices of refraction. See spectrophotometer. (spek TROM et er)

spectrophotometer [*spectro, spectrum* + *photo, light* + *meter, to measure*] An instrument for measuring wavelengths in light spectra for accurate analysis of color and the comparison of luminous intensity. See spectrometer. (spek' troh foh TOM et er)

spectroscope [*spectro, spectrum* + *-scope, to view*] An optical instrument for producing and viewing spectra. See spectrograph. (SPEK truh skohp')

spectroscopy [*spectro, spectrum* + *-scopy, to observe*] The scientific study of spectra using a spectroscope or spectrograph. See spectroscope and spectrograph. (spek TROS kuh pee)

spectrum [*Ltn > specere, to look at* + *-um*] 1.A series of colors, including red, orange, yellow, green, blue, indigo, and violet, that are formed when a beam of sunlight passes through a prism. 2.A series of radiations arranged according to the magnitudes of some common physical property, as wavelength or mass. 3.A continuous range of related qualities, ideas, or activities. (SPEK trum)

specular [*spec, to see* + *-ule* + *-ar*] Pertaining to or resembling a speculum or a mirror. (SPEK yuh lur)

speculate [*spec, to see* + *-ule* + *-ate*] 1.To ponder a given subject. 2.To engage in a business deal involving high risk for the chance of large profit. (SPEK yuh layt')

speculum [*spec, to see* + *-ule* + *-um*] 1.A mirror or reflector in an optical instrument. 2.An instrument inserted into a body passage for medical examination. 3.A patch of color on the wings of ducks and certain other birds. (SPEK yuh lum)

suspect [*sub-, under* + *spect, to look*] 1.To have doubts about. Distrust. 2.To assume guilt without proof. (suh SPEKT {verb}) 3.A person who is suspected. (SUS pekt {noun})

transpicuous [*trans-, through* + *spic, to see* + *-ous*] Easily understood. Transparent. See perspicuous and transparent (def. 2). (tran SPIK yoo us)

sphere   ball

aerosphere [*aero, air & sphere*] The atmosphere surrounding the earth. (EHR oh sfihr')

aspheric [*a-, not & spher(e) & -ic*] Having a nearly perfect spherical shape with only slight aberrations, as a lens. (ay SFIHR ik)

asthenosphere [*a-, without + stheno, strength & sphere*] A zone beneath the earth's surface that lies beneath the lithosphere and consists of several hundred kilometers of weak material that readily yields to persistent stresses. (as THEN uh sfihr')

atmosphere [*atmo, vapor & sphere*] 1.The gaseous mass or envelope surrounding the earth and consisting of five layers that are differentiated by temperature. See lithosphere and hydrosphere. 2.A pervading or surrounding mood, influence, spirit, etc. (AT muh sfihr')

atmospherics [*atmospher(e) & -ics, knowledge*] Natural electromagnetic disturbances in the atmosphere that cause interference in the reception of radio waves. Static. (at' muh SFIHR iks)

bathysphere [*bathy, deep & sphere*] A reinforced spherical diving chamber used for deep-sea observation. (BATH uh sfihr')

biosphere [*bio, life & sphere*] The part of the earth's crust, water, and atmosphere that supports life. See ecosphere. (BEYE uh sfihr')

celestial sphere [*celestial & sphere*] An imaginary, infinite sphere formed by the sky with the earth at its center. (suh LES chul sfihr)

centrosphere [*centro, center & sphere*] 1.The cytoplasm that surrounds a centriole in the centrosome of a cell. 2.The interior central portion of the earth. (SEN truh sfihr')

chromosphere [*chromo, color & sphere*] A gaseous, glowing zone surrounding the photosphere of the sun or other stars. See photosphere. (KROH muh sfihr')

ecosphere [*eco, environment & sphere*] The parts of the universe capable of supporting life. See biosphere. (EK oh sfihr')

ensphere [*en-, in & sphere*] To enclose in, or as if in, a sphere. (en SFIHR)

exosphere [*exo-, outside & sphere*] An atmospheric zone located 300 to 600 miles above the earth that is the outermost, least dense region of the atmosphere. (EKS oh sfihr')

hemisphere [*hemi-, half & sphere*] 1.Half of the earth divided into north and south by the equator or east and west by a meridian. 2.One of the two halves of a sphere formed by a plane passing through its center. (HEM ih sfihr')

hydrosphere [*hydro, water & sphere*] All the water on the surface of the earth. See lithosphere and atmosphere (def. 1). (HEYE druh sfihr')

insphere [*in-, in & sphere*] To enclose in, or as if in, a sphere. Same as ensphere. (in SFIHR)

ionosphere [*ion & sphere*] An atmospheric zone located 50 to 350 miles above the earth with an appreciable content of ions and electrons that cause radio waves to be deflected downward at an angle, thus allowing radio signals to be received at great distances around the curvature of the earth. (eye ON uh sfihr')

lithosphere [*litho, stone & sphere*] The solid outer part of the earth, not including the hydrosphere or atmosphere. See hydrosphere and atmosphere (def. 1). (LITH uh sfihr')

magnetosphere [*magneto, magnetic force & sphere*] An atmospheric zone, extending from about 300 to several thousand miles above the earth, in which charged particles are trapped and their behavior dominated by the earth's magnetic field. (mag NEET uh sfihr')

mesopause [*meso(sphere) & pause*] The outermost boundary of the mesosphere. See tropopause and stratopause. (MEZ uh poz')

mesosphere [*meso-, middle & sphere*] An atmospheric zone, 30 to 50 miles above the earth between the stratosphere and the thermosphere, characterized by decreasing temperature with increasing altitude. (MEZ uh sfihr')

microsphere [*micro-, small & sphere*] A minute sphere. (MEYE kroh sfihr')

oosphere [*oo, egg & sphere*] A large, nonmotile, unfertilized egg that is formed in the oogonium of certain algae and fungi. See oospore and oogonium (def. 2). (OH uh sfihr')

ozonosphere [*ozon(e) & sphere*] An atmospheric zone between 10 and 20 miles in altitude, where most atmospheric ozone is concentrated. It absorbs most of the sun's ultraviolet rays. Ozone layer. (oh ZOH nuh sfihr')

photosphere [*photo, light & sphere*] The luminous, visible surface of the sun or other stars. See chromosphere. (FOHT uh sfihr')

planisphere [*plani, flat & sphere*] 1.A representation of all or part of a sphere on a plane surface. 2.A chart or map that represents the celestial sphere on a plane surface and shows the positions of celestial bodies at a given time and place. (PLAY nih sfihr')

rhizosphere [*rhizo, root & sphere*] The soil that is influenced by and surrounds the roots of a plant. (REYE zoh sfihr')

sferics [*(atmo)s(ph)erics*] Short for atmospherics. See atmospherics. (SFIHR iks)

sphere [*sphere, ball*] 1.A three-dimensional round body with all points on the surface equidistant from the center. 2.Any of the transparent atmospheric zones surrounding a planet or star. 3.The environment or domain within which a person or thing exists. (sfihr)

spherical [*spher(e) & -ical*] 1.Pertaining to a sphere. 2.Resembling a sphere. (SFIHR ih kul)

spherics [*(atmo)spherics*] Short for atmospherics. Same as sferics. See atmospherics. (SFIHR iks)

spheroid [*spher(e) & -oid, resembling*] A body or figure shaped like a sphere, but not a perfect sphere. (SFIHR oid)

spherometer [*spher(e) & meter, to measure*] An instrument for measuring the curvature of a sphere, cylinder, lens, or other curved surface. (sfihr OM et er)

spherule [*spher(e) & -ule, small*] A small sphere. Globule. (SFIHR yool)

spherulite [*spher(e) & -ule, small + -ite, mineral*] A small and usually spherical aggregate of radiating crystals found in obsidian and other vitreous volcanic rocks. (SFIHR yoo leyet')

sphery [*spher(e) & -y*] 1.Resembling a sphere. 2.Pertaining to or resembling a celestial body. (SFIHR ee)

stratopause [*strato(sphere) & pause*] The outermost boundary of the stratosphere. See tropopause and mesopause. (STRAT uh poz')

stratosphere [*strat(um) & sphere*] An atmospheric zone, located 7 to 30 miles above the earth, characterized by few clouds and little temperature change. (STRAT uh sfihr')

thermosphere [*thermo, temperature & sphere*] An atmospheric zone, located 50 to 300 miles above the earth, characterized by notably rising temperature with increasing altitude. (THUR muh sfihr')

tropopause [*tropo(sphere) & pause*] The outermost boundary of the troposphere. See stratopause and mesopause. (TROP uh poz')

troposphere [*tropo, changing & sphere*] An atmospheric zone, located 0 to 7 miles above the earth, characterized by cloud formation, weather conditions, and a rapid decrease in temperature with increasing altitude. (TROP uh sfihr')

unsphere [*un-, not & sphere*] To remove from its position or sphere, as a satellite from its orbit. (un SFIHR)

spor/o, spori   spore, to sow

apospory [*apo-, away + spor, spore + -y*] A situation in which the gametophyte develops directly from the sporophyte without spore formation or meiosis, as in certain bryophytes and pteridophytes. See apogamy. (AP uh spor' ee)

archesporium [*arche, first + spor, spore + -ium*] The cell or cells in a sporangium that ultimately develop into spores. (ahr' kuh SPOR ee um)

arthrospore [*arthro, joint & spore*] A spore formed by filament segmentation in some blue-green algae and in the mycelium of a fungus. (AHR thruh spor')

ascospore [*asco-, sac & spore*] A spore formed in an ascus of an ascomycete fungus. (AS kuh spor')

carpospore [*carpo, fruit & spore*] A nonmotile spore developed from the carpogonium in red algae. (KAHR puh spor')

cryptozoite [*crypto, hidden & (sporo)zoite*] The exoerythrocyte stage of a malaria parasite during which it lives in tissue cells before entering the blood. See sporozoite. (krip' tuh ZOH eyet')

diaspora [*dia-, through + spor, to sow + -a*] The dispersion of a homogeneous group of people. (deye AS pur uh)

Diaspora [*dia-, through + spor, to sow + -a*] The dispersion of colonies of Jews after the Babylonian exile in the sixth century B.C. (deye AS pur uh)

endospore [*endo-, inside & spore*] 1.A spore formed within the cell membrane of a parent cell. 2.The innermost layer of the wall of a spore. See exospore. (EN duh spor')

exospore [*exo-, outside & spore*] The outermost layer of the wall of a spore. See endospore (def. 2). (EKS uh spor')

heterosporous [*hetero, different + spor, spore + -ous*] Producing spores of two or more different kinds, especially microspores and megaspores in seed plants and ferns. Opposed to homosporous. (het' uh roh SPOR us)

homosporous [*homo, same + spor, spore + -ous*] The production of asexual spores of one kind only. Opposed to heterosporous. (hoh' muh SPOR us)

macrosporangium [*macro-, large & sporangium*] In heterosporous plants, a sporangium that produces only megaspores and is borne on a megasporophyll. Same as megasporangium. (mak' roh spuh RAN jee um)

macrospore [*macro-, large & spore*] The usually larger of two kinds of spores in heterosporous plants that gives rise to a female gametophyte. Same as megaspore. (MAK roh spor')

megasporangium [*mega-, large & sporangium*] In heterosporous plants, a sporangium that produces only megaspores and is borne on a megasporophyll. See microsporangium and megasporophyll. (meg' uh spuh RAN jee um)

megaspore [*mega-, large & spore*] The usually larger of two kinds of spores in heterosporous plants that gives rise to a female gametophyte. See microspore. (MEG uh spor')

megasporogenesis [*mega-, large + sporo, spore + -genesis, production*] The production and maturation of a megaspore. See megaspore. (meg' uh spor' uh JEN uh sis)

megasporophyll [*mega-, large + sporo, spore + phyll, leaf*] A leaf or modified leaf that produces only megasporangia. See microsporophyll and megasporangium. (meg' uh SPOR uh fil')

microsporangium [*micro-, small & sporangium*] In heterosporous plants, a sporangium that produces only microspores and is borne on a microsporophyll. See megasporangium and microsporophyll. (meye' kroh spuh RAN jee um)

microspore [*micro-, small & spore*] The usually smaller of two kinds of spores in heterosporous plants that gives rise to a male gametophyte. See megaspore. (MEYE kroh spor')

microsporophyll [*micro-, small + sporo, spore + phyll, leaf*] A leaf or modified leaf that produces only microsporangia. See megasporophyll and microsporangium. (meye' kroh SPOR uh fil')

oospore [*oo, egg & spore*] A fertilized oosphere. See oosphere. (OH uh spor')

sporangiophore [*sporangi(a) & -phore, to bear*] A stalk or filament bearing one or more sporangia. (spuh RAN jee uh for')

sporangium [*spor, spore + angi, vessel + -um*] The reproductive structure or case in which spores are formed. (spuh RAN jee um)

spore [*spor, spore*] A usually asexual reproductive body, produced by most simple plants, bacteria, and certain protozoans, that detaches from the parent and gives rise to a new individual either immediately or at a later, more environmentally favorable time. (spor)

sporicide [*spori, spore + -cide, to kill*] An agent for killing spores. (SPOR uh seyed')

sporiferous [*spori, spore + fer, to bear + -ous*] Spore-bearing. (spuh RIF ur us)

sporocyst [*sporo, spore + cyst, sac*] 1.A one-celled resting body that produces asexual spores. 2.A protective envelope surrounding the spores of a sporozoan. (SPOR uh sist')

sporocyte [*sporo, spore + -cyte, cell*] The spore mother cell that gives rise to four haploid spores during meiosis. (SPOR uh seyet')

sporogenesis [*sporo, spore + -genesis, production*] The formation of or reproduction by spores. (spor' uh JEN uh sis)

sporophore [*sporo, spore* + *-phore, to bear*] A spore-bearing structure or organ in various fungi. (SPOR uh for')

sporophyll [*sporo, spore* + *phyll, leaf*] A leaf or modified leaf that produces sporangia. See microsporophyll and megasporophyll. (SPOR uh fil')

sporophyte [*sporo, spore* + *-phyte, plant*] In plants reproducing by alternation of generations, the spore-producing diploid generation that reproduces asexually by spores. This generation produces a gametophyte. See gametophyte and alternation of generations. (SPOR uh feyet')

sporozoan [*sporo, spore* + *zo, animal* + *-an*] Any of the parasitic protozoans in the class Sporozoa that typically reproduce by spores, as the plasmodium that causes malaria. (spor' uh ZOH un)

sporozoite [*sporo, spore* + *zo, animal* + *-ite*] The infective stage in some sporozoans that results from sexual reproduction and initiates an asexual reproductive cycle in the new host, as in the malaria parasite. See cryptozoite. (spor' uh ZOH eyet')

sporulation [*spor, spore* + *-ule, small* + *-ation*] The process of spore formation. (spor' yuh LAY shun)

teleutospore [*tele, end* & *spore*] A thick-walled, blackish spore that develops during the terminal stage in the life cycle of the rust fungus. Same as teliospore. (tuh LOOT uh spor')

teliospore [*tel, end* & *spore*] A thick-walled, blackish spore that develops during the terminal stage in the life cycle of the rust fungus. (TEE lee uh spor')

tetraspore [*tetra-, four* & *spore*] One of a group of four haploid, asexual spores produced in red algae. (TET ruh spor')

zoospore [*zoo, life* & *spore*] An asexual motile spore that has one or more flagella and is found in certain algae and fungi. (ZOH uh spor')

zygospore [*zygo, pair* & *spore*] A thick-walled resting spore formed by the fusion of two similar gametes, as in some algae and fungi. (ZEYE guh spor')

tax/o   arrangement

ataxia [*a-, without* + *tax, arrangement* + *-ia*] Total or partial loss of the ability to coordinate voluntary muscle action, especially in the extremities. (uh TAK see uh)

chemotaxis [*chemo, chemical* & *taxis*] The movement of a freely moving organism or cell in response to a chemical substance. See chemotropism. (kee' moh TAK sis)

chemotaxonomy [*chemo, chemical* + *taxo, arrangement* + *-nomy, system of laws*] The classification of organisms based on biochemical criteria. See taxonomy. (kee' moh taks ON uh mee)

cytotaxonomy [*cyto, cell* + *taxo, arrangement* + *-nomy, system of laws*] The classification of organisms based on chromosome characteristics and cellular structure. See taxonomy. (seyet' oh taks ON uh mee)

geotaxis [*geo, earth* & *taxis*] The movement of a freely moving organism in response to the earth's gravity. See geotropism. (jee' oh TAK sis)

heliotaxis [*helio, sun* & *taxis*] The movement of a freely moving organism in response to sunlight. See heliotropism and phototaxis. (hee' lee oh TAK sis)

heterotaxis [*hetero, different* + *tax, arrangement* + *-is*] 1.An abnormal structural arrangement of body organs or parts. 2.An abnormal structural arrangement of parts, especially of rock strata. See homotaxis. (het' uh roh TAK sis)

homotaxis [*homo, similar* + *tax, arrangement* + *-is*] Similarity of arrangement or of fossil formations between rock strata located in separate geographical areas. See heterotaxis (def. 2). (hoh' muh TAK sis)

hydrotaxis [*hydro, water* & *taxis*] The movement of a freely moving organism in response to moisture. See hydrotropism. (heye' druh TAK sis)

hypotaxis [*hypo-, less* + *tax, arrangement* + *-is*] The arrangement of clauses in a subordinate relationship, as by conjunctions. See parataxis. (heye' poh TAK sis)

parataxis [*para-, beside* + *tax, arrangement* + *-is*] The arrangement of clauses, phrases, etc., without the use of conjunctions to indicate subordination, as "I came, I saw, I conquered." See hypotaxis. (pehr' uh TAK sis)

phototaxis [*photo, light* & *taxis*] The movement of a freely moving organism in response to light. See phototropism, heliotaxis, and photokinesis. (foht' oh TAK sis)

phyllotaxis [*phyllo, leaf* + *tax, arrangement* + *-is*] The arrangement of leaves on a stem. (fil' uh TAK sis)

stereotaxis [*stereo-, solid* & *taxis*] The movement of a freely moving organism in response to contact with a solid body. See thigmotropism. (stehr' ee oh TAK sis)

syntax [*syn-, together* + *tax, arrangement*] 1.Rules governing the systematic arrangement of words in a grammatical construction according to proper form and relationship. 2.Rules governing the arrangement of components within a system, as in a computer language. (SIN taks)

taxeme [*tax, arrangement* + *-eme, structural unit*] The smallest grammatical feature of the arrangement of elements in a language, as the order of elements in a compound. (TAKS eem)

taxidermy [*taxi, arrangement* + *derm, skin* + *-y*] The art of preparing and mounting the skins of animals to give them a lifelike appearance. (TAKS ih der' mee)

taxis [*tax, arrangement* + *-is*] 1.The movement of a freely moving organism or cell in response to an external stimulus. See tropism. 2.In surgery, the manual movement of a displaced organ or part. (TAK sis)

taxonomy [*taxo, arrangement* + *-nomy, system of laws*] 1.The science of classification. 2.The classification of organisms based on common factors and relationships to each other. (taks ON uh mee)

thermotaxis [*thermo, heat* & *taxis*] 1.The movement of a freely moving organism in response to heat. See thermotropism. 2.The normal regulation of body temperature. (thur' moh TAK sis)

thigmotaxis [*Grk > thigma, touch* & *taxis*] The movement of a freely moving organism in response to contact with a solid body. Same as stereotaxis. (thig' muh TAK sis)

tele, tel, telo   distant, end, complete

biotelemetry [*bio, life* & *telemetry*] The remote monitoring of the physical activities, conditions, or functions of a human or animal. See telemetry. (beye' oh tuh LEM ih tree)

dysteleology [*dys-, bad + teleo, end + log, doctrine + -y*] A philosophical doctrine that considers existence to have no purpose or final cause. See teleology (def. 2). (dis tel' ee OL uh jee)

radio telescope [*radio & tele, distant + -scope, to observe*] A radio antenna system designed to detect and analyze radio waves from celestial bodies. (RAY dee oh' TEL uh skohp')

radiotelegraph [*radio, by radio & telegraph*] A telegraph that uses radio waves instead of wires. See telegraph. (ray' dee oh TEL uh graf')

telecommunication [*tele, distant & communication*] Communication from a distance, as by telephone, radio, television, satellite, etc. (tel' uh kuh myoo' nih KAY shun)

teleconference [*tele, distant & conference*] A conference among individuals at different and usually distant locations conducted through telecommunications. See telecommunication. (TEL uh kon' fer ens)

telegenic [*tele(vision) & gen, to produce + -ic*] Having an attractive appearance on television. (tel' uh JEN ik)

telegnosis [*tele, distant + gnos, knowledge + -is*] Knowledge of distant happenings obtained by supernatural means. Clairvoyance. See precognition and telepathy. (tel' uh NOH sis)

telegony [*tele, distant + -gony, reproduction*] The supposed genetic influence of one sire on subsequent offspring born by the same mother to other sires. (tuh LEG uh nee)

telegram [*tele, distant + gram, to write*] A message transmitted by telegraph and usually delivered in person. (TEL uh gram')

telegraph [*tele, distant + graph, writing*] A device for sending coded messages to a distant location using electric impulses. (TEL uh graf')

telekinesis [*tele, distant + kine, motion + -sis*] The alleged ability to cause movement of an object without the use of physical force, as by psychic forces. See psychokinesis. (tel' uh kih NEE sis)

telemetry [*tele, distant + -metry, science of measuring*] The scientific measurement and transmission of data from a remote source to a receiving station for recording and analysis. (tuh LEM ih tree)

telencephalon [*tel, end + encephal, brain + -on*] The anterior portion of the prosencephalon from which the cerebrum develops. See diencephalon and prosencephalon. (tel' en SEF uh lon')

teleology [*tele, end + -ology, study of*] 1.The branch of cosmology dealing with the study of final causes. 2.The doctrine that attributes purpose or design to natural phenomena in the material world. See dysteleology. (tel' ee OL uh jee)

teleost [*tele, complete + oste, bone*] Any of a group of mostly modern fishes with consolidated internal bony skeletons. (TEL ee ost')

telepathy [*tele, distant + -pathy, feeling*] The alleged communication between minds by supernatural means, as by extrasensory perception. See precognition and telegnosis. (tuh LEP uh thee)

telephone [*tele, distant + -phone, voice*] A device for transmitting and receiving speech sounds or other data from a distant location. (TEL uh fohn')

telephoto [*tele, distant & photo(graphy)*] Pertaining to a camera lens that produces a magnified image of a distant object. (tel' uh FOHT oh)

telephotography [*tele, distant & photography*] 1.The art or technique of photographing distant objects with the aid of a telephoto lens. 2.The process of transmitting text or graphics, as by radio waves or telephone lines. Facsimile. (tel' uh fuh TOG ruh fee)

telescope [*tele, distant + -scope, to view*] An optical instrument for viewing celestial bodies and other objects at great distances. (TEL uh skohp')

telesis [*tele, end + -sis*] The attainment of desired goals through intelligent planning and the skilled use of social and natural processes. (TEL uh sis)

telesthesia [*tel, distant + esthes, sensation + -ia*] The alleged ability to sense things that would normally be beyond the range of the senses. (tel' es THEE zhuh)

telestich [*tele, end & stich {line of verse}*] A poem in which the final letters of successive lines form a word, phrase, or message. See acrostic. (tuh LES tik)

teletypewriter [*tele, distant & typewriter*] An electromechanical typewriter for transmitting and receiving messages over telephone lines. (tel' uh TEYEP reye' ter)

teleutospore [*tele, end & spore*] A thick-walled, blackish spore that develops during the terminal stage in the life cycle of the rust fungus. Same as teliospore. (tuh LOOT uh spor')

television [*tele, distant & vision*] The transmission of visible images electronically to a receiver that converts the electric signals into images on a picture tube or screen. (TEL uh vih' zhun)

telic [*tel, end + -ic*] Directed toward a particular end or purpose. (TEL ik)

teliospore [*tel, end & spore*] A thick-walled, blackish spore that develops during the terminal stage in the life cycle of the rust fungus. (TEE lee uh spor')

telocentric [*telo, end + centr, center + -ic*] Pertaining to a chromosome with the centromere at one end. See acrocentric. (tel' uh SEN trik)

telodynamic [*telo, distant + dynam, power + -ic*] Pertaining to the transmission of power over a distance, specifically mechanical power by cables and pulleys. (tel' uh deye NAM ik)

telomere [*telo, end + -mere, part*] Either of the two extremities of a chromosome. (TEL uh mihr')

telophase [*telo, end & phase*] In mitosis, the fourth and final phase during which the cell divides and a nucleus is formed around each group of daughter chromosomes. See prophase, metaphase, and anaphase. (TEL uh fayz')

the, theo   God

apotheosis [*apo-, from + theo, god + -sis*] 1.The elevating of a human being to the status of a god. Deification. 2.A glorified ideal. (uh poth' ee OH sis)

atheist [*a-, not + the, God + -ist*] One who believes there is no God. See agnostic and infidel (def. 1). (AY thee ist)

henotheism [*heno, one + the, god + -ism*] Belief in or adoption of one particular god without denying the existence of others. (HEN uh thee' iz' um)

monotheism [*mono-, one + the, God + -ism*] The belief in only one God. (MON uh thee iz' um)

pantheism [*pan, all* + *the, God* + *-ism*] 1.The doctrine that identifies God with the laws and forces of nature. 2.Toleration and worship of all the gods. (PAN thee iz' um)

pantheon [*pan, all* + *the, god* + *-on*] 1.A temple built in Rome in 27 B.C. for all the gods. 2.A temple for all the gods. 3.A building containing memorials or tombs of a nation's celebrated dead. (PAN thee on')

polytheism [*poly, many* + *the, god* + *-ism*] The belief in more than one god. (POL ee thee iz' um)

thearchy [*the, god* + *arch, rule* + *-y*] Rule by a god or gods. (THEE ahr' kee)

theism [*the, God* + *-ism*] 1.Belief in the existence of a god or gods. 2.Belief in God as the Creator and Supreme Ruler of the universe. (THEE iz' um)

theocentric [*theo, God* + *centr, center* + *-ic*] Having God as the center of interest and concern. (thee' oh SEN trik)

theocracy [*theo, God* + *-cracy, government*] A government by persons claiming to be representatives of God or a god. See hagiocracy. (thee OK ruh see)

theodicy [*theo, God* + *Grk > dike, justice* + *-y*] A vindication of divine justice while allowing for the existence of evil. (thee OD uh see)

theogony [*theo, god* + *-gony, origination*] An account of the origin and genealogy of the gods. (thee OG uh nee)

theology [*the, God* + *-ology, study of*] The study and interpretation of religion, especially Christianity. (thee OL uh jee)

theomachy [*theo, god* + *-machy, struggle*] Battle with or among the gods. (thee OM uh kee)

theomorphic [*theo, God* + *morph, form* + *-ic*] Having the form or appearance of a god or of God. (thee' oh MOR fik)

theonomous [*theo, God* + *nom, system of laws* + *-ous*] Governed or controlled by God. (thee ON uh mus)

theophany [*theo, God* + *phan, to appear* + *-y*] An appearance of God or a deity to a person. (thee OF uh nee)

theophobia [*theo, God* + *-phobia, fear*] Abnormal fear of the wrath of God. (thee' oh FOH bee uh)

theosophy [*theo, God* + *-sophy, wisdom*] 1.A religious philosophy claiming mystical insight into the divine nature. 2.The philosophy and beliefs of the Theosophical Society, which adhere chiefly to Buddhist and Hindu philosophies and were introduced into the United States in 1875. (thee OS uh fee)

tritheism [*tri-, three* + *the, god* + *-ism*] Belief in three gods; specifically, the belief that the Father, Son, and Holy Ghost are three separate and distinct gods. (TREYE thee iz' um)

therm/o   heat, temperature

aerothermodynamics [*aero, air* + *thermo, heat* + *dynam, energy* + *-ics, study of*] The branch of dynamics dealing with the study of the relationship between heat and mechanical energy in air and other gases. See thermodynamics. (ehr' oh thur' moh deye NAM iks)

bathythermograph [*bathy, deep* + *thermo, heat* + *graph, recording*] An instrument for recording water temperature relative to depth. (bath' uh THUR muh graf')

British thermal unit The amount of heat required to raise the temperature of a pound of water one degree Fahrenheit. (BRIT ish THUR mul YOO nit)

diathermy [*dia-, through* + *therm, heat* + *-y*] The use of high-frequency sound, high-frequency current, or microwaves to produce heat in body tissue for medical treatment and therapy. (DEYE uh thur' mee)

ectotherm [*ecto-, outside* + *therm, temperature*] A cold-blooded animal, such as a fish or reptile, whose body temperature varies with the environment. Same as poikilotherm. (EK tuh thurm')

electrothermal [*electro, electricity* + *therm, heat* + *-al*] Pertaining to the production of heat from electricity. (ih lek' troh THUR mul)

endotherm [*endo-, inside* + *therm, temperature*] A warm-blooded animal, such as a bird or mammal, whose body temperature remains relatively constant. Same as homoiotherm. (EN duh thurm')

endothermic [*endo-, inside* + *therm, heat* + *-ic*] Pertaining to a chemical reaction that causes the absorption of heat. See exothermic. (en' doh THUR mik)

eurytherm [*eury, wide* + *therm, temperature*] An organism capable of existing in a wide range of environmental temperatures. Opposed to stenotherm. (YOOR uh thurm')

exothermic [*exo-, outside* + *therm, heat* + *-ic*] Pertaining to a chemical reaction that causes the liberation of heat, as combustion. See endothermic. (eks' oh THUR mik)

geothermal [*geo, earth* + *therm, heat* + *-al*] Pertaining to heat generated in the interior of the earth. (jee' oh THUR mul)

homoiotherm [*homoio, same* + *therm, temperature*] A warm-blooded animal, such as a bird or mammal, whose body temperature remains relatively constant. See poikilotherm. (hoh MOI uh thurm')

homoiothermic [*homoio, same* + *therm, temperature* + *-ic*] Warm-blooded. See poikilothermic. (hoh moi' uh THUR mik)

hydrothermal [*hydro, water* + *therm, heat* + *-al*] Pertaining to hot water on or beneath the surface of the earth. (heye' druh THUR mul)

hyperthermia [*hyper-, above* + *therm, temperature* + *-ia*] Abnormally high body temperature, sometimes induced for treatment of illness or disease. See hypothermia. (heye' per THUR mee uh)

hypothermia [*hypo-, below* + *therm, temperature* + *-ia*] Abnormally low body temperature. See hyperthermia. (heye' puh THUR mee uh)

isotherm [*iso-, equal* + *therm, temperature*] A line on a map connecting points with equal average temperature for a given time period or equal temperature at a given time. (EYE suh thurm')

isothermal [*iso-, equal* + *therm, temperature* + *-al*] Having equal or constant temperature. (eye' suh THUR mul)

poikilotherm [*Grk > poikilos, varying* + *therm, temperature*] A cold-blooded animal, such as a fish or reptile, whose body temperature varies with the environment. See homoiotherm. (poi KEE luh thurm')

poikilothermic [*Grk > poikilos, varying* + *therm, temperature* + *-ic*] Cold-blooded. See homoiothermic. (poi KEE luh thur' mik)

stenotherm [*steno, narrow* + *therm, temperature*] An organism capable of existing only in a narrow range of environmental temperatures. Opposed to eurytherm. (STEN uh thurm')

therm [*therm, heat*] A unit of heat equal to 100,000 British Thermal Units. (thurm)

thermae [*therm, heat* + *-ae*] Public baths or hot springs, especially those of the ancient Romans. (THUR mee)

thermal [*therm, heat* + *-al*] 1.Pertaining to or resulting from heat. 2.A rising column of warm air. (THUR mul)

thermal barrier [*therm, heat* + *-al* & *barrier*] The speed limitation imposed on an aircraft by aerodynamic overheating. (THUR mul BEHR ee ur)

thermal pollution [*therm, heat* + *-al* & *pollution*] The release of heated fluid into a body of water, resulting in an increased water temperature harmful to the environment. (THUR mul puh LOO shun)

thermic [*therm, heat* + *-ic*] Pertaining to or resulting from heat. Same as thermal (def. 1). (THUR mik)

thermion [*therm, heat* & *ion {electrically charged particle}*] An ion emitted by a heated substance. (THUR meye' un)

thermionics [*thermion* & *-ics, study of*] The scientific study of thermionic phenomena. See thermion. (thur' meye ON iks)

thermistor [*therm, heat* & *(res)istor*] A resistor whose electrical resistance changes with temperature. (thur MIS tur)

thermochemistry [*thermo, heat* & *chemistry*] The branch of chemistry dealing with the study of the relationships between chemical reactions and heat. (thur' moh KEM ih stree)

thermocline [*thermo, temperature* + *-cline, slope*] A layer in a body of water in which the temperature-decrease, as a function of depth, is larger than that of the water below or above it. (THUR muh kleyen')

thermocouple [*thermo, heat* & *couple*] A device for measuring temperature that uses two dissimilar metal conductors connected at both ends so that a voltage measurement taken across the two junctions indicates the difference in temperature between them. (THUR muh kup' ul)

thermoduric [*thermo, heat* + *Ltn > durare, to last* + *-ic*] Able to exist in high temperatures, as certain microorganisms. (thur' moh DUR ik)

thermodynamics [*thermo, heat* + *dynam, energy* + *-ics, study of*] The branch of physics dealing with the study of the relationships between heat and other forms of energy. See aerothermodynamics. (thur' moh deye NAM iks)

thermoelectricity [*thermo, heat* & *electricity*] Electricity produced by heat, as in the thermojunction of a thermocouple. (thur' moh ih lek' TRIS ih tee)

thermoelectron [*thermo, heat* & *electron*] An electron emitted from a substance by the action of heat. (thur' moh ih LEK tron)

thermogenesis [*thermo, heat* + *-genesis, production*] Heat production, especially by oxidation within a human or animal body. (thur' moh JEN uh sis)

thermograph [*thermo, temperature* + *graph, recording*] An instrument for graphically recording variations in temperature. (THUR muh graf')

thermography [*thermo, heat* + *-graphy, writing*] A printing process that produces raised lettering by heating the printed material after dusting it with powder. (thur MOG ruh fee)

thermojunction [*thermo, heat* & *junction*] The junction between the two dissimilar metal conductors of a thermocouple. (thur' moh JUNGK shun)

thermolabile [*thermo, heat* & *labile {subject to change}*] Pertaining to substances that are adversely affected by heat. See thermostable. (thur' moh LAY bul)

thermoluminescence [*thermo, heat* + *Ltn > lumen, light* + *-escence*] Any luminescence of a substance when heated. (thur' moh loo' muh NES ens)

thermolysis [*thermo, heat* + *-lysis, decomposition*] 1.The decomposition of compounds by heat. See pyrolysis. 2.The dissipation of body heat. (thur MOL uh sis)

thermomagnetic [*thermo, heat* & *magnetic*] Pertaining to magnetism that is changed or generated by the action of heat. (thur' moh mag NET ik)

thermometer [*thermo, heat* + *meter, to measure*] An instrument for measuring temperature. (thur MOM et er)

thermomotor [*thermo, heat* & *motor*] A motor that runs on heat. (thur' moh MOHT ur)

thermonuclear [*thermo, heat* & *nuclear*] Pertaining to nuclear reactions that occur at very high temperatures. (thur' moh NOO klee ur)

thermophile [*thermo, heat* + *-phile, a natural liking*] An organism requiring high temperatures for normal development. (THUR muh feyel')

thermoplastic [*thermo, heat* + *plast, to form* + *-ic*] Pertaining to substances that become hard when cooled and soft and pliable when heated. (thur' moh PLAS tik)

thermoreceptor [*thermo, temperature* & *receptor*] A sensory receptor that is sensitive to heat. (thur' moh rih SEP tur)

thermoregulation [*thermo, temperature* & *regulation*] The regulation and control of temperature, specifically internal body temperature. (thur' moh reg' yuh LAY shun)

thermos [*therm, temperature* + *-os*] A device, as a bottle or flask, designed to maintain the temperature of its contents. (THUR mus)

thermoscope [*thermo, temperature* + *-scope, to observe*] An instrument for detecting temperature changes in a substance by observing corresponding volume changes. (THUR muh skohp')

thermosetting [*thermo, heat* & *setting*] Pertaining to plastics that harden permanently when heated. (THUR moh set' ing)

thermosphere [*thermo, temperature* & *sphere*] An atmospheric zone, located 50 to 300 miles above the earth, characterized by notably rising temperature with increasing altitude. (THUR muh sfihr')

thermostable [*thermo, heat* & *stable*] Pertaining to substances that are not adversely affected by heat. See thermolabile. (thur' moh STAY bul)

thermostat [*thermo, temperature* + *stat, stationary*] A device for automatically maintaining a preset temperature. (THUR muh stat')

thermotaxis [*thermo, heat* & *taxis*] 1.The movement of a freely moving organism in response to heat. See thermotropism. 2.The normal regulation of body temperature. (thur' moh TAK sis)

thermotropism [*thermo, heat* + *trop, responding to a stimulus* + *-ism*] The movement or growth of an organism or part in response to heat. See thermotaxis (def. 1). (thur MOT ruh piz' um)

211

therm/o

xerothermic [*xero, dry + therm, heat + -ic*] Characterized by dryness and heat. (zihr' uh THUR mik)

tract   draw, pull

abstract [*abs-, away + tract, draw*] 1.Thought of as being apart from existing realities, material objects, or concrete examples. 2.Difficult to understand. (ab STRAKT)

attract [*at-, to + tract, draw*] 1.To cause to draw to or adhere. 2.To draw by appealing to emotions, interests, admiration, etc. (uh TRAKT)

contract [*con-, together + tract, draw*] 1.A binding agreement between two or more parties. (KON trakt {noun}) 2.To draw together so as to make smaller or shorten. (kun TRAKT {verb})

detract [*de-, down + tract, draw*] To diminish in value or importance. (dih TRAKT)

distract [*dis-, away + tract, draw*] To divert or draw away from the original focus of attention or interest. (dis TRAKT)

extract [*ex-, out + tract, draw*] To draw out or remove. (eks TRAKT)

intractable [*in-, not + tract, draw + -able*] 1.Not easily controlled or managed. Stubborn. 2.Not easily worked or handled. 3.Not easily treated or cured. See tractable. (in TRAK tuh bul)

protract [*pro-, forward + tract, draw*] To draw out or extend in time or space. Prolong. Lengthen. (proh TRAKT)

retract [*re-, back + tract, draw*] 1.To draw back or in. 2.To take back or withdraw, as an offer, statement, etc. See revoke. (rih TRAKT)

subtract [*sub-, beneath + tract, draw*] 1.To take away, as a portion from a whole. 2.To deduct one quantity or number from another. (sub TRAKT)

tractable [*tract, draw + -able*] 1.Easily controlled or managed. Docile. 2.Easily worked or handled. Malleable. See intractable. (TRAK tuh bul)

traction [*tract, pull + -ion*] 1.The act or condition of drawing or pulling. 2.The friction created by a body moving on a surface. (TRAK shun)

tractor [*tract, pull + -or*] 1.A vehicle used for pulling farm equipment. 2.A vehicle with a short chassis used for pulling vans and trailers. (TRAK tur)

troph/o, -trophy   nourishment

atrophy [*a-, without + -trophy, nourishment*] A wasting away or failure to properly develop due to insufficient nutrition, as of organs, tissues, or other body parts. (AT ruh fee)

autotroph [*auto-, self + troph, nourishment*] An organism that produces its own food by using inorganic materials and either photosynthesis or chemosynthesis, as most plants and certain bacteria. See heterotroph. (AWT uh trof')

chemoautotrophic [*chemo, chemical & autotrophic*] Pertaining to an organism that produces its own food using inorganic materials and chemosynthesis, as certain bacteria. See photoautotrophic and autotroph. (kee' moh ot' uh TROF ik)

dystrophy [*dys-, bad + -trophy, nourishment*] Any disorder caused by faulty or inadequate nutrition of a tissue or organ, as muscular dystrophy. (DIS truh fee)

eutrophic [*eu-, good + troph, nourishment + -ic*] Pertaining to a body of water rich in nutrients for supporting plant life, but deficient in oxygen for supporting animal life. See oligotrophic. (yoo TROF ik)

heterotroph [*hetero, other + troph, nourishment*] An organism, as all animals, some bacteria, and certain plants, that depends, either directly or indirectly, on other organisms for food due to its inability to manufacture proteins and carbohydrates from inorganic sources. See autotroph. (HET ur uh trof')

hypertrophy [*hyper-, excessive + -trophy, nourishment*] A usually abnormal enlargement of an organ or body part due to an increase in cell size rather than cell number. (heye PER truh fee)

muscular dystrophy [*muscular & dys-, bad + -trophy, nourishment*] A group of chronic muscle diseases of genetic or unknown origin that cause irreversible muscle deterioration and may result in complete incapacitation. (MUS kyuh lur DIS truh fee)

oligotrophic [*oligo, deficiency + troph, nourishment + -ic*] Pertaining to a body of water deficient in nutrients for supporting plant life, but rich in oxygen for supporting animal life. See eutrophic. (ol' ih goh TROF ik)

photoautotrophic [*photo, light & autotrophic*] Pertaining to an organism that produces its own food using inorganic materials and photosynthesis, as most plants. See chemoautotrophic and autotroph. (foht' oh ot' uh TROF ik)

polytrophic [*poly, many + troph, nourishment + -ic*] Obtaining nourishment from a variety of organic material, as certain bacteria. (pol' ee TROF ik)

prototrophic [*proto-, first + troph, nourishment + -ic*] Pertaining to bacteria with the same nutritional requirements as that of the normal wild type. (proht' uh TROF ik)

trophallaxis [*troph, nourishment + Grk > allaxis, exchange*] The exchange of food substances among members of a colony of social insects, as ants, bees, and termites. (trof' uh LAK sis)

trophic [*troph, nourishment + -ic*] Pertaining to or involving nutrition. (TROF ik)

trophoblast [*tropho, nourishment + blast, cell layer*] The cell layer that forms the outer wall of the blastocyst. It supplies the embryo with nutrients and aids in implanting the embryo in the uterine wall. (TROF uh blast')

trophozoite [*tropho, nourishment + zo, animal + -ite*] In the class Sporozoa, a protozoan that is in the vegetative stage, as contrasted with the reproductive stage. (trof' uh ZOH eyet')

trop/o, -tropy
turning, changing, figure of speech, responding to a stimulus

allotropy [*allo, variation + -tropy, changing*] The property exhibited by certain elements and other substances of existing in more than one form, such as carbon in graphite and diamond. (uh LOT ruh pee)

anatropous [*ana-, back* + *trop, turning* + *-ous*] In the ovary of an angiosperm, having the ovule inverted so that the micropyle lies near the base of the stalk. See orthotropous and campylotropous. (uh NAT ruh pus)

anisotropic [*aniso-, not equal* + *trop, responding to a stimulus* + *-ic*] 1.Having unequal responses to external stimuli. 2.Having properties that vary depending on the direction of measurement. See isotropic. (an eye' suh TROP ik)

apotropaic [*apo-, away* + *trop, turning* + *-ic*] Designed to ward off evil, as a symbol or ritual. (ap' uh troh PAY ik)

campylotropous [*Grk > kampulos, bent* + *trop, turning* + *-ous*] In the ovary of an angiosperm, having the ovule partially inverted so that the micropyle lies horizontal in relation to the stalk. See orthotropous and anatropous. (kam' puh LOT ruh pus)

chemotropism [*chemo, chemical* + *trop, responding to a stimulus* + *-ism*] The movement or growth of an organism or part in response to a chemical stimulus. See chemotaxis. (kih MOT ruh piz' um)

diageotropism [*dia-, through* + *geo, earth* + *trop, turning* + *-ism*] The tendency of certain plants or plant parts to grow or orient themselves at right angles to the direction of the earth's gravitational force. See diatropism. (deye' uh jee OT ruh piz' um)

diatropism [*dia-, through* + *trop, turning* + *-ism*] The tendency of certain plants or plant parts to grow or orient themselves at right angles to the force of a stimulus. See diageotropism. (deye AT ruh piz' um)

entropy [*en-, in* + *-tropy, changing*] 1.A measure of the amount of thermal energy in a thermodynamic system that is unavailable for mechanical work. 2.A measure of the amount of data loss in a transmitted message. See isentropic. (EN truh pee)

esotropia [*eso-, in* + *trop, turning* + *-ia*] A visual condition in which one eye turns inward, resulting in diplopia. Opposed to exotropia. See diplopia. (es' uh TROH pee uh)

exotropia [*exo-, out* + *trop, turning* + *-ia*] A visual condition in which one eye turns outward, resulting in diplopia. Opposed to esotropia. See diplopia. (eks' oh TROH pee uh)

geotropism [*geo, earth* + *trop, responding to a stimulus* + *-ism*] Any growth or movement of an organism in response to the earth's gravity. See geotaxis. (jee OT ruh piz' um)

heliotrope [*helio, sun* + *trop, turning*] 1.A plant with small, fragrant, white or purple flowers. 2.A plant whose stem or flowers turn toward the sun. See helianthus. (HEE lee uh trohp')

heliotropism [*helio, sun* + *trop, responding to a stimulus* + *-ism*] The movement or growth of an organism or part, especially a plant or plant part, in response to sunlight. See heliotaxis and phototropism. (hee' lee OT ruh piz' um)

hydrotropism [*hydro, water* + *trop, responding to a stimulus* + *-ism*] The movement or growth of an organism or part in response to moisture, as the root of a plant. See hydrotaxis. (heye DROT ruh piz' um)

inotropic [*Grk > ino, tendon* + *trop, changing* + *-ic*] Affecting muscular contraction, either positively or negatively. (ee' nuh TROP ik)

isentropic [*iso-, equal & entrop(y) & -ic*] Having constant or equal entropy. See entropy. (eye' sen TROP ik)

isotropic [*iso-, equal* + *trop, turning* + *-ic*] Having properties that are equal regardless of the direction of measurement. See anisotropic (def. 2). (eye' suh TROP ik)

lipotropic [*lipo, fat* + *trop, changing* + *-ic*] Preventing or correcting the accumulation of excess fat in the liver. (lip' oh TROP ik)

neurotropic [*neuro, nerve* + *trop, turning* + *-ic*] Having a natural attraction to nerve tissue, as certain toxins or viruses. See neurotoxin. (noor' oh TROP ik)

nyctitropism [*nycti, night* + *trop, turning* + *-ism*] The propensity of the leaves of certain plants to change positions at night. (nik TIT ruh piz' um)

organotropism [*organ & trop, turning* + *-ism*] The attraction of certain microorganisms, chemicals, toxins, etc., to specific organs or tissues of the body. (or' guh NOT ruh piz' um)

orthotropic [*ortho, vertical* + *trop, turning* + *-ic*] Exhibiting vertical growth, as some plants and plant parts. (or' thuh TROP ik)

orthotropous [*ortho, vertical* + *trop, turning* + *-ous*] In the ovary of an angiosperm, having the ovule vertical so that the micropyle lies in a straight line with and directly opposite the stalk. See campylotropous and anatropous. (or THOT ruh pus)

phototropism [*photo, light* + *trop, responding to a stimulus* + *-ism*] The movement or growth of an organism or part in response to light. See phototaxis, heliotropism, and photokinesis. (foh TOT ruh piz' um)

psychotropic [*psycho, mind* + *trop, changing* + *-ic*] Capable of affecting the mind, as certain drugs used to treat mental disorders. (seye' koh TROP ik)

stereotropism [*stereo-, solid* + *trop, responding to a stimulus* + *-ism*] The movement or growth of an organism or part in response to contact with a solid body. Same as thigmotropism. (stehr' ee OT ruh piz' um)

thermotropism [*thermo, heat* + *trop, responding to a stimulus* + *-ism*] The movement or growth of an organism or part in response to heat. See thermotaxis (def. 1). (thur MOT ruh piz' um)

thigmotropism [*Grk > thigma, touch* + *trop, responding to a stimulus* + *-ism*] The movement or growth of an organism or part in response to contact with a solid body. See stereotaxis. (thig MOT ruh piz' um)

thixotropy [*Grk > thixis, to touch* + *-tropy, changing*] The property of certain gels of liquefying when agitated. (thik SOT ruh pee)

trope [*trop, figure of speech*] 1.The figurative use of a word or phrase. 2.Figure of speech. See tropology (def. 1). (trohp)

tropism [*trop, responding to a stimulus* + *-ism*] The movement or growth of an organism or part in response to an external stimulus. See taxis (def. 1). (TROH piz' um)

tropology [*tropo, figure of speech* + *log, discourse* + *-y*] 1.The figurative use of words in speech or writing. See trope. 2.The interpretation of the Scriptures in a figurative sense rather than a literal sense. (troh POL uh jee)

tropopause [*tropo(sphere) & pause*] The outermost boundary of the troposphere. See stratopause and mesopause. (TROP uh poz')

trop/o, -tropy

tropophilous [*tropo, changing + phil, a natural liking + -ous*] Thriving in a region marked by extreme seasonal climatic changes, as certain plants. See tropophyte. (troh POF uh lus)

tropophyte [*tropo, changing + -phyte, plant*] A plant capable of adapting to changing climatic conditions such as temperature or moisture. See tropophilous. (TROP uh feyet')

troposphere [*tropo, changing & sphere*] An atmospheric zone, located 0 to 7 miles above the earth, characterized by cloud formation, weather conditions, and a rapid decrease in temperature with increasing altitude. (TROP uh sfihr')

vagotropic [*vag(us) & trop, changing + -ic*] Affecting the vagus nerve. (vay' guh TROP ik)

volv, volu, volut　　roll, turn

circumvolution [*circum-, around + volu, turn + -tion*] The act of turning or winding about an axis. See vertiginous (def. 2). (sur' kum vuh LOO shun)

coevolution [*co-, together & evolution*] Evolution involving changes in two or more ecologically interdependent species in relation to each other. See evolve. (koh' ev' uh LOO shun)

convoluted [*con-, together + volut, turn + -ed*] 1.Twisted together or coiled. 2.Complicated. Intricate. (KON vuh loot' id)

convolution [*con-, together + volu, turn + -tion*] 1.A twist, coil, or fold. 2.One of the convoluted ridges on the surface of the brain caused by infolding of the cerebral cortex. Same as gyrus. (kon' vuh LOO shun)

convolve [*con-, together + volv, turn*] To twist or roll together. (kun VOLV)

convolvulus [*con-, together + volv, turn + -ulus*] Any of various erect, trailing, or twining plants of the morning glory family. (kun VOL vyuh lus)

devolve [*de-, down + volv, roll*] 1.To pass down through successive stages. 2.To transfer from one person to another. (dih VOLV)

evolute [*e-, out + volut, roll*] The locus of the centers of curvature of a curve known as the involute. See involute (def. 3). (EV uh loot')

evolution [*e-, out + volut, roll + -ion*] A gradual process of developmental change into a different and usually more complex form. See evolve. (ev' uh LOO shun)

evolve [*e-, out + volv, roll*] To develop gradually. (ih VOLV)

involucre [*in-, in + volu, roll + -crum*] A ring of bracts around the base of a flower, flower cluster, or fruit. (in' vuh LOO kur)

involute [*in-, in + volut, roll*] 1.Complex. Intricate. Convoluted. 2.Rolled inward along the edges, as a leaf. See revolute. 3.Any curve of which a given curve is the evolute. See evolute. (IN vuh loot')

involve [*in-, in + volv, roll*] To include. Engage. (in VOLV)

macroevolution [*macro-, large & evolution*] Large-scale and long-range evolution of organisms, resulting in relatively large and complex changes. See evolve and microevolution. (mak' roh ev' uh LOO shun)

microevolution [*micro-, small & evolution*] Small-scale and short-range evolution of organisms. See evolve and macroevolution. (meye' kroh ev' uh LOO shun)

revolute [*re-, back + volut, roll*] Rolled backward or downward, as the tips or margins of certain leaves. See involute (def. 2). (REV uh loot')

revolution [*re-, again + volu, turn + -tion*] 1.One cycle around an axis or center. 2.A sudden or radical change in a situation. 3.The overthrow of a government. (rev' uh LOO shun)

revolve [*re-, again + volv, turn*] 1.To turn around on, or as if on, an axis. 2.To consider carefully. (rih VOLV)

revolver [*re-, again + volv, turn + -er*] A handgun with a revolving cylinder that has several cartridge chambers, allowing it to be fired repeatedly. (rih VOL vur)

voluble [*volu, roll + -ble*] 1.Characterized by smooth and rapid speech. Fluent. Glib. 2.Talkative. See loquacious. 3.Twining or twisting, as certain plants. (VOL yuh bul)

volume [*volu, roll + -men*] 1.Originally, a scroll. 2.A collection of written or printed sheets bound together to form a book, which is usually one of a complete set. 3.The space occupied within three dimensions. (VOL yoom)

volumeter [*volu(me) & meter, to measure*] An instrument for measuring the volume of liquids, gases, or solids. (VOL yoo mee' ter)

voluminous [*volu, roll + -men + -ous*] 1.Capable of filling volumes. 2.Prolific in speech or writing. 3.Having many coils, folds, or windings. (vuh LOO muh nus)

volute [*volut, turn*] 1.Having a spiral or twisted form. 2.A spiral, scroll-shaped architectural ornament. 3.One of the whorls of a spiral shell. (vuh LOOT)

volvox [*volv, roll + -ox*] Any of various flagellated green algae that form hollow, spherical, multicellular colonies. (VOL voks)

volvulus [*volv, turn + -ulus*] An obstruction caused by abnormal twisting of the intestine upon itself. (VOL vyuh lus)

vers, vert　　turn

adversary [*ad-, toward + vers, turn + -ary*] An opponent. Enemy. (AD vur sehr' ee)

adverse [*ad-, toward + vers, turn*] 1.Not helping or favoring. See inimical (def. 2). 2.Acting in an opposing direction. 3.Turning toward the main stem or axis. See averse (def. 2). (ad VURS)

adversity [*ad-, toward + vers, turn + -ity*] A condition or experience of affliction or hardship. Misfortune. (ad VUR sih tee)

advert [*ad-, toward + vert, turn*] To refer or direct attention in speaking or writing. (ad VURT)

advertent [*ad-, toward + vert, turn + -ent*] Attentive. Heedful. See inadvertent (def. 1). (ad VURT nt)

advertise [*ad-, toward + vert, turn + -ise*] To announce publicly, especially to encourage sales. (AD vur teyez')

ambivert [*ambi-, both + vert, turn*] A person with personality characteristics of both an introvert and an extrovert. See introvert and extrovert. (AM bih vurt')

animadversion [*anim, mind + ad-, to + vers, turn + -ion*] 1.A critical comment or remark. 2.Strong and unfriendly criticism. (an' uh mad VUR zhun)

anniversary [*ann, year + vers, turn + -ary*] The yearly recurrence of a past event, as the date of a wedding. (an' uh VUR suh ree)

averse [*ab-, from* + *vers, turn*] 1.Having a strong feeling of dislike, distaste, opposition, etc. See antipathy. 2.Turning away from the main stem or axis. See adverse (def. 3). (uh VURS)

avert [*ab-, from* + *vert, turn*] 1.Turn away. 2.To ward off or prevent from happening. Avoid. (uh VURT)

bouleversement [*French > bouleverser, to overturn* + *-ment*] 1.A violent disturbance. Convulsion. Confusion. 2.A reversal. (bool' vurs MON)

controversy [*contra-, against* + *vers, turn* + *-y*] An often long and heated dispute between sides holding opposing views. (KON truh vur' see)

convert [*con-, together* + *vert, turn*] To change from one form, belief, party, etc., to another. (kun VURT)

diverse [*dis-, away* + *vers, turn*] Differing in kind, form, or quality. Not alike. (dih VURS)

divert [*dis-, away* + *vert, turn*] 1.To change from one use or course to another. 2.To amuse. Entertain. (dih VURT)

divorce [*dis-, away* + *vert, turn*] 1.The legal ending of a marriage. 2.Any complete disunion or separation. (dih VORS)

evert [*e-, out* + *vert, turn*] Turn outward or inside out. (ih VURT)

extravert [*extra-, outside* + *vert, turn*] A person who directs his interests, thoughts, and feelings primarily outside himself. Same as extrovert. (EKS truh vurt')

extrorse [*extro-, outside* + *vers, turn*] Turned outward or away from the axis. Opposed to introrse. (eks TRORS)

extrovert [*extro-, outside* + *vert, turn*] A person who directs his interests, thoughts, and feelings primarily outside himself. Opposed to introvert. See ambivert. (EKS truh vurt')

inadvertent [*in-, not & advertent*] 1.Not attentive. Heedless. 2.Unintentional. Accidental. See advertent. (in' uhd VURT nt)

introrse [*intro-, inward* + *vers, turn*] Turned inward or toward the axis. Opposed to extrorse. (in TRORS)

introvert [*intro-, inward* + *vert, turn*] A person who directs his interests, thoughts, and feelings primarily upon himself. Opposed to extrovert. See ambivert. (IN truh vurt')

inverse [*in-, in* + *vers, turn*] Reversed in position, relation, nature, or effect. (in VURS)

invert [*in-, in* + *vert, turn*] 1.Turn inside out or upside down. 2.To reverse the position, direction, or condition of. See reverse. (in VURT)

malversation [*mal-, bad* + *vers, turn* + *-ation*] Corrupt or improper conduct in a trusted position, especially in public office. See malfeasance. (mal' vur SAY shun)

obverse [*ob-, toward* + *vers, turn*] 1.Turned toward the observer or opponent. 2.Having the base narrower than the top, as most leaves. 3.Being a counterpart or complement. (ob VURS)

obvert [*ob-, toward* + *vert, turn*] Turn so as to show another side. (ob VURT)

perverse [*per-, wrong* + *vers, turn*] 1.Turned against what is right or sensible. 2.Persistent or obstinate in error. Stubborn. 3.Morally wrong or bad. Corrupt. Wicked. (per VURS)

pervert [*per-, wrong* + *vert, turn*] A person affected with perversion, especially sexual perversion. (PER vurt)

retrorse [*retro-, backward* + *vers, turn*] Turned or directed backward or downward. (rih TRORS)

retroversion [*retro-, backward* + *vers, turn* + *-ion*] 1.A tilting or turning backward. 2.The tilting or turning of an organ, especially the uterus. (ret' roh VUR zhun)

reverse [*re-, back* + *vers, turn*] 1.Turned backward in position, direction, or order. 2.Operating, acting, or arranged contrary to the normal. 3.Change to a former or opposite position or condition. See invert. (rih VURS)

revert [*re-, back* + *vert, turn*] 1.To return to a former practice, belief, or condition. 2.To return to the prior owner or to his or her heirs. (rih VURT)

subvert [*sub-, under* + *vert, turn*] 1.To cause the downfall or destruction of. Ruin. 2.To undermine the principles, morals, or allegiance of. Corrupt. (sub VURT)

tergiversate [*Ltn > tergum, back* + *vers, turn* + *-ate*] 1.To use ambiguities or evasions. Equivocate. See equivocate. 2.To change sides with respect to one's principles, religion, cause, etc. Apostatize. See apostasy. (tur JIV ur sayt')

transverse [*trans-, across* + *vers, turn*] Lying or situated across. Set crosswise. (trans VURS)

traverse [*trans-, across* + *vers, turn*] To travel over, along, or through. (truh VURS)

universe [*uni-, one* + *vers, turn*] 1.The totality of all things observed or postulated. 2.The world or sphere in which something exists. (YOO nuh vurs')

university [*univers(e) & -ity*] An institution of higher learning that offers degrees in specialized fields as well as the arts and sciences. (yoo' nuh VUR sih tee)

vers libre [*vers(e) & French > libre, free*] Free verse. (vehr LEE bruh)

versant [*vers, turn* + *-ant*] 1.The slope of a mountain or mountain range. 2.The general slope of a region. (VUR sunt)

versatile [*vers, turn* + *-ile*] 1.Able to do many things well. 2.Having many uses. (VUR suh tul)

verse [*vers, turn*] 1.A line of metrical composition. A line of poetry. 2.One of the short divisions of a chapter in the Bible. (vurs)

versicle [*vers(e) & -cle, small*] 1.A short verse or sentence, usually from the Psalms, used especially in antiphonal prayer. 2.A short verse. (VUR sih kul)

versicolor [*vers, turn & color*] 1.Having a variety of colors. Variegated. 2.Changing color in different lights. Iridescent. (VUR sih kul' ur)

version [*vers, turn* + *-ion*] 1.An account or description from a certain point of view. 2.A variation of an original. (VUR zhun)

verso [*Ltn > verso folio, the turned page*] A left-hand page of an open book. See recto. (VUR soh)

versus [*vers, turn* + *-us*] 1.Against. 2.As compared to or as the alternative of. (VUR sus)

vertex [*vert, turn*] The highest point. Apex. Summit. (VUR teks)

vertical [*vert, turn* + *-ical*] Perpendicular to a horizontal surface. Upright. (VURT ih kul)

vertiginous [*vertig(o) & -ous*] 1.Affected by or causing vertigo. 2.Turning. Revolving. Whirling. See circumvolution. (vur TIJ uh nus)

vertigo [*vert, turn*] A disorder characterized by dizziness or giddiness. (VURT ih goh')

ver   true

aver [*ad-, to + ver, true*] 1.To declare positively to be true. Affirm. Assert. 2.In law, to state formally as fact. (uh VUR)

inveracity [*in-, not + ver, true + -acity*] Lack of veracity. Untruthfulness. See veracity. (in' vuh RAS ih tee)

veracious [*ver, true + -acious*] Truthful. Accurate. (vuh RAY shus)

veracity [*ver, true + -acity*] Truthfulness. Accuracy. See inveracity. (vuh RAS ih tee)

verdict [*ver, true + dict, to speak*] 1.The formal decision of a judge or jury. 2.An expressed conclusion. (VUR dikt)

verify [*ver, true + -ify*] 1.To prove to be true. Confirm. 2.To test the accuracy of. (VEHR uh feye')

verisimilitude [*ver, true + Ltn > simile, same + -tude*] 1.Appearance of truth. 2.Something that merely resembles the truth. (vehr' uh sih MIL ih tood')

verism [*ver, true + -ism*] Realism in art or literature. (VIHR iz' um)

verity [*ver, true + -ity*] 1.A true statement. 2.A principle, belief, or statement considered to be permanently true. (VEHR ih tee)

voir dire [*French > voir, truth & dire, to say*] A legal oath taken by a prospective witness or juror to test his or her competence. (vwahr DIHR)

xen/o   foreign

axenic [*a-, without + xen, foreign + -ic*] 1.Raised under germ-free conditions, as a laboratory animal. 2.Not contaminated by any other organisms, as a laboratory culture. (ay ZEN ik)

euxenite [*eu-, good + xen, foreign + -ite, mineral*] A lustrous, brownish-black mineral consisting primarily of cerium, erbium, columbium, titanium, uranium, and yttrium. So named for the rare elements it contains. (YOOK suh neyet')

pyroxene [*pyro, fire + xen, foreign*] Any of a group of crystalline mineral silicates that do not contain the hydroxyl radical and are important constituents of igneous and some metamorphic rocks. So named from its being foreign to igneous rocks. (peye ROK seen')

pyroxenite [*pyroxen(e) & -ite, rock*] An igneous rock consisting mainly of pyroxene. (peye ROK suh neyet')

xenia [*xen, foreign + -ia*] On a hybrid plant, the influence or effect produced by the transfer of pollen from one strain to another. (ZEE nee uh)

xenogenesis [*xeno, foreign + -genesis, production*] The supposed generation of offspring completely different from either parent. (zen' uh JEN uh sis)

xenograft [*xeno, foreign & graft*] Tissue taken from a donor of one species and grafted onto a recipient of a different species. Same as heterograft. (ZEN uh graft')

xenolith [*xeno, foreign + lith, stone*] A fragment of rock foreign to the igneous rock in which it is enclosed. (ZEN l ith')

xenophile [*xeno, foreign + -phile, attracted to*] One who is attracted to foreigners or foreign things. (ZEN uh feyel')

xenophobia [*xeno, foreign + -phobia, fear*] Abnormal fear of foreigners or strangers. (zen' uh FOH bee uh)

xer/o, xeri   dry

phylloxera [*phyllo, leaf + xer, dry + -a*] Any of various small insects that attack the roots and leaves of certain plants, especially the grapevine. (fil' ok SIHR uh)

xeric [*xer, dry + -ic*] 1.Characterized by or requiring a small amount of moisture. 2.Pertaining to or adapted to a very dry climate. See hydric (def. 2) and mesic. (ZIHR ik)

xeriscape [*xeri, dry & (land)scape*] A desert landscape. (ZIHR ih skayp')

xeroderma [*xero, dry + derma, skin*] Abnormal dryness and roughness of the skin. (zihr' uh DER muh)

xerography [*xero, dry + -graphy, recording*] A dry photocopying process in which areas on a sheet of plain paper corresponding to areas on the original are sensitized by static electricity and sprinkled with colored resin that adheres and is permanently fused to the paper. (zihr OG ruh fee)

xerophilous [*xero, dry + phil, a natural liking + -ous*] Thriving in an environment having only a small amount of moisture. (zihr OF uh lus)

xerophthalmia [*xer, dry + ophthalm, eye + -ia*] Abnormal dryness of the conjunctiva and cornea of the eyeball due to vitamin A deficiency. (zihr' ahf THAL mee uh)

xerophyte [*xero, dry + -phyte, plant*] A plant that grows only in a dry climate. See hydrophyte and mesophyte. (ZIHR uh feyet')

xerosis [*xer, dry + -osis, abnormal condition*] Abnormal dryness of a body part, especially the skin, conjunctiva, or mucus membranes. (zihr OH sis)

xerothermic [*xero, dry + therm, heat + -ic*] Characterized by dryness and heat. (zihr' uh THUR mik)

zo, zoo   animal, life

anthozoan [*antho, flower + zo, animal + -an*] Any of the marine organisms in the class Anthozoa with no medusoid stage and a dominant polyp stage, including the soft, stony, and horny corals, the sea pens, and the sea anemones. So named from their resemblance to flowers. (an' thuh ZOH un)

Archeozoic [*archeo, ancient + zo, life + -ic*] Designating the first geological era occurring between 5,000,000,000 and 1,500,000,000 years ago and characterized by the earliest datable formation of rocks and one-celled organisms. See Proterozoic. (ahr' kee uh ZOH ik)

azo- [*a-, without + zo, life*] A word root meaning "lifeless" or "containing nitrogen." So named because nitrogen does not support life. (AY zoh)

azoic [*azo-, lifeless + -ic*] Pertaining to the geological periods previous to the existence of life on earth. (ay ZOH ik)

azote [*azo-, containing nitrogen + -ote*] 1.An obsolete term for nitrogen, which does not support animal life. 2.Lifeless. (AY zoht)

azotemia [*azot(e) & -emia, blood condition*] The retention of urea and other nitrogenous waste products in the blood due to chronic kidney insufficiency. (az' oh TEE mee uh)

azotobacter [*azot(e) & bacter(ia)*] Any of various spherical or rod-shaped, nonpathogenic nitrogen-fixing bacteria occurring in soil and water. (ay ZOHT uh bak' ter)

azoturia [*azot(e) & -uria, urine*] An increase of urea or other nitrogenous waste products in the urine. (ay' zoh TOOR ee uh)

bryozoan [*bryo, moss + zo, animal + -an*] Any of the minute aquatic invertebrates of the phylum Bryozoa that form mosslike colonies and are known as moss animals. (breye' uh ZOH un)

Cenozoic [*ceno, recent + zo, animal + -ic*] Designating the fifth and latest geological era occurring from 70,000,000 years ago to the present and characterized by the development of recent varieties of mammals, including man. (see' nuh ZOH ik)

cryptozoite [*crypto, hidden & (sporo)zoite*] The exoerythrocyte stage of a malaria parasite during which it lives in tissue cells before entering the blood. See sporozoite. (krip' tuh ZOH eyet')

entozoon [*ento-, within + zo, animal + -on*] An animal parasite that lives inside the body of its host. See epizoon and endoparasite. (ent' uh ZOH on)

epizoite [*epi-, outside + zo, animal + -ite*] A nonparasitic animal that is attached to the body of another living animal, as for protection. (ep' ih ZOH eyet')

epizoon [*epi-, outside + zo, animal + -on*] An animal parasite that lives on the outside of the body of its host. See entozoon and ectoparasite. (ep' ih ZOH on)

epizootic [*epi-, among + zo, animal + -otic*] Pertaining to a rapidly spreading disease among animals of one kind. See epidemic and epizootiology. (ep' ih zoh OT ik)

epizootiology [*epi-, among + zo, animal + -ology, study of*] The study of the causes, prevention, and control of epidemic diseases among animals. See epidemiology. (ep' ih zoh ot' ee OL uh jee)

hematozoon [*hemato, blood + zo, animal + -on*] An animal parasite living in the blood. (hih mat' oh ZOH on)

holozoic [*holo, whole + zo, animal + -ic*] Feeding on solid organic food, as insectivorous plants and most animals. (hol' uh ZOH ik)

hydrazine [*hydr, hydrogen + azo, containing nitrogen + -ine*] A colorless liquid, N_2H_4, used chiefly as a reducing agent and as a jet and rocket propulsion fuel. (HEYE druh zeen')

hydrazoic acid [*hydr, hydrogen + azo, containing nitrogen + -ic & acid*] A highly volatile liquid, NH_3, used in making explosives. (heye' druh ZOH ik AS id)

hydrozoan [*hydro, water + zo, animal + -an*] Any of the small aquatic animals in the class Hydrozoa, including several corals, marine hydroids, fresh-water hydras, etc. (heye' druh ZOH un)

hylozoism [*hylo, matter + zo, life + -ism*] The philosophical doctrine that all matter has life. (heye' luh ZOH iz' um)

merozoite [*mero, part + zo, animal + -ite*] A cell produced by multiple fission in the asexual reproductive stage of certain sporozoans. (mehr' uh ZOH eyet')

Mesozoic [*meso-, middle + zo, animal + -ic*] Designating the fourth geological era, between the Paleozoic and the Cenozoic eras, occurring between 230,000,000 and 70,000,000 years ago and characterized by the development of birds and mammals. See Cenozoic. (mez' uh ZOH ik)

Metazoa [*meta-, after + zo, animal + -a*] A large zoological division that includes all multicellular animals whose cells are organized into tissues and organs. (met' uh ZOH uh)

Paleozoic [*paleo, ancient + zo, animal + -ic*] Designating the third geological era occurring between 620,000,000 and 230,000,000 years ago and characterized by the first insects, fishes, amphibians, and reptiles. See Mesozoic. (pay' lee uh ZOH ik)

paleozoology [*paleo, ancient + zo, animal + -ology, study of*] The branch of paleontology dealing with the study of ancient animal life through the study of fossil remains. See paleobotany and paleontology. (pay' lee oh' zoh OL uh jee)

polyzoan [*poly, many + zo, animal + -an*] Any of the minute aquatic invertebrates of the phylum Bryozoa that form mosslike colonies and are known as moss animals. Same as bryozoan. (pol' ee ZOH un)

polyzoarium [*polyzo(an) & -arium, a place for*] The skeletal system of a polyzoan colony. (pol' ee zoh EHR ee um)

Proterozoic [*protero-, earlier + zo, life + -ic*] Designating the second geological era occurring between 1,500,000,000 and 620,000,000 years ago and characterized by the appearance of multi-celled organisms. See Paleozoic. (prot' ur uh ZOH ik)

protozoan [*proto-, primitive + zo, animal + -an*] Any of the single-celled or acellular microorganisms with animal-like characteristics that occur in varied form, structure, and habitat. (proht' uh ZOH un)

protozoology [*protozo(a) & -ology, study of*] The branch of zoology dealing with the study of protozoans. (proht' oh zoh OL uh jee)

saprozoic [*sapro, decaying + zo, animal + -ic*] Pertaining to animals that feed on dead and decaying organic matter. See saprophagous and saprophyte. (sap' ruh ZOH ik)

scyphozoan [*Grk > skyphos, cup + zo, animal + -an*] Any of the marine medusoid cnidarians in the class Scyphozoa consisting of mostly jellyfishes and characterized by small or absent polyps. (seye' fuh ZOH un)

spermatozoid [*spermato, sperm + zo, animal + -id*] A male gamete that uses flagella for locomotion and is produced in an antheridium. See antheridium. (spur mat' uh ZOH id)

spermatozoon [*spermato, sperm + zo, animal + -on*] The mature male sex cell found in semen that has a whiplike tail for locomotion and penetrates the female egg to fertilize it. Male gamete. See ovum, gamete, spermatogonium, spermatocyte, and spermatid. (spur mat' uh ZOH on)

sporozoan [*sporo, spore + zo, animal + -an*] Any of the parasitic protozoans in the class Sporozoa that typically reproduce by spores, as the plasmodium that causes malaria. (spor' uh ZOH un)

sporozoite [*sporo, spore + zo, animal + -ite*] The infective stage in some sporozoans that results from sexual reproduction and initiates an asexual reproductive cycle in the new host, as in the malaria parasite. See cryptozoite. (spor' uh ZOH eyet')

trophozoite [*tropho, nourishment + zo, animal + -ite*] In the class Sporozoa, a protozoan that is in the vegetative stage, as contrasted with the reproductive stage. (trof' uh ZOH eyet')

zoanthropy [*zo, animal + anthrop, man + -y*] A form of mental disorder in which the patient believes he is an animal. (zoh AN thruh pee)

zodiac [*zo, animal + Grk > diakos, circle*] Literally, "circle of animals." A portion of the celestial sphere that is divided into twelve equal constellations or signs usually associated with animal or human figures. (ZOH dee ak')

zoo [*zoo, animal*] A place for keeping animals for public viewing. (zoo)

zoogenic [*zoo, animal + gen, cause + -ic*] Originating in or caused by animals, as a disease. (zoh' uh JEN ik)

zoogeography [*zoo, animal + geo, earth + -graphy, science*] The branch of biology dealing with the study of the geographical distribution of animals. See biogeography and phytogeography. (zoh' uh jee OG ruh fee)

zoography [*zoo, animal + -graphy, writing*] The descriptive study of animals. See zoology and phytography. (zoh OG ruh fee)

zooid [*zoo, animal + -id*] 1.Resembling an animal. 2.An individual member of an animal colony. 3.An animal cell capable of independent movement and existence within a living animal organism. (ZOH oid)

zoolatry [*zoo, animal + -latry, worship*] Worship of animals. (zoh OL uh tree)

zoology [*zo, animal + -ology, study of*] 1.The branch of biology dealing with the study of animals. See zoography. 2.The animals of a particular region. Fauna. (zoh OL uh jee)

zoomorphic [*zoo, animal + morph, form + -ic*] Having or representing the form of an animal. (zoh' uh MOR fik)

zoomorphism [*zoo, animal + morph, form + -ism*] The use of animal forms in art or symbolism. (zoh' uh MOR fiz' um)

zoonosis [*zoo, animal + nos, disease + -is*] Any of various diseases of humans that are transmitted by animals under natural conditions. (zoh ON uh sis)

zooparasite [*zoo, animal & parasite*] Any of various parasitic animals. (zoh' uh PEHR uh seyet')

zoophagous [*zoo, animal + phag, to eat + -ous*] Feeding on animal tissue. See carnivorous (def. 1). (zoh OF uh gus)

zoophile [*zoo, animal + -phile, love*] A lover of animals; specifically, one who objects to the use of vivisection in study or research. See vivisection. (ZOH uh feyel')

zoophilia [*zoo, animal + phil, love + -ia*] The engagement in sexual activity with an animal. (zoh' uh FIL ee uh)

zoophilous [*zoo, animal + phil, affinity for + -ous*] Pertaining to plants that can be pollinated by animals other than insects. See anemophilous and entomophilous. (zoh OF uh lus)

zoophobia [*zoo, animal + -phobia, fear*] Abnormal fear of animals. (zoh' uh FOH bee uh)

zoophyte [*zoo, animal + -phyte, plant*] Any of various animals that resemble plants, as a sea anemone or coral. (ZOH uh feyet')

zooplankton [*zoo, animal + Grk > planktos, wandering*] Mostly minute floating aquatic animals. See phytoplankton and microplankton. (zoh' uh PLANK tun)

zooplasty [*zoo, animal + -plasty, forming cells or tissue*] The surgical grafting of tissue from an animal to a human. (ZOH uh plas' tee)

zoospore [*zoo, life & spore*] An asexual motile spore that has one or more flagella and is found in certain algae and fungi. (ZOH uh spor')

zoosterol [*zoo, animal & sterol*] Any of various sterols derived from animals, as cholesterol. See phytosterol. (zoh OS tuh rol')

zootechnics [*zoo, animal + techn, skill + -ics, science*] The science and technology of breeding, rearing, and utilizing animals. (zoh' uh TEK niks)

zootomy [*zoo, animal + -tomy, to cut*] 1.The dissection of animals. 2.The anatomy of animals. (zoh OT uh mee)

zyg/o   pair

azygous [*a-, not + zyg, pair + -ous*] Not occurring as one of a pair. Having no mate. Single. (ay ZEYE gus)

dizygotic [*di-, two + zyg, pair + -otic*] Derived from two eggs fertilized at the same time, as fraternal twins. See monozygotic, zygote, and polyembryony. (deye' zeye GOT ik)

heterozygote [*hetero, different + zyg, pair + -ote*] An organism whose diploid cells contain chromosomes with gene pairs that, at one or more loci, contain different alleles, thus producing gametes of two or more different kinds. See homozygote and zygote. (het' uh roh ZEYE goht')

homozygote [*homo, same + zyg, pair + -ote*] An organism whose diploid cells contain chromosomes with gene pairs that, at one or more loci, contain identical alleles, thus producing gametes that are all identical. See heterozygote and zygote. (hoh' muh ZEYE goht')

monozygotic [*mono-, one + zyg, pair + -otic*] Derived from one fertilized egg, as identical twins. See dizygotic, zygote, and polyembryony. (mon' oh zeye GOT ik)

syzygy [*syn-, together + zyg, pair + -y*] 1.Either of two points on a celestial body's orbit at which it is in conjunction with, or in opposition to, the sun. 2.Either of two points on the moon's orbit where the sun, moon, and earth lie in a straight line. (SIZ uh jee)

zygapophysis [*zyg, pair + apo, from + Grk > phyein, to grow + -sis*] One of two paired natural outgrowths of a vertebra that serve to interlock each vertebra with the ones above and below. (zig' uh POF uh sis)

zygodactyl [*zygo, pair + dactyl, toe*] Having a pair of toes pointing forward and a pair pointing backward, as some birds. (zeye' guh DAK tul)

zygomorphic [*zygo, pair + morph, form + -ic*] Pertaining to organisms or parts that can be divided into symmetrical halves along one axis only. Bilaterally symmetrical. (zeye' guh MOR fik)

zygospore [*zygo, pair & spore*] A thick-walled resting spore formed by the fusion of two similar gametes, as in some algae and fungi. (ZEYE guh spor')

zygote [*zyg, pair + -ote*] 1.The cell, or fertilized ovum, formed by the union of two gametes. 2.The organism that develops from this cell. (ZEYE goht)

The following is a list of words used to complete several synonyms, antonyms, and other words that are normally thought of as belonging together, but do not appear in any other root list.

allograft [*allo, other & graft*] Tissue taken from a donor of a species and grafted onto a recipient that is a member of the same species, but has different genetic composition. See homograft. (AL uh graft')

altruism [*Ltn > alter, other + -ism*] 1.Unselfishness. 2.The ethical doctrine that the general welfare of society is the basis of morality. Opposed to egoism (def. 2). (AL troo iz' um)

anticline [*anti-, opposite + -cline, slope*] An inverted, trough-shaped basin of stratified rock with rock beds sloping upward. See syncline, geosyncline, and geanticline. (AN tih kleyen')

apicoalveolar [*apico, top & alveolar*] Articulated with the tip of the tongue near or touching the alveolar process. (ap' ih koh' al VEE uh lur)

arachnoid [*Grk > arachne, spider + -oid, resembling*] 1.The thin membrane, lying between the dura mater and the pia mater, that forms the middle of the three coverings of the brain and spinal cord. See pia mater and dura mater. 2.Covered with or consisting of long cobweblike hairs. (uh RAK noid')

bulimia nervosa [*Grk > bous, ox + Grk > limos, hunger + -ia & Ltn > nervosus, nervous*] A psychological eating disorder, usually occurring in young women, characterized by compulsive overeating followed by purging, as by self-induced vomiting, fasting, etc. See anorexia nervosa. (boo LEE mee uh nur VOH suh)

central nervous system One of two major divisions of the nervous system consisting of the brain and spinal cord. See peripheral nervous system. (SEN trul NUR vus SIS tum)

cleistothecium [*cleisto, closed + Grk > theke, case + -ium*] A closed fruiting body of ascomycete fungi in which asci are borne and which releases ascospores by decay or rupture of the body wall. See apothecium and perithecium. (kleye' stuh THEE shee um)

Codex Juris Canonici [*Ltn > codex, code & Ltn > juris, law & Ltn > canonicus, canon*] Literally, "code of canon law." The body of canon law that has governed the Catholic Church since 1918 and superseded the Corpus Juris Canonici. See Corpus Juris Canonici. (KOH deks JOOR is kuh NON uh seye')

cum laude [*Ltn > cum, with & Ltn > laude, praise*] Literally, "with praise." Used in diplomas to grant the 3rd highest of three special honors for above-average academic standing from a college or university. See magna cum laude and summa cum laude. (koom LOWD uh)

eccrine [*ec-, out + Grk > krinein, to separate*] Pertaining to the common sweat glands of the human body that secrete sweat without removing cytoplasm from the secreting cells. See apocrine. (EK rin)

ennead [*ennea, nine + -ad, group*] A group or series of nine. (EN ee ad')

exocrine [*exo-, outside + Grk > krinein, to separate*] Pertaining to glands that secrete through a duct, as a salivary or sweat gland. Opposed to endocrine. (EKS uh krin')

exoskeleton [*exo-, outside & skeleton*] A hard external covering that provides protection and support, as the shell of a crustacean. See endoskeleton. (eks' oh SKEL ih tun)

exosmosis [*exo-, outside & osmosis*] 1.Osmosis in an outward direction. 2.Osmosis from a region of higher concentration to a region of lower concentration. Opposed to endosmosis. (eks' os MOH sis)

exotoxin [*exo-, outside & toxin*] A soluble toxin excreted by some bacteria, as in diphtheria or botulism. See endotoxin. (EKS oh tok' sin)

fauna [*Ltn > Faunus, Roman god of nature*] All the animal life of a particular region or period. See flora and biota. (FAW nuh)

haploid [*haplo-, single + -oid*] Pertaining to cells with one complete set of chromosomes, which is half the diploid number. In humans, male and female sex cells are haploid and each contain 23 chromosomes, while most body cells are diploid and contain 46 chromosomes. See diploid (def. 2) and monoploid. (HAP loid)

hypnopompic [*hypno, sleep + Grk > pompe, sending away + -ic*] Pertaining to or associated with the semiconscious state preceding complete wakening from sleep. See hypnagogic. (hip' noh POM pik)

icosahedron [*icosa, twenty + -hedron, surface*] A solid figure with twenty plane surfaces. (eye koh' suh HEE drun)

immigrate [*im-, in + Ltn > migrare, to move + -ate*] To move into a foreign country or region. See emigrate. (IM ih grayt')

maid of honor The principal unmarried woman attending the bride at a wedding. See matron of honor. (mayd uv ON ur)

multilateral [*multi-, many + Ltn > latus, side + -al*] 1.Having many sides. 2.Involving or affecting more than one party, country, etc. See unilateral and bilateral. (mul' tih LAT ur ul)

multiparous [*multi-, more than one + -parous, to produce*] 1.Producing more than one offspring at a time. 2.Having previously given birth at least once. See uniparous. (mul TIP ur us)

multivalent [*multi-, many + -valent, having a specified valence*] Having a valence of three or more. (mul' tih VAY lent)

myriad [*myria, many + -ad, group*] 1.A very large number. 2.Ten thousand. (MIHR ee' uhd)

nonagenarian [*Ltn > nonagenarius, containing ninety*] A person between 90 and 100 years of age. (non' uh juh NEHR ee un)

November [*Ltn > novem, nine + -ber*] The 11th month of the year. So named from the 9th month of the early Roman calendar, which began with March. See September, October, and December. (noh VEM ber)

oblate [*ob-, against + Ltn > ferre, to carry*] Flattened at the poles, as a spheroid formed by revolving an ellipse around its shorter axis. Opposed to prolate. (OB layt)

oviparous [*ovi, egg + -parous, to produce*] Producing eggs that hatch externally, as birds, most reptiles, certain fishes, etc. See ovoviviparous and viviparous. (oh VIP ur us)

ovum [*ov, egg + -um*] The unfertilized, mature female sex cell that is produced in the ovary from an oocyte and, if fertilized by a spermatozoon, develops into a new individual. Female gamete. See spermatozoon, gamete, oogonium (def. 1), and oocyte. (OH vum)

penult [*Ltn > paene, almost + Ltn > ultimus, last*] 1.The next
to the last syllable in a word. 2.The next to the last
item in a series. See penultimate, antepenult, and
antepenultimate. (PEE nult)

penultimate [*Ltn > paene, almost + Ltn > ultimus, last + -ate*]
1.Next to the last. 2.Pertaining to a penult. See penult,
antepenult, and antepenultimate. (pih NUL tuh mut)

pleonasm [*pleo, more + -ism*] The use of successive
synonyms to express an idea, as "cruel and vicious."
See tautology. (PLEE uh naz' um)

prenuptial [*pre-, before + Ltn > nuptiae, wedding + -al*]
Done or occurring before marriage. See postnuptial.
(pree NUP shul)

recto [*Ltn > recto folio, the right side page*] A right-hand
page of an open book. See verso. (REK toh)

saccharide [*sacchar, sugar + -ide*] Any of a large class of
carbohydrates containing sugar, as monosaccharides,
disaccharides, polysaccharides, etc. (SAK uh reyed')

semanteme [*semant(ic) & -eme, structural unit*] The
smallest unit of lexical meaning in a language.
(sih MAN teem')

simile [*Ltn > simile, same*] A figure of speech with an
expressed comparison, as "lips like cherries." See
metaphor. (SIM uh lee)

spermatid [*spermat, sperm + -id*] Any of the four cells
that develop into spermatozoa and result from the
primary and secondary meiotic divisions of a
spermatocyte. See spermatogonium, spermatocyte,
and spermatozoon. (SPUR muh tid)

static [*stat, stationary + -ic*] 1.Pertaining to bodies or
fluids at rest or in equilibrium. 2.Not moving,
changing, or progressing. Inactive. See dynamic and
astatic. (STAT ik)

summa cum laude [*Ltn > summa, highest & Ltn > cum, with
& Ltn > laude, praise*] Literally, "with highest praise."
Used in diplomas to grant the highest of three special
honors for above-average academic standing from a
college or university. See cum laude and magna cum
laude. (SOOM uh koom LOWD uh)

taciturn [*Ltn > tacitus, silent*] Not talkative by nature.
Uncommunicative. Opposed to loquacious.
(TAS ih turn')

toneme [*ton(e) & -eme, structural unit*] A type of phoneme
used in a tone language, such as Chinese, to
distinguish lexical meaning based on variation of tone.
See phoneme. (TOH neem)

utopia [*Grk > ou, not + Grk > topos, place + -ia*] An
imaginary, ideally perfect place, especially socially
and politically. Opposed to dystopia. (yoo TOH pee uh)

9th month of the year named from the 7th month of the early Roman calendar SEPTEMBER 162
10th month of the year named from the 8th month of the early Roman calendar OCTOBER 162
11th month of the year named from the 9th month of the early Roman calendar NOVEMBER 219
12th month of the year named from the 10th month of the early Roman calendar DECEMBER 163
14th century Italian art and literature TRECENTO 43, 116
15th century Italian art and literature QUATTROCENTO 43, 116
16th century Italian art and literature CINQUECENTO 43, 115, 160
17th century Italian art and literature SEICENTO 43, 116, 161
20th century movement that adheres to doctrines of the Reformation NEOORTHODOXY 55, 171, 177
1st Sunday of Lent named for its date 40 days before Easter QUADRAGESIMA 158
1st Sunday before Lent named for its date 50 days before Easter QUINQUAGESIMA 160
2nd Sunday before Lent named for its date 60 days before Easter SEXAGESIMA 161
3rd Sunday before Lent named for its date 70 days before Easter SEPTUAGESIMA 162
abandonment of principles APOSTASY 19
ability and achievement are the basis for advancement MERITOCRACY 24
ability to cause movement of an object without physical force TELEKINESIS 117, 209
ability to change or progress DYNAMIC 69
ability to move objects with the mind PSYCHOKINESIS 117, 195
ability to see things in their true relationship PERSPECTIVE 183, 205
ability to sense things normally beyond the range of the senses TELESTHESIA 78, 209
ability to survive and develop VITALITY 37
able to be molded PLASTIC 168
able to do many things well VERSATILE 215
able to exist in high temperatures THERMODURIC 211
able to read and write LITERATE 68
able to read but not write SEMILITERATE 59, 68
able to use both hands equally well AMBIDEXTROUS 10
able to use only one language MONOLINGUAL 118, 152
able to use only one language MONOGLOT 151
able to use only one language UNILINGUAL 118, 153
able to use two languages BILINGUAL 118, 154
able to use three languages TRILINGUAL 118, 157
able to use several languages MULTILINGUAL 118
able to use several languages LINGUIST 118
abnormal absence of menstruation AMENORRHEA 2, 199
abnormal bleeding from the uterus METRORRHAGIA 199
abnormal closure of teeth MALOCCLUSION 32, 52
abnormal compulsion to lie MYTHOMANIA 141
abnormal condition of the mouth, white patches on mucous membranes LEUKOPLAKIA 118
abnormal condition resulting from taking excessive vitamins HYPERVITAMINOSIS 37, 109
abnormal decrease in blood platelets THROMBOCYTOPENIA 40
abnormal decrease in oxygen to body tissues HYPOXIA 110
abnormal decrease in red blood cells ANAEMIA 2, 98
abnormal decrease in red blood cells ANEMIA 2, 98
abnormal decrease in white blood cells LEUKOPENIA 117
abnormal decrease in the activity of the pituitary gland HYPOPITUITARISM 110
abnormal decrease in the activity of the thyroid gland HYPOTHYROIDISM 110
abnormal decrease of oxygen in the blood HYPOXEMIA 100, 110
abnormal deposits of black pigmentation MELANOSIS 144
abnormal development of cells or tissues DYSPLASIA 33, 167
abnormal digestion DYSPEPSIA 33, 182
abnormal dryness of the eyeball XEROPHTHALMIA 176, 216
abnormal dryness of the skin XERODERMA 61, 216
abnormal dryness of the skin, conjunctiva, or mucus membranes XEROSIS 216
abnormal enlargement of an organ due to an increase in cell size HYPERTROPHY 109, 212
abnormal enlargement of cells CYTOMEGALIC 39, 139
abnormal fetal development TERATOGENIC 88
abnormal formation MALFORMATION 32
abnormal function DYSFUNCTION 33
abnormal function MALFUNCTION 32
abnormal increase in mononuclear leukocytes MONONUCLEOSIS 152
abnormal increase in nonmalignant cells of a tissue HYPERPLASIA 108, 168
abnormal increase in oxygen in the blood and body tissues HYPEROXIA 108
abnormal increase in red blood cells POLYCYTHEMIA 40, 100, 164
abnormal increase in white blood cells LEUKEMIA 100, 117
abnormal increase in white blood cells LEUKOCYTOSIS 40, 117

abnormal increase in the activity of the pituitary gland HYPERPITUITARISM 108
abnormal increase in the activity of the thyroid gland HYPERTHYROIDISM 109
abnormal interest in excrement COPROPHILIA 184
abnormal lack of energy LETHARGY 77
abnormal mixture of male and female characteristics GYNANDROMORPH 13, 166
abnormal new growth of tissue NEOPLASM 168, 171
abnormal overdevelopment of male breasts GYNECOMASTIA 13
abnormal position MALPOSITION 32
abnormal protrusion of the eyeball EXOPHTHALMOS 175
abnormal protrusion of the eyeball EXOPHTHALMUS 175
abnormal reaction to certain substances ALLERGY 77
abnormal redness of the skin ERYTHEMA 77
abnormal rhythm DYSRHYTHMIA 33
abnormal slowness of the heartbeat BRADYCARDIA 40
abnormal structural arrangement of body parts HETEROTAXIS 103, 208
abnormal structural arrangement of rock strata HETEROTAXIS 103, 208
abnormal swallowing of air AEROPHAGIA 8, 183
abnormal twisting of the intestine VOLVULUS 214
abnormally dark pigmentation MELANISM 144
abnormally decreased sensitivity to touch HYPESTHESIA 78, 109
abnormally decreased sensitivity to touch HYPOESTHESIA 78, 109
abnormally decreased tension or tone HYPOTONIC 110
abnormally excessive and frequent fluid bowl movements DIARRHEA 62, 199
abnormally excessive and frequent fluid bowl movements DIARRHOEA 62, 199
abnormally excessive muscular movement HYPERKINESIS 108, 117
abnormally frequent involuntary discharge of semen SPERMATORRHEA 199
abnormally high blood pressure HYPERTENSION 109
abnormally high body temperature HYPERTHERMIA 109, 210
abnormally high fever HYPERPYREXIA 109, 197
abnormally high level of calcium in the blood HYPERCALCEMIA 100, 108
abnormally high level of cholesterol in the blood HYPERCHOLESTEROLEMIA 100, 108
abnormally high level of lipids in the blood HYPERLIPIDEMIA 100, 108, 118
abnormally high level of sugar in the blood HYPERGLYCEMIA 100, 108
abnormally high level of uric acid in the blood HYPERURICEMIA 100, 109
abnormally increased sensitivity to touch HYPERAESTHESIA 78, 108
abnormally increased sensitivity to touch HYPERESTHESIA 78, 108
abnormally increased tension or tone HYPERTONIC 109
abnormally large head MACROCEPHALY 45, 136
abnormally large red blood cell MACROCYTE 40, 136
abnormally low blood pressure HYPOTENSION 110
abnormally low body temperature HYPOTHERMIA 110, 210
abnormally low level of calcium in the blood HYPOCALCEMIA 100, 109
abnormally low level of oxygen in the blood ANOXEMIA 3, 98
abnormally low level of sugar in the blood HYPOGLYCEMIA 100, 110
abnormally rapid breathing HYPERPNEA 109, 193
abnormally rapid breathing POLYPNEA 165, 194
abnormally slow breathing HYPOPNEA 110, 193
abnormally rapid heartbeat TACHYCARDIA 41
abnormally short fingers or toes BRACHYDACTYLOUS 58
abnormally small head MICROCEPHALY 46, 137
abnormally small mature red blood cell MICROCYTE 40, 137
abnormally thin EMACIATE 71
abnormally vivid memory HYPERMNESIA 108
abrupt turn of events PERIPETEIA 52
absence of an organ or body part AGENESIS 1, 84
absence of government ANARCHY 2, 23
absence of life ABIOTIC 1, 34
absence of oxygen in body tissues ANOXIA 3
absence of sensibility to pain ANALGESIA 2, 9
absence of sexual desire ANAPHRODISIA 2
absence of skin pigmentation LEUKODERMA 61, 117
absence of the brain at birth ANENCEPHALY 2, 45
absence of the sense of smell ANOSMIA 3
absence of urine ANURIA 3
absolute certainty APODICTIC 19
absolute sovereignty AUTARCHY 23, 28

ameboid cell AMEBOCYTE 39
ameboid cell in invertebrates AMEBOCYTE 39
amino acid in the urine of birds ORNITHINE 30
among other things INTER ALIA 111
among the members of a single school INTRAMURAL 80
among the members of more than one school EXTRAMURAL 81
amount to AGGREGATE 96
amuse DIVERT 215
analysis of written documents to determine authenticity BIBLIOTICS 34, 131
analyzing mental processes PSYCHOANALYSIS 12, 195
anatomical part resembling a handle MANUBRIUM 141
anatomy of a region of the body TOPOLOGY 130
anatomy of animals ZOOTOMY 204, 218
ancestral line PEDIGREE 181
ancestry of animals PEDIGREE 181
ancient Asian country between the Tigris and Euphrates rivers MESOPOTAMIA 144
ancient Roman central heating system HYPOCAUST 42, 109
ancient Roman nobility PATRICIAN 142
ancient forms of humans PALEOANTHROPIC 14, 25
ancient military device for hurling large stones CATAPULT 12
anemia initially occurring among Mediterranean peoples THALASSEMIA 100
anemia that results from defective blood-producing bone marrow APLASTIC ANEMIA 3, 98, 167
anger at unfair treatment INDIGNANT 6
angle whose vertex is at the center of the circle CENTRAL ANGLE 44
animal attached to another animal EPIZOITE 76, 217
animal cell capable of independent movement ZOOID 218
animal forms in art ZOOMORPHISM 167, 218
animal life of a particular region FAUNA 219
animal whose body temperature remains constant ENDOTHERM 72, 210
animal whose body temperature remains constant HOMOIOTHERM 101, 210
animal whose body temperature varies with the environment ECTOTHERM 73, 210
animal whose body temperature varies with the environment POIKILOTHERM 210
animals and certain plants that feed on insects INSECTIVORE 184
animals for public viewing ZOO 218
animals of a particular region Fauna ZOOLOGY 130, 218
animals that feed on decaying organic matter SAPROZOIC 217
animals that resemble plants ZOOPHYTE 192, 218
animals, the larvae breathe by gills and the adults breathe by lungs AMPHIBIAN 10, 34
animals whose body wall consists of two cell layers DIPLOBLASTIC 38, 155
animals whose embryo consists of three germ cell layers TRIPLOBLASTIC 39, 158
animals whose cells are organized into tissues and organs METAZOA 145, 217
animals with a pair of tentacle-bearing arms BRACHIOPOD 181
animals with a wormlike body that move by ventral cilia GASTROTRICH 83
animals with jointed legs and a segmented body ARTHROPOD 27, 181
animating effect INSPIRE 194
announce ENUNCIATE 71
announce officially and formally PROMULGATE 17
announce officially or publicly PROCLAIM 16
announce publicly to encourage sales ADVERTISE 214
anomalous AMORPHOUS 2, 166
anonymous person ANONYM 3, 174
another aspect of oneself ALTER EGO 29
antenna system to analyze radio waves from celestial bodies RADIO TELESCOPE 201, 209
anterior portion of the head PROCEPHALIC 16, 46
anterior portion of the rhombencephalon METENCEPHALON 46, 145
anterior portion of the prosencephalon TELENCEPHALON 46, 209
anterior segment of an insect PROTHORAX 17
anthology of myths MYTHOGRAPHY 94
anthology of myths about a specific people MYTHOLOGY 127
antibiotic produced by plants in response to a pathogen PHYTOALEXIN 191
antibodies resulting in various autoimmune diseases AUTOIMMUNITY 28
antibody produced by an individual's own body AUTOANTIBODY 28
antibody that reacts with antigens of the same species ISOANTIBODY 104
antigen from one member that can cause antibodies in other members ISOANTIGEN 86, 104
antigen that stimulates the formation of a specific agglutinin AGGLUTINOGEN 84
anticipation and answering in advance PROLEPSIS 16

beyond the earth EXTRATERRESTRIAL 81, 90
beyond the moon SUPERLUNARY 136
beyond the ordinary EXTRAORDINARY 81
beyond the physical SUPERPHYSICAL 193
beyond the physical Supernatural HYPERPHYSICAL 108, 192
beyond the physical world EXTRAMUNDANE 81
beyond the sea ULTRAMARINE 142
beyond the senses EXTRASENSORY 81
beyond what is usual EXTRA 80
Bible BIBLICAL 34
Biblical books excluded from the Hebrew and Protestant Scriptures APOCRYPHA 19, 55
billion cycles Gigacycle GIGAHERTZ 57
binding agreement CONTRACT 212
biochemical reaction that releases energy EXERGONIC 77
biochemical reaction that requires absorption of energy ENDERGONIC 71, 77
biographies written about saints HAGIOGRAPHY 93
biography that psychoanalyzes the subject PSYCHOBIOGRAPHY 36, 94, 195
biological agent that endangers life BIOHAZARD 35
biological internal state of equilibrium HOMEOSTASIS 101
bird named from the yellow hood worn by prothonotaries PROTHONOTARY WARBLER 24
bird with undeveloped wings Kiwi APTERYX 3, 196
birds AVIAN 29
birds ORNITHIC 30
birds of a particular region AVIFAUNA 30
birth NATIVITY 170
birth of Christ NATIVITY 170
bisexual AMBISEXUAL 10
biting mouth-parts in larval stage, sucking mouth-parts in adult stage METAGNATHOUS 145
bitter criticism DIATRIBE 63
black pigment that accounts for dark skin, dark hair, etc. MELANIN 144
black skin and hair MELANOUS 144
black variety of garnet MELANITE 121, 144
blastomere that develops into ectoderm ECTOMERE 38, 73
blessing BENEDICTION 31, 64
blocks projecting like teeth DENTIL 60
blood cell HEMOCYTE 40, 99
blood defect characterized by excessive bleeding HEMOPHILIA 99, 185
blood disease that changes red blood cells to a sickle shape SICKLE CELL ANEMIA 100
blood drawn from a donor, plasma removed, and cells returned to the donor PLASMAPHERESIS 20, 168
blood in the urine HEMATURIA 99
blood or blood vessels HEMAL 99
blood platelet THROMBOCYTE 40
blood poisoning by bacterial toxins TOXEMIA 100
blood poisoning by pathogenic microorganisms SEPTICEMIA 100
blood poisoning by pathogenic microorganisms SAPREMIA 100
blood poisoning by pus-forming microorganisms PYEMIA 100
blood vessels of the brain CEREBROVASCULAR 46
blood-red INCARNADINE 41
bloom EFFLORESCE 18
blooming FLORESCENCE 18
blooming INFLORESCENCE 19
blooming stage of a flower ANTHESIS 18
blooming throughout the season PERPETUAL 183
blue color CYANIC 56
blue dye to extend the range of color sensitivity of photographic film CYANINE 56
blue to red pigment in flowers ANTHOCYANIN 18, 56
blue-green algae CYANOBACTERIA 56
bluish coloration of the skin CYANOSIS 56
bluish-green color AQUA 20
bluish-green color AQUAMARINE 20, 141
bluish-green variety of beryl AQUAMARINE 20, 141
board on which a person rides towed by a motorboat AQUAPLANE 20
boat with three hulls side by side TRIMARAN 157
bodies or fluids at rest STATIC 220
bodily CORPORAL 53
body build derived from the embryonic ectoderm ECTOMORPHIC 73, 166

body build derived from the embryonic mesoderm MESOMORPHIC 143, 166
body build derived from the embryonic endoderm ENDOMORPHIC 72, 166
body of a murder victim CORPUS DELICTI 54
body of a vertebra CENTRUM 44
body of an animal or human CORPUS 54
body of canon law CORPUS JURIS CANONICI 54
body of civil law CORPUS JURIS CIVILIS 54
body of law CORPUS JURIS 54
body of laws PANDECT 176
body of people acting together CORPS 54
body of troops trained for service at sea and on land MARINE 141
body of water containing many islands ARCHIPELAGO 23
body organs essential to life VITALS 37
body temperature, pulse rate, and respiratory rate VITAL SIGNS 37
body with many of the legal powers given to individuals CORPORATION 53
boiling EBULLIENT 70
boldly disrespectful INSOLENT 7
bone cell OSTEOCYTE 40, 178
bone condition in which the bone becomes porous OSTEOPOROSIS 178
bone disorder caused by abnormal conversion of cartilage ACHONDROPLASIA 1, 167
bone tissue due to abnormal growth HYPEROSTOSIS 108, 178
bone-forming cell OSTEOBLAST 39, 178
bones between the wrist and fingers METACARPUS 144
bones between the carpus and phalanges METACARPUS 144
bones between the ankle and toes METATARSUS 145
bones between the tarsus and phalanges METATARSUS 145
bony outgrowth OSTEOPHYTE 178, 191
bony outgrowth on a bone or tooth EXOSTOSIS 178
bony tissue that forms the main body of a tooth DENTIN 60
bony tissue that forms the main body of a tooth DENTINE 60
book collection Library BIBLIOTHECA 34
book containing music named from its being sung on the altar steps GRADUAL 97
book, especially large or scholarly TOME 204
book in a series of volumes TOME 204
book of Common Prayer LITURGY 77
book of alphabetically listed words DICTIONARY 64
book of proper names ONOMASTICON 174
book reading for psychiatric therapy BIBLIOTHERAPY 34
book size, each page one fourth of a printer's sheet QUARTO 159
book size, each page one eighth of a printer's sheet OCTAVO 162
book size, each page one twelfth of a printer's sheet DUODECIMO 156, 163
book size, each page one sixteenth of a printer's sheet SEXTODECIMO 161, 164
book size, each page one eighteenth of a printer's sheet OCTODECIMO 162, 164
book title appearing in red decorative lettering RUBRIC 78
book, usually one of a set VOLUME 214
books containing information on a variety of subjects CYCLOPAEDIA 56
books containing information on a variety of subjects CYCLOPEDIA 56
books containing information on a variety of subjects ENCYCLOPAEDIA 57
books containing information on a variety of subjects ENCYCLOPEDIA 57
bookseller who deals in rare books BIBLIOPOLE 34
born in a particular country NATIVE 170
born out of wedlock ILLEGITIMATE 4, 66
both ears BINAURAL 154
both hands BIMANUAL 141, 154
both male and female sex organs Hermaphroditic BISEXUAL 154
both sexes BISEXUAL 154
bottom waters of the ocean ABYSSAL 1
boundary AMBIT 10
boundary of a circle CIRCUMFERENCE 50
brain CEREBRAL 46
brain ENCEPHALIC 45
brain ENCEPHALON 45
brain and spinal cord CEREBROSPINAL 46
branch out RAMIFY 198
branched RAMATE 198
branches RAMOUS 198

KEYWORDS

chemical element that is highly magnetic DYSPROSIUM 33
chemical reaction that causes absorption of heat ENDOTHERMIC 72, 210
chemical reaction that causes liberation of heat EXOTHERMIC 210
chemical reaction that causes liberation of heat EXOERGIC 77
chemical reactions to form organic compounds CHEMOSYNTHESIS 105
chemistry dealing with plants and animals BIOCHEMISTRY 35
chief angel ARCHANGEL 23
chief clerk PROTHONOTARY 24
chief clerk PROTONOTARY 25
chief enemy ARCHENEMY 23
chief fiend ARCHFIEND 23
chief magistrate in ancient Athens ARCHON 23
chief of a heresy HERESIARCH 23
chief priest ARCHPRIEST 23
chili with meat CHILI CON CARNE 41
chloride containing two atoms of chlorine BICHLORIDE 153
chloride containing two atoms of chlorine DICHLORIDE 154
chloride containing three atoms of chlorine TRICHLORIDE 156
chloride containing four atoms of chlorine TETRACHLORIDE 159
choice between two equally undesirable alternatives DILEMMA 155
choice of words and phrases PHRASEOLOGY 67
choose ELECT 70
choose by vote ELECT 70
Christian festival celebrating the three wise men coming to honor Jesus EPIPHANY 75
Christian sacrament of Holy Communion EUCHARIST 32
Christian statement that begins "I believe in God the Father Almighty" APOSTLES' CREED 54
Christian statement that begins "We believe in one God" NICENE CREED 55
Christmas NATIVITY 170
chromatin more lightly stained and genetically active EUCHROMATIN 32, 48
chromatin more darkly stained and genetically inactive HETEROCHROMATIN 48, 102
chromium CHROME 47
chromium alloy plating CHROME 47
chromium-containing pigment CHROME 47
chromosome other than a sex chromosome AUTOSOME 29, 47
chromosome with the centromere at one end TELOCENTRIC 45, 209
chromosome with the centromere closer to one end ACROCENTRIC 7, 44
chromosomes that determine an individual's sex SEX CHROMOSOME 48
chromosomes that determine an individual's sex HETEROCHROMOSOME 48, 102
chrysoberyl named after Alexander I, Russian Czar ALEXANDRITE 118
Church not governed by external authority AUTOCEPHALOUS 28, 45
church that contains the bishop's throne CATHEDRAL 13
circle of animals ZODIAC 218
circle whose center moves around the circumference of a larger circle EPICYCLE 57, 74
circular motion, especially of ocean currents GYRE 57
circular path GYRAL 57
circular tuba HELICON 57
circumference AMBIT 10
city of brotherly love PHILADELPHIA 185
civil magistrate SYNDIC 107
clarity and correctness in speaking DICTION 64
class given special privileges and status ARISTOCRACY 24
class of wealthy people PLUTOCRACY 24
classes into which knowledge can be placed CATEGORY 12
classification of diseases NOSOLOGY 67
classification of organisms SYSTEMATICS 107, 135
classification of organisms TAXONOMY 173, 208
classification of organisms based on biochemical criteria CHEMOTAXONOMY 173, 208
classification of organisms based on cellular structure CYTOTAXONOMY 39, 173, 208
clause expressing the condition in a conditional sentence PROTASIS 17
clause expressing the conclusion in a conditional sentence APODOSIS 19
clause in a legal document PROVISO 18
clear and distinct Sharp VIVID 38
clear fluid portion of the protoplasm of a cell HYALOPLASM 168
clear from guilt Exonerate VINDICATE 65
clearly apparent Obvious MANIFEST 141
clearly established Indisputable APODICTIC 19

clergy classified according to rank HIERARCHY 23
clever argument that is usually false SOPHISTRY 204
clever but based on a false notion SOPHISTIC 204
clever but misleading argument SOPHISM 204
climate of a small area MICROCLIMATE 137
climate over a large area MACROCLIMATE 136
clinic able to treat many diseases POLYCLINIC 164
close OCCLUDE 52
closed fruiting body of ascomycete fungi CLEISTOTHECIUM 219
closing phase POSTLUDE 15, 136
clumping of red blood cells HEMAGGLUTINATION 99
cluster of stars ASTERISM 27
coal in which the texture of wood is visible LIGNITE 121
coal that burns with much heat and little smoke or flame ANTHRACITE 119
coarse-grained rock PEGMATITE 121
code CRYPTIC 56
code of canon law CODEX JURIS CANONICI 219
code of etiquette PROTOCOL 24
code of moral conduct ETHICS 132
coin named because it was stamped with the figure of a lily FLORIN 18
coin worth two shillings FLORIN 18
coins similar to the Florentine florin FLORIN 18
cold-blooded POIKILOTHERMIC 210
collection of sacred writings HAGIOLOGY 66
collection of selected writings ANTHOLOGY 18
collector of phonograph records DISCOPHILE 185
color blindness MONOCHROMATISM 48, 151
color change METACHROMATISM 48, 144
color distortion CHROMATIC ABERRATION 47
color on the wings of certain birds SPECULUM 205
colored plastid CHROMOPLAST 47, 167
colorless plastid LEUCOPLAST 117, 168
colorless variety of opal HYALITE 120
colors formed when a beam of sunlight passes through a prism SPECTRUM 205
columns along both fronts but none along either side AMPHIPROSTYLE 10, 16
columns along both fronts or along both sides AMPHISTYLAR 10
columns along the front PROSTYLE 17
columns on each end but none along the sides APTERAL 3, 196
columns on every side PERIPTERAL 52, 197
columns surrounding a building PERISTYLE 52
combination of beliefs SYNCRETISM 107
combination of elements to form a whole SYNTHESIS 107
combination of two vowel sounds DIPHTHONG 155
combination of three vowel sounds TRIPHTHONG 158
combination of two different radio frequencies HETERODYNE 70, 102
combine by blending INTERFUSE 81, 112
combine into one UNITE 153
combine into one body INCORPORATE 54
combine with hydrogen HYDROGENATE 22
combined effect greater than the sum of individual effects SYNERGISM 77, 107
combined effect greater than the sum of individual effects SYNERGY 77, 107
combined symptoms SYMPTOMATOLOGY 106, 129
come about Result Culminate EVENTUATE 71
come between INTERVENE 112
come forth EMANATE 71
come forth EMERGE 71
come into opposition between Impede INTERFERE 111
command INJUNCTION 115
command with authority DICTATE 64
commander of a trireme TRIERARCH 24, 157
common axis COAXIAL 30
common center CONCENTRIC 44
common center HOMOCENTRIC 44, 101
common law LEX NON SCRIPTA 66, 96
communication by supernatural means TELEPATHY 80, 209
communication from a distance TELECOMMUNICATION 209

KEYWORDS

decomposition caused by microorganisms BIOLYSIS 35
decomposition resulting from reaction with water HYDROLYSIS 22
decomposition of bony tissue OSTEOCLASIS 178
decomposition of cells CYTOLYSIS 39
decomposition of cells by a lytic agent from another species HETEROLYSIS 103
decomposition of chromatin in a nerve cell CHROMATOLYSIS 47
decomposition of compounds by heat THERMOLYSIS 211
decomposition of fat LIPOLYSIS 118
deduce or infer EDUCE 69, 70
deduct one number from another SUBTRACT 212
deep chasm ABYSS 1
deep-blue color ULTRAMARINE 142
deep-red color RUBY 78
deep-red precious stone RUBY 78
defective articulation of speech DYSARTHRIA 33
degree of a slope GRADE 97
degree of accuracy in reproducing an audio or video signal FIDELITY 81
deliberate deception in speech or conduct Double-dealing DUPLICITY 156
deliberate ill will MALICE 32
deliberate unjustifiable injury or harm MALICE 32
deliberate paradoxical figure of speech CATACHRESIS 12
dental assistant who cleans teeth DENTAL HYGIENIST 60
dentistry dealing with straightening teeth ORTHODONTICS 60, 134, 177
dentistry dealing with bone and tissue surrounding the teeth PERIODONTICS 52, 60, 134
dentistry dealing with diseases of the tooth pulp ENDODONTICS 60, 72, 132
dentistry dealing with extraction of teeth EXODONTICS 60, 132
dentistry dealing with replacement of teeth PROSTHODONTICS 60, 135
deprive of strength EMASCULATE 71
deprive of the power to reproduce EMASCULATE 71
derived from a different species HETEROLOGOUS 102
derived from a verb VERBAL 68
derived from one ancestral form MONOPHYLETIC 152
derived from one fertilized egg MONOZYGOTIC 152, 218
derived from two eggs fertilized at the same time DIZYGOTIC 156, 218
derived from the same organism AUTOLOGOUS 28
descent from the same ancestral line CENOGENESIS 84
descent from more than one ancestral line POLYGENESIS 87, 164
descended from more than one ancestral line POLYPHYLETIC 165
descent through the female line MATRILINEAL 142
descent through the male line PATRILINEAL 142
description from a point of view VERSION 215
description of a specific area CHOROGRAPHY 92
description of diseases NOSOGRAPHY 94
descriptive study of a place TOPOGRAPHY 95
descriptive study of animals ZOOGRAPHY 95, 218
descriptive study of celestial bodies URANOGRAPHY 95
descriptive study of fossils PALEONTOGRAPHY 25, 94
descriptive study of mountains OROGRAPHY 94
descriptive study of plant and animal organs ORGANOGRAPHY 94
descriptive study of plants Descriptive botany PHYTOGRAPHY 94, 191
descriptive study of primitive human cultures ETHNOGRAPHY 92
descriptive study of rainfall HYETOGRAPHY 93
descriptive study of rocks PETROGRAPHY 94
descriptive study of the arts and sciences TECHNOGRAPHY 95
descriptive study of the atmosphere AEROGRAPHY 8, 91
descriptive study of the distribution of mankind ANTHROPOGRAPHY 14, 91
descriptive study of the earth's surface GEOGRAPHY 89, 92
descriptive study of the physical features of a celestial body PHYSIOGRAPHY 94, 193
descriptive study of the universe COSMOGRAPHY 54, 92
desert landscape XERISCAPE 216
deserving to be despised Contemptible DESPICABLE 204
design engraved on a precious stone GLYPTOGRAPH 92
designing and manufacturing of aircraft AVIATION 30
despicable ABJECT 114
destroy gradually ERODE 71
destroy leaving no traces OBLITERATE 68

destruction of one's own prospects SUICIDE 50
destruction of the environment ECOCIDE 50
destructive metabolic process CATABOLISM 12, 144
detailed examination ANALYSIS 11
determine the numerical value of EVALUATE 71
determine the value of Appraise EVALUATE 71
devastating flood Deluge CATACLYSM 12
devastation by fire HOLOCAUST 42
develop gradually EVOLVE 71, 214
developing from kidney tissue NEPHROGENOUS 86, 171
developing from the stem upward toward the apex ACROPETAL 7
development of a diseased condition PATHOGENESIS 79, 87
development of fruit without fertilization PARTHENOCARPY 42
development of two or more embryos from a single ovum POLYEMBRYONY 164
deviate from the main subject DIGRESS 97
deviates from the norm HETEROCLITE 102
deviating from normal behavior ECCENTRIC 44
deviating from the normal rule ANOMALOUS 3, 100
deviation from the normal rule ANOMALY 3, 101
device built on a very small scale MICROMINIATURE 138
device containing a gyroscope with a rotating axis pointing to true north GYROCOMPASS 57, 201
device for carrying air to the lungs AEROPHORE 8, 189
device for coding and decoding speech VOCODER 189
device for detecting vibrations in the earth GEOPHONE 89, 187
device for indicating time HOROLOGE 67
device for maintaining temperature THERMOSTAT 211
device for maintaining a very low temperature CRYOSTAT 55
device for making multiple copies of written material MIMEOGRAPH 93
device for measuring acetic acid ACETOMETER 145
device for measuring acid ACIDIMETER 145
device for measuring alcohol in a liquid ALCOHOLOMETER 145
device for measuring alcohol in the blood DRUNKOMETER 147
device for measuring alkali ALKALIMETER 146
device for measuring distance to the cloud ceiling CEILOMETER 146
device for measuring distance traveled in a taxicab TAXIMETER 150
device for measuring distance traveled in a vehicle ODOMETER 148
device for measuring distance traveled on foot PEDOMETER 149, 181
device for measuring electric charge by the chemical change VOLTAMETER 150
device for measuring electric potential POTENTIOMETER 149
device for measuring temperature that uses two metal conductors THERMOCOUPLE 211
device for measuring wind velocity ANEMOMETER 146
device for monitoring underwater sounds HYDROPHONE 22, 187
device for recording dictation DICTAPHONE 64, 187
device for recording distance traveled ODOGRAPH 94
device for recording telephone conversations DICTOGRAPH 64, 92
device for recording wind velocity ANEMOGRAPH 91
device for reproducing sound from a record PHONOGRAPH 94, 188
device for sending coded messages to a distant location TELEGRAPH 95, 209
device for receiving speech sounds from a distant location TELEPHONE 188, 209
device for varying the aperture of a camera lens DIAPHRAGM 62
device in which bits of colored glass are viewed in symmetrical patterns KALEIDOSCOPE 201
device that converts energy from one form to another TRANSDUCER 63, 69
device that emits electrons when exposed to light PHOTOELECTRIC 190
device to amplify and direct the voice MEGAPHONE 139, 187
device to maintain the temperature of its contents THERMOS 211
device to make multiple copies HECTOGRAPH 43, 93
device to separate materials of different density CENTRIFUGE 44
devices for transmitting data from body functions for analysis BIOINSTRUMENTATION 35
diabetes caused by a disorder of the pituitary gland DIABETES INSIPIDUS 62
diabetes characterized by high concentration of sugar in the blood DIABETES MELLITUS 62
diagnosis by testing blood serum reactions SERODIAGNOSIS 53, 63
diagram of the stars and planets used in astrology HOROSCOPE 201
diagrams displaying numerical relationships GRAPH 92
dialysis of the blood HEMODIALYSIS 63, 99
dictionary LEXICON 66
difference between a color and a reference color CHROMINANCE 47

difference in parts resulting from differences in origin HETEROLOGY 67, 103
difference in position when viewed from two different points PARALLAX 179
different colors HETEROCHROMATIC 48, 102
different forms in the life cycle HETEROMORPHIC 103, 166
different origin HETEROGENOUS 86, 102
different types of individuals within the same species POLYMORPHISM 165, 167
differentiation of cells to form an organism, organ, or part MORPHOGENESIS 86, 167
differing in form HETEROMORPHIC 103, 166
differing in kind HETEROGENEOUS 85, 102
difficult breathing DYSPNEA 33, 193
difficult to describe NONDESCRIPT 96
difficult to read ILLEGIBLE 4
difficult to understand ABSTRACT 212
difficult urination DYSURIA 34
difficulty in swallowing DYSPHAGIA 33, 183
difficulty producing speech sounds DYSPHONIA 33, 187
digest CONSPECTUS 204
digestion PEPTIC 182
digits joined together SYNDACTYL 58, 107
diminish REDUCE 69
diminish in value DETRACT 212
dinosaur of the order Ornithischia that walked on the hind feet ORNITHOPOD 30, 181
dinosaur with a pelvis resembling that of a bird ORNITHISCHIAN 30
diocese in an Eastern Orthodox Church EPARCHY 23, 74
diocese under an archbishop ARCHDIOCESE 23
direct ancestor PROGENITOR 16, 87
direct attention ADVERT 214
direct toward a common center or objective CONCENTRATE 44
directed toward a particular end TELIC 209
director of a symposium SYMPOSIARCH 24, 106
disappear gradually EVANESCE 71
disappearing quickly Fleeting EVANESCENT 71
discharge of material from a cell, as a large molecule, particle, etc. EXOCYTOSIS 39
discharge of pus PYORRHEA 199
discharge of pus PYORRHOEA 199
discharge suddenly EJACULATE 70
disciplinary action in the Roman Catholic Church INTERDICT 65, 111
discipline bodily desires with austerities MORTIFY 169
discontented MALCONTENT 31
discontented person MALCONTENT 31
discontinue a session of a legislature PROROGUE 17
disease caused by vitamin deficiency AVITAMINOSIS 4, 37
disease characterized by small red spots on the skin German measles RUBELLA 78
disease, hardening of tissue in the brain and spinal cord MULTIPLE SCLEROSIS 200
disease marked by abnormal hardening of arterial walls ARTERIOSCLEROSIS 200
disease marked by chronic thickening and hardening of the skin SCLERODERMA 61, 200
disease marked by enlargement of bones in the head, hands, and feet ACROMEGALY 7, 139
disease marked by inflammation of the genital mucous membrane GONORRHEA 88, 199
disease marked by inflammation of the lungs PNEUMONIA 194
disease marked by intestinal inflammation DYSENTERY 33
disease named from the notion that it was caused from bad air MALARIA 31
disease of a joint ARTHROSIS 27
disease of iron metabolism causing bronze skin pigmentation HEMOCHROMATOSIS 48, 99
disease of the brain ENCEPHALOPATHY 45, 79
disease of the eye characterized by a clouding of the lens CATARACT 12
disease of the heart CARDIOPATHY 40, 79
disease of the heart muscle CARDIOMYOPATHY 40, 79, 169
disease of the hip joint COXALGIA 9
disease of the joints ARTHROPATHY 27, 79
disease of the kidneys NEPHROSIS 171
disease of the mind PSYCHOPATHY 79, 196
disease of the muscles MYOPATHY 79, 170
disease of the nervous system NEUROPATHY 79, 172
disease of the retina RETINOPATHY 80
disease of the skin DERMATOSIS 61
disease of the skin that produces pus PYODERMA 61

disease of unknown cause IDIOPATHY 79, 111
disease or illness MALADY 31
disease prevalent over a very large area PANDEMIC 58, 176
disease resulting in softening of the bones OSTEOMALACIA 178
disease transmitted by birds ORNITHOSIS 30
disease-causing agent PATHOGEN 79, 87
diseased condition INFIRMITY 6
diseased condition DYSCRASIA 33
diseases characterized by excessive discharge of urine and persistent thirst DIABETES 61
diseases of the body created by the mind PSYCHOSOMATIC 196
diseases peculiar to women GYNECOPATHY 13, 79
diseases that cause muscle deterioration MUSCULAR DYSTROPHY 34, 212
diseases transmitted by animals ZOONOSIS 218
disguised identity INCOGNITO 5, 53
disjoined DISJUNCT 115
disklike region on a fertilized ovum BLASTODISK 38
disklike region on the surface of a heavily-yolked egg BLASTODISK 38
disliking work Lazy INDOLENT 6
dismiss EJECT 70, 114
dismiss permanently EXPEL 182
disorder caused by inadequate nutrition of a tissue or organ DYSTROPHY 34, 212
disorder characterized by dizziness VERTIGO 215
disorder characterized by recurring cycles of elation and depression CYCLOTHYMIA 56
disorder in which the body cannot tolerate milk GALACTOSEMIA 98
disorder marked by a disregard for moral and social responsibility SOCIOPATH 80
disorder marked by immoral and antisocial behavior PSYCHOPATH 79, 196
disorder of the nervous system marked by convulsive seizures EPILEPSY 75
disorder originally thought to result from neural exhaustion NEURASTHENIA 4, 171
dispersion of people DIASPORA 62, 207
dispersion of Jews DIASPORA 62, 207
display of agility ACROBATICS 7, 130
display different colors when viewed from different directions PLEOCHROISM 48
display two different colors when viewed from two different directions DICHROISM 47, 154
display three different colors when viewed from three different directions TRICHROISM 48, 157
displaying knowledge and culture LITERATE 68
disrespectful IRREVERENT 7
dissection of a dead body NECROTOMY 169, 203
dissection of a plant or animal ANATOMY 11, 202
dissection of animals ZOOTOMY 204, 218
disseminated through the bloodstream HEMATOGENOUS 85, 99
dissimilar species living together in close association of mutual benefit SYMBIOSIS 37, 106
dissipation of body heat THERMOLYSIS 211
distance around CIRCUMFERENCE 50
distance from the center of a polygon to one of its sides APOTHEM 20
distance of an orbiting body from its perihelion or perigee ANOMALY 3, 101
distinctive part SECTOR 202
distinguishing two of three primary colors DICHROMATIC 48, 155
distinguishing all three primary colors TRICHROMATIC 48, 157
distrust SUSPECT 205
disturb greatly Agitate PERTURB 183
divide by cutting through INTERSECT 112, 202
divide into syllables SYLLABIFY 106
divided into four parts by clefts QUADRIFID 158
divided into hundredths CENTESIMAL 43
divided into thousandths MILLESIMAL 115
divided into two parts by a cleft BIFID 154
divided into three parts by clefts TRIFID 157
divination by a book BIBLIOMANCY 34, 140
divination by a rod RHABDOMANCY 140
divination by analysis of the hand Palmistry CHIROMANCY 140
divination by fire PYROMANCY 140, 198
divination by throwing down a handful of earth GEOMANCY 89, 140
divination by water HYDROMANCY 22, 140
divination from birds AUSPICES 29, 204
divination of an object through contact PSYCHOMETRY 149, 196
divination through communication with the dead NECROMANCY 140, 169

KEYWORDS

elements existing in more than one form ALLOTROPY 212
elements of verbal communication that help to communicate meaning PARALANGUAGE 179
elevated platform PODIUM 182
elevating a human being to the status of a god Deification APOTHEOSIS 20, 209
eleven day period by which the solar year leads the lunar year EPACT 74
eleventh sign of the zodiac AQUARIUS 20
eliminate segregation DESEGREGATE 96
elongated bodies in a cell nucleus that contain genes CHROMOSOME 47
embolism caused by air bubbles AEROEMBOLISM 8
embryo develops by structural elaboration rather than by preformation EPIGENESIS 75, 85
embryonic connective tissue in the embryonic mesoderm MESENCHYME 143
embryonic development, implantation of the embryo into the uterine wall BLASTOCYST 38
embryonic development, single layer of cells surrounding a fluid-filled cavity BLASTULA 38
embryonic development, two cell layers, digestive cavity GASTRULA 83
embryonic forebrain PROSENCEPHALON 46
embryonic midbrain MESENCEPHALON 45, 143
embryonic hindbrain RHOMBENCEPHALON 46
embryonic formation and development EMBRYOGENESIS 85
embryonic plant stem located above the cotyledons EPICOTYL 74
embryonic plant stem located below the cotyledons HYPOCOTYL 109
emission of light by a living organism BIOLUMINESCENCE 35
emitting light PHOTOGENIC 87, 190
emitting sparks when struck PYROPHORIC 189, 198
emotional dependence on others ANACLISIS 11
empty INANE 5
empty out EVACUATE 71
enacted after the fact EX POST FACTO 15
enacting laws NOMOTHETIC 173
enclose in a sphere ENSPHERE 206
enclose in a sphere INSPHERE 206
enclosed in parentheses PARENTHETICAL 180
end portion of a long bone that unites with it through ossification EPIPHYSIS 75
ending a marriage DIVORCE 215
endocardium ENDOCARDIAL 41, 72
endoderm ENDOBLAST 38, 71
endoscope for examining a joint ARTHROSCOPE 27, 200
endoscope for examining the abdominal cavity LAPAROSCOPE 201
endoscope for examining the bronchial tubes BRONCHOSCOPE 200
endoscope for examining the ear OTOSCOPE 201
endoscope for examining the fetus FETOSCOPE 201
endoscope for examining the larynx LARYNGOSCOPE 201
endoscope for examining the stomach GASTROSCOPE 83, 201
endoscope for examining the urethra URETHROSCOPE 202
endoscope for examining the urinary bladder CYSTOSCOPE 200
endoscope for examining the vagina and cervix COLPOSCOPE 200
endowed with bodily form INCARNATE 41
endowment of a church PATRIMONY 142
energetic person DYNAMO 69
energy Vigor VITALITY 37
energy of light PHOTODYNAMIC 70, 190
engaged in the field of literature LITERARY 68
engaged in warfare BELLIGERENT 31
enjoyment of life JOIE DE VIVRE 37
enlarge MAGNIFY 140
enlargement of the heart MEGALOCARDIA 41, 139
enlargement of the heart CARDIOMEGALY 40, 139
enlargement of the liver HEPATOMEGALY 100, 139
enlargement of the spleen SPLENOMEGALY 140
enough Sufficient ADEQUATE 76
enroll MATRICULATE 142
entertainment between the acts of a play INTERLUDE 112, 136
enthusiasm Verve ELAN 70
enthusiasm in literary or artistic work VERVE 68
entice to sexual intercourse SEDUCE 69
entire kind GENERIC 85
entire range of a voice or instrument DIAPASON 62

entire universe MACROCOSM 54, 136
enunciate without the vocal cords DEVOCALIZE 188
envelope surrounding the spores of a sporozoan SPOROCYST 207
environment or domain SPHERE 206
enzyme functionally similar to another enzyme ISOENZYME 104
enzyme functionally similar to another enzyme ISOZYME 105
enzyme that aids in blood clotting THROMBOPLASTIN 169
enzyme that begins protein digestion PEPSIN 182
enzyme that catalyzes conversion to an isomeric form ISOMERASE 104
enzyme that catalyzes the hydration or dehydration of a compound HYDRATASE 21
enzyme that converts peptides into amino acids PEPTIDASE 182
enzyme that dissolves blood clots PLASMIN 168
enzyme that functions within the cell that produced it ENDOENZYME 72
enzymes that break down fats LIPASE 118
enzymes that catalyze the removal of hydrogen DEHYDROGENASE 21
enzymes that catalyze the oxidation of hydrogen HYDROGENASE 22
episode that takes place between two things INTERLUDE 112, 136
epitome of the world MICROCOSM 54, 137
equal angles ISOGONIC 91, 104
equal diameters ISODIAMETRIC 63, 104, 148
equal distance apart PARALLEL 179
equal distribution of weight EQUIPOISE 76
equal electric potential ISOELECTRIC 104
equal entropy ISENTROPIC 103, 213
equal force ISODYNAMIC 70, 104
equal in force EQUIPOLLENT 76
equal in value EQUIVALENT 76
equal intervals of time ISOCHRONAL 49, 104
equal magnitude of earthquake shock ISOSEISMAL 105
equal number of electrons ISOELECTRONIC 104
equal number of elements ISOMEROUS 104
equal osmotic pressure ISOTONIC 105
equal osmotic pressure ISOSMOTIC 105
equal pressure ISOPIESTIC 104
equal temperature ISOTHERMAL 105, 210
equal tension ISOTONIC 105
equality of laws ISONOMY 104, 173
equality of measure ISOMETRIC 104, 148
equality of weight EQUIPONDERANCE 76
equally distant EQUIDISTANT 76
equilibrium of the earth's crust ISOSTASY 105
equilibrium resulting from equal pressure ISOSTASY 105
erotic interest in death NECROPHILIA 169, 185
erroneous name MISNOMER 173
error of a lens that prevents light from meeting at a common point ASTIGMATISM 4
error-free INCORRUPT 6, 200
erythroblasts in the circulating blood ERYTHROBLASTOSIS 38, 77
essential parts of something VITALS 37
essential to continuation VITAL 37
essential to life VITAL 37
estimate a value between two known values INTERPOLATE 112
estimate a variable outside its range EXTRAPOLATE 81, 111
estimate an unknown from something known EXTRAPOLATE 81, 111
estrus-producing female sex hormones ESTROGEN 85
etching process that produces tones similar to watercolor washes AQUATINT 20
eucharist LITURGY 77
everlasting fame IMMORTAL 5, 169
everything visible included in one view PANOPTIC 176, 177
everywhere at the same time OMNIPRESENT 176
evidence attesting to one's achievements or trustworthiness CREDENTIALS 54
evil MISCREANT 55
evil influence MALEFIC 32
evil influence MALIGNANT 32, 86
evoke EVOCATIVE 71, 188
evolution involving two or more species COEVOLUTION 214
exactly the same EQUAL 76

expressed conclusion VERDICT 65, 216
expressed in a proverb PROVERBIAL 17, 68
expressed in one language MONOLINGUAL 118, 152
expressed in one language UNILINGUAL 118, 153
expressed in two languages BILINGUAL 118, 154
expressed in three languages TRILINGUAL 118, 157
expressed in several languages MULTILINGUAL 118
expressed in words Oral VERBAL 68
expression that cannot be understood from its elements IDIOM 111
extension of a body part beyond its normal range HYPEREXTENSION 108
extent to which a person cannot be believed CREDIBILITY GAP 55
external covering that provides protection EXOSKELETON 219
external envelope of a flower PERIANTH 18, 51
extinct fish covered with bony plates and scales OSTRACODERM 61
extinct genus of humanoid primates found in Java Java man PITHECANTHROPUS 14
extinct genus of humanoid primates found near Peking, China Peking man SINANTHROPUS 14
extraordinary in a bad way EGREGIOUS 70, 96
extravagant praise PANEGYRIC 177
extreme foolishness LUNACY 136
extremely bad Flagrant EGREGIOUS 70, 96
extremely clean IMMACULATE 5
extremely foolish person LUNATIC 136
extremely great Immense INFINITE 6
extremely large Huge ENORMOUS 71
extremely large Vast COSMIC 54
extremely large ASTRONOMICAL 28, 172
extremely wasteful PROFLIGATE 16
extremities of a chromosome TELOMERE 209
extremity of the scapula ACROMION 7
eye OCULAR 175
eye OPHTHALMIC 176
eye OPTIC 176
eye movements OPTOKINETIC 117, 176
eye weakness or strain ASTHENOPIA 4, 175
eyeball movements OCULOMOTOR 175
eyeglass for one eye MONOCLE 151, 174
eyepiece of an optical instrument OCULAR 175
facial expression ASPECT 204
facial features as a sign of character PHYSIOGNOMY 53, 193
facts that prove a crime CORPUS DELICTI 54
fair Just Impartial EQUITABLE 76
fairness Justness Impartiality EQUITY 76
faithfulness FIDELITY 81
false attribution to a certain writer PSEUDEPIGRAPHY 76, 94, 195
false form PSEUDOMORPH 167, 195
false fruit PSEUDOCARP 42, 195
false pregnancy PSEUDOCYESIS 195
false pregnancy PSEUDOPREGNANCY 195
family name COGNOMEN 173
farsightedness that occurs with advancing age PRESBYOPIA 176
fatal MORTAL 169
father and ruler of a family PATRIARCH 24, 142
father of a family PATERFAMILIAS 142
fatherhood PATERNITY 142
fatherly PATERNAL 142
fathers of the early Christian Church PATRISTIC 142
fats or fatlike materials of a living cell LIPID 118
favorable Auspicious PROPITIOUS 17
favorably inclined Gracious PROPITIOUS 17
fear of England ANGLOPHOBIA 186
fear of Germany GERMANOPHOBIA 186
fear of God THEOPHOBIA 187, 210
fear of Russia RUSSOPHOBIA 187
fear of air AEROPHOBIA 8, 186
fear of animals ZOOPHOBIA 187, 218
fear of being alone MONOPHOBIA 152, 186

feeding on bees APIVOROUS 184
feeding on blood HEMATOPHAGOUS 99, 183
feeding on dead flesh CARRION 41
feeding on dead flesh NECROPHAGOUS 169, 184
feeding on decaying organic matter SAPROPHAGOUS 184
feeding on dung COPROPHAGOUS 183
feeding on fish PISCIVOROUS 184
feeding on flesh CARNIVOROUS 41, 184
feeding on flesh SARCOPHAGOUS 184
feeding on fruit CARPOPHAGOUS 41, 183
feeding on fruit FRUGIVOROUS 184
feeding on grain or seeds GRANIVOROUS 184
feeding on grasses GRAMINIVOROUS 184
feeding on insects CARNIVOROUS 41, 184
feeding on insects INSECTIVOROUS 184
feeding on insects ENTOMOPHAGOUS 183
feeding on leaves PHYLLOPHAGOUS 184, 192
feeding on plants HERBIVOROUS 184
feeding on plants PHYTOPHAGOUS 184, 191
feeding on roots RHIZOPHAGOUS 184
feeding on solid food HOLOZOIC 217
feeding on wood XYLOPHAGOUS 184
feel high regard for RESPECT 205
feeling of dislike ANTIPATHY 79
feeling of high regard Esteem RESPECT 205
feeling of well-being EUPHORIA 33, 189
feeling of ill-being DYSPHORIA 33, 189
feldspar characterized by cleavages that differ slightly from 90 degrees OLIGOCLASE 165
feldspar characterized by perpendicular cleavages ORTHOCLASE 177
feldspar named for its oblique crystals ANORTHITE 3, 119, 177
female aircraft pilot AVIATRIX 30
female benefactor BENEFACTRESS 31
female egg-bearing organ in red algae CARPOGONIUM 41, 88
female gametophyte produced by a megaspore MEGAGAMETOPHYTE 83, 139, 191
female germ cell OOCYTE 40
female patron PATRONESS 143
female reproductive organ in algae and fungi OOGONIUM 88
female reproductive organ of ferns mosses ARCHEGONIUM 23, 88
female reproductive organs in a flower GYNOECIUM 13
female reproductive organ in a flower CARPEL 41
ferns with creeping rhizomes POLYPODY 165, 182
fertilized oosphere OOSPORE 207
festive CONVIVIAL 37
fever PYREXIA 197
fifth element that pervaded all things QUINTESSENCE 160
fifth pair of cranial nerves each of which divides into three branches TRIGEMINAL 157
figurative use of a word TROPE 213
figurative use of words TROPOLOGY 67, 213
figure formed by two intersecting plane surfaces DIHEDRAL 155
figure formed by three intersecting plane surfaces TRIHEDRON 157
figure of speech TROPE 213
figure of speech having the name of one object replaced by another METONYMY 145, 174
figure of speech that uses a part to represent the whole SYNECDOCHE 107
figure of speech that uses exaggeration for rhetorical effect HYPERBOLE 108
figure of speech with an implied comparison METAPHOR 145, 189
figure of speech with an expressed comparison SIMILE 220
figure remaining in a parallelogram, smaller parallelogram removed from one corner GNOMON 53
figure with two sides equal ISOSCELES 104
figures or objects shaped like a half-moon LUNETTE 136
filling volumes VOLUMINOUS 214
film containing microphotographs MICROFILM 137
films that correctly represent all colors PANCHROMATIC 48, 176
films treated to correctly represent all colors except red ORTHOCHROMATIC 48, 177
fine-grained rock APHANITE 3, 119
finger or toe DACTYL 58
fingerprint DACTYLOGRAM 58

foliated rock PHYLLITE 121, 192
follow SUCCEED 42
follow in time POSTDATE 15
following the usual meaning of a word LITERAL 68
fond of good companionship Sociable CONVIVIAL 37
food thought to bestow immortality AMBROSIA 2
foot PODIUM 182
foot and a half long SESQUIPEDALIAN 181
foot-operated lever PEDAL 180
force away REPEL 182
force believed to give the body life Soul SPIRIT 194
force produced by the earth's rotation GEOSTROPHIC 89
force that pulls a rotating body inward towards the center CENTRIPETAL FORCE 44
force that pulls a rotating body outward from center CENTRIFUGAL FORCE 44
forceful, persuasive, and fluent speech ELOQUENT 65, 70
forces that bind quarks together, nonelectrical charges known as colors CHROMODYNAMICS 47, 69, 131
forebrain PROSENCEPHALON 46
forehead METOPIC 145, 175
form into a corporation INCORPORATE 54
form of God THEOMORPHIC 167, 210
form of a beast THERIOMORPHIC 167
form of a root RHIZOMORPHOUS 167
form of an animal ZOOMORPHIC 167, 218
formal authoritative speech ALLOCUTION 65
formal decision of a jury VERDICT 65, 216
formal defense of one's opinions APOLOGIA 19, 66
formal document describing a proposed project PROSPECTUS 17, 205
formal prayer INVOCATION 188
formal speech giving high praise to someone PANEGYRIC 177
formal speech praising a recently deceased person EULOGY 32, 66
formal statement Pronouncement DICTUM 64
formal written or spoken defense APOLOGY 19, 66
formally declare the relinquishment of power ABDICATE 64
formally question a government official INTERPELLATE 112, 182
formation and maturation of spermatozoa SPERMATOGENESIS 87
formation and maturation of spermatozoa SPERMIOGENESIS 87
formation and maturation of the ovum OOGENESIS 86
formation of a single bone by fusion SYNOSTOSIS 107, 178
formation of blood HEMATOSIS 99
formation of gametes GAMETOGENESIS 82, 85
formation of organs ORGANOGENESIS 86
formation of soil PEDOGENESIS 87
formation of words by compounding PARASYNTHESIS 105, 179
formed on the surface of the earth EPIGENE 75, 85
formed below the surface of the earth HYPOGENE 86, 110
forming concepts into a unified whole ESEMPLASTIC 168
forming muscle tissue MYOGENIC 86, 170
forms of a morpheme ALLOMORPH 166
forms of the same phoneme ALLOPHONE 187
forms of an element having the same place in the periodic table ISOTOPE 105
fortified hill of an ancient Greek city ACROPOLIS 7
forward movement PROGRESSION 16, 97
fossil plant PHYTOLITE 121, 191
fossil plant PHYTOLITH 123, 191
fossil plants related to modern horsetails CALAMITE 119
fossil shells named for their resemblance to ram's horns AMMONITE 119
fossilized excrement COPROLITE 120
fountain pen with a fine writing point STYLOGRAPH 95
four areas into which a plane is divided QUADRANT 158
four asexual spores produced in red algae TETRASPORE 160, 208
four beats to the measure QUADRUPLE 159
four channels for sound reproduction QUADRAPHONIC 158, 188
four consonants of the Hebrew name for God YHWH or JHVH TETRAGRAMMATON 159
four equal parts QUARTER 159
four feet QUADRUPED 159, 181
four feet that function as hands QUADRUMANOUS 141, 159

four identical copies QUADRUPLICATE 159
four limbs TETRAPOD 159, 182
four long stamens TETRADYNAMOUS 70, 159
four offspring born at a single birth QUADRUPLET 159
four parts QUADRIPARTITE 159
four sides QUADRILATERAL 158
four times as great QUADRUPLE 159
four wings TETRAPTEROUS 159, 197
fourfold QUADRUPLE 159
fourth degree QUARTIC 159
fourth of the seven canonical hours originally observed at the sixth hour SEXT 161
framework that supports the coffin CATAFALQUE 12
free from illusion Disenchant DISILLUSION 135
free from microorganisms that produce disease ASEPTIC 3
free from restraint EMANCIPATE 71, 141
free of charge PRO BONO 16
free verse VERS LIBRE 215
free-moving cell CORPUSCLE 54
freezing the body for possible revival by future medical cures CRYONICS 36, 55, 131
French intellectuals and writers PHILOSOPHE 185, 204
frequent and indiscriminate sexual relations PROMISCUOUS 17
fresh water polyp HYDRA 21
friction created by a body moving on a surface TRACTION 212
frogs which have no tail ANURAN 3
from the outside EXTRANEOUS 81
front half of half a carcass FOREQUARTER 159
fruit at the tip of the stem ACROCARPOUS 7, 41
fruit flies named from the inability of certain mutants to survive in dry air DROSOPHILA 185
fruit that ripens without splitting open its sheath ACHENE 1
fruit that splits into carpels SCHIZOCARP 42
fruiting only once MONOCARPIC 42, 151
fruiting many times POLYCARPIC 42, 164
full suit of armor PANOPLY 177
function abnormally MALFUNCTION 32
functioning as a noun NOMINAL 174
functioning as a vowel VOCALIC 188
functioning independently AUTONOMOUS 29, 173
functioning involuntarily AUTONOMIC 29, 172
functions and vital processes of an organism PHYSIOLOGY 128, 193
functions of the mind PSYCHE 195
fundamental RADICAL 198
fungus of the skin DERMATOPHYTE 61, 191
fusion of heterogametes ANISOGAMOUS 2, 82, 103
fusion of heterogametes HETEROGAMOUS 82, 102
fusion of pronuclei during fertilization KARYOGAMY 83
future generations POSTERITY 15
gain the favor of Conciliate Appease PROPITIATE 17
galvanometer for detecting electric current GALVANOSCOPE 201
game in which words are formed from randomly chosen letters ANAGRAM 11
gamete that unites with another of the same form ISOGAMETE 83, 104
gamete that unites with another of different form HETEROGAMETE 82, 102
gametophyte, develops directly from the sporophyte without spore formation APOSPORY 19, 207
gangrenous MORTIFY 169
garnet named after Alabanda, an ancient city in Asia Minor ALMANDITE 118
garnet named after Count Uvarov, Russian statesman UVAROVITE 122
garnet named after J.B. de Andrada, Brazilian geologist ANDRADITE 119
garnet named from the gooseberry green variety in Siberia GROSSULARITE 120
garnet with a fiery-red color PYROPE 198
gas from bacterial decomposition of organic waste BIOGAS 35
gaseous element named from the generation of water during its combustion HYDROGEN 21, 86
gaseous element that makes up 21 per cent of the atmosphere OXYGEN 87
gaseous element that makes up 78 per cent of the atmosphere NITROGEN 86
gaseous envelope surrounding the earth consisting of five layers ATMOSPHERE 206
gather together into a group CONGREGATE 96
gears meshed by synchronizing their speed SYNCHROMESH 49, 106
gels liquefying when agitated THIXOTROPY 213

gem with less value than a precious gem SEMIPRECIOUS 59
general view of a subject CONSPECTUS 204
generation of electricity by water power HYDROELECTRIC 21
generation of offspring different from either parent XENOGENESIS 88, 216
genetic composition of an organism GENOTYPE 85
genetic element that can replicate independently of the chromosomes PLASMID 168
genetic element that can replicate in the cytoplasm or with the chromosomes EPISOME 48, 75
genetic influence of one sire on offspring born to other sires TELEGONY 88, 209
gentle disposition BENIGN 31, 84
genuine VERIDICAL 65
genus GENERIC 85
geological era characterized by one-celled organisms ARCHEOZOIC 23, 216
geological era characterized by multi-celled organisms PROTEROZOIC 217
geological era characterized by the first reptiles PALEOZOIC 25, 217
geological era characterized by the development of mammals MESOZOIC 144, 217
geological era characterized by the development of man CENOZOIC 217
geological periods previous to life on earth AZOIC 216
geomorphic rock lined with crystals GEODE 89
germ cell that produces gametes GAMETOCYTE 39, 82
germ-free AXENIC 4, 216
German measles RUBEOLA 78
get rid of completely Exterminate ERADICATE 71, 198
ghost SPECTER 205
ghost SPECTRE 205
giants with a single eye CYCLOPS 56, 175
give a lengthy speech PERORATE 183
give a name to Designate DENOMINATE 173
give assistance to SUPPORT 194
give back RETROCEDE 42, 198
give life to VIVIFY 38
give off EMIT 71
give off vapor through a membrane or pores TRANSPIRE 64, 194
give up Relinquish CEDE 42
given freely PROFUSE 16, 82
giving false information under oath PERJURY 183
gland at the base of the brain that influences body growth Pituitary gland HYPOPHYSIS 110
gland that functions both as an exocrine and an endocrine gland PANCREAS 176
gland that produces gametes GONAD 88
glands located below and in front of each ear PAROTID 180
glands located near the thyroid gland PARATHYROID GLAND 179
glands that secrete directly into the blood ENDOCRINE 72
glands that secrete through a duct EXOCRINE 219
glands that secrete sweat without removing cytoplasm ECCRINE 219
glands in which cytoplasm is lost along with the secretion APOCRINE 19
glassy objects whose exact origin is unknown TEKTITE 122
glorified ideal APOTHEOSIS 20, 209
gnawing mammals including rabbits, hares, and pikas LAGOMORPH 166
Gnostic creator of the material world DEMIURGE 58, 77
go around CIRCUMVENT 51
go back RETROCEDE 42, 198
go back to an earlier and usually worse condition REGRESS 97
go backward to an earlier or less advanced condition RETROGRESS 97, 198
go before ANTECEDE 14, 42
go before PRECEDE 42
go beyond a boundary TRANSGRESS 64, 97
go beyond a limit EXCEED 42
go beyond the limits of TRANSCEND 63
go forward Advance PROCEED 16, 42
go on in an orderly manner PROCEED 16, 42
God as the center of interest THEOCENTRIC 45, 210
goddess of flowers FLORA 18
going back REGRESS 97
going back to a worse condition Deteriorating RETROGRADE 97, 198
going in INGRESS 97
going out EGRESS 70, 97
gold and ivory statues in ancient Greece CHRYSELEPHANTINE 49

golden-brown and yellowish-green algae CHRYSOPHYTE 49, 191
good omen AUSPICIOUS 29, 204
governed by God THEONOMOUS 173, 210
governing in a fatherly manner PATERNALISM 142
government by one person AUTOCRACY 24, 28
government by one person MONOCRACY 24, 151
government by three persons TRIUMVIRATE 158
government by one ruler MONARCHY 23, 151
government by two rulers DIARCHY 23, 154
government by two rulers DYARCHY 23
government by three rulers TRIARCHY 24, 156
government by four rulers TETRARCHY 24, 159
government by five rulers PENTARCHY 24, 160
government by seven rulers HEPTARCHY 23, 162
government by a few rulers OLIGARCHY 23, 165
government by a mob OCHLOCRACY 24
government by elders GERONTOCRACY 24
government by holy persons HAGIARCHY 23
government by holy persons HAGIOCRACY 24
government by priests HIEROCRACY 24
government by representatives of God THEOCRACY 24, 210
government by numerous departments and subdivisions BUREAUCRACY 24
government by technical experts TECHNOCRACY 24
government by the elite ARISTOCRACY 24
government by the military STRATOCRACY 24
government by the people DEMOCRACY 24, 58
government by the wealthy PLUTOCRACY 24
government by women GYNARCHY 13, 23
government by women GYNECOCRACY 13, 24
government in which all share equal power ISOCRACY 24, 104
government in which love of honor is the principal motivator TIMOCRACY 24
government in which officials must be property owners TIMOCRACY 24
government should not interfere with natural economic laws PHYSIOCRACY 24, 193
governmental province EPARCHY 23, 74
governmental subdivision of a province EPARCHY 23, 74
gradual developmental change EVOLUTION 71, 214
gradual improvement PROGRESS 16, 97
grafting tissue from an animal ZOOPLASTY 169, 218
grafting tissue from another person or another species HETEROPLASTY 103, 168
grafting tissue from the same body AUTOPLASTY 29, 167
grammatical construction in which words disagree in sense SYLLEPSIS 106
grammatical construction that agrees in sense rather than syntax SYNESIS 107
grammatical construction that has the same function as its components ENDOCENTRIC 44, 72
grammatical construction that does not have the same function as its components EXOCENTRIC 44
grandiose speech MAGNILOQUENT 65, 140
grant a right or privilege CONCEDE 42
granular metamorphic rock GRANULITE 120
granular rock used in monuments and buildings GRANITE 120
graph that uses parallel bars to represent data BAR GRAPH 91
graphic design DIAGRAM 62
great charter signed in June, 1215 MAGNA CARTA 140
great work MAGNUM OPUS 140
greater than EXCEED 42
greatest work Masterpiece MAGNUM OPUS 140
greatness in size MAGNITUDE 140
Greek translation of the Old Testament supposedly done by seventy scholars SEPTUAGINT 162
green earths used as a pigment TERRE-VERTE 90
green pigment made from chromic oxide CHROME GREEN 47
green pigments composed of blue and chrome yellow CHROME GREEN 47
green pigments in plants CHLOROPHYLL 192
greenish-blue color CYAN 56
group engaged in an activity of dubious legality DEMIMONDE 58
group of two Pair DUAD 156
group of three TRIAD 156
group of three TRIO 157
group of three TRIPLET 158

group of four TETRAD 159
group of four QUARTET 159
group of four QUARTETTE 159
group of four QUADRUPLET 159
group of five PENTAD 160
group of five QUINTET 160
group of five QUINTETTE 160
group of five QUINTUPLET 161
group of six HEXAD 161
group of six SEXTET 161
group of six SEXTETTE 161
group of six SEXTUPLET 161
group of seven HEPTAD 161
group of seven SEPTET 162
group of seven SEPTETTE 162
group of eight OCTAD 162
group of eight OCTET 162
group of eight OCTETTE 162
group of nine ENNEAD 219
group of ten DECADE 163
group of four chromatids formed by longitudinal division of chromosomes TETRAD 159
group of individuals GENUS 85
group of islands ARCHIPELAGO 23
group of states around a common religious center AMPHICTYONY 10
group of things that work together to form a whole SYSTEM 107
group regarded as superior ELITE 70
group united for a common purpose UNION 153
grouped into one UNION 153
growing in pairs DIDYMOUS 155
growing near water SEMIAQUATIC 20, 59
growing on the ground EPIGEAL 75, 88
growing on the lower surface HYPOGENOUS 86, 110
growing on the upper surface EPIGENOUS 75, 85
growing together SYMPHYSIS 106
gypsum named because its brightness was believed to wax and wane with the moon SELENITE 122
gyrocompass GYRO 57
gyroscope GYRO 57
gyrus GYRAL 57
hairlike mineral bodies TRICHITE 122
hairlike projection from the female sex organ in lichens TRICHOGYNE 14
half a day SEMIDIURNAL 59
half a diameter Radius SEMIDIAMETER 59, 63, 150
half of a line of verse HEMISTICH 59
half of the earth HEMISPHERE 59, 206
half the plane surfaces needed for symmetry HEMIHEDRAL 58
halfway between two major tones SEMITONE 59
handcuff MANACLE 141
handgun with a revolving cylinder REVOLVER 214
handwriting CALLIGRAPHY 91
handwriting CHIROGRAPHY 91
handwriting SCRIPT 96
haploid set of chromosomes with its full complement of genes GENOME 48, 85
harass constantly PERSECUTE 183
harass in an injurious manner PERSECUTE 183
hard SCLEROUS 200
hard outer covering SCLERODERMATOUS 61, 200
hard outer plates of an arthropod SCLERITE 200
hardened SCLEROID 200
hardened mass of mycelium in which food is stored SCLEROTIUM 200
hardened tumorlike area of granulation tissue SCLEROMA 200
hardening of tissue or a body part SCLEROSIS 200
hardship Misfortune ADVERSITY 214
harm the reputation of TRADUCE 63, 69
harmless BENIGN 31, 84
harmonious relationship RAPPORT 194
harmony and proportion EURHYTHMY 33

homosexuality HOMOEROTICISM 101
hoofed mammals with an even number of toes ARTIODACTYL 58
hoofed mammals with an uneven number of toes PERISSODACTYL 58
hopeless ABJECT 114
horizontal axis X-AXIS 30
hormone similar to cortisone, contains two more hydrogen atoms HYDROCORTISONE 21, 156
hormone that stimulates buds to flower FLORIGEN 18, 85
hormone that stimulates the release of gastric juices GASTRIN 83
hormones that promote male characteristics ANDROGEN 13, 84
horse named from the quarter-mile tracks on which it was raced QUARTER HORSE 159
hot water of the earth HYDROTHERMAL 22, 210
human MORTAL 169
humans descended from one ancestral line MONOGENISM 86, 151
humans descended from more than one ancestral line POLYGENISM 87, 164
humiliate MORTIFY 169
humorous imitation of a serious literary or musical work PARODY 180
hundredth CENTESIMAL 43
hybrid language spoken in Mediterranean ports LINGUA FRANCA 118
hydra HYDROID 22
hydrate that contains two moles of compound for each mole of water HEMIHYDRATE 21, 59
hydrogen HYDRIC 21
hydrogen and another element HYDRIDE 21
hydrogen and carbon HYDROCARBON 21
hydrotherapy HYDROTHERAPEUTICS 22, 133
hydroxyl group HYDROXY 23
hymn of praise to God DOXOLOGY 55, 66
hymn sung at the beginning of a worship INTROIT 80
hymn sung by alternating groups ANTIPHON 187
hypersensitivity to a substance from a previous inoculation ANAPHYLAXIS 11
hypoxia ANOXIA 3
identical color ISOCHROOUS 48, 104
identity in pitch UNISON 153
igneous rock causing an upward bulge LACCOLITH 123
igneous rock consisting mainly of pyroxene PYROXENITE 121, 198, 216
igneous rock deep in the earth's crust BATHOLITH 123
igneous rocks that originated at great depths as molten matter HYPABYSSAL 109
ignite spontaneously PYROPHORIC 189, 198
igniting spontaneously on contact with an oxidizer HYPERGOLIC 108
illegible handwriting CACOGRAPHY 91
image ICON 111
image created by x-rays RADIOGRAPH 94
imaginary circle around the circumference of the earth EQUATOR 76
imaginary perfect place UTOPIA 220
imaginary dreadful place DYSTOPIA 34
imaginary infinite sphere with the earth at its center CELESTIAL SPHERE 206
immature blood cell HEMATOBLAST 38, 99
immature lymphocyte LYMPHOBLAST 38
immature melanocyte MELANOBLAST 38, 144
immature nerve cell NEUROBLAST 39, 172
immature red blood cell ERYTHROBLAST 38, 77
immeasurably deep ABYSS 1
immeasurably small INFINITESIMAL 6
impairment of muscular movements DYSKINESIA 33, 117
impairment of speech DYSPHASIA 33
impairment of the ability to read DYSLEXIA 33, 66
impairment of the ability to write DYSGRAPHIA 33, 92
impairment of vision without injury or disease AMBLYOPIA 175
important occasion EVENT 71
impossible to get rid of INERADICABLE 6, 71, 198
impossible to get rid of IRRADICABLE 7, 198
impression not based on fact ILLUSION 136
impressive SPECTACULAR 205
improper action IMPROPRIETY 5
improper use of a word or phrase IMPROPRIETY 5
improve human behavior by evaluation of the use of symbols and words GENERAL SEMANTICS 132
in good faith BONA FIDE 81

inflammation of the gallbladder CHOLECYSTITIS 113
inflammation of the gray matter of the spinal cord Polio POLIOMYELITIS 114
inflammation of the gums GINGIVITIS 113
inflammation of the heart CARDITIS 41, 113
inflammation of the ileum ILEITIS 113
inflammation of the intestinal tract ENTERITIS 113
inflammation of the iris IRITIS 113
inflammation of the kidneys NEPHRITIS 113, 171
inflammation of the kidney and its pelvis PYELITIS 114
inflammation of the kidney and its pelvis PYELONEPHRITIS 114, 171
inflammation of the larynx LARYNGITIS 113
inflammation of the liver HEPATITIS 100, 113
inflammation of the lymph nodes LYMPHADENITIS 113
inflammation of the mastoid process MASTOIDITIS 113
inflammation of the meninges MENINGITIS 113
inflammation of the mouth STOMATITIS 114
inflammation of the myocardium MYOCARDITIS 41, 113, 169
inflammation of the nose RHINITIS 114, 199
inflammation of the nose and pharynx RHINOPHARYNGITIS 114, 199
inflammation of the pancreas PANCREATITIS 113
inflammation of the parotid glands PAROTITIS 113, 180
inflammation of the pericardium PERICARDITIS 41, 51, 113
inflammation of the periosteum PERIOSTITIS 52, 113, 178
inflammation of the peritoneum PERITONITIS 52, 113
inflammation of the pharynx PHARYNGITIS 113
inflammation of the prostate gland PROSTATITIS 114
inflammation of the renal glomeruli GLOMERULONEPHRITIS 113, 171
inflammation of the retina RETINITIS 114
inflammation of the sclera SCLERITIS 114, 200
inflammation of the skin DERMATITIS 61, 113
inflammation of the spinal cord MYELITIS 113
inflammation of the stomach GASTRITIS 83, 113
inflammation of the stomach and intestines GASTROENTERITIS 83, 113
inflammation of the thyroid gland THYROIDITIS 114
inflammation of the tissues surrounding a tooth PERIODONTITIS 52, 60, 113
inflammation of the tonsils TONSILLITIS 114
inflammation of the trachea TRACHEITIS 114
inflammation of the urethra URETHRITIS 114
inflammation of the uterus METRITIS 113
inflammation of the uvea UVEITIS 114
inflammation of the uvula UVULITIS 114
inflammation of the vertebrae SPONDYLITIS 114
inflammation of the vagina VAGINITIS 114
inflammation of the vulva VULVITIS 114
inflammation of the vulva and vagina VULVOVAGINITIS 114
inflammation of two or more nerves POLYNEURITIS 114, 165, 172
informal conversation COLLOQUIAL 65
informal meeting COLLOQUIUM 65
ingestion of foreign matter by phagocytes PHAGOCYTOSIS 40, 184
inhale INSPIRE 194
inheritance PATRIMONY 142
inhibiting the growth of malignant cells ANTINEOPLASTIC 167, 170
initiate a quarrel AGGRESS 97
injected under the skin HYPODERMIC 61, 109
injurious treatment by a physician or other professional MALPRACTICE 32
inland water route from Boston, Mass. to Brownsville Texas INTRACOASTAL WATERWAY 80
innate CONGENITAL 84
innate INDIGENOUS 86
innate changes to biological processes BIORHYTHM 36
inner curve of an arch INTRADOS 80
inner layer in the sporangium of a moss ENDOTHECIUM 72
inner layer of a fruit ENDOCARP 42, 72
inner layer of a mature anther ENDOTHECIUM 72
inner layer of the three primary germ cell layers of an embryo ENDODERM 61, 72
inner layer of the three primary germ cell layers of an embryo HYPOBLAST 38, 109
inner lining of the uterus ENDOMETRIUM 72

KEYWORDS

instrument for viewing sounding bodies PHONOSCOPE 188, 201
instrument for viewing spectra SPECTROSCOPE 202, 205
instrument for viewing the sun using one spectral frequency SPECTROHELIOSCOPE 98, 201, 205
instrument for writing minutely MICROGRAPH 93, 138
instrument inserted into a body passage for medical examination SPECULUM 205
instrument similar to a sextant OCTANT 162
instrument that converts sound waves into a small electric current MICROPHONE 138, 187
instrument that reflects the sun's rays in one direction HELIOSTAT 98
instruments that use the interference phenomena of light waves INTERFEROMETER 112, 148
insure against future loss INDEMNIFY 6
intake of fluids by a cell PINOCYTOSIS 40
intellectual CEREBRAL 46
intended to cause pain VINDICTIVE 65
intensely colored CHROMATIC 47
intentional display of emotional behavior HISTRIONICS 133
interconnection between branches ANASTOMOSIS 11
intermediate INTERMEDIARY 112, 143
internal skeleton ENDOSKELETON 72
interpretation of the Scriptures in a figurative sense TROPOLOGY 67, 213
interpreting everything in terms of human beings ANTHROPOCENTRIC 14, 44
intersection of the medians of a triangle CENTROID 44
interval between two successive new moons LUNATION 136
intolerant ILLIBERAL 5
introduce a fluid into INJECT 114
introduce abruptly INTERJECT 112, 114
introduce into a conversation INJECT 114
introduction of a gene into the gene pool of another species INTROGRESSION 80, 97
introduction to a discourse PROLOGUE 17, 67
introduction to a major performance PRELUDE 136
introductory essay PROLUSION 17, 136
introductory event PROLOGUE 17, 67
introductory remarks Preface PROLEGOMENON 16
introductory statement Preface PROEM 16
inverted trough-shaped basin of stratified rock ANTICLINE 219
invocation of a blessing BENEDICTION 31, 64
invocation of evil MALEDICTION 32, 65
ion emitted by a heated substance THERMION 211
irrational distrust of others PARANOIA 179
irreducible constituent of a specified system ATOM 4, 202
irregularity of the heart's normal rhythm ARRHYTHMIA 3
irresistible craving for alcoholic liquors DIPSOMANIA 140
irresistible impulse to start fires PYROMANIA 141, 198
irresistible impulse to steal KLEPTOMANIA 140
isomers in which the atoms differ in spacial arrangement STEREOISOMER 105
issue with authority EMIT 71
itemized list of investments PORTFOLIO 194
jade named from the former belief that it could remedy kidney disorders NEPHRITE 121, 171
jar with a handle on each side AMPHORA 10, 189
jaws aligned ORTHOGNATHOUS 177
jaws projecting forward PROGNATHOUS 16
jellyfishes SCYPHOZOAN 217
jellylike layer between the ectoderm and the endoderm in cnidarians MESOGLEA 143
jellylike layer between the ectoderm and the endoderm in cnidarians MESOGLOEA 143
jellylike state of cytoplasm PLASMAGEL 168
jewish assemblage SYNAGOG 9, 106
jewish assemblage SYNAGOGUE 9, 106
jewish house of worship SYNAGOG 9, 106
jewish house of worship SYNAGOGUE 9, 106
joined together CONJUNCT 114
joined without being a necessary part ADJUNCT 114
joining of bones by ligaments SYNDESMOSIS 107
joining of two bones SYMPHYSIS 106
joining of two individuals PARABIOSIS 36, 178
joining together CONJUNCTION 115
joint between bones ARTHROSIS 27
junction between conductors of a thermocouple THERMOJUNCTION 115, 211

lack of vitality ANEMIA 2, 98
lack of willpower ABULIA 1
lacking a tone center or key ATONAL 4
lacking cerebral functions DECEREBRATE 46
lacking confidence in oneself Shy DIFFIDENT 81
lacking continuity in speech or manner ABRUPT 199
lacking discretion Unwise IMPRUDENT 5
lacking excitement Dull INSIPID 7
lacking in power Ineffective IMPOTENT 5
lacking material substance Spiritual INCORPOREAL 6, 54
lacking meaning Silly INANE 5
lacking moral principles AMORAL 2
lacking muscle tone AMYOTONIA 2, 169
lacking normal pigmentation ACHROMIC 1, 46
lacking physical existence but regarded by the law as existing INCORPOREAL 6, 54
lacking physical strength Weak IMPOTENT 5
lacking sexual organs Sexless ASEXUAL 3
lacking taste INSIPID 7
lake, the cooler lower layer of water HYPOLIMNION 110
lake, the warmer uppermost layer of water EPILIMNION 75
laminated sedimentary rock formed from marine algae STROMATOLITE 122
land AGRARIAN 9
land TERRESTRIAL 90
land and water TERRAQUEOUS 20, 90
language LINGUAL 118
language in a certain region DIALECT 62
language or linguistics LINGUISTIC 118
language peculiar to a group of people IDIOM 111
language structure in terms of morphemes MORPHEMICS 134, 167
language that is the ancestor of another language PROTOLANGUAGE 25
language used among peoples of different languages LINGUA FRANCA 118
language used between nations of the scientific community INTERLINGUA 112, 118
large beads on a rosary PATERNOSTER 142
large bottle of wine MAGNUM 140
large carnivorous dinosaur MEGALOSAUR 139
large cell with a highly lobulated nucleus MEGAKARYOCYTE 40, 139
large constellation in the Southern Hemisphere HYDRA 21
large dinosaurs with four feet SAUROPOD 182
large dose MEGADOSE 139
large dysfunctional erythroblast MEGALOBLAST 38, 139
large molecule MACROMOLECULE 137
large phagocyte MACROPHAGE 137, 184
large stone used in monuments MEGALITH 123, 139
large thick-skinned mammals PACHYDERM 61
large thick-skinned mammals with horns on the snout RHINOCEROS 199
large waterfall CATARACT 12
large wings MACROPTEROUS 137, 197
large-footed birds MEGAPODE 139, 181
large-scale evolution of organisms MACROEVOLUTION 136, 214
large-scale farming AGRIBUSINESS 9
large-scale slaughter HECATOMB 43
larger of two conjugating gametes MACROGAMETE 83, 136
larger spores in heterosporous plants MEGASPORE 140, 207
larger spores in heterosporous plants MACROSPORE 137, 207
last from year to year PERENNATE 73, 182
last stage of the prophase in meiosis DIAKINESIS 62, 117
lasting a long time CHRONIC 49
lasting for two years BIENNIAL 73, 154
lasting for three years TRIENNIAL 74, 157
lasting for four years QUADRENNIAL 73, 158
lasting for five years QUINQUENNIAL 73, 160
lasting for six years SEXENNIAL 74, 161
lasting for seven years SEPTENNIAL 74, 162
lasting for eight years OCTENNIAL 73, 162
lasting for ten years DECENNIAL 73, 163
lasting for fifteen years QUINDECENNIAL 73, 160, 164

line connecting points of equal barometric pressure ISOBAR 31, 104
line connecting points with equal change of barometric pressure ISALLOBAR 31, 103
line connecting points of equal depth below the earth ISOBATH 104
line connecting points of equal magnetic force ISOMAGNETIC 104
line connecting points of equal numerical value ISOPLETH 104
line connecting points of equal value ISOGRAM 104
line connecting points receiving equal rainfall ISOHYET 104
line connecting points with equal average temperature ISOTHERM 105, 210
line connecting points with equal earthquake shock ISOSEISMAL 105
line connecting points with equal magnetic declination ISOGONAL LINE 90, 104
line connecting points with equal magnetic inclination ISOCLINIC LINE 104
line connecting points with equal magnetic intensity ISODYNAMIC 70, 104
line connecting points with zero magnetic declination AGONIC LINE 1, 90
line of descent GENEALOGY 85, 125
line of poetry VERSE 215
line of verse consisting of one metrical foot MONOMETER 148, 152
line of verse consisting of two metrical feet DIMETER 147, 155
line of verse consisting of three metrical feet TRIMETER 150, 157
line of verse consisting of four metrical feet TETRAMETER 150, 159
line of verse consisting of five metrical feet PENTAMETER 149, 160
line of verse consisting of six metrical feet HEXAMETER 148, 161
line of verse consisting of seven metrical feet HEPTAMETER 148, 161
line of verse consisting of eight metrical feet OCTAMETER 148, 162
line of verse lacking part of the last foot CATALECTIC 12
line of verse with the complete number of syllables in the last foot ACATALECTIC 12
line of verse with additional syllables after the last foot HYPERCATALECTIC 13, 108
line of verse with additional syllables after those normal for the meter HYPERMETER 108, 148
line of verse with five syllables PENTASYLLABLE 105, 160
line of verse with six syllables HEXASYLLABLE 105, 161
line of verse with seven syllables SEPTISYLLABLE 105, 162
line of verse with eight syllables OCTOSYLLABLE 105, 162
line of verse with nine syllables ENNEASYLLABLE 105
line of verse with ten syllables DECASYLLABLE 105, 163
line of verse with eleven syllables HENDECASYLLABLE 105, 164
line of verse with twelve syllables DODECASYLLABLE 105, 156, 163
line on a map that shows common linguistic characteristics ISOGRAPH 93, 104
line on a map that shows different dialects ISOGLOSS 104
line that a curve approaches but never meets ASYMPTOTE 4, 105
line that measures the distance through the center of a circle DIAMETER 62, 147
line that passes through the center of an anatomical structure AXIS 30
line through any two nonadjacent angles of a polygon DIAGONAL 62, 90
linear series of body segments METAMERE 145
linguistics expert LINGUIST 118
lipid LIPOID 118
lipids found in nerve tissue CEREBROSIDE 46
liquefy by heating FUSE 81
liquid, N_2H_4, used as a jet fuel HYDRAZINE 21, 217
liquid, NH_3, used in explosives HYDRAZOIC ACID 21, 217
liquid forced through a tube HYDRAULIC 21
liquid packaged with a gas and dispersed through a valve AEROSOL 8
liquidate by paying at intervals AMORTIZE 169
liquor AQUA VITAE 20, 37
liquor AQUAVIT 20, 37
list ENUMERATE 71
list of all the inflected forms of a word PARADIGM 178
list of films FILMOGRAPHY 92
list of martyrs MARTYROLOGY 67
list of persons who have died Obituary NECROLOGY 67, 169
list of recordings DISCOGRAPHY 34, 92
list of sources BIBLIOGRAPHY 34, 91
list of writings BIBLIOGRAPHY 34, 91
literature LITERARY 68
literature having aesthetic value BELLES-LETTRES 68
lithium LITHIC 123
lithographic printing process that uses a photograph PHOTOLITHOGRAPHY 94, 123, 190
little annual rainfall SEMIARID 59

love of wisdom PHILOSOPHY 185, 204
love of women PHILOGYNY 14, 185
love potion PHILTER 185
love potion PHILTRE 185
lover of animals ZOOPHILE 186, 218
lover of archery TOXOPHILITE 186
lover of books BIBLIOPHILE 34, 184
lover of cats AILUROPHILE 184
lover of mankind PHILANTHROPIST 14, 185
lover of music AUDIOPHILE 184
lover of wine OENOPHILE 185
lover of words LOGOPHILE 67, 185
loving music PHILHARMONIC 185
loving one's offspring PHILOPROGENITIVE 16, 87, 185
lower in rank DEGRADE 97
lower in spirit Depress DEJECT 114
lower osmotic pressure HYPOTONIC 110
lower the importance of DOWNGRADE 97
lower the vitality of Weaken DEVITALIZE 37
lowest of the three middle regions of the abdomen HYPOGASTRIUM 83, 109
ludicrous misuse of a word MALAPROPISM 31
luminescence of a substance when heated THERMOLUMINESCENCE 211
luminous circle passing through the sun PARHELIC CIRCLE 98, 180
luminous spot on a lunar halo PARASELENE 179
luminous spot on the parhelic circle opposite the sun ANTHELION 97
luminous spots on the parhelic circle on either side of the sun PARHELION 98, 180
lung disease caused by breathing extremely fine siliceous dust
PNEUMONOULTRAMICROSCOPICSILICOVOLCANOCONIOSIS 139, 194, 201
lung disease caused by breathing mineral or metallic dust PNEUMOCONIOSIS 193
lungs PNEUMONIC 194
lying across TRANSVERSE 64, 215
lying face down PROCUMBENT 16
macroglobulins in the blood MACROGLOBULINEMIA 100, 137
magic potion PHILTER 185
magic potion PHILTRE 185
magistrates EPHOR 74
magnetic properties of a rotating charged particle GYROMAGNETIC 57
magnetism generated by heat THERMOMAGNETIC 211
magnetization of an ancient rock PALEOMAGNETISM 25
magnetohydrodynamics HYDROMAGNETICS 22, 133
magnification that is different from two perpendicular directions ANAMORPHIC 11, 166
main body CORPUS 54
make clear Explain ELUCIDATE 70
make complicated PERPLEX 183
make corrections to by editing EMEND 71
make equal EQUATE 76
make from readily available materials IMPROVISE 5, 16
make holes through PERFORATE 183
make less dangerous DEFUSE 81
make longer ELONGATE 70
make meaningless marks SCRIBBLE 96
make private SECLUDE 52
make something by hand or with machinery MANUFACTURE 141
make uncertain CONFUSE 81
make uncertain PERPLEX 183
make unfit Disqualify INDISPOSE 6
make unwilling INDISPOSE 6
make useful again REVIVE 37
make widespread Disseminate PROMULGATE 17
malaria parasite in tissue cells before entering the blood CRYPTOZOITE 56, 207, 217
male and female reproductive organs in separate individuals DIOECIOUS 155
male and female reproductive organs in the same individual MONOECIOUS 151
male and female sexual characteristics ANDROGYNOUS 13
male female and bisexual flowers on separate plants TRIOECIOUS 157
male gamete produced in an antheridium SPERMATOZOID 217
male gametophyte produced by a microspore MICROGAMETOPHYTE 83, 138, 191

male germ cell SPERMATOCYTE 40
male reproductive organ of ferns, mosses ANTHERIDIUM 18
male reproductive organs in a flower ANDROECIUM 13
malformation of the skull that gives the head a conical shape ACROCEPHALY 7, 45
malformation of the skull that gives the head a conical shape OXYCEPHALY 46
malignant tumor composed of astrocytes ASTROCYTOMA 27, 39
malignant tumor composed of epithelial cells EPITHELIOMA 75
malignant tumor composed of mesothelial tissue MESOTHELIOMA 144
malignant tumor composed of neuroblasts NEUROBLASTOMA 39, 172
malignant tumor composed of striated muscle RHABDOMYOSARCOMA 170
malignant tumor of a bone OSTEOSARCOMA 178
malignant tumor of the liver HEPATOMA 100
malignant tumor of the skin containing dark pigment MELANOMA 144
mammals that feed on insects INSECTIVORE 184
mammals with a single opening for digestive, urinary, and genital organs MONOTREME 152
mammals with forelimbs modified for flight CHIROPTER 196
mammals with no teeth EDENTATE 60, 70
manage cleverly and often unfairly MANIPULATE 141
manage poorly MALADMINISTER 31
management of the income and affairs of a household or government ECONOMY 173
mania involving slightly abnormal elation and overactivity HYPOMANIA 110, 140
manner of expression in speech or writing DICTION 64
manner of using words and phrases in speech or writing PHRASEOLOGY 67
manner of living MODUS VIVENDI 37
manual movement of a displaced organ or part TAXIS 208
manufacture of materials measuring up to 100 nanometers NANOTECHNOLOGY 127
manuscript SCRIPT 96
many branches RAMOSE 198
many carpels POLYCARPELLARY 42, 164
many coils VOLUMINOUS 214
many colors POLYCHROMATIC 48, 164
many colors POLYCHROME 48, 164
many meanings POLYSEMY 165
many nuclei POLYNUCLEAR 165
many pistils POLYGYNY 14, 164
many stamens POLYANDRY 13, 164
many sides MULTILATERAL 219
many types POLYTYPIC 165
many unsaturated chemical bonds POLYUNSATURATED 165
many uses VERSATILE 215
many-headed monster HYDRA 21
mapping an area CHOROGRAPHY 92
marine animals covered with spines ECHINODERM 61
marine animals that bear eight rows of comblike cilia CTENOPHORE 189
marine animals with eight arms OCTOPUS 162
marine organisms named from their resemblance to flowers ANTHOZOAN 18, 216
mark into intervals GRADUATE 97
mark placed above a vowel to indicate a long sound MACRON 137
mark placed above a vowel to indicate sound or quality of pronunciation CIRCUMFLEX 50
mark used to indicate a special phonic value, stress, etc. DIACRITIC 62
mark used to indicate a special phonic value, stress, etc. DIACRITICAL MARK 62
mark used to join elements of a compound word HYPHEN 109
mark used to show the omission of letters APOSTROPHE 20
marks used to enclose a comment or explanation within a sentence PARENTHESIS 180
marked by success AUSPICIOUS 29, 204
market condition, there are so few buyers that any one can impact price OLIGOPSONY 166
market condition, there are so few sellers that any one can impact price OLIGOPOLY 165
market condition, there is only one buyer whose actions can impact price MONOPSONY 152
marriage MATRIMONY 142
married couple lives with the husband's parents PATRILOCAL 142
married couple lives with the wife's parents MATRILOCAL 142
married to only one person at a time MONOGAMY 83, 151
married to two people at the same time BIGAMY 82, 154
married to more than one person at the same time POLYGAMY 83, 164
married woman with a mature appearance and manner MATRON 142
marrying a person of higher social status HYPERGAMY 83, 108

marrying within one's clan ENDOGAMY 72, 82
marrying outside one's clan EXOGAMY 82
mass of living organisms BIOMASS 35
mass of protoplasm without cellular boundaries SYNCYTIUM 40, 107
massive depression in the earth's crust GEOSYNCLINE 89, 105
massive uplift in the earth's crust GEANTICLINE 88
material rather than spiritual or mental PHYSICAL 193
material replacement for body parts BIOMATERIAL 35
materials that can be molded PLASTIC 168
materials that change color when exposed to light PHOTOCHROMIC 48, 190
mathematical expression consisting of one term MONOMIAL 152, 173
mathematical expression consisting of two terms BINOMIAL 154, 173
mathematical expression consisting of three terms TRINOMIAL 157, 174
mathematical expression consisting of two or more terms POLYNOMIAL 165, 174
mature male sex cell Male gamete SPERMATOZOON 217
mature female sex cell Female gamete OVUM 219
mature male or female sex cell GAMETE 82
measles RUBEOLA 78
measure consisting of one foot MONOPODY 152, 181
measure consisting of two feet DIPODY 155, 181
measure consisting of three feet TRIPODY 158, 182
measure consisting of four feet TETRAPODY 159, 182
measure consisting of five feet PENTAPODY 160, 181
measure consisting of six feet HEXAPODY 161, 181
measure consisting of seven feet HEPTAPODY 162, 181
measure of data loss in a message ENTROPY 213
measure of thermal energy unavailable for work ENTROPY 213
measured by the revolutions of the moon LUNAR 136
mechanics dealing with liquids and gases FLUID MECHANICS 132
mechanism for launching aircraft from an aircraft carrier CATAPULT 12
median partition that separates the right and left chest cavities MEDIASTINUM 143
medical history of a patient ANAMNESIS 11
medicine based on biological sciences BIOMEDICINE 35
medicine, especially a purgative PHYSIC 193
medicine that reduces fever ANTIPYRETIC 197
Mediterranean Sea MEDITERRANEAN 90, 143
medusoid stage of a hydrozoan HYDROMEDUSA 22
meeting for discussion of a specific topic SYMPOSIUM 106
meeting or assembly CONVOCATION 188
melanin-containing chromatophore MELANOPHORE 144, 189
member of an animal colony ZOOID 218
member of the 16th century Reformation ANABAPTIST 11
member of the Catholic Church CATHOLIC 13
member of the Democratic Party DEMOCRAT 24, 58
members of the same kind CONGENER 84
membrane lining the abdominal cavity PERITONEUM 52
membrane lining the chambers of the heart ENDOCARDIUM 41, 72
membrane surrounding the vacuole in a plant cell TONOPLAST 169
membrane that covers a muscle APONEUROSIS 19
membrane that covers the eyeball SCLERA 200
men of letters Scholars LITERATI 68
menstruation CATAMENIA 12
mental aspects of sexuality PSYCHOSEXUAL 196
mental balance EQUILIBRIUM 76
mental disorder characterized by belief in one's omnipotence MEGALOMANIA 139, 141
mental disorder characterized by confusion of fact and fantasy PARAMNESIA 179
mental disorder characterized by excitement and violence MANIA 140
mental disorder characterized by extreme depression MELANCHOLIA 144
mental disorder characterized by extreme self-absorption AUTISM 28
mental disorder characterized by feelings of grandeur and persecution PARANOIA 179
mental disorder in which the patient believes he is a wolf LYCANTHROPY 14
mental disorder in which the patient believes he is an animal ZOANTHROPY 14, 218
mental disorder including impaired perception of reality PSYCHOSIS 196
mental disorders that do not include impaired perception of reality NEUROSIS 172
mental disorders that do not include impaired perception of reality PSYCHONEUROSIS 172, 196
mental origin PSYCHOGENIC 87, 195

microscope that focuses a beam of electrons to produce an image ELECTRON MICROSCOPE 137, 200
microscope to make objects appear three-dimensional STEREOMICROSCOPE 139, 202
microscope to study very minute objects ULTRAMICROSCOPE 139, 202
microscopic fragments CRYPTOCLASTIC 56
microscopic organism MICROORGANISM 138
midbrain MESENCEPHALON 45, 143
middle MEDIAL 143
Middle Ages MEDIAEVAL 143
Middle Ages MEDIEVAL 143
middle layer of a fruit MESOCARP 42, 143
middle layer of muscle in the heart MYOCARDIUM 41, 169
middle layer of the three primary germ cell layers of an embryo MESODERM 61, 143
middle of the three coverings of the brain and spinal cord ARACHNOID 219
middle section MIDSECTION 202
middle segment of an insect MESOTHORAX 144
middle state MEDIUM 143
migrating up a river ANADROMOUS 11
migrating down a river CATADROMOUS 12
migrating between salt and fresh waters DIADROMOUS 62
military operations involving naval vessels and ground troops AMPHIBIOUS 10, 34
milk containing bacteria that grow vigorously in dilute acid ACIDOPHILUS MILK 184
million cycles Megacycle MEGAHERTZ 57, 139
million cycles Megahertz MEGACYCLE 139
millipede DIPLOPOD 155, 181
mind PSYCHIC 195
mineral, a hydrous sodium aluminum silicate NATROLITE 121
mineral, an important ore of chromium CHROMITE 47, 120
mineral, an important ore of copper CHALCOCITE 120
mineral, an important ore of copper CHALCOPYRITE 120, 197
mineral, an important ore of iron SIDERITE 122
mineral, an important ore of lead CERUSSITE 119
mineral, an important ore of silver PYRARGYRITE 121, 197
mineral, an ore of copper CUPRITE 120
mineral, an ore of manganese MANGANITE 121
mineral, an ore of strontium STRONTIANITE 122
mineral, an ore of thorium THORITE 122
mineral, an ore of vanadium and lead VANADINITE 123
mineral, blue in color CYANITE 56, 120
mineral content of a rock attributed to outside influences EPIGENESIS 75, 85
mineral enclosed inside another mineral ENDOMORPH 72, 166
mineral enclosing a different mineral PERIMORPH 51, 167
mineral exhibiting the crystalline form of another mineral PSEUDOMORPH 167, 195
mineral formation through gases emitted by solidifying rock magmas PNEUMATOLYSIS 193
mineral found in limestone, marble, and chalk CALCITE 119
mineral known as bloodstone HEMATITE 99, 120
mineral known as rock salt HALITE 120
mineral known as soapstone STEATITE 122
mineral, magnesium carbonate MAGNESITE 121
mineral named after Andalusia, Spain ANDALUSITE 119
mineral named after Anglesey, Wales ANGLESITE 119
mineral named after Aragon in Spain ARAGONITE 119
mineral named after Autun, France AUTUNITE 119
mineral named after Carl W. Scheele, Swedish chemist SCHEELITE 122
mineral named after Col. von Samarski, Russian mine inspector SAMARSKITE 121
mineral named after Deodat de Dolomieu, French mineralogist DOLOMITE 120
mineral named after F.L. Sperry, Canadian mineralogist SPERRYLITE 122
mineral named after Gerard Troost, American mineralogist TROOSTITE 122
mineral named after Ignaz von Born, Austrian mineralogist BORNITE 119
mineral named after Ilmen in the Ural Mountains in Russia ILMENITE 120
mineral named after J. Bohm, German scientist BOEHMITE 119
mineral named after J.J. Gahn, Swedish chemist GAHNITE 120
mineral named after J.W. von Goethe, German scholar and writer GOETHITE 120
mineral named after Jean B. Biot, French mineralogist BIOTITE 119
mineral named after John Gadolin, Finnish chemist GADOLINITE 120
mineral named after Jules Garnier, French geologist GARNIERITE 120
mineral named after Kern County, California KERNITE 120

minute tubular structures in the cytoplasm of cells MICROTUBULE 139
mirror SPECULAR 205
mirror in an optical instrument SPECULUM 205
misapplied name MISNOMER 173
miscellaneous collection OMNIUM-GATHERUM 176
miserably ineffective PATHETIC 79
mislead Deceive DELUDE 135
misleading optical image ILLUSION 136
mitosis, the first phase during which the spindle and chromosomes form PROPHASE 17
mitosis, the chromosomes become aligned along the spindle METAPHASE 145
mitosis, the chromosomes split and move to opposite poles of the spindle ANAPHASE 11
mitosis, the final phase during which the cell divides TELOPHASE 209
mixed together to constitute a whole AGGREGATE 96
mixture for dissolving gold and platinum AQUA REGIA 20
mixture of honey and water HYDROMEL 22
mixture of languages POLYGLOT 164
mixture of lime, sand, and water used as a hard covering PLASTER 168
mixture of neodymium and praseodymium DIDYMIUM 155
model of excellence PARAGON 179
moderate quality Ordinary MEDIOCRE 143
modern NEOTERIC 171
modify equipment already in service RETROFIT 198
mold MATRIX 142
mollusks that have a large head with tentacles around the mouth CEPHALOPOD 45, 181
mollusks that move using a ventral foot GASTROPOD 83, 181
mollusks with a winglike structure in the foot for swimming PTEROPOD 182, 197
mollusks with eight arms, as an octopus OCTOPOD 162, 181
monetary unit equal to one hundredth of a dollar Penny CENT 42
monetary unit equal to one hundredth of a franc CENTIME 43
monetary unit equal to one hundredth of a lira CENTESIMO 43
monetary unit equal to one hundredth of a peso CENTESIMO 43
monetary unit equal to one hundredth of the basic unit CENTAVO 43
monetary unit equal to one hundredth of the basic unit CENTIMO 43
monetary unit equal to one thousandth of a pound MILLIEME 115
monosaccharide with three carbon atoms TRIOSE 157
monosaccharide with four carbon atoms TETROSE 160
monosaccharide with five carbon atoms PENTOSE 160
monosaccharide with six carbon atoms HEXOSE 161
monosaccharide with seven carbon atoms HEPTOSE 162
moon LUNAR 136
moon and the sun LUNISOLAR 98, 136
morally corrupt PROFLIGATE 16
morally wrong Corrupt Wicked PERVERSE 183, 215
more than one husband at a time POLYANDRY 13, 164
more than one wife at a time POLYGYNY 14, 164
more than one meaning EQUIVOCAL 76, 188
more than one possible meaning AMBIGUOUS 10
more than one ring of atoms POLYCYCLIC 57, 164
more than the normal number of fingers or toes POLYDACTYL 58, 164
mosquito that transmits yellow fever AEDES 1
moss animals BRYOZOAN 217
moss animals POLYZOAN 165, 217
mother MATER 142
mother and ruler of a family MATRIARCH 23, 142
mother of a family MATERFAMILIAS 142
motherhood MATERNITY 142
motherliness MATERNITY 142
motherly MATERNAL 142
moths once believed to live in fire PYRALID 197
motor that runs on heat THERMOMOTOR 211
mountain formation OROGENY 86
move back RECEDE 42
move forward PROPEL 17, 182
move forward Propel IMPEL 182
move from one place to another TRANSFER 63
move from one place to another TRANSPLANT 64

musical movement that serves as an introduction to another more important movement PRELUDE 136
mutual agreement SYMPATHY 80, 106
mutually beneficial relationship SYMBIOSIS 37, 106
mythical animal resembling a horse with a single horn on its forehead UNICORN 153
mythical belief in the ability to transform oneself into a wolf LYCANTHROPY 14
mythical subjects in art MYTHOGRAPHY 94
naked Hindu philosophers GYMNOSOPHIST 204
name NOMINAL 174
name ONOMASTIC 174
name as a candidate for office NOMINATE 174
name as a recipient of an award NOMINATE 174
name derived from the name of the father PATRONYMIC 143, 174
name derived from the name of the mother MATRONYMIC 142, 174
name derived from the name of the mother METRONYMIC 174
name in which the genus and the species are given the same name TAUTONYM 174
name of a group of things DENOMINATION 173
name of a place TOPONYM 174
names used in a particular branch of art or science NOMENCLATURE 174
naming something by vocal imitation of its sound ONOMATOPOEIA 174
narcissus bearing clusters of flowers POLYANTHUS 18, 164
nation that cooperates with another in waging war COBELLIGERENT 31
national legislative body of certain nations CONGRESS 97
national self-sufficiency AUTARCHY 23, 28
national self-sufficiency AUTARKY 28
natural NATIVE 170
natural inclination Bent PROPENSITY 17
natural inclination Predisposition PROCLIVITY 16
nature of a proverb PROVERBIAL 17, 68
nature or natural science PHYSICAL 193
navigation of spacecraft ASTRONAVIGATION 28
navigation system that sends signals in all directions OMNIRANGE 176
navigation using the stars Celestial navigation ASTRONAVIGATION 28
near the front ANTERIOR 15
near the back POSTERIOR 15
near the sun HELIACAL 98
nearly perfect spherical shape ASPHERIC 3, 206
needless repetition of an idea in different words TAUTOLOGY 67
neither moral nor immoral AMORAL 2
nerve NEURAL 171
nerve ending sensitive to pressure changes BARORECEPTOR 30
nerve endings in muscle tissue MYONEURAL 170, 171
nerve fibers connecting the cerebral hemispheres CORPUS CALLOSUM 54
nerve fibers connecting different regions of the central nervous system PEDUNCLE 181
nerves and muscles NEUROMUSCULAR 172
nervous system consisting of the brain and spinal cord CENTRAL NERVOUS SYSTEM 219
nervous system consisting of all except the brain and spinal cord PERIPHERAL NERVOUS SYSTEM 52
nervous system that controls involuntary body functions AUTONOMIC NERVOUS SYSTEM 29, 173
nervous system consisting of cranial and sacral nerves PARASYMPATHETIC NERVOUS SYSTEM 79, 105, 179
nervous system consisting of spinal nerves SYMPATHETIC NERVOUS SYSTEM 80, 106
nest of ants FORMICARY 26
nest of wasps VESPIARY 27
neurons that link sensory and motor neurons INTERNEURON 112, 171
neurosis in aircraft pilots AERONEUROSIS 8, 171
new word NEOLOGISM 67, 171
newborn child during the first month after birth NEONATAL 170, 171
next in line IMMEDIATE 5, 143
next to the last PENULTIMATE 220
next to the last item in a series PENULT 220
next to the last syllable in a word PENULT 220
next to the last round SEMIFINAL 59
nickname AGNOMEN 173
nickname COGNOMEN 173
nitric acid AQUA FORTIS 20
nitrogen-fixing bacteria AZOTOBACTER 217
nitrogenous waste products in the blood AZOTEMIA 98, 216
nitrogenous waste products in the urine AZOTURIA 217

no distinguishable head ACEPHALOUS 1, 45
no leader ACEPHALOUS 1, 45
no money Poor IMPECUNIOUS 5
noble MAGNIFICENT 140
non-believer in a particular religion INFIDEL 6, 81
non-believer in a particular theory INFIDEL 6, 81
nonliving material in the protoplasm METAPLASM 145, 168
normal breathing EUPNEA 33, 193
normal digestion EUPEPSIA 32, 182
normal vision HAPLOPIA 175
normally proportioned head ORTHOCEPHALOUS 46, 177
nose RHINAL 199
nose with nostrils directed downward CATARRHINE 12, 199
nose with nostrils directed to the side PLATYRRHINE 199
nosebleed EPISTAXIS 75
not able to be avoided INELUCTABLE 6
not able to be avoided INEVITABLE 6
not able to be called back Final IRREVOCABLE 7, 188
not able to be described INDESCRIBABLE 6, 96
not able to be penetrated IMPERMEABLE 5, 182
not able to combine with other elements INERT 6
not able to meet requirements INCOMPETENT 5
not able to read or write ANALPHABETIC 2
not able to read or write ILLITERATE 5, 68
not accented ATONIC 4
not adequate INADEQUATE 76
not adequate UNEQUAL 76
not adhering to a script UNSCRIPTED 96
not afraid Dauntless INTREPID 7
not alike DIVERSE 215
not ambiguous Unmistakable UNEQUIVOCAL 76, 188
not attentive INADVERTENT 5, 215
not balanced UNEQUAL 76
not bearing fruit ACARPOUS 1, 41
not believable DISCREDIT 55
not believable INCREDIBLE 6, 55
not believable or reasonable IMPLAUSIBLE 5
not belonging to the nature of a thing EXTRINSIC 81
not capable of being annulled INDEFEASIBLE 6
not capable of being appeased IMPLACABLE 5
not capable of being atoned for INEXPIABLE 6
not capable of being conquered INVINCIBLE 7
not capable of being corrected INCORRIGIBLE 6
not capable of being disproved IRREFUTABLE 7
not capable of being disturbed Calm IMPERTURBABLE 5, 182
not capable of being erased INDELIBLE 6
not capable of being explained INEXPLICABLE 6
not capable of being expressed in words INEFFABLE 6
not capable of being felt by touching Intangible IMPALPABLE 5
not capable of being imitated INIMITABLE 6
not capable of being measured or understood Extreme ABYSMAL 1
not capable of being mixed IMMISCIBLE 5
not capable of being overcome Insurmountable INSUPERABLE 7
not capable of being penetrated IMPERVIOUS 5, 182
not capable of being persuaded Unyielding INEXORABLE 6
not capable of being rejected IRRECUSABLE 7
not capable of being repaired IRREPARABLE 7
not capable of being satisfied INSATIABLE 7
not capable of being taken away INALIENABLE 5
not capable of being taken by force IMPREGNABLE 5
not capable of being touched Impalpable INTANGIBLE 7
not capable of being understood Inconceivable INCOMPREHENSIBLE 5
not capable of being weighed or evaluated IMPONDERABLE 5
not capable of error INFALLIBLE 6
not capable of failure INFALLIBLE 6
not capable of producing the desired effect INEFFICACIOUS 6

not capable of sexual intercourse IMPOTENT 5
not capable of sin or wrongdoing IMPECCABLE 5
not causing disease NONPATHOGENIC 79, 86
not changeable IMMUTABLE 5
not changing or progressing STATIC 220
not characterized by repeated cycles APERIODIC 3, 51
not compatible INCONGRUOUS 5
not conforming to established beliefs UNORTHODOX 55, 178
not conforming to established beliefs, especially in theology HETERODOX 55, 102
not considerate Selfish ASOCIAL 3
not contaminated by other organisms AXENIC 4, 216
not corrupt INCORRUPT 6, 200
not cyclic ACYCLIC 1, 56
not disturbed by IMPERVIOUS 5, 182
not easily controlled Stubborn INTRACTABLE 7, 212
not easily disturbed Calm EQUABLE 76
not easily noticed INCONSPICUOUS 6, 205
not easily subdued INDOMITABLE 6
not easily taught or disciplined Recalcitrant INDOCILE 6
not easily treated INTRACTABLE 7, 212
not easily understood Obscure INSCRUTABLE 7
not easily worked INTRACTABLE 7, 212
not entirely aquatic SEMIAQUATIC 20, 59
not entirely aquatic SUBAQUATIC 20
not entirely terrestrial SEMITERRESTRIAL 59, 90
not entirely transparent SEMITRANSPARENT 59, 63
not equal UNEQUAL 76
not exercising forceful, persuasive, or fluent speech INELOQUENT 6, 65, 71
not exhibiting equality in measurements ANISOMETRIC 2, 103, 146
not fit to be eaten INEDIBLE 6
not fitting Unfit INEPT 6
not forming an angle AGONIC 1, 90
not generous Stingy ILLIBERAL 5
not genuine APOCRYPHAL 19, 55
not happy Unfortunate INFELICITOUS 6
not harmful INNOCUOUS 7
not having a common center ECCENTRIC 44
not having previously given birth UNIPAROUS 153
not helping ADVERSE 214
not in agreement INCONSONANT 6
not in good taste Improper INDECOROUS 6
not lawful or acceptable ILLEGITIMATE 4, 66
not leading to a definite result INCONCLUSIVE 5, 52
not legal ILLEGAL 4, 66
not legally qualified INCOMPETENT 5
not living INANIMATE 5
not noble IGNOBLE 4
not occurring at regular intervals APERIODIC 3, 51
not occurring at the same rate ASYNCHRONOUS 4, 49, 105
not occurring at the same time ASYNCHRONOUS 4, 49, 105
not one of a pair Single AZYGOUS 4, 218
not permitted ILLICIT 5
not permitting the passage of fluid IMPERMEABLE 5, 182
not pertinent EXTRANEOUS 81
not proportionate INCOMMENSURATE 5
not readily grasped by the mind Vague IMPALPABLE 5
not readily grasped by the mind Vague INTANGIBLE 7
not satisfactorily adapted MALADAPTED 31
not satisfactorily adjusted MALADJUSTED 31
not showing meanness or pettiness in feelings or conduct MAGNANIMOUS 140
not spiritual CORPOREAL 53
not spiritual Worldly CARNAL 41
not steady ASTATIC 4
not subject to death IMMORTAL 5, 169
not subject to decay INCORRUPT 6, 200
not suitable Inappropriate INAPT 5

occurring twice in a three month period BIQUARTERLY 154, 159
occurring at the end of a three month period QUARTERLY 159
occurring twice a year BIANNUAL 73, 153
occurring twice a year SEMIANNUAL 59, 73
occurring twice a year SEMIYEARLY 59
occurring once every two weeks BIWEEKLY 154
occurring once every three weeks TRIWEEKLY 158
occurring once every two months BIMONTHLY 154
occurring once every three months TRIMONTHLY 157
occurring once a year ANNUAL 73
occurring once every two years BIENNIAL 73, 154
occurring once every two years BIYEARLY 154
occurring once every three years TRIENNIAL 74, 157
occurring once every four years QUADRENNIAL 73, 158
occurring once every five years QUINQUENNIAL 73, 160
occurring once every six years SEXENNIAL 74, 161
occurring once every seven years SEPTENNIAL 74, 162
occurring once every eight years OCTENNIAL 73, 162
occurring once every ten years DECENNIAL 73, 163
occurring once every fifteen years QUINDECENNIAL 73, 160, 164
occurring once every twenty years VICENNIAL 74
occurring once every fifty years SEMICENTENNIAL 43, 59, 74
occurring once every one hundred years CENTENNIAL 43, 73
occurring once every one hundred and fifty years SESQUICENTENNIAL 43, 74
occurring once every two hundred years BICENTENNIAL 42, 73, 153
occurring once every three hundred years TERCENTENARY 43, 74
occurring once every three hundred years TRICENTENNIAL 43, 74, 156
occurring once every four hundred years QUADRICENTENNIAL 43, 73, 158
occurring once every five hundred years QUINCENTENNIAL 43, 73, 160
occurring once every six hundred years SEXCENTENARY 43, 74, 161
oceanic sediment produced from land TERRIGENOUS 88, 90
oculomotor nerve OCULOMOTOR 175
ode sung by a single voice MONODY 151
offensively arrogant INSOLENT 7
offensively bold Saucy IMPUDENT 5
offer PROFFER 16
officer in the Roman army commanding one hundred men CENTURION 43
official chair of a bishop CATHEDRA 13
official chair of a position CATHEDRA 13
official copy TRANSCRIPT 63, 96
official in charge of an institution PROVOST 18
official public order EDICT 65, 70
offspring PROGENY 16, 87
offspring of a mortal and a god DEMIGOD 58
offspring of one person POSTERITY 15
often encountered Ubiquitous OMNIPRESENT 176
omen observed in birds AUSPICES 29, 204
omission of an unstressed vowel at the beginning of a word APHESIS 19
omission of conjunctions for rhetorical effect ASYNDETON 4, 105
omission of letters from the beginning of a word APHAERESIS 19
omission of letters from the beginning of a word APHERESIS 19
omission of letters from the middle of a word SYNCOPE 107
omission of letters from the end of a word APOCOPE 19
omit ELIDE 70
omit a vowel or syllable in pronunciation ELIDE 70
on the alert Watchful QUI VIVE 37
one axis UNIAXIAL 30, 153
one axis MONAXIAL 30, 151
one carpel MONOCARPELLARY 42, 151
one color MONOCHROMATIC 48, 151
one color HOMOCHROMATIC 48, 101
one cycle MONOCYCLIC 57, 151
one cycle around an axis REVOLUTION 214
one day only EPHEMERAL 74
one direction only UNIDIRECTIONAL 153
one ear only MONAURAL 151

one eighth of a circle OCTANT 162
one foot MONOPODE 152, 181
one form MONOMORPHIC 152, 166
one fourth of a circle QUADRANT 158
one hundred CENTURY 43
one hundred soldiers CENTURY 43
one hundredth part PERCENT 43
one husband at a time MONANDRY 13, 151
one leaf UNIFOLIATE 153
one leaflet UNIFOLIOLATE 153
one legislative chamber UNICAMERAL 153
one logarithmic scale and one arithmetic scale SEMILOGARITHMIC 59
one magnetic pole UNIPOLAR 153
one meaning Unambiguous Unequivocal UNIVOCAL 153, 188
one million deaths MEGADEATH 139
one million tons of TNT MEGATON 140
one million ohms MEGOHM 140
one million volts MEGAVOLT 140
one million watts MEGAWATT 140
one millionth of a farad MICROFARAD 137
one millionth of a gram MICROGRAM 138
one millionth of a second MICROSECOND 138
one millionth of an ampere MICROAMPERE 137
one morpheme MONOMORPHEMIC 152, 166
one of a kind UNIQUE 153
one of the axes in a three-dimensional Cartesian coordinate system X-AXIS 30
one of the axes in a three-dimensional Cartesian coordinate system Y-AXIS 30
one of the axes in a three-dimensional Cartesian coordinate system Z-AXIS 30
one of two halves of a sphere HEMISPHERE 59, 206
one predominate melody HOMOPHONIC 102, 187
one revolution of the moon around the earth LUNAR MONTH 136
one ring of atoms MONOCYCLIC 57, 151
one sex only UNISEXUAL 153
one side only UNILATERAL 153
one sixth of a circle SEXTANT 161
one thousand million Billion MILLIARD 115
one thousand paces MILLIARY 115
one thousand years MILLENARIAN 73, 115
one thousand years during which Christ will rule on earth MILLENNIUM 73, 115
one unvarying tone MONOTONE 152
one who believes the existence of God is unknown AGNOSTIC 1, 53
one who believes there is no God ATHEIST 4, 209
one who denies the existence of God INFIDEL 6, 81
one who goes before Predecessor ANTECESSOR 14, 42
one who takes part in a conversation INTERLOCUTOR 65, 112
one wife at a time MONOGYNY 14, 152
one-fourth part QUARTER 159
one-fourth part QUARTERN 159
one-of-a-kind SUI GENERIS 87
only member of its group MONOTYPIC 152
opal deposited around geysers GEYSERITE 120
opal that is transparent or translucent when wet HYDROPHANE 22
open-minded PERVIOUS 183
opening into the archenteron of the gastrula BLASTOPORE 38
operate in water and on land AMPHIBIOUS 10, 34
operate on water and on land AMPHIBIAN 10, 34
operate in water, on land, or in the air TRIPHIBIAN 10, 37, 158
operate with the hands MANIPULATE 141
operated by compressed air PNEUMATIC 193
operating contrary to normal REVERSE 215
operating without external assistance AUTOMATIC 29
opponent ADVERSARY 214
oppose authority REBEL 31
opposing direction ADVERSE 214
opposition between laws ANTINOMY 172
oral examination VIVA VOCE 37, 188

oral instruction given to catechumens CATECHESIS 12
orbit nearest the moon PERILUNE 51, 136
orbit nearest the sun PERIHELION 51, 98
orbit farthest from the moon APOLUNE 19, 136
orbit farthest from the sun APHELION 19, 98
orbit of the moon nearest the earth PERIGEE 51, 89
orbit of the moon farthest from the earth APOGEE 19, 88
order and harmony COSMOS 54
order in which minerals crystallize PARAGENESIS 87, 179
order of events CHRONOLOGY 49, 124
order the use of PRESCRIBE 96
orderly and harmonious system COSMOS 54
organ that becomes the adult kidney in lower fishes PRONEPHROS 17, 171
organ that becomes the adult kidney in fishes and amphibians MESONEPHROS 143, 171
organ that becomes the adult kidney in mammals, reptiles, and birds METANEPHROS 145, 171
organelles in plant cells that perform photosynthetic or storage functions PLASTID 168
organic compounds that consist of carbon combined with hydrogen and oxygen CARBOHYDRATE 20
organic substances necessary for normal metabolism VITAMIN 37
organism existing in a narrow range of temperatures STENOTHERM 211
organism existing in a wide range of temperatures EURYTHERM 210
organism living on the outer body of a host ECTOCOMMENSAL 73
organism requiring high temperatures THERMOPHILE 185, 211
organism that causes a plant disease PHYTOPATHOGEN 79, 87, 191
organism that depends on other organisms for food HETEROTROPH 103, 212
organism that lives on another organism PARASITE 179
organism that produces its own food AUTOTROPH 29, 212
organism that produces its own food using chemosynthesis CHEMOAUTOTROPHIC 29, 212
organism that produces its own food using photosynthesis PHOTOAUTOTROPHIC 29, 190, 212
organism whose genetic material is in a membrane-bound nucleus EUCARYOTE 32
organism whose genetic material is in a membrane-bound nucleus EUKARYOTE 32
organism whose genetic material is not in a membrane-bound nucleus PROKARYOTE 16
organism whose reproductive cells are similar to its somatic cells HOLOGAMOUS 83
organism with gene pairs that contain identical alleles HOMOZYGOTE 102, 218
organism with gene pairs that contain different alleles HETEROZYGOTE 103, 218
organisms attached to aquatic plants PERIPHYTON 52, 191
organisms characterized by a reddish eyespot EUGLENA 32
organisms that can be divided into symmetrical halves ZYGOMORPHIC 167, 218
organisms with the same genetic characteristics BIOTYPE 36
organized militarily PARAMILITARY 179
orifice that connects the stomach to the esophagus CARDIAC 40
origin RADIX 198
origin and development of a single organism ONTOGENY 86
origin and development of a species of organisms PHYLOGENY 87
origin and development of mental processes PSYCHOGENESIS 87, 195
origin and development of plants PHYTOGENESIS 87, 191
origin from a father PATERNITY 142
origin of something GENESIS 85
origin of the gods THEOGONY 88, 210
original draft named from being the first sheet glued onto a manuscript PROTOCOL 24
original from which others develop PROTOTYPE 25
original model ARCHETYPE 23
original model PROTOTYPE 25
originating externally EXOGENOUS 85
originating from within ENDOGENOUS 72, 85
originating in muscle tissue MYOGENIC 86, 170
originating in the heart CARDIOGENIC 40, 84
originating in the kidney NEPHROGENOUS 86, 171
originating in the nervous system NEUROGENIC 86, 172
originating outside the organism EXOGENOUS 85
originating outside the organism HETEROGENOUS 86, 102
originating within the organism AUTOGENOUS 28, 84
originating within the organism ENDOGENOUS 72, 85
ornament carved in low relief ANAGLYPH 11
ornamental flower garden PARTERRE 90
orthochromatic ISOCHROMATIC 48, 104
osmosis from higher to lower concentration EXOSMOSIS 219

osmosis from lower to higher concentration ENDOSMOSIS 72
osmosis in an inward direction ENDOSMOSIS 72
osmosis in an outward direction EXOSMOSIS 219
out of many, one Motto of the United States E PLURIBUS UNUM 70
out of place Absurd INCONGRUOUS 5
outburst of melodious sound DIAPASON 62
outer boundary of a closed plane figure PERIMETER 51, 149
outer boundary of an area PERIMETER 51, 149
outer calyx EPICALYX 74
outer curve of an arch EXTRADOS 80
outer layer in the sporangium of a moss AMPHITHECIUM 10
outer layer of a fruit EPICARP 42, 74
outer layer of a fruit EXOCARP 42
outer layer of cells in plants EPIDERMIS 61, 74
outer layer of the cerebrum CEREBRAL CORTEX 46
outer layer of the three primary germ cell layers of an embryo ECTODERM 61, 73
outer layer of the three primary germ cell layers of an embryo EPIBLAST 38, 74
outer portion of the cytoplasm ECTOPLASM 73, 167
outermost boundary above which the air is too thin for aircraft AEROPAUSE 8
outermost boundary of the troposphere TROPOPAUSE 207, 213
outermost boundary of the stratosphere STRATOPAUSE 206
outermost boundary of the mesosphere MESOPAUSE 144, 206
outermost layer of a spore EXOSPORE 207
outermost of the three coverings of the brain and spinal cord DURA MATER 142
outermost part of an area PERIPHERY 52
outermost part of the stele PERICYCLE 51, 57
outlaw PROSCRIBE 17, 96
outside a cell EXTRACELLULAR 80
outside a spacecraft EXTRAVEHICULAR 81
outside the center PERIPHERAL 52
outside the cranium EXTRACRANIAL 46, 80
outside the curriculum EXTRACURRICULAR 80
outside the due process of law EXTRAJUDICIAL 81
outside the jurisdiction of a court EXTRAJUDICIAL 81
outside the marriage EXTRAMARITAL 81
outside the nucleus of a cell EXTRANUCLEAR 81
outside the uterus EXTRAUTERINE 81
outside the vascular system EXTRAVASCULAR 81
outside the walls of a city EXTRAMURAL 81
outspoken VOCAL 188
oval-shaped structure attached to the back side of each testis EPIDIDYMIS 75
overemotional behavior DRAMATICS 131
overflowing with enthusiasm Exuberant EBULLIENT 70
overspread SUFFUSE 82
overthrow of a government REVOLUTION 214
ovule vertical so the micropyle lies opposite the stalk ORTHOTROPOUS 178, 213
ovule inverted so the micropyle lies near the base of the stalk ANATROPOUS 11, 213
ovule partially inverted so the micropyle lies horizontal CAMPYLOTROPOUS 213
own distinct form IDIOMORPHIC 111, 166
ownership of real estate by an institution who cannot sell it MORTMAIN 141, 169
oxide containing one oxygen atom MONOXIDE 152
oxide containing two oxygen atoms DIOXIDE 155
oxide containing three oxygen atoms TRIOXIDE 157
oxide containing four oxygen atoms TETROXIDE 160
oxide containing five oxygen atoms PENTOXIDE 160
oxygen and hydrogen mixture OXYHYDROGEN 23
page size, one fourth of a printer's sheet QUARTO 159
page size, one eighth of a printer's sheet OCTAVO 162
page size, one twelfth of a printer's sheet DUODECIMO 156, 163
page size, one sixteenth of a printer's sheet SEXTODECIMO 161, 164
page size, one eighteenth of a printer's sheet OCTODECIMO 162, 164
pain along the nerves NEURALGIA 9, 171
pain in a joint ARTHRALGIA 9, 27
pain in a muscle MYALGIA 9, 169
pain in the big toe PODAGRA 181
pain in the ear Earache OTALGIA 10

pain in the heart CARDIALGIA 9, 40
pain in the hip joint COXALGIA 9
pain in the kidneys NEPHRALGIA 9, 171
pain in the uterus METRALGIA 9
pain-relieving effect similar to morphine ENDORPHINS 72, 166
painful longing for the past NOSTALGIA 9
painful menstruation DYSMENORRHEA 33, 199
painted by mixing the colors with wax before burning in ENCAUSTIC 42
painting done in watercolors AQUARELLE 20
painting scenes from everyday life GENRE 85
painting that rejected impressionism POSTIMPRESSIONISM 15
painting that sought to make impressionism more formal NEOIMPRESSIONISM 170
pair DUO 156
pair of toes pointing forward and a pair pointing backward ZYGODACTYL 58, 218
paired natural outgrowths of a vertebra ZYGAPOPHYSIS 20, 218
pairing of chromosomes in meiosis SYNAPSIS 106
paragraph appended below the signature as an afterthought P.S. POSTSCRIPT 15, 96
parallel rows on a vertical axis ORTHOSTICHOUS 178
parallel structure in writing PARALLELISM 179
paralysis of a single limb MONOPLEGIA 152
paralysis of corresponding parts on both sides of the body DIPLEGIA 155
paralysis of one side of the body HEMIPLEGIA 59
paralysis affecting the lower extremities PARAPLEGIA 179
paralysis affecting all four extremities QUADRIPLEGIA 159
paralysis caused by prenatal brain defect or injury during birth CEREBRAL PALSY 46
parasite in the blood HEMATOZOON 99, 217
parasite that lives inside its host ENDOPARASITE 72
parasite that lives inside its host ENTOZOON 217
parasite that lives outside its host EPIZOON 76, 217
parasite that lives on the outer surface of its host ECTOPARASITE 73
parasites that spend their life cycle on the same species of host AUTOECIOUS 28
parasites that spend their life cycle on different species of hosts HETEROECIOUS 102
parasitic animals ZOOPARASITE 218
parasitic protozoan that causes malaria PLASMODIUM 168
pardon for political offenses AMNESTY 2
part of a building below ground level HYPOGEUM 89, 110
part of a cell nucleus that stains readily CHROMATIN 47
part of a cell nucleus that does not stain readily ACHROMATIN 1, 46
part of a circle bounded by two radii and the included arc SECTOR 202
part of a drama in which a character talks to himself SOLILOQUY 65
part of a plant embryo that develops into the root RADICLE 198
part of a play during which the characters are introduced PROTASIS 17
part of a play following the protasis and preceding the catastasis EPITASIS 75
part of a play following the epitasis and preceding the catastrophe CATASTASIS 12
part of a play following the catastasis CATASTROPHE 12
part of a sentence that expresses what is said about the subject PREDICATE 65
part of a theater under the balcony Parquet circle PARTERRE 90
part of an ode that follows the strophe and antistrophe EPODE 76
part of speech that expresses action VERB 68
part of the earth that supports life BIOSPHERE 36, 206
part of the mind most aware of reality EGO 29
part of the universe capable of supporting life ECOSPHERE 206
part representative of a whole Sample SPECIMEN 205
partial paralysis PARESIS 180
partially parasitic HEMIPARASITE 59
partially parasitic SEMIPARASITE 59
partially permeable SEMIPERMEABLE 59, 183
partition that separates the abdominal and chest cavities DIAPHRAGM 62
partly automatic and partly operated by hand SEMIAUTOMATIC 29, 59
parts of different kinds HETEROGENEOUS 85, 102
parts of the same kind HOMOGENEOUS 86, 101
pass by degrees GRADATE 97
pass down through stages DEVOLVE 214
pass into or through INTERFUSE 81, 112
pass through a porous substance PERCOLATE 182
pass through pores TRANSUDE 64

person or thing intensely disliked ANATHEMA 11
person recently converted NEOPHYTE 171, 191
person sent to represent a government EMISSARY 71
person skilled in the use of words VERBALIST 68
person suspected SUSPECT 205
person to carry baggage PORTER 194
person to whom a debt is owed CREDITOR 55
person trained as a crew member of a spacecraft ASTRONAUT 27
person trained to live and work underwater AQUANAUT 20
person who advocates government by the people DEMOCRAT 24, 58
person who assigns names NOMENCLATOR 174
person who attempts to predict the future PROPHET 17
person who believes that Christians are free from moral law ANTINOMIAN 172
person who destroys religious images ICONOCLAST 111
person who directs his interests outside himself EXTRAVERT 81, 215
person who directs his interests outside himself EXTROVERT 81, 215
person who directs his interests upon himself INTROVERT 80, 215
person who dissects cadavers for anatomical demonstrations PROSECTOR 17, 202
person who dresses in the manner of the opposite sex TRANSVESTITE 64
person who elects to undergo sex change surgery TRANSSEXUAL 64
person who enjoys good food and drink BON VIVANT 37
person who gives aid BENEFACTOR 31
person who gives up allegiance to his or her native land EXPATRIATE 142
person who has completed a course of study GRADUATE 97
person who has recently risen above his class PARVENU 182
person who initiates candidates into religious mysteries MYSTAGOGUE 9
person who interferes wrongly Intruder INTERLOPER 112
person who interprets the Bible literally BIBLICIST 34
person who is very foolish or stupid IDIOT 111
person who lives at the expense of others PARASITE 179
person who practices clever but misleading reasoning SOPHIST 204
person who precipitates an event without being affected CATALYST 12
person who prepares the dead for burial MORTICIAN 169
person who presents a proposal PROPONENT 17
person who receives benefits BENEFICIARY 31
person who refuses to recognize authority REBEL 31
person who seeks to destroy established beliefs ICONOCLAST 111
person who seems like a god DEMIGOD 58
person who speaks for God PROPHET 17
person who speaks in favor of something ADVOCATE 188
person who supports someone PATRON 142
person who supports something Advocate PROPONENT 17
person who takes dictation or copies manuscript Secretary AMANUENSIS 141
person who violates the legal rights of others INTERLOPER 112
person who withdraws from society RECLUSE 52
person with an excessive enthusiasm for something MANIAC 141
person with appreciation for beauty AESTHETE 78
person with appreciation for beauty ESTHETE 78
person with characteristics of both an introvert and extrovert AMBIVERT 10, 214
person with heart disease CARDIAC 40
person with superior knowledge of a subject Connoisseur COGNOSCENTE 53
person with whom secrets are shared CONFIDANT 81
personal belongings PARAPHERNALIA 179
personal shame IGNOMINY 4, 173
personified INCARNATE 41
persons classified according to rank HIERARCHY 23
persons from many parts of the world COSMOPOLITAN 54
persons of literary achievement LITERATI 68
pet name HYPOCORISM 109
phagocyte in connective tissue HISTIOCYTE 40
pharmacist APOTHECARY 20
philosophy of Aristotle who taught while walking around PERIPATETIC 52
philosophy of the Theosophical Society THEOSOPHY 204, 210
phoneme used in a tone language TONEME 220
photoengraving on zinc plates PHOTOZINCOGRAPHY 94, 190
photograph of a microscopic image MICROGRAPH 93, 138

photograph taken through a microscope PHOTOMICROGRAPH 94, 139, 190
physical and chemical properties PHYSICOCHEMICAL 193
physical appearance of the body PHYSIQUE 193
physical therapy PHYSIOTHERAPY 193
picture created by a shadow SHADOWGRAPH 95
picture that represents a word PICTOGRAPH 94
pictures on the inside wall of a circular room CYCLORAMA 56, 176
pictures presented to appear as a continuous scene PANORAMA 177
pierce through TRANSFIX 63
pigeonhole in a dovecote COLUMBARIUM 26
pigment essential for vision in dim light Visual purple RHODOPSIN 78, 176
pigment important for color vision Visual violet IODOPSIN 175
pigment in freshwater fishes that resembles rhodopsin PORPHYROPSIN 176
pigment in plants that regulates growth PHYTOCHROME 48, 191
pigment that produces the yellow color of urine UROCHROME 48
pigment-producing bacterium CHROMOGEN 47, 84
pigments responsible for the yellow to orange coloration in autumn leaves XANTHOPHYLL 50, 192
pioneer of an important belief APOSTLE 19
pipe carrying a fluid DUCT 69
piscina SACRARIUM 26
pity PATHOS 79
place between Insert INTERPOSE 112
place for an audience AUDITORIUM 26
place for cremation of corpses CREMATORIUM 26
place for fishing PISCARY 26
place for keeping aquatic animals and plants AQUARIUM 20, 26
place for keeping bees APIARY 26
place for keeping birds AVIARY 26, 29
place for keeping dead bodies MORTUARY 26, 169
place for keeping dried plants HERBARIUM 26
place for keeping insects INSECTARY 26
place for keeping small land animals and plants TERRARIUM 27, 90
place for keeping the ashes of the cremated dead CINERARIUM 26
place for studying live animals and plants VIVARIUM 27, 38
place for the bones of the dead OSSUARY 26
place for the study and exhibition of trees ARBORETUM 26
place in office INDUCT 69
place in which souls make atonement for their sins PURGATORY 197
place reserved in front of the choir ANTECHOIR 15
place where things meet JUNCTION 115
plan together secretly to commit an unlawful act CONSPIRE 194
plane figure with all angles equal ISOGON 90, 104
plane figure with all sides equal EQUILATERAL 76
plane figure with three angles TRIANGLE 156
plane figure with four angles QUADRANGLE 158
plane figure with four angles QUADRILATERAL 158
plane figure with four angles TETRAGON 91, 159
plane figure with five angles PENTAGON 91, 160
plane figure with six angles HEXAGON 90, 161
plane figure with seven angles HEPTAGON 90, 161
plane figure with eight angles OCTAGON 91, 162
plane figure with nine angles NONAGON 91
plane figure with ten angles DECAGON 90, 163
plane figure with eleven angles HENDECAGON 90, 163
plane figure with twelve angles DODECAGON 90, 156, 163
plane figure with fifteen angles QUINDECAGON 91, 160, 164
plane figure with three or more angles POLYGON 91, 164
plane figure with opposite sides parallel and equal PARALLELOGRAM 179
plane that divides something into two equal parts MEDIAN 143
planned military movement MANEUVER 141
plant adapting to changing climatic conditions TROPOPHYTE 192, 214
plant and animal life of a particular region BIOTA 36
plant bearing red and pink flowers CARNATION 41
plant cell that differs from surrounding cells IDIOBLAST 38, 111
plant growing on another plant EPIPHYTE 75, 191
plant growing within another plant ENDOPHYTE 72, 191

290

plant grown for flowers and colored leaves AMARANTH 1, 18
plant growth hormones that promote cell division CYTOKININ 39
plant having the buds below the surface GEOPHYTE 89, 191
plant life of a particular region FLORA 18
plant not visible to the naked eye MICROPHYTE 138, 191
plant origin PHYTOGENIC 87, 191
plant part able to grow into a new plant PHYTON 191
plant part attached to the central axis AXILE 30
plant parts at right angles to a stimulus DIATROPISM 63, 213
plant parts at right angles to the earth's gravitational force DIAGEOTROPISM 62, 88, 213
plant parts, turn downward due to rapid growth on the upper side EPINASTY 75
plant parts, turn upward due to rapid growth on the lower side HYPONASTY 110
plant stem with its growing point at the apex ACROGEN 7, 84
plant structure bearing gamete-producing organs GAMETOPHORE 82, 189
plant substance promoting cell division KINETIN 117
plant that feeds on insects CARNIVORE 41, 184
plant that gets food from decaying organic matter SAPROPHYTE 191
plant that gets food from other organisms HETEROPHYTE 103, 191
plant that grows in a dry climate XEROPHYTE 192, 216
plant that grows in moderately moist soil MESOPHYTE 144, 191
plant that grows in water HYDROPHYTE 22, 191
plant that grows in water HYGROPHYTE 191
plant that grows in salty soil HALOPHYTE 191
plant that grows on rocks LITHOPHYTE 123, 191
plant that grows on snow or ice CRYOPHYTE 55, 191
plant that has no known wild ancestor CULTIGEN 84
plant that produces its own food AUTOPHYTE 29, 190
plant that produces seeds SPERMATOPHYTE 192
plant tissue composed of lignified cells with thick walls SCLERENCHYMA 200
plant tissue composed of soft thin-walled cells PARENCHYMA 179
plant visible to the naked eye MACROPHYTE 137, 191
plant whose flowers turn toward the sun HELIOTROPE 98, 213
plant with finely divided fernlike leaves Yarrow MILFOIL 115
plant with purple flowers HELIOTROPE 98, 213
plant without seed leaves ACOTYLEDON 1
plant-eating animal HERBIVORE 184
plants and animals that form an ecological community BIOCENOSIS 35
plants bearing numerous small white flowers Baby's breath GYPSOPHILA 185
plants comprising the mosses and liverworts BRYOPHYTE 190
plants including ferns that have no flowers or seeds PTERIDOPHYTE 191
plants named for their liver-shaped leaves HEPATICA 100
plants referred to as mums, most commonly yellow CHRYSANTHEMUM 18, 49
plants, the gamete-producing generation that reproduces sexually GAMETOPHYTE 82, 191
plants, the spore-producing generation that reproduces asexually SPOROPHYTE 192, 208
plants with a differentiated vascular system TRACHEOPHYTE 192
plants with yellow flowers named from the shape of the seed COREOPSIS 175
plants without differentiated leaves, stems, and roots THALLOPHYTE 192
plastic surgery of the nose RHINOPLASTY 168, 199
plastics that harden permanently when heated THERMOSETTING 211
plastid containing chlorophyll CHLOROPLAST 167, 192
Platonic creator of the material universe DEMIURGE 58, 77
play on words Pun PARONOMASIA 174, 180
playwright DRAMATURGE 77
plead in behalf of another INTERCEDE 42, 111
pleasant sound EUPHONIOUS 33, 187
plentiful Abundant Copious PROFUSE 16, 82
pleurisy and pneumonia PLEUROPNEUMONIA 193
pneumonia PNEUMONIC 194
pneumonia resulting in inflammation of the lungs and bronchial tubes BRONCHOPNEUMONIA 193
poem in honor of a bride and bridegroom EPITHALAMIUM 75
poem in which a short verse follows a longer one EPODE 76
poem in which the first letters in each line form a word ACROSTIC 8
poem in which the final letters of successive lines form a word TELESTICH 209
poem mourning someone's death MONODY 151
poem or speech following a play EPILOGUE 66, 75
poem with the same end rhyme in all lines MONORHYME 152

point above the center of an earthquake EPICENTER 44, 74
point beneath the center of a nuclear explosion HYPOCENTER 44, 109
point out INDICATE 65
point where altitudes of a triangle intersect ORTHOCENTER 44, 177
poison created within the body AUTOTOXIN 29
poisoning by substances within the body AUTOINTOXICATION 28
poisonous to plants PHYTOTOXIC 191
pollen-bearing part of a flower ANTHER 18
pollinated by insects ENTOMOPHILOUS 185
pollinated by animals other than insects ZOOPHILOUS 186, 218
pollinated by wind-borne pollen ANEMOPHILOUS 184
polyp stage of a hydrozoan HYDROID 22
polyps in a hydroid colony named from their resemblance to a flower HYDRANTH 18, 21
polysaccharide that is the main carbohydrate reserve in animal tissue GLYCOGEN 85
ponder a subject SPECULATE 205
poor imitation PARODY 180
poor nutrition MALNUTRITION 32
popular saying Maxim DICTUM 64
portion of a written document dealing with a specific point PARAGRAPH 94, 179
portion of an embryonic somite from which skeletal muscle is derived MYOTOME 170, 203
portion of an embryonic somite from which the skin is derived DERMATOME 61, 203
portion of the brain below the posterior part of the cerebrum CEREBELLUM 46
portion of the brain below the thalamus HYPOTHALAMUS 110
portion of the brain that consists of two hemispheres CEREBRUM 46
portion of the small intestine named for the width of twelve fingers DUODENUM 156, 163
portion of the stomach that connects to the esophagus CARDIA 40
position in a ranking GRADE 97
possession by one party MONOPOLY 152
posterior portion of the prosencephalon DIENCEPHALON 45, 155
posterior portion of the rhombencephalon MYELENCEPHALON 46
pour or spread around CIRCUMFUSE 50, 81
pour out DIFFUSE 81
pour out EFFUSE 81
powder from hemoglobin HEMATIN 99
power ENERGY 77
power structure formed by pro-slavery forces SLAVOCRACY 24
power to endure VITALITY 37
powerful explosive DYNAMITE 69
powerful person in business or industry MAGNATE 140
powerlessness PARALYSIS 179
practice of acquitting a person through the oaths of others COMPURGATION 197
practice of foot massage in the treatment of disorders REFLEXOLOGY 129
precede in time ANTEDATE 15
preceding event ANTECEDENT 14, 42
precipitation formed in the atmosphere HYDROMETEOR 22
precursor of a vitamin PROVITAMIN 18, 37
precursor of pepsin PEPSINOGEN 87, 182
precursor of plasmin PLASMINOGEN 87, 168
precursor of trypsin TRYPSINOGEN 88
predecessor PROGENITOR 16, 87
predict PROGNOSTICATE 16, 53
prediction PROGNOSTIC 16, 53
prediction of the cause of a disease PROGNOSIS 16, 53
predictions and advice HOROSCOPE 201
predominantly maternal hereditary traits MATRICLINOUS 142
predominantly paternal hereditary traits PATRICLINOUS 142
prehistoric drawing PICTOGRAPH 94
preliminary attempt PROLUSION 17, 136
preliminary instruction PROPAEDEUTIC 17
premature contraction of the heart EXTRASYSTOLE 81, 105
preparation of wood for microscopic examination XYLOTOMY 204
prescribed form for public worship LITURGY 77
present as proof ADDUCE 68
present for the first time INTRODUCE 69, 80
pressure or weight BARIC 30
pressures greater than normal atmospheric pressure HYPERBARIC 31, 108

pretend PROFESS 16
pretend illness MALINGER 32, 86
prevent from ever happening PRECLUDE 52
prevent from happening Avoid AVERT 215
preventing excess fat in the liver LIPOTROPIC 118, 213
preventing growth of cells CYTOSTATIC 39
primary threadlike structure in mosses PROTONEMA 25
primates resembling humans but more primitive PROTOHUMAN 25
primitive arrangement of vascular tissue in roots and stems PROTOSTELE 25
primitive digestive cavity of a gastrula ARCHENTERON 23
primitive female germ cell OOGONIUM 88
primitive male germ cell SPERMATOGONIUM 88
primroses bearing multi-flowered umbels POLYANTHUS 18, 164
principal married woman attending the bride MATRON OF HONOR 142
principal unmarried woman attending the bride MAID OF HONOR 219
principal stops of an organ DIAPASON 62
principle considered to be permanently true VERITY 216
principle that governs the universe LOGOS 67
printing from a plane surface PLANOGRAPHY 94
printing from a stone or zinc plate LITHOGRAPHY 93, 123
printing that produces raised lettering by heating THERMOGRAPHY 95, 211
printing with logotypes LOGOGRAPHY 67, 93
prior to enactment RETROACTIVE 198
private mark Trademark IDIOGRAPH 93, 111
problems named from the opened box releasing all that is evil PANDORA'S BOX 177
process by which knowledge is acquired COGNITION 52
process of a nerve cell that carries impulses away from the cell body AXON 30
process of a nerve cell that carries impulses toward the cell body DENDRITE 26, 120
process of deformation of the earth's surface DIASTROPHISM 62
process of equating EQUATION 76
process of extracting metals using high temperatures PYROMETALLURGY 198
process of removing metals from ores HYDROMETALLURGY 22
process of unfolding EFFLORESCENCE 18
process that forms organic compounds in the presence of light PHOTOSYNTHESIS 105, 190
proclaim or affirm PREDICATE 65
produce Beget PROCREATE 16
produce heat in body tissue for medical treatment DIATHERMY 62, 210
produce offspring Breed PROPAGATE 17
produce offspring Reproduce PROCREATE 16
produce very low temperatures CRYOGEN 55, 84
produced by aerobes AEROBIC 8, 34
produced by heat PYROGENIC 87, 197
produced by living organisms BIOGENIC 35, 84
produced by motion KINETIC 117
produced by radioactivity RADIOGENIC 87
produced by the blood HEMATOGENOUS 85, 99
produced by the earth TERRIGENOUS 88, 90
produced by the liver HEPATOGENIC 85, 100
produced by the voice VOCAL 188
producing colored pictures from stone or zinc plates CHROMOLITHOGRAPHY 47, 92, 123
producing current when exposed to light PHOTOVOLTAIC 190
producing eggs that hatch externally OVIPAROUS 219
producing eggs that hatch internally OVOVIVIPAROUS 37
producing live young rather than eggs VIVIPAROUS 38
producing fever PYRETIC 197
producing immunity IMMUNOGENIC 86
producing male offspring only ANDROGENOUS 13, 84
producing offspring PROGENITIVE 16, 87
producing many offspring PHILOPROGENITIVE 16, 87, 185
producing many offspring at a single birth POLYTOCOUS 165
producing one offspring at a time UNIPAROUS 153
producing more than one offspring at a time MULTIPAROUS 219
producing offspring of one sex only MONOGENIC 86, 151
producing poisons TOXICOGENIC 88
producing pus PYOGENIC 87
producing putrefaction or decay SAPROGENIC 87

public official in ancient Greek states DEMIURGE 58, 77
public secretary SCRIBE 96
publication in many newspapers at once SYNDICATE 65, 107
punctuation that indicates less separation than a colon SEMICOLON 59
pupa of a butterfly CHRYSALIS 49
purchase issues of a periodical SUBSCRIBE 96
pure essence QUINTESSENCE 160
pure water AQUA PURA 20
purity of color CHROMA 47
purple color AMETHYST 2
pursue PROSECUTE 17
put forward for consideration Propose PROPOUND 17
put into as if by pouring Instill Inspire INFUSE 81
put into effect by formal proclamation PROMULGATE 17
put into use INVOKE 188
put off until a later time PROCRASTINATE 16
put out Banish EXCLUDE 52
pyrrhotite named after Domenico Troili, Italian scientist TROILITE 122
quality of remaining calm Composure EQUANIMITY 76
quality that arouses feelings of pity PATHOS 79
quantities raised to the second power QUADRATIC 158
quantity under a radical sign RADICAND 198
quantity whose value depends on its application PARAMETER 149, 179
quartz named from the belief that it prevented intoxication AMETHYST 2
quartz stained ruby red RUBASSE 78
question closely CATECHIZE 12
question formally INTERROGATE 112
quotation to introduce the theme EPIGRAPH 75, 92
rabies named from the victim's inability to swallow liquids HYDROPHOBIA 22, 186
radial elements that make up the compound eye of an arthropod OMMATIDIUM 175
radiation of a single wavelength MONOCHROMATIC 48, 151
radiations arranged according to some common physical property SPECTRUM 205
radical change REVOLUTION 214
radical that consists of one atom of hydrogen and one atom of oxygen HYDROXYL 23
radioactive isotope RADIOISOTOPE 105
radius of a celestial body SEMIDIAMETER 59, 63, 150
raise the grade of AGGRADE 96
raise the importance of UPGRADE 97
raise the spirits of ELATE 70
raised piece of land TERRACE 90
raising birds AVICULTURE 30
raising only one crop MONOCULTURE 151
ramose RAMOUS 198
range of related qualities SPECTRUM 205
rapid spread of something EPIDEMIC 58, 74
rapidly circulating air about a low pressure center CYCLONE 56
rapidly spreading disease among animals EPIZOOTIC 76, 217
rapidly spreading disease among people EPIDEMIC 58, 74
ratio of one and one half to one HEMIOLA 59
ratio of red blood cells to total volume HEMATOCRIT 99
reach a decision about CONCLUDE 52
read thoroughly PERUSE 183
readily stained CHROMATIC 47
readily stained CHROMOPHIL 47, 184
realism in art or literature VERISM 216
reasoning with two premises and a conclusion SYLLOGISM 67, 106
rebirth PALINGENESIS 87
reborn REDIVIVUS 37
recalling to memory ANAMNESIS 11
receptacle that attaches to the carpels in flowering plants CARPOPHORE 41, 189
receptor sensitive to heat THERMORECEPTOR 211
record of events in the order of occurrence CHRONICLE 49
record of the history of a family GENEALOGY 85, 125
recording images by exposure of sensitized surfaces to light PHOTOGRAPHY 94, 190
recording of radiant energy variations BOLOGRAPH 91
records of the activities of an organization ANNALS 73

recruit into the armed forces INDUCT 69
recurring time period CYCLE 56
red RUBIOUS 78
red blood cell ERYTHROCYTE 39, 77
red blood cells ERYTHROID 77
red coloring matter in blood HEMACHROME 48, 98
red or pink color Ruddy FLORID 18
red pigment containing basic lead chromate CHROME RED 47
red pigment in hemoglobin HEME 99
red variety of chalcedony CARNELIAN 41
red variety of tourmaline RUBELLITE 78, 121
reddening Blushing RUBESCENT 78
reddish color Ruddy RUBICUND 78
reddish color ERYTHROID 77
reddish-brown RUBIGINOUS 78
reddish-yellow pigment of bile BILIRUBIN 78
redness of feathers or hair ERYTHRISM 77
reduce the strength of Debilitate ENERVATE 71
reducing fever ANTIPYRETIC 197
refer to indirectly ALLUDE 135
refinement or worldly knowledge SOPHISTICATED 204
reflect light in one color and transmit light in another color DICHROISM 47, 154
refuse to accept REJECT 114
refuse to notice IGNORE 4, 53
refusing to compromise INTRANSIGENT 7, 63
regard with extreme dislike Loathe DESPISE 205
regeneration of a body part MORPHALLAXIS 166
region consisting of large cities MEGALOPOLIS 139
region in a plant where tissue develops into specific parts of an organ HISTOGEN 86
region that contains the heart HEMAL 99
region's indigenous plants and animals AUTOCHTHONOUS 28
region's original inhabitants Aboriginal AUTOCHTHONOUS 28
regions under the ocean HYDROSPACE 22
regrettable object of public display SPECTACLE 205
regular customer PATRON 142
regular intervals PERIODIC 51
regulation of body temperature THERMOREGULATION 211
regulation of body temperature THERMOTAXIS 208, 211
rehabilitation or prevention of disability, injury, and disease PHYSICAL THERAPY 193
related rock formations TERRANE 90
related through the father PATERNAL 142
related through the mother MATERNAL 142
release from slavery Liberate EMANCIPATE 71, 141
release from slavery Liberate MANUMIT 141
release of heated fluid into water, harmful to the environment THERMAL POLLUTION 211
religious belief, the essence of God the Father and God the Son is the same HOMOOUSIAN 101
religious belief, the essence of God the Father and God the Son is similar HOMOIOUSIAN 101
religious belief, the essence of God the Father and God the Son is different HETEROOUSIAN 103
religious body DENOMINATION 173
religious image ICON 111
religious philosophy claiming mystical insight into divine nature THEOSOPHY 204, 210
religious philosophy that emphasizes the study of the nature of man ANTHROPOSOPHY 14, 204
religious writings excluded from the New Testament APOCRYPHA 19, 55
remote monitoring of a human or animal BIOTELEMETRY 36, 146, 208
removal of living tissue for examination BIOPSY 36, 175
remove a person from his or her native land EXPATRIATE 142
remove all traces of Obliterate ERASE 71
remove anything undesirable PURGE 197
remove by suction ASPIRATE 194
remove from a country by force Exile DEPORT 194
remove from danger EVACUATE 71
remove from its sphere UNSPHERE 207
remove hydrogen DEHYDROGENATE 21
remove objectionable passages from a publication EXPURGATE 197
remove the clitoris CIRCUMCISE 50
remove the foreskin CIRCUMCISE 50

remove water from DEHYDRATE 21
repeated cycles PERIODIC 51
repetition of a word at the beginning of successive phrases ANAPHORA 11, 189
repetition of a word at the end of successive phrases EPISTROPHE 75
repetition of the same initial sound in two or more words of a phrase ALLITERATION 68
repetition of the last word of one clause at the beginning of the next ANADIPLOSIS 11, 154
repetition of unnecessary conjunctions for rhetorical effect POLYSYNDETON 105, 165
represent speech sounds using phonetic symbols TRANSCRIBE 63, 96
representation of a sphere on a plane surface PLANISPHERE 206
representation of ideas IDEOGRAPHY 93
representation of something in the future as existing presently PROLEPSIS 16
representation of the birth of Christ NATIVITY 170
representative of the world COSMOPOLITAN 54
reproduction by budding BLASTOGENESIS 38, 84
reproduction by egg and sperm OOGAMY 83
reproduction by fission SCHIZOGENESIS 87
reproduction by spores SPOROGENESIS 87, 207
reproduction from a single individual ASEXUAL 3
reproduction in which an egg develops without fertilization PARTHENOGENESIS 87
reproductive aperture GONOPORE 88
reproductive cycles that alternate between asexual and sexual DIGENESIS 84, 155
reproductive organs of either male or female UNISEXUAL 153
reproductive process in plants that does not require fertilization APOMIXIS 19
reputation in good standing CREDIT 55
requiring a small amount of moisture XERIC 216
requiring moderate moisture MESIC 143
requiring substantial moisture HYDRIC 21
resembles the truth VERISIMILITUDE 216
resembling a bird ORNITHOID 30
resembling a celestial body SPHERY 206
resembling a circle CYCLOID 56
resembling a human ANDROID 13
resembling a human ANTHROPOID 14
resembling a leaf PHYLLOID 192
resembling a sphere SPHERICAL 206
resembling a sphere SPHERY 206
resembling a tree ARBOREAL 26
resembling a tree ARBORESCENT 26
resembling a tree DENDROID 26
resembling a woman GYNECOID 13
resembling an animal ZOOID 218
resembling an ape ANTHROPOID 14
resembling bone OSTEOID 178
resembling fat LIPOID 118
resembling melanin MELANOID 144
resembling melanosis MELANOID 144
resembling skin DERMOID 61
resembling stone LITHOID 123
residence for monks apart from the rest of the world MONASTERY 151
resistor whose resistance changes with temperature THERMISTOR 211
respiratory pigment essential in cell respiration CYTOCHROME 39, 47
respiratory pigment in muscle fibers MYOGLOBIN 170
respiratory pigment in red blood cells HEMOGLOBIN 99
respiratory pigment similar to hemoglobin HEMOCYANIN 56, 99
responsive to sexual stimulation EROGENOUS 85
resting body that produces asexual spores SPOROCYST 207
restoration to life ANABIOSIS 11, 34
restore new life to REVIVIFY 37
restore vitality to REVITALIZE 37
restore water to REHYDRATE 23
restraint MANACLE 141
result of medical treatment IATROGENIC 86, 111
retention of the immature characteristics of youth NEOTENY 171
retired because of old age SUPERANNUATED 74
return a person to his or her native land REPATRIATE 143
return to a former practice REVERT 215

roses bearing numerous large flowers FLORIBUNDA 18
rosy-pink color CARNATION 41
round building with an arena at the center AMPHITHEATER 10
round building with an arena at the center AMPHITHEATRE 10
roundabout expression CIRCUMLOCUTION 50, 65
roundabout way of speaking CIRCUMLOCUTION 50, 65
roundabout way of speaking or writing PERIPHRASIS 52
rule by a god THEARCHY 24, 210
rule by a mob MOBOCRACY 24
rule of conduct RUBRIC 78
rule of the seas THALASSOCRACY 24
ruler of one of four provinces TETRARCH 24, 159
Russian astronaut COSMONAUT 54
sac surrounding the heart PERICARDIUM 41, 51
saclike structure at the head of a sperm cell ACROSOME 8
sacred book of Christianity BIBLE 34
sacred writing SCRIPTURE 96
sacred writings of a religion BIBLE 34
sacrifice of 100 oxen HECATOMB 43
sacrificial offering consumed by fire HOLOCAUST 42
sadness named from the belief that it resulted from too much black bile MELANCHOLY 144
sail around the earth CIRCUMNAVIGATE 51
saint who is the special guardian PATRON SAINT 143
salt of chromic acid CHROMATE 47
same chemical combining weight EQUIVALENT 76
same form ISOMORPHIC 104, 166
same form UNIFORM 153
same kind HOMOGENEOUS 86, 101
same name HOMONYMOUS 101, 174
same origin ISOGENOUS 86, 104
same sound HOMOPHONIC 102, 187
same text printed on alternate lines in different languages INTERLINEAR 112
sample taken for medical analysis SPECIMEN 205
sanctuary in a church SACRARIUM 26
sanctum open only to priests ADYTUM 1
satellite synchronous with the earth's rotation GEOSYNCHRONOUS 49, 89, 105
satellite synchronous with the earth's rotation GEOSTATIONARY 89
say in advance PREDICT 65
saying attributed to Jesus but not in the Gospels LOGION 67
sayings attributed to Jesus but not in the Bible AGRAPHA 1, 91
saying farewell VALEDICTION 65
scatter among other things INTERSPERSE 112
scene viewed through a small aperture DIORAMA 63
scene with figures placed against a painted background DIORAMA 63
school graduated from ALMA MATER 142
schoolteacher who instructs in a pedantic manner PEDAGOG 9, 180
schoolteacher who instructs in a pedantic manner PEDAGOGUE 9, 180
science dealing with atomic nuclei NUCLEONICS 134
science dealing with correct reasoning LOGIC 67
science dealing with electronics in aviation AVIONICS 131
science dealing with electrons ELECTRONICS 132
science dealing with energy ENERGETICS 77, 132
science dealing with energy and forces MECHANICS 133
science dealing with flight AERONAUTICS 8, 130
science dealing with living organisms and their environment BIOECOLOGY 35, 124
science dealing with logical analysis ANALYTICS 11, 130
science dealing with miniaturized electronic circuits MICROELECTRONICS 134, 137
science dealing with musical sounds HARMONICS 133
science dealing with natural drugs PHARMACOGNOSY 53
science dealing with nonliving matter and energy PHYSICS 134, 193
science dealing with space flight ASTRONAUTICS 27, 130
science dealing with specialized orthopedic devices ORTHOTICS 134, 178
science dealing with the chemical composition of the universe COSMOCHEMISTRY 54
science dealing with the collection of numerical data STATISTICS 135
science dealing with the control of fluids FLUIDICS 132
science dealing with the distribution of personnel and equipment LOGISTICS 133

scientific measurement of geologic time GEOCHRONOMETRY 49, 88, 147
scientific measurement of light intensity PHOTOMETRY 149, 190
scientific measurement of skulls CRANIOMETRY 46, 146
scientific measurement of the head CEPHALOMETRY 45, 146
scientific use of water to treat injury or disease HYDROTHERAPY 22
scientist specializing in physics PHYSICIST 193
screen decorated with icons in an Eastern Orthodox Church ICONOSTASIS 111
scroll VOLUME 214
sea MARINE 141
sea MARITIME 141
sea not open to all nations MARE CLAUSUM 141
sea open to all nations MARE LIBERUM 141
sea shared by two or more nations MARE NOSTRUM 141
seaman MARINER 141
seasickness MAL DE MER 31, 141
second legal marriage DEUTEROGAMY 82
second legal marriage DIGAMY 82, 155
secret CRYPTIC 56
secrete sweat PERSPIRE 183, 194
secretions in the body AUTACOID 28
seeming reasonable but lacking merit SPECIOUS 205
selected literary passages ANALECTS 11
self The individual as a whole EGO 29
self-amputation of a damaged appendage AUTOTOMY 29, 202
self-assured but overconfident of knowledge SOPHOMORIC 204
self-centered EGOCENTRIC 29, 44
self-educated person AUTODIDACT 28
self-esteem EGO 29
self-fertilization in plants AUTOGAMY 28, 82
self-fertilization in protozoans AUTOGAMY 28, 82
self-generating AUTOGENOUS 28, 84
self-governing AUTONOMOUS 29, 173
self-governing with regard to certain affairs SEMIAUTONOMOUS 29, 59, 173
self-government AUTONOMY 29, 173
self-induced hypnosis AUTOHYPNOSIS 28
self-pollination ENDOGAMY 72, 82
self-propelled vehicle AUTOMOBILE 29
selfish EGOTISTICAL 29
selfish person EGOIST 29
selfish person EGOTIST 29
selfishness Conceit EGOISM 29
selfishness Conceit EGOTISM 29
seller of eyeglasses OPTICIAN 176
seller of flowers FLORIST 18
semicircular arrangement HEMICYCLE 57, 58
seminar by several lecturers COLLOQUIUM 65
send from one place to another TRANSMIT 64
sensation of body movement KINESTHESIA 78, 117
sensation produced by another sense SYNAESTHESIA 78, 106
sensation produced by another sense SYNESTHESIA 78, 107
sensitive to light PHOTOSENSITIVE 190
sensitive to the rights of blacks NEGROPHILE 185
sensitive to the rights of homosexuals HOMOPHILE 101, 185
sensory nerve fibers that respond to small variations EPICRITIC 74
sensory nerves that respond only to gross variations PROTOPATHIC 25, 79
sensual CARNAL 41
separate Individual RESPECTIVE 205
separate branch of the military CORPS 54
separate into parts to study the whole ANALYZE 11
separate petals POLYPETALOUS 165
separate sepals POLYSEPALOUS 165
separation of a whole into elements for individual study ANALYSIS 11
separation of particles DIALYSIS 62
separation of two adjacent vowels DIERESIS 63
sequence of numbers with a constant relation PROGRESSION 16, 97
sequence of terms in which adjacent terms have the same ratio GEOMETRIC PROGRESSION 16, 89, 97, 147

short-lived EPHEMERAL 74
shortening a word by omitting identical successive sounds or syllables HAPLOLOGY 67
shorter arms of a cross-shaped church TRANSEPT 63
show disapproval OBJECT 114
show faith Trust CONFIDE 81
showing a courageous spirit in forgiving MAGNANIMOUS 140
showing a strong inclination toward revenge VINDICTIVE 65
showing disapproval DYSLOGISTIC 32, 33, 66
showing good will BENEVOLENT 31
showing ill will MALICIOUS 32
showing great knowledge and understanding PROFOUND 16
showing keen judgment Shrewd PERSPICACIOUS 183, 205
showing parts in the same ratio HOMOLOGRAPHIC 93, 101
showing unwillingness to believe INCREDULOUS 6, 55
shrinking of the cytoplasm through osmosis PLASMOLYSIS 168
shrub that bears rose-colored flowers RHODORA 78
shut out EXCLUDE 52
sigh SUSPIRE 194
sign before a quantity indicating the root to be extracted RADICAL SIGN 198
sign of something INDICATE 65
sign of things to come PROGNOSTIC 16, 53
signal to a computer to execute a higher priority program INTERRUPT 112, 200
signature by one person for another ALLOGRAPH 91
silicate of soda found in igneous rocks SODALITE 122
silvery heavy liquid Mercury HYDRARGYRUM 21
similar in structure HOMOLOGOUS 101
similar meaning SYNONYMOUS 107, 174
similarity ANALOGY 11, 66
similarity PARALLELISM 179
similarity between members of different species ISOMORPHISM 104, 166
similarity between rock strata in separate areas HOMOTAXIS 102, 208
similarity between things otherwise dissimilar ANALOGY 11, 66
similarity in crystalline form but differing in chemical composition HOMEOMORPHISM 101, 166
similarity in form HOMOMORPHISM 101, 166
similarity in function between parts of different origin ANALOGY 11, 66
similarity of crystalline structure ISOMORPHISM 104, 166
similarity of parts in organisms of common origin HOMOLOGY 67, 101
similarity of size, form, or arrangement SYMMETRY 106, 150
simple molecule that can combine with other molecules to form a polymer MONOMER 152
simple organisms that have characteristics of both animals and plants PROTIST 24
simultaneous combination of contrasting musical rhythms POLYRHYTHM 165
simultaneous communication in opposite directions DUPLEX 156
simultaneous communication in opposite directions DIPLEX 155
simultaneous conflicting feelings Undecided AMBIVALENT 10
simultaneous occurrence CONJUNCTION 115
simultaneous use of two or more keys in a musical composition POLYTONALITY 165
singer VOCALIST 188
single cell UNICELLULAR 153
single nucleus MONONUCLEAR 152
single nucleus UNINUCLEATE 153
single path of development UNILINEAR 153
single piece of stone MONOLITH 123, 152
single piece of type containing more than one letter LOGOTYPE 67
single quantity UNIT 153
single unit UNIFY 153
single vowel sound MONOPHTHONG 152
single-celled microorganism MONAD 151
single-celled microorganisms PROTOZOAN 25, 217
six beats to the measure SEXTUPLE 161
six offspring born at a single birth SEXTUPLET 161
six times as great SEXTUPLE 161
six-pointed star HEXAGRAM 161
sixfold SEXTUPLE 161
sixteenth note SEMIQUAVER 59
sixty-fourth note HEMIDEMISEMIQUAVER 58, 59
sixth letter of the early Greek alphabet DIGAMMA 155

skeletal system of a polyzoan colony POLYZOARIUM 26, 165, 217
skill of performing aerial maneuvers AEROBATICS 8, 130
skill of performing gymnastic feats ACROBATICS 7, 130
skilled performer of gymnastic feats ACROBAT 7
skill of using available means for gaining success TACTICS 135
skillful action MANEUVER 141
skim the surface of the water HYDROPLANE 22
skin Cutaneous DERMAL 61
skin covering the inner canthus normally in people of Asian descent EPICANTHUS 74
skin grafting DERMATOPLASTY 61, 167
skin immediately below the epidermis DERMIS 61
skin innervated from a single spinal nerve root DERMATOME 61, 203
skin that covers the dermis EPIDERMIS 61, 74
skull CRANIAL 46
skull CRANIATE 46
skull CRANIUM 46
skull and the brain CRANIOCEREBRAL 46
sky EMPYREAN 197
slaughter of many people CARNAGE 41
slope GRADIENT 97
slope backward RECEDE 42
slope of a mountain VERSANT 215
slope of a region VERSANT 215
slow the progress of IMPEDE 180
slow-moving TARDIGRADE 97
slow-moving animals TARDIGRADE 97
sluggish INERT 6
small aquatic animals HYDROZOAN 23, 217
small area with uniform environmental conditions BIOTOPE 36
small calcified body within the pulp cavity of a tooth DENTICLE 60
small celestial bodies that orbit the sun between Jupiter and Mars ASTEROID 27
small cup for serving black coffee DEMITASSE 58
small cup of black coffee DEMITASSE 58
small duct DUCTULE 69
small flint tool MICROLITH 123, 138
small flower FLORET 18
small gap across which a nerve impulse passes SYNAPSE 106
small glandular cavity CRYPT 55
small harbor for boats MARINA 141
small opening for the pollen tube MICROPYLE 138
small particle of meteoric dust MICROMETEORITE 138
small particles of chromatin arranged to form a chromosome CHROMOMERE 47
small phagocyte MICROPHAGE 138, 184
small photograph MICROPHOTOGRAPH 93, 138, 189
small rootlike structure RADICLE 198
small sheet of microfilm containing microphotographs MICROFICHE 137
small sphere SPHERULE 206
small spherical aggregate of radiating crystals SPHERULITE 122, 206
small spherical bacteria MICROCOCCUS 137
small teeth MICRODONT 60, 137
small tooth DENTICLE 60
small tremor of the earth's crust MICROSEISM 138
small volcanic vent SPIRACLE 194
small-flowered epiphytic orchids EPIDENDRUM 26, 74
small-scale evolution of organisms MICROEVOLUTION 137, 214
smaller of two conjugating gametes MICROGAMETE 83, 137
smaller spores in heterosporous plants MICROSPORE 138, 207
smallest component of an element having all the properties of the element ATOM 4, 202
smallest unit of a writing system GRAPHEME 92
smallest unit of speech sound in a language PHONEME 187
smallest meaningful unit of a language that cannot be further divided MORPHEME 167
smallest meaningful vocabulary item of a language LEXEME 66
smallest unit of lexical meaning in a language SEMANTEME 220
smallest grammatical feature of the arrangement of elements in a language TAXEME 208
smooth and rapid speech Fluent VOLUBLE 214
smooth continuous gliding from one note to another PORTAMENTO 194

snooperscope attached to a rifle SNIPERSCOPE 201
sociable GREGARIOUS 96
social and economic factors SOCIOECONOMIC 173
social gathering after separation REUNION 153
softening Soothing EMOLLIENT 71
soil that surrounds the roots of a plant RHIZOSPHERE 206
soldier trained to jump from an aircraft using a parachute PARATROOPER 179
sole ruler MONARCH 23, 151
solid figure with four plane surfaces TETRAHEDRON 159
solid figure with five plane surfaces PENTAHEDRON 160
solid figure with six plane surfaces HEXAHEDRON 161
solid figure with seven plane surfaces HEPTAHEDRON 161
solid figure with eight plane surfaces OCTAHEDRON 162
solid figure with ten plane surfaces DECAHEDRON 163
solid figure with eleven plane surfaces HENDECAHEDRON 163
solid figure with twelve plane surfaces DODECAHEDRON 156, 163
solid figure with twenty plane surfaces ICOSAHEDRON 219
solid figure with twenty-four plane surfaces TRISOCTAHEDRON 158, 163
solid figure with four or more plane surfaces POLYHEDRON 164
solid ground Dry land TERRA FIRMA 90
solid part of the earth LITHOSPHERE 123, 206
solidity, uniformity, and intractability MONOLITHIC 123, 152
solution in which water is the dispersing medium HYDROSOL 22
something known COGNITION 52
something out of its proper place in time ANACHRONISM 11, 49
something that promotes well-being BENEFIT 31
something that represents something else SYMBOL 106
soothes or relieves pain ANODYNE 3
soul passes into another body METEMPSYCHOSIS 145, 195
soul reappears in another body REINCARNATION 41
sound PHONIC 187
sound reproduction that uses one source of sound MONAURAL 151
sound reproduction that uses two sources of sound BINAURAL 154
sounding box with one string for determining musical intervals MONOCHORD 151
space behind a parapet where guns are mounted TERREPLEIN 90
space between two things INTERVAL 112
space occupied within three dimensions VOLUME 214
speak ill of MALIGN 32, 86
speak in favor of something ADVOCATE 188
speak or read aloud DICTATE 64
speaking or writing several languages POLYGLOT 164
speaking the truth Veracious VERIDICAL 65
special mood or atmosphere surrounding a place AMBIANCE 10
special mood or atmosphere surrounding a place AMBIENCE 10
species that occur in the same area SYMPATRIC 106, 143
species that occurs in separate areas ALLOPATRIC 142
speech pattern of an individual IDIOLECT 63, 111
speech sound PHONE 187
speech sound that does not form a syllable NONSYLLABIC 105
speech sound with the sound of a vowel but the function of a consonant SEMIVOWEL 59
speech sounds of a language PHONETICS 134, 187
speech that uses grandiose words GRANDILOQUENCE 65
speech transcription based on pronunciation PHONOGRAPHY 94, 188
speed five times the speed of sound HYPERSONIC 109
speed limitation by aerodynamic overheating THERMAL BARRIER 211
speeds near the speed of sound TRANSONIC 64
spelling in which the same letter can represent different sounds HETEROGRAPHY 93, 102
spelling that varies from the current standard HETEROGRAPHY 93, 102
spermatozoa produced by the male SPERMATOPHORE 189
sphere SPHERICAL 206
sphere in which something exists UNIVERSE 153, 215
sphere of pure fire EMPYREAN 197
spherical chamber for deep-sea observation BATHYSPHERE 206
spiral HELIX 57
spiral form VOLUTE 214
spiral scroll-shaped architectural ornament VOLUTE 214

spirit PSYCHE 195
spirit or soul PNEUMA 193
spiritual apathy ACEDIA 1
spiritual interpretation of words ANAGOGE 9, 11
spiritual knowledge GNOSTIC 53
spitting up blood HEMOPTYSIS 99
splitting along a traverse circular line CIRCUMSCISSILE 51
spoken language PHONETIC 187
spokesperson PROLOCUTOR 17, 65
spokesperson for a cause PROPHET 17
sporangium that produces only megaspores MACROSPORANGIUM 137, 207
sporangium that produces only megaspores MEGASPORANGIUM 140, 207
sporangium that produces only microspores MICROSPORANGIUM 138, 207
spore developed from the carpogonium in red algae CARPOSPORE 41, 207
spore formation SPORULATION 208
spore formed by filament segmentation ARTHROSPORE 27, 207
spore formed by the fusion of two similar gametes ZYGOSPORE 208, 218
spore formed in an ascus ASCOSPORE 207
spore formed within a parent cell ENDOSPORE 72, 207
spore mother cell SPOROCYTE 40, 207
spore that develops during the terminal stage of the rust fungus TELIOSPORE 208, 209
spore that develops during the terminal stage of the rust fungus TELEUTOSPORE 208, 209
spore-bearing SPORIFEROUS 207
spore-bearing structure SPOROPHORE 189, 208
spores of one kind only HOMOSPOROUS 102, 207
spores of two different kinds HETEROSPOROUS 103, 207
sporophyte, develops directly from the gametophyte without fertilization APOGAMY 19, 82
sports requiring skill and strength ATHLETICS 130
spread Disseminate PROPAGATE 17
spread from within SUFFUSE 82
spread over or through PERFUSE 82, 183
spread throughout PERMEATE 183
spread throughout PERVADE 183
spring holiday for planting trees ARBOR DAY 26
spurious religious writings PSEUDEPIGRAPHY 76, 94, 195
square QUADRATIC 158
square dance performed by four couples QUADRILLE 158
staining readily with chromium salts CHROMAFFIN 47
stalk bearing reproductive organs GONOPHORE 88, 189
stalk bearing sporangia SPORANGIOPHORE 189, 207
stalk that bears the gynoecium GYNOPHORE 13, 189
stalk that supports the floral parts ANTHOPHORE 18, 189
stalklike part PEDUNCLE 181
stamens and pistils maturing at different times DICHOGAMOUS 82
stamens and pistils maturing at the same time HOMOGAMOUS 83, 101
stamens and pistils on the same flower MONOCLINOUS 151
stamens and pistils on the same flower SYNOECIOUS 107
stamens united with pistils GYNANDROUS 13
staminate and pistillate flowers in the same cluster ANDROGYNOUS 13
staminate and pistillate flowers in the same cluster SYNOECIOUS 107
staminate and pistillate flowers on the same plant MONOECIOUS 151
staminate and pistillate flowers on different plants DIOECIOUS 155
standing upright ORTHOSTATIC 178
stanza or epigram consisting of one line MONOSTICH 152
stanza consisting of two lines DISTICH 155
stanza or poem consisting of three lines TRISTICH 158
stanza or poem consisting of four lines TETRASTICH 160
stanza or poem consisting of five lines PENTASTICH 160
stanza or poem consisting of six lines HEXASTICH 161
stanza or poem consisting of seven lines HEPTASTICH 162
star continually visible above the horizon CIRCUMPOLAR 51
star-shaped ASTEROID 27
star-shaped figure produced in crystal structures ASTERISM 27
star-shaped neuroglial cells ASTROCYTE 27, 39
star-shaped sign used to indicate footnote references, omissions, etc. ASTERISK 27
star-shaped structure formed around the centrosome during mitosis ASTER 27

state formally as fact AVER 216
state in lower mammals that resembles pregnancy PSEUDOPREGNANCY 195
state located between the Gulf of Mexico and the Atlantic Ocean FLORIDA 18
state of balance EQUIPOISE 76
state of balance between opposing forces EQUILIBRIUM 76
state of drowsiness preceding sleep HYPNAGOGIC 9
state preceding complete wakening HYPNOPOMPIC 219
statement based on incomplete evidence CONJECTURE 114
statement expressing regret for an error APOLOGY 19, 66
statement of religious beliefs CREED 55
statement of the equality of two mathematical expressions EQUATION 76
statement that is self-contradictory and false PARADOX 55, 178
statement that is true but seems unbelievable PARADOX 55, 178
statistical data of populations DEMOGRAPHICS 58, 92, 131
statistical data pertaining to human life VITAL STATISTICS 37
statistical study of the vocabulary of languages LEXICOSTATISTICS 66, 133
statute law LEX SCRIPTA 66, 96
staying for a short time TRANSIENT 64
steep ABRUPT 199
stem around which leaves and branches are arranged AXIS 30
stem that functions as a leaf CLADOPHYLL 192
stem that functions as a leaf PHYLLOCLADE 192
stem that functions as the missing leaf blade that it replaces PHYLLODE 192
steps or seats raised one above another GRADIN 97
sterols derived from animals ZOOSTEROL 218
sterols derived from plants PHYTOSTEROL 191
stick out Project PROTRUDE 17
sticking out Bulging PROTUBERANT 17
stimulate to activity INSPIRE 194
stimulates the flow of saliva SIALAGOGUE 9
stimulating the secretion of milk LACTOGENIC 86
stomach GASTRIC 83
stomach and intestines GASTROINTESTINAL 83
stone LITHIC 123
Stone Age beginning with very crudely chipped flint EOLITHIC 123
Stone Age beginning with crudely chipped stone tools PALEOLITHIC 25, 123
Stone Age between Paleolithic and Neolithic MESOLITHIC 123, 143
Stone Age characterized by advanced stone tools and farming NEOLITHIC 123, 170
stone composed of granite and cement GRANOLITH 123
stonelike granules in a statocyst STATOLITH 123
stonelike particle in the inner ear OTOLITH 123
stony iron meteorite SIDEROLITE 122
stony meteorite AEROLITE 8, 118
stony meteorite AEROLITH 8, 123
stony meteorite that contains chondrules CHONDRITE 120
stop progress INTERCEPT 111
stoppage of blood flow HEMOSTASIS 99
stopping blood circulation HEMOSTASIS 99
stopping blood flow HEMOSTATIC 100
story of one's life written by another BIOGRAPHY 35, 91
story of one's life written by oneself AUTOBIOGRAPHY 28, 35, 91
straight line whose motion generates a figure GENERATRIX 85
strait with violent currents EURIPUS 33
strands resulting from chromosome reduplication CHROMATID 47
stratified rock, both sides have the same downward slope ISOCLINE 104
streaming movement of protoplasm CYCLOSIS 56
striated ganglionic masses in each cerebral hemisphere CORPUS STRIATUM 54
strict adherence to promises FIDELITY 81
strive to attain something ASPIRE 194
strong criticism ANIMADVERSION 214
strong downpour Deluge CATARACT 12
strong feeling of dislike AVERSE 215
strong laxative PURGATIVE 197
structural makeup of a plant or animal ANATOMY 11, 202
structural similarities due to common origin HOMOGENOUS 86, 101
structural similarities due to evolution HOMOPLASTIC 102, 168

structure in cytoplasm thought to determine hereditary characteristics PLASMAGENE 87, 168
structure in which spores are formed SPORANGIUM 207
structure of rock masses in the earth's crust GEOTECTONIC 89
structure that attaches to the spindle fiber during mitosis CENTROMERE 44
structure that contains the centrioles and divides during mitosis CENTROSOME 44
structure that forms the center of an aster during mitosis CENTRIOLE 44
structure that folds over the glottis during swallowing EPIGLOTTIS 75
structure that is the result of mineral-rich water dripping from the roof STALACTITE 122
structure that is the result of mineral-rich water dripping to the floor STALAGMITE 122
structure that supports the radula to break up food ODONTOPHORE 60, 189
structures surrounding the mouth of certain invertebrates PERISTOME 52
stubbornly persistent Obstinate PERTINACIOUS 183
student in the second year SOPHOMORE 204
student who delivers the farewell speech VALEDICTORIAN 65
study and treatment of aging persons GERIATRICS 110, 132
study and treatment of behavioral disorders in children ORTHOPSYCHIATRY 111, 177, 195
study and treatment of diseases of children PEDIATRICS 111, 134, 180
study and treatment of diseases of the mind and nervous system NEUROPSYCHIATRY 111, 172, 195
study and treatment of diseases peculiar to women GYNIATRICS 13, 110, 133
study and treatment of disorders of the feet PODIATRY 111, 181
study and treatment of disorders of the hands and feet CHIROPODY 181
study and treatment of mental disorders PSYCHIATRY 111, 195
study and treatment of obesity BARIATRICS 30, 110, 131
study of China SINOLOGY 129
study of Russian government KREMLINOLOGY 126
study of a body moving at speeds greater than the speed of sound SUPERSONICS 135
study of a place TOPOLOGY 130
study of a species and its environment AUTECOLOGY 28, 124
study of air and other gases PNEUMATICS 134, 193
study of air-borne biological materials AEROBIOLOGY 8, 34, 123
study of algae ALGOLOGY 124
study of algae PHYCOLOGY 128
study of ancient Assyrians ASSYRIOLOGY 124
study of ancient Egypt EGYPTOLOGY 125
study of ancient animal life through fossil remains PALEOZOOLOGY 25, 128, 217
study of ancient plant life through fossil remains PALEOBOTANY 25
study of ancient plant and animal life through fossil remains PALEONTOLOGY 25, 128
study of ancient plants and animals and their environment PALEOECOLOGY 25, 128
study of ancient inscriptions EPIGRAPHY 75, 92
study of ancient peoples ARCHAEOLOGY 23, 124
study of ancient peoples ARCHEOLOGY 23, 124
study of ancient writing PALEOGRAPHY 25, 94
study of anesthesia ANESTHESIOLOGY 2, 78, 124
study of animal behavior ETHOLOGY 125
study of animals ZOOLOGY 130, 218
study of ants MYRMECOLOGY 127
study of architecture ARCHITECTONICS 23, 130
study of atmospheric conditions on living organisms BIOMETEOROLOGY 35, 124
study of atmospheric phenomena METEOROLOGY 126
study of atoms ATOMICS 131, 202
study of atoms, molecules, and other elementary particles MICROPHYSICS 134, 138, 192
study of automatic control systems AUTONETICS 29, 131
study of bacteria BACTERIOLOGY 124
study of beauty AESTHETICS 78, 130
study of beauty ESTHETICS 78, 132
study of biological control systems BIOCYBERNETICS 35, 131
study of biological data BIOMETRICS 35, 131, 146
study of biological improvement of humans before or after birth EUPHENICS 32, 132
study of birds ORNITHOLOGY 30, 127
study of birds' eggs OOLOGY 127
study of blood HEMATOLOGY 99, 126
study of blood and lymph vessels ANGIOLOGY 124
study of blood circulation HEMODYNAMICS 70, 99, 133
study of body movement KINESIOLOGY 117, 126
study of body movements in communication Body language KINESICS 117, 133
study of bones OSTEOLOGY 127, 178

study of breeding THREMMATOLOGY 130
study of causes ETIOLOGY 125
study of caves SPELEOLOGY 129
study of celestial bodies ASTROGEOLOGY 27, 88, 124
study of cell chemistry CYTOCHEMISTRY 39
study of cells CYTOLOGY 39, 125
study of cells using photometry CYTOPHOTOMETRY 39, 147, 189
study of chemical reactions and heat THERMOCHEMISTRY 211
study of children PEDOLOGY[1] 128, 180
study of church architecture ECCLESIOLOGY 125
study of climate in a small area MICROCLIMATOLOGY 127, 137
study of climate over a large area MACROCLIMATOLOGY 126, 136
study of climate on living organisms BIOCLIMATOLOGY 35, 124
study of climates CLIMATOLOGY 124
study of clouds NEPHOLOGY 127
study of coins NUMISMATICS 134
study of colors CHROMATICS 47, 131
study of control systems CYBERNETICS 131
study of correct word pronunciation ORTHOEPY 177
study of cosmetics COSMETOLOGY 124
study of crime CRIMINOLOGY 125
study of death and dying THANATOLOGY 129
study of demons DEMONOLOGY 125
study of dialects DIALECTOLOGY 62, 125
study of diseased tissue HISTOPATHOLOGY 79, 126
study of diseases PATHOLOGY 79, 128
study of diseases of the mind PSYCHOPATHOLOGY 79, 129, 196
study of diseases of the nervous system NEUROPATHOLOGY 79, 127, 172
study of diseases peculiar to women GYNECOLOGY 13, 126
study of drugs PHARMACOLOGY 128
study of drugs and mental behavior PSYCHOPHARMACOLOGY 129, 196
study of early races of mankind PALEETHNOLOGY 25, 128
study of earthquakes SEISMOLOGY 129
study of electric currents and magnetic forces ELECTRODYNAMICS 69, 132
study of electricity in motion ELECTROKINETICS 117, 132
study of embryos EMBRYOLOGY 125
study of enzymes ENZYMOLOGY 125
study of epidemic diseases among people EPIDEMIOLOGY 58, 74, 125
study of epidemic diseases among animals EPIZOOTIOLOGY 76, 125, 217
study of ethical ramifications of research BIOETHICS 35, 131
study of ethical terms METAETHICS 133, 144
study of excrement SCATOLOGY 129
study of extraterrestrial living organisms EXOBIOLOGY 36, 125
study of extraterrestrial living organisms ASTROBIOLOGY 27, 34, 124
study of family histories GENEALOGY 85, 125
study of fermentation and enzyme action ZYMOLOGY 130
study of fermentation processes ZYMURGY 77
study of ferns PTERIDOLOGY 129
study of final causes TELEOLOGY 129, 209
study of fingerprints DACTYLOGRAPHY 58, 92
study of firearms and ammunition BALLISTICS 131
study of fishes ICHTHYOLOGY 126
study of fluids at rest or in equilibrium HYDROSTATICS 22, 133
study of fluids in motion HYDRODYNAMICS 21, 70, 133
study of food, nutrition, and diet SITOLOGY 129
study of force, mass, and motion DYNAMICS 69, 131
study of forces and matter in equilibrium STATICS 135
study of forces on the motion of material bodies KINETICS 117, 133
study of forces within the earth GEODYNAMICS 70, 89, 132
study of formal debate FORENSICS 132
study of freezing points CRYOSCOPY 55, 200
study of friction TRIBOLOGY 130
study of fruit growing POMOLOGY 128
study of fruits and seeds CARPOLOGY 41, 124
study of fungi MYCOLOGY 127
study of gemstones GEMMOLOGY 125

study of gemstones GEMOLOGY 125
study of genetic factors and drug response PHARMACOGENETICS 87, 134
study of geographical and political factors GEOPOLITICS 89, 92, 132
study of glaciers GLACIOLOGY 126
study of grasses AGROSTOLOGY 9, 124
study of handwriting GRAPHOLOGY 93, 126
study of health maintenance HYGIENICS 133
study of hearing disorders AUDIOLOGY 124
study of heat and mechanical energy in air AEROTHERMODYNAMICS 9, 69, 130, 210
study of heat and other forms of energy THERMODYNAMICS 70, 135, 211
study of heredity GENETICS 85, 132
study of heredity using cytology and genetics CYTOGENETICS 39, 84, 131
study of historical changes in a language DIACHRONIC 49, 62
study of history CLIOMETRICS 131, 146
study of history through psychology PSYCHOHISTORY 195
study of how time affects life CHRONOBIOLOGY 36, 49, 124
study of human anatomical measurements ANTHROPOMETRY 14, 146
study of human character ETHOLOGY 125
study of human knowledge EPISTEMOLOGY 75, 125
study of human populations DEMOGRAPHY 58, 92
study of human settlements EKISTICS 132
study of human social behavior SOCIOLOGY 129
study of hymns HYMNOLOGY 126
study of ideas IDEOLOGY 126
study of immunity IMMUNOLOGY 126
study of immunity in relation to heredity IMMUNOGENETICS 86, 133
study of insects ENTOMOLOGY 125
study of lakes LIMNOLOGY 126
study of language LINGUISTICS 118, 133
study of language during a given time period SYNCHRONIC 49, 106
study of last things ESCHATOLOGY 125
study of lepidopterans LEPIDOPTEROLOGY 126, 197
study of linguistic tones in a language TONETICS 135
study of liquids in motion HYDROKINETICS 22, 117, 133
study of living organisms and life processes BIOLOGY 35, 124
study of malformations TERATOLOGY 129
study of mammals MAMMALOGY 126
study of man ANTHROPOLOGY 14, 124
study of man's origin ANTHROPOGENESIS 14, 84
study of mathematical systems METAMATHEMATICS 134, 145
study of meanings in a language SEMANTICS 135
study of meanings in context PRAGMATICS 134
study of mental and physical processes PSYCHOPHYSIOLOGY 129, 193, 196
study of mental forces and their relation to human behavior PSYCHODYNAMICS 70, 135, 195
study of metals METALLOGRAPHY 93
study of microscopic forms of life MICROBIOLOGY 36, 127, 137
study of microscopic fossils MICROPALEONTOLOGY 25, 127, 138
study of minerals MINERALOGY 127
study of miracles THAUMATOLOGY 129
study of mollusks MALACOLOGY 126
study of moral obligation DEONTOLOGY 125
study of mosses and liverworts BRYOLOGY 124
study of mountains OROLOGY 127
study of muscles MYOLOGY 127, 170
study of music MUSICOLOGY 127
study of music of two or more cultures ETHNOMUSICOLOGY 125
study of myths MYTHOLOGY 127
study of nature COSMOGRAPHY 54, 92
study of newborn children NEONATOLOGY 127, 170, 171
study of numbers MATHEMATICS 133
study of numbers NUMEROLOGY 127
study of nutrition DIETETICS 131
study of oceans OCEANOGRAPHY 94
study of oceans OCEANOLOGY 127
study of organisms and their environment ECOLOGY 125
study of organisms living free from germs except those known GNOTOBIOTICS 36, 53, 132

study of parasites PARASITOLOGY 128
study of people and their working environment ERGONOMICS 77, 132, 173
study of phenomena PHENOMENOLOGY 128
study of physical therapy PHYSIATRICS 111, 134, 193
study of place names TOPONYMY 174
study of plant communities and their environment PHYTOSOCIOLOGY 128, 191
study of plant and animal communities and their environment SYNECOLOGY 107, 129
study of plant and animal organs ORGANOLOGY 127
study of plant diseases PHYTOPATHOLOGY 79, 128, 191
study of plants Botany PHYTOLOGY 128, 191
study of plants in a region FLORISTICS 19, 132
study of poetry POETICS 134
study of poisons TOXICOLOGY 130
study of political elections PSEPHOLOGY 128
study of pollen PALYNOLOGY 128
study of postage stamps PHILATELY 185
study of prehistoric man PALEOANTHROPOLOGY 14, 25, 128
study of primates PRIMATOLOGY 128
study of primitive peoples AGRIOLOGY 124
study of projectiles in flight BALLISTICS 131
study of proper names ONOMASTICS 134, 174
study of proper names ONOMATOLOGY 127, 174
study of protozoans PROTOZOOLOGY 25, 128, 217
study of psychic phenomena beyond physical law PARAPSYCHOLOGY 128, 179, 195
study of psychological behavior and language PSYCHOLINGUISTICS 118, 135, 195
study of public worship LITURGICS 77, 133
study of punishment PENOLOGY 128
study of pure motion without reference to force or mass KINEMATICS 117, 133
study of rainfall HYETOLOGY 126
study of reality named from Aristotle's writings after physics METAPHYSICS 134, 145, 192
study of recurring natural phenomena PHENOLOGY 128
study of reflexes REFLEXOLOGY 129
study of refracted light DIOPTRICS 63, 131, 175
study of related languages to determine their divergence GLOTTOCHRONOLOGY 49, 126
study of religion THEOLOGY 130, 210
study of religious dogmas DOGMATICS 131
study of reptiles and amphibians HERPETOLOGY 126
study of rheumatic diseases RHEUMATOLOGY 129
study of right triangles TRIGONOMETRY 91, 150, 157
study of rings in trees for dating DENDROCHRONOLOGY 26, 49, 125
study of rock strata STRATIGRAPHY 95
study of rocks PETROLOGY 128
study of rocks and minerals LITHOLOGY 123, 126
study of rules of conduct ETHICS 132
study of serums SEROLOGY 129
study of sexual behavior SEXOLOGY 129
study of shells and mollusks CONCHOLOGY 124
study of sign language SEMEIOLOGY 129
study of sign language SEMIOLOGY 129
study of signs and symbols and their relationships to their users PRAGMATICS 134
study of signs and symbols apart from their users SYNTACTICS 107, 135
study of signs and symbols and their representations SEMANTICS 135
study of signs and symbols and their representations SEMASIOLOGY 129
study of signs and symbols in a language SEMIOTICS 135
study of skull characteristics CRANIOLOGY 46, 125
study of sleep HYPNOLOGY 126
study of small-scale atmospheric phenomena MICROMETEOROLOGY 127, 138
study of snakes OPHIOLOGY 127
study of social behavior SOCIOBIOLOGY 37, 129
study of social effects on language usage SOCIOLINGUISTICS 118, 135
study of soils PEDOLOGY² 128
study of sound PHONICS 134, 187
study of sound and hearing ACOUSTICS 130
study of spacial separation among individuals PROXEMICS 135
study of specific factors in an economy MICROECONOMICS 134, 137, 173
study of spectra SPECTROSCOPY 202, 205

study of speech sounds PHONETICS 134, 187
study of spelling ORTHOGRAPHY 94, 177
study of static electricity ELECTROSTATICS 132
study of style as a method of analyzing literary works STYLISTICS 135
study of suicide SUICIDOLOGY 129
study of symbols SYMBOLOGY 106, 129
study of syphilis SYPHILOLOGY 129
study of the absorption, excretion, etc., of drugs PHARMACOKINETICS 117, 134
study of the actions of drugs PHARMACODYNAMICS 70, 134
study of the anatomy of the nervous system NEUROANATOMY 12, 171, 203
study of the anus and rectum PROCTOLOGY 128
study of the atmosphere AEROLOGY 8, 124
study of the biology of the mind PSYCHOBIOLOGY 36, 128, 195
study of the chemical composition of the earth GEOCHEMISTRY 88
study of the chemical structure of the nervous system NEUROCHEMISTRY 172
study of the composition of the earth GEOGNOSY 53, 89
study of the connection between heavenly bodies and human affairs ASTROLOGY 27, 124
study of the conversion of food into energy by living organisms BIOENERGETICS 35, 77, 131
study of the depth measurement of water BATHYMETRY 146
study of the deterioration of hereditary qualities CACOGENICS 84, 131
study of the deterioration of hereditary qualities DYSGENICS 33, 84, 132
study of the ear OTOLOGY 128
study of the ear, nose, and throat OTOLARYNGOLOGY 128
study of the ear, nose, and throat OTORHINOLARYNGOLOGY 128, 199
study of the earth above sea level HYPSOGRAPHY 93
study of the earth in ancient times PALEOGEOGRAPHY 25, 89, 94
study of the earth's age GEOCHRONOLOGY 49, 88, 125
study of the earth's magnetism GEOMAGNETISM 89
study of the earth's surface GEOMORPHOLOGY 89, 126, 166
study of the effects of below-normal temperatures on living organisms CRYOBIOLOGY 36, 55, 125
study of the effects of light on plants and animals PHOTODYNAMICS 70, 134, 190
study of the effects of physical stimuli on mental processes PSYCHOPHYSICS 135, 193, 196
study of the effects of radiation on living organisms RADIOBIOLOGY 36, 129
study of the endocrine system ENDOCRINOLOGY 72, 125
study of the equilibrium of air AEROSTATICS 8, 130
study of the eye OPHTHALMOLOGY 127, 176
study of the fetus FETOLOGY 125
study of the flow of matter RHEOLOGY 129
study of the form and structure of plants and animals MORPHOLOGY 127, 167
study of the functions and activities of tissue HISTOPHYSIOLOGY 126, 192
study of the functions of organisms or their parts PHYSIOLOGY 128, 193
study of the functions of the nervous system NEUROPHYSIOLOGY 127, 172, 193
study of the geographical distribution of animals ZOOGEOGRAPHY 89, 95, 218
study of the geographical distribution of plants PHYTOGEOGRAPHY 89, 94, 191
study of the geographical distribution of plants GEOBOTANY 88
study of the geographical distribution of plants and animals BIOGEOGRAPHY 35, 88, 91
study of the heart CARDIOLOGY 40, 124
study of the improvement of a species by genetic control EUGENICS 32, 85, 132
study of the improvement of well-being by improvement of living conditions EUTHENICS 33, 132
study of the industrial arts TECHNOLOGY 129
study of the integration of mind and body PSYCHOBIOLOGY 36, 128, 195
study of the interaction between sound waves and light waves ACOUSTOOPTICS 130, 175
study of the kidneys NEPHROLOGY 127, 171
study of the larynx LARYNGOLOGY 126
study of the measurement of life span BIOMETRY 36, 146
study of the measurement of planes and solids GEOMETRY 89, 147
study of the measurement of positions of celestial bodies ASTROMETRY 27, 146
study of the measurement of the growth of part of an organism ALLOMETRY 146
study of the molecular structure of biological systems MOLECULAR BIOLOGY 36, 127
study of the moon SELENOLOGY 129
study of the morphemes of a language MORPHEMICS 134, 167
study of the motion of air AERODYNAMICS 8, 69, 130
study of the mouth STOMATOLOGY 129
study of the nature and structure of the Church ECCLESIOLOGY 125
study of the nature of being ONTOLOGY 127
study of the nervous system NEUROLOGY 127, 172

study of the nose RHINOLOGY 129, 199
study of the origin of the universe COSMOGONY 54, 88
study of the overall forces in an economy MACROECONOMICS 133, 136, 173
study of the overall sound pattern of a language PHONOLOGY 128, 188
study of the phonemes of a language PHONEMICS 134, 187
study of the physical characteristics of the body SOMATOLOGY 129
study of the physical properties of celestial bodies ASTROPHYSICS 28, 130, 192
study of the physics of the earth GEOPHYSICS 89, 132, 192
study of the physiography of the moon SELENOGRAPHY 95
study of the production and distribution of wealth ECONOMICS 132, 173
study of the races of mankind ETHNOLOGY 125
study of the relations between language and other cultural factors METALINGUISTICS 118, 133, 145
study of the size and shape of the earth GEODESY 89
study of the skin DERMATOLOGY 61, 125
study of the skull as being indicative of mental faculties PHRENOLOGY 128
study of the stomach GASTROLOGY 83, 125
study of the stomach and intestines GASTROENTEROLOGY 83, 125
study of the structure of the earth's crust TECTONICS 135
study of the systematization of knowledge ARCHITECTONICS 23, 130
study of the true meaning and history of a word ETYMOLOGY 125
study of the universe ASTRONOMY 28, 172
study of the upper atmosphere AERONOMY 8, 172
study of the urinary tract UROLOGY 130
study of the writing system and speech sounds of a language GRAPHEMICS 92, 133
study of thermionic phenomena THERMIONICS 135, 211
study of ticks and mites ACAROLOGY 123
study of tissue structure HISTOLOGY 126
study of trees DENDROLOGY 26, 125
study of tumors ONCOLOGY 127
study of types TYPOLOGY 130
study of urban areas URBANOLOGY 130
study of values AXIOLOGY 124
study of veins PHLEBOLOGY 128
study of venereal diseases VENEREOLOGY 130
study of viruses VIROLOGY 130
study of vision and light OPTICS 134, 176
study of volcanoes VOLCANOLOGY 130
study of volcanoes VULCANOLOGY 130
study of water in the atmosphere HYDROMETEOROLOGY 22, 126
study of water on and beneath the earth's surface HYDROLOGY 22, 126
study of water on the earth's surface HYDROGRAPHY 22, 93
study of weights and measures METROLOGY 126, 148
study of whales CETOLOGY 124
study of winds ANEMOLOGY 124
study of word formation MORPHOLOGY 127, 167
study of words LEXICOLOGY 66, 126
study of worms HELMINTHOLOGY 126
study of written records PHILOLOGY 67, 185
study of x-rays ROENTGENOLOGY 129
study of x-rays and other radiation RADIOLOGY 129
style of public speaking ELOCUTION 65, 70
style of speaking LOCUTION 65
style of speaking or writing VERBIAGE 68
subdivision Portion SECTION 202
subdivisions of a period in geologic time EPOCH 76
subject to death MORTAL 169
subject to the laws of another HETERONOMOUS 103, 173
subjunctive mood SUBJUNCTIVE 115
subordinate ruler TETRARCH 24, 159
substance causing mutation MUTAGEN 86
substance converted into a pigment CHROMOGEN 47, 84
substance emitting light PHOSPHORESCENCE 189
substance for cleaning teeth DENTIFRICE 60
substance from which an enzyme is produced ZYMOGEN 88
substance that causes an allergy ALLERGEN 84
substance that causes hallucinations HALLUCINOGEN 85

substance that causes the production of an antibody ANTIGEN 84
substance that increases the rate of a chemical reaction CATALYST 12
substance that retards a chemical reaction ANTICATALYST 12
substance that transmits impulses between nerve cells NEUROTRANSMITTER 63, 172
substances adversely affected by heat THERMOLABILE 211
substances not adversely affected by heat THERMOSTABLE 211
substances that become soft when heated THERMOPLASTIC 169, 211
substances that form a gel with water HYDROCOLLOID 21
substitution of an inoffensive term for an offensive one EUPHEMISM 32
substitution of an offensive term for an inoffensive one DYSPHEMISM 32, 33
succeed in accomplishing MANAGE 141
sudden ABRUPT 199
sugar that cannot be further decomposed by hydrolysis MONOSACCHARIDE 152
sugars that yield two monosaccharides DISACCHARIDE 155
sugars that yield three monosaccharides TRISACCHARIDE 158
sugars that yield a small number of monosaccharides OLIGOSACCHARIDE 166
sugars that yield more than three monosaccharides POLYSACCHARIDE 165
suggestion given during hypnosis for execution after awakening POSTHYPNOTIC 15
suitable ELIGIBLE 70
suitable for writing letters EPISTOLARY 75
suitable to a particular purpose EXPEDIENT 180
sum of the processes necessary for life METABOLISM 144
sum total AGGREGATE 96
sun SOLAR 98
sun as the center HELIOCENTRIC 44, 98
sun god HELIOS 98
sunflowers HELIANTHUS 18, 98
superior Distinguished EMINENT 71
supernatural being Ghost SPIRIT 194
supernatural mental abilities PSYCHIC 195
supply with oxygen AERATE 8
supporting base PEDESTAL 180
supporting tissue of the brain and spinal cord NEUROGLIA 172
suppression of blood flow ISCHEMIA 100
suppression of one gene by another EPISTASIS 75
surface features of a region TOPOGRAPHY 95
surgery involving the nervous system NEUROSURGERY 172
surgery of the brain to treat mental disorders PSYCHOSURGERY 196
surgery that uses extreme cold to destroy tissue CRYOSURGERY 55
surgery using a microscope and very small instruments MICROSURGERY 139
surgical clamp used to stop bleeding HEMOSTAT 100
surgical connection of tubular structures to form a channel ANASTOMOSIS 11
surgical creation of an opening for an artificial excretory passage OSTOMY 203
surgical creation of an opening into the colon COLOSTOMY 203
surgical creation of an opening into the ileum ILEOSTOMY 203
surgical cutting into the skull CRANIOTOMY 46, 203
surgical cutting of a bone OSTEOTOMY 178, 203
surgical cutting of a nerve NEUROTOMY 172, 203
surgical cutting of a spinal nerve root RHIZOTOMY 203
surgical cutting of the vagus nerve VAGOTOMY 204
surgical fixation of a joint ARTHRODESIS 27
surgical fracturing of a bone OSTEOCLASIS 178
surgical incision into a lobe of the brain LOBOTOMY 203
surgical incision into the abdominal wall LAPAROTOMY 203
surgical incision into the chest wall THORACOTOMY 204
surgical incision into the trachea TRACHEOTOMY 204
surgical incision of a kidney NEPHROTOMY 171, 203
surgical incision of a tonsil TONSILLOTOMY 204
surgical incision of an ovary OVARIOTOMY 203
surgical incision of the bladder to remove a stone LITHOTOMY 123, 203
surgical incision of the sclera SCLEROTOMY 200, 204
surgical incision of the uterus HYSTEROTOMY 203
surgical incision of the vulva EPISIOTOMY 203
surgical opening of a vein PHLEBOTOMY 203
surgical opening of a vein VENESECTION 202
surgical removal of a breast MASTECTOMY 203

surgical removal of a kidney NEPHRECTOMY 171, 203
surgical removal of a lobe LOBECTOMY 203
surgical removal of a lung PNEUMONECTOMY 193, 203
surgical removal of a mastoid MASTOIDECTOMY 203
surgical removal of a nerve NEURECTOMY 171, 203
surgical removal of a varicose vein VARICOTOMY 204
surgical removal of a vertebral lamina LAMINECTOMY 203
surgical removal of an ovary OOPHORECTOMY 189, 203
surgical removal of an ovary OVARIECTOMY 203
surgical removal of dead bone or tissue NECROTOMY 169, 203
surgical removal of hemorrhoids HEMORRHOIDECTOMY 99, 199, 203
surgical removal of part of an organ, bone, or other structure RESECTION 202
surgical removal of skin to eliminate wrinkles Face lift RHYTIDECTOMY 203
surgical removal of the appendix APPENDECTOMY 202
surgical removal of the fallopian tube SALPINGECTOMY 203
surgical removal of the gallbladder CHOLECYSTECTOMY 202
surgical removal of the larynx LARYNGECTOMY 203
surgical removal of the liver HEPATECTOMY 100, 203
surgical removal of the parathyroid glands PARATHYROIDECTOMY 179, 203
surgical removal of the pituitary gland HYPOPHYSECTOMY 110, 203
surgical removal of the prostate gland PROSTATECTOMY 203
surgical removal of the spleen SPLENECTOMY 204
surgical removal of the stomach GASTRECTOMY 83, 203
surgical removal of the thyroid gland THYROIDECTOMY 204
surgical removal of the tonsils TONSILLECTOMY 204
surgical removal of the uterus HYSTERECTOMY 203
surgical removal of the vagina VAGINECTOMY 204
surgical removal of the vas deferens VASECTOMY 204
surgical removal of the vitreous humor VITRECTOMY 204
surgical restructuring of an eyelid Eye lift BLEPHAROPLASTY 167
surgical restructuring of bone OSTEOPLASTY 168, 178
surgically move an organ from one individual to another TRANSPLANT 64
surgically reconstructing blood vessels ANGIOPLASTY 167
surround by a defensive obstruction CIRCUMVALLATE 51
surround with a fluid CIRCUMFUSE 50, 81
surrounded by dry land MEDITERRANEAN 90, 143
surrounding AMBIENT 10
surrounding CIRCUMAMBIENT 10, 50
surrounding Adjacent on all sides CIRCUMJACENT 50
surrounding Flowing around CIRCUMFLUENT 50
surrounding mood ATMOSPHERE 206
surrounding substance in which something exists MEDIUM 143
surrounding the North or South Pole CIRCUMPOLAR 51
swirling motion Vortex GYRE 57
syllables of a language SYLLABARY 106
symbol representing a speech sound in printing PHONOTYPE 188
symbol representing a speech sound in shorthand PHONOGRAM 187
symbolic representation using images ICONOGRAPHY 93, 111
symbols each representing a speech sound PHONETIC ALPHABET 187
symphony orchestra PHILHARMONIC 185
symptoms occurring together SYNDROME 107
system of measurement that uses the meter, kilogram, and second METER-KILOGRAM-SECOND 115, 148
systematic arrangement of words SYNTAX 107, 208
systematic list of items CATALOG 12, 66
systematic list of items CATALOGUE 12, 66
systematic rhythmic exercises CALISTHENICS 131
table showing precomputed positions of a celestial body EPHEMERIS 74
tail fin having symmetrical lobes HOMOCERCAL 101
tail fin having two unequal lobes HETEROCERCAL 102
take away SUBTRACT 212
take away Subtract DEDUCT 68
take back, as a license REVOKE 188
take back, as an offer RETRACT 212
take between the starting point and destination INTERCEPT 111
take charge MANAGE 141
take control of an office ACCEDE 42

thousand twenty four binary digits KILOBIT 115
thousand twenty four bytes KILOBYTE 115
thousand volts KILOVOLT 115
thousand watts KILOWATT 115
thousandth MILLESIMAL 115
threadlike core of a chromosome CHROMONEMA 47
threatening possibility SPECTER 205
threatening possibility SPECTRE 205
three axes TRIAXIAL 30, 156
three branches TRIFURCATE 157
three colors TRICHROMATIC 48, 157
three contiguous letters representing a single speech sound TRIGRAPH 95, 157
three contiguous vowels representing a single vowel sound TRIPHTHONG 158
three focal lengths TRIFOCAL 157
three forms TRIMORPH 157, 167
three horns TRICORN 157
three identical copies TRIPLICATE 158
three in one, especially the Trinity TRIUNE 153, 158
three leaves TRIFOLIATE 157
three legislative chambers TRICAMERAL 156
three letters TRILITERAL 68, 157
three lobes TRILOBATE 157
three offspring born at a single birth TRIPLET 158
three parts TRIPARTITE 157
three persons who share authority TRIUMVIRATE 158
three sides TRILATERAL 157
three successive lines of verse usually rhyming TRIPLET 158
three teeth TRIDENTATE 60, 157
three terms into which colleges divide the academic year TRIMESTER 157
three times as great TRIPLE 158
three-dimensional effect of sound reproduction STEREOPHONIC 188
three-dimensional round body SPHERE 206
three-dimensional vision STEREOPSIS 176
three-legged support TRIPOD 158, 182
three-part name designating the genus, species, and subspecies TRINOMIAL 157, 174
three-wheeled vehicle operated by pedals and carrying two passengers PEDICAB 180
threefold TRIPLE 158
thrifty Frugal PROVIDENT 18
thriving at low temperatures CRYOPHILIC 55, 185
thriving at relatively low temperatures PSYCHROPHILIC 185
thriving in a small amount of moisture XEROPHILOUS 186, 216
thriving in a moist environment HYGROPHILOUS 185
thriving in a salty environment HALOPHILIC 185
thriving in extreme climatic changes TROPOPHILOUS 186, 214
thriving in light PHOTOPHILOUS 185, 190
through the mouth PERORAL 183
through the skin PERCUTANEOUS 182
throw forward PROJECT 16, 114
throw into something INJECT 114
throw out forcefully EJECT 70, 114
tidal movements caused by the moon LUNITIDAL 136
time between one event and another INTERIM 112
time between repeated cycles PERIOD 51
time required to stimulate tissue with twice the rheobase CHRONAXY 49
timing mechanism in living organisms BIOLOGICAL CLOCK 35
tiny filaments of a nerve cell body NEUROFIBRIL 172
tissue around a tooth PERIODONTAL 52, 60
tissue around the back and sides of a fingernail or toenail PERIONYCHIUM 52
tissue between the layers of the cranium DIPLOE 155
tissue formation HISTOGENESIS 86
tissue grafted on the same body AUTOGRAFT 28
tissue grafted onto a different species HETEROGRAFT 102
tissue grafted onto a different species XENOGRAFT 216
tissue grafted onto the same species HOMOGRAFT 101
tissue grafted onto the same species but different genetic composition ALLOGRAFT 219
tissue of a body organ as distinguished from connective tissue PARENCHYMA 179

tissue of a leaf between the lower and upper epidermis MESOPHYLL 144, 192
tissue regeneration NEOGENESIS 86, 170
tissue surrounding a kidney PERINEPHRIUM 51, 171
tissue that performs protective functions EPITHELIUM 76
tissue that surrounds and nourishes the embryo in seed plants ENDOSPERM 72
toastmaster SYMPOSIARCH 24, 106
tone that is eight tones above or below a given tone OCTAVE 162
tongue LINGUA 118
tongue LINGUAL 118
tongue-shaped LINGULATE 118
too small for an optical microscope SUBMICROSCOPIC 139, 202
tooth-shaped DENTIFORM 60
tooth-shaped DENTOID 60
tooth-shaped ODONTOID 60
toothache ODONTALGIA 9, 60
total opposition to current flow IMPEDANCE 180
totality of all things UNIVERSE 153, 215
toward the axis ADAXIAL 30
toward the head CEPHALAD 45
toxic substances of plant origin PHYTOTOXIC 191
toxin excreted by bacteria EXOTOXIN 219
toxin produced in bacteria and released upon disintegration ENDOTOXIN 72
toxin that destroys certain cells, as snake venom CYTOTOXIN 39
toxin that destroys nerve tissue, as rattlesnake venom NEUROTOXIN 172
toxin that destroys red blood cells, as cobra venom HEMOTOXIN 100
tract of land TERRITORY 90
tract of land with regard to its physical features TERRAIN 90
trademark LOGO 67
trademark LOGOTYPE 67
trailing along the ground PROCUMBENT 16
tranquilizer ATARACTIC 4
tranquilizing effect ATARACTIC 4
transfer blood into a person TRANSFUSE 64, 82
transfer from one person to another DEVOLVE 214
transfer of pollen from one strain to another XENIA 216
transition into menopause PERIMENOPAUSE 51
translate secret code Decode DECRYPT 56
transmission of a photograph by radio waves RADIOPHOTOGRAPHY 95, 190
transmission of disease to other parts of the body METASTASIS 145
transmission of power over a distance TELODYNAMIC 70, 209
transmission of visible images TELEVISION 209
transmit TRAJECT 63, 114
transmitted through the female line HOLOGYNIC 13
transmitter and receiver TRANSCEIVER 63
transmitting light without color separation ACHROMATIC 1, 46
transmitting text by telephone lines TELEPHOTOGRAPHY 95, 190, 209
transparent DIAPHANOUS 62
transposition of letters within a word METATHESIS 145
travel over TRAVERSE 64, 215
traveling amusement show CARNIVAL 41
traveling around PERIPATETIC 52
traveling bag that opens into two halves PORTMANTEAU 194
traveling on foot PEDESTRIAN 180
treating disease using an agent that has a similar effect HOMEOPATHY 79, 101
treating disease using an agent that produces the opposite effect ALLOPATHY 79
treating disease using natural remedies HOMEOPATHY 79, 101
treating disease using natural remedies NATUROPATHY 79
treating disease with water HYDROPATHY 22, 79
treatise on poetic theory POETICS 134
treatment of disease by exposure to sunlight HELIOTHERAPY 98
treatment of disorders of the musculoskeletal system ORTHOPAEDICS 134, 177, 180
treatment of disorders of the musculoskeletal system ORTHOPEDICS 134, 177, 180
treatment that uses skeletal manipulation OSTEOPATHY 79, 178
treatment using low temperatures CRYOTHERAPY 55
tree named from the seeds being hidden by scales within the cones CRYPTOMERIA 56
tree of life ARBORVITAE 26, 37

tree-climbing plants often grown as ornamental house plants PHILODENDRON 26, 185
treelike ARBOREOUS 26
treelike structure of nerve tissue in the cerebellum ARBOR VITAE 26, 37
trees named from the covering of the buds EUCALYPTUS 32
trees named from the seed capsule shaped like a cup HYDRANGEA 21
trees with pink and purple flowers RHODODENDRON 26, 78
triangular TRIGONAL 91, 157
trillion cycles TERAHERTZ 57
trough-shaped basin of stratified rock SYNCLINE 106
true identity concealed INCOGNITO 5, 53
true sexual reproduction AMPHIMIXIS 10
true statement VERITY 216
trustee FIDUCIARY 81
truthful Accurate VERACIOUS 216
truthfulness Accuracy VERACITY 216
tube for carrying body fluid DUCT 69
tube that carries food to the stomach ESOPHAGUS 183
tube that carries food to the stomach OESOPHAGUS 184
tubular muscular system, as the alimentary canal PERISTALSIS 52
tumor composed of blood vessels HEMANGIOMA 99
tumor composed of bony tissue OSTEOMA 178
tumor composed of fatty tissue LIPOMA 118
tumor composed of muscle tissue MYOMA 170
tumor composed of nerve tissue NEUROMA 172
tumor composed of striated muscle RHABDOMYOMA 170
tumor consisting of tissues derived from the ectoderm DERMOID 61
tumor of the skin composed of a yellowish mass of tissue cells XANTHOMA 50
tumorlike mass of blood HEMATOMA 99
turn around on an axis REVOLVE 214
turn away AVERT 215
turn outward EVERT 71, 215
turn to show another side OBVERT 215
turn upside down INVERT 215
turned against what is right PERVERSE 183, 215
turned backward RETROFLEX 198
turned backward in position REVERSE 215
turned backward or downward RETRORSE 199, 215
turned inward INTRORSE 80, 215
turned outward EXTRORSE 81, 215
turned toward the observer OBVERSE 215
turning VERTIGINOUS 215
turning about an axis CIRCUMVOLUTION 51, 214
turning away from the main axis AVERSE 215
turning toward the main axis ADVERSE 214
turning backward RETROVERSION 199, 215
turning of an organ RETROVERSION 199, 215
twelfths DUODECIMAL 156, 163
twelve disciples APOSTLE 19
twining plants CONVOLVULUS 214
twist CONVOLUTION 214
twist together CONVOLVE 214
twisted together CONVOLUTED 214
twisting, as certain plants VOLUBLE 214
two axes BIAXIAL 30, 153
two beats to the measure DUPLE 156
two branches BIFURCATE 154
two branches BIRAMOUS 154, 198
two centromeres DICENTRIC 44, 154
two colors DICHROMATIC 48, 155
two contiguous letters representing a single speech sound DIGRAPH 92, 155
two dialects BIDIALECTAL 61, 153
two directions BIDIRECTIONAL 154
two distinct adult color phases DICHROMATIC 48, 155
two distinct types of animals of the same species DIMORPHISM 155, 166
two distinct types of plant parts DIMORPHISM 155, 166
two equal but opposite electrical charges separated by a small distance DIPOLE 155

two focal lengths BIFOCAL 154
two forms DIMORPHIC 155, 166
two forms of female HETEROGYNOUS 13, 102
two germ layers DIPLOBLASTIC 38, 155
two heads BICEPHALOUS 45, 153
two heads DICEPHALOUS 45, 154
two identical copies DUPLICATE 156
two leaves BIFOLIATE 154
two leaves DIPHYLLOUS 155, 192
two legislative chambers BICAMERAL 153
two liquids, one suspended in the other EMULSION 71
two lobes BILOBATE 154
two magnetic poles BIPOLAR 154
two morphemes BIMORPHEMIC 154, 166
two opposing opinions BIPOLAR 154
two or more centers of power within a political system POLYCENTRISM 45, 164
two or more forms during the life cycle PLEOMORPHISM 167
two overlapping characters having a special sound DIGRAPH 92, 155
two parties BIPARTISAN 154
two parts BINARY 154
two parts BIPARTITE 154
two points on a celestial body's orbit SYZYGY 108, 218
two points on the moon's orbit SYZYGY 108, 218
two sets of teeth DIPHYODONT 60, 155
two sides BILATERAL 154
two similar parts DUAL 156
two stamens DIANDROUS 13, 154
two symmetrical sides BILATERAL 154
two teeth BIDENTATE 60, 153
two times during the year when day and night are of equal length EQUINOX 76
two-footed animal BIPED 154, 180
two-legged support BIPOD 154, 181
two-part name designating the genus and species BINOMIAL 154, 173
twofold Double DUPLE 156
twofold Double DUPLEX 156
type species of a genus GENOTYPE 85
typewriter for transmitting messages TELETYPEWRITER 209
typewritten copy TYPESCRIPT 96
umbrella for protection from the sun PARASOL 98, 179
unable to repay Insolvent BANKRUPT 199
unaccented syllables at the beginning of a line of verse ANACRUSIS 11
unaltered crystalline growth IDIOMORPHIC 111, 166
unauthorized ILLEGAL 4, 66
unbelieving INCREDULOUS 6, 55
unclear AMBIGUOUS 10
under the skin Subcutaneous HYPODERMIC 61, 109
under the tongue SUBLINGUAL 118
underground chamber HYPOGEUM 89, 110
underground room CRYPT 55
underlying nature HYPOSTASIS 110
undermine the principles of Corrupt SUBVERT 215
understanding of another person's feelings EMPATHY 79
undifferentiated cells or tissues BLASTEMA 38
undifferentiated living substance BLASTEMA 38
undifferentiated embryonic ectoderm ECTOBLAST 38, 73
undifferentiated embryonic mesoderm MESOBLAST 39, 143
undifferentiated embryonic endoderm ENDOBLAST 38, 71
unequal INEQUALITY 6, 76
unequal number of elements HETEROMEROUS 103
unequal responses to stimuli ANISOTROPIC 3, 103, 213
unfair apportionment MALAPPORTIONMENT 31
unfair distribution MALDISTRIBUTION 31
unfavorable Harmful INIMICAL 6
unfavorable Unlucky INAUSPICIOUS 5, 205
unfertilized egg of certain algae and fungi OOSPHERE 206
unfriendly Hostile INIMICAL 6

unified organization MONOLITH 123, 152
uniform color ISOCHROMATIC 48, 104
unintentional INADVERTENT 5, 215
union of two similar gametes ISOGAMY 83, 104
union of two dissimilar gametes ANISOGAMY 2, 82, 103
union of two dissimilar gametes HETEROGAMY 82, 102
union of two gametes SYNGAMY 83, 107
unit MONAD 151
unit for measuring sound volume equal to one tenth of a bel DECIBEL 163
unit of electrical energy equal to one kilowatt for one hour KILOWATT-HOUR 115
unit of electromagnetic energy PHOTON 190
unit of force DYNE 69
unit of heat equal to 100, 000 British Thermal Units THERM 211
unit of illumination equal to one lumen per square centimeter PHOT 189
unit of length equal to the distance from the earth to the sun ASTRONOMICAL UNIT 28, 172
unit of measure of the refractive power of a lens DIOPTER 63, 175
unit of sound energy PHONON 188
unit of sound volume measured by comparing with a reference tone PHON 187
unit of storage containing 1, 048, 576 bits MEGABIT 139
unit of storage containing 1, 048, 576 bytes MEGABYTE 139
unit of viscosity equal to one hundredth of a poise CENTIPOISE 43
unit of volume equal to one-fourth of a gallon QUART 159
unit of weight equal to one hundred pounds Hundredweight CENTAL 42
unit of work energy needed to raise one kilogram one meter KILOGRAMMETER 115, 148
unit of work equal to a force of one dyne acting through a distance of one centimeter ERG 77
unite by lacing together INTERLACE 112
united into one body CORPORATE 53
united petals GAMOPETALOUS 82
united petals MONOPETALOUS 152
united petals SYMPETALOUS 106
united sepals GAMOSEPALOUS 82
united sepals MONOSEPALOUS 152
united sepals SYNSEPALOUS 107
uniting two adjacent vowels SYNALEPHA 106
uniting two adjacent vowels to form a diphthong SYNERESIS 107
universal wisdom PANSOPHY 177, 204
universe COSMIC 54
universe including all galaxies METAGALAXY 144
universe regarded as an orderly and harmonious system COSMOS 54
unknown field of knowledge TERRA INCOGNITA 7, 53, 90
unknown land TERRA INCOGNITA 7, 53, 90
unknown origin CRYPTOGENIC 56, 84
unknown source ANONYMOUS 3, 174
unpaired X chromosome MONOSOME 48, 152
unpaired sex chromosome MONOSOME 48, 152
unselfishness ALTRUISM 219
untruthfulness INVERACITY 7, 216
upper lateral regions of the abdomen HYPOCHONDRIUM 109
uppermost of the three middle regions of the abdomen EPIGASTRIUM 75, 83
uproot ERADICATE 71, 198
uproot and replant TRANSPLANT 64
upward slope UPGRADE 97
urge into action IMPEL 182
urge irresistibly COMPEL 182
use ambiguities TERGIVERSATE 215
use ambiguous expressions to mislead EQUIVOCATE 76, 188
use of a proper name to designate a class it is typical of ANTONOMASIA 173
use of a title in place of a proper name ANTONOMASIA 173
use of successive synonyms to express an idea PLEONASM 220
use of very long words SESQUIPEDALIAN 181
use the mind Think CEREBRATE 46
used by both eyes BINOCULAR 154, 174
used by one eye only MONOCULAR 151, 174
utter suddenly Exclaim EJACULATE 70
vague feeling of uneasiness MALAISE 31
valence of one MONOVALENT 152

very skillful Adroit AMBIDEXTROUS 10
very talkative Garrulous LOQUACIOUS 65
very unusual UNIQUE 153
vibrating disk in a microphone DIAPHRAGM 62
view of a wide area PANORAMA 177
view of the earth in which the entire surface is at mean sea level GEOID 89
vigor DYNAMISM 69
vigor VERVE 68
vigorous DYNAMIC 69
vindication of divine justice THEODICY 210
violate the law TRANSGRESS 64, 97
violent disturbance BOULEVERSEMENT 215
violent political or social upheaval CATACLYSM 12
violent upheaval occurring in nature CATACLYSM 12
virus that destroys bacteria BACTERIOPHAGE 183
viruses in the blood VIREMIA 100
viruses responsible for the common cold RHINOVIRUS 199
visible surface of the sun PHOTOSPHERE 190, 206
visible to the naked eye MACROSCOPIC 137, 201
vision OPTICAL 176
vision of death THANATOPSIS 176
visual condition characterized by the inability to see well in bright light HEMERALOPIA 175
visual condition characterized by the inability to see well in dim light NYCTALOPIA 175
visual condition in which objects appear double DIPLOPIA 155, 175
visual condition in which one eye turns inward ESOTROPIA 213
visual condition in which one eye turns outward EXOTROPIA 213
visual condition in which the image is not the same size in both eyes ANISEIKONIA 2, 103, 111
visual condition in which the image is the same size in both eyes ISEIKONIA 103, 111
visual condition in which the refractive power is equal in both eyes ISOMETROPIA 104, 148, 175
visual condition in which the refractive power is not equal in both eyes ANISOMETROPIA 2, 103, 146, 175
visual condition resulting from abnormal refraction of the eye AMETROPIA 2, 146, 175
visual condition resulting in distant vision blurred and near vision clear MYOPIA 175
visual condition resulting in distant vision clear and near vision blurred HYPERMETROPIA 108, 148, 175
visual condition resulting in distant vision clear and near vision blurred HYPEROPIA 108, 175
visual condition resulting in perfect vision EMMETROPIA 147, 175
visual defect named from blindness to red, the first primary color PROTANOPIA 4, 24, 176
visual defect named from blindness to green, the second primary color DEUTERANOPIA 4, 175
visual defect named from blindness to blue, the third primary color TRITANOPIA 4, 158, 176
vitamin found in all living cells BIOTIN 36
vividly expressive ELOQUENT 65, 70
vocabulary of a language LEXICAL 66
vocabulary of a language LEXIS 66
vocabulary of a language or particular subject LEXICON 66
vocabulary of a particular subject TERMINOLOGY 67
vowels VOCALIC 188
walk about PERAMBULATE 182
walk around CIRCUMAMBULATE 50
walk through to inspect PERAMBULATE 182
walking horizontal PRONOGRADE 97
walking on the entire sole of the foot PLANTIGRADE 97
walking on the toes DIGITIGRADE 97
walking vertical ORTHOGRADE 97, 177
wall of earth to protect soldiers Rampart PARAPET 179
ward off evil APOTROPAIC 20, 213
warlike Combative BELLIGERENT 31
warlike Pugnacious BELLICOSE 31
warm-blooded HOMOIOTHERMIC 101, 210
wasting away due to insufficient nutrition ATROPHY 4, 212
water AQUA 20
water and another substance chemically combined HYDRATE 21
water containing decomposing organic matter and no free oxygen POLYSAPROBIC 36, 165
water rich in nutrients for supporting plant life EUTROPHIC 33, 212
water deficient in nutrients for supporting plant life OLIGOTROPHIC 166, 212
water on the earth HYDROSPHERE 22, 206
water pipe for fighting fires HYDRANT 21
water-bearing rock formation AQUIFER 20

watercraft that skims the surface HYDROPLANE 22
watery AQUEOUS 20
watery fluid in the chambers of the eye AQUEOUS HUMOR 20
way of entering Entrance INGRESS 97
way of going out Exit EGRESS 70, 97
way something appears to the eye ASPECT 204
way something appears to the mind ASPECT 204
weak acid used as a bleach HYPOCHLOROUS ACID 109
weak androgenic steroid ANDROSTERONE 13
weakness ADYNAMIC 1, 69
weakness INFIRMITY 6
well-informed about literature LITERARY 68
well-known Distinguished PROMINENT 17
well-known Notorious PROVERBIAL 17, 68
well-respected elderly man PATRIARCH 24, 142
well-respected elderly woman MATRIARCH 23, 142
werewolf LYCANTHROPE 14
white amino acid that results from the hydrolysis of protein LEUCINE 117
white blood cell LEUKOCYTE 40, 117
white blood cell easily stained with basic dyes BASOPHIL 184
white blood cell easily stained with eosin dyes EOSINOPHIL 185
white blood cell easily stained with neutral dyes NEUTROPHIL 185
white blood cell in the lymphatic system LYMPHOCYTE 40
white blood cell with a single nucleus MONOCYTE 40, 151
white blood cells that have very minute granules in the cytoplasm AGRANULOCYTE 1, 39
white blood cells that vary according to granules in the cytoplasm GRANULOCYTE 39
white mineral substances TERRA ALBA 90
white opaque spot on the cornea LEUKOMA 117
whitish discharge from the vagina LEUKORRHEA 118, 199
who goes there QUI VIVE 37
whorl of a spiral shell VOLUTE 214
wide circulation ENCYCLICAL 56
widespread damage named from an unfavorable aspect of the stars DISASTER 28
widespread disaster CATASTROPHE 12
wild uproar PANDEMONIUM 176
wind caused by downward flowing air KATABATIC 13
wind caused by upward flowing air ANABATIC 11
wing-shaped PTERYGOID 197
wishing harm or evil on another MALEVOLENT 32
with praise for academic standing CUM LAUDE 219
with great praise for academic standing MAGNA CUM LAUDE 140
with highest praise for academic standing SUMMA CUM LAUDE 220
withdraw formally from an organization SECEDE 42
within a blood vessel INTRAVASCULAR 80
within a cell INTRACELLULAR 80
within a galaxy INTRAGALACTIC 80
within a molecule INTRAMOLECULAR 80
within a muscle INTRAMUSCULAR 80
within a species INTRASPECIFIC 80
within a state INTRASTATE 80
within a vein INTRAVENOUS 80
within an artery INTRAARTERIAL 80
within layers of skin INTRACUTANEOUS 80
within layers of skin INTRADERMAL 61, 80
within the cranium INTRACRANIAL 46, 80
within the eyeball INTRAOCULAR 80, 174
within the heart INTRACARDIAC 41, 80
within the nucleus of a cell INTRANUCLEAR 80
within the uterus INTRAUTERINE 80
within the walls of a city INTRAMURAL 80
without a brand name GENERIC 85
without a calyx or corolla ACHLAMYDEOUS 1
without a center ACENTRIC 1, 44
without a mouth ASTOMATOUS 4
without a name ANONYMOUS 3, 174
without a name INNOMINATE 7, 173

without a stem ACAULESCENT 1
without a tail ACAUDATE 1
without a written language NONLITERATE 68
without color ACHROMATIC 1, 46
without color ACHROMIC 1, 46
without concern Carefree INSOUCIANT 7
without crystalline form AMORPHOUS 2, 166
without delay IMMEDIATE 5, 143
without fault PERFECT 182
without fault or error IMMACULATE 5
without fault or error IMPECCABLE 5
without feet APODAL 3, 181
without fever AFEBRILE 1
without form AMORPHOUS 2, 166
without gaining or losing heat ADIABATIC 1, 61
without gills ABRANCHIATE 1
without honor Base IGNOBLE 4
without imagination Dull PEDESTRIAN 180
without individuality ANONYMOUS 3, 174
without interest or enthusiasm PERFUNCTORY 183
without intervention Direct IMMEDIATE 5, 143
without knowledge IGNORANT 4, 53
without knowledge or awareness INCOGNIZANT 5, 53
without leaves APHYLLOUS 3, 192
without light APHOTIC 3, 189
without limits INFINITE 6
without liveliness Dull INANIMATE 5
without petals APETALOUS 3
without regard to Regardless IRRESPECTIVE 7, 205
without regret IMPENITENT 5
without sin IMMACULATE 5
without symmetry ASYMMETRY 4, 105, 146
without teeth EDENTATE 60, 70
without teeth EDENTULOUS 60, 70
without the ability to move INERT 6
without variation UNIFORM 153
without water ANHYDROUS 2, 20
without wings APTEROUS 3, 196
woman who manages the domestic affairs of an institution MATRON 142
womb MATRIX 142
women of dubious social standing DEMIMONDE 58
wooded ARBOREOUS 26
word composed of a sequence of letters without regard to its meaning VOCABLE 188
word derived from the same root as another Cognate PARONYM 174, 180
word element pronounced as a single sound SYLLABLE 106
word for word AD VERBUM 67
word for word VERBATIM 68
word for word and letter for letter VERBATIM ET LITERATIM 68
word formed by combining two other words PORTMANTEAU WORD 194
word formed by rearranging letters ANAGRAM 11
word formed from the first letter from each word of a series ACRONYM 7, 174
Word of God LOGOS 67
word of mouth Orally VIVA VOCE 37, 188
word or phrase rather than an inflected form PERIPHRASTIC 52
word or phrase that modifies another word or phrase ADJUNCT 114
word, phrase, etc., inserted into a passage PARENTHESIS 180
word, phrase, or form of expression LOCUTION 65
word puzzle LOGOGRIPH 67
word referred to by a relative pronoun ANTECEDENT 14, 42
word root meaning eleven HENDECA- 163
word root meaning lifeless or containing nitrogen AZO- 4, 216
word root meaning not equal ANISO- 2, 103
word root meaning ovary OOPHOR- 189
word root meaning synchronous SYNCHRO- 49, 106
word root meaning twelve DODECA- 156, 163
word root meaning twelve DUODEC- 156, 163

word that connects other words CONJUNCTION 115
word that is irregular in inflection HETEROCLITE 102
word that modifies a noun or pronoun ADJECTIVE 114
word used in a new sense NEOLOGISM 67, 171
word used in place of a noun PRONOUN 17
word used to characterize a person or thing EPITHET 76
word used to help form a verbal unit Helping verb AUXILIARY VERB 67
word used to modify a verb, adjective, or another adverb ADVERB 67
word with a similar meaning to another word SYNONYM 107, 174
word with the opposite meaning of another word ANTONYM 174
word with no meaning VERBALISM 68
word with one syllable MONOSYLLABLE 105, 152
word with two syllables DISYLLABLE 105, 156
word with three syllables TRISYLLABLE 108, 158
word with four syllables TETRASYLLABLE 108, 160
word with four or more syllables POLYSYLLABLE 105, 165
word with only one meaning UNIVOCAL 153, 188
words addressed to an absent person for rhetorical effect APOSTROPHE 20
words beyond what is necessary VERBIAGE 68
words in their exact sense LITERAL 68
words of a language VOCABULARY 188
words pronounced the same, always differ in meaning HOMONYM 101, 174
words pronounced the same, always differ in meaning HOMOPHONE 101, 187
words spelled the same, always differ in meaning HOMOGRAPH 93, 101
words spelled the same, always differ in meaning and pronunciation HETERONYM 103, 174
words to avoid repetition of words used previously ANAPHORA 11, 189
words used by an individual VOCABULARY 188
wordy DIFFUSE 81
wordy PROLIX 17
wordy VERBOSE 68
work out in detail ELABORATE 70
workable VIABLE 37
working of miracles THAUMATURGY 77
worship of all the gods PANTHEISM 177, 210
worship of animals ZOOLATRY 117, 218
worship of demons DEMONOLATRY 117
worship of idols IDOLATRY 117
worship of images ICONOLATRY 111, 117
worship of the Virgin Mary to an excessive degree MARIOLATRY 117
worship of the dead NECROLATRY 117, 169
worship of the sun HELIOLATRY 98, 117
worshiping beings in a combined animal and human form THERIANTHROPIC 14
worthy of belief CREDITABLE 55
worthy to be chosen ELIGIBLE 70
writ issued to bring a prisoner before a court HABEAS CORPUS 54
write at the top SUPERSCRIBE 96
write beforehand PRESCRIBE 96
write illegibly SCRIBBLE 96
write letters or words in another alphabet TRANSLITERATE 64, 68
write on a surface INSCRIBE 96
write one's name at the end of a document SUBSCRIBE 96
write spoken material TRANSCRIBE 63, 96
writer SCRIBE 96
writer of glossaries GLOSSOGRAPHER 92
writer who does scripts SCRIPTWRITER 96
writing dictionaries LEXICOGRAPHY 66, 93
writing of history HISTORIOGRAPHY 93
writing prose using line lengths determined by sense STICHOMETRY 150
writing room SCRIPTORIUM 26, 96
writings about the lives of saints HAGIOLOGY 66
writings and pictures intended to arouse sexual excitement PORNOGRAPHY 94
writings having lasting and widespread interest LITERATURE 68
writings of a specific period or country LITERATURE 68
writings of dubious authenticity APOCRYPHA 19, 55
writings on a particular subject CORPUS 54
written above SUPERSCRIPT 96

KEYWORDS

amnesia 2
amnesty 2
amoral 2
amorphous 2, 166
amortize 169
amphiarthrosis 10, 27
amphibian 10, 34
amphibiotic 10, 34
amphibious 10, 34
amphibole 10
amphibolite 10, 119
amphibology 10, 66
amphibrach 10
amphictyony 10
amphimacer 10, 136
amphimixis 10
amphipod 10, 181
amphiprostyle 10, 16
amphisbaena 10
amphistylar 10
amphitheater 10
amphitheatre 10
amphithecium 10
amphora 10, 189
amphoteric 10
amyotonia 2, 169
anabaena 11
Anabaptist 11
anabatic 11
anabiosis 11, 34
anabolism 11, 144
anachronism 11, 49
anaclisis 11
anacoluthon 2
anacrusis 11
anadiplosis 11, 154
anadromous 11
anaemia 2, 98
anaerobe 2, 9, 34
anaerobic 2, 9, 34
anaesthesia 2, 78
anaglyph 11
anagoge 9, 11
anagram 11
analcite 2, 119
analects 11
analgesia 2, 9
analgesic 2, 9
analogy 11, 66
analphabetic 2
analysis 11
analytics 11, 130
analyze 11
anamnesis 11
anamorphic 11, 166
anapest 11
anaphase 11
anaphora 11, 189
anaphrodisia 2
anaphylaxis 11
anaplasia 11, 167
anaptyxis 11
anarchy 2, 23
anarthria 2
anastomosis 11
anastrophe 11

anathema 11
anatomy 11, 202
anatropous 11, 213
ancestry 14, 42
andalusite 119
andesite 119
andradite 119
androecium 13
androgen 13, 84
androgenous 13, 84
androgynous 13
android 13
androphobia 13, 186
androsterone 13
anecdote 2
anemia 2, 98
anemograph 91
anemology 124
anemometer 146
anemophilous 184
anencephaly 2, 45
aneroid 2
aneroid barometer 2, 30, 146
anesthesia 2, 78
anesthesiology 2, 78, 124
angiography 91
angiology 124
angioplasty 167
anglesite 119
Anglophile 184
Anglophobia 186
anhydride 2, 20
anhydrite 2, 20, 119
anhydrous 2, 20
animadversion 214
aniseikonia 2, 103, 111
aniso- 2, 103
anisogamous 2, 82, 103
anisogamy 2, 82, 103
anisometric 2, 103, 146
anisometropia 2, 103, 146, 175
anisotropic 3, 103, 213
ankerite 119
annals 73
anniversary 73, 214
anno domini 73
annual 73
annual ring 73
annuity 73
annus mirabilis 73
anodyne 3
anomalous 3, 100
anomaly 3, 101
anomie 3, 172
anomy 3, 172
anonym 3, 174
anonymous 3, 174
anorexia 3
anorexia nervosa 3
anorthite 3, 119, 177
anorthosite 3, 119, 177
anosmia 3
anoxemia 3, 98
anoxia 3
ante meridiem 14
antebellum 14, 31

antecede 14, 42
antecedent 14, 42
antecessor 14, 42
antechamber 15
antechoir 15
antedate 15
antediluvian 15
antemeridian 15
antemortem 15, 169
antenatal 15, 170
antependium 15
antepenult 15
antepenultimate 15
anterior 15
anteroom 15
anthelion 97
anther 18
antheridium 18
anthesis 18
anthocyanin 18, 56
anthodium 18
anthology 18
anthophore 18, 189
anthozoan 18, 216
anthracite 119
anthropocentric 14, 44
anthropogenesis 14, 84
anthropography 14, 91
anthropoid 14
anthropology 14, 124
anthropometry 14, 146
anthropomorphism 14, 166
anthropopathism 14, 79
anthropophagy 14, 183
anthroposophy 14, 204
antibiosis 34
anticatalyst 12
anticline 219
antigen 84
antineoplastic 167, 170
antinomian 172
antinomy 172
antipathy 79
antiphon 187
antipsychotic 195
antipyretic 197
antonomasia 173
antonym 174
anuran 3
anuria 3
aorist 3
apathy 3, 79
apatite 119
aperiodic 3, 51
apetalous 3
aphaeresis 19
aphanite 3, 119
aphasia 3
aphelion 19, 98
apheresis 19
aphesis 19
aphonia 3, 187
aphorism 19
aphotic 3, 189
aphyllous 3, 192
apiary 26

autogyro 28, 57
autohypnosis 28
autoimmunity 28
autointoxication 28
autologous 28
autolysis 29
automatic 29
automobile 29
automysophobia 186
autonetics 29, 131
autonomic 29, 172
autonomic nervous system 29, 173
autonomous 29, 173
autonomy 29, 173
autophyte 29, 190
autoplasty 29, 167
autopsy 29, 175
autoradiograph 29, 91
autosome 29, 47
autotomy 29, 202
autotoxin 29
autotroph 29, 212
autunite 119
auxiliary verb 67
aver 216
averse 215
avert 215
avian 29
aviary 26, 29
aviation 30
aviator 30
aviatrix 30
aviculture 30
avifauna 30
avionics 131
avitaminosis 4, 37
axenic 4, 216
axial 30
axile 30
axiology 124
axis 30
axle 30
axon 30
azo- 4, 216
azoic 216
azote 216
azotemia 98, 216
azotobacter 217
azoturia 217
azygous 4, 218
bacteremia 98
bactericide 50
bacteriology 124
bacteriophage 183
ballistics 131
balneology 124
bankrupt 199
bar 30
bar graph 91
bariatrics 30, 110, 131
baric 30
barite 30, 119
barograph 30, 91
barometer 30, 146
baroreceptor 30
baryon 30

basophil 184
batholith 123
bathometer 146
bathymetry 146
bathysphere 206
bathythermograph 91, 210
bauxite 119
belles-lettres 68
bellicose 31
belligerent 31
benediction 31, 64
benefactor 31
benefactress 31
beneficent 31
beneficiary 31
benefit 31
benevolent 31
benign 31, 84
biannual 73, 153
biathlon 153
biaxial 30, 153
Bible 34
biblical 34
biblicist 34
bibliography 34, 91
bibliolatry 34, 117
bibliomancy 34, 140
bibliomania 34, 140
bibliopegy 34
bibliophile 34, 184
bibliophobia 34, 186
bibliopole 34
bibliotheca 34
bibliotherapy 34
bibliotics 34, 131
bicameral 153
bicentennial 42, 73, 153
bicephalous 45, 153
biceps 153
bichloride 153
bichromate 47, 153
biconcave 153
biconvex 153
bicuspid 153
bicycle 56, 153
bidentate 60, 153
bidialectal 61, 153
bidirectional 154
biennial 73, 154
biennium 73, 154
bifid 154
bifocal 154
bifoliate 154
bifurcate 154
bigamy 82, 154
bilabial 154
bilateral 154
bilingual 118, 154
bilirubin 78
billion 116, 154
bilobate 154
bimanual 141, 154
bimonthly 154
bimorphemic 154, 166
binary 154
binaural 154

binocular 154, 174
binomial 154, 173
bioassay 35
bioastronautics 28, 35, 131
biocatalyst 12, 35
biocenosis 35
biochemistry 35
biocide 35, 50
bioclimatology 35, 124
bioconversion 35
biocybernetics 35, 131
biodegradable 35, 97
bioecology 35, 124
bioelectric 35
bioenergetics 35, 77, 131
bioengineering 35
bioethics 35, 131
biofeedback 35
biogas 35
biogenesis 35, 84
biogenic 35, 84
biogeography 35, 88, 91
biography 35, 91
biohazard 35
bioinstrumentation 35
biological clock 35
biology 35, 124
bioluminescence 35
biolysis 35
biomass 35
biomaterial 35
biomathematics 35, 131
biome 35
biomechanics 35, 131
biomedicine 35
biometeorology 35, 124
biometrics 35, 131, 146
biometry 36, 146
bionics 36, 131
bionomics 36, 131, 173
biophysics 36, 131, 192
biopsy 36, 175
biorhythm 36
bioscience 36
biosocial 36
biosphere 36, 206
biostatistics 36, 131
biosynthesis 36, 105
biota 36
biotechnology 36, 124
biotelemetry 36, 146, 208
biotic 36
biotin 36
biotite 119
biotope 36
biotron 36
biotype 36
bipartisan 154
bipartite 154
biped 154, 180
bipinnate 154
biplane 154
bipod 154, 181
bipolar 154
biquarterly 154, 159
biramous 154, 198

craniotomy 46, 203
cranium 46
credence 54
credentials 54
credibility gap 55
credible 55
credit 55
creditable 55
creditor 55
credo 55
credulous 55
creed 55
crematorium 26
criminology 125
cryobiology 36, 55, 125
cryogen 55, 84
cryogenics 55, 84, 131
cryolite 55, 120
cryometer 55, 146
cryonics 36, 55, 131
cryophilic 55, 185
cryophyte 55, 191
cryoprobe 55
cryoscope 55, 200
cryoscopy 55, 200
cryostat 55
cryosurgery 55
cryotherapy 55
crypt 55
cryptanalysis 11, 56
cryptic 56
cryptoclastic 56
cryptocrystalline 56
cryptogam 56, 82
cryptogenic 56, 84
cryptogram 56
cryptography 56, 92
cryptomeria 56
cryptozoite 56, 207, 217
crystallography 92
ctenophore 189
cultigen 84
cum laude 219
cunnilingus 118
cuprite 120
curriculum vitae 37
cyan 56
cyanic 56
cyanine 56
cyanite 56, 120
cyanobacteria 56
cyanosis 56
cybernetics 131
cyberphobia 131, 186
cycle 56
cycloid 56
cyclometer 56, 147
cyclone 56
cyclopaedia 56
cyclopedia 56
cyclops 56, 175
cyclorama 56, 176
cyclosis 56
cyclostome 56
cyclothymia 56
cynophobia 186

cystoscope 200
cytochemistry 39
cytochrome 39, 47
cytogenesis 39, 84
cytogenetics 39, 84, 131
cytokinesis 39, 117
cytokinin 39
cytology 39, 125
cytolysis 39
cytomegalic 39, 139
cytomegalovirus 39, 139
cytopathic 39, 79
cytophotometry 39, 147, 189
cytoplasm 39, 167
cytostatic 39
cytotaxonomy 39, 173, 208
cytotoxin 39
dactyl 58
dactylogram 58
dactylography 58, 92
dactylology 58, 66
decade 163
decagon 90, 163
decagram 163
decahedron 163
decalcomania 140
decaliter 163
Decalog 66, 163
Decalogue 66, 163
decameter 147, 163
decapod 163, 181
decare 163
decasyllable 105, 163
decathlon 163
December 163
decemvir 163
decennial 73, 163
decennium 73, 163
decerebrate 46
decibar 30, 163
decibel 163
decigram 163
decile 163
deciliter 163
decillion 116, 163
decimal 163
decimeter 147, 163
decrypt 56
decuple 163
dedicate 64
deduce 68
deduct 68
defuse 81
degrade 97
degression 97
dehydrate 21
dehydrogenase 21
dehydrogenate 21
deject 114
dekagram 163
dekaliter 163
dekameter 147, 163
delude 135
demagog 9, 58
demagogue 9, 58
demigod 58

demimonde 58
demisemiquaver 58, 59
demitasse 58
demiurge 58, 77
democracy 24, 58
democrat 24, 58
demographics 58, 92, 131
demography 58, 92
demonolatry 117
demonology 125
dendriform 26
dendrite 26, 120
dendrochronology 26, 49, 125
dendroid 26
dendrology 26, 125
denominate 173
denomination 173
densimeter 147
densitometer 147
dental 60
dental hygienist 60
dentate 60
denticle 60
dentiform 60
dentifrice 60
dentigerous 60
dentil 60
dentin 60
dentine 60
dentistry 60
dentition 60
dentoid 60
denture 60
deontology 125
deport 194
deportment 194
dermal 61
dermatitis 61, 113
dermatogen 61, 84
dermatology 61, 125
dermatome 61, 203
dermatophyte 61, 191
dermatoplasty 61, 167
dermatosis 61
dermis 61
dermoid 61
describe 96
desegregate 96
despicable 204
despise 205
detract 212
deuteranopia 4, 175
deuterogamy 82
Deuteronomy 173
devitalize 37
devocalize 188
devolve 214
diabetes 61
diabetes insipidus 62
diabetes mellitus 62
diachronic 49, 62
diacritic 62
diacritical 62
diacritical mark 62
diadromous 62
diagenesis 62, 84

MAIN ENTRY INDEX

gyre 57
gyro 57
gyrocompass 57, 201
gyromagnetic 57
gyroplane 57
gyroscope 57, 201
gyrus 57
habeas corpus 54
hagiarchy 23
hagiocracy 24
hagiography 93
hagiology 66
halite 120
hallucinogen 85
halophilic 185
halophyte 191
haphephobia 186
haploid 219
haplology 67
haplopia 175
harmonics 133
hecatomb 43
hectare 43
hectogram 43
hectograph 43, 93
hectoliter 43
hectometer 43, 147
heliacal 98
helianthus 18, 98
helical 57
helicoid 57
helicon 57
helicopter 57, 196
heliocentric 44, 98
heliograph 93, 98
heliolatry 98, 117
heliometer 98, 147
Helios 98
heliostat 98
heliotaxis 98, 208
heliotherapy 98
heliotrope 98, 213
heliotropism 98, 213
helium 98
helix 57
helminthology 126
hemachrome 48, 98
hemacytometer 40, 98, 148
hemagglutination 99
hemal 99
hemangioma 99
hematic 99
hematin 99
hematinic 99
hematite 99, 120
hematoblast 38, 99
hematocrit 99
hematogenesis 85, 99
hematogenous 85, 99
hematology 99, 126
hematolysis 99
hematoma 99
hematophagous 99, 183
hematopoiesis 99
hematosis 99
hematozoon 99, 217

hematuria 99
heme 99
hemeralopia 175
hemicellulose 58
hemicycle 57, 58
hemidemisemiquaver 58, 59
hemihedral 58
hemihydrate 21, 59
hemimetabolic 59, 144
hemimorphic 59, 166
hemiola 59
hemiparasite 59
hemiplegia 59
hemipterous 59, 196
hemisphere 59, 206
hemistich 59
hemochromatosis 48, 99
hemocyanin 56, 99
hemocyte 40, 99
hemocytometer 40, 99, 148
hemodialysis 63, 99
hemodynamics 70, 99, 133
hemoflagellate 99
hemoglobin 99
hemoglobinuria 99
hemolymph 99
hemolysis 99
hemophilia 99, 185
hemophobia 99, 186
hemoptysis 99
hemorrhage 99, 199
hemorrhoid 99, 199
hemorrhoidectomy 99, 199, 203
hemostasis 99
hemostat 100
hemostatic 100
hemotoxin 100
hendeca- 163
hendecagon 90, 163
hendecahedron 163
hendecasyllable 105, 164
henotheism 209
hepatectomy 100, 203
hepatic 100
hepatica 100
hepatitis 100, 113
hepatogenic 85, 100
hepatoma 100
hepatomegaly 100, 139
hepatotoxic 100
heptad 161
heptagon 90, 161
heptahedron 161
heptameter 148, 161
heptaploid 161
heptapody 162, 181
heptarchy 23, 162
heptastich 162
Heptateuch 162
heptavalent 162
heptose 162
herbarium 26
herbicide 50
herbivore 184
herbivorous 184
heresiarch 23

hermeneutics 133
herpetology 126
heterocercal 102
heterochromatic 48, 102
heterochromatin 48, 102
heterochromosome 48, 102
heteroclite 102
heterocyclic 57, 102
heterodox 55, 102
heterodyne 70, 102
heteroecious 102
heterogamete 82, 102
heterogamous 82, 102
heterogamy 82, 102
heterogeneous 85, 102
heterogenesis 86, 102
heterogenous 86, 102
heterogony 88, 102
heterograft 102
heterography 93, 102
heterogynous 13, 102
heterolecithal 102
heterologous 102
heterology 67, 103
heterolysis 103
heteromerous 103
heteromorphic 103, 166
heteronomous 103, 173
heteronym 103, 174
Heteroousian 103
heterophyllous 103, 192
heterophyte 103, 191
heteroplasty 103, 168
heteroploid 103
heteropterous 103, 196
heterosexual 103
heterosis 103
heterosporous 103, 207
heterotaxis 103, 208
heterothallic 103
heterotroph 103, 212
heterozygote 103, 218
hexachord 161
hexad 161
hexadecimal 161, 164
hexagon 90, 161
hexagram 161
hexahedron 161
hexameter 148, 161
hexaploid 161
hexapod 161, 181
hexapody 161, 181
hexastich 161
hexasyllable 105, 161
Hexateuch 161
hexavalent 161
hexose 161
hierarchy 23
hierocracy 24
hindquarter 159
histiocyte 40
histogen 86
histogenesis 86
histology 126
histopathology 79, 126
histophysiology 126, 192

MAIN ENTRY INDEX

revive 37
revivify 37
revoke 188
revolute 214
revolution 214
revolve 214
revolver 214
rhabdomancy 140
rhabdomyoma 170
rhabdomyosarcoma 170
rheology 129
rheometer 149
rheumatoid arthritis 27, 114
rheumatology 129
rhinal 199
rhinitis 114, 199
rhinoceros 199
rhinology 129, 199
rhinopharyngitis 114, 199
rhinoplasty 168, 199
rhinovirus 199
rhizobium 36
rhizocarpous 42
rhizogenic 87
rhizomorphous 167
rhizophagous 184
rhizopod 182
rhizosphere 206
rhizotomy 203
rhodamine 77
rhodium 77
rhodochrosite 48, 77, 121
rhododendron 26, 78
rhodolite 78, 121
rhodonite 78, 121
rhodopsin 78, 176
rhodora 78
rhombencephalon 46
rhyolite 121
rhythmics 135
rhytidectomy 203
rigor mortis 169
robotics 135
rodenticide 50
roentgenography 95
roentgenology 129
rubasse 78
rubefacient 78
rubella 78
rubellite 78, 121
rubeola 78
rubescent 78
rubicund 78
rubidium 78
rubiginous 78
rubious 78
rubric 78
ruby 78
rupture 200
Russophile 185
Russophobia 187
saccharide 220
saccharimeter 149
saccharometer 149
sacrarium 26
salimeter 149

salinometer 149
salpingectomy 203
salpingitis 114
samarskite 121
sanatorium 26
sanitarium 26
sapremia 100
saprobe 37
saprogenic 87
saprolite 121
saprophagous 184
saprophyte 191
saprozoic 217
sarcocarp 42
sarcophagous 184
sarcoplasm 168
sauropod 182
scapolite 122
scatology 129
scenography 95
scheelite 122
schizocarp 42
schizogenesis 87
schizopod 182
sclera 200
sclerenchyma 200
sclerite 200
scleritis 114, 200
scleroderma 61, 200
sclerodermatous 61, 200
scleroid 200
scleroma 200
sclerometer 149, 200
scleroprotein 200
sclerosis 200
sclerotium 200
sclerotomy 200, 204
sclerous 200
scolecite 122
scotopia 176
scribble 96
scribe 96
script 96
scriptorium 26, 96
Scripture 96
scriptwriter 96
scyphozoan 217
seborrhea 199
secede 42
seclude 52
sectile 202
section 202
sector 202
seduce 69
segregate 96
seicento 43, 116, 161
seismograph 95
seismology 129
seismometer 149
selenite 122
selenography 95
selenology 129
semanteme 220
semantics 135
semasiology 129
semeiology 129

semiannual 59, 73
semiaquatic 20, 59
semiarid 59
semiautomatic 29, 59
semiautonomous 29, 59, 173
semicentennial 43, 59, 74
semicolon 59
semiconductor 59
semidiameter 59, 63, 150
semidiurnal 59
semifinal 59
semiliterate 59, 68
semilogarithmic 59
semilunar 59, 136
semimonthly 59
semiology 129
semiotics 135
semiparasite 59
semipermeable 59, 183
semiprecious 59
semiprofessional 59
semiquaver 59
semiterrestrial 59, 90
semitone 59
semitransparent 59, 63
semivowel 59
semiweekly 59
semiyearly 59
sensitometer 150
September 162
septendecillion 116, 162, 164
septennial 74, 162
septet 162
septette 162
septicemia 100
septillion 116, 162
septisyllable 105, 162
septuagenarian 162
Septuagesima 162
Septuagint 162
septuple 162
serigraphy 95
serodiagnosis 53, 63
serology 129
sesquicentennial 43, 74
sesquipedalian 181
sex chromosome 48
sexagenarian 161
Sexagesima 161
sexcentenary 43, 74, 161
sexdecillion 116, 161, 164
sexennial 74, 161
sexology 129
sext 161
sextant 161
sextet 161
sextette 161
sextile 161
sextillion 116, 161
sextodecimo 161, 164
sextuple 161
sextuplet 161
sferics 135, 206
shadowgraph 95
sialadenitis 114
sialagogue 9

thermoplastic 169, 211
thermoreceptor 211
thermoregulation 211
thermos 211
thermoscope 202, 211
thermosetting 211
thermosphere 207, 211
thermostable 211
thermostat 211
thermotaxis 208, 211
thermotropism 211, 213
thigmotaxis 208
thigmotropism 213
thixotropy 213
thoracotomy 204
thorite 122
thremmatology 130
thrombocyte 40
thrombocytopenia 40
thrombophlebitis 114
thromboplastin 169
thyroidectomy 204
thyroiditis 114
tiltmeter 150
timocracy 24
tocology 130
tocophobia 187
tome 204
tomography 95, 204
toneme 220
tonetics 135
tonometer 150
tonoplast 169
tonsillectomy 204
tonsillitis 114
tonsillotomy 204
topography 95
topology 130
toponym 174
toponymy 174
toreutics 135
toxemia 100
toxicogenic 88
toxicology 130
toxophilite 186
tracheitis 114
tracheophyte 192
tracheotomy 204
tractable 212
traction 212
tractor 212
traduce 63, 69
traject 63, 114
trajectory 63, 114
transact 63
transceiver 63
transcend 63
transcribe 63, 96
transcript 63, 96
transducer 63, 69
transduction 63, 69
transect 63, 202
transept 63
transfer 63
transfigure 63
transfix 63

transform 63
transfuse 64, 82
transgress 64, 97
transient 64
transit 64
transition 64
transitive 64
translate 64
transliterate 64, 68
translucent 64
transmarine 64, 141
transmit 64
transmute 64
transnational 64
transonic 64
transparent 64
transpicuous 64, 205
transpire 64, 194
transplant 64
transport 64, 194
transpose 64
transsexual 64
transude 64
transuranic 64
transverse 64, 215
transvestite 64
traverse 64, 215
trecento 43, 116
tredecillion 116, 164
tremolite 122
triad 156
trialogue 67, 156
triangle 156
triarchy 24, 156
triathlon 156
triaxial 30, 156
tribology 130
tribrach 156
tricameral 156
tricentennial 43, 74, 156
triceps 156
trichite 122
trichloride 156
trichogyne 14
trichopteran 197
trichotomy 156, 204
trichroism 48, 157
trichromatic 48, 157
triclinic 157
tricorn 157
tricuspid 157
tricycle 57, 157
tridentate 60, 157
triennial 74, 157
triennium 74, 157
trierarch 24, 157
trifecta 157
trifid 157
trifocal 157
trifoliate 157
trifurcate 157
trigeminal 157
trigonal 91, 157
trigonometry 91, 150, 157
trigraph 95, 157
trihedron 157

trilateral 157
trilingual 118, 157
triliteral 68, 157
trillion 116, 157
trilobate 157
trilobite 157
trilogy 67, 157
trimaran 157
trimer 157
trimester 157
trimeter 150, 157
trimetrogon 91, 150, 157
trimonthly 157
trimorph 157, 167
trinomial 157, 174
trio 157
trioecious 157
triose 157
trioxide 157
tripartite 157
triphibian 10, 37, 158
triphthong 158
triplane 158
triple 158
triplet 158
triplicate 158
triploblastic 39, 158
triploid 158
tripod 158, 182
tripody 158, 182
trireme 158
trisaccharide 158
trisect 158, 202
triskaidekaphobia 158, 164, 187
trisoctahedron 158, 163
trisomic 158
tristich 158
trisyllable 108, 158
tritanopia 4, 158, 176
tritheism 158, 210
tritone 158
triumvirate 158
triune 153, 158
trivalent 158
triweekly 158
troilite 122
troostite 122
trope 213
trophallaxis 212
trophic 212
trophoblast 39, 212
trophozoite 212, 217
tropism 213
tropology 67, 213
tropopause 207, 213
tropophilous 186, 214
tropophyte 192, 214
troposphere 207, 214
trypsinogen 88
tubuliflorous 19
tungstite 122
turbidimeter 150
typescript 96
typography 95
typology 130
tyrannicide 50

SECONDARY ROOT INDEX

cleisto, closed 82, 219
climat, climate 35, 124, 126, 127, 136, 137
clin, slope 16, 104, 157
-cline, slope 88, 89, 104, 105, 106, 151, 211, 219
clino, slope 146
clin, to lean 11, 102, 142
co-, together 31, 173, 214
co-, with 30
-coccus, bacteria 88, 137, 155, 193
-coel, cavity 38
col, colon 113
col-, together 65, 66, 135
coleo, sheath 196
coll, glue 21, 24
collo, glue 84
colo, colon 203
-colous, inhabiting 90
columba, dove 26
com-, together 5, 182, 194, 197
con-, completely 42, 52, 204
con-, together 6, 37, 44, 68, 81, 84, 96, 97, 114, 115, 188, 194, 204, 212, 214, 215
con-, with 41
conch, shell 124
coni, dust 139, 193, 194, 201
contra-, against 64, 215
contra-, opposite 64
copro, dung 183, 184
copro, excrement 120
cor-, with 199
corn, horn 153, 157
crat, government 24, 58
crystall, crystal 56
crystallo, crystal 92
cteno, comb 189
-cule, small 123
cupr, copper 120
cyno, dog 186
cyst, bladder 113, 202
cysto, bladder 200
cyst, sac 38, 207
de-, away 37, 64, 68, 81, 135, 194
de-, derived from 173
de-, down 6, 96, 97, 114, 204, 205, 212, 214
de-, from 140
de-, remove 21, 46, 56, 96, 188
desm, ligament 107
deuter, second 4, 175
deutero, second 82, 173
dicho, apart 82, 203
dif-, away 81
dign, worthy 6
dihydro-, addition of two hydrogen atoms 21, 156
dire, to say 216
dis-, apart 96, 115, 194, 200, 202
dis-, away 6, 97, 135, 182, 212, 215
dis-, lack of 105, 147, 152
dis-, negative 28
dis-, not 55
disco, disk 34, 92, 185

dolicho, long 45
-drome, course 8
-drome, to run 107
-dromous, moving 11, 12, 62
dy-, two 23
ec, out 83, 99, 100, 110, 171, 179, 189, 193, 199, 202, 203, 204
ec-, out 44, 219
ecclesi, church 125
echino, spiny 61
eco, environment 25, 28, 35, 50, 107, 124, 125, 128, 129, 206
ef-, out 6, 18, 81
electro, electric 21, 41, 45, 69, 92, 132, 169, 200
electro, electricity 70, 117, 132, 147, 210
em-, intensive 79, 197
-eme, structural unit 66, 92, 167, 187, 208, 220
en-, at 77, 132
en-, in 27, 42, 45, 56, 57, 58, 74, 147, 166, 175, 180, 206, 213
en-, into 9, 56, 61, 145, 195
-enchyma, type of cell tissue 143, 179, 200
ennea, nine 105, 219
enter, intestine 33, 83, 113, 125, 143
ento-, within 217
entom, insect 125
entomo, insect 183, 185, 186
eo-, early 123
ept, fit 6
eroto, sexual desire 28, 85, 101, 140
eso-, in 213
-ess, feminine 31, 143
-et, diminutive 18
-ette, diminutive 136
ethn, race 25, 125, 128
ethno, race 44, 92, 125
etio, cause 125
-etum, place 26
eury, wide 183, 196, 210
ev, age 143
ex-, out 42, 52, 142, 175, 182, 194, 197, 212
exo-, out 60, 132, 213
exo-, outside 36, 39, 42, 44, 77, 82, 85, 125, 178, 206, 207, 210, 219
fac, to do 6, 32, 182
fac, to make 78
fic, to do 31, 32
fic, to make 16, 140, 176, 198
fact, to do 31, 32
fact, to make 141
femto-, quadrillionth (10^{-15}) 147
fer, to bear 18, 20, 207
fer, to carry 50, 63, 64, 189
feto, fetus 125, 201
fibro, fiber 38
fid, split 154, 157, 158
flex, to bend 50, 129, 198
fluor, fluorine 21, 120
fluoro, fluorescence 147, 201
foli, leaf 115, 153, 154, 157, 183, 194
fore-, before 159

fug, to flee 44
-fy, to make 140, 153, 198
galacto, milk 199
Germano, German 185, 186
geront, old age 126
geronto, old age 24
-gerous, bearing 60
giga-, billion (10^9) 57
gingiv, gum 113
glauco, bluish-green 120
gloss, language 104
gloss, tongue 110
glosso, language 92
glot, language 151, 164
glott, tongue 75
glotto, language 49, 126
glyc, sugar 100, 108, 110
glyco, sugar 85
glyco, glycogen 21, 85, 170
gnath, jaw 16, 145, 177
gram, to draw 104, 160, 161
gram, to record 58
gram, to write 11, 56, 62, 67, 75, 111, 152, 179, 187, 209
gramma, letter 159
grani, grain 184
grano, granite 123
gymno, naked 186, 204
hagi, holy 23
hagio, holy 24, 66, 93
hal, salt 120
halo, salt 185, 191
haplo-, single 67, 175, 219
-hedral, surface 58, 155
-hedron, surface 122, 156, 157, 158, 159, 160, 161, 162, 163, 164, 219
hemer, day 74, 175
hen, one 109, 163, 168
heno, one 209
hier, holy 23
hiero, holy 24
hist, tissue 126
histio, tissue 40
histo, tissue 79, 86, 126, 192
hol, whole 13, 59
holo, whole 13, 38, 42, 83, 93, 144, 217
hyal, glass 120
hyalo, transparent 168
hyet, rain 104, 126
hyeto, rain 93
hygro, moisture 93, 148, 185, 191, 201
hylo, matter 217
hymeno, membrane 196
hypn, sleep 9, 15, 126
hypno, sleep 219
hypso, high 93, 148
hyster, womb 203
hystero, womb 203
ichthy, fish 126
icosa, twenty 219
ideo-, idea 93, 126

-ify, to make 6, 37, 38, 68, 106, 169
il-, at 136
im-, in 182, 194, 219
immuno, immunity 86, 126, 133
in-, in 41, 52, 69, 81, 97, 114, 115, 170, 194, 205, 206, 214, 215
in-, into 54
in-, on 19, 96, 188
in-, to 65
it, go 7, 63, 64, 80
-ium, chemical element 47, 77, 78
kai, and 158, 164, 187
kary, nucleus 16, 32, 51, 107
karyo, nucleus 40, 83, 117, 139, 168
kerat, cornea 113
keto, ketone 86
-kinin, hormone 39
klepto, to steal 140
labio, lip 60, 154
labor, work 70
lacto, milk 86
-lagnia, lust 9
lago, hare 166
lalo, talk 186
laparo, abdominal wall 201, 203
laryng, larynx 113, 126, 128, 199, 203
laryngo, larynx 201
lect, choose 62
leg, choose 70
lepido, scale 121, 126, 196, 197
-lepsy, seizure 12, 75
lepto, thin 45
lign, wood 121
lob, lobe 154, 157, 203
lobo, lobe 203
luc, light 64
lymph, lymph 113
lympho, lymph 38, 40
lysi, dissolving 148
-lysis, decomposition 11, 12, 22, 29, 35, 39, 47, 62, 103, 118, 190, 193, 198, 211
-lysis, destruction 99
-lysis, loosening 168, 179
-lyze, decomposition 11
-machy, struggle 67, 210
magnet, magnetic force 25, 57
magneto, magnetic force 23, 70, 93, 133, 148, 206
malac, mollusks 126
malac, soft 178
mammo, breast 93
mangan, manganese 121
mast, breast 13, 113, 203
meli, honey 22, 62
men, month 12, 157
men, menstruation 9, 23
meno, menstruation 2, 33, 199
mening, meninges 113
mer, part 56, 103, 104, 152, 155, 157, 165
-mere, part 38, 44, 47, 145, 209
merg, to dip 71

-poiesis, production 77, 99, 118
-polis, city 7, 54, 139, 169
pon, to put 15, 17, 18
porphyr, violet 176
pos, place 112
pos, to put 64
pre-, before 15, 30, 42, 52, 53, 65, 68, 73, 96, 116, 136, 170, 188, 220
presby, old 176
primo, first 87
proct, rectum 128
pros, in front of 46
prostat, prostate gland 114, 203
protero-, earlier 217
psychro, cold 149, 185, 187
pterid, fern 129
pterido, fern 191
ptysis, spitting 99
pulmon, lung 40
py, pus 100
pyo, pus 61, 87, 199
pycno, dense 149
pyel, renal pelvis 114
pyelo, renal pelvis 114, 171
quattr, four 116, 164
quattro, four 43, 116
radio, by radio 95, 190, 209
radio, radiation 29, 36, 91, 94, 105, 129, 149, 201
re-, again 37, 41, 53, 57, 153, 194, 214
re-, against 31
re-, back 7, 23, 42, 52, 55, 69, 82, 96, 97, 114, 129, 143, 182, 188, 194, 202, 205, 212, 214, 215
red-, again 37
reg, rule 20, 50
rhabdo, rod 140, 170
rheo, flow 129, 149
rhizo, root 36, 42, 87, 167, 182, 184, 203, 206
roentgen, x-rays 95, 129
rog, to ask 17, 112
Russo, Russian 185, 187
sacchar, sugar 220
sacchari, sugar 149
saccharo, sugar 149
sacr, sacred 26
sali, salt 149
salping, fallopian tube 114, 203
sapr, putrid 100
sapro, putrid 87
sapro, decaying 37, 184, 191, 217
sapro, decomposed 36, 121, 165
sarco, flesh 42, 168, 184
-sarcoma, malignant tumor 170, 178
saur, lizard 139, 197
sauro, lizard 182
scat, excrement 129
schizo, fission 87
schizo, split 42, 182
se-, apart 42, 52, 96
se-, away 69
sebo, fat 199

secut, follow 17, 183
seism, earthquake 105, 129, 138
seismo, earthquake 95, 149
selen, moon 122, 129, 179
seleno, moon 95
sero, serum 53, 63, 129
sesqui-, one and a half 43, 74, 181
sial, saliva 9, 114
sider, iron 122
sidero, iron 122
silico, silica 139, 194, 201
Sino, Chinese 14, 129
sito, food 129
socio, social 37, 80, 118, 128, 129, 135, 150, 173, 191
soli, alone 65
somat, body 129, 196
somato, body 168
-some, body 8, 44, 47, 138
some, chromosome 158
somni, sleep 7
son, sound 6, 64, 109, 135, 153
sperm, seed 72
spermat, sperm 220
spermato, seed 192
spermato, sperm 40, 87, 88, 189, 199, 217
spermi, sperm 50
spermio, sperm 87
sphygmo, pulse 95, 150
spiro, coil 57
splen, spleen 204
spleno, spleen 140
spondyl, vertebrae 114
-stasis, stable state 101, 105, 145
-stasis, stoppage 75, 99
-stasis, stationary 110, 111
stat, standing 178
stat, stoppage 100
stat, stationary 4, 8, 22, 39, 55, 98, 130, 132, 133, 135, 198, 211, 220
stato, stationary 123, 202
steat, fat 122
steno, abbreviated 95
steno, narrow 184, 211
stereo-, solid 208, 213
stereo-, three-dimensional 95, 105, 139, 176, 188, 202
stetho, chest 202
sthen, strength 4, 131, 169, 171, 175
stheno, strength 4, 206
-stichous, having rows 178
stomat, mouth 4, 11, 114, 129
-stome, mouth 52, 56
styl, column 10, 17, 52
stylo, style 95
sub-, below 45, 96
sub-, beneath 42, 115, 136, 212
sub-, under 20, 82, 90, 114, 118, 139, 141, 194, 202, 205, 215
sub-, up 194
sub-, nearly 20
super-, above 96, 135

NOTES

NOTES